An Introduction to Women's Studies

Gender in a Transnational World

An Introduction to Women's Studies

Gender in a Transnational World

Inderpal Grewal
Women Studies, San Francisco State University

and

Caren Kaplan
Women's Studies, University of California at Berkeley

Boston   Burr Ridge, IL   Dubuque, IA   Madison, WI   New York   San Francisco   St. Louis
Bangkok   Bogotá   Caracas   Kuala Lumpur   Lisbon   London   Madrid   Mexico City
Milan   Montreal   New Delhi   Santiago   Seoul   Singapore   Sydney   Taipei   Toronto

McGraw-Hill Higher Education

*A Division of The **McGraw-Hill** Companies*

AN INTRODUCTION TO WOMEN'S STUDIES:
GENDER IN A TRANSNATIONAL WORLD

Published by McGraw-Hill, an imprint of The McGraw-Hill
Companies, Inc., 1221 Avenue of the Americas, New York, NY,
10020. Copyright © 2002 by The McGraw-Hill Companies, Inc.
All rights reserved. No part of this publication may be reproduced
or distributed in any form or by any means, or stored in a database
or retrieval system, without the prior written consent of The
McGraw-Hill Companies, Inc., including, but not limited to, in any
network or other electronic storage or transmission, or broadcast
for distance learning. Some ancillaries, including electronic and
print components, may not be available to customers outside the
United States.

This book is printed on acid-free paper.

1 2 3 4 5 6 7 8 9 0 DOC/DOC 0 9 8 7 6 5 4 3 2 1

ISBN 0-07-109380-X

Editorial director: *Jane Karpacz*
Sponsoring Editor: *Beth Kaufman*
Development editor: *Terri Wise*
Senior marketing manager: *Daniel M. Loch*
Associate project manager: *Catherine R. Schultz*
Senior production supervisor: *Michael R. McCormick*
Media producer: *Lance Gerhart*
Senior designer: *Pam Verros*
Associate supplement coordinator: *Joyce J. Chappetto*
Cover design: *Asylum Studios*
Cover photographs: *©Photodisc/©Stone*
Typeface: *10/12 Times Roman*
Compositor: *Carlisle Communications, Ltd.*
Printer: *R. R. Donnelley & Sons Company*

Library of Congress Cataloging-in-Publication Data
Grewal, Inderpal.
    An introduction to women's studies : gender in a transnational world / Inderpal Grewal,
  Caren Kaplan.
      p.   cm.
    Includes index.
    ISBN 0-07-109380-X (alk. paper)
    1. Women's studies. 2. Sex differences—Political aspects. 3. Women in popular culture.
  4. Gender identity—Political aspects. I. Kaplan, Caren, 1955– II. Title.

HQ1180.G74   2002
305.4'071—dc21   2001042748

www.mhhe.com

ABOUT THE AUTHORS

Inderpal Grewal is Professor and Chair of Women Studies at San Francisco State University. A former high school teacher in India, she received her Ph.D. in English from the University of California at Berkeley. She is also a founder of Narika, an agency that addresses the needs of South Asian women in the United States, and she works with activist groups that focus on Asian women and immigration issues. She has authored a monograph and co-edited several books and journal issues, often with her long-time collaborator Caren Kaplan. Her special interests include the history of British imperialism, South Asian women in diaspora, and the new transnational feminist activism.

Caren Kaplan is Associate Professor and Chair of the Department of Women's Studies at the University of California at Berkeley. She received her Ph.D. in the History of Consciousness program at the University of California at Santa Cruz. The author of a monograph as well as the co-editor of several books, she has collaborated with Inderpal Grewal for many years on essays and edited collections. Her special interests are the history of Western and international feminism, feminist theory, and aspects of imperialism and globalization such as travel, tourism, and information technologies.

B R I E F   C O N T E N T S

C O N T E N T S

ACKNOWLEDGMENTS

This book represents a truly collaborative effort. We began working together close to fifteen years ago and we have been writing and editing projects together ever since. This book in particular reflects our long-standing experiences as teachers and administrators in women's studies departments. Teaching the introductory course on an almost yearly basis, we found that we agreed on the limitations of the usual course design. We also agreed that the introductory course should be one of the most exciting and engaging classes in the women's studies curriculum—for both teachers and students. This book represents a labor of love on our part, as it overtook several years of our lives. We are immensely proud of this project and what we learned by doing it.

We have been helped by so many people along the way. First, we want to thank Beth Kaufman, our primary editor at McGraw-Hill. When we were unsure about undertaking this project, Beth had a good answer to our every worry. Once we signed on to the project, Beth continued to support us in every way. Her vision and commitment to women's studies as a field is exemplary. We also want to thank Terri Wise, our developmental editor at McGraw-Hill, for her outstanding editorial assistance in the process of bringing this book to publication. Terri's expertise made our jobs much easier. Other folks at McGraw-Hill we worked with, such as Cara Harvey, Kelly Delso, Cathy Schultz, Dan Loch, and Christina Lembo, have helped us as well.

We have also been greatly aided by stellar research assistants. In the first stage of the project, Cynthia Golembeski did a herculean job of digging and collecting materials. Gillian Harkins picked up the ball and never let it drop as she helped us with research and production of the manuscript. We thank her for her good humor and moral support. We also want to thank Valerie Larson and Ben Ansell for their help with research. Phoebe Southwood helped us with a database early in the project and we thank her for her care and efforts. Finally, a special thanks goes to Deborah Cohler, our editorial assistant in the final stage of the project. Deb's meticulous work, sense of humor, and intelligent engagement with the theory and content of the project made it possible for us to complete this book. We cannot thank her enough for her help and companionship.

Both our universities supported this project in many ways. At San Francisco State University, Inderpal would like to thank Dean of Humanities Nancy McDermid and Associate Dean Susan Shimanoff for their interest in and support of this project. A summer stipend and course release from the university greatly aided this project. Jenna Gretsch and Lisa Warren kept the Women Studies Department office running smoothly and helped in all kinds of ways. Inderpal would also like to thank her colleagues in the Women Studies Department, Minoo Moallem, Chinosole, and M. A. Jaimes-Guerrero. At the University of California at Berkeley, Caren would like to thank the Undergraduate Research Assistant Program for a summer grant that funded a research assistant as well as the Beatrice Bain Research Group and Designated Emphasis in Women, Gender, and Sexuality Studies staff, Phoebe Southwood and Gee Gee Lang, as well as the Women's Studies Department staff, Carla Atkins Patterson and Althea Grannum-Cummings. She would like to thank Dean George Breslauer for his support as well as her colleagues in the Women's Studies department, Norma Alarcón, Wendy Brown, Evelyn Nakano Glenn, Barrie Thorne, and Trinh T. Minh-ha.

Many colleagues suggested ideas, specific pieces, or approaches for this project. We want to thank Tani Barlow, Amrita Basu, Lauren Berlant, Chung-moo Choi, Lawrence Cohen, Cathy Davidson, Carolyn Dinshaw, Judith Farquhar, Elena Glasberg, Yukiko Hanawa, Donna Haraway, Gretchen Jones, Miranda Joseph, Suad Joseph, Laura Kang, Kim Kono, Rachel Lee, Lydia Liu,

Minoo Moallem, Donald Moore, Ambra Pirri, Allan Pred, Jasbir Puar, Priti Ramamurthy, Erica Rand, Brinda Rao, Sherene Razack, Lisa Rofel, Mary Ryan, Marilyn Schuster, Ella Shohat, Eric Smoodin, Jenny Terry, Susan Van Dyne, Ginette Verstraete, Leti Volpp, Robyn Wiegman, and Ken Wissoker.

We would like to thank the following reviewers for their comments on the manuscript in various stages of its development: Lisa Bowleg—Georgetown University, Nupur Chaudhuri—Kansas State University, Carolyn DiPalma—University of South Florida, Sophie Ho—Purdue University, Patricia Huckle—San Diego State University, Lisa Koogle—Russell Sage College, Joyce Ladenson—Michigan State University, and Eve Oishi—California State University, Long Beach.

We have been grateful for suggestions and feedback at forums where we presented our project in process, in particular, the meeting on international feminism at the University of Washington in Seattle in February 2000 (organized by Tani Barlow and Alys Weinbaum), a panel organized by Robyn Wiegman at the 1999 NWSA meetings, a seminar at the University of California at Irvine sponsored by Women's Studies, and a symposium at Smith College in January 2000. Minoo Moallem, Deborah Cohler, and Chinosole each taught the course as we designed it at San Francisco State University and gave us extremely valuable feedback. Our teaching assistants for the course were invaluable in helping us revise and rethink our project. Thanks to Lee Ann Assalone, Iliana Cordero, Valerie Larsen, Chris Guzaitis, and Sima Sakhshari at SFSU and thanks to Kim Kono, Christina Grijalva, and Jennifer Hosek at UCB. Our students in the course in both universities have been our greatest support and inspiration. Over a series of years we "test-drove" the textbook in our introductory classes and our students gave us the best feedback of all—their attention, their best efforts, and their embrace of learning to think about women and gender in a transnational frame.

In particular, we would like to thank our colleagues and friends whose work and comradeship means so much to us. Minoo Moallem has been friend, interlocutor, and inspiration for many years. Robyn Wiegman's intellectual and collegial support has meant much to us as we have worked on the project. Ella Shohat's warm support and interest is always sustaining to us. We are grateful, as always, to Tani Barlow for keeping things interesting in women's studies, challenging our ideas, and giving us her friendship and support.

Caren would like to thank both her first women's studies teacher, Jill Lewis, and her other significant scholarly and pedagogical influence, Lester Mazor, for showing her how to combine courage, intelligence, and a passion for justice into a pedagogical practice. Jim Clifford, Donna Haraway, and Hayden White influenced many of the ideas that underscore this project. She would also like to thank her friends Sig Roos, Ruthie Rohde, and Meredith Miller for their long-term friendship. Margie Cohen's interest and support has meant a great deal. Thanks to Roberta Smoodin, Mitch and Heidi Kaplan, and Henry Flax and David Norton for making family matter. Doris and Arthur Kaplan showed their usual patience and support. Their interest in this and all the other work she does makes all the difference in the world. Finally, but not least, Caren thanks Eric Smoodin for reading and talking about everything, and helping in every way.

Inderpal would like to thank her family. She hopes all her nieces and nephews will take "Intro to Women Studies" in their college years: Elena and Emily Grewal; Aneel, Rajneet, and Simar Chahal; Gurmehar and Mankaran Grewal; Anthony and Vinnie Jessel; and Kyle Adams. She is also grateful to so many family members who put up with her working hours—both Jessels and Grewals. In addition, she thanks all those in the Park Day community and those friends who supported her so much, especially Pat Abe, Dan Calef, Bobbi Shern Nikles, Roland Nikles, Sharon Ruffman, Marilyn Ancel, Lois Segal, Mona Halaby, Michelle Mercer, and Bruce Golden. Without Maia Lohuaru and Ana Franco, this work would not be completed. The "Narika girls" put up with her missing many events—even though she heard all about it later! And last, but never least, thanks to Alfred Jessel, who makes it all possible.

In closing, we would like to dedicate this book to our two best helpers and jokers, Kirin and Sonal Jessel. They took a keen interest in the book and kept our spirits up with their questions and commentary. "When will you be done?" they asked year after year. "Soon," we said, year after year. As we have worked on this project, we have watched them grow into strong, smart, energetic girls who view awareness of gender issues as a natural part of their education. We are thinking about their future as we write and do our work.

INTRODUCING WOMEN'S STUDIES: GENDER IN A TRANSNATIONAL WORLD

At the turn of the century, after three decades of women's studies and feminist activism, what lies ahead for feminist teachers and students? In this book we will explore the many issues and topics that have grown out of women's studies over the last three decades, as well as the new economic and social conditions that we face in the world today. Women's studies in the United States looks quite different now from its beginnings in the early 1970s. At that time, hardly any feminist scholarships existed in academic departments and much of the writing of earlier feminists had been neglected or ignored in college and university classrooms. As women's studies classes grew in number throughout the 1970s, 80s, and 90s, they became part of a vibrant popular feminist movement linked to transformations in society at large, such as legal, social, economic, political, and cultural change. For instance, advances in approaches to sexual assault and harassment were made in the legal arena, changing workplaces and homes. Current attitudes toward the family, women's work and mothering, and sexuality would have been almost unthinkable in the 1950s and early 60s. Feminists have played a major role in these changes and women's studies classrooms have assisted in the formulation of new ideas and the analysis and discussion of the role of women in society.

In the late 1970s and 1980s, women's studies responded to challenges by changing its curriculum and content. For example, the earlier homophobia that marked some programs was answered by new emphasis on the study of sexuality and lesbian cultures.

Teachers addressed the race and class bias of early women's studies programs and projects by changing curricular content to include the study of women of color and working class women. During this time period and throughout the 1990s, the curriculum expanded to include women with disabilities, women from multiple ethnicities, as well as transgender and bisexual communities. Across several decades and through debate and struggle as well as success and achievement, women's studies courses reflected an increasingly diverse and multicultural world.

However, one emphasis was still missing or marginalized: an international perspective on women's lives and concerns. Until recently, there were only two ways of addressing international issues in the women's studies classroom. The first method, popular since the 1970s, was to point to the similarities among women around the world and across time periods. This "common world of women" approach focused on topics such as motherhood and family structure. While this well-meaning approach seemed to propose a world of people without prejudices of skin color or national biases, all linked through biology or cultural activities that seem to be the lot of women the world over, it did not recognize that women are also divided by class, race, nationality, sexuality, and other signs of power. The second approach was a more hierarchical one that viewed Western culture as modern and other cultures as hoping or needing to catch up to the West in Western terms. This "women and development" approach posed an important set of questions about poverty, education, and health. However, many feminists could not avoid acknowledging that development programs in the poorest nations did not result in improvements in women's lives. Instead, women's power and influence in the household deteriorated as a result of modernization policies such as population control, increased industrialization, and the use of technology in agriculture. Given the problems with these two approaches, are there better ways for women's studies to introduce the study of women within and beyond the boundaries of the United States?

In writing and compiling this book, our hope is to encourage women's studies to invent new ways to internationalize our curricula. Without throwing out the valuable work from the past or ignoring our local concerns and agendas, we believe that it is the right time to alter our frameworks and diversify, once again, the subject matter of women's studies. The field has shown, over several decades of dialogue and debate, that it can change and become stronger. When the world changes, a field such as women's studies must engage these changes and lead the way in analyzing and discussing women and gender in new ways.

The goal of this introductory textbook is to encourage people to be more aware of the connections between their lives and what they learn about the rest of the world from their families, teachers, communities, and the media. For example, how do women's studies students understand world events in the newspaper? In 1999, an article and accompanying photograph appeared in national newspapers describing a visit by then-First Lady Hillary Clinton and her daughter Chelsea to Egypt for a women's rights conference. Hillary Clinton was quoted as supporting women's rights to education, health care, and political participation in so-called developing countries. The photograph showed mother and daughter with scarves covering their heads in accordance with Islamic tradition. We asked our students to write about this article and to focus on the significance of the main quotations and the ways the two women were dressed. Were there any connections between political and social issues in the United States and the presence of the spouse of the President at a women's rights conference in North Africa? In particular, we asked our students to think about how they might have read this article before they took the class. Most students reported that either they would have ignored the article altogether or, if they were interested in Hillary Clinton, they would

have accepted her endorsement of women's human rights and the need for development in Egypt and other "Third World" countries at face value. What they learned in the class was that things can be more complicated. Thus, Hillary Clinton may indeed support women's rights around the world, but it is in the best interest of the United States to represent this as a foreign need rather than one that could also be necessary for some women at home. Similarly, the adoption of modest headgear could signal her attempt to please her Egyptian hosts—but it also could be seen as a sign of her willingness to play the role of a "traditional" wife in the midst of her husband's impending impeachment trial. For women's studies students and teachers, there are many interesting things to notice and discuss about this article and photograph, some related to international issues and many connected to other topics closer to home in the United States.

This example from our class meetings shows that "internationalizing" the women's studies curricula does not mean focusing on the foreign, the strange, or exotic women in distant places. Nor does it mean an inattention is paid to women in the United States. Rather, to begin to think more internationally means that we learn to make connections between the lives and cultures of women in diverse places without reducing all women's experiences into a "common culture." We can begin by asking why we see certain items in the news and not others. How does information reach us? What local and national influences shape our view of the world in which we live? What do we think we need to know or learn about? How can we discover what other people think about us and why? These are just a few of the many questions raised in a course that internationalizes women's studies.

The next compelling set of concerns for our students is the increasingly global world in which we all live. Our jobs, our shopping habits, our recreation, the food we eat, are all determined to a greater or lesser degree by a global economy. The spread of this global economy around the world is known as globalization. This globalized economy is new in many ways, and we must learn more about the trade agreements and the international bodies that govern the financial world. But the seeds of this economy were sown much earlier. Starting in the sixteenth century, European expansion and colonization led to a world linked no longer simply through trade but also through military might and imperial rule. The inequalities produced by colonial expansion created a new map of the world. "West" and "East" came to refer to Europe and its "others" (all regions and cultures Europeans had encountered since the Crusades of the eleventh to the thirteenth centuries). In the twenty-first century, the legacies of these encounters remain within the difference between what is called the "North" (industrialized countries of North America and Europe) and the "South" (the so-called underdeveloped or rural countries of Latin America, Africa, and Asia, among others). Divisions between the so-called Third World and the First World reflect the aftereffects of earlier colonial and imperial policies. For instance, European colonization created a difference between those who were seen as "barbaric" or "uncivilized" and those who believed themselves to be "civilized" and superior. This difference was often expressed in racial, cultural, or national terms. In addition, throughout this time period, differences between men and women were tied to differences of race and class. Differences between women from "barbaric" cultures and those from "civilized" cultures become key to understanding gender then and today. These histories of gender in relation to race, class, nationality, culture, religion, sexuality, and other factors are a crucial part of the women's studies curriculum in what we call a transnational world, where inequality and differences rather than commonalities can be highlighted.

A transnational approach to women's studies requires some new methods. The term *transnational* means a number of different things. First of all, it means, literally, moving across national boundaries. Throughout this book we refer to the ways in which people, goods, money, and media images cross national boundaries in new ways that start to change our very idea of what we mean by national and local identities. Second, the term *transnational* enables us to see how this transformation of national boundaries depends not only on political changes but also on economic and cultural shifts. In women's studies we can look at these changes from an interdisciplinary perspective, drawing on many fields of study to begin to understand these complex conditions. Third, the term *transnational* refers to new forms of international alliances and networks across national boundaries that are enabled by new media and technologies as well as contemporary political, economic, and cultural move-

ments. These transnational networks are often aided by nongovernmental organizations and new social movements. Fourth, it is very important to stress that these new international communities and identities do not simply create an ideal world where women are all the same and equal. Rather, a transnational approach pays attention to the inequalities and differences that arise from new forms of globalization as well as from older histories of colonialism and racism. A transnational approach, as we use it in this book, emphasizes the world of connections of all kinds that do not necessarily create similarities. Rather, the transnational world in which we are all living is a world of powerful possibilities and challenges.

How to Use This Book

Women's studies scholarship is so industrious and interdisciplinary that the field seems to shapeshift every few years. This changing and dynamic quality of women's studies is exactly what excites those of us who participate in it. Yet it poses a problem for the authors of textbooks who need to present an overview of the field: How do you harness this growing entity that we call "women's studies"? This challenge confronts anyone who contemplates the introductory course. What to put in and what to leave out? Our decisions are difficult and often partial. Some people resort to disciplinary approaches to narrow down materials, creating a more "sociological" or "humanities-based" design. Others limit the course to the United States. Everyone worries about the introductory course: is it representative or inclusive enough? We addressed this problem by working together, combining our knowledge and experience as researchers and teachers. We also consulted students, friends, and colleagues in many fields. In many ways, we compounded our problems, since the materials for our book increased exponentially. But we also renewed our commitment to the intellectual and political challenge of the introductory course as a kind of laboratory for interdisciplinary work. And we rediscovered the pleasure of learning new ideas and content. In the process, the course has become more effective overall and interesting to teach. We hope that whether you are an instructor or a student, using this textbook will bring you a great deal of pleasure and new knowledge.

It is impossible to include everything we think is important to introduce the study of women and gender in a transnational frame. We have had to make difficult decisions. Even so, there is a lot of material in this book. Although we have taught the sections in this book exactly as you find them in the table of contents, we expect that people will use them as the foundation for a class and then add other materials that make sense based on their own expertise. We have ordered the sections in such a way that they build on each other, but we encourage users of the book to move around in it and find the paths through the materials that make the most sense. The instructor's manual also provides helpful suggestions and additional materials.

To help you decide how you want to use the book, we have written introductions to each of the four parts. These introductions provide you with primary concepts, questions, and terms as well as the rationale for the sections. In addition, our short comments precede each excerpted piece to situate the author or topic in a more specific way. We have included key words to clarify and define concepts and events as well as to identify historical figures. Summary questions follow each section to facilitate class discussion and reading comprehension. Many of our colleagues have asked us why we chose to use excerpts instead of leaving pieces intact. Our first answer is length! In attempting to use pieces that refer us to many different places and time periods, we found that we needed a variety of examples of scholarly and popular work. Our solution was to edit pieces and use only part of each one. Our comments at the start of each piece are a way to place them in a larger context and link them together. Nevertheless, we encourage people to read the entire article or book if they like. If a piece interests you, you can find the full citation in the bibliography at the end of the book.

As we have worked on this project, we have been thinking a great deal about the different kinds of people who choose to teach and to take courses in women's studies. Since our goal for the course is to provide an interdisciplinary introduction to the field, we have thought a lot about how to encourage our colleagues across many disciplines to use this book. For some, a book outside of their discipline may seem inadequate. Yet, in putting together a book on international and transnational issues, we have found that we need many disciplines as well as contributions from interdiscipli-

nary fields. Such an approach allows us to see how gender comes to mean different things in different places in the modern world and how emerging feminist movements can draw upon this history in their organizing and theorizing. In the years we have worked on this textbook, we have read work in many fields. We have tried to include as many approaches as we could. There are certainly some topics and approaches that are not represented in this book and some locations or regions that we have not mentioned. Similarly, there may be important issues we have not been able to include. This book is a place to begin the study of women and gender in a transnational world. There is much more to be said. We hope that this book will inspire you to add materials and bring your own interests and concerns to the introduction of women's studies.

The Sections of the Book

I. Women's Bodies in Science and Culture

How to begin the study of women and gender in a transnational world? There are many points of entry to this interdisciplinary field. We decided to begin this textbook at the point that works for us and for many of our students: the rise of Western science and the emergence of modern notions of sexual and racial difference. If we understand this history, we can see how terms and concepts that we take for granted, such as *sex, gender,* and *race,* change their meaning and significance over time. Therefore, we begin this textbook by asking questions about the history of scientific and medical knowledge as a way to demonstrate that all kinds of information about bodies, male and female, raced or classed or ethnicized, come from a social or cultural source. How some of these sources gain power and credibility, influencing ideas about men and women and society in general, and how some do not is a key part of women's studies. The spread of these ideas and explanations about sex, gender, and race is influenced by economic, political, and cultural changes on a global scale.

The pieces excerpted in this section introduce the history of science and medicine in a way that shows how different people are studied and defined according to methods that place some populations and groups in very unequal relations to others. In particular, we look at the notion of scientific objectivity as it has been applied to human biology and the rise of sex differences as the primary explanation for human diversity. We also examine the participation of women in science and technology. The rise of eugenics and other racialized sciences of population control is included in this section to provide links among the history of racism and European colonialism, biological notions of sexual difference and social class, and stakes in controlling or influencing reproduction. Crucial to the history of women's bodies in science and medicine are the new local and global forms of education and organizing activities. These activities have altered the relationship between gender, science, and medicine.

II. Gendered Identities: Individuals, Communities, Nations, Worlds

Identity is a crucial part of feminist analysis. In the first part of the book, we show how science and medical knowledge create powerful identities of gender, race, class, and ethnicity in the modern period. In Part Two, we assemble materials that show how specific identities become crucial to the operation of the nation-state; that is, how the political structure that has become the dominant form of government around the world produced a new kind of political entity—the individual citizen, who can vote, own property, and participate in national life. What role have women played in the formation of nation and state in modern times? How does gender shape and inform politics on a local level in communities as well as on a larger scale? Just as the economic system of capitalism brought about new needs for technologies and scientific practices, the emergence of democratic nation-states in Europe and its former colonies has prompted new roles and identities for people, such as the citizen and the individual. In this part of the book, we explore the ways that the modern state requires national, ethnic, and gendered identities in order to operate. Just as every person in the modern world must possess a nationality, it seems that each person must be able to be identified fully and clearly as male or female. Since most people also hold identities in relation to families and other groups, we can see that there are many possible identities that can influence the power and agency that women hold in the world.

III. Representations, Cultures, Media, and Markets

Representation and gender are key issues in women's studies. Over the last thirty years, feminists have studied how women have been portrayed in art and popular culture in many periods of time. Stereotypes, both negative and positive, have been examined in areas such as politics, media, art, literature, advertising, and film. Thus, we have come to understand femininity and masculinity through the ways that culture conveys dominant notions of gender, race, class, and sexuality. In addition, the points of view and the work of many women who have been marginalized or oppressed have been sought out and recovered.

Recasting these issues in a transnational framework, we need to consider the industries that produce knowledge and ways of seeing. For example, images of women who appear to be "exotic" or "primitive" or "natural" cannot be viewed only as gendered but must be seen as part of the history of capitalism and modern imperialism. The power to produce and disseminate information in the context of modern European colonization has enabled the proliferation of various kinds of stereotypes linked not only to race but also to religion, nationality, sexuality, and class. In women's studies, therefore, we can learn about industrialization and the expansion of capitalism through communication technologies and media such as print, cinema, and the Internet. The globalization of advertising and media brings with it newly gendered meanings of the body, beauty, family, and culture. In this part of the book, we aim to provide not only a view of the various representations of gender that proliferate in the world but also an understanding of the production and consumption of these images and ideas.

IV. Gendering Globalization and Displacement

This part of the book discusses displacement in the context of globalization; that is, how the movements of goods, services, finance, people, and ideas have changed in the modern period. Since globalization shapes contemporary ideas about gender and links gendered roles across national boundaries, we examine both economic and cultural aspects of the emergence of this modern global world. What do we mean by "modern" and by "global"? The phenomenon that we are examining here has been in the making for at least five centuries. From the fifteenth century, colonization and conquest began to change the ways in which people everywhere lived and worked, along with their sense of identity and belonging. The dramatic increase in prosperity in Europe brought about by colonization was linked directly to the impoverishment and genocide of people in the colonized zones. This prosperity and the search for more resources and markets encouraged more circulations of people and goods. Travel for trade and for war led to the development of transportation routes that, in later periods, enabled tourism as well as migration and urbanization. The forced displacement of millions of people through slavery and indentured labor contributed to the profits of the industrialized nations. These displacements continue to leave a legacy in which forms of culture and identity rooted in a place of origin become the basis for nationalist social and political movements.

In closing the book with this section, we want to focus on the ways that gender comes to matter in these diverse displacements. How has this history affected different women and in what ways? If some women have traveled for leisure, others have traveled to work in fields or homes or factories. When women are displaced by war or famine, they may face specific challenges and risks. Slavery and involuntary displacement

have affected women in particular ways. In looking at many forms of displacement across this long modern period, we ask: Has globalization created a common world for women? In Part Four, we provide examples of the ways in which the idea of a common world for women remains in tension with the continuing inequalities that globalization generates. These tensions are signs of connection or links between women as well as points of opportunity for deeper understanding and social change.

Conclusion

We end this book with a brief consideration of why feminism still matters in the new century. If we accept that women's studies and feminist approaches will always be changing in relation to current conditions and needs, then part of our task in this field is to recognize and comment on contemporary issues and debates, such as the effects of globalization. In our view, the task posed at this point in time is how to think transnationally. The world in which we live is not simply bounded by the borders of one community or nation. We will better understand feminist futures if we acknowledge the ways in which we are part of a complex and connected world, a world that is undoubtedly transnational.

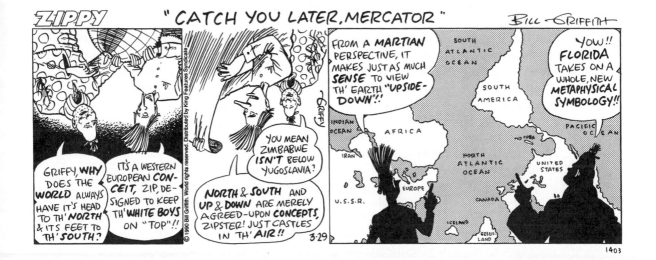

1403

Women's Bodies in Science and Culture

Why start an introduction to women's studies textbook with a discussion of science and medicine? If we begin our study of women's lives by considering what makes women and men distinct in different cultures and time periods, we first have to ask what counts as difference. Many people think that biology answers such a question once and for all. But science (including biology) has a history. People produce ideas and methods for science based on their sense of what is needed and important for their society. None of these ideas is neutral. The categories that science creates are often seen as truths that cannot be challenged. Yet studying the history of science shows us that ideas and methods have always changed. Feminists are interested in tracing the ways that women and men have been identified, described, and categorized by science in any given location and time period. In the case of sex difference, we need to learn the history of how categories of male and female (i.e., gender categories) are created and used by the sciences. Moreover, we need to see how gender is intertwined with and often dependent on other categories, such as racial and class difference.

When we use the word "science" we tend to think of value-neutral information that describes precisely and objectively how nature works. But even a superficial knowledge of different cultures and time periods suggests that such a view of science is limited to a Western perspective. In the modern period, this Western notion of science has become extremely powerful and widespread. For this very reason, in this section we will focus on Western science and its modes of thinking about and describing the world. Other ways of thinking and of describing the natural world, for instance Chinese or Native American medicine, remain in use in many places but do not appear to have power and legitimacy in the West. These other kinds of practices become marked as "traditional" or "alternative," while Western science is believed to be "modern" and legitimate. In recognizing the history of the rise of the "new" science in Europe and the loss of legitimacy of other kinds of scientific practices, we are not suggesting that any form of science is good or bad in and of itself. Rather, we want to question how dominant ways of thinking about science and medicine have created the ideas about differences between men and women that we live with today.

One of the primary hallmarks of Western science is the division of the world between nature and culture. In this division, nature stands for the untouched and unchanging natural world, while culture stands for the changing ways of human beings across time and space. In this framework, it is assumed that science studies nature and seeks to unlock its secrets. Once unlocked, the secrets of nature come to have the status of "truth." Along with the attributes of objectivity and truth, this form of science brings with it views on differences between men and women, and races, sexualities, and economic and social classes. Along the way, entire cultures and diverse modes of living and understanding became consigned to the past and designated as nonmodern or traditional. How and when did this kind of science arise?

Western science arose in Europe during the transition from the Middle Ages to the modern period. During this period of economic and cultural expansion, Europe gained power and authority through the new sciences that supported entire new industries and technologies. The "new" science opposed practices of magic and superstition, marking anything that was not seen as "rational" as unscientific and false. Thus, the healing practices of women, of people from non-European cultures, and of past cultures were viewed increasingly as naive superstition and any knowledges based on these ways of healing were dismissed as myth. Once capitalism established itself in Europe through the Industrial Revolution and colonization, the "new" science and its medical versions became authoritative methods that created truths and certainties about the so-called natural world. When Europeans met people from other cultures as they traded and began to colonize areas of the world, they learned from and borrowed many ideas about mathematics, agriculture, astronomy, and healing. These practices were based on observation and long-established traditions and could well be called "scientific." However, at the end of the Middle Ages, as Western science gained strength through its association with new industries and technologies, the scientific practices of non-Western or premodern cultures were disregarded or devalued.

For example, in Europe itself during this time period, the "new" science increasingly viewed earlier methods of birth control and childbirth as unscientific. More and more often, reproduction and childbirth were seen to be the appropriate subject for the new scientific "experts," who were mostly men, and less and less the province of midwives and women themselves. With the professionalization of medicine, special practitioners (doctors and scientists) claimed the expertise to treat people's bodies as their objects of study. This process of professionalization and medicalization was to the advantage of males who became professionals in these new sciences and to the disadvantage of women who had served as healers and midwives and whose knowledge had given them higher status in their societies. Similarly, in places that encountered European traders and colonizers, forms of healing and medicine that were not Western were also dismissed as "unscientific" and useless.

Although women have participated in science in many ways throughout time and across cultures, as the "new" science grew more and more dominant, its primary ideas and methods of training and implementation became even more politically charged and unequal. It is hard to imagine today that differences between the sexes could be explained by anything other than biology. Yet, until the "new" science of the modern period in the West, different cultures explained differences between men and women in varied ways. For instance, Islamic humoralism differentiated between male and female bodies by their possession of cold and hot attributes rather than two different kinds of reproductive systems. Even in Europe until the late eighteenth century, bodies were believed to have one sex. In this belief system, women's bodies were viewed as a slightly inferior version of men's. However, once difference between the sexes took on a meaning influenced by the "new" science, with male bodies believed to be completely different from and superior to female bodies, the position of women in society in general, and in science and medicine in particular, became increasingly marginal or subject to male control.

These histories deepen our understanding of what might be at stake in producing information about sexual and racial difference (among others) in the modern period. Therefore, feminist scientists historicize their fields not to discredit science and medicine but to help us see that these fields are always produced by people—by human beings—who are not neutral, objective, or uninvested in what they do. All science tries to solve problems or raise new questions by identifying new problems to explore. But problems or questions are cultural; they are human-made—that is, political. They are filled with many agendas and purposes and they are never pure. In this view of science, we can interpret political and cultural struggles for control and power through the rise of science and medicine. This struggle for control has been termed "biopower"—the way biology and medicine are used by governments and other social interests to further the goals of those who are in power.

What views of women emerge from the sciences of "biopower"? How does difference turn into inequality in this time period? In Europe and the United States, the rising belief in scientific explanations that proposed biological differences as the foundation of racial and sexual difference (such as social Darwinism, Malthusianism, and eugenics) placed different women in new kinds of unequal relationships. While social Darwinism explained the origin and evolution of the human species through "scientific" studies of hierarchies of development and civilization, Malthusianism argued that increasing population was the greatest threat to the welfare of Western civilization. Eugenics brought together many strands of scientific research to lobby for the preservation of pure and superior human stock and the management and control, if not outright elimination, of those deemed *by science* to be inferior. These new ideas divided women along the lines of race and class as well as culture and nation. In particular, by the middle of the nineteenth century in Western culture, white, well-to-do women came to stand as the symbol of ideal motherhood to propagate the race and the nation, thereby preserving Western civilization.

This notion of ideal motherhood became normative in certain societies to the detriment of all those women who were neither white nor middle class nor heterosexual. Normative femininity became associated with qualities that supported the two-sex model of biological differences; normal women were perceived to be less intelligent, less assertive, and less able than men even as they were supposed to be exceptional in the domestic realm of home and mothering. Nonnormative femininity became associated with perversion, marginality, and nonreproductive sex and increasingly came to be seen as a pathology—something to be cured by biomedicine. The challenge for late nineteenth- and early twentieth-century middle-class feminists in the West was to capture one of the characteristics of nonnormative femininity—nonreproductive sex—and make it normative, part of middle-class life and marriage. In this process, the middle-class feminists cut themselves off from the social movements for women's health in general and allied themselves with eugenicists, whose projects were often overtly racist and classist.

Margaret Sanger, who is viewed by many as the "mother" of the birth-control movement, is an interesting example of the meeting of Malthusian eugenics, social Darwinian hierarchies, and the U.S. suffrage movement. Sanger's family was poor and working class and her sister was a domestic servant, like many other Irish immigrants at the close of the nineteenth century. Yet, during a period of labor unrest and increasing popular support for eugenics, Sanger directed her argument for birth control to the group that seemed to have the most potential to win political power: white, middle-class women. However, Sanger's campaign for birth control was viewed as very controversial. It was believed that birth control would degrade middle-class, white women, making them immodest and turning them into bad mothers. Proponents of birth control such as Sanger tried to advocate contraception within the confines of marriage and respectability, thereby severing ties with socialist groups, who were concerned with working women's health and safety rather than respectability. Then as now, health care for poor women was so inadequate that multiple pregnancies meant a declining standard of living. Turn-of-the-century organizers, like Emma Goldman, who tried to link basic health care to birth control, were arrested and charged with behaving indecently and corrupting public morals.

Margaret Sanger was arrested too. These experiences convinced her that advocating birth control for middle-class women as a way to enhance their sexuality and increase their independence was not going to work in a conservative political climate. Sanger turned away from the socialists and the labor organizers who were trying to improve health care and living conditions for the poor. Increasingly, she allied herself with the eugenicists who were organizing against the new waves of immigrants. These immigrants included people from Eastern and Southern Europe—Jews, Greeks, and Italians—as well as people from Asia, who were believed to be racially inferior. Instead of "birth control," the watchword became "population control." Population control attempted to restrain the sexuality and reproduction of the poor, non-whites, and colonized peoples. For middle-class women in the so-called developed nations, birth control was and continues to be viewed as a medical and personal right. It remains, therefore, controversial, expensive, and tightly regulated by governments and the medical profession.

The split in approach and politics between "birth control" and "population control" can be seen in debates about sterilization around the world. In Europe and the United States, middle-class women and men still find it difficult to obtain sterilization procedures. Once a middle-class woman, especially a white middle-class woman, has had children, it is uncommon for her to be offered sterilization as an option to control fertility. Meanwhile, many women deemed inferior by virtue of their race or class are forced into government-sponsored sterilization programs that were put into place by eugenicists in the 1930s and continue into the present day.

Across the world, especially in the so-called Third World, where population control is a high priority for governments and Western aid agencies, sterilization has been advocated through coercive means. Since the 1960s, aid programs to the so-called developing countries have been linked to population control and most governments have complied. For a poor country to become "developed"—that is, to become "modern"—it must show that population control is part of the way a nation-state can look after the welfare of its people. Even in the so-called developed countries, in poor and disenfranchised communities, sterilization is offered more often than the full range of possible forms of birth control. The question for feminists in women's studies is, what kinds of reproductive control and rights are available and to whom?

Internationally, women's health serves both as an indicator of the general health of a given society and as a distinct set of issues on its own. If maternal and child health are poor, it may be a sign of a general lack of health care and services or it may be a sign that women's status and power are very low. One of the biggest problems women around the world face is the way that biomedicine has turned women's ability to menstruate, to become pregnant, and to give birth into a medical condition that requires scientific intervention and control. Consequently, governments become increasingly interested in women's reproductive capacities and come to play a larger and often more intrusive role in women's lives. So we have to understand these technologies not as neutral techniques and approaches but as tools of a particular society with specific agendas and aims. Who sets these agendas and aims?

Can we imagine an approach to women's reproductive capacities that views them not as a disease or a medical problem to be solved but as a set of physical properties that have some distinct characteristics requiring some specialized attention and assistance? Or can we imagine women's reproductive capacities as somewhat different from men's but also linked? This view would acknowledge that men's and women's "biology" probably share many more features than not and that reproduction is also a shared rather than a distinct set of concerns. What changes in science or medicine would enable us to ask these questions?

To put this somewhat differently, can we refuse or reject Western science and medicine, with their legacy of social and political inequalities? There are many debates among feminists on this topic. Some feminists believe that we should embrace "alternative" medicine and science. However, this approach can lead us to romanticize the practices of the past or of another culture without fully appreciating or understanding how these practices work in their own contexts. Other feminists argue that science and medicine should be studied to better understand how, in all cultures, forms of power shape perceptions of gender in relation to many other differences. Moreover, some feminists point out that in many locations "traditional" and "modern" practices of healing coexist, sometimes in contention and sometimes in cooperation. Who practices what and where is up to us to find out.

For instance, some non-Western healing traditions have always had many followers around the world. In many places, Western medicine is available only to the wealthy while the poor can afford only local healers. Since the 1970s, many governments have slashed their health care budgets and do not choose to fund health services. And even the wealthy turn to alternative medicine when faced with the sometimes invasive and debilitating techniques of Western medical technology. Moreover, many countries have never fully implemented Western medicine or its scientific approaches. China, for instance, developed its own science of the body through a state-sponsored medical system based on acupuncture and its remedies and treatments. However, we must not think that everything outside Western medicine and science is a utopian alternative. For example, Chinese medicine has its own hierarchies and inequities, in which gender and class differences are quite apparent.

As the example of the use of alternative medicine suggests, at this historical moment we are experiencing a profound dissatisfaction with the methods of modern Western biopower. Through the feminist study of the history of Western science, we have come to understand that modern life exacts a high price. The technology and industrialization that have been seen as the ways to become modern and developed have led to widespread environmental damage and vast social inequities. Disparities between the lives of the rich and the poor are greater than ever. Around the globe, poverty is a female condition. Feminists continue to ask why women are in this situation and how the industrialization and technology that promised so much delivered so little.

Because feminists have been at the forefront of researching, studying, and organizing activities against the worst effects of environmental destruction and industrialization as well as against the excesses and inequities of Western biomedicine, many feminist projects emphasize education and health advocacy. Some feminists argue for more transnational forms of organizing against what are seen as globalizing technologies of biomedicine such as sterilization, fertility treatments, and sex selection through amniocentesis. Through United Nations conferences, nongovernmental organizations, and other international agencies, feminists have worked for rules and regulations that address the health and education needs of women around the world. Other feminists believe there are too many differences between women to organize globally around single issues. They emphasize local strategies based on the needs of specific communities. Our viewpoint is that a knowledge of the history of science must inform all these kinds of organizing activities.

In women's studies we recognize that there are many ways of learning about the situation of women in different places and times. Feminist work generates new perspectives on established fields such as science and medicine without making claims for absolute truth. As the readings in Part One will demonstrate, there are many disciplines and fields available to aid us in understanding the history of Western biopower and the gender politics of the modern world. The feminist study of gender in this historical context reveals the ways that changes in science alter our views of and ideas about bodies, gender, race, and many other important categories.

Sex Differences Across Cultures

Sex and the Body

NELLY OUDSHOORN

Nelly Oudshoorn is a historian of science. This excerpt from her work presents a historical view of how differences between male and female bodies have been understood in scientific and biological thought in European culture since the sixteenth century. Oudshoorn shows us that knowledge about gender changes with time and place.

... The myriad ways in which scientists have understood sex provide many illuminating countermoves to the argument that sex is an unequivocal, ahistorical attribute of the body that, once unveiled by science, is valid everywhere and within every context. Early medical texts in particular challenge our present-day perceptions of male and female bodies. For our postmodern minds it is hard to imagine that for two thousand years, male and female bodies were not conceptualized in terms of differences. Medical texts from the ancient Greeks until the late eighteenth century described male and female bodies as fundamentally similar. Women had even the same genitals

Nelly Oudshoorn, "Sex and the Body," *Beyond the Natural Body: An Archaeology of Sex Hormones,* New York: Routledge, 1994: 6–11.

as men, with one difference: "theirs are inside the body and not outside it." In this approach, characterized by Thomas Laqueur as the "one-sex model," the female body was understood as a "male turned inside herself," not a different sex, but a lesser version of the male body (Laqueur 1990). Medical textbooks of this period show drawings of the female genitals that stress their resemblance to male genitalia so vividly that one could believe them to be representations of the male penis. For thousands of years the "one-sex model" dominated biomedical discourse, even to such an extent that medical texts lacked a specific anatomical nomenclature for female reproductive organs. The ovary, for instance, did not have a name of its own, but was described as the female testicle, thus referring again to the male organ. The language we are now familiar with, such as vagina and clitoris, simply did not exist (Laqueur 1990: 5,96).

This emphasis on similarities rather than differences is also present in the texts of anatomists who studied parts of the body other than the reproductive organs. For Vesalius, the father of anatomy, "sex was only skin deep, limited to differences in the outline of the body and the organs of reproduction. In his view, all other organs were interchangeable between the sexes" (Schiebinger

Key Terms

biomedical The biology of bodies; basis of medical knowledge.

discourse A concept drawn from the work of Michel Foucault, the French historian and philosopher of the late twentieth century, that refers to a dominant or powerful way of thinking.

gender The assignment of masculine and feminine characteristics to bodies in cultural contexts.

sex The categories of male and female and the biological characteristics and properties of bodies placed in these categories.

1989: 189). In his beautiful drawings of the skeleton in *Epitome,* an anatomical atlas that appeared in 1543, Vesalius did not give a sex to the bony structure of the body (Schiebinger 1989: 182). This (as we would now perceive it) "indifference" of medical scientists to bodily differences between the sexes does not seem to be a consequence of ignorance of the female body. Since the fourteenth century, the dissection of women's bodies *was* part of anatomical practice (Schiebinger 1989: 182). According to Laqueur, the stress on similarities, representing the female body as just a gradation of one basic male type, was inextricably intertwined with patriarchal thinking, reflecting the values of an overwhelmingly male public world in which "man is the measure of all things, and woman does not exist as an ontologically distinct category" (Laqueur 1990: 62).

It was only in the eighteenth century that biomedical discourse first included a concept of sex that is more familiar to our present-day interpretations of the male and the female body. The long-established tradition that emphasized bodily similarities over differences began to be heavily criticized. In the mid-eighteenth century, anatomists increasingly focused on bodily differences between the sexes and argued that sex was not restricted to the reproductive organs, or as one physician put it: "the essence of sex is not confined to a single organ but extends, through more or less perceptible nuances, into every part" (Schiebinger 1989: 189). The first part of the body to become sexualized was the skeleton. If sex differences could be found in "the hardest part of the body," it would be likely that sex penetrated "every muscle, vein, and organ attached to and molded by the skeleton" (Schiebinger 1989: 191). In the 1750s, the first female skeletons appeared in medical textbooks. Londa Schiebinger has described how anatomists paid special attention to those parts of the skeleton that would become socially significant, amongst which was the skull. The depiction of the female skull was used to prove that women's intellectual capacities were inferior to those of men (Schiebinger 1986). The history of medicine in this period contains many illustrations of similar reflections of the social role of women in the representation of the human body. Anatomists of more recent centuries "mended nature to fit emerging ideals of masculinity and femininity" (Schiebinger 1989: 203).[1] In nineteenth-century cellular physiology the

medical gaze shifted from the bones to the cells. Physiological "facts" were used to explain the passive nature of women. The biomedical sciences thus functioned as an arbiter in sociopolitical debates about women's rights and abilities (Laqueur 1990: 6, 215).

By the late nineteenth century medical scientists had extended this sexualization to every imaginable part of the body: bones, blood vessels, cells, hair, and brains (Schiebinger 1989: 189). Only the eye seems to have no sex (Honegger 1991: 176). Biomedical discourse thus shows a clear shift in focus from similarities to differences.[2] The female and the male body now became conceptualized in terms of opposite bodies with "incommensurably different organs, functions, and feelings" (Laqueur 1990: viii).

Following this shift, the female body became the medical object par excellence (Foucault 1976), emphasizing woman's unique sexual character. Medical scientists now started to identify the "essential features that belong to her, that serve to distinguish her, that make her what she is" (Laqueur 1990: 5). The medical literature of this period shows a radical naturalization of femininity in which scientists reduced woman to one specific organ. In the eighteenth and nineteenth centuries scientists set out to localize the "essence" of femininity in different places in the body. Until the mid-nineteenth century, scientists considered the uterus as the seat of femininity. This conceptualization is reflected in the statement of the German poet and naturalist Johann Wolfgang von Goethe (1749–1832): Der Hauptpunkt der ganzen weiblichen Existenz ist die Gebaermutter (The main point [or the essence] of the entire female existence is the womb) (Medvei 1983: 213).

In the middle of the nineteenth century, medical attention began to shift from the uterus to the ovaries, which came to be regarded as largely autonomous control centers of reproduction in the female animal, while in humans they were thought to be the "essence" of femininity itself (Gallagher and Laqueur 1987: 27). In 1848, Virchow (1817–1885), often portrayed as the founding father of physiology, characterized the function of the ovaries:

It has been completely wrong to regard the uterus as the characteristic organ. . . . The womb, as part of

the sexual canal, of the whole apparatus of reproduction, is merely an organ of secondary importance. Remove the ovary, and we shall have before
us a masculine woman, an ugly half-form with the
coarse and harsh form, the heavy bone formation,
the moustache, the rough voice, the flat chest, the
sour and egoistic mentality, and the distorted outlook . . . in short, all that we admire and respect in
woman as womanly, is merely dependent on her
ovaries.

(Medvei 1983: 215)

The search for the female organ par excellence was not
just a theoretical endeavor. The place in the body where
the "essence" of femininity was located became the object of surgical interventions. The ovaries, perceived as
the "organs of crises", became the paradigmatic object
of the medical specialty of gynecology that was established in the late nineteenth century (Honegger 1991:
209, 211). The medical attention given to the ovaries resulted in the widespread practice of surgical operations
for removal of the ovaries in many European countries,
as well as in the United States. In the 1870s and 1880s,
thousands of women were subjected to this drastic procedure for the treatment of menstrual irregularities and
various neuroses (Corner 1965: 4).

Early in the twentieth century, the "essence" of femininity came to be located not in an organ but in chemical substances: sex hormones. The new field of sex
endocrinology introduced the concept of "female" and
"male" sex hormones as chemical messengers of femininity and masculinity. This hormonally constructed
concept of the body has developed into one of the dominant modes of thinking about the biological roots of sex
differences. Many types of behavior, roles, functions
and characteristics considered as typically male or female in Western culture have been ascribed to hormones.[3] In this process, the female body, but not the
male body, has become increasingly portrayed as a body
completely controlled by hormones. At this moment,
the hormones estrogen and progesterone are the most
widely used drugs in the history of medicine. These substances are a popular means of controlling fertility and
are used for numerous other purposes: as menstruation
regulators or abortifacients, in pregnancy tests, and as
specific medications for female menopause. Hormones
are produced by pharmaceutical companies and delivered to women through a worldwide distribution network, including Third World countries (Wolffers et al.
1989: 27). This was not so a century ago. Our grandmothers did not know of any hormones: estrogen and
progesterone as such did not exist in the nineteenth century. The concept of hormones was coined in 1905, and
it took two decades before pharmaceutical companies
began the mass production of hormones. Nowadays millions of women take hormonal pills and many of us have
adopted the hormonal model to explain our bodies.

[. . .] Feminist studies have pointed out that cultural
stereotypes about women and men play an important
role in shaping scientific theories. The major question
that emerges then is: to what extent do scientists use
cultural notions in their research practice?

NOTES

1. Ludmilla Jordanova gave another striking example in her
analysis of the representation of the female and male body in the
wax models used for making anatomical drawings in the biomedical
sciences in France and Britain in the eighteenth and nineteenth centuries. She described how these wax models depict male figures as
active agents and females as the passive objects of sexual desire.
These female figures, or "Venuses," lie on the velvet or silk cushions, whereas male figures are usually upright, and often in positions
of motion, thus reflecting the cultural stereotypes of the active male
and the passive female (Jordanova 1980: 54).

2. This shift seems to have been caused by epistemological and
sociopolitical changes rather than by scientific progress. In *Making
Sex,* Thomas Laqueur described this shift in the context of changes
in the political climate. The French Revolution and new liberal
claims in the seventeenth century led to new ideals about the social
relationships between men and women, in which the complementarity between the sexes was emphasized. This theory of complementarity "taught that men and women are not physical and moral
equals but complementary opposites." Women now became viewed
as "fundamentally different from, and thus incomparable to, men"

(Laqueur 1990: 32, 216, 217). The theory of sexual complementarity was meant to keep women out of competition with men, designing separate spheres for men and women. In this theory, which came to be known as the "doctrine of the two spheres," the sexes were expected to complement, rather than compete with, each other.

The shift from studying similarities to differences was not caused by new scientific findings; on the contrary, Laqueur described how scientific literature provided many new discoveries which could have strengthened the one-sex model. The new field of embryology, for instance, claimed that reproductive organs "begin from one and the same embryonic structure," offering support to the earlier belief in the similarity between male and female reproductive systems (Laqueur 1990: 169). However, Laqueur does not present a simple causal model for scientific and political changes: "these social and political changes are not, in themselves, explanations for the reinterpretation of bodies . . . none of these things caused the making of a new sex body. Instead, the remaking of the body is itself intrinsic to each of these developments" (Laqueur 1990: 11).

3. See Briscoe (1978); Fausto-Sterling (1985); Fried (1982); Messent (1976); Money and Ehrhardt (1972); Rogers (1976).

SOURCES

Briscoe, A. M. (1978). "Hormones and Gender," in E. Tobach and B. Rosoff (eds), *Genes and Gender,* New York: Gordian.

Corner, G. W. (1965). "The Early History of Oestrogenic Hormones," *Proceedings of the Society of Endocrinology* 33: 3–18.

Fausto-Sterling, A. (1985). *Myths of Gender: Biological Theories about Women and Men,* New York: Basic Books.

Foucault, M. (1976). *Histoire de la sexualite, 1: La Volonte de savoir.* Gallimard.

Fried, B. (1982). "Boys Will Be Boys Will Be Boys: The Language of Sex and Gender," in R. Hubbard, M. S. Henefin, B. Fried (eds), *Biological Woman: The Convenient Myth,* Cambridge: Schenkman.

Gallagher, C., and Laqueur, T., (eds) (1987). *The Making of the Modern Body: Sexuality and Society in the Nineteenth Century,* Berkeley, Los Angeles, and London: University of California Press.

Honegger, C. (1991). *Die Ordnung der Geslechter: Die Wissenschaften vom Menschen und das Weib,* Frankfurt and New York: Campus Verlag.

Jordanova, Ludmilla. (1980) ."Natural Facts: A Historical Perspective on Science and Sexuality," in C. MacCormack, and M. Strathern (eds), *Nature, Culture and Gender,* New York: Cambridge University Press.

Laqueur, T. (1990). *Making Sex: Body and Gender from the Greeks to Freud,* Cambridge, Mass., and London: Harvard University Press.

Medvei, V. C. (1983). *A History of Endocrinology,* The Hague: MTP Press.

Messent, P. R. (1976). "Female Hormones and Behavior," in B. Lloyd, J. Archer (eds), *Exploring Sex Differences,* London and New York: Academic Press.

Money, J., and Ehrhardt, A. (1972). *Man and Woman, Boy and Girl,* Baltimore, MD: Johns Hopkins University Press.

Rogers, L. (1976). "Male Hormones and Behaviour," in B. Lloyd and J. Archer (eds), *Exploring Sex Differences,* London and New York: Academic Press.

Schiebinger, L. (1986). "Skeletons in the Closet: The First Illustrations of the Female Skeleton in the Nineteenth-Century Anatomy," *Representations* 14: 42–83.

Schiebinger, L. (1989). *The Mind Has No Sex? Women in the Origins of Modern Science.* Cambridge, Mass., and London: Harvard University Press.

Wolffers, I., Hardon, A., and Janssen, J. (1989). *Marketing Fertility: Women, Menstruation and the Pharmaceutical Industry,* Amsterdam: Wemos.

The Egg and the Sperm
EMILY MARTIN

Emily Martin is a feminist anthropologist. In this excerpt, she shows how scientific knowledge, believed to be factual and objective, reflects biases against women that are shared by the societies in which this knowledge is produced.

Egg and Sperm: A Scientific Fairy Tale

At a fundamental level, all major scientific textbooks depict male and female reproductive organs as systems for the production of valuable substances, such as eggs and sperm.[1] In the case of women, the monthly cycle is described as being designed to produce eggs and prepare a suitable place for them to be fertilized and grown—all to the end of making babies. But the enthusiasm ends there. By extolling the female cycle as a productive enterprise, menstruation must necessarily be viewed as a failure. Medical texts describe men-

Emily Martin, "The Egg and the Sperm: How Science Has Constructed a Romance Based on Stereotyped Male–Female Roles," in *Gender and Scientific Authority,* Eds. Barbara Laslett et al., Chicago: University of Chicago Press, 1996: 324–8, 337–9.

struation as the "debris" of the uterine lining, the result of necrosis, or death of tissue. The descriptions imply that a system has gone awry, making products of no use, not to specification, unsalable, wasted, scrap. An illustration in a widely used medical text shows menstruation as a chaotic disintegration of form, complementing the many texts that describe it as "ceasing," "dying," "losing," "denuding," "expelling."[2]

Male reproductive physiology is evaluated quite differently. One of the texts that sees menstruation as failed production employs a sort of breathless prose when it describes the maturation of sperm: "The mechanisms which guide the remarkable cellular transformation from spermatid to mature sperm remain uncertain. . . . Perhaps the most amazing characteristic of spermatogenesis is its sheer magnitude: the normal human male may manufacture several hundred million sperm per day."[3] In the classic text *Medical Physiology,* edited by Vernon Mountcastle, the male/female, productive/destructive comparison is more explicit: "Whereas the female *sheds* only a single gamete each month, the seminiferous tubules *produce* hundreds of millions of sperm each day" (emphasis mine).[4] The fe-

Key Terms

cybernetic The science of systems, human and mechanical, characterized by flexibility and self-regulation.
darwinism The ideas of Charles Darwin, who in the second half of the nineteenth century wrote that "natural selection" was the process in which nature ensured the survival of the best and the strongest.

psychodynamic Changing mental activities.
social darwinism The use of Darwin's ideas of natural selection to control populations or manipulate the survival of one group over another.
stereotype A way of thinking about a group or person based on a set of behaviors or qualities that are believed to be fixed and unchanging.

male author of another text marvels at the length of the microscopic seminiferous tubules, which, if uncoiled and placed end to end, "would span almost one-third of a mile!" She writes, "In an adult male these structures produce millions of sperm cells each day." Later she asks, "How is this feat accomplished?"[5] None of these texts expresses such intense enthusiasm for any female processes. It is surely no accident that the "remarkable" process of making sperm involves precisely what, in the medical view, menstruation does not: production of something deemed valuable.[6]

One could argue that menstruation and spermatogenesis are not analogous processes and, therefore, should not be expected to elicit the same kind of response. The proper female analogy to spermatogenesis, biologically, is ovulation. Yet ovulation does not merit enthusiasm in these texts either. Textbook descriptions stress that all of the ovarian follicles containing ova are already present at birth. Far from being *produced,* as sperm are, they merely sit on the shelf, slowly degenerating and aging like overstocked inventory: "At birth, normal human ovaries contain an estimated one million follicles [each], and no new ones appear after birth. Thus, in marked contrast to the male, the newborn female already has all the germ cells she will ever have. Only a few, perhaps *400,* are destined to reach full maturity during her active productive life. All the others degenerate at some point in their development so that few, if any, remain by the time she reaches menopause at approximately 50 years of age."[7] Note the "marked contrast" that this description sets up between male and female: the male, who continuously produces fresh germ cells, and the female, who has stockpiled germ cells by birth and is faced with their degeneration.

Nor are the female organs spared such vivid descriptions. One scientist writes in a newspaper article that a woman's ovaries become old and worn out from ripening eggs every month, even though the woman herself is still relatively young: "When you look through a laparoscope . . . at an ovary that has been through hundreds of cycles, even in a superbly healthy American female, you see a scarred, battered organ."[8]

To avoid the negative connotations that some people associate with the female reproductive system, scientists could begin to describe male and female processes as homologous. They might credit females with "producing" mature ova one at a time, as they're needed each month, and describe males as having to face problems of degenerating germ cells. This degeneration would occur throughout life among spermatogonia, the undifferentiated germ cells in the testes that are the long-lived, dormant precursors of sperm.

But the texts have an almost dogged insistence on casting female processes in a negative light. The texts celebrate sperm production because it is continuous from puberty to senescence, while they portray egg production as inferior because it is finished at birth. This makes the female seem unproductive, but some texts will also insist that it is she who is wasteful.[9] In a section heading for *Molecular Biology of the Cell,* a bestselling text, we are told that "Oogenesis is wasteful." The text goes on to emphasize that of the seven million oogonia, or egg germ cells, in the female embryo, most degenerate in the ovary. Of those that do go on to become oocytes, or eggs, many also degenerate, so that at birth only two million eggs remain in the ovaries. Degeneration continues throughout a woman's life: by puberty 300,000 eggs remain, and only a few are present by menopause. "During the 40 or so years of a woman's reproductive life, only 400 to 500 eggs will have been released," the authors write. "All the rest will have degenerated. It is still a mystery why so many eggs are formed only to die in the ovaries."[10]

The real mystery is why the male's vast production of sperm is not seen as wasteful.[11] Assuming that a man "produces" 100 million (10^8) sperm per day (a conservative estimate) during an average reproductive life of 60 years, he would produce well over two trillion sperm in his lifetime. Assuming that a woman "ripens" one egg per lunar month, or 13 per year, over the course of her 40-year reproductive life, she would total 500 eggs in her lifetime. But the word "waste" implies an excess, too much produced. Assuming two or three offspring, for every baby a woman produces, she wastes only around 200 eggs. For every baby a man produces, he wastes more than one trillion (10^{12}) sperm.

How is it that positive images are denied to the bodies of women? A look at language—in this case, scientific language—provides the first clue. Take the egg and the sperm.[12] It is remarkable how "femininely" the egg behaves and how "masculinely" the sperm.[13] The egg is seen as large and passive.[14] It does not *move* or *journey,* but passively "is transported," "is swept,"[15] or even "drifts"[16] along the fallopian tube. In utter contrast, sperm are small, "streamlined,"[17] and invariably active. They "deliver" their genes to the egg, "activate the developmental program of the egg,"[18] and have a "velocity" that is often remarked upon.[19] Their tails are "strong" and efficiently powered.[20] Together with the forces of ejaculation, they can "propel the semen into the deepest recesses of the vagina."[21] For this they need "energy," "fuel,"[22] so that with a "whiplashlike motion and strong lurches"[23] they can "burrow through the egg coat"[24] and "penetrate" it.[25]

At its extreme, the age-old relationship of the egg and the sperm takes on a royal or religious patina. The egg coat, its protective barrier, is sometimes called its "vestments," a term usually reserved for sacred, religious dress. The egg is said to have a "corona,"[26] a crown, and to be accompanied by "attendant cells."[27] It is holy, set apart and above, the queen to the sperm's king. The egg is also passive, which means it must depend on sperm for rescue. Gerald Schatten and Helen Schatten liken the egg's role to that of Sleeping Beauty: "a dormant bride awaiting her mate's magic kiss, which instills the spirit that brings her to life."[28] Sperm, by contrast, have a "mission,"[29] which is to "move through the female genital tract in quest of the ovum."[30] One popular account has it that the sperm carry out a "perilous journey" into the "warm darkness," where some fall away "exhausted." "Survivors" "assault" the egg, the successful candidates "surrounding the prize."[31] Part of the urgency of this journey, in more scientific terms, is that "once released from the supportive environment of the ovary, an egg will die within hours unless rescued by a sperm."[32] The wording stresses the fragility and dependency of the egg, even though the same text acknowledges elsewhere that sperm also live for only a few hours.[33]

[. . .]

Can we envision a less stereotypical view? Biology itself provides another model that could be applied to the egg and the sperm. The cybernetic model—with its feedback loops, flexible adaptation to change, coordination of the parts within a whole, evolution over time, and changing response to the environment—is common in genetics, endocrinology, and ecology and has a growing influence in medicine in general.[34] This model has the potential to shift our imagery from the negative, in which

the female reproductive system is castigated both for not producing eggs after birth and for producing (and thus wasting) too many eggs overall, to something more positive. The female reproductive system could be seen as responding to the environment (pregnancy or menopause), adjusting to monthly changes (menstruation), and flexibly changing from reproductivity after puberty to nonreproductivity later in life. The sperm and egg's interaction could also be described in cybernetic terms. J. F. Hartman's research in reproductive biology demonstrated fifteen years ago that if an egg is killed by being pricked with a needle, live sperm cannot get through the zona.[35] Clearly, this evidence shows that the egg and sperm *do* interact on more mutual terms, making biology's refusal to portray them that way all the more disturbing.

We would do well to be aware, however, that cybernetic imagery is hardly neutral. In the past, cybernetic models have played an important part in the imposition of social control. These models inherently provide a way of thinking about a "field" of interacting components. Once the field can be seen, it can become the object of new forms of knowledge, which in turn can allow new forms of social control to be exerted over the components of the field. During the 1950s, for example, medicine began to recognize the psychosocial *environment* of the patient: the patient's family and its psychodynamics. Professions such as social work began to focus on this new environment, and the resulting knowledge became one way to further control the patient. Patients began to be seen not as isolated, individual bodies, but as psychosocial entities located in an "ecological" system: management of "the patient's psychology was a new entrée to patient control."[36]

The models that biologists use to describe their data can have important social effects. During the nineteenth century, the social and natural sciences strongly influenced each other: the social ideas of Malthus about how to avoid the natural increase of the poor inspired Darwin's *Origin of Species.*[37] Once the *Origin* stood as a description of the natural world, complete with competition and market struggles, it could be reimported into social science as social Darwinism, in order to justify the social order of the time. What we are seeing now is similar: the importation of cultural ideas about passive females and heroic males into the "personalities" of gametes. This amounts to the "implanting of social imagery on representations of nature so as to lay a firm basis for reimporting exactly that same imagery as natural explanations of social phenomena."[38]

Further research would show us exactly what social effects are being wrought from the biological imagery of egg and sperm. At the very least, the imagery keeps alive some of the hoariest old stereotypes about weak damsels in distress and their strong male rescuers. That these stereotypes are now being written in at the level of the *cell* constitutes a powerful move to make them seem so natural as to be beyond alteration.

The stereotypical imagery might also encourage people to imagine that what results from the interaction of egg and sperm—a fertilized egg—is the result of deliberate "human" action at the cellular level. Whatever the intentions of the human couple, in this microscopic "culture" a cellular "bride" (or femme fatale) and a cellular "groom" (her victim) make a cellular baby. Rosalind Petchesky points out that through visual representations such as sonograms, we are given "*images* of younger and younger, and tinier and tinier, fetuses being 'saved.' " This leads to "the point of visibility being 'pushed back' *indefinitely.*"[39] Endowing egg and sperm with intentional action, a key aspect of personhood in our culture, lays the foundation for the point of viability being pushed back to the moment of fertilization. This will likely lead to greater acceptance of technological developments and new forms of scrutiny and manipulation, for the benefit of these inner "persons": court-ordered restrictions on a pregnant woman's activities in order to protect her fetus, fetal surgery, amniocentesis, and rescinding of abortion rights, to name but a few examples.[40]

Even if we succeed in substituting more egalitarian, interactive metaphors to describe the activities of egg and sperm, and manage to avoid the pitfalls of cybernetic models, we would still be guilty of endowing cellular entities with personhood. More crucial, then, than what *kinds* of personalities we bestow on cells is the very fact that we are doing it at all. This process could ultimately have the most disturbing social consequences.

One clear feminist challenge is to wake up sleeping metaphors in science, particularly those involved in descriptions of the egg and the sperm. Although the literary convention is to call such metaphors "dead," they are not so much dead as sleeping, hidden within the scientific content of texts—and all the more powerful for it.[41] Waking up such metaphors, by becoming aware of when we are projecting cultural imagery onto what we study, will improve our ability to investigate and understand nature. Waking up such metaphors, by becoming aware of their implications, will rob them of their power to naturalize our social conventions about gender.

NOTES

1. The textbooks I consulted are the main ones used in classes for undergraduate premedical students or medical students (or those held on reserve in the library for these classes) during the past few years at Johns Hopkins University. These texts are widely used at other universities in the country as well.

2. Arthur C. Guyton, *Physiology of the Human Body,* 6th ed. (Philadelphia: Saunders College Publishing, 1984), 624.

3. Arthur J. Vander, James H. Sherman, and Dorothy S. Luciano, *Human Physiology: The Mechanisms of Body Function,* 3d ed. (New York: McGraw-Hill, 1980), 483–84.

4. Vernon B. Mountcastle, *Medical Physiology,* 14th ed. (London: Mosby, 1980), 2:1624.

5. Eldra Pearl Solomon, *Human Anatomy and Physiology* (New York: CBS College Publishing, 1983), 678.

6. For elaboration, see Emily Martin, *The Woman in the Body: A Cultural Analysis of Reproduction* (Boston: Beacon, 1987), 27–53.

7. Vander, Sherman, and Luciano, 568.

8. Melvin Konner, "Childbearing and Age," *New York Times Magazine* (December 27, 1987), 22–23, esp. 22.

9. I have found but one exception to the opinion that the female is wasteful: "Smallpox being the nasty disease it is, one might expect nature to have designed antibody molecules with combining sites that specifically recognize the epitopes on smallpox virus. Nature differs from technology, however: it thinks nothing of wastefulness. (For example, rather than improving the chance that a spermatozoon will meet an egg cell, nature finds it easier to produce millions of spermatozoa.)" (Niels Kaj Jerne, "The Immune System,"

Scientific American 229, no. 1 [July 1973]: 53). Thanks to a *Signs* reviewer for bringing this reference to my attention.

10. Bruce Alberts et al., *Molecular Biology of the Cell* (New York: Garland, 1983), 795.

11. In her essay "Have Only Men Evolved?" (in *Discovering Reality: Feminist Perspectives on Epistemology, Metaphysics, Methodology, and Philosophy of Science,* ed. Sandra Harding and Merrill B. Hintikka [Dordrecht: Reidel, 1983], 45–69, esp. 60–61), Ruth Hubbard points out that sociobiologists have said the female invests more energy than the male in the production of her large gametes, claiming that this explains why the female provides parental care. Hubbard questions whether it "really takes more 'energy' to generate the one or relatively few eggs than the large excess of sperms required to achieve fertilization." For further critique of how the greater size of eggs is interpreted in sociobiology, see Donna Haraway, "Investment Strategies for the Evolving Portfolio of Primate Females," in *Body/Politics,* ed. Mary Jacobus, Evelyn Fox Keller, and Sally Shuttleworth (New York: Routledge, 1990), 155–56.

12. The sources I used for this article provide compelling information on interactions among sperm. Lack of space prevents me from taking up this theme here, but the elements include competition, hierarchy, and sacrifice. For a newspaper report, see Malcolm W. Browne, "Some Thoughts on Self Sacrifice," *New York Times* (July 5, 1988), C6. For a literary rendition, see John Barth, "Night-Sea Journey," in his *Lost in the Funhouse* (Garden City, N.Y.: Doubleday, 1968), 3–13.

13. See Carol Delaney, "The Meaning of Paternity and the Virgin Birth Debate," *Man* 21, no. 3 (September 1986): 494–513. She discusses the difference between this scientific view that women contribute genetic material to the fetus and the claim of long-standing Western folk theories that the origin and identity of the fetus comes from the male, as in the metaphor of planting a seed in soil.

14. For a suggested direct link between human behavior and purportedly passive eggs and active sperm, see Erik H. Erikson, "Inner and Outer Space: Reflections on Womanhood," *Daedalus* 93, no. 2 (Spring 1964): 582–606, esp. 591.

15. Guyton (n. 2 above), 619; and Mountcastle (n. 4 above), 1609.

16. Jonathan Miller and David Pelham, *The Facts of Life* (New York: Viking Penguin, 1984), 5.

17. Alberts et al., 796.

18. Ibid., 796.

19. See, e.g., William F. Ganong, *Review of Medical Physiology,* 7th ed. (Los Altos, Calif.: Lange Medical Publications, 1975), 322.

20. Alberts et al. (n. 10 above), 796.

21. Guyton, 615.

22. Solomon (n. 5 above), 683.

23. Vander, Sherman, and Luciano (n. 3 above), 4th ed. (1985), 580.

24. Alberts et al., 796.

25. All biology texts quoted above use the word "penetrate."

26. Solomon, 700.

27. A. Beldecos et al., "The Importance of Feminist Critique for Contemporary Cell Biology," *Hypatia* 3, no. 1 (Spring 1988): 61–76.

28. Gerald Schatten and Helen Schatten, "The Energetic Egg," *Medical World News* 23 (January 23, 1984): 51–53, esp. 51.

29. Alberts et al., 796.

30. Guyton (n. 3 above), 613.

31. Miller and Pelham (n. 17 above), 7.

32. Alberts et al. (n. 11 above), 804.

33. Ibid., 801.

34. William Ray Arney and Bernard Bergen, *Medicine and the Management of Living* (Chicago: University of Chicago Press, 1984).

35. J. F. Hartman, R. B. Gwatkin, and C. F. Hutchison, "Early Contact Interactions between Mammalian Gametes *In Vitro,*" *Proceedings of the National Academy of Sciences (U.S.)* 69, no. 10 (1972): 2767–69.

36. Arney and Bergen, 68.

37. Ruth Hubbard, "Have Only Men Evolved?" (n. 11 above), 51–52.

38. David Harvey, personal communication, November 1989.

39. Rosalind Petchesky, "Fetal Images: The Power of Visual Culture in the Politics of Reproduction," *Feminist Studies* 13, no. 2 (Summer 1987): 263–92, esp. 272.

40. Rita Arditti, Renate Klein, and Shelley Minden, *Test-Tube Women* (London: Pandora, 1984); Ellen Goodman, "Whose Right to Life?" *Baltimore Sun* (November 17, 1987); Tamar Lewin, "Courts Acting to Force Care of the Unborn," *New York Times* (November 23, 1987), A1 and B10; Susan Irwin and Brigitte Jordan, "Knowledge, Practice, and Power: Court Ordered Cesarean Sections," *Medical Anthropology Quarterly* 1, no. 3 (September 1987): 319–34.

41. Thanks to Elizabeth Fee and David Spain, who in February 1989 and April 1989, respectively, made points related to this.

REFERENCES

Darwin, C. (1871). *The Descent of Man, and Selection in Relation to Sex.* London: John Murray. 2 vols.

Ellis, H. H. (1894). *Man and Woman.* London: Walter Scott.

Freud, S. (1953–74). *The Standard Edition of the Complete Psychological Works of Sigmund Freud,* ed. James Strachey. London: Hogarth Press.

Gallop, J. (1982). *Feminism and Psychoanalysis. The Daughter's Seduction.* London: Macmillan.

Krafft-Ebing, R. von (1931). *Psychopathia Sexualis.* Brooklyn: Physicians and Surgeons Book Co.

L'Esperance, J. (1977). "Doctors and Women in Nineteenth Century Society: Sexuality and Role." In J. Woodward and D. Richards (eds.) *Health Care and Popular Medicine in Nineteenth Century England.* London: Croom Helm.

Weeks, J. (1981). *Sex, Politics and Society. The Regulation of Sexuality since 1800.* London: Longman.

——— (1985). *Sexuality and Its Discontents. Meanings, Myths and Modern Sexualities.* London: Routledge & Kegan Paul.

A Welcoming Soil: Islamic Humoralism
CAROL LADERMAN

We have read thus far about European histories of gender and biology. Now we turn, through the work of medical anthropologist Carol Laderman, to the knowledge produced in medieval Islam and Christianity about bodies that are gendered depending on how hot or cold and wet or dry they are. In medieval Islam, it was believed that bodies had "humors" and the possession of particular humors characterized male and female bodies. The spread of Islam through many parts of the world has ensured that the legacy of these ideas led to quite different ways of thinking about gender than we see in the European traditions.

Medieval Islamic Humoral Theory

. . . According to medieval humoral theory, foods, diseases, medicines, and many other aspects of nature could be scientifically classified according to their inherent qualities of heat, cold, dryness, and moisture. Heat and cold did not refer, necessarily, to thermal qualities; that is, squash hot off the stove was still considered to be extremely cold. Not only were foods, and

Carol Laderman, "A Welcoming Soil: Islamic Humoralism on the Malay Penninsula," in *Paths and Asian Medical Knowledge,* Charles Leslie and Allan Young, eds. University of California Press, 1992: 276–77.

so forth, rated as to humoral degrees, but their precise positions were often calculated as well, for example, in terms of "the beginning of the third degree" or "the end of the second." Health handbooks, such as the *Regimen Sanitatis Salernitanum* (Harington 1920) and the *Tacuinum Sanitatis* (Cogliati 1976) (translated into Latin from the work of Ibn Botlan), advised readers as to the effects of foods, their usefulness and dangers, and the means of neutralizing them. For example, cucumbers, which are cold and humid in the third degree, are useful in cooling fevers but may cause pain in the loins and stomach. They can be neutralized by the addition of honey and oil (both "hot"). Spinach, cold and humid in the second degree, should be fried with "hot" salt and spices to balance its humoral qualities.

Although medieval Islamic humoral theory emphasized the importance of balance for the maintenance of health, the ideal human body was not located on the humoral scale midway between the cold and hot, wet and dry polarities, but was hot and moist in the second degree (McVaugh 1975). (Temperance should lie between the first degree hot and first degree cold.) Heat that is not natural to the body could imperil it by causing putrefaction. Internal heat, however, was not only believed to increase the virility and courage of its possessor, it was considered "the great instrument with which the system . . . destroys hot things which are inimical to life

Key Terms

humors Fluids in the body that were believed to produce certain characteristics, including masculinity and femininity.

renaissance The revival of arts and literature in Western Europe since the fifteenth century.

. . . and protects also against injurious cold." Cold "produces only weakness and damage. It is for this reason that heat is called the innate heat while cold is not termed the innate cold" (Shah 1966).

Medieval physicians, such as Avicenna (Krueger 1963), Averroes (Blumberg 1961), Ibn Ridwan (Dols 1984), Ibn Botlan (Cogliati 1976), and Maimonides (1981), advised their patients to live prudent lives, since moderation in all things produced innate heat. Moderate amounts of sleep, a moderate degree of wakefulness, moderate exercise, moderate mental exertion, moderate quantities of food, moderate use of hot baths, moderate indulgence in pleasurable activities, moderation in the expression of emotions—all of these are beneficial to human well-being. Excess of any kind is destructive to health since it disturbs the innate heat. Thus, extremes of atmospheric temperature or topical applications, either hot or cold, are destructive to innate heat, excessive activity disperses it, excessive repose suppresses it, excessive food and drink smother it, insufficient food depletes it, strong emotions and too much pleasure destroy it—all are productive of cold, the absence of health. (Anger, in fact, was considered to deplete the innate heat by causing it to boil within the heart.) The predominance of heat and moisture ensures long life, since death is nothing more than cold and dryness.

When one considers the negative connotations of cold in medieval Islamic medical theory, it is not surprising to learn that women, the imperfect half of humanity, are naturally colder than men, and moister, since "their greater cold leads to the excessive formation of excrements" (Krueger 1963). Females are deficient in heat from the time of their conception. They are produced from the imperfect semen of their fathers' left testicles and deposited in the left side of their mothers' wombs, both of which are naturally colder than those on the right (Maclean 1980; Maimonides 1970). Women's slower metabolism burns food less efficiently. The residue changes to fat, which is stored to nourish their unborn babies and, later, used in milk production. The female form, broader in the hips and narrower in the shoulders than the male, is due to deficiency of heat, the driving force that sends matter up toward the head. Women's brains, therefore, lack the mental characteristics of heat: courage, liberality, moral strength, and honesty. Their lesser amounts of innate heat make women weaker and more vulnerable to sickness, particularly in their womanly parts and functions. They were advised to avoid sitting on cold stones, staying too long in a cold bath, and drinking cold water, since this would further deplete their innate heat and cause the uterus to ache, or even to slip its moorings (Rowland 1981). A cold, wet womb is a sterile womb, since "just as a wet soil and too much rain [it] will destroy seeds" (Elgood 1970).

The production of male seed was encouraged by the external application of heat and by a diet which emphasized foods that increase heat and excluded foods that increase cold. Although medieval and Renaissance theoreticians were careful to measure humoral qualities in precise degrees, a layman could arrive at a rough estimation by using this rule of thumb: those foods which taste sweet, salty, bitter, or sharp were heating, as are oils, fats, alcohol, and the flesh of animals, while those foods which are sour, astringent, or tasteless were cooling.

Once the seed was planted, it could still be imperiled by the mother's coldness. Miscarriage and premature labor were usually attributed to a disproportionate measure of cold and damp within the womb. Childbirth further depleted a woman's innate heat, putting her into a colder-than-normal condition for the duration of the postpartum period.

The intensely pleasurable sex act was considered to be fraught with danger for the male. Intercourse depleted his body of hot, moist semen, decreasing his body's strength and rendering his brain dry (Gorlin 1961). Averroes counseled moderation in sexual activity, explaining that those whose lust is excessive often die young, while Maimonides (1981) warned that only "one in a thousand dies of other diseases, the rest of the thousand of sexual overindulgence." Men were advised to avoid cold water and fruits after intercourse and to shun old women and women who had recently delivered, since both were extremely cold and would rob the man of his innate heat. The young mother would regain her heat in time, but the old, of both sexes, were permanently cold, a cold that increased with age, ending with death, the total absence of heat. A man who aspired to a long and healthy life, therefore, should locate himself in a warm climate, conduct himself with moderation in all things, avoid cold foods except in hot weather (unless they were balanced by heating ingredients), and marry a young wife.

Many of the precepts of medieval Islamic theory were incorporated into the Malay medical system, and continue to be salient today, but acceptance was selective. Some beliefs have remained essentially unchanged, others have been modified, and still others were never accepted, since they reversed the hot and cold polarities of pre-Islamic, aboriginal cosmology. . . .

REFERENCES

Blumberg, H. (1961). *Averroes' Epitome of Parva Naturalis.* Cambridge, Mass.: The Mediaeval Academy of America.

Cogliati, Arano L. (1976). *The Medieval Health Handbook (Tacuinum Sanitatis).* New York: George Braziller.

Dols, M. W. (1984). *Medieval Islamic Medicine.* Berkeley, Los Angeles, London: University of California Press.

Elgood, C. (1970). *Safavid Medical Practice.* London: Luzac and Co., Ltd.

Gorlin, E., ed. (1961). *Maimonides "On Sexual Intercourse."* Brooklyn: Rambash Publishing Co.

Harington, Sir J. (1920). *The School of Salernum: Regimen Sanitatis Salernitanum.* New York: P. B. Hoeber.

Krueger, H. C. (1963). *Avicenna's Poem on Medicine.* Springfield, IL: Charles C. Thomas.

Maclean, I. (1980). *The Renaissance Notion of Woman.* London: Cambridge University Press.

Maimonides. (1970). *Medical Aphorisms,* F. Rosner and S. Munter, ed. and trans. New York: Yeshiva University Press.

————. (1981). *The Book of Knowledge,* trans. H. M. Russell and Rabbi J. Weinberg, Edinburgh: Royal College of Physicians.

McVaugh, M. (1975). Discussion of medicinal degrees at Montpellier by Henry of Winchester. *Bulletin of the History of Medicine* 9:57.

Rowland, B. (1981). *The Medieval Woman's Guide to Health.* Kent, Ohio: Kent State University Press.

Shah, M. H. (1966). *The General Principles of Avicenna's Canon of Medicine.* Karachi: Naveed Clinic.

Androgynous Males and Deficient Females: Biology and Gender Boundaries in Sixteenth- and Seventeenth-Century China

CHARLOTTE FURTH

Charlotte Furth, a historian of China, explains that gender in sixteenth- and seventeenth-century China was based on a yin-yang dichotomy in which male and female were characterized by the ability to reproduce. This philosophy of opposites is different from the Western or Islamic systems of gendered opposites since it emphasizes reproductive capacity rather than behavior or essence per se.

Biological Sex and its Boundaries in Medicine: The False Male and the False Female

Biological anomaly—the appearance in one individual of physical characteristics which are sexually dysfunctional or thought appropriate to the opposite sex—seems to challenge accepted norms in a particularly

Charlotte Furth, "Androgynous Males and Deficient Females: Biology and Gender Boundaries in Sixteenth- and Seventeenth-Century China," *Late Imperial China* 9.2 (December 1988): 3–9, 12–16.

disturbing way. However, in Chinese biological thinking, based as it was on yin-yang cosmological views, there was nothing fixed and imutable about male and female as aspects of yin and yang. These two aspects of primary ch'i are complementary and interacting, so that each at all times dynamically influences the other and each enjoys times of ascendancy in the periodic rhythms of things. In medicine, yin and yang permeate the body and pattern its functions, and here as elsewhere they are interdependent, mutually reinforcing, and capable of turning into their opposites. This natural philosophy would seem to lend itself to a broad and tolerant view of variation in sexual behavior and gender roles.

In Chinese accounts of human biology we can see these classic cosmological notion at work in the standard interpretations of conception and sexual differentiation. "What is it that congeals at the time of sexual union to make the fetus? Though it is none other than the [male] essence (*ching*) and [female] blood (*hsueh*), made up of material dregs that exist in the world below, a tiny bit of pre-existent (*hsien t'ien*) true ch'i, moved to germinate by the feelings of desire, subtly mediates between them."

❧ *Key Terms* ❧

gender inversion When the gender characteristics or roles of one sex are assigned to the opposite sex.

yin-yang In Chinese thought, the two complementary forces or principles whose interplay makes up all phenomena.

This is the account in *Systematic Aid for the Disorders of Yin,* an authoritative seventeenth-century gynecological text.[1] Here female blood is not on a grosser material level than male semen; both are body fluids in one aspect and partake of heavenly ch'i in another. The sex of the child is determined simply by the relative ascendancy of yin or yang ch'i present at the moment of conception. In medical literature these forces are at times envisaged as internal to the bodies of the partners, as reproductive vitality. At times they are imagined as environmental influences, since yin and yang qualities inhering in such things as time of day, date or month or season of year, direction, moment in menstrual cycle of a woman, wind, weather—all are part of the total environmental force-field bearing on the event.

Thus we can see that human males are not "pure yang" or females "pure yin," and sexual differentiation depends upon the momentary balance of fluid forces in dynamically interacting relationship with one another. This fluidity further suggested to medical authorities ways to explain certain kinds of biological anomalies in human beings. Disorderly configurations of yin-yang influences at the time of conception were held responsible for multiple births and for physical and functional defects. "Scattered" or "dispersed" ch'i produces twins; "deficient" yang or yin ch'i produces sterile individuals; "contrary," "variegated," or "disordered" ch'i (*po ch'i, luan ch'i*) produces "*fei nan fei nü*" (those who are neither male nor female; or false males and false females).[2]

"Old mothers and young fathers produce overripe daughters; vigorous mothers and feeble (*shuai*) fathers produce weakling sons."[3] This is how medical authorities categorized the milder, borderline cases of biological insufficiency in men and women. Believing that individuals with subnormal reproductive capacities still had the potential for fruitfulness, doctors recommended that such girls be married early, while weddings be delayed for these boys. Only time would tell whether in fact such individuals were among those whose yin and yang ch'i was so fatally aberrant as to make them barren.

Serious anomaly began with barrenness in the functionally normal and extended to those with reproductively "useless bodies." Li Shih-chen's *Systematic Materia Medica* provides the best synthesis of the traditions concerning this in medicine and natural philosophy:

Normally ch'ien and k'un [active and latent aspects of the cosmos] make [human beings into] fathers and mothers; but there are five kinds of false males [*fei nan*] who cannot become fathers and five kinds of false females [*fei nü*] who cannot become mothers. Can it indeed be the case that defective males are deficient in yang ch'i while defective females have blocked yin ch'i? The false females are the corkscrew, the striped, the drum, the horned, and the pulse. . . . The false males are the natural eunuch, the bullock [casterated], the leaky, the coward, and the changeling.[4]

As explained by Li and other medical writers who repeated these classifications, four of the five terms applied to women refer to genital abnormalities of the sort that would make sexual penetration impossible. The fifth or "pulse" is a woman with highly erratic menses. One of five physical abnormalities, the "drum" (or in other versions "small door"), was well known in popular lore as a "stone maiden"—one whose hymen is impenetrable.[5]

By contrast with false females, false males are largely the functionally impotent, not the physically marred. The "coward" for example is "he who sees the enemy and refuses to engage."[6] The "leaky" is a male subject to uncontrolled or excessive seminal losses—a serious disorder in light of the medical view of reproductive fluids as measurable "vital essences" (*ching*) whose conservation is essential to both potency and longevity. Even the "natural eunuch" (*t'ien yen*)—a category defined in the ancient *Nei ching* medical classic as a male whose beard does not grow—in Li Shih-chen's later formulation is simply one "whose yang is impotent and of no use." Among males clear-cut physical anomaly is reserved for the "changeling."

"The changeling (*pien*) body is both male and female, what the common people call 'those with two forms' (*erh hsing*). The dynastic history of the Chin [Western Chin AD 265–419] considered them the product of disordered ch'i and called them 'human anomalies' (*jen k'o*). There are three types: those who can [both] serve men as women and serve women as men; those who are yin half the month and yang the other half; and those who can act as wife but not as husband. All of these have useless bodies."[7]

Although superficially parallel, false males and false females in fact were gendered classifications, the product of social assumptions about men and women. In accounts of borderline deficiency, an oversexed ("overripe") girl is produced by an excess of her youthful father's "yang ch'i." Vigorous mothers, if unchecked, weaken the sexual vitality of their sons. Yin energy doesn't lead to fecundity in girls but to weakness in men, and medical authorities don't identify any pathology of undersexed females or oversexed males. Similarly females fail biologically because of physical deformity; men are those whose sexual adequacy is defined in terms of performance. Moreover, the changelings with "two forms" are classed with males and described as capable of bisexual roles, in a manner that echos old Chinese legends of hermaphrodites as fantastic beings with superabundant erotic capabilities.[8] All of these asymmetries reflect the assumption that sexual action or initiative is a male attribute. Finally, false females merely fail to attain the proper role of women; only false males, in particular the eunuch and the changeling, are not merely deficient but appear to move toward the opposite, feminine, sexual pole.

Medical authority, then, defined the sexually normal in terms of reproductive capabilities alone. From one end of this spectrum the sterile person, even though she or he looks ordinary and is capable of intercourse, is classed among those with a basic biological defect. From the other end, the physically anomalous person is fully human but simply useless. Beyond this no kind of sex act or object of desire was singled out in medical literature as pathological. Commonplace medical recommendations for moderation and restraint in sexual activity had the sole aim of conserving reproductive vitality. They included no catalog of "perversions," and procreative efficacy alone defined the sexually healthy.[9]

In keeping with this there was no category of homosexual as a kind of false male. Medical literature appeared in harmony with Ming social images of homosexual behavior as a kind of male dissipation. As such potentially it could distract from family responsibilities and was perhaps imprudent in its wasteful expenditure of vital essence, but it was not in principle incompatible with proper male sexuality.[10] There is only the "coward," who rejects the family duty of pa-

ternity, and the castrati, who are incapable of it. One finds here neither the Christian notion of "unnatural" sexual acts nor its modern medicalized outgrowth, the concept of perversion as the manifestation of a psychologically deviant personality.

In the foregoing medical analysis, reproductive incapacity occurs at a deep biological level. It is part of "native endowment" bestowed by Heaven and suggests that the physical boundaries between the sexes, including phenomena which blur those boundaries, are fixed inalterably before birth. But yin and yang constantly change and interact both in the human body and in the environment at large, and throughout life human beings are never free from their influences.

Li Shih-chen's essay on "human anomaly" (*jen k'uei*) which stands as at the last chapter of his *Systematic Materia Medica,* was in fact a wide-ranging inquiry into biological processes as they govern human reproduction and produce our species norms. If false males and false females were shaped by events at work at conception, other sexual anomalies appeared spontaneously in adults. Can it be, he asked, that women sometimes grow beards, and men's breasts secrete milk; or that males have given birth, and adults have changed from one sex to the other? As a natural philosopher, Li was working within a long-standing Chinese view of cosmological pattern that sought to incorporate anomaly rather than reject the irregular as inconsistent with the harmony of natural pattern. Where patterns are seen as temporal processes, regularities are probabilities, not absolutes, and the "strange" as a unique event, like snow in summer, will—as the philosopher Chu Hsi put it in the Sung dynasty—occasionally intrude on the scene without undermining the intelligibility of the whole.

At the same time, anomaly posed problems for Li Shih-chen which had not troubled Chu Hsi five centuries earlier. As John Henderson has argued, late Ming thinkers were beginning to question the tradition of "correlative thinking" which assumed that natural, moral, and cosmological phenomena were rendered intelligible by an underlying pattern of affinities (*kan ying*).[11] Where the older view accommodated omens and magic as well as the rich lore of numerical and qualitative correspondences to make the anomalous a sign of unseen order, Li Shih-chen struck a newer note with these questions about "strange" reproductive events: he was dissatisfied with available explanations of the mechanisms involved. Nonetheless, this was a skepticism about the limits of human understanding more than a query about the believability of events. As food for seventeenth-century natural philosophy, the "strange" was a challenge to conventional canons of intelligibility, not superstition to be dismissed. Li Shih-chen concluded that changes of sex were among the possible "transformations of yin and yang."[12]

—Males Who Become Female

From time to time in late Ming China stories circulated of men who were transformed into women and women who were transformed into men. They gained visibility when they surfaced in the form of reports to government authorities of omens, where they played a ritual role in court politics. Like epidemics, natural disasters, astronomical events, and multiple births of males, these had traditionally been understood in light of the theory of cosmological correlations as signs, for good or ill, of the health of the Heavenly Mandate. A zealous quarrier of historical curiosities could find a number of instances of such omens in the dynastic histories of the medieval period, especially the Wei and Chin dynasties (AD 220–419). Literati writings over the centuries also occasionally noted such things. But the "Omen" (Wu hsing) sections of the Sung and Yuan dynastic histories contained no such accounts.[13]

Then, beginning in the fifteenth century, such stories began to crop up in the informal literature. It was reported in the "Omen" section that a female changed into a male in Kansu in 1548, while in Shansi in 1568, a male changed into a female.[14] Li Shih-chen took particular note of this second case, noting that its reliability was attested by the recent nature of the event and the rank of the circuit intendant who reported it to the throne. His account reads as follows:

> In the second year of the Lung-ching emperor, the Shansi governor, Shih Sung-hsu, reported that in Ching-lo county a man named Li Liang-yü was married for four years to a woman named Chang. Later due to poverty he divorced his wife and went to work as a laborer. In the first month of the first year of the Lung-ching reign he suffered a stomach

ache that came and went. On the ninth day of the second month of the second year he suffered sharp protracted pain. By sometime in the fourth month he could no longer feel his testicles [shen nang], which shrank, withdrew within his body, and became a vagina. The following month he began to menstruate and to dress like a woman. At the time he was 28 years old.[15]

[. . .]

The case of Li Liang-yü was commented upon by the emperor, one of the greatest natural philosophers of the day (Li Shih-chen), and at least three authors of pi chi (Li Hsu, Shen Te-fu, Wang Shih-chen). In addition, several seventeenth-century short stories depict a male who assumes a feminized physical and social identity and may be taken as commentaries on the inversion of sexual roles, even if it cannot be proved that they were directly inspired by the scandal itself. The stories include a particularly brilliant one by Li Yü, "A Male 'Mother Mencius.' "[16] Li Yü gives a quasinaturalistic interpretation of the phenomenon. The hero castrates himself, and thereby is transformed from an ordinary youth involved in a homosexual love affair to a feminized inhabitant of the inner quarters.

By treating his castratus protagonist sympathetically as lover, wife, foster mother, and chaste widow on the model of the mother of Mencius, Li Yü shocks his readers with an account of gender inversion which is psychologically as well as socially radical. The narrative clearly establishes the line separating such an individual from the ordinary "dragon yang" (lung yang) homosexual male, who in the story is made to joke about "the seven disagreeable things about a woman."[17] At the same time, conventional heterosexual attitudes are parodied at the end in a deadpan satire of a moralist's homily: "Cast your vital essence (ching shen) in a useful place. Isn't it beneficial to increase the Empire's household registers and produce progeny for your ancestors? Why would you take your 'golden fluid' and throw it away in some filthy receptacle?"[18]

The Li Yü story is framed by a narrator's social analysis of a "southern wind" (nan feng, punning on nan feng, "male fashion") of gender transgression currently sweeping China. It suggests that in the permissive atmosphere of the late Ming, homosexual activity threatened to break out of its accustomed pattern as a sporadic masculine dissipation to entangle men in what most would see as degrading, eunuchlike female roles.

The issue of the new "southern wind" was also raised by both Shen Te-fu and Hsieh Chao-che in their essays. Shen contrasted what he saw as the normal pattern of homosexual activity, "laughable but also pitiful," with a new "southern wind" of homosexual profligacy. For men to take males as lovers was to be expected among unmarried and impoverished bachelors, or in the all-male environment of shipboard, barracks, prison, or monastery. But the new fashionable sodomy [nan seh] was practiced by upper-class "gentlemen of ambition," spreading from its original home in the far south (Fukien) to the Yangtze delta regions, penetrating the entertainment quarters of Nanking and only half-resisted even in the north.[19] Hsieh Chao-che saw it as a revival of practices which had died out since the Sung under the influence of neo-Confucianism. In his words, "The whole country has gone crazy." (chü kuo ju k'uang).[20]

Li Liang-yü was extraordinary, even for the sixteenth and seventeenth centuries. No other case like his appeared in either formal or informal literature of the Ming that I have seen. Later the Ch'ing dynastic history included two reports of male-to-female sex change, but details are lost. However, I have found three late Ming accounts of males who were said to have given birth, in contexts which suggest that many associated this phenomenon also with current fashions in sodomy. A traditional explanation for male pregnancy, as for other kinds of anomalous birth was spirit possession, which is the interpretation offered in the case reported by Li Hsu.[21] However, another man claimed that someone had spied upon him while he was bathing,[22] while a third was said to have borne twin sons by his homosexual lover, a military officer from Fukien.[23] Hsieh Chao-che reported an incident in which male pregnancy was portrayed as a lesson to sodomites: "In our own dynasty when Chao Wen-hsiang was at Soochow a report came in that a male had given birth. He did not reply [to this announcement] but looked straight at his disciples and said, 'Be warned! Recently buggery [nan se] has become more commonplace than fornication with females. It will certainly lead to this sort of thing.' "[24] Nonetheless, however they understood the mechanisms

involved, those who reported such anomalies did not question that this strange thing happened to certain people as men.[25]

In sum, late Ming male gender identity was not easily compromised by the sexually "strange." Social role normally overshadowed the sexual in gender construction, and the result for males was that mutability of bodies and diversity of objects of desire need not render male gender problematic. Relations between older and younger partners or between genteel and servile ones did not upset established notions of social hierarchy. Even male pregnancy was capable of being interpreted not as the result of possession by demonic influences but as an enlargement, however risky, of male powers. Broad and flexible notions of what was sexually compatible with maleness stopped only at the extreme: only the eunuch could be seen as a concubine. [. . .]

As a symbol of the sexual itself as a source of threat to social order, Li's case pointed to the subversive potential of late Ming sexual politics: the homosexual fashion that threatened elite moral legitimacy and the eunuch power that eroded bureaucratic authority.

[. . .]

⌒Females Who Become Male

By contrast with Li Liang-yü, the case reported in the Ming history of a female who turned into a male attracted little literati notice as a scandal. We learn from the omen section of the dynastic history only that in 1549 this happened to a "young woman, seventeen [sui]," daughter of a member of a guard unit (Wei) near Ta-t'ung in Kansu.[26] However, three other cases were discussed in seventeenth century pi chi, all involving adolescent girls, all also in the northwest in Kansu. The most circumstantial, by Wang Shih-chen (1634–1711), reads as follows:

The case of Li Liang-yü of Shansi, who turned into a woman in the Chia-ching era, has already been recorded in earlier histories. But recently I saw in the "Miscellany of the Hall of Benevolence and Reciprocity" an account of two most strange events concerning Chuang-liang [a county in Kansu]. A woman named Chuang, widow of a soldier in the Red Deer Regiment, had a daughter. She was already promised in marriage when at age twelve, she suddenly turned into a male. Ashamed, she [sic] told no one, until her marriage took place and her husband appealed to the local magistrate to dissolve the union and return her to her father's household, permitting him to marry again. However, the girl's [sic] mother-in-law, finding her compliant and agreeable, pitied her and took her back. Today his name is "Chuang Ch'i-sheng" ["prosperity begins"], and he works in the district library.[27]

Wang reported a second similar case in Chuang-liang ten years later, while T'an Ch'ien (1594–1658) picked up a report of a case in P'ing-liang, Kansu, dating from 1514, in which it was claimed that a young woman changed sex, grew a beard, married, and fathered children. As a male, this individual's personal name was Kao-lei ("distant thunder").[28]

If these Ming accounts are supplemented by the ten reports of female-to-male sex change that appeared in the Ch'ing dynastic history,[29] and by seventeenth- and eighteenth-century narratives by P'u Sung-ling, Yuan Mei, and others, there is ample evidence for a pattern in the reported events and in their social interpretation. Although the official Ch'ing cases do not come from Kansu, but from scattered locations all over China, five of them (half) give the individual's age. She was young—typically an adolescent, though one of the five involved a child of seven who underwent the change, it was said, after recovering from smallpox.

The narratives constructed around these events show a common set of themes. The youngster's marriage provokes a crisis; the approaching wedding day may even lead to illness, and one narrative of such a case presents it as a "miracle cure" of the well-known mid-Ch'ing doctor, Yeh Kuei.[30] There are rejected brides; but families gain a son. There is a new, auspicious name, and a happy ending, especially if the stock theme of heirless parents figures in. The event is not explained or described, but presented as a rebirth mediated by some extraordinary power. P'u Sung-ling encapsulated all the idealized elements of this topos in his narrative, "Transformed into a Boy" ("Hua nan") in *Liao chai:*

In Soochow . . . a girl one night was sitting in the family courtyard. Suddenly she was struck on the forehead by a meteorite from the sky. She fell down as if dead. Her parents were old and had no son; they wept bitterly. But she revived, and on being restored to life announced, laughing, "now I am a male." They investigated and indeed it was so. The parents did not consider him a monster (*yao jen*) but welcomed this violent and sudden gift of a son.[31]

Accounts of females who turn into males differ markedly, then, from those which describe such a transformation in the opposite direction. We do not know whether as an omen, female-to-male change was considered auspicious, along the lines of male multiple births. But socially it could be welcomed by the individuals and families that experienced it. Instead of being given elaborate rationalizations from the cosmological repertory as in the case of Li Liang-yü, female-to-male changes were explained simply. They were also subject to less questioning, scrutiny, and skepticism. However, there is no reason for thinking that this was because of any biologically based intuition that one kind of claim was likely to be less valid than another. In both directions the phenomenon was presented and interpreted as a change, not as a case of mistaken identity.[32]

Significantly, narratives of female-to-male changes were marked by a total suppression of the sexual in favor of the social. In spite of the fact that the actual feelings hinted of in these tales were more often the "feminine" ones of modesty and shame, the transition to male gender was presented as a psychologically unproblematic shift of role. Thus the discourse about transformations of sex subtly genderized the different protagonists' relationship to their bodily changes. Girls become male passively and modestly, like good girls; their new gender was accomplished through social placement untouched by sexual feelings. The male has taken an active role in his transformation, and narrators imply erotic motivation and moral complicity in subverting orthodox relationships.

NOTES

1. Wu Chih-wang, *Chi yin kang mu* [Systematic Aid for the Disorders of Yin], pref 1620. Shanghia 1958 ed.: 179. This text, heavily derivative of the Ming medical master Wang K'en-t'ang, was reprinted dozens of times in the Ch'ing dynasty.

2. *Chi yin kang mu,* 183–85. See also the standard eighteenth-century medical encyclopedia, Wu Ch'ien, et al., *I tsung chin chien* [Golden Mirror of Medicine], published 1742. Peking 1981 ed. 3:47. A frequently cited classical authority on reproductive anomaly was Ch'u Ch'eng (fl. Southern Ch'i dynasty AD 479–501). See *Ch'u shih i shu* [Posthumous Essay of Master Ch'u], reprinted in T'ao Tsung-i, *Shuo fu,* Taipei: Hsin hsing shu chü, 1963.

3. Ch'i Chung-fu, *Nü k'o pai wen* [One Hundred Questions on Medicine for Women]. Pref 1220. This work was widely reprinted in the late Ming. See *hsia* chüan: 1a. See also *Chi yin kang mu:* 183; and Shen Chin-ao (1717–1767), *Fu k'o yü ch'ih* [Jade Rule of Medicine for Women], published 1774.

4. Li Shih-chen, *Pen ts'ao kang mu* [Systematic Materia Medica], pub 1596. See chüan 52, "Jen k'uei" ["human anomaly"].

5. A variant of "stone maiden" (*shih nü*) is "solid maiden" (*Shih nü*). Shen Yao-feng,[fl late eighteenth century?] author of *Shen shih nü k'o chi yao* [Master Shen's Essentials of Medicine for Women], 1850 preface by Wang Shih-hsiung, has a slightly different list of "false males and false females." Interestingly, he suggests that "drums" can be cured in infancy by surgery. Hong Kong 1956 reprint: 19.

6. *Pen ts'ao kang mu,* chüan 52.

7. *Pen ts'ao kang mu,* chüan 52. Another classification of "false males," derived from Buddhism, may be found in Shen Te-fu, *Wan-li yeh huo pien,* pref 1606. Reprinted Peking 1959, 1980; Hsieh Chao-che, *Wu tsa tsu.* Reprinted in the *Pi-chi hsiao-shuo ta-kuan pa pien,* vols 6 and 7. 922. It was presented as a typology of "natural eunuchs" and not used by medical men.

8. The annals of the Chin dynasty, alluded to by Li Shih-chen, present one common Chinese version of the hermaphrodite as erotic wizard. It was said of a palace favorite of the emperor Hui-ti [AD 290–307] that he assumed the form of a woman for one half the month and of a man for the other half. Judith Zeitlin quotes a Southern Sung miscellany, *Lu chun hsin hua,* which uses the same topos. A dissolute "maidservant" seduces her mistress. "Though I am a woman, both forms are present in me. When I encounter a woman I assume a male form: when I encounter a male, then I become a woman again," Zeitlin 1987:10.

9. Typical late Ming medical advice on sexuality and health may be found in Wan Ch'üan, *Wan Mi-chai shu* [Works of Wan Mi-chai], Wan-li edition, "Yang sheng" ["Long Life"] section; and in Kung T'ing-hsien, *Wan ping hui chun* [Rejuvenation from All Ills], publ 1587.

10. See Shen Te-fu:622; Hsieh Chao-che, chüan 5:3533; chüan 8:3743–45; 3780–81. Useful information may be found in two secondary works: "Wei hsing shih kuan chai" [pseud], *Chung-kuo t'ung-hsing-lien mi shih* [Secret History of Homosexual Love in China], 2 vols, Hong Kong, n.d.; and "Xiaomingxiong" [pseud], *Zhongguo tongxing'ai shilu* [Veritable Record of Chinese Homosexuality], Hong Kong 1984. Michel Foucault (1978) has shaped our understanding of the social construction of sexuality in Europe by his analysis of the nineteenth-century emergence of the "homosexual" and "lesbian" as personality types. As the power to define sexual norms shifted from the church to the emerging sciences and professions, sexual transgressions ceased to be defined as discrete carnal acts and came to be associated with deep-rooted personal dispositions constituting a social identity.

11. Henderson 1984. See also the review by Willard Peterson in the *Harvard Journal of Asiatic Studies* 46.2 (December 1986). In a related discussion of late imperial astronomy, Nathan Sivin (1986) has argued that considerations of "cosmic indeterminancy" led astronomers to doubt the possibility of perfectly accurate prediction.

12. *Pen ts'ao kang mu,* chüan 52.

13. The *Chin shih,* 3:907–8, with three cases, represented a high point of official reporting of sex change as omens. The annalist assumed these occurred under the influence of the homosexual fashion at the court of the emperor Hui-ti [AD 290–307]. Later official histories largely dropped the issue, though there is one report of a male birth in the *Sung shih,* 5:1369. Reports of sex change in the "Omen" sections of the Ming and Ch'ing dynastic histories are summarized in Ch'en 1982:349, 388.

14. *Ming shih,* 2:441–2.

15. *Pen ts'ao kang mu,* chüan 52.

16. Li Yü, "Nan Meng mu chiao ho san ch'ien" [A Male 'Mother Mencius' Teaches the 'Three Removals'], *Li Yü ch'üan chi,* 13:5381–5454. See also P'u Sung-ling, "Jen yao" in *Liao chai chih i,* 3:1711–13. Late Ming pornographic short stories with similar homosexual themes are analyzed in McMahon 1984, 1987.

17. "They wear makeup, substituting the false for the true; they bind feet and pierce ears to make themselves beautiful; their breasts stick out and hang down like tumorous swellings; they can't go out, but are tied to home like a melon to its vine; they are bound to their children and have no freedom; their monthly blood flow soaks the matting and stains their lower garments; babies come one after another with no end in sight." "Nan Meng mu," 5389.

18. "Nan Meng mu," 5453.

19. Shen Te-fu:622.

20. Hsieh Chao-che, 8:3744–45, 3780–81.

21. *Chieh-an lao-jen man pi:*22.

22. *Ch'ing pai lei ch'ao,* "i pin" section, 25:2, reporting a case of 1644.

23. Wang Shih-chen (1634–1711), *Ch'ih pei ou t'an* 2:182. P'u Sung-ling has a version of this story in *Liao chai chih i* 2:1037.

24. Hsieh Chao-che 5:3533.

25. Religion supported folklore concerning male pregnancy, since "*nei tan*" internal alchemy taught seekers of immortality to cultivate an "immortal embryo" within. In the late Ming or even today, any visitor to temples dedicated to the "five hundred lohan" would find images of pregnant monks, skin peeled back to reveal the child. See Needham 1983. A comic burlesque is found in the magical pregnancies of Tripitaka and Chu Pa-chieh in chapter 53 of *Journey to the West.* My thanks to Ann Waltner for calling my attention to this reference.

26. *Ming shih,* 2:442.
27. Wang Shih-chen, *Ch'ih pei ou t'an,* chüan *hsia:* 185.
28. T'an Chi'en, *Tsao lin tsa tsu,* "I chi" section:6.
29. *Ch'ing shih kao* 14.41:19b24b.
30. Yang Chih-i and Chu Chen-sheng 1961:185–86.
31. P'u Sung-ling, 2:1060. Yuan Mei. *Tzu pu yü,* chüan 17:8b/9a has a similar anecdote.

32. This contrasts with the commentaries on reports of female-to-male sex change found in European sources from Pliny to Montaigne. These were taken as credible evidence of the mutability of bodies based on the Galenic belief that female reproductive organs are homologous with male, only turned outside in. However, these European authorities believed that such transformations worked only in one direction, "up the great chain of being." See Laqueur 1986:13–14.

REFERENCES

Ch'en, Pan-kuan. (1982). *Erh-shih-liu shih i-hsueh shih-liao hui-pien* [Documentary Collection of Materials on Medicine in the Twenty-six Dynastic Histories]. Peking: Chung-i yen-chiu yuan.

Duden, Barbara. (1987). *Repertory on Body History: An Annotated Bibliography.* Pasadena, Calif.: Humanities Working Paper 125, California Institute of Technology.

Elvin, Mark. (1984). "Female Virtue and the State in China," *Past and Present* 104.

Foucault, Michel. (1978). *The History of Sexuality. Vol. 1: An Introduction.* Trans. Robert Hurley. New York: Pantheon Books.

Fu I-ling. (1963). *Ming tai chiang-nan shih min ching chi shih t'an* [Investigation of the Urban Economic Life of Ming Dynasty Chiang-nan]. Shanghai: Jen-min ch'u-pan she.

Henderson, John B. (1984). *The Development and Decline of Chinese Cosmology.* New York: Columbia University Press.

Illich, Ivan. (1982). *Gender.* New York: Pantheon Books.

Imperato-McGinley, J., et al. (1979). "Androgens and the Evolution of Male Gender Identity Among Male Pseudohermaphrodites with Five-alpha Reductose Deficiency." *New England Journal of Medicine* 300 (22): 1233–37.

H. Jones and N. Scott. (1958). *Hermaphroditism, Genital Anomalies, and Related Endocrine Disorders.* Baltimore: Williams and Wilkins.

Laqueur, Thomas. (1986). "Orgasm, Generation, and the Politics of Reproductive Biology," *Representations* 14 (Spring).

Li Yü. (1970). *Li Yü chüan chi* [Collected Works of Li Yü]. Helmut Martin, compiler. 15 vols., Taipei.

Mammitzsch, Hans-Richard. (1968). *Wei Chung-hsien: A Reappraisal of the Eunuch and the Factional Strife at the Late Ming Court.* University of Hawaii PhD thesis.

Mann, Susan. (1987). "Widows in the Kinship, Class and Community Structures of Qing Dynasty China." *Journal of Asian Studies* 46.1 (February).

McMahon, Keith. (1987). "Eroticism in Late Ming, Early Qing Fiction." *T'oung Pao* LXXIII.

McMahon, Keith. (1984). *The Gap in the Wall: Containment and Abandon in Seventeenth-century Chinese Fiction.* Princeton University PhD thesis.

Meijer, M. J. (1985). "Homosexual Offences in Ch'ing Law." *T'oung Pao* LXXI.

Ming shih, 28 vols., 332 chüan. (1974 reprint). Taipei: Chung-hua shu-chü ch'u-pan she.

Money, John, and Ehrhardt, Anke. (1972). *Man and Woman, Boy and Girl: The Differentiation and Dimorphism of Gender Identity from Conception to Maturity.* Baltimore and London: The Johns Hopkins University Press.

Needham, Joseph. (1983). *Science and Civilization in China. Vol. 5, Pt. 5: Spagyrical Discovery and Invention: Physiological Alchemy.* Cambridge: Cambridge University Press.

Ng, Vivien W. (1987). "Ideology and Sexuality: Rape Laws in Qing China." *Journal of Asian Studies* 46.1 (February).

P'u Sung-ling. (1962). *Liao chai chih i* [Strange Stories from a Chinese Studio]. 3 vols., Shanghai.

Schipper, Kristofer. (1982). *Le corps Taoiste: corps physique—corps social.* Paris: Fayard.

Sivin, Nathan. (1986). "On the Limits of Empirical Knowledge in the Traditional Chinese Sciences." In J. T. Fraser, N. Lawrence, and F. C. Haber, eds., *Time, Science, and Society in China and the West,* Amherst: University of Massachusetts Press.

Van Gulik, R. H. (1951). *Erotic Colour Prints of the Ming Period.* 3 vols. Tokyo: privately printed.

Van Gulik, R. H. (1974). *Sexual Life in Ancient China.* Leiden: E. J. Brill.

Wakeman, Frederick. (1985). *The Great Enterprise.* 2 vols. Berkeley: University of California Press.

"Wei hsing shih kuan chai" [pseud]. n.d. *Chung-kuo t'ung-hsing-lien mi shih* [Secret History of Homosexual Love in China]. 2 vols. Hongkong: Yu-chou ch'u-pan she.

"Xiaomingxiong" ("Samshasha") [pseud]. (1984). *Zhongguo tongxing'ai shihlu* [Veritable Record of Homosexual Love in China]. Hongkong.

Yang Chih-i and Chu Chen-sheng. 1961. *Ku-chin ming i kuai ping ch'i chih mi-chi shih-lu* [Veritable Record of the Precious Raft of Marvelous Cures of Strange Illnesses by Famous Doctors Ancient and Modern]. Taipei.

Zeitlin, Judith T. 1987. "Over the Borderline: Transvestites and Transsexuals in Seventeenth-Century Chinese Literature." Unpublished manuscript.

Social Construction Theory: Problems in the History of Sexuality

CAROLE S. VANCE

Carole Vance, a feminist scholar of sexuality, argues that ideas about gender and sexuality must not be understood as "natural" or unchanging "truths" but as "social constructions," that is, as ideas produced in societies in a particular time and place.

Carole S. Vance, "Social Construction Theory: Problems in the History of Sexuality," in *Homosexuality, Which Homosexuality?* Dennis Altman et al, London: GNP Publishers, 1989: 13, 14, 16–17, 18, 23, 29–30, 31.

Social construction theory in the field of sexuality proposed an extremely outrageous idea. It suggested that one of the last remaining outposts of the "natural" in our thinking was fluid and changeable, the product of human action and history rather than the invariant result of the body, biology, or an innate sex drive. [. . .]

Essentialism can take several forms in the study of sexuality: a belief that human behaviour is "natural," predetermined by genetic, biological, or physiological mechanisms and thus not subject to change; or the

Key Terms

biological determinism The belief that biology determines fundamentally all behavior and actions.
constructionist Argues against essentialized views of identity in favor of historical and cultural approaches and methods.
deconstruction The notion of deconstruction is used in different ways by scholars and researchers in various fields. Feminist and early gay and lesbian historians and social scientists drew upon the notion of deconstruction to develop a cultural analysis of sex, sexuality, and gender. This term has also been used by Jacques Derrida, the contemporary French historian of philosophy, who challenges essentialism and biological determinism

by questioning the foundational assumptions of so-called natural beliefs in Western culture. In the Derridean school of thought, no meaning is ever fixed; they are always dependent on cultural and linguistical context.
essentialist Argues that the characteristics of persons or groups are largely similar in all human cultures and historical periods, since they are significantly influenced by biological factors.
sexual identity The labeling of persons based on sexual practices.**sexual subjects** A term used to refer to the individuals and groups that become categorized and recognizable through dominant ideas and discourses about sexuality and desire.

notion that human behaviours which show some similarity in form are the same, an expression of an underlying human drive or tendency. Behaviours that share an outward similarity can be assumed to share an underlying essence and meaning.

The development of science and social science in Euro-America in the past century can be characterized by a general movement away from essentialist frameworks toward perspectives that, although called by various names, are constructionist. These new frameworks have challenged the "natural" status of many domains, presenting the possibility of a truly *social* inquiry as well as suggesting that human actions have been and continue to be subject to historical forces and, thus, to change. Gender and sexuality have been the very last domains to have their natural, biologized status called into question. For all of us, essentialism was our first way of thinking about sexuality and still remains the hegemonic one in the culture.

[. . .]

Some critics contend that social construction theory implies that sexual identity, or more to the point, lesbian and gay identity, is somehow fictional, trivial, unimportant or not real, because it is socially constructed. The punch line "it's *only* socially constructed" is a characteristic remark of these critics, revealing their belief that only biologically determined phenomena could have any significance in human social life. This is an odd position for historians and social scientists to take. Social construction approaches call attention to the paradox between the historically variable ways in which culture and society construct seemingly stable reality and experience: here, the ways in which the prevailing sexual system seems natural and inevitable to its natives, and for many individuals the expression of some deeply felt essence. To explain how reality is constructed does not imply that it is not real for the persons living it—or trivial, unimportant, or ephemeral—though it is also true that the insight of construction, when absorbed by the natives (that is, us) has the potential to subvert the natural status of the sexual system and cause us to question and rethink our experience of essential identity.

Other variants of this misreading suggest that individual sexual identity is easily changeable, much like a new outfit plucked from the closet at whim; that individuals have conscious control over sexual identity; and that large-scale cultural formations regarding sexuality are easily changed. Since social constructionists have said nothing of the kind, one is at first puzzled by the enormity of this misunderstanding, but the explanation for it is perhaps to be found in the special status of sex in our culture and our thought (Rubin 1984).

An analogy from anthropology is useful here. It is commonplace for anthropologists to say that human behaviour is socially or culturally constructed, by which we mean that human behaviour is learned and not intrinsic or essentially determined. But to suggest that any feature of human life, for example, national or ethnic identity, is socially constructed is not to say that it is trivial. Nor is it to say that entire cultures can transform themselves overnight, or that individuals socialized in one cultural tradition can acculturate at whim to another.

This criticism of social construction confuses the individual level with the cultural level: that sexuality is constructed at the level of culture and history through complex interactions which we are now trying to understand does not mean that individuals have an open-ended ability to construct themselves, or to reconstruct themselves multiple times in adulthood. (This is not to deny individuals experiences of sexual malleability and change, which are probably considerably more extensive than our cultural frames and our own biographical narratives admit.) The specialness of sex is highlighted by this comparison, since a quite ordinary and accepted insight about cultural construction in most areas of human life seems very difficult to understand without distortion when applied to sexuality. When we come to sex, our minds grind to a halt: normal distinctions become incomprehensible, and ordinary logic flies out the window.

[. . .]

At minimum, all social construction approaches adopt the view that physically identical sexual acts may have varying social significance and subjective meaning depending on how they are defined and understood in different cultures and historical periods. Because a sexual act does not carry with it a universal social meaning, it follows that the relationship between sexual acts and sexual identities is not a fixed one, and it is projected from the observer's time and place to others at great peril. Cultures provide widely different categories, schemata, and labels for framing sexual and affective experiences. The relationship of sexual act and identity to sexual community is equally variable and complex. These distinctions, then, *between* sexual acts, identities, and communities are widely employed by constructionist writers. [. . .]

Social construction's greatest strength lies in its violation of our folk knowledge and scientific ideologies that would frame sexuality as "natural," determined by biology and the body. This violation makes it possible, indeed compels us to raise questions that a naturalizing discourse would obscure and hide. Social constructionists have been even-handed in this endeavour, dethroning the body in all fields—in heterosexual history as well as in lesbian and gay history. At first, we greeted this development with good cheer, happy to be rid of the historical legacy of nineteenth-century spermatic and ovarian economies, women's innate sexual passivity, and the endless quest to find the hormonal cause of homosexuality. Yet the virtue of social construction may also be its vice.

Has social construction theory, particularly variants which see "sexual impulse," "sex drive," or "lust" as created, made no room for the body, its functions and physiology? As sexual subjects, how do we reconcile constructionist theory with the body's visceral reality and our own experience of it? If our theory of sexuality becomes increasingly disembodied, does it reach the point of implausibility, even for us? And if we wish to incorporate the body within social construction theory, can we do so without returning to essentialism and biological determinism?

[. . .]

The tension here is identical to a tension felt within feminism, which simultaneously holds two somewhat contradictory goals. One goal is to attack the gender system and its primacy in organizing social life, but the second goal is to defend women as a group. Defending women or advancing their interest (in equal pay, abortion rights, or child care, for example) emphasizes their status as a special group with a unique collective interest, distinct from men, thus replaying and perhaps reinforcing the very gender dichotomy crucial to the system of gender oppression.

The same irresolvable tension exists within the lesbian and gay movement, which on the one hand attacks a naturalized system of sexual hierarchy which categorizes and stabilizes desires and privileges some over others, and on the other hand defends the interest of "lesbian and gay people," which tends to reify identity and essential nature in a political process I've described. There is no solution here, since to abandon either goal for the other would be foolish. Real, live lesbians and gays need to be defended in an oppressive system, and the sexual hierarchy, which underlies that oppression, needs to be attacked on every level, particularly on the intellectual and conceptual levels, where naturalized systems of domination draw so much of their energy. There is no easy solution here, but even an awareness of this tension can be helpful, since it powerfully contributes to the larger political and emotional climate in which social construction theory is received, and rightly so. [. . .]

Social construction theory offered many radical possibilities in theorizing about sexuality. To take the next steps, we need to continue and deepen our discussion about its very real problems. These problems will not be resolved through theoretical discussion alone, though such discussions offer clarification, but through the course of continued research and investigation.

To the extent social construction theory strives for uncertainty through questioning assumptions rather than seeking closure, we need to tolerate ambiguity and fluidity. The future is less closed than we feared, but perhaps more open than we hoped. All movements of sexual liberation, including lesbian and gay, are built on imagining: imagining that things could be different, other, better than they are. Social construction shares that imaginative impulse and thus is not a threat to the lesbian and gay movement, but very much of it.

Clearly, the tension between deconstructing systems of sexual hierarchy and defending lesbians and gays will be an ongoing one. In that case, we need to find a way to acknowledge more openly and respond more appropriately to the emotional responses social construction theory engenders, deeply felt responses about identity, community, solidarity, politics, and survival—in short, our lives.

REFERENCE

Rubin, Gayle. "Thinking Sex: Notes for a Radical Theory of the Politics of Sexuality." *Pleasure and Danger: Exploring Female Sexuality.* Carole S. Vance, ed. London: Pandora Press, 1984: 267–319.

REFLECTING ON THE SECTION

This section addresses the history of science and biology to show how femininity and masculinity are naturalized (assumed to have a basis in nature). What are some of the important differences among these various ways of understanding the gendering of bodies? How are language and metaphor used in each version of science and medicine to distinguish between male and female roles? What are some possible consequences for women of this use of descriptive language? For men? Current scientific ideas about male and female bodies and cultural definitions of masculinity and femininity all have histories. Studying the different models that biologists and medical practitioners in different cultures and time periods have used to conceptualize human bodies can help us realize that these ideas are not essential. Vance's essay describes this way of thinking about bodies as a social constructivist theory: a belief that the cultural context in which a person, act, or behavior is situated determines the way gender will be perceived and experienced. In contrast, essentialists assert that bodies possess qualities that do not change over time and space. Which theory of identity is more familiar to you? What parts of the readings in this section have supported your previous conception of sex differences and sexuality? What parts have challenged essentialist or constructivist ideas that have been taught to you?

The Rise of Western Science

Magic
LINDA GORDON

Linda Gordon, a feminist historian, argues that the association of objectivity and truth with the form of knowledge that we call "science" in the West was created by its differentiation from "magic." Gordon says that magic and science have the same root; the impulse to control and explain the environment. Since magic was linked to women's practices of healing, the rise of science discredited both magic and women's historical role as healers and experts on natural phenomena.

In the ancient and modern preindustrial worlds, magic was an important part of the technology of birth control. There were sacrifices to gods, incantations, potions and philters, dances and pantomimes. Some modern Western scientists have dismissed these methods, since most of them, apparently, do not work. But many "scientific" methods of birth control do not always work. Furthermore, there may be psychogenic causes for infertility—that is, mental states may cause physiological changes that prevent conception. It is possible that magical birth control did work when its user believed in it.

Linda Gordon, "Magic," *Woman's Body, Woman's Right,* Penguin, 1976: 29–33.

It is altogether incorrect to oppose magic to science. Magical rituals themselves arose out of impulses to explain and control the environment; magic and science had the same roots and may even have once been identical. Superstitions are often good examples of "scientific" or rational magic. Perhaps the first attempts to prevent conception were inspired by observing the circumstances that had actually pertained during an act of intercourse that proved sterile and then trying to reproduce those circumstances. Whatever the efficacy, the attempt is rational. Furthermore, superstitions like this are much easier formed than broken. They quickly gain the honored place of tradition whether they work or not. Consider the situation of a woman whose menstrual period is late. Wishing not to have a child, she might try some magical recipe for causing abortion. If, a week later, her menstrual period comes, she might recognize the possibility of mere coincidence, that her good fortune had nothing to do with the potion she drank; but if she found herself in the same predicament another time, it would be *rational,* not merely superstitious, for her to take the potion again—just in case.

Another kind of magic is based on symbolism. In many primitive cultures human needs and patterns are

Key Terms

civilized The term used to describe some cultures as more rational, scientific, and modern than others, leading to practices of cultural superiority.

high culture A term to describe elite culture (as differentiated from mass culture or popular culture).

primitive The term used to describe some cultures as irrational, closer to nature or to animals, and outside of history and modern time.

projected onto other creatures and objects. Eastern European peasants, for example, turn the wheel of the grain mill backward four times at midnight; this being a reverse process, it is supposed to prevent conception. A Serbian woman closes the door with the legs of a newly born infant; she is thus closing the house, and herself, to further conception.[1] Both ancient Roman women and modern German peasant women believed that tea made from the seeds of fruitless willow trees would make them sterile[2] Knots, a widespread symbol of sterility, are often tied in order to prevent conception.[3]

A cluster of magical beliefs found all over Europe centers around the use of the fingers, possibly as phallic symbols. A fourteenth-century writer, Frater Rudolphus, told women to sit or lie on as many fingers as they wished to have years without children. Modern Serbian peasant women would place as many fingers in a child's first bath as they wished free years. In another variant, a bride was supposed to sit on the desired number of fingers while riding in her wedding coach. Among Bosnians, a woman was supposed to slide the desired number of fingers into her girdle as she mounted a horse—and if she slid both hands inside the girdle she would be sterile forever! A more grotesque variant had it that the woman desiring sterility should carry the finger of a premature child.[4]

Another form of magical contraception was, simply, asking the gods, usually called prayer. If one believes in the existence and power of any gods, clearly this too is a rational way to try to prevent conception. And yet, ironically, this, which is still widely practiced in the "civilized" world, is probably the least "scientific" of all methods, because it is passive and powerless, instead of active and power-seeking. The magical methods that are based on trying to find out what makes conception or birth happen and then stopping it, even if they are mistaken, are far more scientific.

To the extent that magic systematically breaks away from the passivity of the human role in most religions it can be seen as humanistic and scientific, at least within its historical context. Medicine is an outgrowth of magic both logically and historically. The first doctors were magician priests, the "medicine men" or "witch doctors." In peasant societies women usually dominated the medical profession; they were the midwives and the practitioners of herbal medicine for the last thousand to fifteen hundred years of Western history. Under the influence of the Christian churches in medieval and early modern Europe, their magic fell into disrepute among the ruling classes (though not among the masses of poor people); they were called witches, were accused of having acquired their powers from the devil, rather than from their own brain power, and were hanged and burnt by the thousands.

There were many reasons for this persecution. Witches threatened the stability of the society, partly because they did not conform to their assigned roles as women, and partly because their practice represented a resurfacing of the paganism below the Christian veneer. The content of their witchcraft was also threatening to the churches. As the dogma of Christianity was then conceived, medicine itself was inimical to orthodoxy, and the witches were practicing medicine. They prescribed potions and incantations and performed massages and douches for all kinds of ailments and conditions. They gave abortions and made women temporarily sterile. They generally violated the passive spirit—the acceptance of God's will—that the shepherd churches wished to encourage in their sheep.

There is a widespread misconception that witches and other folk healers used magical remedies out of their inability to diagnose or cure. Anthropologists contributed a related misunderstanding, that many "primitive" cultures used superstitious forms of birth control because they did not understand the process of conception. On the contrary, magical remedies were often prescribed and used together with physiologically effective ones, both in "primitive" and in "high" cultures. The ancient Greek physician Aëtios prescribed well-constructed pessaries to be used along with wearing as an amulet the tooth of a child.[5] Papuan women who wear a rope around their waists in order not to conceive also wash their vaginas carefully after intercourse.[6] (One might call that hedging one's bets.) Belief in imitative, or symbolic, magic by no means implies ignorance of material forces, any more than religion implies ignorance of the laws of physics.

NOTES

1. This greater power was often found in matrilineal societies—where descent is figured through the mother—and in matrilocal societies—where a married couple goes to live in the wife's native place. Both matrilineality and matrilocality tend to divide the loyalties, obligations, and power of men between their family of marriage and their family of birth, divisions that frequently result in men's periodic absences and greater autonomy for the women. It is not that patrilineal and patrilocal societies do not practice birth control—they do. But men's concern is more often with over-all population problems, whereas women tend also to worry about their own need for more space between births.

2. Norman E. Himes, *Medical History of Contraception* ([1936] New York: Gamut Press, 1963), pp. 175, 177.

3. Apthekar, Herbert, *Anjea: Infanticide, Abortion, and Contraception in Savage Society.* New York: William Godwin, 1931, p. 119.

4. Himes, Norman Edwin, *Medical History of Contraception,* New York: Schocken Books, 1970, pp. 6, 9, 20, 174.

5. Ibid, p. 175.

6. Quoted in ibid., p. 95.

7. Ibid., p. 20.

Reading B

Feminist Approaches to Technology
SHEILA ROWBOTHAM

Sheila Rowbotham, a feminist historian, argues that much of the knowledge we now label as "technology" came from the world outside of Europe and North America, thereby disputing the widespread belief that the West is the source of advanced knowledge. Rowbotham reminds us that women in premodern or non-European societies produced technologies that have made important contributions to science.

Women as historical actors have begun to be restored to the history of western science; they have come into view, in Londa Schiebinger's phase "manoeuvring

Sheila Rowbotham, "Feminist Approaches to Technology: Women's Values or a Gender Lens?" *Women Encounter Technology: Changing Patterns of Employment in the Third World,* Swasti Mitter and Sheila Rowbotham, ed. New York: Routledge, 1995: 52–9.

Key Terms

alchemy The search for a way to change metals into gold in the European Middle Ages.

ideology Following from the philosophy of Karl Marx, the nineteenth-century German political philosopher, ideology refers to the ideas of the dominant classes that are imposed on less powerful people.

Shakers Eighteenth- and nineteenth-century religious group originating in England and migrating to the United States, they received their name from the trembling induced by spiritual experiences. Known for their tight-knit communities and their belief in a deity possessing both male and female characteristics.

within the gender boundaries prescribed by society" (1989a: p. 7). Such manoeuvring surely also existed outside western science, for even in very ancient times women can be found studying science in many cultures. Margaret Alic describes women doctors in Egypt before 3000 BC, while ancient Babylonian women perfumers developed the chemical techniques used among alchemists in Alexandria in the first century AD (Alic 1986: pp. 20–22). She observes that the Dark Ages,

> were not as bleak a time for women as one might expect. In the Byzantine Empire a succession of women rulers pursued scientific interests. In China women engineers and Taoist adepts pushed science and technology forward at a steady rate. With the rise of Islam and the subsequent conquest and unification of the Arab regions, translations and elaborations of ancient Greek works formed the basis of Arab science. A diverse and tolerant culture, the early Moslem empire preserved and expanded upon the knowledge of antiquity. Women studied at the medical school in Baghdad and female alchemists followed the teachings of Maria the Jewess. If Moslem women scholars are not recorded in the historical text, their existence is at least testified to by stories from the Arabian Nights. (p. 47)

She goes on to tell the legend of the Arab slave girl Tawaddud, who outwitted readers of the Koran, doctors of law and medicine, scientists, and philosophers with her wisdom and learning.

Rather than viewing history in terms of an undifferentiated structure of patriarchy, it is possible to see women emerging intellectually in some periods and forced into retreat in others. Historians have begun to examine what David Noble has described as differences within the "recurring fact" of female subordination. As he says, "There have been significant variations of experience, variations that have shaped particular cultures and lives" (Noble 1992: 4).

This nuanced view of history makes it possible to enquire into the actual social circumstances which have enabled women to enter the world of science and technology, for it has not simply been an ideological struggle but a practical one. Several broad features can be outlined. First, it has certainly been an advantage to be a member of the upper classes. Class has created a certain space for gender maneuvering. For example, one of the most celebrated Byzantine women scholars, Anna Comnena (1083–1148), was the daughter of Emperor Alexius. Her father's many wars provided her with material for her favourite subject, military technology, and her book *The Alexiad* contains "detailed descriptions of weapons and military tactics" (Alic 1986: 48). In medieval Europe the "ladies of Salerno" contributed to the eleventh-century revival based on translating ancient Greek medical writing from Arabic into Latin. They were a group of noble Italian women who were able to enter the universities in this period.

According to legend an upper-class scholar called Trotula wrote on medicine, dealing with subjects such as skin diseases and cosmetics, birth control, gynecology, lice, toothache, and even slimming. In a work attributed to her this advice was given: "The obese person was to be smeared with cow dung and wine and placed in a steam cabinet or in heated sand four times per week" (Alic 1986: 53).

The patronage of royal and aristocratic women, which played a significant part in scientific innovation in early modern Western science, can be observed elsewhere. An early example is to be found in Japan, where the Empress Shotoku-Tenno ordered the printing of one million charms in 767. These were distributed in 770, the earliest printed documents produced in any country (Sarton 1927: 529).

Science and Daily Life

There were, however, other ways of entering science for women from less privileged backgrounds. An important influence upon science has been the tradition of practical experiments associated with craft skills, and women have contributed both through the workshop and through the household. Way back in the second millennium BC, cuneiform tablets name two women chemists, Tappūti-Bēlatēkallim and Ninu. Although women had a low status in ancient Sumerian culture, they could engage in business. Margaret Alic writes:

> The perfume industry was very important in ancient Babylon since aromatic substances were used in

medicine and religion as well as for cosmetics. The apparatus and recipes of perfumery were similar to those used in cooking. Women perfumers developed the chemical techniques of distillation, extraction, and sublimation.

(Alic 1986: 21)

The textile crafts, where women are to be found in many cultures spinning wool, silk and linen, are also female trades closely linked to household duties. Irfan Habib describes how, in 1301–2, Amir Khusrau advised his daughter in Delhi to be content with the needle and spindle, which he compared to her spear and arrow, a source of wealth and a means of hiding one's body (Habib, 1992: p. 12).[1] Nearly fifty years later another poet, 'Islami, was grumbling at Raziyya's presumption on becoming Sultan though a woman, and urging women to sit with the charka rather than assuming sovereignty (ibid.: 13). Irfan Habib comments:

> To these two poets one feels truly grateful in spite of their unacceptably reactionary views on the place of woman: their admonitions have enabled us to fix the generalization of the spinning wheel at least in India in the first half of the fourteenth century.

Unfortunately the poets were not concerned with a gendered account of technological innovation or implementation.

In China the memory has survived of Huang Tao P'o, a famous woman textile technologist of the thirteenth century who brought knowledge of cotton growing, spinning, and weaving from Hainan to the Yangtze (Needham 1981: 111). In Hainan she is remembered still as the inventor of the loom.[2]

Who is remembered and revered is not a matter of chance but bound up with how science is defined and what model of the relationship between science and technology is adopted; it indeed depends on how knowledge is constituted. The recognition that "technology" means much more than applied science, that it is itself a creative area of culture which involves the tacit know-how based on doing, has opened up a much broader approach to the history and sociology of science and technology, which has enabled feminists to redefine the parameters of women's contribution to

technology. This understanding is by no means new: the fifteenth-century French writer and defender of women, Christine de Pisan, located women's technological creativity in precisely these areas of human culture. The rediscovery of how the domestic sphere has interacted historically with certain kinds of technological and scientific know-how has recently begun to blur the boundaries between formal and informal knowledge. Women's cultural traditions have been passed on orally or through household manuals rather than through the academy. Medicine is an obvious example. Long before the invention of penicillin, Elizabeth Stone, in nineteenth-century Wisconsin, specialized in treating lumberjacks' wounds with poultices of mouldy bread in warm milk or water (Stanley 1983: 14).

In medieval Europe women were active in many areas of craft production, but from the sixteenth century they were to be excluded from many trades. Still, Maria Winkelmann, the daughter of a Lutheran minister, born near Leipzig in 1670, was able to receive an advanced training in astronomy by serving as an unofficial apprentice in the house of the self-taught Christopher Arnold. Astronomy in late seventeenth-century Germany was organized partly along guild lines and partly through study at the university. The practical observation work occurred, however, largely outside the university. Maria Winkelmann was able to pursue her work by marrying Germany's leading astronomer, Gottfried Kirch. This enabled her to continue as an assistant to Kirch in Berlin. She became celebrated for her scientific work, which included the discovery of a previously unknown comet in 1702. Together she and her husband worked on astronomy which contributed to the production of an astronomically accurate calendar (Schiebinger 1989b: 21–38).

Family connections have been important to women entering scientific study from early times. Hypatia of Alexandria, born AD 370 when the city was in turmoil as the Roman Empire was converting to Christianity, was the daughter of the mathematician and astronomer Theon. As well as theoretical writing, Hypatia was interested in mechanics and practical technology. She designed a plane astrolabe for measuring the positions of stars, planets, and the sun to calculate time and the ascendant sign of the zodiac, and a graduated brass hydrometer for determining the density of a liquid. She was murdered by fanatical and jealous Christian monks hostile to her learning (Alic 1986: 44).

The persistent appearance of women as practitioners of alchemy was not only because of ideological affinities. Alchemy presents an example of a craft form through which women could be technologically creative. Maria the Jewess was a prominent early alchemist. She invented a water bath in the first century AD which resembled a double boiler and was used to heat a substance slowly or maintain it at a constant temperature. The French still call a double boiler a *bain-marie*. She also invented distilling apparatus. Maria compared the thickness of the metal in part of the still to a "pastrycook's cooper frying pan" and recommended flour paste for sealing joints (Alic 1986: 37). It is possible to see here the connection between domestic craft and technology, present in much of women's inventiveness, which the hierarchical model of technology as applied science or a narrow definition of technology as physical objects would obliterate. Another creative link has been to the reproduction of life. Cleopatra, a later Alexandrian alchemist, brought imagery of conception and birth into her writing and studied weights and measures in an attempt to quantify experiments. However, in the third century the Roman emperor Diocletian persecuted Alexandrian alchemists. Consequently alchemy was to be culturally rerouted. As Margaret Alic says, 'The Arabs rescued the science and ancient alchemy reached Europe during the Middle Ages, but by that time it had degenerated into mystical mumbo-jumbo' (Alic 1986: 41).

Interest in alchemy was to appear again during the thirteenth-century scientific revival. In fourteenth-century Paris, Perrenelle Lethas married the well-to-do scribe Nicholas Flamnel. Together they discovered an ancient alchemical manuscript. They laboured together experimenting with mercury and silver, trying to create gold.

—∾Separate Communities

Women can be found studying science and making practical contributions through medicine or technological innovation within the separate space of intellectual or religious communities. An early example was the famous mathematician Pythagoras of Samos, c.

582–500 BC, who formed a community in the Greek colony of Croton in southern Italy between 540 and 520 BC, in which there were at least twenty-eight women teachers and students. The most famous of these was Theano, who married Pythagoras when he was an old man. She and her daughters were renowned as healers and believed that the human body in microcosm reflected the macro universe. When the community was forcibly dispersed she took Pythagoras's philosophical and mathematical ideas with her through Greece into Egypt (Alic 1986: 22–24).

Some medieval European convents provided women with education in medicine, sanitation, and nutrition. Hildegard, born 1098, was a learned abbess in Germany who studied scientific ideas and developed ideas of links between the body and the universe. Hildegard lived in a period when the influence of the ancient Greeks was being translated from Arabic into Latin, and her writing indirectly expressed these influences, which were to continue to affect scientific thought into the Renaissance (ibid.: 62–67).

The Shakers also provided a communal situation in which women were able to contribute to technological inventions. Catherine Greene's contribution to devising the cotton gin is uncertain, though, according to a Shaker writer, Eli Whitney once publicly admitted her help (Shaker Manifesto 1890: 10). One certain breakthrough is the invention of the circular saw, c. 1810, by Sister Tabitha Babbitt of the Harvard Massachusetts Shakers.

> After watching the brothers sawing, she concluded that their back and forth motion wasted half their effort, and mounted a notched metal disc on her spinning wheel to demonstrate her proposed improvements. . . . Sister Tabitha intended the blade to be turned by water power. (p. 19, footnote)

The entry points for women into the world of science and technology in cultures which have been hostile to their participation have thus been through the power of aristocratic wealth and patronage; through learning within a practical craft situation or housewifery; through their family networks; and through groups and communities set apart from society. These social and material circumstances have entwined with ideological factors. Cultures which have respected experience have enabled women to practice skills gained through doing rather than academic knowledge. Oppositional ideologies have also contained a critique of elitist knowledge, which has sometimes been sympathetic to the claims of women, even though these have been subordinated in relation to a hegemonic academy. Nonetheless, given conducive social conditions, women have contributed to invention and drawn on aspects of their experience as well as upon formal learning.

—◦ Access and Exclusion

It is misleading to present a unified or steady progress for women as a homogenous group even within Western science, for as cultural gates opened through education and the upper-class women's salons, which were to become spaces for exchanging ideas from the seventeenth century, they were also closing. The formal academies created in the late seventeenth century tended to be exclusively male. The Académie Royale des Sciences was founded in 1666 and closed the intellectual paths opened by Cartesian women like Elisabeth of Bohemia, Catherine Descartes, and Madeleine de Scudery (Schiebinger 1992: 9). The Berlin Academy of Sciences did admit Maria Winkelmann, but she was denied a post in the observatory. She wrote: "Now I go through a severe desert, and because . . . water is scarce . . . the taste is bitter" (cited in Schiebinger 1989b).

The professionalization of science made it harder for women who were practitioners through craft and family connections. However, the popularity of science also inspired upper-class European women to take up the study. Many of these gained a reputation for eccentricity, like Mad Madge, the Duchess of Newcastle, who broke into the Royal Society of London in 1667, or Lady Mary Montagu, who brought the knowledge of inoculation to Britain from Turkey in the eighteenth century and was described as having "a tongue like a viper and a pen like a razor" (Alic 1986: 0). Later examples come from an enlightened and radical milieu. Dr. James Miranda Stuart Barry, a protégé of James Barry who was a follower of Mary Wollstonecraft, dressed as a man to become a doctor at Edinburgh in 1812 and pursued a successful career as an army surgeon (ibid.: 105). Ada Byron Lovelace developed a concept for an analyt-

ical engine and studied cybernetics in the 1840s, reviving old ideas of microcosm and macrocosm. Unfortunately this early pioneer of the computer imagined that she had found an infallible system for winning at the horse races, and with Charles Babbage lost a great deal of money (ibid.: 157–163).

Professionalization meant that education became of crucial importance. Access to colleges in the nineteenth century was an important demand among women who sought entry into the public sphere of scientific debate. In the early nineteenth century in America, educational ideas which emphasized science with a practical application for industry included women. For example, Amos Eaton, founder of RPI, was a proponent of women's education and opposed to "the monkish policy" of the universities (Noble 1992: 266). Vassar College, Smith College, and Wellesley College were established to educate women scientifically as well as in other subjects. Oberlin was the first coeducational school. It modeled itself on manual labour schools, in particular the Oneida Academy, which grew out of a community and combined religious instruction with science and practical training in agriculture and mechanical arts. In the 1850s the People's College movement in upstate New York also took a practical approach to education, while Wesleyan University, a Methodist institution, was initially coeducational with an orientation to industrial scientific education. MIT was also coeducational (ibid.: 267–270). Women moved into higher education in the United States in the late nineteenth and early twentieth century in large numbers. However, a reaction became evident in the latter part of the nineteenth century, when arguments about "women's nature," in terms of physical and psychological difference, were used as reasons to exclude them. Wesleyan College eliminated coeducation, and women's enrollment at MIT fell off. From the institutes of technology a concerted male opposition consolidated akin to that of the academies of the earlier era.

Recent research has then effected a remarkable recovery of women excluded from conventional histories of Western science, which has in turn brought about a deeper exploration of the relationship between gender and science. This work can lead us to an examination of both the barriers which have prevented women from gaining access and the circumstances which have made it possible for women to learn about scientific ideas and contribute to technology themselves; questions which have a significant and direct relevance to the contemporary position of women. However, such an assessment of the possibility of women gaining power to shape the design and purpose of technology would need to refer not only to the internal tensions within scientific thought but also to the wider social context. This necessary connection has tended to fall into the background in the focus upon the scientific milieu itself which has characterized much of the new gender-sensitive history of science and technology.

REFERENCES

Alic, Margaret. (1986). *Hypatia's Heritage: A History of Women in Science from Antiquity to the Late 19th Century.* London: The Women's Press.

Habib, Irfan. (1992). "Pursuing the History of Indian Technology. Pre-modern Modes of Transmission of Power," *Social Scientist,* Vol. 20, Nos. 2–3, March/April.

Needham, Joseph. (1981). *Science in Traditional China.* Cambridge, Mass.: Harvard University Press.

Noble, David F. (1992). *A World without Women, The Christian Clerical Culture of Western Science.* New York: Alfred A. Knopf.

Sarton, George. (1927). *Introduction to the History of Science, Vol.I, From Homer to Omar Khayyam.* Baltimore: Carnegie Institution of Washington, The Williams and Wilkins Co.

Schiebinger, Londa. (1989b). "Maria Winkelmann: The Clash between Guild Traditions and Professional Science," in Arina Angermen, Geete Biinena, Annemieke Keunen, Vefte Poels and Jacqueline Zikzee (eds), *Current Issues in Women's History.* London: Routledge.

Schiebinger, Londa. (1992). Why Science Is Sexist, *Women's Review of Books,* Vol. X, No. 3, December.

Shaker Manifesto. (1890). cited by Autumn Stanley in "Women Hold Up Two-thirds of the Sky: Notes for the Revised History of Technology," in Joan Rothschild (ed), *Machina Ex Dea: Feminist Perspectives on Technology.* New York: Pergamon Press, 1983.

Stanley, Autumn. (1983). "Women Hold Up Two-thirds of the Sky: Notes for a Revised History of Technology," in Joan Rothschild (ed.), *Machine Ex Dea, Feminist Perspectives on Technology.* New York: Pergamon Press.

NOTES

1. I am grateful to Navsharan G. Singh for this reference.

2. I am grateful to Tongjiang Long for this information.

Reading C

The Biological Connection
ANNE FAUSTO-STERLING

Anne Fausto-Sterling, feminist biologist and historian of science, argues that science is founded on many sexist assumptions. This should not lead us to disregard scientific knowledge. Rather, we must understand that science reveals the personal beliefs and feelings of researchers, so we must take those ideologies and sentiments into account.

Science, according to definition, is knowledge based on truth, which appears as fact obtained by systematic study and precise observation. To be scientific is to be unsentimental, rational, straight-thinking, correct, rigorous, exact. Yet in both the nineteenth and twentieth centuries scientists made strong statements about the social and political roles of women, claiming all the while to speak the scientific truth. Feminists, too, have used scientific arguments to bolster their cause.[1] Furthermore, research about sex differences frequently contains gross procedural errors. In a 1981 article one well-known psychologist cited "ten ubiquitous methodological problems" that plague such work.[2] The list contains striking errors in logic—such as experiments done only on males from which the investigators draw conclusions about females, and the use of limited (usually white, middle-class) experimental populations from which a scientist draws conclusions about *all* males or females. Perhaps the most widespread methodological problem is pinning the results of a study on gender when differences could be explained by other variables. Many researchers note, for example, that boys do better than girls on college entrance tests in mathematics. For years scientists concluded from such results that boys are bet-

Anne Fausto-Sterling, "The Biological Connection," *Myths of Gender,* New York: Basic Books, 1992: 8–10.

ter at math than are girls. Recently, however, several investigators have pointed out that girls take fewer math courses in high school; thus, college entrance exams pit boys with more training in math against girls with less training. Sex and course taking are confounded, and the conclusion that boys are inherently better at math remains without clear-cut support.

What is the untrained onlooker to make of all this? Are these examples of "science corrupted," as one historian has called the misrepresentation of women in scientific studies,[3] or do such cases provide evidence for a rather different view of science—one in which the scientists themselves emerge as cultural products, their activities structured, often unconsciously, by the great social issues of the day? During the past 15 years scholars in women's studies have looked hard at virtually every field of intellectual inquiry, all the while feeling more and more like the child in the story about the emperor's new clothes. Examining the same material that for years great intellects had deemed solid, whole, flawless, they have found themselves asking, naïvely at first, but then with greater factual and theoretical sophistication, "But where are the women?" and, "If you take women into account, doesn't that change the whole conclusion?" Scientific inquiry, particularly as it pertains to sex and gender, has been no exception.

If science as an overall endeavor is completely objective and functions independently of the prevailing social winds, then scientists who commit gross errors of method and interpretation are simply bad at their jobs. The problem with this view is that flaws in research design often show up in the work of intelligent, serious men and women who have been trained at the best institutions in the country. By all conventional measures—publication record, employment in universities, invitations to scholarly conferences   they are good scientists, highly regarded by their peers. Here, then, we face an apparent paradox. Some of the most recognized scientists in their fields have built a reputation on what others, myself included, now claim to be bad work. One could resolve the paradox simply by denouncing the entire scientific enterprise as intellectually corrupt, but I find this an unacceptable position. I believe that the majority of scientists not only are highly capable but try in good faith to design careful, thoughtful experiments. Why, then, do they seem to fail so regularly when it comes to research on sex differences?

The answer may be found if, rather than simply dismissing these researchers as bad at their trade, we think about what they do as "conventional science." In analyzing male/female differences these scientists peer through the prism of everyday culture, using the colors so separated to highlight their questions, design their experiments, and interpret their results. More often than not their hidden agendas, nonconscious and thus unarticulated, bear strong resemblances to broader social agendas. Historians of science have become increasingly aware that even in the most "objective" of fields—chemistry and physics—a scientist may fail to see something that is right under his or her nose because currently accepted theory cannot account for the observation.[4] Although no one can be entirely successful, all serious scientists strive to eliminate such blind spots. The prospects for success diminish enormously, how-ever, when the area of research touches one very personally. And what could be more personally significant than our sense of ourselves as male or female? In the study of gender (like sexuality and race) it is inherently impossible for any individual to do unbiased research.

What, then, is to be done? We could call for a ban on all research into sex differences. But that would leave questions of genuine social and scientific interest unanswered. We could claim an agnostic position—that all research is good for its own sake—but no one really believes that. Scientists make judgments all the time about the importance of particular lines of research, and those deemed frivolous or otherwise insignificant fail to receive funding. We ought, therefore, neither to impose research bans nor to claim agnosticism. Instead, we ought to expect that individual researchers will articulate—both to themselves and publicly—exactly where they stand, what they think, and, most importantly, what they *feel* deep down in their guts about the complex of personal and social issues that relate to their area of research. Then let the reader beware. The reader can look at the data, think about the logic of the argument, figure out how the starting questions were framed, and consider alternate interpretations of the data. By definition, one cannot see one's own blind spots; therefore one must acknowledge the probability of their presence and provide others with enough information to identify and illuminate them.

NOTES

1. Sayers, *Biological Politics, Feminist and Anti-feminist Perspectives,* New York: Tavisrock, 1982.

2. C. N. Jacklin, "Methodological Issues in the Study of Sex-related Differences," *Developmental Review* 1(1981): 266–73.

3. S. S. Mosedale, "Science Corrupted: Victorian Biologists Consider 'The Woman Question,'" *Journal of the History of Biology* 11(1978): 1–55.

4. T. S. Kuhn, *The Structure of Scientific Revolutions* (Chicago: University of Chicago Press, 1962).

Women's Brains

STEPHEN JAY GOULD

Stephen Jay Gould, scientist and historian of science, tells us that scientific research in race and gender was influenced by biases and prejudices. Looking at the nineteenth-century science of craniometry, Gould argues that much of the information produced about women's brain size might have been useful but the interpretations were extremely prejudiced against women as a group.

In the prelude to *Middlemarch,* George Eliot lamented the unfulfilled lives of talented women:

> Some have felt that these blundering lives are due to the inconvenient indefiniteness with which the Supreme Power has fashioned the natures of women: if there were one level of feminine incompetence as strict as the ability to count three and no more, the social lot of women might be treated with scientific certitude.

Eliot goes on to discount the idea of innate limitation, but while she wrote in 1872, the leaders of European anthropometry were trying to measure "with scientific certitude" the inferiority of women. Anthropometry, or

Stephen Jay Gould, "Women's Brains" in *The Panda's Thumb: More Reflections in Natural History,* New York: W. W. Norton, 1980: 152–59.

measurement of the human body, is not so fashionable a field these days, but it dominated the human sciences for much of the nineteenth century and remained popular until intelligence testing replaced skull measurement as a favored device for making invidious comparisons among races, classes, and sexes. Craniometry, or measurement of the skull, commanded the most attention and respect. Its unquestioned leader, Paul Broca (1824–80), professor of clinical surgery at the Faculty of Medicine in Paris, gathered a school of disciples and imitators around himself. Their work, so meticulous and apparently irrefutable, exerted great influence and won high esteem as a jewel of nineteenth-century science.

Broca's work seemed particularly invulnerable to refutation. Had he not measured with the most scrupulous care and accuracy? (Indeed, he had. I have the greatest respect for Broca's meticulous procedure. His numbers are sound. But science is an inferential exercise, not a catalog of facts. Numbers, by themselves, specify nothing. All depends upon what you do with them.) Broca depicted himself as an apostle of objectivity, a man who bowed before facts and cast aside superstition and sentimentality. He declared that "there is no faith, however respectable, no interest, however legitimate, which must not accommodate itself to the progress of human knowledge and bend before truth." Women, like it or not, had smaller brains than men and,

---

Key Terms

anthropometry The science of the measurement of the human body.

craniometry The science of the measurement of the human skull.

therefore, could not equal them in intelligence. This fact, Broca argued, may reinforce a common prejudice in male society, but it is also a scientific truth. L. Manouvrier, a black sheep in Broca's fold, rejected the inferiority of women and wrote with feeling about the burden imposed upon them by Broca's numbers:

> Women displayed their talents and their diplomas. They also invoked philosophical authorities. But they were opposed by *numbers* unknown to Condorcet or to John Stuart Mill. These numbers fell upon poor women like a sledge hammer, and they were accompanied by commentaries and sarcasms more ferocious than the most misogynist imprecations of certain church fathers. The theologians had asked if women had a soul. Several centuries later, some scientists were ready to refuse them a human intelligence.

Broca's argument rested upon two sets of data: the larger brains of men in modern societies, and a supposed increase in male superiority through time. His most extensive data came from autopsies performed personally in four Parisian hospitals. For 292 male brains, he calculated an average weight of 1,325 grams; 140 female brains averaged 1,144 grams for a difference of 181 grams, or 14 percent of the male weight. Broca understood, of course, that part of this difference could be attributed to the greater height of males. Yet he made no attempt to measure the effect of size alone and actually stated that it cannot account for the entire difference because we know, a priori that women are not as intelligent as men (a premise that the data were supposed to test, not rest upon):

> We might ask if the small size of the female brain depends exclusively upon the small size of her body. Tiedemann has proposed this explanation. But we must not forget that women are, on the average, a little less intelligent than men, a difference which we should not exaggerate but which is, nonetheless, real. We are therefore permitted to suppose that the relatively small size of the female brain depends in part upon her physical inferiority and in part upon her intellectual inferiority.

In 1873, the year after Eliot published *Middlemarch,* Broca measured the cranial capacities of prehistoric skulls from L'Homme Mort cave. Here he found a difference of only 99.5 cubic centimeters between males and females, while modern populations range from 129.5 to 220.7. Topinard, Broca's chief disciple, explained the increasing discrepancy through time as a result of differing evolutionary pressures upon dominant men and passive women:

> The man who fights for two or more in the struggle for existence, who has all the responsibility and the cares of tomorrow, who is constantly active in combating the environment and human rivals, needs more brain than the woman whom he must protect and nourish, the sedentary woman, lacking any interior occupations, whose role is to raise children, love, and be passive.

In 1879, Gustave Le Bon, chief misogynist of Broca's school, used these data to publish what must be the most vicious attack upon women in modern scientific literature (no one can top Aristotle). I do not claim his views were representative of Broca's school, but they were published in France's most respected anthropological journal. Le Bon concluded:

> In the most intelligent races, as among the Parisians, there are a large number of women whose brains are closer in size to those of gorillas than to the most developed male brains. This inferiority is so obvious that no one can contest it for a moment; only its degree is worth discussion. All psychologists who have studied the intelligence of women, as well as poets and novelists, recognize today that they represent the most inferior forms of human evolution and that they are closer to children and savages than to an adult, civilized man. They excel in fickleness, inconstancy, absence of thought and logic, and incapacity to reason. Without doubt there exist some distinguished women, very superior to the average man, but they are as exceptional as the birth of any monstrosity, as, for example, of a gorilla with two heads; consequently, we may neglect them entirely.

Nor did Le Bon shrink from the social implications of his views. He was horrified by the proposal of some American reformers to grant women higher education on the same basis as men:

A desire to give them the same education, and, as a consequence, to propose the same goals for them, is a dangerous chimera. . . . The day when, misunderstanding the inferior occupations which nature has given her, women leave the home and take part in our battles; on this day a social revolution will begin, and everything that maintains the sacred ties of the family will disappear.

Sound familiar?[o]

I have reexamined Broca's data, the basis for all this derivative pronouncement, and I find his numbers sound but his interpretation ill-founded, to say the least. The data supporting his claim for increased difference through time can be easily dismissed. Broca based his contention on the samples from L'Homme Mort alone—only seven male and six female skulls in all. Never have so little data yielded such far-ranging conclusions.

In 1888, Topinard published Broca's more extensive data on the Parisian hospitals. Since Broca recorded height and age as well as brain size, we may use modern statistics to remove their effect. Brain weight decreases with age, and Broca's women were, on average, considerably older than his men. Brain weight increases with height, and his average man was almost half a foot taller than his average woman. I used multiple regression, a technique that allowed me to assess simultaneously the influence of height and age upon brain size. In an analysis of the data for women. I found that, at average male height and age, a woman's brain would weight 1,212 grams. Correction for height and age reduces Broca's measured difference of 181 grams by more than a third, to 113 grams.

I don't know what to make of this remaining difference because I cannot assess other factors known to in-

fluence brain size in a major way. Cause of death has an important effect: degenerative disease often entails a substantial diminution of brain size. (This effect is separate from the decrease attributed to age alone.) Eugene Schreider, also working with Broca's data, found that men killed in accidents had brains weighing, on average, 60 grams more than men dying of infectious diseases. The best modern data I can find (from American hospitals) records a full 100-gram difference between death by degenerative arteriosclerosis and by violence or accident. Since so many of Broca's subjects were elderly women, we may assume that lengthy degenerative disease was more common among them than among the men.

More importantly, modern students of brain size still have not agreed on a proper measure for eliminating the powerful effect of body size. Height is partly adequate, but men and women of the same height do not share the same body build. Weight is even worse than height, because most of its variation reflects nutrition rather than intrinsic size—fat versus skinny exerts little influence upon the brain. Manouvrier took up this subject in the 1880s and argued that muscular mass and force should be used. He tried to measure this elusive property in various ways and found a marked difference in favor of men, even in men and women of the same height. When he corrected for what he called "sexual mass," women actually came out slightly ahead in brain size.

Thus, the corrected 113-gram difference is surely too large: the true figure is probably close to zero and may as well favor women as men. And 113 grams, by the way, is exactly the average difference between a 5 foot 4 inch and a 6 foot 4 inch male in Broca's data. We would not (especially us short folks) want to ascribe greater intelligence to tall men. In short, who knows what to do with Broca's data? They certainly don't permit any confident claim that men have bigger brains than women.

To appreciate the social role of Broca and his school, we must recognize that his statements about the brains of women do not reflect an isolated prejudice toward a single disadvantaged group. They must be weighed in the context of a general theory that supported contemporary social distinctions as biologically ordained. Women, blacks, and poor people suffered the same disparagement, but women bore the brunt of

---

[o]When I wrote this essay, I assumed that Le Bon was a marginal, if colorful, figure. I have since learned that he was a leading scientist, one of the founders of social psychology, and best known for a seminal study on crowd behavior, still cited today (*La psychologie des foules,* 1895), and for his work on unconscious motivation.

Broca's argument because he had easier access to data on women's brains. Women were singularly denigrated but they also stood as surrogates for other disenfranchised groups. As one of Broca's disciples wrote in 1881: "Men of the black races have a brain scarcely heavier than that of white woman." This juxtaposition extended into many other realms of anthropological argument, particularly to claims that, anatomically and emotionally, both women and blacks were like white children—and that white children, by the theory of recapitulation, represented an ancestral (primitive) adult stage of human evolution. I do not regard as empty rhetoric the claim that women's battles are for all of us.

Maria Montessori did not confine her activities to educational reform for young children. She lectured on anthropology for several years at the University of Rome, and wrote an influential book entitled *Pedagogical Anthropology* (English edition 1913). Montessori was no egalitarian. She supported most of Broca's work and the theory of innate criminality proposed by her compatriot Cesare Lombroso. She measured the circumference of children's heads in her schools and inferred that the best prospects had bigger brains. But she had no use for Broca's conclusions about women. She discussed Manouvrier's work at length and made much of his tentative claim that women, after proper correction of the data, had slightly larger brains than men. Women, she concluded, were intellectually superior, but men had prevailed heretofore by dint of physical force. Since technology has abolished force as an instrument of power, the era of women may soon be upon us: "In such an epoch there will really be superior human beings, there will really be men strong in morality and in sentiment. Perhaps in this way the reign of women is approaching, when the enigma of her anthropological superiority will be deciphered. Woman was always the custodian of human sentiment, morality, and honor."

This represents one possible antidote to "scientific" claims for the constitutional inferiority of certain groups. One may affirm the validity of biological distinctions but argue that the data have been misinterpreted by prejudiced men with a stake in the outcome, and that disadvantaged groups are truly superior. In recent years, Elaine Morgan has followed this strategy in her *Descent of Woman,* a speculative reconstruction of human prehistory from the woman's point of view—and as farcical as more famous tall tales by and for men.

I prefer another strategy. Montessori and Morgan followed Broca's philosophy to reach a more congenial conclusion. I would rather label the whole enterprise of setting a biological value upon groups for what it is: irrelevant and highly injurious. George Eliot well appreciated the special tragedy that biological labeling imposed upon members of disadvantaged groups. She expressed it for people like herself—women of extraordinary talent. I would apply it more widely—not only to those whose dreams are flouted but also to those who never realize that they may dream—but I cannot match her prose. In conclusion, then, the rest of Eliot's prelude to *Middlemarch:*

> The limits of variation are really much wider than anyone would imagine from the sameness of women's coiffure and the favorite love stories in prose and verse. Here and there a cygnet is reared uneasily among the ducklings in the brown pond, and never finds the living stream in fellowship with its own vary-footed kind. Here and there is born a Saint Theresa, foundress of nothing, whose loving heartbeats and sobs after an unattained goodness tremble off and are dispersed among hindrances instead of centering in some long-recognizable deed.

The Ethics of Genetic Research on Sexual Orientation

UDO SCHUKLENK, EDWARD STEIN, JACINTA KERIN, AND WILLIAM BYNE

The authors examine the scientific research that seeks to substantiate the claim that homosexuality has a genetic basis. They believe that the biases that inform the science of the "gay gene" will lead to increasing discrimination against gays and lesbians.

Ethical Concerns

We have several ethical concerns about genetic research on sexual orientation. Underlying these concerns is the fact that even in our contemporary societies, lesbians, gay men, and bisexuals are subject to widespread discrimination and social disapprobation. Against this background, we are concerned about the particularly gruesome history of the use of such research. Many homosexual people have been forced to undergo "treatments" to change their sexual orientation, while others have "chosen" to undergo them in

Udo Schuklenk, Edward Stein, Jacinta Kerin, William Byne, "The Ethics of Genetic Research on Sexual Orientation," *The Hastings Center Report,* Hastings Center, Hastings-on-Hudson, July/August 1997: 1–4.

order to escape societal homophobia. All too often, scientifically questionable "therapeutic" approaches destroyed the lives of perfectly healthy people. "Conversion therapies" have included electroshock treatment, hormonal therapies, genital mutilation, and brain surgery.[1] We are concerned about the negative ramifications of biological research on sexual orientation, especially in homophobic societies. In Germany, some scholars have warned of the potential for abuse of such genetic research, while others have called for a moratorium on it to prevent the possible abuse of its results in homophobic societies. These warnings should be taken seriously.

We are concerned that people conducting research on sexual orientation work within homophobic frameworks, despite their occasional claims to the contrary. A prime example is the German obstetrician Gunter Dorner, whose descriptions of homosexuality ill-conceal his heterosexism. Dorner writes about homosexuality as a "dysfunction" or "disease" based on "abnormal brain development." He postulates that it can be prevented by "optimizing" natural conditions or by "correcting abnormal hormonal concentrations prenatally"

Key Terms

gay gene Trend in current genetic research to locate the biological source of homosexuality.
homophobia A bias or prejudice against all nonheterosexual identities and practices, usually displayed through violence or discrimination against gay, lesbian, bisexual, and transgender people.

polymorphism The occurrence of something in several different forms.
sociobiology Late twentieth-century science of human behavior based on biological determinism. Often used to justify discrimination based on race and gender.

(emphasis added).[2] Another example is provided by psychoanalyst Richard Friedman, who engages in speculation about nongay outcomes given proper therapeutic intervention.[3] Research influenced by homophobia is likely to result in significantly biased accounts of human sexuality; further, such work is more likely to strengthen and perpetuate the homophobic attitudes on which it is based.

—Sexual Orientation Research Is Not Value Neutral

Furthermore, we question whether those who research sexual orientation can ever conduct their work in a value-neutral manner. One might expect that the majority of American sex researchers would treat homosexuality not as a disease, but rather as a variation analogous to a neutral polymorphism. To consider whether or not this is the case, one must look at the context in which interest in sexual orientation arises. Homophobia still exists to some degree in all societies within which sexual orientation research is conducted. The cultures in which scientists live and work influence both the questions they ask and the hypotheses they imagine and explore. Given this, we believe it is unlikely that the sexual orientation research of any scientist (even one who is homosexual) will escape some taint of homophobia.

This argument is importantly different from the claim that objective research can be used unethically in discriminatory societies. The latter logic implies that what should be questioned is the regulation of the application of technology, not the development of the technology in the first place. While we do provide arguments for questioning the efficacy of such regulations should they be developed, our deeper concerns are directed toward the institutional and social structures that constrain sex research. Attention to these contextual details shows that research into sexual orientation is different from research into most other physical/behavioral variations. Since sexual orientation is the focus of intense private and public interest, relevant inquiry cannot be studied independently of societal investment. It is naive to suggest that individual researchers might suddenly find themselves in the position of neutral inquirers. Social mores both constrain

and enable the ways in which an individual's research is focused.

We are not claiming that all researchers are homophobic to some degree whether or not they are aware of it. Nor are we talking about the implicit or explicit intentions of individual sexual orientation researchers. Rather, we are seeking to highlight that the very motivation for seeking the "origin" of homosexuality has its source within social frameworks that are pervasively homophobic. Recognition that scientific projects are constituted by, and to some degree complicit in, social structures does not necessarily entail that all such science should cease. At the very least, however, it follows that sexual orientation research and its use should be subject to critique. Such a critique will call into question the claim that, by treating homosexuality as a mere variation of human behavior, researchers are conducting neutral investigations into sexual orientation. . . .

—Normativity of Naturalness and Normality

Why is there a dispute as to whether homosexuality is natural or normal? We suggest it is because many people seem to think that nature has a prescriptive normative force such that what is deemed natural or normal is necessarily good and therefore ought to be. Everything that falls outside these terms is constructed as unnatural and abnormal, and it has been argued that this constitutes sufficient reason to consider homosexuality worth avoiding.[4]

Arguments that appeal to "normality" to provide us with moral guidelines also risk committing the naturalistic fallacy of mistakenly deduces from the way things are to the way they ought to be. For instance, Dean Hamer and colleagues commit this error in their *Science* article when they state that "it would be fundamentally unethical to use such information to try to assess or alter a person's current or future sexual orientation, either heterosexual or homosexual, or other normal attributes of human behavior."[5] Hamer and colleagues believe that there is a major genetic factor contributing to sexual orientation. From this they think it follows that homosexuality is normal and thus worthy of preservation. Thus they believe that genetics can tell us what is normal, and that the content of what is normal tells us what ought to be. This is a typical example of a naturalistic fallacy.

Normality can be defined in a number of ways, but none of them direct us in the making of moral judgments. First, normality can be reasonably defined in a descriptive sense as a statistical average. Appeals to what is usual, regular, and/or conforming to existing standards ultimately collapse into statistical statements. For an ethical evaluation, it is irrelevant whether homosexuality is normal or abnormal in this sense. All sorts of human traits and behaviors are abnormal in a statistical sense, but this is not a sufficient justification for a negative ethical judgment about them.

Second, "normality" might be defined in a functional sense, where what is normal is something that has served an adaptive function from an evolutionary perspective. This definition of normality can be found in sociobiology, which seeks biological explanations for social behavior. There are a number of serious problems with the sociobiological project.[6] For the purposes of this argument, however, suffice it to say that even if sociobiology could establish that certain behavioral traits were the direct result of biological evolution, no moral assessment of these traits would follow. To illustrate our point, suppose any trait that can be reasonably believed to have served an adaptive function at some evolutionary stage is normal. Some questions arise that exemplify the problems with deriving normative conclusions from descriptive science. Are traits that are perpetuated simply through linkage to selectively advantageous loci less "normal" than those for which selection was direct? Given that social contexts now exert "selective pressure" in a way that nature once did, how are we to decide which traits are to be intentionally fostered?

[. . .]

U.S.-Specific Arguments

In the United States, several scholars and lesbian and gay activists have argued that establishing a genetic basis for sexual orientation will help make the case for lesbian and gay rights. The idea is that scientific research will show that people do not choose their sexual orientations and therefore should not be punished or discriminated against due to them. This general argument is flawed in several ways.[7] First, we do not need

to prove that a trait is genetically determined to argue that it is not amenable to change at will. This is clearly shown by the failure rates of conversion "therapies."[8] These failures establish that sexual orientation is resistant to change, but they do not say anything about its ontogeny or etiology. Sexual orientation can be unchangeable without being genetically determined. There is strong observational evidence to support the claim that sexual orientation is difficult to change, but this evidence is perfectly compatible with nongenetic accounts of the origins of sexual orientations. More importantly, we should not embrace arguments that seek to legitimate homosexuality by denying that there is any choice in sexual preference because the implicit premise of such arguments is that if there was a choice, then homosexuals would be blameworthy.

Relatedly, arguments for lesbian and gay rights based on scientific evidence run the risk of leading to impoverished forms of lesbian and gay rights. Regardless of what causes homosexuality, a person has to decide to identify publicly as a lesbian, to engage in sexual acts with another woman, to raise children with her same-sex lover, or to be active in the lesbian and gay community. It is when people make such decisions that they are likely to face discrimination, arrest, or physical violence. It is decisions like these that need legal protection. An argument for lesbian and gay rights based on genetic evidence is impotent to protect such decisions because it focuses exclusively on the very aspects of sexuality that might not involve choices.

Another version of this argument focuses on the specifics of U.S. law. It claims that scientific evidence will establish the immutability of sexual orientation, which, according to one current interpretation of the equal protection clause of the Fourteenth Amendment of the U.S. Constitution, is one of three criteria required of a classification for it to evoke heightened judicial scrutiny. This line of argument has serious internal problems.[9] Like a good deal of American bioethical reasoning, it also has limited or no relevance to the global context. Since the results of the scientific research are not confined within American borders, justifications that go beyond U.S. legislation are required.

The same sort of problem occurs in other defenses of sexual orientation research that discuss possible ramifications in U.S.-specific legislative terms. For instance, Timothy Murphy claims that, even if a genetic probe predictive of sexual orientation were available, mandatory testing would be unlikely.[10] He bases this claim on the fact that in some states employment and housing discrimination against homosexual people is illegal. In many countries, however, the political climate is vastly different, and legal antigay discrimination is widespread. And there is evidence that scientific research would be used in a manner that discriminates against homosexuals.[11] For example, in Singapore, homosexual sex acts are a criminal offense. The Singapore Penal Code sections 377 and 377A threaten sentences ranging from two years to life imprisonment for engaging in same-sex acts. Not coincidentally in light of our concerns, a National University of Singapore psychiatrist recently stated that "presymptomatic testing for homosexuality should be offered in the absence of treatment,"[12] implying that homosexuality is a condition in need of a cure.

[. . .]

The Value of Knowing the Truth

Finally, various scholars appeal to the value of the truth to defend research on sexual orientation in the face of ethical concerns. Scientific research does, however, have its costs, and not every research program is of equal importance. Even granting that, in general, knowledge is better than ignorance, not all risks for the sake of knowledge are worth taking. With respect to sexual orientation, historically, almost every hypothe-sis about the causes of homosexuality led to attempts to "cure" healthy people. History indicates that current genetic research is likely to have negative effects on lesbians and gay men, particularly those living in homophobic societies.[13]

A Global Perspective

Homosexual people have in the past suffered greatly from societal discrimination. Historically, the results of biological research on sexual orientation have been used against them. We have analyzed the arguments offered by well-intentioned defenders of such work and concluded that none survive philosophical scrutiny. It is true that in some countries in Scandinavia, North America, and most parts of Western Europe, the legal situation of homosexual people has improved, but an adequate ethical analysis of the implications of genetic inquiry into the causes of sexual orientation must operate from a global perspective. Sexual orientation researchers should be aware that their work may harm homosexuals in countries other than their own. It is difficult to imagine any good that could come of genetic research on sexual orientation in homophobic societies. Such work faces serious ethical concerns so long as homophobic societies continue to exist. Insofar as socially responsible genetic research on sexual orientation is possible, it must begin with the awareness that it will not be a cure for homophobia and that the ethical status of lesbians and gay men does not in any way hinge on its results.

NOTES

1. Jonathan Ned Katz, *Gay American History* (New York: Thomas Crowell, 1976), pp. 197–422.

2. Gunter Dorner, "Hormone-Dependent Brain Development and Neuroendocrine Prophylaxis," *Experimental and Clinical Endocrinology* 94 (1989): 4–22.

3. Richard C. Friedman, *Male Homosexuality: A Contemporary Psychoanalytic Perspective* (New Haven: Yale University Press, 1988), p. 20.

4. Michael Levin, "Why Homosexuality Is Abnormal," *Monist* 67 (1984): 251–83.

5. Dean Hamer et al., "A Linkage between DNA Markers on the X Chromosome and Male Sexual Orientation," *Science* 261 (1993), p. 326.

6. Philip Kitcher, *Vaulting Ambition: Sociobiology and the Quest for Human Nature* (Cambridge, Mass.: MIT Press, 1985).

7. Edward Stein, "The Relevance of Scientific Research Concerning Sexual Orientation to Lesbian and Gay Rights," *Journal of Homosexuality* 27 (1994): 269–308.

8. Charles Silverstein, "Psychological and Medical Treatments of Homosexuality," in *Homosexuality: Research Implications for*

Public Policy, J. C. Gonsiorek and J. D. Weinrich, eds. (Newbury Park, Calif.: Sage, 1991), pp. 101–14.

9. Janet Halley, "Sexual Orientation and the Politics of Biology: A Critique of the New Argument from Immutability," *Stanford Law Review* 46 (1994): 503–68.

10. Timothy Murphy, "Abortion and the Ethics of Genetic Sexual Orientation Research," *Cambridge Quarterly of Healthcare Ethics* 4 (1995), p. 341.

11. Paul Billings, "Genetic Discrimination and Behavioural Genetics: The Analysis of Sexual Orientation in Intractable Neurological Disorders," *Human Genome Research and Society,* Norio Fujiki and Darryl Macer, eds. (Christchurch and Tsukuba: Eubios Ethics

Institute, 1993), p. 37; Paul Billings, "International Aspects of Genetic Discrimination," in *Human Genome Research and Society,* Norio Fujiki and Darryl Macer, eds. (Christchurch and Tsukuba: Eubios Ethics Institute, 1992), pp. 114–17.

12. L. C. C. Lim, "Present Controversies in the Genetics of Male Homosexuality," *Annals of the Academy of Medicine Singapore* 24 (1995): 759–62.

13. For further elaborations on this argument, see Edward Stein, Udo Schuklenk, and Jacinta Kerin, "Scientific Research on Sexual Orientation," in *Encyclopedia of Applied Ethics,* Ruth Chadwick, ed. (San Diego: Academic Press, 1997).

REFLECTING ON THE SECTION

This section's readings all address the supposed objectivity of scientific research. For instance, Linda Gordon asks us to consider how "science" has come to be differentiated from "magic." This distinction, as the history of Western science reveals, left out the contributions and bodies of knowledge of women and much of the non-Western world. Yet rather than dismissing science, Fausto-Sterling argues we must understand it to be constructed through debates about cultural beliefs and values. Gould and Schuklenk et. al. show how racism, misogyny, and homophobia led to some scientific ideas that have now been dismissed by most scientists. What types of innovations, studies, and practices have you thought of as "medical" or "scientific"?

Do Gordon's and Rowbotham's essays challenge or change your own beliefs or assumptions? How does considering the roles of women in societies in greater specificity add to or broaden definitions of "science"? Do you think that such a broadening challenges how we think about science today? What kinds of research practices do the authors in this section propose? Do you think that any of the interventions in research on gender, sexual orientation, and race that these two essays propose would avoid some of the pitfalls outlined in the readings in this section?

The Making of Race, Sex, and Empire

The Social Construction of Race

IAN F. HANEY LÓPEZ

Legal scholar Ian F. Haney López describes the way that biological arguments about race continue to be used in the legal system even though scientific research has concluded that there is no biological basis for race. The concept of race remains powerful and becomes perpetuated through legal, scientific, and political institutions.

—Biological Race

There are no genetic characteristics possessed by all Blacks but not by non-Blacks; similarly, there is no gene or cluster of genes common to all Whites but not to non-Whites.[1] One's race is not determined by a single gene or gene cluster, as is, for example, sickle-cell anemia. Nor are races marked by important differences in gene frequencies (the rates of appearance of certain gene types). The data compiled by various scientists demonstrate, contrary to popular opinion, that intragroup differences exceed intergroup differences. That is, greater genetic variation exists *within* the populations typically labeled Black and White than *between* these populations.[2] This finding refutes the supposi-

Ian F. Haney López, "The Social Construction of Race," 29 Harvard Civil Rights—Civil Liberties Law Review 1 (1994): 11–12, 13–15, 16–17, 27–33.

tion that racial divisions reflect fundamental genetic differences.

Rather, the notion that humankind can be divided along White, Black, and Yellow lines reveals the social rather than the scientific origin of race. The idea that there exist three races, and that these races are "Caucasoid," "Negroid," and "Mongoloid," is rooted in the European imagination of the Middle Ages, which encompassed only Europe, Africa, and the Near East. This view found its clearest modern expression in Count Arthur de Gobineau's *Essay on the Inequality of Races,* published in France in 1853–55.[3] The peoples of the American continents, the Indian subcontinent, East Asia, Southeast Asia, and Oceania—living outside the imagination of Europe and Count Gobineau—are excluded from the three major races for social and political reasons, not for scientific ones. Nevertheless, the history of science has long been the history of failed efforts to justify these social beliefs.[4] Along the way, various minds tried to fashion practical human typologies along the following physical axes: skin color, hair texture, facial angle, jaw size, cranial capacity, brain mass, frontal lobe mass, brain surface fissures and convolutions, and even body lice. As one scholar notes, "[t]he nineteenth century was a period of exhaustive and—as it turned out—futile search for criteria to define and describe race differences."[5]

Key Term

reify/reification To make something into an object, especially an object that can be traded or sold at a market.

To appreciate the difficulties of constructing races solely by reference to physical characteristics, consider the attempt to define race by skin color. On the basis of white skin, for example, one can define a race that includes most of the peoples of Western Europe. However, this grouping is threatened by the subtle gradations of skin color as one moves south or east, and becomes untenable when the fair-skinned peoples of Northern China and Japan are considered. In 1922, in *Ozawa v. United States,*[6] the Supreme Court nicely explained this point. When Japanese-born Takao Ozawa applied for citizenship he asserted, as required by the Naturalization Act, that he was a "white person." Counsel for Ozawa pointedly argued that to reject Ozawa's petition for naturalization would be "to exclude a Japanese who is 'white' in color." This argument did not persuade the Court: "Manifestly, the test [of race] afforded by the mere color of the skin of each individual is impracticable as that differs greatly among persons of the same race, even among Anglo-Saxons, ranging by imperceptible gradations from the fair blond to the swarthy brunette, the latter being darker than many of the lighter hued persons of the brown or yellow races."[7] In rejecting Ozawa's petition for citizenship, the Court recognized that race is not a function of skin color alone. If it were, some now secure in their White status would have to be excluded, and others firmly characterized as non-Whites would need to be included. As the *Ozawa* Court correctly tells us, "mere color of the skin" does not provide a means to racially divide people. [. . .]

The rejection of race in science is now almost complete. In the end, we should embrace historian Barbara Field's succinct conclusion with respect to the plausibility of biological races: "Anyone who continues to believe in race as a physical attribute of individuals, despite the now commonplace disclaimers of biologists and geneticists, might as well also believe that Santa Claus, the Easter Bunny and the tooth fairy are real, and that the earth stands still while the sun moves."[8]

Racial Illusions

Unfortunately, few in this society seem prepared to relinquish fully their subscription to notions of biological race. This includes Congress and the Supreme Court. Congress's anachronistic understanding of race is exemplified by a 1988 statute that explains that "the term 'racial group' means a set of individuals whose identity as such is distinctive in terms of physical characteristics or biological descent."[9] The Supreme Court, although purporting to sever race from biology, also seems incapable of doing so. In *Saint Francis College v. Al-Khazraji,*[10] the Court determined that an Arab could recover damages for racial discrimination under 42 U.S.C. § 1981. Writing for the Court, Justice White appeared to abandon biological notions of race in favor of a sociopolitical conception, explaining: "[. . .] Clear-cut categories do not exist. The particular traits which have generally been chosen to characterize races have been criticized as having little biological significance. It has been found that differences between individuals of the same race are often greater than the differences between the 'average' individuals of different races [. . .]."[11] Despite this seeming rejection of biological race, Justice White continued: "The Court of Appeals was thus quite right in holding that § 1981, 'at a minimum,' reaches discrimination against an individual 'because he or she is genetically part of an ethnically and physiognomically distinctive subgrouping of *homo sapiens.*'"[12] By adopting the lower court's language of genetics and distinctive subgroupings, Justice White demonstrates the Court's continued reliance on blood as a metonym for race. [. . .] During oral argument in *Metrobroadcasting v. FCC,* Justice Scalia again revealed the Court's understanding of race as a matter of blood. Scalia attacked the argument that granting minorities broadcasting licenses would enhance diversity by blasting "the policy as a matter of 'blood,'" at one point charging that the policy reduced to a question of 'blood . . . blood, not background and environment.'"[13] [. . .]

Racial Formation

Race must be viewed as a social construction. That is, human interaction rather than natural differentiation must be seen as the source and continued basis for racial categorization. The process by which racial meanings arise has been labeled racial formation.[14] In this formulation, race is not a determinant or a residue of some other social phenomenon, but rather stands on its own as an amalgamation of competing societal forces. Racial formation includes both the rise of racial groups and their constant reification in social thought. I draw upon this theory but use the term "racial fabrication" in order to highlight four important facets of the social construction of race. First, humans rather than abstract social forces produce races. Second, as human constructs, races constitute an integral part of a whole social fabric that includes gender and class relations. Third, the meaning-systems surrounding race change quickly rather than slowly. Finally, races are constructed relationally, against one another, rather than in isolation. Fabrication implies the workings of human hands, and suggests the possible intention to deceive. More than the industrial term "formation," which carries connotations of neutral constructions and processes indifferent to individual intervention, referring to the fabrication of races emphasizes the human element and evokes the plastic and inconstant character of race. An archaeological exploration of the racial identity of Mexicans [. . .] will illustrate these four elements of race.

In the early 1800s, people in the United States ascribed to Latin Americans nationalities and, separate from these, races. Thus, a Mexican might also be White, Indian, Black, or Asian. By the 1840s and 1850s, however, U.S. Anglos looked with distaste upon Mexicans in terms that conflated and stigmatized their race and nationality. This animus had its source in the Anglo-Mexican conflicts in the Southwest, particularly in Texas and California. In the newly independent Texas, war propaganda from the 1830s and 1840s purporting to chronicle Mexican "atrocities" relied on racial disparagements. Little time elapsed following the U.S. annexation of Mexican territory in 1848 before laws began to reflect and reify Anglo racial prejudices. Social prejudices quickly became legal ones, highlighting the close ties between race and law. In 1855, for example, the California Legislature targeted Mexicans as a racial group with the so-called Greaser Act. Ostensibly designed to discourage vagrancy, the law specifically applied to "all persons who are commonly known as 'Greasers' or the issue of Spanish and Indian blood . . . and who go armed and are not peaceable and quiet persons."[15]

Typifying the arrogant belligerence of the times are the writings of T. J. Farnham:

No one acquainted with the indolent, mixed race of California will ever believe that they will populate, much less, for any length of time, govern the country. The law of Nature which curses the mulatto here with a constitution less robust than that of either race from which he sprang lays a similar penalty upon the mingling of the Indian and white races in California and Mexico. They must fade away; while the mixing of different branches of the Caucasian family in the States will continue to produce a race of men, who will enlarge from period to period the field of their industry and civil domination, until not only the Northern States of Mexico, but the Californias also, will open their glebe to the pressure of its unconquered arm. The old Saxon blood must stride the continent, must command all its northern shores, must here press the grape and the olive, here eat the orange and the fig, and in their own unaided might, erect the altar of civil and religious freedom on the plains of the Californias.[16]

Farnham's racist hubris illustrates the four important points about the nature of racial fabrication enumerated earlier.

First, the transformation of "Mexican" from a nationality to a race came about through the dynamic interplay of myriad social forces. As the various strains in this passage indicate, Farnham's racialization of Mexicans does not occur in a vacuum, but in the context of dominant ideology, perceived economic interests, and psychological necessity. In unabashedly proclaiming the virtue of raising industry and harnessing nature, Farnham trumpeted the dominant Lockean ideology of the time, an ideology which served to confirm the superiority of the industrialized Yankees and the inferiority of the pastoral Mexicans and Indians, and to justify the expropriation of their lands.[17] By lauding the commercial and economic interests of colonial expansion, Farnham also appealed to the freebooting capitalist spirit of America, recounting to his East Coast readers the riches which lay for their taking in a California populated only by mixed-breed Mexicans. Finally, Farnham's assertions regarding the racial character of these Mexicans reflected the psychological need to justify conquest: the people already in California, Farnham assured his readers, would "fade away" under Nature's curse, and in any event, were as a race "unfit" to govern their own land. As suggested, racial fabrication must be viewed as a complex process subject to manifold social forces.

Second, because races are constructed, ideas about race form part of a whole social fabric into which other relations, among them gender and class, are also woven. Farnham's choice of martial and masculine imagery is not accident but a reflection of the close symbiosis in the construction of racial and gender hierarchies during the nineteenth century.[18] This close symbiosis was reflected, for example, in distinct patterns of gender racialization during the era of frontier expansion—the native men of the Southwest were depicted as indolent, slothful, cruel, and cowardly Mexicans, while the women were described as fair, virtuous, and lonely Spanish maidens. Consider the following leaden verse:

> The Spanish maid, with eye of fire,
> At balmy evening turns her lyre
> And, looking to the Eastern sky,
> Awaits our Yankee chivalry
> Whose purer blood and valiant arms,
> Are fit to clasp her budding charms.
>
> The man, her mate, is sunk in sloth—
> To love, his senseless heart is loth:
> The pipe and glass and tinkling lute,
> A sofa, and a dish of fruit;
> A nap, some dozen times by day;
> Somber and sad, and never gay.[19]

This doggerel depicts the Mexican women as Spanish, linking their sexual desirability to European origins, while concurrently comparing the purportedly slothful Mexican man to the ostensibly virile Yankee. Social renditions of masculinity and femininity are inseverably a part of racial constructs, just as racial stereotypes invariably embody some elements of sexual identity. The archaeology of race soon becomes the excavation of gender and sexual identity.

Farnham's appeal to industry also reveals the close interconnection between racial and class structures. The observations of Arizona mine owner Sylvester Mowry reflect this linkage: "The question of [resident Mexican] labor is one which commends itself to the attention of the capitalist: cheap, and under proper management, efficient and permanent. [. . .] They have been peons for generations. They will remain so, as it is their natural condition."[20] When Farnham wrote in 1840 before U.S. expansion into the Southwest, Yankee industry stood in counterpoint to Mexican indolence. When Mowry wrote in 1863, after fifteen years of U.S. regional control, Anglo capitalism stood in a fruitful managerial relationship to cheap, efficient Mexican labor. The nearly diametric change in the conception of Mexicans held by Anglos, from indolent to industrious, reflects the emergence of an Anglo economic elite in the Southwest and illustrates the close connection between class relations and ideas about race. [. . .] The syncretic nature of racial, gender, and class constructs suggests that a global approach to oppression is not only desirable, it is *necessary* if the amelioration of these destructive social hierarchies is to be achieved.

Third, comparing the stereotypes of Mexicans propounded by Farnham and Mowry demonstrates the relatively rapid rate at which racial systems of meaning can change. In 1821, when Mexico gained its independence, its residents were not generally considered a race. Twenty years later, as Farnham's writing shows, Mexicans were denigrated in explicitly racial terms as indolent cowards. And twenty years after that, Mowry lauds Mexicans as naturally industrious and faithful. The rapid emergence of Mexicans as a race, and the equally quick transformations wrought in their perceived racial character, exemplify the plasticity of race. Accretions of racial meaning are not sedimentary products which once deposited remain solid and unchanged, or subject only to a slow process of abrasion, erosion, and buildup. Instead, the processes of racial fabrication continuously melt down, mold, twist, and recast races: races are not rocks, they are plastics.

NOTES

1. *See generally* Leon Kamin et al., *Not in Our Genes: Biology, Ideology, and Human Nature* (1984); Alan Almquist & John Cronin, "Fact, Fancy and Myth on Human Evolution," 29 *Current Anthropology* 520 (1988); *and* Bruce Bower, "Race Falls from Grace," 140 *Science News* 380 (1991).

2. See Richard C. Lewontin, "The Apportionment of Human Diversity," 6 *Evolutionary Biology* 381, 397 (1972). See generally L. L. Cavalli-Sforza, "The Genetics of Human Populations," 231 *Scientific American* 80 (Sept. 1974).

3. Thomas F. Gossett, *Race: The History of an Idea in America* 342–47 (1975).

4. See generally Stephen Jay Gould, *The Mismeasure of Man* (1981); William Stanton, *The Leopard's Spots: Scientific Attitudes toward Race in America 1815–59* (1960); and Nancy Stepan, *The Idea of Race in Science: Great Britain, 1800–1960* (1982).

5. Gossett, *supra* note 3, at 65–83. Charles Darwin proposed several of these axes, arguing at one point that "[w]ith civilized nations, the reduced size of the jaws from lessened use, the habitual play of different muscles serving to express different emotions, and the increased size of the brain from greater intellectual activity, have together produced a considerable effect on their general appearance in comparison with savages." *Id.* at 78 (quoted without attribution to a specific source). Darwin also supposed that the body lice of some races could not live on the bodies of members of other races, thus prompting him to suggest that "a racial scale might be worked out by exposing doubtful cases to different varieties of lice." *Id.* at 81. Leonardo da Vinci is another icon of intellectual greatness guilty of harboring ridiculous ideas regarding race. Da Vinci attributed racial differences to the environment in a novel manner, arguing that those who lived in hotter climates worked at night and so absorbed dark pigments, while those in cooler climates were active during the day and correspondingly absorbed light pigments. *Id.* at 16.

6. 260 U.S. 178 (1922).

7. *Id.* at 197.

8. See Barbara Jeanne Fields, "Slavery, Race and Ideology in the United States of America," 181 *New Left Rev.* 95–96 (1990).

9. Genocide Convention Implementation Act of 1987, 18 U.S.C. § 1093 (1988).

10. 481 U.S. 604 (1987).

11. *Id.* at 610, n.4.

12. *Id.* at 613.

13. Neil Gotanda, "A Critique of 'Our Constitution Is Color-Blind,' " 44 *Stanford Law Review* 1, 32 (1991) (citing Ruth Marcus, "FCC Defends Minority License Policies: Case before High Court Could Shape Future of Affirmative Action," *Washington Post,* Mar. 29, 1990, at A8).

14. Omi & Winant, at 61. Michael Omi and Howard Winant *Racial Formation in the United States: From the 1960's to the 1980's* New York: Routledge 1986.

15. Cal. Stat. 175 (1855), *excerpted in* Robert F. Heizer & Alan J. Almquist, *The Other Californians: Prejudice and Discrimination under Spain, Mexico, and the United States to 1920,* at 151 (1971). The recollections of "Dame Shirley," who resided in a California mining camp between 1851 and 1852, record efforts by the ascendant Anglos to racially denigrate Mexicans. "It is very common to hear vulgar Yankees say of the Spaniards, 'Oh, they are half-civilized black men!' These unjust expressions naturally irritate the latter, many of whom are highly educated gentlemen of the most refined and cultivated manner." L. A. K. S. Clappe, *The Shirley Letters from the California Mines, 1851–1852,* at 158 (1922), quoted in Heizer & Almquist, *supra* at 141.

16. T. J. Farnham, *Life, Adventures, and Travel in California* 413 (1840), quoted in Heizer & Almquist, *supra* note 15, at 140.

17. See generally Robert A. Williams, "The Algebra of Federal Indian Law: The Hard Trail of Decolonizing and Americanizing the White Man's Indian Jurisprudence," 1986 *Wisconsin Law Review* 219.

18. See Nancy Leys Stepan, "Race and Gender: The Role of Analogy in Science," in *Anatomy of Racism* 38 (David Theo Goldberg ed., 1990).

19. Reginald Horsman, *Race and Manifest Destiny: The Origins of American Racial Anglo-Saxonism* 233 (1981) (citation omitted).

20. Sylvester Mowry, *The Geography of Arizona and Sonora* 67 (1863), quoted in Ronald Takaki, *Iron Cages: Race and Class in Nineteenth Century America* 163 (1990).

Malthusianism

LINDA GORDON

Linda Gordon, a feminist social historian, discusses Malthusianism, which was the economic and philosophical basis for eugenics. Gordon reveals that Malthus's ideas about population and poverty came from his biases against the poor and reflected his own interests in the welfare of the capitalist class to which he belonged.

In Britain in the nineteenth century, population growth and the possibility of its control became for the first time a public controversy. The development of a secular, capitalist "science" of economics helped remove population from the area of ineluctable natural events to an area that seemed open to human manipulation. Industrialism created a contradiction between Protestant-bourgeois attitudes of sexual prudery and fears of overpopulation. On the one hand, the bourgeoisie,

Linda Gordon: "Malthusianism," *Woman's Body, Woman's Right: Birth Control in America,* Penguin, 1976: 73–77.

dominated increasingly by industrialists, was threatened by unrest among the urban and especially the rural poor, whose economic position had been worsened by industrialization.[1] On the other hand, the bourgeoisie had created over a three-century period a culture that severely repressed sexual activity in order to inculcate discipline and self-repression into its work force. Bourgeois culture by the late eighteenth century was especially hostile to women's autonomy and imposed limitations on women partly through an ideology that made motherhood dominant among women's roles and linked it inseparably to sex. Birth control would have destroyed that linkage, and secular and religious authorities condemned it absolutely. Thus the goals of population control and sexual control were somewhat at odds.

If the bourgeoisie was divided on the question of reproductive control because of its sexual attitudes, it was also divided in attitudes toward overall social control. Capitalist political theory had a "radical" and a

---

Key Terms

bourgeois/bourgeoisie Characteristics of the middle class or members of the middle class, especially identified with commercial and entrepreneurial interests.

eugenics The "science" of eugenics was based on Darwinian ideas of selecting the most "superior" races to reproduce while discouraging or eliminating those races believed to be inferior.

laissez-faire economics Economic principle of noninterference in the workings of the market.

Malthusianism The ideas proposed by Thomas Malthus in the late eighteenth century in England, in which the central belief was that population increases, caused by individual inability to exercise sexual restraint, lead to poverty.

natural law Laws derived from divine command in the Christian tradition in late medieval and early modern Europe.

utopianism Proposing or advocating ideals for the reorganization of society.

Liberal version by the late eighteenth century. "Radical" meant a democratic and somewhat more egalitarian version of Liberalism; above all, the radical streams of political thought were optimistic, asserting the possibility of the perfection of society. The Liberal tradition, by contrast, was more pessimistic. By the early nineteenth century Liberals had absorbed much of the cynicism of the Hobbesian conservatives, a cynicism appropriate to them now that they represented a dominant class. Liberals speculated that inequality and widespread poverty were inevitable and necessary to the maintenance of a high culture. Their laissez-faire economics was often but a rewording of natural-law arguments against tampering with the ordained order.

This political division was almost immediately carried into the population issue. The response to Malthus was divided doubly, between radical and Liberal attitudes toward social control, and between concern for sexual control and concern for population control. These differences made the Malthusian controversy complex. A tendency among historians to oversimplify that controversy has lumped together all Malthus's supporters in one group and all his opponents in another. In reality, a complex set of responses made Malthusianism a tradition open to many different interpretations.

Malthus's ideas on population were part of his general work as a political economist of the developing industrial-capitalist system, which he defended primarily against its mercantilist opponents. Malthus was a Liberal, and the economic forms he defended, such as the transformation of virtually all the nation's men into wage laborers, were attacked more from the Right than from the Left. Malthus appears in history as doing battle chiefly with the radicals in large part because his work on population has continued controversial. Yet in the first edition of Malthus's *Essay,* then a mere pamphlet, it is clear that the population issue was but one among many points on which Malthus disagreed with Godwin and other advocates of revolutionary utopianism.

In all his views, even as they changed, Malthus identified himself with the capitalist class and identified its welfare with the welfare of his nation. He wrote that it was impossible "to remove the want of the lower classes of society . . . the pressure of distress on this part of a community is an evil so deeply seated, that no human ingenuity can reach it."[2] An opponent of the ex-

isting British Poor Laws,* he wrote in the second edition in 1803:

> A man who is born into the world already possessed, if he cannot get subsistence from his parents on whom he has a just demand, and if the society do not want his labor, has no claim of *right* to the smallest of good, and, in fact, has no business to be where he is. At nature's mighty feast there is no vacant cover for him. She tells him to be gone, and will quickly execute her own orders, if he do not work upon the compassion of some of her guests. If these guests get up and make room for him, other intruders immediately appear demanding the same favor. . . .[3]

In his attacks on any hint of the traditional right of subsistence in the Poor Laws, Malthus was helping the British bourgeoisie to destroy local traditions of welfare and community responsibility, and thereby to create a working class defenseless against incorporation into industry. His work was ultimately influential in securing the passage of the Poor Law of 1834, a measure reflecting the interests of the industrial capitalists almost exclusively: it abolished "outdoor relief," forcing the poor to enter workhouses or, as their only alternative, to take low-paying factory jobs.[4] The Law of 1834 has been called Malthusian, and certainly Malthus supplied the original (and tenacious) theory that welfare provisions themselves contribute to overpopulation by encouraging reproduction among the poor,[5] a false attack still hurled at welfare legislation today.

The most important contribution of Malthusian population theory to that body of political thought lay in its assumptions, not in its calculations or policy recommendations. His formula that population increases geometrically and subsistence arithmetically does not stand up.[6] His prediction that deliberate birth limitation could not work was already being proven false in France, where birth rates had been falling for many decades.[7] Much more long-lasting as a theory, however, was the idea that overpopulation itself is the major cause of poverty. Indeed, this idea is the kernel of Malthusianism. It made "natural" disasters such as war and famine take on social meaning—they were popu-

*Legislation providing for state support of the needy.

lation regulators whether so intended or not. In the particular historical period in which Malthus offered his interpretation of population and poverty, the theory justified employers' interests in offering the lowest possible wages. Indeed, the theory presented the capitalist system of forcing laborers into jobs at subsistence wages as somehow inevitable, as being determined by natural laws such as those that governed reproduction. Malthusian population theory tended to draw attention away from the organization of labor and the distribution of resources. Periodic overpopulation was presented as universal; Malthus did not notice, or did not care to mention, that the rich did not suffer from overpopulation and famine.

By denying a class analysis of poverty, Malthusian theory denied the validity of class antagonism as a strategy for change. Demands made by the poor of the rich were illegitimate; only through self-help and sexual restraint could the poor help themselves. Malthus saw this sexual restraint as doubly valuable: not only would it reduce population but it would also stimulate industriousness. (Malthus operated on the basis of a crude theory of sublimation, an assumption that the frustration of the sex urge would induce men to put more energy into their work.) Yet at the same time Malthus was suspicious of sexual restraint, as of all forms of birth control, not merely out of religious scruples but because of his primary concern for the class interests of industrialists: "Prudential habits with regard to marriage, carried to a considerable extent among the labouring class of a country mainly dependent upon manufactures and commerce, might injure it."[8] As Marx pointed out, Malthus in fact understood overpopulation as a product of the economic system, of the "Trinity of capitalistic production: over-production, over-population, over-consumption," but would not admit it.[9] Instead Malthus, while denying a class analysis to those who might use it against the system, put forward the perspective of the industrial capitalist class as if it were universal truth.

Two assumptions, then, are central to Malthusianism: that overpopulation causes poverty and that individual failings in the form of lack of restraint cause overpopulation. These two assumptions are equally central to neo-Malthusianism and reveal the historical connection that gives the two "isms" the same name. In birth-control history Malthusianism and neo-Malthusianism were in opposition. Malthus was opposed to contraception, which he considered a vice. "Neo-Malthusian," to the contrary, was a name applied to early advocates of contraception. But both shared the view that overpopulation caused poverty, and it was on that premise that the neo-Malthusians concluded that population control could prevent poverty. Both also shared the recommendation of self-help, as opposed to class struggle, as a remedy for poverty.

Neo-Malthusianism

Neo-Malthusianism in its origins was the radical version of Malthusian population theory. Based on optimistic premises, the neo-Malthusians believed not only that population could be controlled but that its control could provide a key to the creation of a perfect society. It is sometimes said that they turned Malthus on his head. But they only reversed his religious opposition to contraception; they did not reverse his basic assumptions about the driving forces in the world, as Marx was later to do to Hegel.

Nevertheless, the neo-Malthusians had important differences with Liberals. Primarily they accepted contraception. Anticlericalism, antimysticism and even anti-Christianity made the radicals more prepared to challenge both the conservative interpretation that Providence determined family size and the Liberal one that only restraint could do it. Also associated with radicalism was a positive, even adulatory, attitude toward science and technology which inclined them favorably toward contraceptive technology. Perhaps most important was the radicals' greater acceptance of the scientific attitude that nature could be controlled and manipulated by human effort; surely it was this urge that led the neo-Malthusians, when they encountered some traditional contraceptive formulas, to recommend them enthusiastically to the poor as a cure for their poverty.

NOTES

1. Eric Hobsbawm and George Rude, *Captain Swing* (New York: Pantheon, 1968), pp. 42–43.

2. Thomas Malthus, *An Essay on Population,* 1st ed. ([1798] London: Macmillan, 1926), p. 95.

3. Ibid., 2d ed. (1803), pp. 531–32.

4. Maurice Dobb, *Studies in the Development of Capitalism* (London: George Routledge & Sons, 1946), pp. 274–75; Kenneth Smith, *The Malthusian Controversy* (London: Routledge & Kegan Paul, 1951), p. 297. These comments should not be construed to mean that Malthus supported only "official" bourgeois economics. He also, for example, defended the unproductive consumption of the aristocracy.

5. J. R. Poynter, *Society and Pauperism* (London: Routledge & Kegan Paul, 1969), pp. 225–27, 324.

6. Ronald L. Meek, Foreword to *Marx and Engels on Malthus* (London: Lawrence & Wishart, 1953), passim.

7. Indeed, in a later edition of his *Essay,* Malthus was forced to acknowledge that deliberate reproductive restraint might be workable. See Gertrude Himmelfarb, "The Specter of Malthus," *Victorian Minds* (New York: Knopf, 1968), pp. 102–105.

8. Malthus, *Principles of Political Economy* (London, 1836), p. 254.

9. Karl Marx, *Capital* (New York: Modern Library, n.d.), 1:696*n.*

Carol Simpson/Impact Visuals

FIGURE 1.1   "TRADITIONAL AMERICAN VALUES"

Imperialism and Motherhood

ANNA DAVIN

Anna Davin, a historian of Europe and imperialism, details the use of Malthusianism and eugenics by the British government to encourage population growth among the British with the goal of producing more soldiers. Davin argues that such policies focused on teaching women to be better mothers in order to increase the population of whites as a race able to colonize the world.

⟶ Population and Power

Around the beginning of the twentieth century infant life and child health took on a new importance in public discussion, reinforced by emphasis on the value of a healthy and numerous population as a national resource. During the nineteenth century most political economists had tended to believe with Thomas Malthus that excessive population was dangerous, leading to the exhaustion of resources, and consequently to war, epidemic disease, and other natural checks on growth. This argument was strengthened by Darwinist notions of the struggle for existence as an essential part of the survival of the race.[1] In the last decades of the century it was

Anna Davin, "Imperialism and Motherhood," *History Workshop Journal* (Spring 1978): 9–11, 11–14.

used both by the radical neo-Malthusians, who recommended contraception as an artificial check on population and therefore a preventive of poverty (which they attributed to overpopulation, arguing for instance that wages were kept down by the competition for employment); and also by the advocates of what was coming to be known as eugenics, who wanted a selective limitation of population growth, to prevent the "deterioration of the race" and decline as an imperial nation through the proliferation of those they regarded as "unfit" (to breed).[2] There was however another view, early expressed by Charles Kingsley (in 1858), that overpopulation was impossible "in a country that has the greatest colonial empire that the world has ever seen." He believed that "since about four-fifths of the globe cannot be said to be as yet in any wise inhabited or cultivated," "it was a duty, one of the noblest of duties, to help the increase of the English race as much as possible," and he urged the members of the Ladies' Sanitary Association, whom he was addressing, to fight against infant mortality.[3]

Later enthusiasts for empire also tended to see population as crucial, especially after the publication of an influential work by J. R. Seeley, *The Expansion of England,* in 1883, and they were disturbed by the falling

---

Key Terms

empire The territories that belong to a single imperial sovereign state.

imperialism The policy of expansion of power and domination of a nation by direct territorial occupation or indirect control over political and economic life.

nationalism Allegiance to a nation-state; a movement to achieve independence or sovereignty for a territorial entity or a cultural group.

birth rate which each census after 1881 confirmed. The maintenance of empire, argued the prominent conservative journalist J. L. Garvin in 1905:

> would be best based upon the power of a white population, proportionate in numbers, vigour, and cohesion to the vast territories which the British democracies in the Mother Country and the Colonies control.

If the British population did not increase fast enough to fill the empty spaces of the empire, others would. The threat was not from the indigenous populations, whom he does not mention, but from rival master races. The respective white populations of the United States, Germany, and the British Isles, he said, were 73 million, 61 million, and 54 million, and Britain's rate of increase was the slowest, as well as starting from the lowest base. And others protected their industry by tariffs so that they could make the most of their larger labour forces:

> Germany and America absorb into their industrial system year by year a number of new workers twice and three times as large as we can find employment for. These states, therefore, gain upon us in manpower and money-power alike; in fighting-power and budget-power; and in strict consequence sea-power itself must ultimately be shared between them.[4]

The birth rate then was a matter of national importance: population was power. Children, it was said, belonged "not merely to the parents but to the community as a whole"; they were "a national asset," "the capital of a country"; on them depended "the future of the country and the Empire"; they were "the citizens of tomorrow."[5] This appreciation of their value was certainly strengthened by concern as to their supply. From the mid-seventies the birth rate had been declining, and this trend once recognized caused much anxiety, especially when it was realized that a substantial proportion of those born did not survive. The infant mortality rate for England and Wales in 1899 was 163—that is, out of every 1,000 children born, 163 died before reaching their first birthday. This was higher than the average for the decade (154), which in turn was higher than the

average for the 1880s (142). Rates were highest in the poorest, most populous districts.[6] And as Alexander Blyth, Medical Officer of Health for Marylebone, pointed out in 1907:

> Over-production lessens, under-production enhances the value of commodities. Considering the life of an infant as a commodity its money value must be greater than 35 years ago. It is of concern to the nation that a sufficient number of children should annually be produced to more than make good the losses by death; hence the importance of preserving infant life is even greater now than it was before the decline of the birth rate.[7]

The influential author of the first comprehensive and authoritative treatise on infant mortality (*Infant Mortality: A Social Problem,* 1906), George Newman, who at this point was also a London Medical Officer of Health (for Finsbury), expressed similar concern in its preface:

> there is an annual loss to England and Wales of 120,000 lives by the death of infants. In past years there has been a similar drain upon the national resources of life. But it should not be forgotten that this loss of life is now operating in conjunction with a diminished income.[8]

Similar statements (and metaphors) abounded at that time.

Infant mortality was not of course a new problem: Sir John Simon in his reports as medical officer to the Privy Council had already in mid-century identified it as an index of the general sanitary condition; and in the 1890s, when unlike other indices of health it seemed to be getting worse (although the new theories of bacteriology offered fresh hope of solution), Medical Officers of Health were anxiously observing and analyzing it: as the new local monitors of public health they were in the best position to collate statistical information and to compare different factors and attempts at prevention.[9] Some municipalities were already in the 1890s distributing leaflets on infant care and providing instruction to mothers through visits to their homes. Such efforts were given new impetus not only by the epidemics of infant diarrhea during the hot summers of 1898–1900 but also by the climate of opinion in the 1900s, when in the wake of the disastrous Boer War fears for national standards of physique reached a peak.[10] Concern for the health of older children (which again had begun to preoccupy some doctors and teachers in the 1880s and 1890s) also greatly intensified, and the official investigations which resulted brought no reassurance.[11] Various measures followed, at both national and local levels. Laws designed to improve the conditions of infancy and childbirth were passed: midwives were required to have training (1902—though with delayed execution), local authorities were empowered to provide meals for needy children (1906), and obliged to organize medical inspection (though not treatment) in schools (1907), births had to be notified within six weeks so that health visitors could be sent round (1907), while the Children Act of 1908 made detailed provision across the spectrum of child welfare. Municipal authorities experimented with schemes to supply hygienic milk cheaply for weaned infants (at risk from the contaminated and adulterated milk normally on sale in working-class districts), and with prizes for healthy babies or for babies which survived their first year; they distributed endless leaflets and sent out battalions of health visitors. The Local Government Board organized two conferences on infant mortality, in 1906 and 1908, and conducted enquiries (through its medical department under Arthur Newsholme) into different aspects of infant mortality.[12]

Besides all this official activity, voluntary societies for the promotion of public health and domestic hygiene mushroomed in these years: the Institute of Hygiene (1903), the Infants' Health Society (1904), the National League for Physical Education and Improvement (1905), the Food Education Society (1908), the National League for Health, Maternity and Child Welfare (1905), the Eugenics Education Society (1908), the Women's League of Service for Motherhood (1910), and so on.[13] The officers and members of such societies were overwhelmingly ladies and gentlemen, sometimes of some prominence, who gave financial support, their names, and often their time and energy. Local branches would unite the socially conscious gentry of a neighbourhood—doctors, clergymen, social workers, medical officers of health, councillors, teachers, nurses and health visitors, but most of all ladies whose work was

voluntary and who would have no other job. Membership of such societies often overlapped with local authorities, and they would be called on to give evidence to official enquiries and also advice in the formation and execution of social policy. Their influence, in spite of their voluntary status, should not be underestimated. These new organizations, along with the older established societies of medical, social, statistical, and sanitary bent, were all in the 1900s eagerly taking up the issues of child welfare and domestic hygiene.

Their debates (reported in the national press, the medical press, and the journals of the societies) present immediate clues to all the interest and activity, in their constant references to national and imperial interest. The crucial factors seem to be that competition (both economic and political) from recently industrialized Germany and the United States appeared more and more threatening, and Japan too loomed as an impending rival. A poor military performance in the Boer War had dramatized fears of national inadequacy and exposed the poor health of the working class in Britain, from which were drawn both soldiers and sailors to defend the empire and workers to produce goods with which to dominate the world economically. At the same time the findings of the 1901 census confirmed that the birth rate was still falling, and medical statistics suggested that infant mortality was actually rising. The result was a surge of concern about the bearing and rearing of children—the next generation of soldiers and workers, the Imperial race.

—Motherhood

Middle-class convention of the time took for granted that the proper context of childhood was the family, and the person most responsible the mother. So if the survival of infants and the health of children was in question, it must be the fault of the mothers, and if the nation needed healthy future citizens (and soldiers and workers) then mothers must improve. This emphasis was reinforced by the influential ideas of eugenists: good motherhood was an essential component in their ideology of racial health and purity. Thus the solution to a national problem of public health and of politics was looked for in terms of individuals, of a particular role—the mother, and a social institution—the family.

This obscured to an extent which now seems astonishing the effects on child health of poverty and environment. It also contributed substantially to a shift in the dominant ideology. The family remained the basic institution of society, and woman's domestic role remained supreme, but gradually it was her function as mother that was being most stressed, rather than her function as wife. (Even the recommended reasons for marriage changed: in a manual of the 1860s the young woman was advised to seek as partner for life someone able to support her, willing to protect her, ready to help her, and qualified to guide and direct her—no mention of children—while a 1914 book on young women and marriage gave as the three main objects for marriage the reproduction of the race, the maintenance of social purity, and the mutual comfort and assistance of each married couple.)[14]

Moreover, the relationship between family and state was subtly changing. Since parents were bringing up the next generation of citizens the state had an interest in how they did it.[15] Child-rearing was becoming a national duty, not just a moral one: if it was done badly the state could intervene, if parental intentions were good but there were difficulties the state should give help, and if it was done well parents should be rewarded at least by approval for their patriotic contribution. Arguments of this kind were gaining weight, overriding the old individualist protests about parental rights (already undermined by compulsory education) and the danger of "demoralizing" people by helping them. They were used to justify not only contemporary measures such as the power given to Poor Law Guardians to remove children from unsuitable parents (Poor Law Act 1899) or the provision of school meals, but also the campaigns for maternity insurance (benefit to help with the expenses of childbirth, which was included in Lloyd George's 1911 Health Insurance Act) and for "the endowment of motherhood," the forerunner of family allowances. State responsibility was however a generalized supervision, very much in the background as a safety net. The real everyday responsibilities belonged to the mother.

Because of the declining birth rate motherhood had to be made to seem desirable; because high infant mortality was explained by maternal inadequacy the standards of mothers must be improved. A powerful ideology of motherhood emerged in relation to these problems of the early twentieth century, though it was firmly rooted of course in nineteenth-century assumptions about women, domesticity, and individualism. Motherhood was to be given new dignity: it was the duty and destiny of women to be the "mothers of the race," but also their great reward. But just as it was the individual mother's duty and reward to rear healthy members of an imperial race, so it was her individual ignorance and neglect which must account for infant deaths or sick children. Thus moral blackmail, exploiting the real difficulties and insecurities of many mothers, underpinned their new lofty status. Nor did their elevation mean an end to subordination. To be good mothers they now needed instruction, organized through the various agencies of voluntary societies and local government, in the skills of what came to be known as mothercraft, as they were being defined by the medical profession. Doctors, district nurses, health visitors, were all asserting their superior knowledge and authority, establishing moral sanctions on grounds of health and the national interest, and denigrating traditional methods of child care—in particular care by anyone except the mother: neighbours, grandmothers, and older children looking after babies were automatically assumed to be dirty, incompetent, and irresponsible. The authority of state over individual, of professional over amateur, of science over tradition, of male over female, of ruling class over working class, were all involved in the redefining of motherhood in this period, and in ensuring that the mothers of the race would be carefully guided, not carried away by self-importance.

The ideology of motherhood transcended class, even though its components had different class origins. Emphasis on the importance of women not "shirking" motherhood related to the belief that middle- and upper-class women were pursuing new opportunities in education and employment rather than marrying, or were marrying but restricting the number of their children, either tendency boding ill for the race. Emphasis on maternal ignorance related more to working-class women, who must by definition be ignorant, or at the very least irresponsible, since it was taken for granted that if you knew what you should be doing you would do it, and if in spite of that knowledge you didn't, it must be from fecklessness. It is perhaps significant that doctors were such prominent exponents of the ideology. On the one hand their experience of normal working-class life was usually minimal, since doctors' fees were beyond the working-class budget except in case of emergency. On the other, as guardians of health they appeared to have some responsibility for such problems as the preservation of infant life, and mothers made useful scapegoats, relieving them of blame. Failure to breast-feed, taking an infant to the minder in the cold early morning before clocking in at the mill, going out to work at all, were all signs of maternal irresponsibility, and infant sickness and death could always be explained in such terms. Even as careful a statistician as Arthur Newsholme, in his report on infant mortality for the medical department of the Local Government Board in 1910, ended up ignoring the evidence of his own tables as to regional variation and the excessive incidence of infant mortality wherever particular features of working-class urban life were concentrated (most of all overcrowding and the failure of local authorities to introduce a waterborne sewage system in place of middens and ash privies), and sounding off interminably about the "ignorance and fecklessness of mothers."[16]

This article, then, is an attempt to explore the context in which a new definition of woman's role developed in Britain in the early years of the twentieth century, and to suggest some of the pressures which contributed to the formation of an ideology of motherhood whose influence still touches us today.

NOTES

In the notes below, works and sources referred to only once or twice are given in full on the first occasion. Those referred to frequently are abbreviated as follows:

School for Mothers—Evelyn Bunting, ed., *The School for Mothers*, 1907.

Rearing an Imperial Race—C. E. Hecht, ed., *Rearing an Imperial Race*, 1913, proceedings of National Food Reform League conference on Diet, Cookery, and Hygiene in Schools.

McCleary, *Infant Welfare Movement*—G. F. McCleary, *The Early History of the Infant Welfare Movement*, 1933.

Newman, *Infant Mortality*—George Newman, *Infant Mortality, A Social Problem*, 1906.

Newsholme, *Fifty Years*—Arthur Newsholme, *Fifty Years in Public Health*, 1935.

Pritchard, *Infant Education*—Eric Pritchard, *Infant Education*, 1907.

Saleeby, *Race Culture*—C. W. Saleeby, *Parenthood and Race Culture*, 1909.

Maternity—Margaret Llewellyn Davies, ed., *Maternity, Letters from Working Women*, collected by the Women's Co-operative Guild, 1915. (New ed Virago 1978 with introduction by Gloden Dallas.)

BMJ—*British Medical Journal* (the authoritative weekly publication of the British Medical Association (BMA), voice of the medical establishment).

PP—Parliamentary Papers (printed government papers available in research libraries).

PRO—Public Record Office (now at Kew).

1. As for instance in T. H. Huxley, "The Struggle for Existence," in *The Nineteenth Century*, Feb. 1888.

2. The eugenists drew both on ideas of "the survival of the fittest," as developed by Francis Galton and Karl Pearson, and on Mendel's theories of heredity as they came into currency at the turn of the century.

3. Charles Kingsley, *The Massacre of the Innocents*, address given at the first public meeting of the Ladies' National Association for the Diffusion of Sanitary Knowledge in 1858. Printed as a Ladies' Sanitary Association pamphlet.

4. J. L. Garvin, "The Maintenance of Empire," in C. S. Goldman, ed., *The Empire and the Century*, 1905, pp. 72–81. Japan had also now established itself as a sea power by its skillful defeat of the much bigger Chinese navy in the 1894–95 Sino-Japanese war. Compare J. Crichton Browne's presidential address to the Medical Section of the International Congress for the Welfare and Protection of Children, 1902, pp. 6, 9.

5. E. Cadbury, M. C. Matheson and G. Shann, *Women's Work and Wages*, 1906, pp. 228–29; *BMJ* 30 July 1904, p. 231, address by Sir William Selby Church, President of the Royal College of Physicians, at annual meeting of BMA; T. J. Macnamara, Liberal MP, "In Corpore Sano," *Contemporary Review*, Feb. 1905, p. 238; inaugural address by Earl Beauchamp to the International Congress for the Welfare and Protection of Children, 1902, p. 4.

6. McCleary, *Infant Welfare Movement*, p. 146.

7. Alexander Wynter Blyth, preface to Eric Pritchard, *Infant Education*, 1907. Pritchard was a prominent St. Marylebone doctor whose energies and powers of propaganda were devoted to saving infant lives for the nation through the mothers; he believed that infants could "live and thrive in spite of poverty and bad sanitation" but would not "survive bad mothercraft." Eric Pritchard, "Schools

for Mothers," Proceedings of Infant Mortality Conference at Liverpool, 1914, p. 54.

8. Newman, *Infant Mortality,* p. v. George Newman (1870–1948) became first Chief Medical Officer to the Board of Education 1907; during World War I served on various important health committees; from 1919 was first Chief Medical Officer at new Ministry of Health. Married but no children. See *Dictionary of National Biography* and text throughout.

9. Jeanne Brand, *Doctors and the State,* 1965, is a useful text for the history of Medical Officers of Health.

10. See G. R. Searle, *The Quest for National Efficiency,* 1971.

11. For earlier concern see James Crichton Browne, "Education and the Nervous System" in Malcolm Morris, ed., *The Book of Health,* 1883; J. C. Browne, Report to Education Department upon Alleged Over-pressure of Work in Public Elementary Schools (PP. 1884 lxi (293)); Francis Warner, "Physical and Mental Condition of 50,000 Children" in *Journal of Royal Statistical Society,* lvi, 1893; Childhood Society's Report on the scientific study of the mental and physical conditions of childhood, 1895; and the campaign of the Women's Industrial Council against children's employment outside school, as in *Women's Industrial News,* April 1896, and Edith Hogg, "School Children as Wage-Earners," *The Nineteenth Century* Aug. 1897. Also J. C. Browne, *Physical Efficiency in Children,* 1902; Royal Commission on Physical Training (Scotland) PP. 1903, xxx; Interdepartmental Committee on Physical Deterioration PP. 1904, xxxii.

12. See McCleary, *Infant Welfare Movement,* 1933, and *Development of the British Maternity and Child Welfare Services,* 1945,

and (less detailed) George Newman, *English Social Services,* 1941. For results attributed to the young infant welfare movement by John Burns and his assurance of the Local Government Board's "paternal interest in milk, the mothers and the babies," see Proceedings of National Conference on Infant Mortality 1908, p. 12, and compare p. 28.

13. There is a useful list of voluntary societies "engaged in health propaganda of a public nature," with a few details in each, in Newman's *Public Education in Health,* 1924, pp. 18–22.

14. J. W. Kirton, *Cheerful Homes: How to Get and Keep Them* (undated) pp. 11–12; Mary Scharlieb, *What It Means to Marry or Young Women and Marriage,* 1914, pp. 36–37. (Kirton devotes only 23 out of 288 pages to children—"Our Precious Darlings"; Annie S. Swann in *Courtship and Marriage,* 1894, gives them 38 out of 144 pages; and Scharlieb 60 out of 140, besides frequent mention.)

15. See Gertrude Tuckwell, *The State and Its Children,* 1894; John Gorst, *The Children of the Nation,* 1906, Reginald Bray, *The Town Child,* 1907; H. Llewellyn Heath, *The Infant, the Parent and the State,* 1907; ed. Kelynack, *Infancy,* 1910, etc.

16. PP. 1910, xxxix (Cd. 5263) pp. 71–73. Arthur Newsholme (1857–1943) was Medical Officer of Health for Brighton from 1888, then from 1908 till he retired in 1919 Principal Medical Officer to the Local Government Board, appointed by John Burns. He was an accepted authority on medical statistics and believed strongly in state medicine. Married but no children. See *Dictionary of National Biography* and text throughout.

Race Culture: Recent Perspectives on the History of Eugenics

FRANK DIKKOTER

Historian Frank Dikkoter describes how the concept of race gained power through the scientific theory of eugenics. Although Nazi ideology was the most extreme example of so-called social eugenics, Dikkoter argues that population control in the poorer parts of the world today is still based on similar assumptions and ideas.

Far from being a politically conservative and scientifically spurious set of beliefs that remained confined to the Nazi era, eugenics belonged to the political vocabulary of virtually every significant modernizing force between the two world wars. It was part of such widely discussed issues as evolution, degeneration, civilization, and modernity, and touched on a wide variety of emerging fields like maternity, psychiatry, criminology, public health, and sex education. It was supported by scientific societies, pressure groups, and political institutions in such different countries as India, Brazil, and Sweden. Widely seen to be a morally acceptable and scientifically viable way of improving human heredity, its main tenets were embraced by social reformers, established intellectuals, and medical authorities from one end of the political spectrum to the other, including British conservatives and Spanish anarchists.[1] Even after World War II, liberal intellectuals such as Aldous Huxley and Hermann Müller expressed their revulsion at Nazi practices while restating their belief in a "humane" and "scientific" way of geneti-

Frank Dikkoter, "Race Culture: Recent Perspectives on the History of Eugenics," *American Historical Review* (April 1998): 467–68, 470, 472–73, 476–77.

cally improving the human race. In the People's Republic of China today, eugenics has become official policy, but foreign critics sometimes forget the extent to which developed countries were in the thrall of similar ideas until a few decades ago.

Eugenics was not so much a clear set of scientific principles as a "modern" way of talking about social problems in biologizing terms: politicians with mutually incompatible beliefs and scientists with opposed interests could all selectively appropriate eugenics to portray society as an organic body that had to be guided by biological laws. Eugenics gave scientific authority to social fears and moral panics, lent respectability to racial doctrines, and provided legitimacy to sterilization acts and immigration laws. Powered by the prestige of science, it allowed modernizing elites to represent their prescriptive claims about social order as objective statements irrevocably grounded in the laws of nature. Eugenics promoted a biologizing vision of society in which the reproductive rights of individuals were subordinated to the rights of an abstract organic collectivity.

[. . .]

Although tens of thousands of people defined as mentally retarded have been consistently abused, locked up, and sterilized, on occasion even castrated, historians have had relatively little to say about this marginalized social group. The last decade has seen a thriving literature specifically concerned with questions of gender and race, and this timely focus has opened up new and exciting perspectives in the history of eugenics, although people with learning disabilities still have to gain a clearer place in these studies.

While it is true that the overwhelming majority of people alleged to be mentally retarded and forced to undergo sterilization were women, the notion of "gender"—an analytical concept far too often used as a synonym for "women"—may not quite capture the ways in which individuals from very different personal and social backgrounds were systematically banned from society by being labeled "morons," "retardants," or "cretins." Women themselves, nevertheless, were keen participants in eugenics movements, the best-known cases being Margaret Sanger and Marie Stopes. In Scandinavia, women's organizations played an active and vocal role in the public support of sterilization laws.

[. . .]

After World War I, eugenic ideas were systematically developed by specific societies and organizations, in particular in Brazil, seen as a racially diverse and economically underdeveloped country by a small European intelligentsia who believed that eugenic policies were a key to national revival. In contrast to Brazil, Argentina was a more scientifically advanced society and a wealthier place in which non-European population groups had long been reduced by campaigns of extermination and conquest. Marked by a context of large-scale European immigration, debates on eugenics were more focused on which European "races" and social "classes" best represented the racial foundation of Argentine nationality. In Mexico, following a revolution in 1910 that started to transform the social and political landscape, eugenics was associated with a revolutionary representation of the population as a superior and "cosmic" race in which all different groups in the nation merged.

[. . .]

Eugenist discourse may have been widespread, but it also encountered resistance. In Britain, leading scientists such as J. B. S. Haldane, Julian Huxley, Lancelot Hogben, and Herbert Jennings turned against eugenics and denounced the race and class prejudice it cultivated. If the decline in eugenics within scientific circles often preceded Nazi atrocities, the cruelty of German policies eventually led to a strong reaction, supported by a long-standing and influential anti-eugenics coalition among people of both secular and religious backgrounds.[2] In France, moreover, widespread reluctance to interfere in the private lives of families, opposition from religious and liberal groups, and the professional duty of family doctors to respect the confidentiality of their patients combined to marginalize eugenic proposals.

[. . .]

Open democracies with a vibrant civil society, such as Britain and the Netherlands, were generally less inclined to adopt extreme eugenic proposals than authoritarian regimes in Germany and the People's Republic of China.[3]

While most historians note an erosion of faith in eugenics after World War II, some also point out how recent medical innovations in reproductive technologies, including human gene therapy, the Human Genome Project, and in vitro fertilization, could lead to a resurgence in eugenic ideas.[4] This certainly was the case in the 1970s in the Soviet Union, when parts of the liberal intelligentsia started proposing a form of "socialist eugenics," portraying themselves as a genetically superior elite destined by DNA to rule over the dysgenic fray. The systematic invocation of human genetics in political theories justifying social inequality even caused a prominent geneticist to denounce the abuse of science in an official organ of the Central Committee.[5] Eugenic arguments also continue to surface regularly in the United States, as illustrated by a proposal in 1991 by state representative David Duke, a former grand wizard in the Ku Klux Klan. His proposal for a law offering mostly African-American female welfare recipients in Louisiana cash payments for the use of the contraceptive device Norplant strongly echoes earlier eugenic reforms. In some Scandinavian countries, sterilizations continued to be practiced on a widespread scale until 1970. Forced sterilizations for eugenic reasons were also performed decades after the end of World War II in parts of Switzerland.[6]

The recent revelation by a Swiss historian that the canton of Vaud passed a sterilization law for mentally handicapped patients in 1928 caused widespread consternation in the international media, in contrast to the relatively muted reception given to eugenic legislation passed in the People's Republic of China. In Gansu province alone, a 1988 law proscribes marriage for mentally retarded people until they have undergone sterilization surgery; according to the figures announced by Gansu provincial authorities, thousands of people have been sterilized since the law was implemented. Eugenic legislation, passed under the rubric of "maternal and infant health," was also accepted at the national level in 1995. More generally, eugenist discourse in the People's Republic permeates virtually every field related to human reproduction, from birth control to sex education. Directly indebted to the eugenic vision elaborated in many countries between the two world wars, medical and economic explanations are used to curb the reproduction of marginalized people described as "unfit," while abstractions like the "nation," "future generations," and the "gene pool" are raised above the rights and needs of individuals and

their families. A greater focus on less developed areas of the world that have not received detailed attention, an emphasis on the highly prevalent yet dispersed nature of eugenic ideas in developed countries, and attention to the different inflections of eugenics in a variety of historical contexts would contribute to a more general appreciation of the history of eugenics, in which China would appear not so much a lonely exception as an integral part of more global trends that have deeply marked and continue to affect the twentieth century.

[. . .]

NOTES

1. The reference to Spain is from Richard Cleminson, "Eugenics by Name or Nature? The Spanish Anarchist Sex Reform of the 1930s," *History of European Ideas* 18 (1994): 729–40; two recent articles provide useful overviews of the field, Robert Nye, "The Rise and Fall of the Eugenics Empire: Recent Perspectives on the Impact of Bio-Medical Thought in Modern Society," *Historical Journal* 36 (1993): 687–700; P. J. Pauly, "The Eugenics Industry—Growth or Restructuring?" *Journal of the History of Biology* 26 (Spring 1993): 131–45.

2. Elazar Barkan, *The Retreat of Scientific Racism: Changing Concepts of Race in Britain and the United States between the Two World Wars* (Cambridge, 1992).

3. See also Paul Weindling, *Health, Race, and German Politics between National Unification and Nazism, 1870–1945* (Cambridge,

1989), an important book highlighting the significant changes in broader social, political, and disciplinary fields from the Weimar Republic to the Nazi era.

4. See the new preface in Daniel J. Kevles's classic book *In the Name of Eugenics: Genetics and the Uses of Human Heredity* (1985; Cambridge, 1995).

5. N. Dubinin, "Nasledovanie Biologicheskoe i Sotsial'noe," *Kommunist* 11 (1980): 62–74.

6. On Switzerland, see Philippe Ehrenström, "Stérilisation opératoire et maladie mentale: Une étude de cas," *Gesnerus* 48 (1991): 503–16; and Frank Preiswerk, "Auguste Forel (1848–1931): Un projet de régénération sociale, morale et raciale," *Annuelles: Revue d'histoire contemporaine* 2 (1991): 25–50.

New Technologies of Race
EVELYNN M. HAMMONDS

Physicist and feminist scholar of science and technology, Evelynn Hammonds shows us that the new techniques of morphing and other computer-generated visuals of racial mixing draw upon the ideologies of eugenics and biologically based notions of race and gender to imagine the future.

On 18 July 1950 the *New York Times* announced "No Scientific Basis for Race Bias Found by World Panel of Experts." The article reported on the findings of a distinguished group of scientists, working under the auspices of the United Nations Educational, Scientific and Cultural Organization (UNESCO), who had reached a consensus that there "was no scientific justification for race discrimination."

The Statement presented four premises: that mental capacities of all races are similar; that no evidence for biological deterioration as a result of hybridization existed; that there was no correlation between

Evelynn M. Hammonds, "New Technologies of Race," in *Processed Lives: Gender and Technology in Everyday Life,* Jennifer Terry and Melodie Calvert, eds. New York: Routledge, 1997: 108–9, 111, 113–21.

national or religious groups and any race; and fourth, that race was less a biological fact than a social myth.[1]

The UNESCO document was a highly politicized statement [. . .] In many respects it reflected the desire of some scientists to redress the excesses of Nazism, where biological notions of racial difference and racial inferiority had been used to justify the extermination of Jews and homosexuals, rather than offering a balanced account of the contemporary scientific debates over the role of environment, heredity, and culture in the observed differences between the races.

Several historians of science have argued that the publication of the UNESCO document signaled the end of mainstream scientific support for racial science. The division of the human species into biological races, which had been of cardinal significance to scientists for over a hundred years, was no longer viable as a research topic. Race, which in the pre-1950s period had been used to explain individual character and temperament, the structure of social communities, and the fate of human societies, was no longer central to the work of anthropologists or biologists. Even if one does not entirely accept this assessment, and it is debatable

Key Terms

miscegenation A term used to describe the "mixture" of races through reproduction. In the United States, laws against miscegenation (between Caucasians and persons of African descent) were upheld until the 1960s.

morphological differences Distinctions among organisms based on form and structure.

whether most scientists did, it is argued that, at the very least, the belief in the fixity, reality, and hierarchy of human races—in the chain of superior and inferior human types—which had shaped the activities of scientists for most of the twentieth century had ceased to be a central feature of biological and anthropological research. Gone were the detailed cranial measurements, the tables of racial comparisons, the construction of racial typologies, and the reconstruction of racial histories in mainstream scientific journals. Instead, as Nancy Stepan argues, in their place we find discussions of populations, gene frequencies, selection, and adaptation. The biological study of human diversity is now permeated with the language of genetics and evolution. "Race," Stepan asserts, "lost its reality and naturalness, to such an extent that probably the majority of scientists even go so far as to consider the very word 'race' unnecessary for purposes of biological inquiry."[2]

I suggest that these scientists and historians of science have misread the observed shift in biology and anthropology from studies of gross morphological studies of racial difference to studies of populations and gene frequencies. In the United States, race has always been dependent upon the visual. I argue that the notion of race—as both a social and a scientific concept—is still deeply embedded in morphology, but it is the meaning given to morphological differences that has been transformed. Race, defined biologically in terms of morphological differences between certain pure types (white, African, Asian, etc.) and in particular the mixing of these pure racial types, has been re-inscribed in the new computer technology of "morphing" and, as such, separated from its previous antecedents in the history of antimiscegenation, and racial oppression.[3] "Morphing," a computer software term for "making one thing appear to turn into another," denotes shape-changing while carrying along with it a change in identity. In this technology, persons of different races are not produced as a result of sexual intercourse between persons of two different races but by a computer-generated simulation of the mixing of genetic characteristics that are presumed to be determinants of morphological differences between pure racial types. Morphing is not simply, as Emily Martin notes, "a car transformed into a tiger or Arnold Schwarzenegger turning into a pool of liquid metal in *Terminator 2*," but it is also the technological production of new racial types, as in Michael Jackson's *Black or White* video, where whites turn into aborigines as easily as he himself morphs into a black panther. Miscegenation then becomes an instance of border crossing between the human and the "other." The "other" includes the nonhuman and also the more familiar "other," nonwhite humans. In such a case, technological artistry masks the imbrication of power, which is never articulated, in such transformations of white into nonwhite, and the nonwhite into animal. These transformations serve as late-twentieth-century versions of the Great Chain of Being. Morphing, with its facile device of shape-changing, interchangeability, equivalency, and feigned horizontality in superficial ways, elides its similarity with older hierarchical theories of human variation. However, as I will discuss, the new technology of race, morphing, is at the center of an old debate about miscegenation and citizenship in the United States.

[. . .]

⟞*What Color Is Black?*

The 13 February 1995 cover story of *Newsweek* magazine was entitled "What Color Is Black? Science, Politics and Racial Identity." Interestingly, inside, the title of the lead article changed slightly to "What Color Is Black? What Color Is White?" The cover displayed a short description of the article:

> The answers aren't simple. Immigration is changing the hue of America. Intermarriage has spawned a generation proud of its background, eager for its place at the American table. As always, race drives American domestic policy on issues from legislative districts to census counts. And path-breaking scientists insist that three racial categories are woefully inadequate for the myriad variations of our species.[4]

Immigration followed by intermarriage are said to be the driving forces behind this "new" aspect of race relations in America. The article appeared 28 years after the last state antimiscegenation law was struck down.[5] It appeared 45 years after the UNESCO document on race, yet it asserted on the one hand that race is a biological concept—"race is a notoriously slippery concept that

FIGURE I.2 "WHAT COLOR IS BLACK?",
NEWSWEEK, 13 FEBRUARY 1995

But *Newsweek*'s cover offered a representation of race—pictures of people of color of various shades in photographs cropped to emphasize shape of head, nose and lips—at odds with its text, which emphasized that science was unable to provide a definitive or rather comfortable answer about the social meaning of racial difference (see Figure I.2). Here we see the visual display of a variety of people of color which made race seem "real," while the scientists' commentary emphasized that the reliance upon categories based on groupings of physical types had no meaning for the scientific study of race and, by implication, the sociopolitical debates as well. Interestingly, in *Newsweek*'s typology the persons who are raced are those who are not white. No photographs depicting differences among whites or between whites and people of color are displayed, suggesting that the differences among those classified as Black (or African American) are what is at issue.

[. . .]

Newsweek followed on the heels of a much more novel approach to the topic, where biology was supplanted by computer technology in the representation of racial difference—*Time* magazine's special issue in the fall of 1993, "The New Face of America: How Immigrants Are Shaping the World's First Multicultural Society." The cover featured a slightly tanned woman, with brown straight hair, somewhat almond-shaped eyes, and slightly full lips (see Figure I.3). The sidebar read, "Take a good look at this woman. She was created by a computer from a mix of several races. What you see is a remarkable preview of . . . The New Face of America."[8] The introduction to the issue, by managing editor Jim Gaines revealed the true identity of the cover girl.

eludes any serious attempt at definition: it refers mostly to observable differences in skin color, hair texture, and the shape of one's eyes or nose"—while also pointing out that most scientists argue that race is a mere social construct.[6] After reporting the current scientific data about racial differences for several pages, the authors conclude:

> Changing our thinking about race will require a revolution in thought as profound, and profoundly unsettling, as anything science has ever demanded. What these researchers are talking about is changing the way in which we see the world—and each other. But before that can happen, we must do more than understand the biologist's suspicion about race. We must ask science, why is it that we are so intent on sorting humanity into so few groups—us and Other—in the first place.[7]

> The woman on the cover of this special issue of *Time* does not exist—except metaphysically. Her beguiling if mysterious visage is the product of a computer process called morphing—as in metamorphosis, a striking alteration in structure or appearance. When the editors were looking for a way to dramatize the impact of interethnic marriage, which has increased dramatically in the U.S. during the last wave of immigration, they turned to morphing to create the kind of offspring that might result from seven men and seven women of various ethnic and racial backgrounds.[9]

FIGURE I.3   "THE NEW FACE OF AMERICA",
TIME **MAGAZINE, FALL 1993**

The picture was generated by an Asian-American computer specialist, dubbed a cybergeneticist, whose efforts are described as "in the spirit of fun and experiment." This cover girl, Eve, whom Donna Haraway has dubbed "SimEve," has an interesting lineage: she is 15 percent Anglo-Saxon, 17.5 percent Middle Eastern, 17.5 percent African, 7.5 percent Asian, 35 percent Southern European, and 7.5 percent Hispanic. This breakdown of her racial heritage would be familiar to DuBois and any other early twentieth-century biologist or anthropologist. Eve was produced with the same software package, Morph 2.0, used in *Terminator 2* and the Michael Jackson video. *Time*'s cybergeneticist also produced a chart showing forty-nine different combinations of the progeny from seven males and seven females (see Figure I.4). Most of the images or "morphies" on the chart are a straight 50/50 combination of the physical characteristics of their progenitors, though the editors note that an entirely

different image could be produced by using different combinations of features. Interestingly, after eyes, the most important parental feature is the neck, which they found often determined the gender of the offspring. The volume of specific features is also important. For example, if an African man has more hair than a Vietnamese woman, his hair will dominate. Of course, such manipulations of features produced some truly unexpected results as well. One of their "tentative unions" produced a distinctly feminine face—sitting atop a muscular neck and hairy chest. "Back to the mouse on that one," the editors wrote. In this case the implicit norms governing morphing appear to forbid any monstrous combinations paralleling late-nineteenth-century rhetoric against the progeny of interracial unions, which claimed that such hybrid persons were unnatural. With the *Time* cover we wind up with not a true composite but a preferred or filtered composite of mixed figures, with no discussion of the assumptions or implications underlying the choices.

Despite their tone and the explicit efforts to separate the morphed images from the conflicted meanings they represent, the editors of *Time* came up against their own desires:

> Little did we know what we had wrought. As onlookers watched the image of our new Eve begin to appear on the computer screen, several staff members promptly fell in love. Said one: "It really breaks my heart that she doesn't exist. . . ." We sympathized with our lovelorn colleagues, but even technology has its limits. This is a love that must forever remain unrequited.[10]

This is truly the drama of miscegenation in cyberspace. The history of white men crossing racial boundaries to have sexual relations with African, Asian, Mexican, and Native-American women—and then refusing to acknowledge their offspring in order to reserve the right to determine how whiteness would be defined as a characteristic of citizenship—is simultaneously implied and disavowed. Race mixing in its newest form shapes our future, not the past; bits and bytes replace the flesh and blood that provoked the guilt, hatred, and violence of our country's history of racial domination. Hierarchies of domination have not disappeared

FIGURE I.4   *TIME*'S "MORPHIES"

as female reproduction is replaced by a masculine technophilic reproduction because stereotypical racial typologies remain in place.[11] I say this because no woman of color has ever symbolized citizenship in United States history, only the denial of citizenship. Women of color were among the last groups to achieve the right to vote and all the attendant rights of citizenship that flow from it. Donna Haraway argues that SimEve forever excites a desire that cannot be fulfilled and as such is an example of the dream of technological transcendence of the body. But I think SimEve carries a different meaning in the light of the history of miscegenation. Because she is a cyber, she is the representation of the desire to deny kinship and retain masculine power based on the maintenance of racial difference.

NOTES

Author's note: I want to thank Jennifer Terry for her insightful comments on this chapter.

1. Elazar Barkan, *The Retreat of Scientific Racism: Changing Concepts of Race in Britain and the United States between the World Wars* (Cambridge: Cambridge University Press, 1992), p. 341.

2. Nancy Stepan, *The Idea of Race in Science* (Hamden, CT: Archon Press, 1982), p. 171.

3. These pure racial types are defined in terms of morphological differences such as hair texture, skin color, shape of eyes corresponding to geographical origin (white Anglo-Saxon, African, etc.).

4. "What Color Is Black? What Color Is White?" *Newsweek,* 13 February 1995, p. 3.

5. In 1967, the U.S. Supreme Court struck down the final existing antimiscegenation laws in *Loving v. Virginia.*

6. *Newsweek,* 13 February 1995, p. 64.

7. Ibid., p. 69.

8. "The New Face of America," *Time* magazine, Special Issue, Fall 1993.

9. Ibid., p. 2.

10. Ibid., p. 2.

11. Donna Haraway, "Universal Donors in a Vampire Culture: It's All in the Family. Biological Kinship Categories in the Twentieth-Century United States," in William Cronon (ed.) *Uncommon Ground: Toward Reinventing Nature* (New York: Norton, 1995).

REFLECTING ON THE SECTION

This section's readings illustrate the relationship between science and culture. In particular, they examine the relationship of race to gender through legal, medical, scientific, and popular examples. Scientific movements such as Malthusianism, eugenics, and social Darwinism emerged from a cultural context in which inequalities of race, class, and gender became part of established scientific and medical practices.

In what ways can we see the legacies of these ideas even today? It is impossible to understand the ways in which motherhood became tied to notions of social health and national interests without considering the impact of European imperialism. As Anna Davin argues, ideal motherhood came to be seen as something that a nation-state would foster and protect, often at the expense of poor and nonwhite women. Thus, nationalism became racialized as women were encouraged to produce white citizens and soldiers. Moving to the current moment, Evelynn M. Hammonds illustrates how modern technologies like computer simulations, or "morphing," draw upon the histories of eugenics, imperialism, and fears of miscegenation. In what ways does the nation-state still tell us what ideal motherhood might be? Do new technologies repeat the histories presented in this section, or do they provide solutions?

Medicine in a Historical Perspective

"And So I Grew Up"

NONGENILE MASITHATHU ZENANI

Nongenile Masithathu Zenani is a practicing doctor/healer in South Africa. While she grew up without a formal education, she was initiated into her profession by a healer and, over the initial opposition of her husband, came to play an important role as a respected doctor in her community.

. . . Then difficulties arose. The subject regarding my vocation to be a doctor came up again, it became more persistent as my nervousness and chest troubles intensified. Now, whenever a person who had done something came into my sight—if this person had done something bad—my body would itch, I would become uncomfortable; I would become excitable, nervous, I would experience intense pains in my chest. I could not stay with a person who had done something bad.

This became more and more evident in me, and caused my husband considerable anxiety. He wanted to send me to more doctors then, to determine what was wrong with me. And he did take me to the doctors, he took me by night. We went to a doctor, and my husband had me examined there. The doctor explained that my body pores were those of "white death." My blood was repelled by anything evil or dirty. I am therefore a "white" person. The doctor advised that I be treated to ensure my strength against the things that trouble the blood.

My husband said, "Well, I give her to you, Doctor. Treat her, because this is painful to me too."

Nongenile Masithathu Zenani, " 'And So I Grew Up': The Autobiography of Nongenile Masithathu Zenani." Researched and translated by Harold Scheub, in *Life Histories of African Women,* ed. Patricia W. Romero. London: Ashfield Press, 1988: 43–45.

The doctor then charged a fee for pounding herbs, but he did not charge for the diagnosis. I was to do the pounding.

My husband produced the money, a pound, and left me with the doctor, saying that he would come to visit me frequently, but that I would be under the care of this doctor.

I stayed with that doctor then, and time passed for me there. He treated me in every way, purging me, washing me, feeding me a medicine that pained my body. And my trouble ceased.

The pains in my chest ended, my anxieties were calmed. He made me dance, also a part of the treatment—he did everything.

Then, during the year, as his place was visited by sick people who had come to be treated, this doctor told me to go and take care of a person who had come to be examined. I was sent to another house; I went and examined that person. I finished that, and the doctor asked me to prepare some medicine for this patient. I did that. I treated him, and he became well. The doctor then rewarded me with doctor's white beads, a string of beads that was tied to my head, on the cranium—the first string of beads, beads of initiation. These were tied on.

The second time I completed an examination, a set of doctor's beads was put around my neck. Then my husband came again, he arrived to find me wearing these sets of beads. During his presence, a sick person came; I went to examine him, and I finished the job while my husband was still there.

Time passed, we went on like that—until I was treating my own patients. I would diagnose some of their diseases, they would come to me and I would treat them, and they would get well. And some of them would also become doctors, those with symptoms similar to mine. Various kinds of people came to me—a person with one kind of ache, a person who was barren, a person burdened by some illness. There were all kinds of people, all sorts, and "Well, it's about time that she should go and set up her own practice, at her own house. She should treat her own people, because she's now got quite a clientele here."

That was the decision of the doctor. I returned then, and remained at my own house.

There were some difficulties, which might have caused great confusion had they not changed in time: while I was establishing my practice, traveling all over the countryside treating people, my husband became very angry. Why did I not come home anymore? I seem to be going to so many homesteads to treat patients, and I don't return to my own home! I might be gone as long as a week, even *two* weeks. That bothered him, we were annoying each other now, and it began to seem like a bad situation for our marriage. Eventually, it became clear that I wanted my husband to return the

lobola.[1] I could no longer be his wife, because I would not be able to treat people as a white doctor does— people come to European doctors' offices to be treated, but the Xhosa doctor goes to the people, and thus must travel throughout the area. We are fetched, and go all over the countryside. When a doctor is called, she must go to treat people wherever they happen to be. Now if my husband demands that I operate in a manner that is unnatural, in a way that is not the way I have been created, then it is better if I depart from him for a period of ten years.

I did leave him, then I returned. He was suffering because of my absence. He begged me, saying that he had done a childish thing, not realizing what he had been doing. He feared that his wife would be carried away from him by certain people.

So I did come back, and from that time there were no misunderstandings in our relationship . . . though another difficulty might have arisen.

NOTE

1. *Lobola* is the complex contractual arrangement made between the bride and groom and their families. Here, Mrs. Zenani is referring to the *lobola* cattle, a symbolic part of the exchange. [Scheub]

Exorcising the Midwives

BARBARA EHRENREICH AND DIERDRE ENGLISH

Barbara Ehrenreich and Dierdre English, feminist scholars of Western patriarchy, describe how, in the United States at the turn of the twentieth century, Western medicine took away power, authority, and a livelihood from midwives and women healers in favor of mostly male physicians.

There was one last matter to clean up before the triumph of (male) scientific medicine would be complete, and that was the "midwife problem." In 1900, 50 percent of the babies born were still being delivered by midwives. Middle- and upper-class women had long since accepted the medical idea of childbirth as a pathological event requiring the intervention and supervision of a (preferably regular) physician. It was the "lower" half of society which clung to the midwife and her services: the rural poor and the immigrant working class in the cities. What made the midwives into a "problem" was then not so much the matter of direct competition; the regular doctors were not interested in taking the midwife's place in a Mississippi sharecropper's shack or a sixth-story walk-up apartment in one of New York's slums. (Although one exceptionally ve-nal physician went to the trouble of calculating all the fees "lost" to doctors on account of midwifery):[1] It makes sense to speak of "competition" only between people in the same line of business; and this was not the case with the midwives and the doctors.

The work of a midwife cannot be contained in a phrase like "practicing medicine." The early-twentieth-century midwife was an integral part of her community and culture. She spoke the mother's language, which might be Italian, Yiddish, Polish, Russian. She was familiar not only with obstetrical techniques, but with the prayers and herbs that sometimes helped. She knew the correct ritual for disposing of the afterbirth, greeting the newborn or, if necessary, laying to rest the dead. She was prepared to live with the family from the onset of labor until the mother was fully recovered. If she was a southern black midwife, she often regarded the service as a religious calling:

> "Mary Carter," she [an older midwife] told me, "I'm getting old and I done been on this journey for 45 years. I am tired. I won't give up until the Lord replace me with someone. When I asked the Lord, he showed me you."
>
> The [young] midwife responded, "Uh, uh, Aunt Minnie, the Lord didn't show you me." She say, "Yes Sir, you got to serve. You can't get from under it."

Barbara Ehrenreich and Dierdre English, "Exorcising the Midwives," *For Her Own Good: 150 Years of the Experts' Advice to Women,* Garden City, NY: Anchor Press, 1978: 84–88.

Key Term

midwife Historically, a female who assists women during childbirth.

She did serve because, repeatedly, "Something come to me, within me, say, 'Go ahead and do the best you can.' "[2]

All of this was highly "unscientific," not to mention unbusinesslike. But the problem, from the point of view of medical leaders, was that the midwife was in the way of the development of modern institutional medicine. One of the reforms advanced by medicine's scientific elite was that students should be exposed somewhere along the line not only to laboratories and lectures but to live patients. But which live patients? Given the choice, most people would want to avoid being an object of practice for inexperienced medical students. Certainly no decent woman in 1900 would want her delivery witnessed by any unnecessary young males. The only choice was the people who had the least choice—the poor. And so the medical schools, the most "advanced" ones anyway, began to attach themselves parasitically to the nearest "charity" hospital. In an arrangement which has flourished ever since, the medical school offered its medical trainees as staff for the hospital; the hospital in turn provided the raw "material" for medical education—the bodies of the sick poor. The moral ambiguities in this situation were easily rationalized away by the leaders of scientific medicine. As a doctor on the staff of Cornell Medical College put it:

> There are heroes of war, who give up their lives on the field of battle for country and for principle, and medical heroes of peace, who brave the dangers and horrors of pestilence to save life; but the homeless, friendless, degraded, and possibly criminal sick poor in the wards of a charity hospital, receiving aid and comfort in their extremity and contributing each one his modest share to the advancement of medical science, render even greater service to humanity.[3]

Medical science now called on poor women to make their contribution to that "most beneficent and disinterested of professions." Obstetrics-gynecology was America's most rapidly developing specialty, and midwives would just have to get out of the way. Training and licensing midwives was out of the question, for, as one doctor argued, these measures would

decrease the number of cases in which the stethoscope, pelvimeter, and other newly developed techniques could be used to increase obstetrical knowledge.[4]

A Dr. Charles E. Zeigler was equally blunt in an article addressed to his colleagues in the *Journal of the American Medical Association:*

> It is at present impossible to secure cases sufficient for the proper training in obstetrics, since 75 percent of the material otherwise available for clinical purposes is utilized in providing a livelihood for midwives.[5]

Note the curious construction here: "the material . . . is utilized . . ." The woman who was seen by her midwife as a neighbor, possibly a friend, was, in the eyes of the developing medical industry, not even a customer: she has become inert "material."

The public campaign against midwives was, of course, couched in terms of the most benevolent concern for the midwives' clientele. Midwives were "hopelessly dirty, ignorant, and incompetent, relics of a barbaric past."[6]

> They may wash their hands, but oh, what myriads of dirt lurk under the fingernails. Numerous instances could be cited and we might well add to other causes of pyosalpinx "dirty midwives." She is the most virulent bacteria of them all, and she is truly a micrococcus of the most poisonous kind.[7]

Furthermore, the midwife and, as we shall see, dirtiness in general, were un-American. Overturning almost 300 years of American history, obstetricians A. B. Emmons and J. L. Huntington argued in 1912 that midwives are

not a product of America. They have always been here, but only incidentally and only because America has always been receiving generous importations of immigrants from the continent of Europe. We have never adopted in any State a system of obstetrics with the midwife as the working unit. It has almost been a rule that the more immigrants arriving in a locality, the more midwives will flourish there, but as soon as the immigrant is assimilated, and becomes part of our civilization, then the midwife is no longer a factor in his home.[8]

In the rhetoric of the medical profession, the midwife was no more human than her clientele. She was a foreign "micrococcus" brought over, as was supposedly the case with other germs, in the holds of ships bearing immigrant workers. The elimination of the midwife was presented as a necessary part of the general campaign to uplift and Americanize the immigrants—a mere sanitary measure, beyond debate.

Certainly the midwives were "ignorant" according to the escalating standards of medical education; possibly some also deserved the charge of being "dirty" and "incompetent." The obvious remedy for these shortcomings was education and some system of accountability, or supervision. England had solved its "midwife problem" without rancor by simply offering training and licensing to the midwives. Even the least literate midwife could be trained to administer silver nitrate eyedrops (to prevent blindness in babies whose mothers have gonorrhea) and to achieve certain standards of cleanliness. But the American medical profession would settle for nothing less than the final solution to the midwife question: they would have to be eliminated—outlawed. The medical journals urged their constituencies to join the campaign:

> surely we have enough influence and friends to procure the needed legislation. Make yourselves heard in the land; and the ignorant meddlesome midwife will soon be a thing of the past.[9]

In fact, the doctors were not prepared, in any sense of the word, to take over once the midwives were eliminated. For one thing, there were simply not enough obstetricians in the United States to serve the masses of poor and working-class women, even if the obstetricians were inclined to do so. According to historian Ben Barker-Benfield, "even a hostile obstetrician admitted in 1915 that 25 percent of births in New York State outside New York City would be deprived *entirely* of assistance when the midwife was eliminated."[10]

Then too, obstetricians introduced new dangers into the process of childbirth. Unlike a midwife, a doctor was not about to sit around for hours, as one doctor put it, "watching a hole"; if the labor was going too slow for his schedule he intervened with knife or forceps, often to the detriment of the mother or child. Teaching hospitals had an additional bias toward surgical intervention since the students did have to practice something more challenging than normal deliveries. The day of the totally medicalized childbirth—hazardously overdrugged and overtreated—was on its way.[11] By the early twentieth century it was already clear even to some members of the medical profession that the doctors' takeover was a somewhat dubious episode in the history of public health. A 1912 study by a Johns Hopkins professor found that most American doctors at the time were *less* competent than the midwives they were replacing.[12] The physicians were usually less experienced than midwives, less observant, and less likely to even be *present* at a critical moment.

But, between 1900 and 1930, midwives were almost totally eliminated from the land—outlawed in many states, harassed by local medical authorities in other places. There was no feminist constituency to resist the trend. In the 1830s, women in the Popular Health Movement had denounced the impropriety—and dangers—of male assistance at births. But this time, when *female* assistance at births was in effect being turned into a crime, there was no outcry. Middle-class feminists had no sisterly feelings for the "dirty" immigrant midwife. They had long since decided to play by the rules laid down by the medical profession and channel their feminist energies into getting more women into (regular) medical schools. Elizabeth Blackwell, for example, believed that no one should assist in childbirth without a complete medical education.

There may have been some resistance to the male takeover within the immigrant communities, but we have no evidence of this. Most women no doubt accepted male, institutional care in the interests of their children. With the elimination of midwifery, all women—not just those of the upper class—fell under the biological hegemony of the medical profession. In the same stroke, women lost their last autonomous role as healers. The only roles left for women in the medical system were as employees, customers, or "material."

NOTES

1. Frances E. Kobrin, "The American Midwife Controversy: A Crisis of Professionalization," *Bulletin of the History of Medicine,* July/August 1966, p. 350.

2. Molly C. Dougherty, "Southern Lay Midwives as Ritual Specialists," paper presented at the American Anthropological Association Annual Meeting, Mexico City, 1974.

3. Austin Flint, M.D., "The Use and Abuse of Medical Charities in Medical Education," *Proceedings of the National Conference on Charities and Corrections,* 1898, p. 331.

4. Quoted in Ann H. Sablosky, "The Power of the Forceps: A Study of the Development of Midwifery in the United States," Master's Thesis, Graduate School of Social Work and Social Research, Bryn Mawr College, May 1975, p. 15.

5. Quoted in Ursula Gilbert, "Midwifery as a Deviant Occupation in America," unpublished paper, 1975.

6. G. J. Barker-Benfield, *The Horrors of the Half-Known Life* (New York: Harper & Row, 1976), p. 63.

7. Sablosky, op. cit., p. 16.

8. Barker-Benfield, op. cit., p. 69.

9. Sablosky, op. cit., p. 17.

10. Barker-Benfield, op. cit., p. 69.

11. See Doris Haire, "The Cultural Warping of Childbirth," *International Childbirth Education Association News,* Spring 1972; Suzanne Arms, *Immaculate Deception* (San Francisco: San Francisco Book Co., 1976).

12. Kobrin, op. cit.

Reading C

Women and Medicine

DAVID ARNOLD

David Arnold is a historian who studies the practice of Western medicine in colonial India. Arnold argues that

David Arnold, "Women and Medicine," *Colonizing the Body,* Berkeley: University of California Press, 1993: 254–61, 262–64, 265–66.

the British colonizers sought to "civilize" Indians by introducing Western science and medicine. In the effort to eliminate the so-called superstitions of Indian healers and midwives, the British created women's hospitals and promoted the education of women doctors. Yet

Key Terms

caste In Indian Hinduism, castes are hereditary social classes, usually based on occupation, that are enforced by custom, law, and religion.

colonial hegemony European domination in political, economic, and cultural spheres, sometimes perpetuated by members of the elite groups in colonized areas.

colonial medicine The form of Western medicine practiced in the colonies, which increased the power and authority of the colonizers.

purdah The segregation of women from men; practiced through veiling or separate living quarters.

colonial medicine increased the power and authority of the British and decreased the autonomy and significance of local healers and medical practices.

Women's health occupies a special place in the history of Western medicine and colonial hegemony. From a present-day perspective, it is striking how little consideration was given to women's health in colonial India before the 1860s and 1870s, but it is also remarkable how rapidly thereafter it assumed a prominent and emblematic position in debates over the nature and authority of Western medicine.

In the early nineteenth century, in an essentially male-oriented and male-operated system of medicine, women appeared only as adjuncts and appendages to the health of men. The primary arenas of state medicine in the first half of the nineteenth century—the army, the jails, even the hospitals—were primarily male domains in which women played little part. Even when they were present—as prisoners, as soldiers' wives and daughters—their specific needs were largely ignored. Sickness and mortality among the wives of European soldiers were duly noted in the sanitary commissioners' annual reports from the 1860s onward, but with scant comment, and the declining number of British Army wives in India (there were barely 3,000 by 1890) strengthened the almost exclusively male orientation of military medicine. Indian soldiers' wives received hardly a mention in the sanitary reports. The one state medical measure before the 1880s which did have a direct bearing on women was the Contagious Diseases Act of 1868, but this was clearly designed to address the problem of venereal disease among British soldiers rather than the health of prostitutes (or soldiers' wives). There appears to have been no serious discussion of venereal disease as it affected women in India before the 1920s. The diseases that preoccupied colonial medicine in the nineteenth century were epidemic diseases, the communicable diseases of the cantonment, civil lines, and plantations, the diseases that threatened European lives, military manpower, and male productive labor.[1]

When women were mentioned in early nineteenth-century medical texts, either it was in a gesture of exclusion—remarking how little European doctors knew about the diseases of Indian women because of the physical inaccessibility of females in purdah—or, if they were European women, they were incorporated in the environmentalist paradigm which had such a powerful hold over European conceptions of health and disease at the time. Within this paradigm, women served as markers of the rapid and destructive effects of a tropical climate on European constitutions.

As far back as 1773 John Clark described the effects of India's climate as being that it "relaxes the solids, dissolves the blood, and predisposes to putrefaction." He found these effects most evident among European women, whose "lively bloom and ruddy complexions" were "soon converted into a languid paleness; they become supine and enervated, and suffer many circumstances peculiar to the sex, from mere heat of climate and relaxation of the system."[2] William Twining in the 1830s similarly dwelt upon the greater physical hardships Western women endured in India, numbering among these the problems attending menstruation and childbirth, the frequency of miscarriages, and maternal mortality. The converse of this assumption of European vulnerability was a belief that Indian women were more attuned to their environment. Twining, for instance, thought hysteria rare among Indian women because of "the modified scale of sympathies" between body and climate, which saved Indians from many of the complaints which afflicted Europeans.[3]

As the century progressed, there were subtle shifts in European attitudes. There was a declining (though certainly not negligible) sense of European vulnerability, and the seemingly more secure health status of women was one perceptual marker of this. [. . .] The old language of constitutions and exoticism gradually gave way to a more confident belief in the value of personal hygiene and sanitation. With the growth of the European community in the second half of the century (and the increasing number of white women) Western doctors sought to be reassuring about the prospects for European survival—and safe childbearing—in India. But, significantly, women's health was still not seen to be a state responsibility. It was left to a host of medical manuals and family health guides to inform and instruct—occasionally, as in 1871, with a government prize as an incentive to their publication.[4] Attending white women in labor might have been one of the more common and lucrative parts of a civil surgeon's private practice (and perhaps a reason why they did not welcome the idea of women doctors for India), but it was not seen to be the responsibility of state medicine as such.

However, Indian women were by no means irrelevant to the emerging discourses and evolving practices of colonial medicine. Their very elusiveness was an implicit challenge to the hegemonic ambitions of Western medicine. Moreover, Western medicine could claim little success if it was effectively shunned by half the indigenous population. Equally, women in India—as elsewhere—were taken to represent a society's true nature and worth. As has often been pointed out, this gender agenda was set early in the century by James Mill when he remarked in his *History of British India* that "the condition of women is one of the most remarkable circumstances in the manners of nations. Among rude people, the women are generally degraded; among civilized people they are exalted." He added, in case his reader should be left in any doubt, that "nothing can exceed the habitual contempt which the Hindus entertain for their women."[5] The campaign against *sati,* the suppression of female infanticide, and the later debates over widow remarriage and the age of consent were all powerfully informed by this equation of Indian—more especially Hindu—society with barbaric behavior toward women.

Nor were the women themselves the only focus for this critical attention. Another was the zenana, the women's quarters in Hindu and Muslim households. This, provokingly, was "uncolonized space"—in Western eyes an abode of ignorance and superstition, a place of dirt, darkness, and disease.[6] From the 1860s, Christian missions were established with the aim of penetrating the zenana, using women missionaries to enter where no male outsider would be allowed, and employing education and health as the means of gaining access to the hearts and minds of secluded women. For Western medicine the zenana became a battlefield, increasingly implicated in resistance to Western medicine and a site where disease and ignorance about health and hygiene needed urgently to be defeated—not just for the benefit of the women themselves but also for the health of their children and husbands. As Western medicine and public health crossed the threshold and entered the Hindu home, so "new" dis-

eases, like neonatal tetanus and tuberculosis (seen very much as a zenana disease by the early twentieth century), came to the fore.[7]

One of the most striking examples of the growing attempt to incorporate women into a colonizing medical discourse and practice were moves to replace or reform the traditional Indian midwives, or *dais.* Attention began to be drawn to them from the 1860s and 1870s as European women doctors and missionaries learned more about their crude and often dangerous techniques and as the scale of infant mortality in India began to be recognized. The dais' activities were freely labeled "barbaric." Thus, in the course of an appeal for funds to provide medical aid for the women of India in 1890, Lady Dufferin referred to "the condition of those women who, debarred from all skilled medical relief, are subjected to the barbarous practice of ignorant midwives."[8] [. . .]

One colonial response to the horrors perpetrated by the dais was to seek to oust the traditional specialists and replace them with "modern" agents and institutions. Women were encouraged to give birth not in their own homes (in darkened rooms and squalid outhouses) but in lying-in or maternity hospitals, like the one opened in Madras in 1844. But, in one of those characteristic inversions which aligned what was most esteemed in Western medicine with what was most impure and degrading in Hindu society, such practices ran counter to the Hindu perception of birth as a highly polluting state and, indeed, to the seclusion of women practiced by many high-caste Hindu families and by Muslim purdah women. Although the Lying-in Hospital in Madras was open to all, in practice it catered either to low-class Europeans and Anglo-Indians (who occupied a separate ward) or, in greater numbers, to the local "Pariahs," or Untouchables, who showed few apparent objections to it on caste or religious grounds. In 1858, 833 "Pariah" women were admitted to the hospital compared to 87 "East Indians" (Anglo-Indians) and only 19 Hindus and 18 Muslims.[9]

High-caste Hindu and purdah Muslim women shunned the hospital entirely, and the tendency for their hospitals and dispensaries to be seen as "low-caste" institutions, out of bounds to the higher castes and communities, was one of the greatest problems confronting European women doctors throughout this period. Even when the Victoria Hospital for Caste and Gosha Women was opened in Madras in 1890 in an attempt to overcome this cultural resistance, it at first attracted very few inpatients because "respectable caste people still look upon a residence in any hospital as a degradation."[10] The general reluctance of women to enter hospitals had not greatly changed by World War I, even among the middle classes. In 1913 some 3,687 births in Madras city took place in hospitals, but this represented less than a fifth of registered births in the city.[11] In rural areas there were hardly any comparable facilities at all, even if women and their families had been willing to use them. [. . .]

─ഗ *Women Doctors for India*

A series of separate initiatives was launched in the 1870s and 1880s to provide women doctors for India. One of the earliest of these came from Mary Scharlieb, the wife of an English barrister in Madras. Reacting to what she learned of the dais and their methods, she had herself trained as a midwife but, feeling that this was not enough, persuaded the provincial surgeon general, Dr. Edward Balfour, to allow her to attend classes at the Madras Medical College in 1875. Perhaps not surprisingly, Scharlieb ran into considerable opposition from a skeptical and resentful male medical establishment in India. The *Indian Medical Gazette,* the unofficial voice of the IMS, did not disguise its strong views on the matter. It claimed, first, that there was no proven demand for women doctors in India and, second, that while women were "physically, mentally, and morally fitted for the profession of nursing," they were quite unsuited to the demands and skills required of doctors. As far as the *Gazette* was concerned, opening medical education in India to women was a dangerous and wholly unwarranted experiment.[12] Nonetheless, Mary Scharlieb succeeded in qualifying and, after further medical training in England, ran a successful medical practice in Madras for five years before ill health forced her to return to England.[13]

In 1881 the maharani of Panna sent a message to Queen Victoria through a missionary doctor, Elizabeth Bielby, asking that more be done to provide medical help for Indian women. Dr. Frances Hoggan (one of the first British women to qualify as a doctor) followed up this plea by proposing that a medical department be set up in India, run exclusively by and for women. She argued that the IMS had failed to provide the medical services needed by India's women and that only women doctors could overcome their objections to being examined and treated by male surgeons and physicians. In her view, the "shrinking" of women patients from male doctors was not a "prejudice" to be disregarded; it was a "natural" attitude which "religion and custom alike consecrate." It was the "right of Indian women" to expect this sentiment to be "respected and not outraged."[14]

The state's own initiative, when it eventually came, was characteristically halfhearted. On hearing of the medical needs of Indian women (from Mary Scharlieb and others), Queen Victoria urged the new vicereine, Lady Dufferin, to do what she could to promote medical aid for India's women. A fund was duly established in 1885, commonly called the Dufferin Fund but formally known as the National Association for Supplying Female Medical Aid to the Women of India. Its main objectives were to provide medical instruction, including teaching and training in India, for women as doctors, hospital assistants, nurses, and midwives; to organize medical relief for women and children, including the establishment of hospitals, dispensaries, and wards under female superintendence; and to supply trained female nurses and midwives.[15]

In recent years the Dufferin Fund has been either eulogized or derided. It has, for instance, been described as "a lucid example of British paternalism in India" and cited as evidence of the general failure of "imperial reform initiatives" in women's health before the 1920s.[16] But it would be foolish to ignore the considerable impact the fund had on women's health and medical education, just as it would be reckless not to see its practical limitations and its political significance within an expanding colonial order. The increase in the number of women (and, with them, of children as well) attending hospitals and dispensaries in the first years of the fund represented a significant widening of the bounds of Western medicine, often through the creation of hospitals and dispensaries solely for women and children.

[. . .]

Nonetheless, it is necessary to look critically at the nature and significance of the Dufferin Fund. The history of the fund reveals deep contradictions in state attitudes toward women's health. At the level of imperial rhetoric, the work of the Dufferin Fund was proudly acclaimed for bringing the benefits of Western civilization to Indian women and, as Lord Curzon put it in 1899, lifting the veil of purdah "without irreverence."[17][. . .]

And yet, for all the viceregal rhetoric, it is indicative of the secondary importance that was actually attached to medical work for women that it was left to wives of viceroys and governors, that the Dufferin Fund operated through a series of volunteer branch committees with only a weak central structure, rather than being taken up as official business. The government offered its goodwill but would not take up the work itself.

[. . .]

Again, although Hoggan and others claimed that women doctors were naturally best suited to practice among members of their own sex, this gender-before-race argument ignored the fervent politicization of women's bodies in late-nineteenth-century India. In an age of Hindu revivalism and nationalist self-assertion, debate over such issues as the Age of Consent Bill of 1891 (which aimed to raise the permissible age of sexual intercourse within marriage from ten to twelve) brought the "women's question" firmly within the domain of Indian, especially Indian male, political discourse.[18] European women doctors were walking into a minefield. Some, like Edith Pechey in Bombay, took a defiant position, lecturing the Hindus of Bombay in 1890 on the evils of child marriage, a practice, she warned them, "so barbarous in its immediate effects and so disastrous to you as a race in its remoter action that it should at once be put a stop to."[19] Others, more unwittingly, became a target for accusations of racial arrogance and cultural ignorance; some were suspected of being undercover agents for the evangelizing work of the Zenana Missions (indeed, the Dufferin Fund found it difficult to distance itself from the activities of missionary women doctors).

It did not help that newly arrived women doctors rarely had any knowledge of the "languages, customs, and habits" of the people among whom they were to work, and it was not until 1890 that the Central Committee of the Dufferin Fund recognized the importance of doctors' knowing enough of a local language to be able to communicate directly with their patients rather than through interpreters.[20] Hindu newspapers in Bengal in the 1890s launched a sustained attack on the Dufferin Fund and white women doctors, denouncing zenana hospitals as an insult to the Indian traditions of childbearing and dismissing the doctors themselves as "half-educated good-for-nothings."[21] How far the sentiments voiced by male newspaper editors reflected the attitudes of women themselves is more difficult to assess, but in a society where men controlled women's access to health care, male hostility had obvious implications.

GLOSSARY

ayah	nursemaid	*sastra*	Hindu religious text
Ayurveda	Hindu system of medicine	*sati*	immolation of Hindu widow on her husband's funeral pyre
bhadralok	"respectable" middle class in Bengal		
dai	Indian midwife	*sirkar*	government
devi	goddess	*thagi*	crime committed by a Thag (or Thug)
ghura	earthenware pot	*tika*	mark
hakim	Yunani practitioner	*tikadar*	inoculator ("mark-maker")
kaviraj	Ayurvedic practitioner (in Bengal)	*vaidya*	Ayurvedic practitioner
lakh	100,000	Yunani	Muslim system of medicine
mela	fair, festival	zamindar	landholder
puja	worship	zenana	women's quarters
raiyatwari	a land revenue system based on individual peasant proprietors (*raiyats*)		

NOTES

1. Margaret I. Balfour and Ruth Young, *The Work of Medical Women in India,* Oxford: Oxford University Press, 1929.

2. John Clark, *Observations on the Diseases in Long Voyages to Hot Countries and Particularly on Those Which Prevail in the East Indies,* London: Wilson and Nicol, 1773.

3. William Twining, *Clinical Illustrations of the More Important Diseases of Bengal with the Results of an Enquiry into Their Pathology and Treatment,* Calcutta: Baptist Mission Press, 2nd Edition, 1835, 2 vols. Calcutta: Mission Press, 1832.

4. W. J. Moore, *A Manual of Family Medicine for India.* 2nd ed. London: Churchill, 1877.

5. James Mill, *A History of British India,* 5th ed. London: Madden, 1858.

6. Janaki Nair, 1990. "Uncovering the Zenana: Visions of Indian Womanhood in Englishwomen's Writings, 1813–1940," *Journal of Women's History* 2:8–34.

7. In 1919, one-quarter of all infant mortality in the United Provinces was attributed to tetanus. *United Provinces Sanitary Commission Annual Report* 1919. On TB in India, see Kailas Chunder Bose, "Tuberculosis," *Proceedings of the First All-India Sanitary Conference* 1911, 133–36.

8. Dufferin Fund Annual Report, 1890, 112.

9. *Madras Annual Report on Civil Dispensaries* 1858, 37; J. L. Ranking, Report of the Lying-in Hospital and Dispensary for Women and Children, Madras: Government Press, 1868.

10. *Dufferin Fund Annual Report,* 1890, 197.

11. *Administration Report of the Corporation of Madras Health Department* 1913, 28.

12. *Indian Medical Gazette,* Oct. 1875, 274–75; July 1882, 184.

13. Mary Scharlieb, *Reminiscences,* London: Williams and Norgate, 1924.

14. Frances Elizabeth Hoggan, "Medical Women for India," *Contemporary Review* 42:267–75, 1882.

15. *Dufferin Fund Annual Report,* 1890, 8.

16. Dagmar Engels, *Beyond Purdah,* Delhi: Oxford University Press, 1996. For a more balanced account, see Balfour and Young, 1929.

17. *Indian Medical Gazette,* Apr. 1899, 134.

18. For the debates and issues of the period, see Charles Heimsath, *Indian Nationalism and Hindu Social Reform,* Princeton: Princeton University Press, 1954; Dagmar Engels, " The Age of Consent Act of 1891: Colonial Ideology in Bengal," *South Asia Research* 3: 107–31.

19. Edythe Lutzker, *Edith Pechey Phipson, M.D.: The Story of England's Foremost Pioneering Woman Doctor,* New York: Exposition Press, 1973.

20. *Dufferin Fund Annual Report,* 1890, 15; see the Native Newspaper Reports for the period for Bombay, e.g., *Mahratta,* 10 Apr. 1886, *Subodh Patrika* 4 Apr. 1886; *Jame Jamshed,* 21 Aug. 1886.

21. Engels, 1996.

Sexual Surgery in Late-Nineteenth-Century America

BEN BARKER-BENFIELD

Ben Barker-Benfield, a historian of Western medicine, traces the beginnings of gynecology in the West in the nineteenth century to focus on the use of clitoridectomy as a cure for women's "unruly" or "unfeminine" behavior or for illnesses characterized as "female complaints." Barker-Benfield highlights the history of race and class in the selection of patients who were experimented upon the early years of gynecology. His work shows that clitoridectomy, or female circumcision, has a history in the West and cannot be thought of as a solely African or Islamic custom.

Clitoridectomy was the first operation performed to check woman's mental disorder. Invented by the English gynecologist Isaac Baker Brown (33, 34) in 1858, it was first performed in America in the late 1860s and continued to be performed in the United States at least until 1904, and perhaps until 1925. After publishing his results in 1866, the English inventor was severely censured by his profession; he died two years later and the performance of clitoridectomy in England died with him (35). Analysis of Baker Brown's cases shows a significant incidence of female hostility toward men

Ben Barker-Benfield, "Sexual Surgery in Late-Nineteenth Century America," *International Journal of Health Services,* Vol 15.2, 1975: 285–87, 288–89, 293–95.

and the role men demanded women play, and suggests that he regarded woman's sexual independence, whether construed to have stemmed from nymphomania or from misandry, as a sickness to be treated.

In the United States, however, clitoridectomy coexisted with and then was superseded by the circumcision of females of all ages up to the menopause (it removed all or part of the "hood" of the clitoris); circumcision continued to be performed until at least 1937. Both clitoridectomy and circumcision aimed to check what was thought to be a growing incidence of female masturbation, an activity which men feared inevitably aroused women's naturally boundless but usually repressed sexual appetite for men. Men needed to deploy their sperm elsewhere for social and economic success—in the gynecologic curbing of female sexual appetite, for example. There is, by the way, ample evidence that gynecologists saw their knives' cutting into women's generative tract as a form of sexual intercourse.

Female castration, or oophorectomy, or normal ovariotomy, was a much more widespread and frequently performed operation than clitoridectomy. Invented by Robert Battey of Rome, Georgia, in the United States in 1872, it flourished between 1880 and 1910, then slackened its pace in the 1910s; women were still being castrated for psychologic disorders as late as 1946. One estimate in 1906 was that for every one of

---

Key Terms

clitoridectomy This practice consists of the surgical removal of the clitoris as well as other parts of the labia or genitalia.

female circumcision The initiation of a female into a group (usually an age group) through ceremonies and the practice of clitoridectomy.

the 150,000 doctors in the United States there was one castrated woman; some of these doctors boasted that they had removed from 1,500 to 2,000 ovaries apiece. Female castration was largely superseded by other similar operations, including hysterectomy, which had co-existed as an alternative and auxiliary to castration since about 1895. And of course there is evidence today of "excessive," "promiscuous ," and "careless" surgical treatment in America, particularly that accorded women and children. The examples frequently cited include hysterectomy, mastectomy, tonsillectomy, infant circumcision, hemorrhoidectomy, and oophorectomy, the latter indicated by apparently physical conditions. Such emphasis on surgical therapy perhaps sustains the argument that the operations reflect beliefs especially true of American psychology. The operations (performed overwhelmingly by men) are distinct from those performed in other countries in frequency and in concentration. For example, in the United States in 1965, 516 hysterectomies and 278 breast operations were performed for each 100,000 of the female population. The respective figures in England and Wales in 1966 were only 213.2 and 171.7. The contrast should be compared to the relative positions of midwives in each country. They have been driven out by doctors, obstetricians, and legislators in the United States, whereas in England (as in most countries in the world), most babies are delivered by midwives (9, 36–42).

Women were castrated and clitoridectomized in England, Germany, and France, although both operations seem to have ceased earlier in England and France than in America. There was continual interpenetration of ideas between Europe and America, although Americans tended to receive rather than to give; and, of course, there was a fundamental historical relationship between the new world and the old. American attitudes toward Europe embodied a constellation of powerful feelings, including guilt, hostility, and a sense of cultural and historical inferiority. The factor with which I have been concerned, and which I have in some sense isolated from that skein, is the effect of the social pressures on men on male attitudes toward women. The history of female castration in European countries must be woven into the fabric of those societies' histories, including the effects of the progress of democracy in each place.

The Social Context for Female Castration

From one perspective, the castration of women starting in the 1870s (performed overwhelmingly on noninstitutionalized outpatients, and only later—in the 1890s—on inmates of mental institutions) was part of the general anxiety about the racial future of white America. Jefferson had suggested a racial-improvement breeding program in *Notes on Virginia* (43). From the post-Civil War period until World War II there was an accelerating eugenic program in the United States, carried out on the bodies of the insane and epileptic. In the period I have been studying, such sterilization was actually implemented on the bodies of women, not men. Ruth Caplan (1) has described how late-nineteenth-century treatment of the insane combined sterilization, isolation, and dehumanization. Perhaps the same can be said for a growing number of Americans' experiences of urban and industrial life. The purging of criminals, paupers, deaf mutes, retarded, and so on (the period is remarkable for its bizarre and vast compendia of physiologic curiosities and abnormalcies) was a major contribution to the process of dehumanization (44).

Social leaders and molders—doctors, clergymen, popular novelists, and politicians—saw America as a beleagured island of WASP righteousness, surrounded by an encroaching flood of dirty, prolific immigrants, and sapped from within by the subversive practices of women. Their masturbation, contraception, and abortion were exhausting society's procreative power. These males saw society as a body invaded by foreign germs, its native blood corrupted and used up from outside and within. These metaphors emerge in the work of Todd, Gardner, and a myriad of their contemporaries (see references 9, parts 3 and 4; 14; 21; 22; 45; 46).

Whatever its metaphor, this vision was shared by gynecologists attempting to purge midwives away from the perverted sources of new life, snipping off the clitorises of girls and women addicted to masturbation and removing the ovaries of women deemed unfit to breed, or too rebellious in themselves to be tolerated. The anxieties intensified toward the end of the century, the critical zenith of the "search for order." The separation and subordination of blacks was formalized at a national level in 1896, and their segregation, castration, and lynching coincided with the growing nativism, the lynching of immigrants, the extirpation of resistant Filipinos and Indians, and the peak of the castration of women (47, 48). Such treatment manifested the aggrandizement of the white skin and penis, a process manifesting the hypostasis of physiologic identity in lieu of other forms of identity (dynastic, class, craft) stripped from men by industrialism and by democracy: the stripping went on less extremely and more slowly in Europe. The only source of identity remaining to men other than body was the less certain form of money, with which body was confused. (For the argument that body (and money) were the only sources of identity left because of democracy, see references 9:10, Vol. 2, pp. 239–240: 32).)

[. . .]

—◦Who the Patients Were

The women on whom these operations were performed were rich enough, or in rich enough hands, to afford the new gynecologic care (56). It is true that the poorest class of women in America had played a crucial part in launching gynecologic surgery and the careers built upon it. Sims was the inventor of the first successful operation for the cure of the vesicovaginal fistula; his greatest influence in medical history was the encouragement of an extremely active, adventurous policy of surgical interference with woman's sexual organs in the interest, above all, of making woman produce babies. He also castrated women. (Castration and impregnation were both regarded as ways to control woman's dangerous sexuality.) Early in his career Sims bought a number of slaves suffering from vesicovaginal fistulae expressly for his surgical experiment, housing them in a private hospital in his backyard. With the support of some of the wealthiest and most influential men and women in New York City, he later established the Woman's Hospital there. It maintained the supply of human material upon which Sims, his colleagues, their pupils, and guests could experiment. Most of the first patients were destitute Irish immigrant women, whose fistulae and general health were so bad that they allowed Sims and his fellows to keep them there indefinitely, even as the slaves' medical and social condition enabled Sims to make them literally "his" patients. One of the first of these Irish indigents,

Mary Smith, endured 30 operations between 1856 and 1859, precisely the number the slave Anarcha had endured between 1845 and 1849. Like his contemporaries—and rivals—Sims constantly devised new operations and instruments, discarding them when they caused too many accidents. The hospital's patients were treated free. Sims and other gynecologic surgeons made their money by applying the hospital discoveries in private practice, where they charged "stupendous" fees. The conclusion is inescapable that the hospital was instituted for the same reason that Sims garnered diseased black women into his backyard: to provide guinea pigs before he and the others could convincingly offer care to the wives of the wealthy (9, Ch. 10). It may be that the fact that the first American clitoridectomy patient I have come across (57) was the only working-class one (she was a seamstress) can be explained in the same way.

But the chief targets of gynecologic surgery aimed specifically at sexual discipline were the wives and daughters of rich, or at least middle-class, men. These women might also be guinea pigs. Battey's first castration (58) was of a young private patient who seems to have been of the same leisured class that supplied the rest of his patients. According to Dr. Palmer Dudley (56) in 1900, "the hardworking, daily-toiling woman is not as fit a subject for gynecologic surgery as the woman so situated in life as to be able to conserve her strength and, if necessary, to take a prolonged rest, in order to secure the best results." If her sick condition derived from postindustrial worklessness, it also depended on it for cure. The greatest amount of sexual surgery was performed on the nonworking female dependents of men economically "well situated in life." The operations were performed throughout the country in urban centers small and large where gynecologists practiced, from Ottumwa and Keokuk in Iowa, to New Orleans, from Young's Crossroads, South Carolina, to New York, Philadelphia, and Boston, to Los Angeles, San Francisco, and Portland, Oregon.

[. . .]

Doctors in the nineteenth century claimed to direct society morally, and exhorted ministers and politicians to do so according to medical precepts. Women were being orderly in asking the appropriate social authorities to help. After Cushing's castration of her, that woman "previously sunk into a state of profound melancholia on account of her belief that her masturbation eternally damned her, told him that 'a window has been opened in heaven.' " Gynecologists were answering women's prayers. But their sexual values condemned gynecologists to sustain the belief that being female was a disease. Doctors' attempts to restore to women a measure of willpower was a sisyphean rock of their own making. As men generally (including doctors) confined women to the butterfly existence that made them sick, more demanding, in need of more confinement (to bed, asylum, or both) and so on, so doctors created symptoms they attempted to cure, their therapy expressing the same assumptions of the male identity which found it necessary to exclude and subordinate women (as they excluded the "feminine" in themselves). Doctors and gynecologists prescribed addictive drugs for displaced and disordered women; if drugs did not work, the same doctor, or another one, castrated the patient, deeming her drug addiction a symptom of her sick condition; if that operation did not work, she was put back on drugs. If only one ovary was extirpated at first, or both ovaries but not the tubes, or ovaries and tubes but not the uterus, the cycle of drugs and operations could drag on and on. It was extended when surgeons began to cure castrated women by transplanting other women's ovaries into them. This kind of circle permitted men to ignore the commitment to male insanity they believed their competitive and obsessive lifestyle entailed. Castration destroyed woman's one remaining thread of identity, her hope for motherhood, in the way critics of the operation described. Many castrated women were left hopeless, sunk into despair on a scale almost beyond imagination (9, Ch. 9; 28;81).

But by the same standard of social beliefs generating disease, castration could and did work. If the nature of the doctor's authority, and its expression in his treatment, and the nature of the patient's belief, and its expression in her disorder, were all pitched just right, then she might be restored to an "order" she would be willing to accept. Clearly the missing factors in all of these cases could have been crucial. Perhaps one reason for the success in a few cases was the gynecologic surgeon's necessary decisiveness, which made him more likely to conform to the putatively authoritative role of the male than the dreadfully pressured democrat, unsupported by such expertise. Disorderly women were handed over to the gynecologists for castration and other kinds of radical treatment by husbands or fathers unable to enforce their minimum identity guarantee—the submission of woman. The handed-over woman then underwent a period of intense discipline by anesthesia and knife, or the S. Weir Mitchell kind of discipline, developed concurrently with castration (which Mitchell also performed). Mitchell's "rest-cure" consisted of the patient's descent to womblike dependence, then rebirth, liquid food, weaning, upbringing, and reeducation by a model parental organization—a trained female nurse entirely and unquestionably the agent firmly implementing the orders of the more distant and totally authoritative male, i.e. the doctor in charge. The patient was returned to her menfolk's management, recycled, and taught to make the will of the male her own (82).

Some women refused castration, standing on their right to motherhood and the value of maternal identity, which they shared with men, whatever the difference in their reasons. On the other hand, many women went much further than simply allowing their men to submit them to the knife. By and large, women share beliefs about roles and social order: If such beliefs drove them inevitably to disorder, they went to the proper authorities. One "maiden lady" in 1877 demanded of William Goodell and Weir Mitchell that they remove her womb and ovaries, once they had told her of such operations (52, 83).

The sequence of such a gynecologist–patient dialectic is clear: men invented, or heard of, the new operations, and decided to try them; they informed women, or women's menfolk. The news got abroad. So some proponents of castration could declare innocently that the patient came in to beg to be castrated. Edes (73) said in 1898 that such pleas reflected the "professional medical errors of a previous medical generation." In 1897 B. Sherwood-Dunn (61) considered the doctor's responsibility in such cases: "The fact . . . that women come to us pleading to have their ovaries removed, a thing which happens to every man in practice, is all the more reason why we should stand between them" and the deleterious results. On the same occasion, Dr. Henry Carstens admitted that (61)

" . . . a woman does not always come to us to have [her ovaries] removed, but because she has some morbid condition which causes her to apply to the physician, and the doctor, thinking it is the tubes and ovaries that are at fault, removes them. In many cases a wrong diagnosis is made." Gynecologists remained convinced that they knew best, and either tortured the notion of the participation of the patient's will, or simply reneged on a preoperation agreement if a woman managed to extract one—not to remove both ovaries, for example—once the patient was unconscious under the knife (73).

The conflict in a woman confronted with the Hobson's choice of castration must have been a terrible one, torn as she was by the differing male demands on her. She was troublesome enough to her husband or father (with his persistent apprehensions of her sperm-sucking propensities (32) and the menace of her menstruation) to have him present her for castration. At the same time, she would have been aware of the male demand for race preservation, his woman's-ovaries man's-route-to-the-future of the WASP nation. Gynecologists accused WASP women of undermining that future by aborting and contracepting. And as a corollary, woman would have been aware of the social calumny that followed her castration; castrated women were commonly known as "its" (56, 84). To paraphrase Freud, what did men want? And woman would have been torn, too, by her own lifetime's interiorization of such feelings. They were hers, together with her feelings about her body's submission to the doctor's surgical appetite.

In 1904 one doctor noted the power of social beliefs in spreading these operations. Female patients were "fully convinced that directly or indirectly, all their grief emanates from the pelvis, and oftentimes this idea is fostered and materially augmented by their friends" (77). Women were "the sex." The gynecologic phenomena herein described were symbiotic between patient and doctor, reflecting and refracting the largest contours of social beliefs and expectations. Another doctor, this time in 1906, reported a case where a patient had repeatedly requested that the right ovary and the uterus be removed. She was refused because no conditions existed warranting such a procedure. But usually friends, relatives, and doctors would confirm a woman's tracing her trouble to her sex organs. . . . Another doctor had laid part of the responsibility for the almost automatic mutilation of woman's sexual organs to women's own appropriation of such operations as a "fashionable fad" and as a "mark of favor," an image suggesting that some women understood and responded to the surgeon's invasion of their bodies as a form of courtship and copulation (85). It may be noted that clitoridectomists and castrators tested women for indications of the disease of desire by inducing orgasm, manipulating clitoris or breasts. Some women considered their scars "as pretty as the dimple in the cheek of sweet sixteen," and so adopted the views of Goodell and other gynecologists that castration made women more attractive sexually. Van de Warker placed the major portion of responsibility for the operations on the medical profession, but he also described the collaboration of passive, careless, and wealthy women. A man of his times, he bewailed the destruction of what he regarded as nationally owned ovaries.

Nonetheless, one cannot help being moved by the critically distinct perspectives supplied by the handful of radically thoughtful doctors like Van de Warker. Historical change seems to come about, as William James remarked somewhere, by adding as little as possible of the new onto as much as possible of the old. Van de Warker was ashamed that medical reform had always come from outside medical ranks. But given the symbiotic nature of the relation he described, given gynecologic persistence in castration in the face of massive evidence against the operation, and given its significance as the prominent tip of an iceberg of social beliefs, it was reasonable to assume that the iron circuit could only be broken from outside.

REFERENCES

1. Caplan, R. *Psychiatry and the Community in Nineteenth Century America,* p. 140, New York, 1969.

2. Dain, N. *Concepts of Insanity in the United States, 1789–1865,* pp. 10, 12, 26, 65, University Press, New Brunswick, N.J., 1964.

3. Meigs, C. *Woman: Her Diseases and Remedies,* Ed. 2, p. 54. Blanchard and Lee, 1851.

4. Brigham, A. *Remarks on the Influence of Mental Cultivation and Mental Excitement upon Health,* Ed. 2, pp. vii, 80–81. Marsh, Capen, and Lyon, Boston, 1833.

5. Jarvis, E. "On the Comparative Liability of Males and Females to Insanity, and Their Comparative Curability and Mortality when Insane." *American Journal of Insanity* 7: 155, 1850.

6. Ray, I. *Mental Hygiene,* p. 54. Hafner Publishing Company, New York, 1968 (facsimile of 1863 edition).

7. Jarvis, F. "On the Supposed Increase of Insanity." *American Journal of Insanity* 8: 349, 1852.

8. Ray, I. "The Insanity of Women Produced by Desertion or Seduction." *American Journal of Insanity* 23: 267, 1866.

9. Barker-Benfield, B. *The Horrors of the Half-Known Life,* Ch. 6 and Pt. 3, Harper & Row, New York, forthcoming.

10. de Tocqueville, A. *Democracy in America,* Vols. 1 and 2. Random House, Vintage edition, New York, 1945.

11. Meyer, D. *The Positive Thinkers,* pp. 51–56. Doubleday, Garden City, N.Y., 1965.

12. Wiebe, R. H. *The Search for Order,* pp. xiii, 1, 5–6, 8, 52. Hill and Wang, American Century edition, New York, 1968.

13. Gardner, A. K. *History of the Art of Midwifery,* p. 4. Stringer and Townshend, New York, 1852. (Also published as introduction to Gardner's edition of W. Tyler Smith's *The Modern Practice of Midwifery,* Robert M. DeWitt, New York, 1852.)

14. Gardner, A. K. *Our Children,* p. 210. Belknap and Bliss, Hartford, 1872.

15. Shryock, R. H. *Medicine in America,* pp. 189–190. Johns Hopkins University Press, Baltimore, 1966.

16. Shryock, R. H. *Medicine and Society in America: 1660–1860,* p. 147. Cornell University Press, Great Seal edition, Ithaca, N.Y., 1962.

17. Fishbein, M. *A History of the American Medical Association,* pp. 82–85. W. B. Saunders, Philadelphia, 1947.

18. Smith, H. N. *Virgin Land,* Ch. X. Vintage, New York, 1950.

19. Vest, G. In *Up from the Pedestal: Selected Writings in the History of American Feminism,* ed. A. Kraditor, p. 195. Quadrangle Books, Chicago, 1968.

20. Gardner, A. K. New York Medical College for Women. *Frank Leslie's Illustrated Newspaper* 30(759): 71, April 19, 1870.

21. Todd, J. *Woman's Rights,* p. 12. Lee and Shepard, Boston, 1867.

22. Gardner, A. K. *Conjugal Sins,* p. 195. J. S. Redfield, New York, 1870.

23. Marcy, H. O. "The Early History of Abdominal Surgery in America." *Transactions of the Section on Obstetrics and Diseases of Women and Children of the American Medical Association,* pp. 248–266, 1909.

24. *Transactions of the American Medical Association* 10:31, 1857.

25. Gardner, A. K., and Barker, F. "Remarks on Puerperal Fever." *Transactions of the New York Academy of Medicine,* 1858.

26. Thomas, T. G. *Diseases of Women,* Preface to 1st Edition. H. C. Lea, Philadelphia, 1868.

27. Storer, H. R. *The Causation, Course and Treatment of Reflex Insanity in Women,* p. 79, Lee and Shepard, Boston, 1871.

28. Barker-Benfield, B. *Sexual Surgery,* forthcoming.

29. Sims, J. M. *Clinical Notes on Uterine Surgery,* pp. 131–35, 206–7. William Wood, New York, 1866.

30. Baldwin, W. O. In *The Story of My Life,* by J. M. Sims, p. 433. D. Appleton, New York, 1885.

31. Chadwick, J. R. Obstetrics and Gynecological Literature, 1876–1881. *Transactions of the American Medical Association* 32: 255, 1881.

32. Barker-Benfield, B. "The Spermatic Economy." In *The American Family in Social-Historical Perspective,* edited by M. Gordon, St. Martin's Press, New York, 1973.

33. Baker Brown, I. *On the Curability of Certain Forms of Insanity, Epilepsy, Catalepsy.* Robert Hardwicke, London, 1866.

34. Meeting to Consider the Proposition of the Council for the Removal of Mr. I. Baker Brown, *Br. Med. J.* 1: pp. 395–410, 1867.

35. Tait, I., Masturbation. *The Medical News* 53(1):3, July 7, 1888.

36. Bunker, J. "Surgical Manpower: A Comparison of Operations and Surgeons in the United States and in England and Wales." *New Engl. J. Med.* 282(3):135–44, 1970.

37. Bunker, J. "When to Operate?" *Saturday Review,* pp. 30–31, August 22, 1970.

38. Norris, F. S. "We Need Women Doctors." Letter to the Editor, *Washington Evening Star,* December 15, 1970.

39. Bolande, R. P. "Ritualistic Surgery: Circumcision and Tonsillectomy." *New Engl. J. Med.* 280(11): 591–97, 1969.

40. Klemesrude, J. "Those Who Have Been There Aid Breast Surgery Patients." *New York Times,* February 8, 1971.

41. Weiss, E., and English, O. S. *Psychosomatic Medicine,* Ed. 3, Ch. 19, W. B. Saunders, Philadelphia, 1957.

42. *Maternity Care in the World: Report of a Joint Group of the International Federation of Gynecology and Obstetrics and the International Confederation of Midwives,* pp. 173, 317. Pergamon Press, London, 1966.

43. Jefferson, T. *Notes on Virginia,* p. 133. Harper Torchbook, New York, 1964.

44. Myerson, A., Ayer, J. B., Putnam, T. J., Keeler, C. E., and Alexander, I. *Eugenical Sterilization: A Reorientation of the Problem.* Macmillan, New York, 1936.

45. Engelmann, G. J. "The Increasing Sterility of American Women." *Transactions of the Section on Obstetrics and Diseases of Women and Children of the American Medical Association,* pp. 271–95, 1901.

46. Higham, J. *Strangers in the Land,* Ch. 6. Atheneum, New York, 1968.

47. Brown, R. M. "Historical Patterns of Violence in America." In *Violence in America,* Gurr and Graham, ed. pp. 47–49. Signet, New York, 1969.

48. Beisner, R. I., *Twelve against Empire: The Anti-Imperialists, 1898–1900,* pp. 45–46. McGraw-Hill, New York, 1968.

49. Gilliam, D. T. "Oophorectomy for the Insanity and Epilepsy of the Female: A Plea for Its More General Adoption." *Transactions of the American Association of Obstetricians and Gynecologists* 9: 320, 1896.

50. Goodell, W. "Clinical Notes on the Extirpation of the Ovaries for Insanity." *American Journal of Insanity* 38: 295, 1882.

51. Flexner, E. *Century of Struggle,* Chs. 11–13, 15, 16. Atheneum, New York, 1968.

52. Goodell, W. *Lessons in Gynecology,* pp. 270–76. D. G. Brinton, Philadelphia, 1879.

53. Van de Warker, E., "The Fetich of the Ovary." *American Journal of Obstetrics and Diseases of Women and Children* 54: 369, 1906.

54. Meyer, J. "A Case of Insanity, Caused by Diseased Ovaries, Cured by Their Removal—A Phenomenal Triumph for Operative Treatment." *Transactions of the American Association of Obstetricians and Gynecologists* 7: 503–4, 1894.

55. Brockman, D. C. "Oophorectomy for Grave Functional Nervous Diseases Occurring during Menstruation." *Transactions of the Western Surgical and Gynecological Association,* pp. 104–10, 1900.

56. Dudley, A. P. "Results of Ovarian Surgery." *Transactions of the Section on Obstetrics and Diseases of Women and Children of the American Medical Association,* pp. 188–89, 1900.

57. "Case of Excessive Masturbation." *American Journal of Obstetrics and Diseases of Women and Children* 6: 294–95, 1873–1874.

58. Battey, R. "Normal Ovariotomy Case." *Atlanta Medical and Surgical Journal* 10(6): 323–25, 1872.

59. Gardner, A. K. "The Physical Decline of American Women." *The Knickerbocker* 55(1): 37–52, 1860. (Also appended to *Conjugal Sins,* p. 218, J. S. Redfield, New York, 1870.)

60. Battey, R. "Normal Ovariotomy." *Atlanta Medical and Surgical Journal* 11(1): 20–21, 1873.

61. Dunn, B. S. "Conservation of the Ovary." *Transactions of the American Association of Obstetricians and Gynecologists* 10: 209–24, 1897.

62. Engelmann, G. J. "Cliterodectomy [sic]." *The American Practitioner* 25: 3, 1882.

63. Transactions of the Woman's Hospital Society. *Am. J. Obstet. Gynecol.* 43: 721, 1901.

64. Cushing, E. W. "Melancholia, Masturbation: Cured by Removal of Both Ovaries." In Report of the Annual Meeting of the Gynecological Society of Boston. *J.A.M.A.* 8: 441–42, 1887.

65. Block, A. J. "Sexual Perversion in the Female." *New Orleans Medical and Surgical Journal* 22(1): 6, 1894.

66. Church, A. "Removal of Ovaries and Tubes in the Insane and Neurotic." *American Journal of Obstetrics and the Diseases of Women and Children* 28:494–95, 1893.

67. Discussion of A. Church's "Removal of Ovaries and Tubes in the Insane and Neurotic." *American Journal of Obstetrics and the Diseases of Women and Children* 28: 569–73, 1893.

68. Pratt, E. H. "Circumcision of Girls." *Journal of Orificial Surgery* 6(9): 385–86, 1898.

69. Manton, W. P. "The Legal Question in Operations of the Insane." *Transactions of the American Association of Obstetricians and Gynecologists* 6: 246, 1893.

70. Burnham, J. "Psychoanalysis and American Medicine: 1894–1918." *Psychological Issues* 5(4): 73–81, 1967.

71. Hamilton, A. "The Abuse of Oophorectomy in Diseases of the Nervous System." *New York Medical Journal* 57: 180–183, 1893.

72. Edes, R. "Points in the Diagnosis and Treatment of Some Obscure Common Neuroses." *J.A.M.A.* 27: 1077–82, 1896.

73. Edes, R. "The Relations of Pelvic and Nervous Diseases." *J.A.M.A.* 31: 1133–36, 1898.

74. Warner, Quoted in Report of the Annual Meeting of the Gynecological Society of Boston. *J.A.M.A.* 8: 441–42, 1887.

75. Cokenower, J. A plea for conservative operations on the ovaries. *Transactions of the Section on Obstetrics and Diseases of Women and Children of the American Medical Association,* p. 298, 1904.

76. Report of the Annual Meeting of the Gynecological Society of Boston. *J.A.M.A.* 8: 441–442, 1887.

77. Byford, H. T. *Manual of Gynecology,* Ed. 2, pp. 180–185. P. Blakiston, Philadelphia, 1897.

78. Polak, J. O. Final results in conservative surgery of the ovaries. *Transactions of the Section on Obstetrics and Diseases of Women and Children of the American Medical Association,* p. 340, 1909.

79. Kelly, H. The ethical side of the operation of oophorectomy. *American Journal of Obstetrics* 27: 208–209, 1898.

80. MacLean, D. Sexual mutilation. *California Medical Journal* 15: 382–384, 1894.

Unmasking Tradition
ROGAIA ABUSHARAF

Anthropologist Rogaia Abusharaf studies women in Sudan. Abusharaf urges us to consider the role of late-twentieth-century female circumcision in specific cultural and socioeconomic contexts in order to understand why the practice continues. Only then, she argues, can meaningful strategies for change be found.

I will never forget the day of my circumcision, which took place forty years ago. I was six years old. One morning during my school summer vacation, my mother told me that I had to go with her to her sisters' house and then to visit a sick relative in Halfayat El Mulook [in the northern part of Khartoum, Sudan]. We did go to my aunts' house, and from there all of us went straight to [a] red brick house [I had never seen].

While my mother was knocking, I tried to pronounce the name on the door. Soon enough I realized that it was Hajja Alamin's house. She was the midwife who performed circumcisions on girls in

Rogaia Abusharaf, "Unmasking Tradition." *The Sciences*, March/April 1998: 23–77.

my neighborhood. I was petrified and tried to break loose. But I was captured and subdued by my mother and two aunts. They began to tell me that the midwife was going to purify me.

The midwife was the cruelest person I had seen. . . . [She] ordered her young maid to go buy razors from the Yemeni grocer next door. I still remember her when she came back with the razors, which were enveloped in purple wrapping with a crocodile drawing on it.

The women ordered me to lie down on a bed [made of ropes] that had a hole in the middle. They held me tight while the midwife started to cut my flesh without anesthetics. I screamed till I lost my voice. The midwife was saying to me, "Do you want me to be taken into police custody?" After the job was done I could not eat, drink, or even pass urine for three days. I remember one of my uncles who discovered what they did to me threatened to press charges against his sisters. They were afraid of him and they decided to bring me back to the midwife. In her sternest voice she ordered me to squat on the floor and urinate. It seemed like the most difficult

---

Key Terms

FGM (female genital mutilation) This term is used among those working to eradicate female circumcision to arouse public outrage and organize opposition to the practice. The FGM argument usually poses female circumcision as a human rights violation as well as the mutilation and abuse of a woman's body and sexual parts.

genital cutting A term used in contrast to "FGM" as a more neutral description of clitoridectomy and female circumcision to avoid hasty value judgments without adequate historical and cultural context.

thing to do at that point, but I did it. I urinated for a long time and was shivering with pain.

It took a very long time [before] I was back to normal. I understand the motives of my mother, that she wanted me to be clean, but I suffered a lot.

—from a 1989 interview with
Aisha Abdel Majid, a Sudanese woman
working as a teacher in the Middle East

Aisha Abdel Majid's story echoes the experience of millions of African women who have undergone ritualized genital surgeries, often as young girls, without anesthesia, in unsanitary conditions, the surgical implement a knife, a razor blade, or a broken bottle wielded by a person with no medical training. The pain and bleeding are intense; the girls sometimes die. Survivors are prone to a host of medical complications that can plague them throughout their lives, including recurrent infections, pain during intercourse, infertility and obstructed labor that can cause babies to be born dead or brain-damaged.

Female circumcision, also known as genital mutilation, is a common practice in at least 28 African countries, cutting a brutal swath through the center of the continent—from Mauritania and the Ivory Coast in the west to Egypt, Somalia, and Tanzania in the east. The ritual also takes place among a few ethnic groups in Asia. Where it is practiced, female circumcision is passionately perpetuated and closely safeguarded; it is regarded as an essential coming-of-age ritual that ensures chastity, promotes cleanliness and fertility, and enhances the beauty of a woman's body. In Arabic the colloquial word for circumcision, *tahara,* means "to purify." It is estimated that between 100 million and 130 million women living today have undergone genital surgeries, and each year two million more—mostly girls from four to twelve years old—will be cut.

Last December genital mutilation became illegal in Egypt, thanks to a closely watched court decision, and women's groups in Africa and abroad hope that the landmark ruling will bolster eradication efforts worldwide. But most people working for change recognize that government action, though an important and useful symbol, is ultimately not the answer. Barbaric though the ritual may seem to Westerners, female circumcision is deeply enmeshed in local traditions and

beliefs. Treating it as a crime and punishing offenders with jail time would in many cases be unfair. Mothers who bring their daughters for the operation believe they are doing the right thing—and indeed, their children would likely become social outcasts if left uncut. You cannot arrest an entire village.

Make no mistake: I believe that genital mutilation must end if women are to enjoy the most basic human rights. But it does little good for a Westerner, or even an African-born woman such as myself, to condemn the practice unilaterally. We must learn from history: when colonial European powers tried to abolish the surgery in the first half of this century, local people rejected the interference and clung even more fiercely to their traditions. Without an understanding of indigenous cultures, and without a deep commitment from within those cultures to end the cutting, eradication efforts imposed from the outside are bound to fail. Nothing highlights the problem more clearly than the two terms used to describe the procedure: is it circumcision, an "act of love," as some women call it, or mutilation? Contradictory though the answer might seem, it is both.

Because genital cutting is considered an essential aspect of a woman's identity, abolishing it has profound social implications. Think of the politics and emotions in Western countries that have swirled around issues such as abortion, the right of homosexuals to be parents, and the ethics of human cloning. Any change that requires a readjustment of long-established social mores makes people highly uncomfortable.

The justifications for female circumcision vary. Some ethnic groups in Nigeria believe that if a woman's clitoris is not removed, contact with it will kill a baby during childbirth. Other people believe that, unchecked, the female genitalia will continue to grow, becoming a grotesque penislike organ dangling between a woman's legs. Vaginal secretions, produced by glands that are often removed as part of the surgery, are thought to be unclean and lethal to sperm.

Circumcision is also intended to dull women's sexual enjoyment, and to that end it is chillingly effective. In a survey conducted in Sierra Leone, circumcised women reported feeling little or no sexual responsiveness. The clitoris is always at least partially removed during the operation, and without it orgasm becomes practically impossible. Killing women's desire is thought to keep them chaste; in fact, genital cutting is so closely associated with virginity that a girl who is spared the ordeal by enlightened parents is generally assumed to be promiscuous, a man-chaser.

Such beliefs may seem absurd to outsiders. But in the nineteenth century respected doctors in England and the United States performed clitoridectomies on women as a supposed "cure" for masturbation, nymphomania, and psychological problems. Today some girls and women in the West starve themselves obsessively. Others undergo painful and potentially dangerous medical procedures—facelifts, liposuction, breast implants, and the like—to conform to cultural standards of beauty and femininity. I am not trying to equate genital cutting with eating disorders or cosmetic surgery; nevertheless, people in the industrialized world must recognize that they too are influenced, often destructively, by traditional gender roles and demands.

Local custom determines which kind of genital surgery girls undergo. Part or all of the clitoris may be removed; that is called clitoridectomy. A second kind of operation is excision, in which the clitoris and part or all of the labia minora, the inner lips of the vagina, are cut away. Clitoridectomy and excision are practiced on the west coast of Africa, in Chad and the Central African Republic, and in Kenya and Tanzania.

The most drastic form of genital surgery is infibulation, in which the clitoris and labia minora are removed, and then the labia majora, the outer lips of the vagina, are stitched together to cover the urethral and vaginal entrances. The goal is to make the genital area a blank patch of skin. A Sudanese woman in her sixties I interviewed told me that the midwife performing the surgery is often reminded by a girl's kinswomen to "make it smooth and beautiful like the back of a pigeon." A new opening is created for the passage of urine and menstrual blood and for sex—but the opening is made small, to increase the man's enjoyment. After the operation a girl's legs may be tied together for weeks so that skin grows over the wound. Women who have undergone infibulation must be cut open before childbirth and restitched afterward. Infibulation is practiced in Mali, Sudan, Somalia, and parts of Ethiopia and northern Nigeria.

Genital surgery is usually performed by a midwife, either at her home, in the girl's home, or in some cases in a special hut where a group of girls is sequestered during the initiation period. Midwives often have no medical training and little anatomical knowledge; if a girl struggles or flinches from the pain, the surgical instrument may slip, causing additional damage. There is also concern that unsterilized circumcision instruments may be spreading the AIDS virus. Among affluent Africans there is a growing trend to have the operation performed by physicians in private clinics—sometimes as far away as Europe—where general anesthesia is administered and conditions are hygienic.

The word *circumcision* (literally, "cutting around"), which was borrowed from the male operation, is a striking misnomer when applied to the procedures performed on women. Male circumcision, in which the foreskin of the penis is removed, is not associated with health problems, nor does it interfere with sexual functioning or enjoyment. By contrast, the immediate complications of female genital surgery include tetanus and other infections, severe pain, and hemorrhaging, which can in turn lead to shock and death. In July 1996 the Western press reported that an 11-year-old Egyptian girl had died following a circumcision performed by a barber. The following month a 14-year-old girl died, also in Egypt. Countless other deaths go unreported.

Long-term complications of genital surgery are also common, particularly for women who have been infibulated. Scar tissue blocking the urethral or vaginal opening can lead to a buildup of urine and menstrual blood, which, in turn, can cause chronic pelvic and urinary-tract infections. The infections can lead to back pain, kidney damage, severe uterine cramping, and infertility. If sebaceous glands in the skin become embedded in the stitched area during the surgery, cysts the size of grapefruits may form along the scar. Nerve endings can also become entrapped in the scar, causing extreme pain during sex.

Childbirth poses many special dangers for the infibulated woman. The baby's head may push through the perineum, the muscular area between the vagina and the anus. Sometimes a fistula, or abnormal passage, between the bladder and the vagina develops because of damage caused by obstructed labor. Women who develop fistulas may suffer frequent miscarriages because of urine seeping into the uterus. In addition, they smell of urine and often become outcasts.

Not surprisingly, depression and anxiety are also frequent consequences of genital surgery—whether spurred by health problems, fears of infertility, or the loss of a husband's attention because of penetration difficulties.

In spite of its grim nature, female circumcision is cloaked in festivity. Girls are feted and regaled with gifts after the operation. In some societies the experience includes secret ceremonies and instruction in cooking, crafts, child care, and the use of herbs. After circumcision adolescent girls suddenly become marriageable, and they are allowed to wear jewelry and womanly garments that advertise their charms. Among the Masai of Kenya and Tanzania, girls undergo the operation publicly; then the cutting becomes a test of bravery and a proof that they will be able to endure the pain of childbirth. Circumcision gives girls status in their communities. By complying, they also please their parents, who can arrange a marriage and gain a high bridal price for a circumcised daughter.

The consequences of not undergoing the ritual are equally powerful: teasing, disrespect and ostracism. Among the Sabiny people of Uganda, an uncircumcised woman who marries into the community is always lowest in the pecking order of village women, and she is not allowed to perform the public duties of a wife, such as serving elders. Uncut women are called girls, whatever their age, and they are forbidden to speak at community gatherings. The social pressures are so intense that uncircumcised wives often opt for the operation as adults.

Girls, too, can be driven to desperation. A Somali woman identified as Anab was quoted in a report by a local women's group:

When girls of my age were looking after the lambs, they would talk among themselves about their circumcision experiences and look at each other's genitals to see who had the smallest opening. Every time the other girls showed their infibulated genitals, I would feel ashamed I was not yet circumcised. Whenever I touched the hair of infibulated girls, they would tell me not to touch them since I was [still] "unclean." . . . One day I could not stand it anymore. I took a razor blade and went to an isolated place. I tied my clitoris with a thread, and while pulling at the thread with one hand I tried to cut part of my clitoris. When I felt the pain and saw the blood coming from the cut I stopped. . . . I was seven years old.

Yet despite the peer pressure and the benefits to be gained from being circumcised, the prospect of the operation can loom threateningly over a girl's childhood, poisoning everyday activities and filling her with fear and suspicion. Memuna M. Sillah, a New York City college student who grew up in Sierra Leone, described in a recent story in *Natural History* how as a child, whenever her mother sent her on an unusual errand, she feared that it might be a trick, that this might be the moment when strange women would grab her and cut her flesh. And Taha Baashar, a Sudanese psychologist, has reported the case of a seven-year-old girl who suffered from insomnia and hallucinations caused by fear of the operation. The problems reportedly improved when the girl was promised she would not be circumcised.

The origins of female circumcision are uncertain. Folk wisdom associates it with ancient Egypt, though the examination of mummies has so far provided no corroboration. Ancient Egyptian myths stressed the bisexuality of the gods, and so circumcision may have been introduced to clarify the femininity of girls. (In some African countries the clitoris is considered a masculine organ, and in the fetus, of course, both clitoris and penis develop from the same precursor tissue.) At any rate, the ritual certainly dates back more than 1,000 years: the eighth-century poet El Farazdaq denounced the tribe of Azd in the Arabian peninsula in one of his lampoons, writing that their women had never experienced the pain of circumcision and were therefore "of inferior stock."

Although female circumcision is practiced by Africans of all religions—Muslims, Christians and Ethiopian Jews, as well as followers of animist religions, such as the Masai—it is particularly associated with Islam. Many Muslims believe the ritual is a religious obligation. In fact, however, female circumcision is not mentioned in the Koran, and it is unknown in predominantly Muslim countries outside of Africa, such as Saudi Arabia and Iraq. What seems likely is that when Islam came to Africa, its emphasis on purity became associated with the existing practice of genital cutting—much the way early Christianity assimilated existing pagan rituals such as decorating evergreen trees.

Female circumcision came to European attention long ago. An early historical record can be found in the writings of Pietro Bembo, the sixteenth-century Italian cardinal:

> They now . . . sailed into the Red Sea and visited several areas inhabited by blacks, excellent men, brave in war. Among these people the private parts of the girls are sewn together immediately after birth, but in a way not to hinder the urinary ways. When the girls have become adults, they are given away in marriage in this condition and the husbands' first measure is to cut open with a knife the solidly consolidated private parts of the virgin. Among the barbarous people virginity is held in high esteem.

Other Europeans also wrote about genital cutting in accounts that were read by generations of foreign travelers to Africa. But despite some attempts by Christian missionaries and colonial powers to intervene, genital mutilation remained largely unknown abroad until the 1950s, when nationalist struggles gave rise to the women's movement in Africa. It was then that local activists and medical professionals began publicly condemning the practice.

After college I lived in Khartoum and worked for two years at a development corporation. A secretary I became friendly with there, whom I will call Shadia, confided in me that she found intercourse painful because of the effects of her circumcision. She and her husband had agreed, she told me, that any daughters of theirs would not be cut.

Two years ago I returned to Sudan to visit friends, and I looked up Shadia. We had not seen each other for a decade. We embraced; I asked about her children and she pulled out a photograph. I gasped. The three girls, the youngest of whom was about six, were dressed in jewelry and fancy clothes, their hands and feet patterned with henna, and around their shoulders they wore traditional maroon-and-gold satin shawls called *firkas*. It was unmistakably a picture from a circumci-

sion celebration. How could my friend have had such a change of heart? I was shocked.

Shadia explained. One day while she was at work her mother-in-law, who lived with the family, had secretly taken the girls to be circumcised, in defiance of their parents' wishes. When Shadia's husband, a truck driver, returned home, he was so distraught that he left the house and did not return for a week. Shadia was also heartbroken but she consoled herself that the girls had "only" been given clitoridectomies; at least they had not been infibulated, as she had. "It could have been worse," she told me resignedly.

Entrenched customs die hard, and the task facing anticircumcisionists is daunting. They can take heart, however, from the precedents: foot binding and widow burning, once widespread in China and India, respectively, have been abolished.

International efforts to end genital mutilation began in 1979, when the World Health Organization published statements against it. Then, after a gathering of African women's organizations in Dakar, Senegal, in 1984, the Inter-African Committee against Traditional Practices Affecting the Health of Women and Children was formed; since then, affiliates in 23 African countries have been working to end the practice. In 1994 the International Conference on Population and Development in Cairo adopted the first international document to specifically address female genital mutilation, calling it a "basic rights violation" that should be prohibited.

A variety of projects have aimed to end genital cutting:

- *Alternative initiation rituals:* In 1996 in the Meru district of Kenya, 25 mother–daughter pairs took part in a six-day training session, during which they were told about the health effects of circumcision and coached on how to defend the decision not to be cut. The session culminated in a celebration in which the girls received gifts and "books of wisdom" prepared by their parents.
- *Employment for midwives:* In several African countries, programs have aimed at finding other ways for midwives and traditional healers to make a living. A soap factory set up near Umbada, Sudan, with help from Oxfam and UNICEF is one example.

• *Health education:* Many African governments have launched public information campaigns. In Burkina Faso, for instance, a national committee has held awareness meetings and distributed teaching materials. A documentary film, *Ma fille ne sera pas excisée* ("My daughter will not be excised"), has been shown on national television. And in Sierra Leone, health workers found that when it was explained to women that genital surgery had caused their physical ailments, they were more willing to leave their daughters uncut.

So far the success of such pilot projects remains uncertain. The available statistics are disheartening: in Egypt, Eritrea, and Mali the percentages of women circumcised remain the same among young and old. Attitudes, however, do seem to be shifting. In Eritrea men and women under 25 are much more likely than people in their forties to think the tradition should be abandoned. And in recent years in Burkina Faso, parents who are opposed to circumcision but who fear the wrath of aunts or grandmothers have been known to stage fake operations.

Refugees and immigrants from Africa who arrive in Australia, Canada, Europe, or the United States have brought genital mutilation more immediately to Western attention. On the basis of the 1990 U.S. Census, the Centers for Disease Control and Prevention in Atlanta, Georgia, has estimated that at least 168,000 girls and women in the United States either have been circumcised or are at risk. In the past four years the U.S. Congress and nine state governments have criminalized the practice, and similar laws have been passed in several European countries. So far in the United States, no one has been prosecuted under the new laws.

Meanwhile, Fauziya Kassindja, a 20-year-old woman from Togo, spent more than a year behind bars, in detention centers and prisons in New Jersey and Pennsylvania, after fleeing to the United States in 1994 to avoid circumcision. Her mother, who remained in Togo, had sacrificed her inheritance and defied the family patriarch to help her escape. A U.S. immigration judge initially denied Kassindja's claim of persecution, saying her story lacked "rationality." Later, his ruling was overturned, and Kassindja was granted political asylum.

Western ignorance and incredulity regarding female circumcision have made life difficult and even dangerous for immigrant Africans. I recently met an infibulated Sudanese woman living in New England who was having trouble finding a gynecologist trained to treat her. "I am six months pregnant and I don't know what to expect," she told me fearfully. While pressing for an end to the practice, advocates must not ignore its victims. Perhaps exchange programs should be arranged for American gynecologists and obstetricians, to enable them to learn appropriate prenatal care from their African counterparts.

Every society has rules to which its members are expected to conform. But for African women, belonging exacts too high a price. Whereas African men often have more than one wife and freely engage in extramarital sex, "the acceptable image of a woman with a place in society [is] that of one who is circumcised, docile, fertile, marriageable, hardworking, asexual, and obedient," writes Olayinka Koso-Thomas, a Nigerian physician.

The irony is that, in a society that forces women to reconstruct their bodies in order to be socially and sexually acceptable, most men prefer sex with uncircumcised women. In a study of 300 Sudanese men, each of whom had one wife who had been infibulated and one or more who had not, 266 expressed a strong sexual preference for the uninfibulated wife. A second irony is that circumcision does not guarantee a woman a secure marriage; in fact, the opposite may be true. Infibulated women are more prone to fertility problems, which in Africa is grounds for being cast off by a husband. One study has shown that infibulated women in Sudan are more than twice as likely as other women to be divorced.

It might seem odd that women, not men, are the custodians of the ritual—in fact, a Sudanese man recently made headlines by filing a criminal lawsuit against his wife for having their two daughters circumcised while he was out of the country. Why do women subject their daughters to what they know firsthand to be a wrenchingly painful ordeal? Many are simply being practical. "I think that it is very important for the virginity of women to be protected if they want to get husbands who respect them," a 55-year-old Sudanese mother of five girls told me. To get married and have children is a survival strategy in a society plagued by poverty, disease, and illiteracy. The socioeconomic dependence of women on men colors their attitude toward circumcision.

But male oppression is not the biggest problem women face in Africa. Africans—men and women alike—must still cope with the ugly remnants of colonialism, the fact that they and their land have been exploited by Western nations and then abandoned. They are struggling to build democratic systems and economic stability from scratch. For African feminists, Western outrage about genital mutilation often seems misplaced. On a continent where millions of women do not have access to the basics of life—clean water, food, sanitation, education, and health care—genital mutilation is not necessarily the top priority.

Studies have shown that the more educated women are, the less willing they are to have their daughters circumcised. I have no doubt that when African women have taken their rightful places in the various spheres of life, when they have gained social equality, political power, economic opportunities, and access to education and health care, genital mutilation will end. Women will make sure of that.

REFLECTING ON THE SECTION

This section examines the role that women play in the practice of medicine. Think about the different values and associations of words such as doctor, midwife, healer, nurse, health care practitioner, and witch doctor, What, when, and who are associated with different terms? What can we learn about the role that gender plays in particular cultures through these terms?

Nongenile Masithathu Zenani reveals the difficulties of becoming a healer given the obstacles placed before her, while Ehrenreich and English show us the ways in which the professionalization of medicine produced new kinds of masculine control over women's bodies. In the process, they argue, the work of midwives was devalued and discredited. In the context of European colonization, the example of nineteenth-century India clearly shows how the rise of Western medicine was linked to the exercise of control over colonized people, particularly women. Thus, Western medicine's supposed benefits came with loss of power for women medical practitioners and greater male control over women's bodies.

Barker-Benfield analyzes the rise of gynecology in Europe and the United States, especially the sexual surgeries that were designed to control women's behavior and attitudes. Why do you think that these histories of clitoridectomy and ovariectomy have been largely forgotten while African or Islamic female circumcision has become so notorious? Abusharaf urges Western feminists to consider the history of colonialism in relation to female genital cutting in order to avoid mandating or legislating behavior for people in other parts of the world. Taken together, Barker-Benfield and Abusharaf raise troubling questions about the ways in which societies attempt to control women's behavior through surgical practices—yet they take great pains to avoid reducing all examples of such surgeries to a generalized sameness. How are such contemporary practices as cosmetic surgery, hysterectomies, and anorexia nervosa similar to and different from the sexual surgeries that Abusharaf describes? What sort of action or study does Abusharaf call for in her essay?

Population Control and Reproductive Rights: Technology and Power

Contested Terrain: The Historical Struggle for Fertility Control

SUSAN DAVIS

Susan Davis reminds us that fertility control has been used in various societies throughout history. In the United States since the middle of the nineteenth century, the struggle to resist what Davis calls "male control over women's fertility" has been fought by a diverse group of people, from socialists to upper-class women. Based on this history, Davis argues for "reproductive freedom" instead of "population control" or abortion rights alone.

For centuries women have used an enormous variety of fertility control methods, attesting to the importance of such control to women. Yet reproduction has also been an ideological battleground on which men, women, and the state have struggled for control over women. Determining who has such control is one measure of the reigning ideology of any culture.

Susan E. Davis, "Contested Terrain: The Historical Struggle for Fertility Control," in *Women under Attack: Victories, Backlash, and the Fight for Reproductive Freedom,* Susan E. Davis, ed. Boston: South End Press, 1988: 7–14.

⌐ Early Fertility Control

As far back as 1850 B.C.E., Egyptian women used vaginal pessaries (suppositories killing or blocking sperm), as did Indian, African, and Middle Eastern women. Vaginal douches of many kinds have been used around the world: Aristotle recommended the use of oil of cedar or olive oil; women of Sumatra used tannic acid. The Old Testament refers to vaginal sponges. Djuka tribes of (Dutch) Guyana used condoms to catch semen inside the vagina, and instructions for manufacturing condoms for men appear in North American home remedy books in the nineteenth century. Among Australians of the Parapitshuri Sea region, ovaries were surgically removed from girls chosen to be collective prostitutes for the men of the tribe.

The "rhythm method" and natural decreased fertility brought on by extended breast-feeding were used by Inuit and other Native American, Ancient Egyptian, and modern European women. Numerous home remedy abortifacients, either taken orally or inserted into the

---

uterus, included those suggested by Greek physicians in the time of Nero and those detailed by German folk medicine. Inserting instruments into the uterus and scraping fetal tissue are documented among sources as varied as tenth-century Persian physicians and twentieth-century Greenland Inuit tribes. Attempts to self-induce abortion—by jumping from heights, lifting heavy weights, taking hot baths, etc.—were also common. According to a survey of anthropological literature, 125 out of 200 tribes studied reported use of abortion.

To limit population and maintain desired sex ratios, some cultures have also practiced infanticide. Aristotle and Plato suggested it for eugenic purposes. An ancient Roman law entitled the father to decide whether to keep a child, attesting to men's power over reproduction. Infanticide has also been documented among Australian, and Native American and Polynesian peoples, and specifically for female newborns among Chinese, Indians, North Africans, and Tahitians.

More Recent U.S. History

Until the mid-nineteenth century, the U.S. government had no systematic legal position on birth control or abortion. The Catholic Church did not prohibit abortion before "quickening"—fetal movement beginning around the fourth month of gestation—until 1869.

The Industrial Revolution produced great changes. People moved from the countryside, where more children meant more agricultural production, into urban areas, where children cost more than they produced. Enormous hardships on the job, overcrowding and lack of resources at home, cruel practices of child labor, as well as the rigors of endless childbearing on women's health influenced many women, including Black women slaves, to try to limit the size of their families. The ideology of the period stressed planning and investment of resources. Concomitantly, women sought to invest their limited energy and resources in smaller numbers of children. Use of abortion and often unreliable birth control was widespread among women of all social classes.

By the 1870s, three diverse forces joined together to outlaw abortion and establish male control over women's fertility. Growing ranks of licensed physicians sought to monopolize women's health care by eliminating women's access to birth control and abor-

tion and by outlawing midwives, the primary reproductive health care providers until that point. Eager for more workers to be (re)produced, industrialists favored this result. Support also came from eugenicists, who wanted greater procreation by middle-class women of northern European descent and less among immigrants from southern and eastern Europe.

The Family Limitation Movement

The progressive political movements in the first quarter of the twentieth century were complex and dynamic. The suffragist movement, whose leadership was primarily white and middle class, was deeply conflicted about broader social issues, including fertility control. The working-class movement for unionization and socialism was equally conflicted about feminism and fertility control, as well as generally exclusionary and sexist toward women. Nonetheless, it was in the context of working-class organizations that the first wave of the modern fertility control movement began.

Social activists Emma Goldman and Margaret Sanger held mass street meetings in New York City. Sanger wrote a popular column for women in the Socialist Party daily newspaper, *The Call*. Many members of the left-wing International Workers of the World and the Socialist Party printed and distributed Sanger's famous "Family Limitation" leaflet, instructing tens of thousands of women in birth-control techniques. These organizers articulated the idea that reproductive self-control was critical to equality between the sexes and to improving women's position in society.

This movement was set back by two factors. The first was the aggressive prosecution of family limitation movement activists, especially Margaret Sanger, through the Comstock Law, which prohibited "obscene" material (including birth-control information) from being distributed by mail. Long jail sentences imposed severe strains on the leadership and limited organizing. Yet these women might have braved the storm more heroically had they had more support from the suffrage and working-class movements.

Just when persecutions of family limitation movement leaders began in earnest, the socialist movement came under sharp attack from the government and the workers' movement split on the question of political direction. The left wing, which supported the family limitation movement, wanted to continue a trade union, mass movement approach to social change. The right wing favored an electoral approach and backed away from too much confrontation with the government it sought to join. It opposed the family limitation movement, viewing it as a threat to the working-class family and an "unimportant," nonpolitical issue.

By the 1920s, Margaret Sanger and her more moderate feminist colleagues sought the protection of the medically based, industrialist-funded population control movement, dominated by eugenicists. They sought to impose fertility control (though not abortion) on U.S. women, particularly those poor and Black, for whom they thought it was "socially appropriate" to limit fertility. This same group subsequently sought to use modern contraceptive techniques to control population growth in colonial regions of Asia, Africa, and especially Latin America. U.S. investors and government leaders were increasingly worried by the desires of Third World peoples for freedom and self-determination. They theorized that liberation movements could be undermined by coercing Third World women into using birth control. Testing new contraceptive technologies on women without their consent became a common practice. Many women did receive the contraceptives and sterilization they needed, but often at great cost to their health and political freedom.

For family limitation activists, half a dream was better than none. They supported organizations like Sanger's American Birth Control League, the forerunner of Planned Parenthood, which lobbied for government endorsement and funding. By the 1960s, the birth-control movement was controlled by the government, technocrats, doctors, and international capitalists.

—ᴄᴏ Europᴇan Parallᴇls

At the same time that U.S. women struggled for access to fertility control, European women demanded the same rights. For example, after the Russian Revolution of 1917, a national governmental women's bureau led by Alexandra Kollontai fought for women's rights as family members and political activists. It demanded the legalization of abortion and distribution of contraceptives, as well as a host of other social changes offering women more freedom, such as collective kitchens, child care, and an end to the sexual double standard. Abortion was legalized in 1920 as a temporary health care measure, but was repealed in 1935 in a general attack on progressive social laws and policies. In Germany, the women's movement, allied with the progressive workers' movement, lacked an independent feminist approach and was soundly defeated by Nazi population policymakers, who outlawed abortion and instituted eugenics and genocide as a central platform of social control.

—ᴄᴏ The Second Wave

In the years preceding 1968, the lives of North American women shifted significantly. Living standards improved and white women began to join the paid workforce in larger numbers. The development of the highly reliable birth-control pill allowed young women to become more sexually active. The emphasis on birth control for Third World and poor North American women by the now-established population control organizations had an ironic double effect: While racist in intent and effect, it was also liberating to have birth control publicly accepted and available. Abortion remained a necessity, although its illegality kept it expensive and dangerous.

Many women who participated in the civil rights and antiwar movements in the 1960s questioned their position in society, particularly traditional expectations about sexuality and reproduction. Women began to articulate the need to control their reproductive capacity if they were to be liberated. They rediscovered feminist theorists who linked reproductive and sexual freedom to the quality of women's lives and to their political, economic, and social power.

Distribution of gynecological information, contraceptives, and illegal abortion referrals became increasingly politicized. Women rallied to expose the cruel reality of women's abortion experiences: Abortion rarely involved anesthesia or sanitary conditions and was usually a humiliating and life-threatening experience. Estimates range from 200,000 to one million illegal abortions performed annually. Many deaths were the direct result of botched abortions, primarily among poor women, a significant portion of whom were women of color.

By 1968 abortion was a major issue in the emerging women's movement, including demands for reform or repeal of laws limiting abortion. Moderate and liberal feminists sought support from the legal and medical establishments to reform abortion laws. Radical and socialist feminists aimed at repeal of all abortion laws and eradication of the legal and medical establishment's control over abortion. Their goal was "free abortion on demand" so that *all* women, regardless of income, could control their reproductive capacity. Driven by the slogan "the personal is political," they organized mass mobilizations and independent women's organizations. Their politics included issues of sexual preference, antiracism, antimilitarism, and working-class involvement in a call for women's liberation. Despite political differences, all feminists united to make abortion a central national issue.

The social and economic climate had also changed. When male workers were in demand in the 1900s, an antibirth birth-control and antiabortion policy prevailed. Now lower-paid women workers were needed for service jobs and the burgeoning computer revolution. Many doctors were also outraged by the medical complications and deaths associated with illegal abortion. Others were eager to control yet another aspect of women's health care and garner the profits from legalized, medically controlled abortion. Public opinion was also changing; by 1969, over 60 percent of the U.S. populations in every religious group endorsed abortion as a private issue to be decided by individual women.

By 1970, Colorado, Hawaii, and New York had reformed abortion laws. Hundreds of women poured into New York from all over the country seeking safe, legal, inexpensive abortions. Skirmishes on the legislative and judicial fronts were waged everywhere. Finally, in 1973 the U.S. Supreme Court decided in *Roe v. Wade* that the right to choose an abortion belonged to a woman and her doctor, at least during the first three months of pregnancy. This judicial solution would soon open new arenas for struggle.

The Movement for Reproductive Freedom

After the *Roe v. Wade* decision, many women discarded their picket signs, believing the struggle was

over, even though women in different parts of the country did not have ready access to abortions. Later that year, the issue of sterilization abuse received attention when it was reported that federal funds had been used to sterilize two Black teenagers without their knowledge or consent. In response to this and other abuses, a multinational group of activists formed the Committee to End Sterilization Abuse (CESA) in New York City. Their research revealed the racist population-control policy begun in the 1940s that led to the sterilization of over a third of all women of childbearing age in Puerto Rico. A highly successful campaign of propaganda and withholding of other fertility control had been conducted by a coalition of government, big business, and medical forces. Additional studies documented that disproportionately high numbers of Black and Native American women in the United States were also being sterilized.

In response to the Hyde Amendment, radical and socialist feminists in New York City formed the

FIGURE 1.5   THE PRICE OF AN ABORTION

Committee for Abortion Rights and Against Sterilization Abuse (CARASA). Abortion rights and freedom from sterilization abuse were seen as two sides of the same coin, since poor women, denied funding for abortion, might be coerced into sterilization—which, by contrast, was funded 90 percent by the government. Countering racist population-control policies was intended to build unity across race and class lines, which

had been one of the failings of the family limitation movement. Lesbian activists soon urged the movement to broaden its agenda to include a redefinition of family and to analyze reproduction as it affects the social, economic, and political needs of other groups of women. This process led to the comprehensive, radical demand for reproductive freedom.

Reading B

Reproductive Rights
ANGELA DAVIS

Activist and scholar Angela Davis argues that racist sterilization abuse is an important part of the debate on reproductive rights in the United States. She gives historical examples of the way the domestic population policy of the U.S. government stems from eugenics.

The abortion rights activists of the early 1970s should have examined the history of their movement. Had they done so, they might have understood why so many of their Black sisters adopted a posture of suspicion toward their cause. They might have understood how important it was to undo the racist deeds of their predecessors, who had advocated birth control as well as compulsory sterilization as a means of eliminating the "unfit" sectors of the population. Consequently, the young white feminists might have been more receptive to the suggestion that their campaign for abortion rights include a vigorous condemnation of sterilization abuse, which had become more widespread than ever.

It was not until the media decided that the casual sterilization of two Black girls in Montgomery, Al-

abama, was a scandal worth reporting that the Pandora's box of sterilization abuse was finally flung open. But by the time the case of the Relf sisters broke, it was practically too late to influence the politics of the abortion rights movement. It was the summer of 1973 and the Supreme Court decision legalizing abortions had already been announced in January. Nevertheless, the urgent need for mass opposition to sterilization abuse became tragically clear. The facts surrounding the Relf sisters' story were horrifyingly simple. Minnie Lee, who was 12 years old, and Mary Alice, who was 14, had been unsuspectingly carted into an operating room, where surgeons irrevocably robbed them of their capacity to bear children.[1] The surgery had been ordered by the HEW-funded Montgomery Community Action Committee (funded by the U.S. Department of Health, Education, and Welfare) after it was discovered that Depo-Provera, a drug previously administered to the girls as a birth-prevention measure, caused cancer in test animals.[2]

After the Southern Poverty Law Center filed suit on behalf of the Relf sisters, the girls' mother revealed that she had unknowingly "consented" to the operation, having been deceived by the social workers who handled

Angela Davis, "Reproductive Rights," *Women, Race and Class,* New York: Vintage Books, 1983: 215–21.

her daughters' case. They had asked Mrs. Relf, who was unable to read, to put her "X" on a document, the contents of which were not described to her. She assumed, she said, that it authorized the continued Depo-Provera injections. As she subsequently learned, she had authorized the surgical sterilization of her daughters.[3]

In the aftermath of the publicity exposing the Relf sisters' case, similar episodes were brought to light. In Montgomery alone, 11 girls, also in their teens, had been similarly sterilized. HEW-funded birth control clinics in other states, as it turned out, had also subjected young girls to sterilization abuse. Moreover, individual women came forth with equally outrageous stories. Nial Ruth Cox, for example, filed suit against the state of North Carolina. When she was 18—eight years before the suit—officials had threatened to discontinue her family's welfare payments if she refused to submit to surgical sterilization.[4] Before she assented to the operation, she was assured that her infertility would be temporary.[5]

Nial Ruth Cox's lawsuit was aimed at a state which had diligently practiced the theory of eugenics. Under the auspices of the Eugenics Commission of North Carolina, so it was learned, 7,686 sterilizations had been carried out since 1933. Although the operations were justified as measures to prevent the reproduction of "mentally deficient persons," about 5,000 of the sterilized persons had been black.[6] According to Brenda Feigen Fasteau, the American Civil Liberties Union (ACLU) attorney representing Nial Ruth Cox, North Carolina's recent record was not much better.

> As far as I can determine, the statistics reveal that since 1964, approximately 65 percent of the women sterilized in North Carolina were Black and approximately 35 percent were white.[7]

As the flurry of publicity exposing sterilization abuse revealed, the neighboring state of South Carolina had been the site of further atrocities. Eighteen women from Aiken, South Carolina, charged that they had been sterilized by a Dr. Clovis Pierce during the early 1970s. The sole obstetrician in that small town, Pierce had consistently sterilized Medicaid recipients with two or more children. According to a nurse in his office, Dr. Pierce insisted that pregnant welfare women would "have to submit [sic!] to voluntary sterilization" if they wanted him to deliver their babies.[8] While he was ". . . tired of people running around and having babies and paying for them with my taxes,"[9] Dr. Pierce received some $60,000 in taxpayers' money for the sterilizations he performed. During his trial he was supported by the South Carolina Medical Association, whose members declared that doctors ". . . have a moral and legal right to insist on sterilization permission before accepting a patient, if it is done on the initial visit."[10]

Revelations of sterilization abuse during that time exposed the complicity of the federal government. At first the Department of Health, Education, and Welfare claimed that approximately 16,000 women and 8,000 men had been sterilized in 1972 under the auspices of federal programs.[11] Later, however, these figures underwent a drastic revision. Carl Shultz, director of HEW's Population Affairs Office, estimated that between 100,000 and 200,000 sterilizations had actually been funded that year by the federal government.[12] During Hitler's Germany, incidentally, 250,000 sterilizations were carried out under the Nazis' Hereditary Health Law.[13] Is it possible that the record of the Nazis, throughout the years of their reign, may have been almost equaled by U.S. government-funded sterilizations in the space of a single year?

Given the historical genocide inflicted on the native population of the United States, one would assume that Native American Indians would be exempted from the government's sterilization campaign. But according to Dr. Connie Uri's testimony in a Senate committee hearing, by 1976 some 24 percent of all Indian women of childbearing age had been sterilized.[14] "Our bloodlines are being stopped," the Choctaw physician told the Senate committee, "Our unborn will not be born . . . This is genocidal to our people."[15] According to Dr. Uri, the Indian Health Services Hospital in Claremore, Oklahoma, had been sterilizing one out of every four women giving birth in that federal facility.[16]

Native American Indians are special targets of government propaganda on sterilization. In one of the HEW pamphlets aimed at Indian people, there is a sketch of a family with *ten children* and *one horse* and another sketch of a family with *one child* and *ten horses*. The drawings are supposed to imply that more children mean more poverty and fewer children mean wealth. As if the ten horses owned by the one-child family had been magically conjured up by birth control and sterilization surgery.

The domestic population policy of the U.S. government has an undeniably racist edge. Native American, Chicana, Puerto Rican, and Black women continue to be sterilized in disproportionate numbers. According to a National Fertility Study conducted in 1970 by Princeton University's Office of Population Control, 20 percent of all married Black women have been permanently sterilized.[17] Approximately the same percentage of Chicana women had been rendered surgically infertile.[18] Moreover, 43 percent of the women sterilized through federally subsidized programs were Black.[19]

The astonishing number of Puerto Rican women who have been sterilized reflects a special government policy that can be traced back to 1939. In that year President Roosevelt's Interdepartmental Committee on Puerto Rico issued a statement attributing the island's economic problems to the phenomenon of overpopulation.[20] This committee proposed that efforts be undertaken to reduce the birth rate to no more than the level of the death rate.[21] Soon afterward an experimental sterilization campaign was undertaken in Puerto Rico. Although the Catholic Church initially opposed this experiment and forced the cessation of the program in 1946, it was converted during the early 1950s to the teachings and practice of population control.[22] In this period over 150 birth control clinics were opened, resulting in a 20 percent decline in population growth by the mid-1960s.[23] By the 1970s, over 35 percent of all Puerto Rican women of childbearing age had been surgically sterilized.[24] According to Bonnie Mass, a serious critic of the U.S. government's population policy,

> . . . if purely mathematical projections are to be taken seriously, if the present rate of sterilization of 19,000 monthly were to continue, then the island's population of workers and peasants could be extinguished within the next 10 or 20 years . . . [establishing] for the first time in world history a systematic use of population control capable of eliminating an entire generation of people.[25]

During the 1970s, the devastating implications of the Puerto Rican experiment began to emerge with unmistakable clarity. In Puerto Rico the presence of corporations in the highly automated metallurgical and pharmaceutical industries had exacerbated the problem of unemployment. The prospect of an ever-larger army of unemployed workers was one of the main incentives for the mass sterilization program. Inside the United States today, enormous numbers of people of color—and especially racially oppressed youth—have become part of a pool of permanently unemployed workers. It is hardly coincidental, considering the Puerto Rican example, that the increasing incidence of sterilization has kept pace with the high rates of unemployment. As growing numbers of white people suffer the brutal consequences of unemployment, they can also expect to become targets of the official sterilization propaganda.

The prevalence of sterilization abuse during the latter 1970s may have been greater than ever before. Although the Department of Health, Education, and Welfare issued guidelines in 1974, which were ostensibly designed to prevent involuntary sterilizations, the situation has nonetheless deteriorated. When the American Civil Liberties Union's Reproductive Freedom Project conducted a survey of teaching hospitals in 1975, it discovered that 40 percent of those institutions were not even aware of the regulations issued by HEW.[26] Only 30 percent of the hospitals examined by the ACLU were even attempting to comply with the guidelines.[27]

The 1977 Hyde Amendment added yet another dimension to coercive sterilization practices. As a result of this law passed by Congress, federal funds for abortions were eliminated in all cases but those involving rape and the risk of death or severe illness. According to Sandra Salazar of the California Department of Public Health, the first victim of the Hyde Amendment was a 27-year-old Chicana woman from Texas. She died as a result of an illegal abortion in Mexico shortly after Texas discontinued government-funded abortions. There have been many more victims—women for whom sterilization has become the only alternative to the abortions that are currently beyond their reach. Sterilizations continue to be federally funded and free, to poor women, on demand.

Over the last decade the struggle against sterilization abuse has been waged primarily by Puerto Rican, Black, Chicana, and Native American women. Their cause has not yet been embraced by the women's movement as a whole. Within organizations representing the interests of middle-class white women, there has been a certain reluctance to support the demands of the campaign against sterilization abuse, for these women are often denied their individual rights to be sterilized when they desire to take this step. While women of color are urged, at every turn, to become permanently infertile, white women enjoying prosperous economic conditions are urged, by the same forces,

to reproduce themselves. They therefore sometimes consider the "waiting period" and other details of the demand for "informed consent" to sterilization as further inconveniences for women like themselves. Yet whatever the inconveniences for white middle-class women, a fundamental reproductive right of racially oppressed and poor women is at stake. Sterilization abuse must be ended.

NOTES

1. Herbert Aptheker, "Sterilization, Experimentation, and Imperialism," *Political Affairs,* Vol. LIII, No. 1 (January 1974), p. 38. See also Anne Braden, "Forced Sterilization: Now Women Can Fight Back," *Southern Patriot,* September 1973.

2. *Ibid.*

3. Jack Slater, "Sterilization, Newest Threat to the Poor," *Ebony,* Vol. XXVIII, No. 12 (October 1973), p. 150.

4. Braden, *op. cit.*

5. Les Payne, "Forced Sterilization for the Poor?" *San Francisco Chronicle,* February 26, 1974.

6. Harold X, "Forced Sterilization Pervades the South," *Muhammed Speaks,* October 10, 1975.

7. Slater, *op. cit.*

8. Payne, *op. cit.*

9. *Ibid.*

10. *Ibid.*

11. Aptheker, *op cit.,* p. 40.

12. Payne, *op. cit.*

13. Aptheker, *op. cit.,* p. 48.

14. Arlene Eisen, "They're Trying to Take Our Future—Native American Women and Sterilization," *The Guardian,* March 23, 1972.

15. *Ibid.*

16. *Ibid.*

17. Quoted in a pamphlet issued by the Committee to End Sterilization Abuse, Box A244, Cooper Station, New York 10003.

18. *Ibid.*

19. *Ibid.*

20. Linda Gordon, *Woman's Body, Woman's Right: Birth Control in America* (New York: Penguin Books, 1976), p. 338.

21. *Ibid.*

22. Bonnie Mass, *Population Target: The Political Economy of Population Control in Latin America* (New York: Penguin Books, 1976), p. 92.

23. *Ibid.*

24. Gordon, *op. cit.,* p. 401. See also pamphlet issued by CESA.

25. Mass, *op. cit.,* p. 108.

26. Rahemah Aman, "Forced Sterilization," *Union Wage,* March 4, 1978.

27. *Ibid.*

Biotechnology and the Taming of Women's Bodies
SOHEIR MORSY

Soheir Morsy, a feminist anthropologist, says that women in the non-Western world and poor women in the West have been subject to population-control policies and have served as the objects for pharmaceutical experimentation for contraceptive technologies. New techniques such as biotechnology, especially in the area of fertility control, can be understood only as a continuation of colonial power. Many groups have emerged to resist these new technologies.

The International Discourse on "Population"

While the international discourse on "Population" has been cleansed of the overtly racist language of the past, it still betrays a concerted effort to impose control over women's bodies at home and abroad. . . . For all the rhetoric of freedom of choice, which one would assume to include the choice of remaining childless, the anguish endured by women of the north in pursuit of conception suggests that motherhood remains central to the cultural construction of womanhood.

Soheir Morsy, "Biotechnology and the Taming of Women's Bodies," in *Processed Lives: Gender and Technology in Everyday Life,* Jennifer Terry and Melodie Calvert, eds. New York: Routledge, 1997: 168–72.

Among women of the global south the promotion of new forms of contraceptive technology, such as the five-year, surgically implantable device marketed under the commercial name of Norplant, proceeds within the framework of demographically informed "family planning" programs which target "breeders," be they in Indonesia, Thailand, Brazil, Egypt, or inner-city Baltimore. Before Norplant, other forms of contraceptive technology, such as IUDs, including the infamous Dalkon Shield, had been shamelessly promoted as the epitome of progress, and as Science's contribution to women's liberation, no less. For example,

French experts, indignant about the subjection of women among Muslims, declared that women in Africa had suffered greatly from "millenary inequality." The IUD was presented as the only means that could free women from their husbands and from society in general . . . [N]ot surprisingly, nothing was said about the means of their economic independence.

In the meantime, within France itself, population experts were earnestly striving to keep French-women from having the right to take the pill.

(Moreau-Bisseret 1986: 75)

As purposeful instruments of population control, the new professional provider-dependent contracep-

---

Key Terms

biotechnology The application to industry of advances made in the techniques and instruments of research in the biological sciences, in particular genetic cloning and engineering.

social reproduction The way that society reproduces and continues its hierarchies and power relations through institutions such as the family, schools, and the military.

tive technologies are a far cry from the safe and woman-controllable means of fertility regulation which feminists have long struggled for. Beyond the rhetoric appropriated from feminists by the international population establishment, the recent exposure of the potential for racist social engineering inherent in the "magical" Norplant technology underscores the dark side of international "family planning" (Hartmann 1995) and the practice of "choice" among poor women of the United States (ACLU 1990, 1991, 1992, 1995) who are "sentenced to Norplant" (Baker 1991).

For the United States, the belated discovery that the "Norplant miracle" has been nothing less than a "Norplant nightmare"[1] is hardly surprising for those familiar with the experience of women of the south who served as "bodies of choice" for Norplant experimental trials (Hartmann 1995; Morsy 1993; UBINIG 1988). Surprise is also muted if we recall that Norplant technology originated as the brainchild of William Shockley, the infamous eugenicist and advocate of scientific racism. Shockley's vision of controlling the population of allegedly low-IQ blacks and working-class whites, who tended to have large families, is no secret (Rose and Hamner 1976).

—Antifertility "Vaccines": Another "Miracle" of Biotechnology

While Norplant has been approved for use in a number of countries; including the United States, ignoring reasoned objections from feminists, including medical professionals in this country and elsewhere, the antifertility vaccines are still in the phase of clinical trials but already discredited within the framework of an international campaign. Launched by the Amsterdam-based Women's Global Network for Reproductive Rights in November of 1993, the International Campaign for a Stop of Research on Antifertility "Vaccines," mushroomed into a worldwide effort. By May of 1994 some 369 groups and organizations in 35 countries had joined the campaign.[2] For opponents of the "vaccines" a central issue is the potential for their abuse. In this regard Judith Richter (a feminist health activist who has been in the forefront of the international opposition to the antifertility "vaccines") considers abuse potential in terms of inherent features of the technology (prolonged

duration of effectiveness, difficulty of voluntary reversibility by the user, and ease of administration— "vaccination" on a mass scale) which increase the likelihood of uninformed, misinformed, and coercive administration of the contraceptive (Richter 1994).

As described in the literature of the campaign, and elaborated in the work of Judith Richter (1993), the stated aim of the immunological contraceptive technology is to bring on temporary infertility by turning the immune system against bodily elements which are essential for biological reproduction. Of the variety of antifertility "vaccines," which are mainly for women, the one on which research is most advanced is that which aims to neutralize the human pregnancy hormone HCG (human chorionic gonadotrophin). This is a hormone which is produced in the body of a woman shortly after conception (fertilization).

A biological trigger mechanism is central to making HCG work as a contraceptive device. The hormone is altered and attached to a bacterial or viral carrier (such as a diphtheria or tetanus toxoid). With this biological ploy, the immune system is tricked into mistaking the natural pregnancy hormone for an infectious germ and reacting against it accordingly. As a result, the body's secretion of pregnancy-related substances is impeded and the fertilized egg is expelled. Variations on this scheme of immunological tampering include interference with the production of sperm, the maturation of egg cells, the fertilization process itself, and the implantation and development of the early embryo.

Within the framework of the campaign, the Women's Global Network for Reproductive Rights has compiled contrasting evaluations of the "vaccines," which document women's criticism, researchers' promises, and promoters' arguments:

- Women observe that we have no control over this new technology, while researchers flaunt it as long-acting.
- Women express concern that the action of this new technology cannot be stopped upon a woman's request. To promoters, on the other hand, the technology is valued as a new antigenic weapon against reproductive process.
- Women fear lifelong sterility; researchers pride themselves on the technology's effectiveness as an instrument for fertility control.

- Women see no advantage over existing contraceptive methods; researchers emphasize "no user failure."
- Whereas women foresee adverse effects of tampering with a delicate immunological system, promoters focus on the ease of administration on a mass scale, pointing to the established familiarity with antidisease vaccines among targeted populations.
- Women's questioning of immunological risks is countered by assertions of safety: no adverse effects on hormones and metabolism is the assertion offered in response.
- Women reject the false comparison with vaccines against diseases; promoters argue in favor of contraceptive choice.
- Feminist activists raise questions about the impact on HIV of immunological tampering; promoters are content with the technology's usefulness for women in Third World countries.
- Women say we don't need a bad choice contraceptive . . . besides, pregnancy is not a disease, and the contraceptive effect of this technology is unreliable . . . Promoters say the antifertility vaccines do not interrupt sexual intercourse.

The noninterruption of sexual intercourse is regarded as an improvement over Norplant, from which prolonged bleeding may cause such disruption. This has been noted as an impediment to Norplant acceptability among Muslim women, for whom menstrual bleeding is considered polluting and therefore a barrier to sexual intercourse.

—◦ Conclusion

Feminist assessment of the new forms of biotechnology (e.g., Klein 1989; Rose and Hamner 1976; Yanoshik and Norsigian 1989) has gone a long way toward deconstructing the notions of "progress" and "development" which often accompany the promotion of this type of technology. In the process, due emphasis has been placed on the power structures of which biotechnology is born, within the framework of which it is promoted internationally, and to the reproduction of which it contributes.

[. . .] Yanoshik and Norsigian (1989: 62) observe that

[B]ecause western medicine, the population control establishment, and the pharmaceutical industry are more interested in controlling population and making money than in ensuring users' safety or creating woman-centered options, the effects of many of the contraceptive technologies have proven catastrophic. Millions of women's lives have been adversely affected by following advice or order to use such "miracle" technologies, oral contraceptives, Depo-Provera, or hormonal implants.

Other researchers have also revealed the technological management of biological reproduction as simultaneously a mechanism of *social* reproduction. Biotechnology is thus recognized as harboring the potential for reinforcement of dominant values ranging from "appropriate" definitions of healthy offspring and "professional" judgment, to the mystification of state power.

As technological fixes increasingly become integrated within a framework of medicalization, this confuses the international politics of women's reproductive rights. In attending to the serious political challenge represented by this development and to related technology-assisted mystification, it is crucial not to lose sight of the importance of shared, popularized scientific knowledge as an instrument of resistance. More generally, there is a continued need for informed international feminist solidarity based on mutual respect and appreciation of local priorities of struggle.

NOTES

1. *Norplant Nightmare* is the title of a documentary aired on 26 February 1996 by the Washington, D.C.-based ABC affiliate WJAL. Contradicting the notion of a "Norplant Miracle," the program highlighted the plight of women who have suffered from Norplant's adverse side effects, and the difficulties surrounding its removal. The documentary also brought attention to the lawsuits which have been filed against the manufacturer on behalf of adversely affected users of this new contraceptive technology.

2. Additional information on the campaign, and a list of signatories, may be obtained from the Coordinating Office of the Women's Global Network for Reproductive Rights, NZ Voorburgwal 32, 1012 RZ Amsterdam, The Netherlands.

REFERENCES

ACLU. (1990). *Annual Report*. New York: Reproductive Freedom Project.

Baker, B. (1991). "Sentenced to Norplant." *The Network News* (of the National Women's Health Network, Washington, DC) January/February.

Hartmann, B. (1995). *Reproductive Rights and Wrongs: The Global Politics of Population Control*. Revised edition. Boston, MA: South End Press.

Klein, R. (1989). *The Exploitation of a Desire: Women's Experiences with In Vitro Fertilization*. Deakin University, Australia: Women's Studies Summer Institute.

Moreau-Bisseret, N. (1986). "A Scientific Warranty for Sexual Politics: Demographic Discourse on 'Reproduction' (France)." *Feminist Issues* 6(1): 67–85.

Morsy, S. A. (1993). "Bodies of Choice: Norplant Experimental Trials on Egyptian Women," in B. Mintzes, A. Hardon, and J. Hanhart (eds) *Norplant under Her Skin*. Amsterdam: Wemos; Women's Health Action Foundation, pp. 89–114.

Richter, J. (1993). *Vaccination against Pregnancy: Miracle or Menace?* Amsterdam: HAI (Health Action International)/Bielefeld, Germany: BUKO Pharma-Kampagne.

Richter, J. (1994). "Beyond Control: About Antifertility 'Vaccines,' Pregnancy Epidemics and Abuse," In R. Snow and G. Sen (eds), *Power and Decision Making: The Social Control of Reproduction*. Cambridge, MA: Harvard University Press.

Rose, H., and Hamner, J. (1976). "Women's Liberation: Reproduction and the Technological Fix," in H. Rose and S. Rose (eds) *The Political Economy of Science: Ideology of/in the Natural Sciences*. London: Macmillan Press.

UBINIG. (1988). *Norplant: The Five-Year Needle*. Dakkar, Bangladesh: UBINIG.

Yanoshik, K., and Norsigian, J. (1989). "Contraception, Control, and Choice," In K. S. Ratcliff (ed.) *Healing Technology: Feminist Perspectives*. Ann Arbor, Mich: University of Michigan Press, pp. 61–92.

Family Matters

BETSY HARTMANN

Betsy Hartmann argues that the assumption that population control threatens the environmental future is based on Western ethnocentrism and a lack of knowledge about various parts of the world. Hartmann points out that population rates have slowed worldwide and that some women may still have valid reasons for choosing to have large families.

On the surface, fears of a population explosion are borne out by basic demographic statistics. In the twentieth century the world has experienced an unprecedented increase in population. In 1900 global population was 1.7 billion, in 1950 it reached 2.5 billion, and today roughly 5.7 billion people inhabit the earth. Three-quarters of them live in the so-called

Betsy Hartmann, "Family Matters," in *Reproductive Rights and Wrongs,* Boston: South End Press, 1997: 5–12.

Third World. The United Nations predicts that world population will eventually stabilize at about 11.6 billion between 2150 and 2200, though such long-term demographic projections are notoriously imprecise.

Initially, this rapid increase in population was due in part to some very positive factors: Advances in medicine, public health measures, and better nutrition meant that more people lived longer. However, in other cases, notably in Africa, it may have been a response to colonialism, as indigenous communities sought to reconstitute themselves after suffering high death rates from slavery, diseases introduced from Europe, and oppressive labor conditions. In many countries colonialism also disrupted traditional methods of birth spacing.[1]

In most industrialized countries, the decline in mortality rates was eventually offset by declines in birth rates, so that population growth began to stabilize in what is called the "demographic transition." Most in-

---

Key Terms

child mortality rate The number of deaths of children aged one is four per thousand children in this age group in a given year.

(Crude) birth rate The number of births per thousand people in a given year.

(Crude) mortality or death rate The number of deaths per thousand people in a given year.

demography The statistical study of births, deaths, and diseases in populations.

infant mortality rate The number of deaths of infants under one year of age per thousand live births in a given year.

multinational corporation A business with branches and affiliates in several different countries.

population growth rate The rate at which a population is growing or declining in a given year from natural increase and net migration, computed as a percentage of the base population.

replacement-level fertility The level of fertility at which women on the average are having only enough daughters to "replace" themselves in a given population.

dustrialized countries have now reached the "replacement level" of fertility, and in some the population is actually declining.

Today birth rates are also falling in virtually every area of the Third World. In fact, the *rate* of world population growth has been slowing since the mid-1960s. Population growth rates are highest in sub-Saharan Africa—about 2.9 percent in 1994—but are considerably less than that in Asia (1.9 percent) and Latin America (2.0 percent). It is also important to remember that despite higher rates of growth, Africa contains a relatively small share of the world's population— India will have more births in 1994 than all 50 sub-Saharan nations combined.

The United Nations estimates that by 2045 most countries will have reached replacement-level fertility. The reason population growth still seems to be "exploding" is that a large proportion of the present population is composed of men and women of child bearing age. Half of the world's people are under the age of 25. Barring major catastrophes, an inevitable demographic momentum is built into our present numbers, but this should be a subject of rational planning, not public paranoia. The truth is that the population "explosion" is gradually fizzling out.

Nevertheless, there is still considerable discrepancy between birth rates in the industrialized world and birth rates in many Third World countries, particularly in sub-Saharan Africa. Conventional wisdom has it that Third World people continue to have so many children because they are ignorant and irrational—they exercise no control over their sexuality, "breeding like rabbits." This "superiority complex" of many Westerners as well as some Third World elites is one of the main obstacles in the way of meaningful discussion of the population problem. It assumes that everyone lives in the same basic social environment and faces the same set of reproductive choices. Nothing is further from the truth.

In many Third World societies, having a large family is an eminently rational strategy of survival. Children's labor is a vital part of the family economy in many peasant communities of Asia, Africa, and Latin America. Children help in the fields, tend animals, fetch water and wood, and care for their younger brothers and sisters, freeing their parents for other tasks. Quite early in life, children's labor makes them an asset

rather than a drain on family income. In Bangladesh, for example, boys produce more than they consume by the age of 10 to 13 and by the age of 15 their total production has exceeded their cumulative lifetime consumption. Girls likewise perform a number of valuable economic tasks, which include helping their mothers with cooking and the post-harvest processing of crops.[2]

In urban settings children often earn income as servants, messenger boys, and the like, or else stay home to care for younger children while their parents work. Among the Yoruba community in Nigeria, demographer John Caldwell found that even urban professional families benefit from many children through "sibling assistance chains." As one child completes education and takes a job, he or she helps younger brothers and sisters move up the educational and employment ladder, and the connections and the influence of the family spread.[3]

In recent years, however, urbanization has been associated with fertility decline in a number of countries for both positive and negative reasons. For those with ample resources, living in an urban area can mean greater access to education, health and family planning services, and the kind of information and media that promote a smaller family norm. Since the debt crisis and economic recession of the 1980s, however, the quality of life of the urban poor has deteriorated in many countries. High unemployment or work in insecure, low-wage occupations mean that poor people simply do not have enough financial resources to support a large family. Brazil has experienced such a distress-related fertility decline. The government's failure to institute agrarian reforms in rural areas forced people to flee the poverty of the countryside, only to face the harsh realities of urban slums.[4]

Security is another crucial reason to have many children. In many Third World societies, the vast majority of the population has no access to insurance schemes, pension plans, or government social security. It is children who care for their parents in their old age; without them one's future is endangered. The help of grown children can also be crucial in surviving the periodic crises—illness, drought, floods, food shortages, land disputes, political upheavals—which, unfortunately, punctuate village life in most parts of the world.[5]

By contrast, parents in industrialized countries and their affluent counterparts among Third World urban elites have much less need to rely on children for either labor or old-age security. The economics of family size changes as income goes up, until children become a financial burden instead of an asset. When children are in school, for example, they no longer serve as a source of labor. Instead parents must pay for their education, as well as for their other needs, which cost far more in a high-consumption society than in a peasant village. And there is often no guarantee that parents' investment will buy the future loyalty of a grown child. As economist Nancy Folbre notes, "The 'gift' of education, unlike a bequest, cannot be made contingent upon conformity to certain expectations. Once given, it can hardly be revoked."[6]

In industrialized societies personal savings, pension plans, and government programs replace children as the basic forms of social security. These social changes fundamentally alter the value of children, making it far more rational from an economic standpoint to limit family size. Folbre also argues that as the value of children decreases, male heads of households are more willing to allow their wives to work outside the home, since the contribution of their wages to the family economy now exceeds the value of their household work.[7] This further spurs fertility decline.

Son preference can be another important motive for having large families. The subordination of women means that economically and socially daughters are not valued as highly as sons in many cultures, particularly in South Asia, China, and parts of the Middle East. Not only does daughters' domestic work have less prestige, but daughters typically provide fewer years of productive labor to their parents, because in many societies, they marry and leave home to live with their in-laws shortly after puberty.

Son preference, combined with high infant and child mortality rates, means that parents must have many children just to ensure that one or two sons survive. A computer simulation found that in the 1960s an Indian couple had to bear an average of 6.3 children to be confident of having one son who would survive to adulthood.[8] Son preference can also lead to skewed sex ratios, so that there are more males than females in a given population. Although at birth boys outnumber girls by a ratio of about 105 to 100, this discrepancy soon disappears, all else being equal, because biologi-

cally girls have better survival rates beginning in the first months after birth. In China, much of South Asia, and parts of North Africa, however, discrimination against girls means that there continue to be fewer girls than boys, and women than men, in the population. Discrimination takes many forms, from more typical forms of unbenign neglect, such as giving girls less food and health care, to female infanticide and sex-selective abortion. According to one estimate, more than 100 million women are "missing" throughout the world as the result of such discrimination. The situation is particularly serious in North India and China.[9]

High infant and child mortality rates are major underlying causes of high birth rates. Each year in developing countries more than 12 million children die before reaching their fifth birthday. The average infant mortality rate is more than 71 deaths per 1,000 live births in developing countries as a whole, and over 100 in sub-Saharan Africa. By comparison, it is only 14 in industrialized countries.[10] In recent decades there has been some progress in reducing infant and child mortality, but not nearly enough.

High infant mortality means that parents cannot be sure their children will survive to contribute to the family economy and to take care of them in their old age. The poor are thus caught in a death trap: They have to keep producing children in order that some will survive. Most countries that have achieved a low birth rate have done so only after infant and child mortality has declined.

High infant mortality is primarily caused by poor nutrition, both of the mother and of the child. In situations of chronic scarcity, women often eat last and least, with a profound impact on infant health. Inadequately nourished mothers typically give birth to underweight babies, and low birth weight has been identified as the "greatest single hazard for infants," increasing their vulnerability to developmental problems and their risk of death from common childhood illnesses.[11] Severely undernourished women also give lower-quality breast milk; for a woman to breast-feed successfully without damaging her health, she must increase her calorie and nutrient intake by up to 25 percent, an impossibility for many poor women.[12]

Breast-feeding, in fact, has relevance to the population issue on several different but interconnected levels. In many countries, increases in infant mortality have been linked to the switch from breast-feeding to bottle-feeding. Infant formula lacks the antibodies in breast milk that help to protect babies from disease. Poor women, moreover, often cannot afford a steady supply of formula and dilute it with too much water.

Proper sterilization of bottles, nipples, and drinking water is also problematic in poor households. As a result, Third World infants breast-fed for less than six months are *five* times more likely to die in the second six months of life than those who have been breast-fed longer. Overall the mortality rate for bottle-fed infants in the Third World is roughly double that for breast-fed infants.[13]

Intensive sales campaigns by multinational corporations, such as the Swiss-based Nestlé Company and American Home Products, bear a large share of the responsibility for the shift from breast- to bottle-feeding. Advertisements with pictures of plump, smiling white babies and the penetration of local health establishments by company representatives have helped convince women that they will have healthier children if they switch to formula. An international campaign against these formula "pushers" finally led the World Health Organization (WHO) in 1980 to establish a voluntary code of conduct, setting standards for the advertising and marketing of formula. Every country signed on, except for the United States.

Although the code has brought improvements in terms of mass advertising, the companies still widely promote formula through health establishments. A study of breast-feeding in four Third World cities found that formula marketers had close commercial ties with physicians, pharmacists, and midwives, and that as a result, women who used Western-type health and maternity services tended to introduce formula earlier.[14] The WHO code is clearly not strong enough.

The decline in breast-feeding is also due to the fact that more women are now employed outside the home in occupations and workplaces that actively discourage the practice or do not offer support. Extended maternity leave with pay, on-site day care, and flexible scheduling would greatly facilitate breast-feeding, but unfortunately, in most countries, these are not high so-

cial priorities despite their obvious benefits to women and children.

In addition to giving protection against infection, another key advantage of breast-feeding is that it happens to be one of the world's most effective natural contraceptives. It frequently causes lactational amenorrhea, the suppression of ovulation and menstruation by the release of the hormone prolactin. Each month of breast-feeding adds up to three weeks to the interval between births, and women who breast-feed often, whenever the baby wants, delay the return to fertility even longer.[15]

Hence, a decline in breast-feeding without a corresponding use of effective contraception means that pregnancies are more closely spaced, and the close spacing of births is itself a major cause of infant mortality. The relationship can also go the other way: A child's death means a woman stops breast-feeding and resumes fertility sooner, with a higher risk of the next child's death. This vicious biological circle may be one of the key reasons high infant mortality and high fertility go hand in hand.[16]

The last (but not least) cause of high birth rates is the subordination of women. Male dominance in the family, patriarchal social mores, the systematic exclusion of women from the development process, and the absence of decent birth-control services combine to force many women into having more children than they want. The social environment, in effect, leaves them little or no reproductive choice.

Behind the demographic statistics, then, lies a reality unfamiliar to many middle-class people, who do not have to worry from day to day about who will help in the fields, who will take care of them when they are old and sick, or how many children they need to have in order to ensure that a few survive to adulthood. High birth rates are often a distress signal that people's survival is endangered. Yet the proponents of population control put the argument the other way around, insisting that people are endangering their own survival— and the survival of future generations—by having so many children. This is the basis of the Malthusian philosophy that has defined the dimensions of the population problem for so long.

NOTES

1. See, for example, Marc H. Dawson, "Health, Nutrition, and Population in Central Kenya, 1890–1945," in Dennis D. Cordell and Joel W. Gregory, eds., *African Population and Capitalism: Historical Perspectives* (Boulder: Westview Press, 1987). Basic demographic statistics taken from U.S. Bureau of the Census, Report WP/94, World Population Profile: 1994 (Washington, D.C.: Government Printing Office, 1994) and William K. Stevens, "Feeding a Booming Population without Destroying the Planet," *New York Times,* 5 April 1994.

2. Mead T. Cain, "The Economic Activities of Children in a Village in Bangladesh," *Population and Development Review,* vol. 3, no. 3 (September 1977).

3. John C. Caldwell, *Theory of Fertility Decline* (London: Academic Press, 1982), p. 69.

4. Thais Corall, "Brazil: A Failed Success Story," paper presented to the Conference on Multilateral Population Assistance, Oslo, Norway, 25 May 1994.

5. See Mead T. Cain, "Risk and Insurance: Perspectives on Fertility and Agrarian Change in India and Bangladesh," *Population and Development Review,* vol. 7, no. 3 (September 1981) and, by the same author, "Fertility as an Adjustment to Risk," Population Council, Center for Policy Studies Working Papers, No. 100 (New York: October 1983). Also see Caldwell, *Theory of Fertility Decline.*

6. Nancy Folbre, "Of Patriarchy Born: The Political Economy of Fertility Decisions," *Feminist Studies,* vol. 9, no. 2 (Summer 1983), p. 274. For more on the costs of children, and the political economy of who bears those costs, see Folbre, *Who Pays for the Kids: Gender and the Structures of Constraint* (London and New York: Routledge, 1994).

Also see Caldwell, *Theory of Fertility Decline,* for more on how education changes the value of children. Japan provides an interesting example of how the role of children as a source of security changes. In 1950, at the beginning of Japan's industrial boom, a survey showed that over half the population expected to be supported by children in their old age. By 1961, after a decade of rapid growth, this figure had already declined to 27 percent, and the birth rate had also fallen dramatically. Japan example from William W. Murdoch, *The Poverty of Nations: The Political Economy of Hunger and Population* (Baltimore: Johns Hopkins University Press, 1980), p. 29.

7. Folbre, "Of Patriarchy Born."

8. Indian example from Frances Moore Lappé and Joseph Collins, *Food First: Beyond the Myth of Scarcity* (New York: Ballantine Books, 1979), p. 32.

9. Amartya Sen, "More Than 100 Million Women Are Missing," *New York Review of Books,* 20 December 1990.

10. United Nations Development Program (UNDP), *Human Development Report 1993* (New York: Oxford University Press, 1993), Tables 3 and 4, pp. 140–43.

11. José Villar and José M. Belizan, "Women's Poor Health in Developing Countries: A Vicious Circle," in Patricia Blair, ed., *Health Needs of the World's Poor Women* (Washington, D.C.: Equity Policy Center, 1981).

12. Isabel Nieves, "Changing Infant Feeding Practices: A Woman-Centered View," in Blair, ed., *Health Needs.*

13. Ann Wigglesworth, "Space to Live," background article, *The State of World Population 1983.* Press File, prepared by the New Internationalist Publications Cooperative for the UNFPA (Oxford: 1983); Lappé and Collins, *Food First,* p. 337.

14. Beverly Winikoff, *The Infant Feeding Study: Summary,* report submitted to Agency for International Development by the Population Council (New York: Population Council, n.d.).

15. Maggie Jones, "The Biggest Contraceptive in the World," *New Internationalist,* no. 110 (April 1982).

16. See Wigglesworth, "Space to Live"; James P. Grant, *State of the World's Children 1982–83* (New York: UNICEF, 1983); and Kathleen Newland, *Infant Mortality and the Health of Societies,* Worldwatch Paper No. 47 (Washington, D.C.: Worldwatch Institute, December 1981).

Call for a New Approach
COMMITTEE ON WOMEN, POPULATION AND THE ENVIRONMENT

This committee of organizers, health practitioners, and scholars from different countries around the world issued a statement in 1992 calling for a "new approach" to reproductive freedom and to allied issues such as environmental degradation, racism, and poverty. They argue that to halt population growth, we must improve women's economic, social, and health status.

The Committee on Women, Population and the Environment is an alliance of women activists, community organizers, health practitioners, and scholars of diverse races, cultures, and countries of origin working for women's empowerment and reproductive freedom and against poverty, inequality, racism, and environmental degradation. Issued in 1992, their statement, "Women, Population and the Environment: Call for a New Approach" continues to gather individual and organizational endorsements from around the world.

Committee on Women, Population and the Environment, "Call for a New Approach," in *Reproductive Rights and Wrongs*, Betsy Hartmann, Ed. Boston: South End Press, 1997: 311–13.

Call for a New Approach

We are troubled by recent statements and analyses that single out population size and growth as a primary cause of global environmental degradation.

We believe the major causes of global environmental degradation are:

- Economic systems that exploit and misuse nature and people in the drive for short-term and short-sighted gains and profits.
- The rapid urbanization and poverty resulting from migration from rural areas and from inadequate planning and resource allocation in towns and cities.
- The displacement of small farmers and indigenous peoples by agribusiness, timber, mining, and energy corporations, often with encouragement and assistance from international financial institutions, and with the complicity of national governments.
- The disproportionate consumption patterns of the affluent the world over. Currently, the industrialized nations, with 22 percent of the world's population,

Key Terms

family planning programs An important element of population control movements in which governments take responsibility for reducing family size.

global demilitarization A social movement that calls for an end to weapons and military deployment across the world.

nonrenewable resources Resources (such as oil) of which there is a finite quantity.

structural adjustment policies (SAPs) Many countries have high levels of indebtedness to the World Bank and the International Monetary Fund (entities that were created in the twentieth century to promote neoliberal, free-market economic policies around the world). Structural adjustment policies require nations to change their economic strategies to prioritize the repayment of these loans over other needs.

consume 70 percent of the world's resources. Within the United States, deepening economic inequalities mean that the poor are consuming less, and the rich more.

- Technologies designed to exploit but not to restore natural resources.
- Warmaking and arms production which divest resources from human needs, poison the natural environment, and perpetuate the militarization of culture, encouraging violence against women.

Environmental degradation derives thus from complex, interrelated causes. Demographic variables can have an impact on the environment, but reducing population growth will not solve the above problems. In many countries, population growth rates have declined, yet environmental conditions continue to deteriorate.

Moreover, blaming global environmental degradation on population growth helps to lay the groundwork for the re-emergence and intensification of top-down, demographically driven population policies and programs which are deeply disrespectful of women, particularly women of color, and their children.

In Southern countries, as well as in the United States and other Northern countries, family planning programs have often been the main vehicles for dissemination of modern contraceptive technologies. However, because so many of their activities have been oriented toward population control rather than women's reproductive health needs, they have too often involved sterilization abuse; denied women full information on contraceptive risks and side effects; neglected proper medical screening, follow-up care, and informed consent; and ignored the need for safe abortion and barrier and male methods of contraception. Population programs have frequently fostered a climate where coercion is permissible and racism acceptable.

Demographic data from around the globe affirm that improvements in women's social, economic, and health status and in general living standards are often keys to declines in population growth rates. We call on the world to recognize women's basic right to control their own bodies and to have access to the power, resources, and reproductive health services to ensure that they can do so.

National governments, international agencies, and other social institutions must take seriously their obli- *gation to provide the essential prerequisites for women's development and freedom. These include:*

1. Resources such as fair and equitable wages, land rights, appropriate technology, education, and access to credit.
2. An end to structural adjustment programs, imposed by the IMF, the World Bank, and repressive governments, which sacrifice human dignity and basic needs for food, health, and education to debt repayment and "free-market," male-dominated models of unsustainable development.
3. Full participation in the decisions which affect our own lives, our families, our communities, and our environment, and incorporation of women's knowledge systems and expertise to enrich these decisions.
4. Affordable, culturally appropriate, and comprehensive health care and health education for women of all ages and their families.
5. Access to safe, voluntary contraception and abortion as part of broader reproductive health services which also provide pre- and postnatal care, infertility services, and prevention and treatment of sexually transmitted diseases, including HIV and AIDS.
6. Family support services that include child care, parental leave, and elder care.
7. Reproductive health services and social programs that sensitize men to their parental responsibilities and to the need to stop gender inequalities and violence against women and children.
8. Speedy ratification and enforcement of the U.N. Convention on the Elimination of All Forms of Discrimination against Women as well as other U.N. conventions on human rights.

People who want to see improvements in the relationship between the human population and the natural environment should work for the full range of women's rights; global demilitarization; redistribution of resources and wealth between and within nations; reduction of consumption rates of polluting products and processes and of nonrenewable resources; reduction of chemical dependency in agriculture; and environmentally responsible technology. They should support local, national, and international initiatives for democracy, social justice, and human rights.

The Human Genome Diversity Project: Implications for Indigenous Peoples

DEBRA HARRY

Researcher and activist Debra Harry describes the Human Genome Diversity Project, the scientific quest to map the genetic diversity of the human species. Harry asks: Who stands to benefit from this exhaustive and expensive effort and how will the information be handled or used? Histories of colonialism and racism link this project to eugenics and other forms of social engineering.

We reported on the Human Genome Diversity Project in *Abya Yala News*'s Fall/Winter 1993 issue. Indigenous opposition to the project has been growing since that time, and the project has yet to respond adequately to fundamental ethical problems such as those raised in this article.

The Human Genome Diversity Project (HGD Project) proposes to collect blood and tissue samples from

Debra Harry, "The Human Genome Diversity Project: Implications for Indigenous Peoples," *Abya Yala News,* South and Meso American Indian Rights Center (SAIIC), Vol. 8.4 (Winter 1994): 1–5. 14 March 1995.

hundreds of different Indigenous groups worldwide for genetic study. On the assumption that these groups are headed for extinction, scientists are rushing to gather DNA samples before they disappear. Then, they say, at least the human genetic diversity will be preserved in gene banks as "immortalized cell lines." But why the tremendous interest in saving the genes of Indigenous people and not the people themselves? Who really stands to benefit from this endeavor? What are the dangers and long-term implications of biotechnology and genetic engineering? These are questions Indigenous people must ask themselves in order to protect their interests in the face of such a mysterious and well-funded effort.

Issues of Concern

HGD Project scientists claim to be searching for answers to questions about human evolution. However, Indigenous peoples already possess strong beliefs and knowledge regarding their creation and histories; furthermore, this is not a priority concern for Indigenous

---

Key Terms

genetic engineering The artificial manipulation, modification, and recombination of DNA in order to modify an organism or population of organisms.
genome The inherited genetic material that directs the development of cells in an organism.

indigenous Native to a specific land or region.
intellectual property Knowledge that can be bought and sold and, thus, patented.

people. The HGD Project's assumptions that the origins and/or migrations of Indigenous populations will be "discovered" and scientifically "answered" is insulting to groups who already have strong cultural beliefs regarding their origins. What will be the impact of a scientific theory of evolution and migration that is antithetical to an Indigenous group's common beliefs? Will these new theories be used to challenge aboriginal territorial claims, or rights to land?

Medical Benefits?

The often repeated claim that medical applications will be developed to treat diseases suffered by Indigenous peoples is a complete misrepresentation of the Project and serves to coerce the participation of subjects based on the false hope for medical miracles. The Project's mandate is simply to collect, database, and maintain genetic samples and data, not to develop medical applications.

The HGD Project will make the genetic samples available to "the public." However, it is not clear who will have access to the data and actual genetic samples. It appears that the HGD Project will maintain an open-access policy. This means that once genetic materials are stored in gene banks, they will be available in perpetuity, with minimal control, to anyone requesting access. Scientists need only demonstrate the validity of their scientific research in order to gain access to the samples. Medical applications are in fact likely to result from the eventual research, manipulation, and commercialization of the genetic materials. But they will most likely come in the form of pharmaceuticals or expensive genetic therapy techniques. Possible benefits will go only to those who can afford the high costs of such treatments.

The proposition that medical benefits will result from genetic sampling is further suspect, since no aspect of the project will take into account the role that existing and historical socioeconomic and environmental conditions play in the health of Indigenous communities.

If an Indigenous population were interested in researching a genetic question specific to its group, it would not need the HGD Project to do so. Genetic research technology and expertise are widely available. The enticement of potential medical benefits is an empty promise which will be used to gain access to communities for the collection of samples.

Commercialization, Ownership, and Intellectual Property Rights

The HGD Project raises inevitable questions regarding both ownership of the genetic samples themselves and who stands to profit from the commercialization of products derived from the samples. The Project puts Indigenous peoples' most fundamental property—their own genes—in the hands of anyone who wants to experiment with them. In doing so, the Project opens the door to widespread commercialization and potential misuse of the samples and data.

The Project will enable "bioprospectors" to stake legal claims on the natural genetic resource base of Indigenous peoples. Some of those claims will strike it rich, in the form of profitable patents. As in the case of future medical applications, the direct benefits from the HGD gene banks will go to those who can afford to invest in research, manipulation, and commercialization of the genetic data. Patent law will be the primary vehicle which enables scientists to secure exclusive rights to the genetic samples. Patent laws grant a limited property right to the patent holder and exclude others from using the patented item for a specific period of time, usually for a 17-year period.

Patenting Human Genes

Since 1980, when the U.S. Supreme Court ruled that the creation of an oil-eating microbe is patentable, there has been a disturbing trend in U.S. patent law that extends patent protection to life forms. Since then, the U.S. Patent and Trademark Office (PTO) has granted patents for newly created microorganisms, living animals, and human tissues and genes, breaking the long-standing policy that animate life forms were not patentable. The National Institutes of Health, and others, have secured patent rights for fragmented gene sequences, many with unknown function and physical significance. This trend has enabled research institutions and corporations to secure patents for almost 5 percent of the entire human genome and has spurred a rush for ownership of the remaining 95 percent of the human genome.

Does anyone have the right to own a life form or to commodify parts of the human body? While many debate the ethical and moral implications of patenting life forms, in 1993 U.S. Secretary of Commerce Ron Brown filed a patent claim on the cell line of a 26-year-old Guayami woman from Panama. Her cell line was of interest because some Guayami people carry a unique virus, and their antibodies may prove useful in AIDS and leukemia research. Fortunately, international protest and action by the Guayami General Congress and others led to the withdrawal of the patent claim by the U.S. Secretary of Commerce in November 1993.

Patent claims have also been filed by the Secretary of Commerce for the cell lines of Indigenous people from the Solomon Islands. The Solomon Islands Government has demanded withdrawal of the patent applications and repatriation of the genetic samples, citing an invasion of sovereignty, lack of informed consent, and moral grounds as the reasons for protest. In early March 1994, Secretary Ron Brown rejected these requests, stating that "there is no provision for considerations related to the source of the cells that may be the subject of a patent application." In other words, according to existing patent law, the source of a genetic sample is irrelevant.

Indigenous people must be aware that it may be extremely difficult or impossible to recover or repatriate samples of our blood, tissues, or body parts once they are removed from our bodies and stored elsewhere. In 1984 John Moore filed a lawsuit claiming that his blood cells had been misappropriated while he was undergoing treatment for leukemia at the University of California, Los Angeles Medical Center. During his treatment, Moore's doctor developed a cell line which proved valuable in fighting bacteria and cancer. The UCLA Board of Regents filed a patent claim on this cell line, from which they developed commercially valuable antibacterial and cancer-fighting pharmaceuticals. Moore claimed that he was entitled to share in profits derived from commercial uses of these cells and any other products resulting from research on any of his biological materials. In a significant 1990 California Supreme Court decision, the court established that "donors" do not have an intellectual property right in the tissues removed from their body.

Sample Collection

The HGD Project will seek the consent of the individuals and populations to be sampled. Questions of what constitutes "informed consent" and how it will be secured remain to be answered. The HGD Project has secured a grant from the J. D. and C. T. MacArthur Foundation (despite the expressed opposition of Native leaders) in order to develop a model protocol for the collection of genetic samples from Indigenous groups.

The concept of "informed consent" raises many unanswered questions in the minds of Indigenous peoples, such as: Who is authorized to give consent? Should consent be required only from the individual being sampled or also include the governing body of that particular Indigenous nation? Can consent be granted by government officials of the nation-state in which the Indigenous nation is located? How will permission be obtained for collection of samples from the dead, or for use of fetal and placental tissues as sources for genetic samples? How will the project be explained in the local language? Will the full scope of the project and the short- and long-term implications and potential uses of the samples be fully disclosed? Will donors be fully informed of the potential for profits that may be made from their genetic samples?

Other Potential for Misuse

With genetic engineering technology today, it is possible to manipulate the "blueprints" of living organisms. Gene technology makes it possible to isolate, splice, insert, rearrange, recombine, and mass-reproduce genes.

Andrew Kimbrell, *The Human Body Shop,* 1994.

Though genetic engineering still seems like science fiction to many people, it is a reality. Through genetic engineering, scientists are capable of reprogramming the genetic codes of living things to meet societal or economic goals. Transgenic experiments can mix plant genome with that of animals, and human genome with that of plants or animals. The ethical and legal questions raised by genetic engineering technology are numerous and unanswered. Nonetheless, this area remains virtually unregulated. While the HGD Project itself does not plan to do genetic engineering, no safe-guards exist to prevent others from doing so with the HGD genetic samples.

Genetic manipulation raises serious ethical and moral concerns for Indigenous peoples, for whom any violation of the natural order of life is abhorrently wrong. Scientists are genetically manipulating existing life forms, altering the course of natural evolution, and creating new life forms. Genes are living organisms which reproduce, migrate, and mutate. The full implications of genetically altered life forms released into the environment cannot possibly be anticipated.

─ᐧRecommendations

Indigenous organizations need to alert all Indigenous peoples to the work of the Human Genome Organiza-tion (the body governing the HGDP) in order to prevent the taking of their genetic materials by this project, or by freelance scientists, and to assist groups in reclaim-ing any genetic materials that have already been taken.

Indigenous people must engage in community edu-cation and discussion about the full scope of this proj-ect and the potential dangers of genetic manipulation

before they decide whether to participate. It is impera-tive that our communities become fully aware of the Project's implications and begin documenting pro-posed or current sample collecting. We need to form an international Indigenous research group to determine the extent of existing international protections for hu-man materials and to develop additional policies which insure the protection of our intellectual, cultural, and biological property rights.

Indigenous people must call for a worldwide mora-torium on the collection, databasing, transformation, and commercialization of cell lines and genetic materi-als of Indigenous peoples until international standards and regulation are put into place which fully protect the environment and the interests of Indigenous peoples.

For more information, contact:
Debra Harry, P.O. Box 72, Nixon, Nevada 89424, phone (702) 574-0309. Email: Debra_Harry@Together.org or dharry@igc.apc.org.
Jeannette Armstrong, En'owkin Centre, 257 Brunswick Street, Penticton, BC V2A 1P2 (604) 493-7181.
RAFI-Canada (Rural Advancement Foundation Interna-tional), Suite 504-71 Bank Street, Ottawa, Ontario KIP 5N2, phone (613) 567-6880.

REFLECTING ON THE SECTION

Susan Davis reminds us that women and men have sought to control reproduction using various technolo-gies for thousands of years. To understand part of this long history, Angela Davis argues persuasively that racism tilted U.S. medical technology and social poli-cies toward population control and racial genocide rather than reproductive freedom. In a similar vein, Soheir Morsy calls our attention to problems with the contraceptive technologies that are available to women in the Third World and suggests new approaches that might be less harmful. The Committee on Women, Population, and the Environment has taken on the task of organizing against coercive forms of population control and advocating for new approaches.

How are the histories of race and imperialism em-bedded within the global policies of population con-trol? In what ways can we argue that overpopulation may not always lead to poverty or be the primary cause of poverty? How do the history of race relations in the United States and the history of colonization and im-perialism globally affect reproductive rights, the de-velopment of reproductive technologies, and the funding and implementation of population policies? What are the specific roles of women in these tech-nologies and strategies? Do new technologies such as genetic cloning or mapping reinforce or challenge the role of science in producing inequalities in modern times?

Strategizing Health Education

Global Aspects of Health and Health Policy in Third World Countries

MAUREEN LARKIN

Maureen Larkin, a scholar of health studies, compares the First and Third Worlds to discuss similarities and contrasts in the areas of health and development. Larkin explains that development strategies for health care will not be effective if they do not address globalization and the colonial legacies that create inequality and poverty.

Introduction

The health of populations is shaped by complex interactions between humans and their socioeconomic, physical, and cultural environments. The epidemiological profile (patterns of health and disease) of populations changes over time in intricate and uneven ways as the relationship to these environments change. This is exemplified in the major epidemiological transitions achieved in Western countries over the past 150 years,

Maureen Larkin, "Global Aspects of Health and Health Policy in Third World Countries," in *Globalization and the Third World,* Ray Kiely and Phil Newfleet, eds. London: Routledge, 1998: 92–99, 106–10.

which accompanied the socioeconomic changes associated with the transition to an industrial capitalist society.

Over this period, major changes took place in patterns of health and disease and the life expectancy of populations. Significantly, major infectious diseases such as tuberculosis and others such as the food- and water-borne diseases that were the major causes of death in the nineteenth century were wiped out, resulting in a substantial decline in mortality rates. As time went on, these diseases have come to be replaced by chronic conditions such as heart disease and cancers, which are linked to changing lifestyles and increased longevity (McKeown 1976).

While much debate surrounds the saliency of particular factors and processes involved in these transitions, research indicates that the key influences on health in this period were the preventive roles played by access to adequate nutrition, clean water, and sanitation.

Medical science at this time lacked effective cures for the major causes of mortality. However, these changes cannot be assumed to have been a simple automatic outcome of industrial growth. Rather, a variety of mediating

---

Key Terms

First World/Third World Terms applied to so-called advanced (wealthy) and disadvantaged (impoverished) areas of the world.

globalization The phenomenon of linking markets and currencies around the world. Also used to suggest homogenization (or Westernization) of cultures.

nongovernmental organization (NGO) An organization devoted to issues of social welfare that is not directly linked to any government.

processes of a political and ideological nature were at play to shape the developmental process and the accompanying health outcomes. Mobilising agents, ideologies, reform movements (such as sanitary movements and trade unions), and local government were an integral part of the change process, exerting pressure on employers and the state for a more equitable distribution of economic growth (Szreter 1988). Moreover, improvements in health were not equally distributed throughout the population; differentials in health status between different socioeconomic groups were marked and continue to be so up to the present day (*Black Report* 1980).

This brief synopsis suggests important similarities and contrasts which can be drawn between First and Third World countries in relation to health and development. In varying and uneven ways, many of these countries are now undergoing forms of capitalist industrial development. Their health profiles are similarly distributed in uneven forms. In the poorer regions—such as sub-Saharan Africa, parts of Latin America, Asia and the Middle East—can be found health and disease profiles which are not dissimilar to those which prevailed in the developed world a century ago, with high mortality rates and low life expectancy (World Bank 1993). Infant and child mortality are particularly high and are linked to the complex interaction of infectious diseases with malnutrition and poverty.

Alongside this, in the newly industrialising countries (NICs) and for the elites and middle classes throughout the Third World, are to be found patterns similar to those in the developed world today, with increased life expectancy and a growing prevalence of chronic disease and disability (Phillips and Verhasselt 1994).

The picture is therefore a mixed one, with old and new patterns of disease to be found telescoped together in the urban slums and rich suburbs of many Third World countries. It is estimated, for example, that infant mortality rates in slum areas can be three times as high as city averages in many cities (Basta in Phillips and Verhasselt 1994).

What this suggests is that the forms of development which are taking place, and how they are working themselves through, are highly complex and there are no easy parallels to be drawn between these and Western forms of development. In Britain capitalist industrial development combined with general social development to provide the basic prerequisites for health—such as access to nutrition, clean water, and sanitation facilities—as well as reforms in the fields of housing, health, and welfare services. But this was achieved over an extended period of time and under very different historic, economic, and political conditions from those of the Third World today.

Capitalism developed gradually in Britain over several centuries, transforming it into an industrial society in the eighteenth and nineteenth centuries. Indeed, it took over 100 years to develop the necessary institutional reforms to provide for the health and welfare needs of the population. In contrast to this, the various forms of development taking place in the Third World today are considerably speeded up as modern technology and communications insert themselves into cultures and communities in complex and uneven ways. Over a matter of decades, what were formerly largely agricultural subsistence communities are rapidly being transformed by globalised forms of production and consumption practices [. . .]

This, combined with their very different historic backgrounds and the dominant position of Western countries in what are now global markets, means that the future direction and possibilities for the poorer countries are highly uncertain. [. . .] This uncertainty is intensified by the increasing tendency for dominant countries to use their market power and financial leverage to dictate the context and form of development which can take place.

The health problems and prospects within the poorer regions of the Third World are intricately caught up in these developmental processes. It is within and through the complex web of influences at play that health and health issues come to be defined, shaped, and experienced. However, these processes can no longer be understood solely within the confines of particular countries or nation-states. As Western technologies, cultures, and ideologies spread around the globe and insert themselves into the Third World, so increasingly development and health issues become caught up in and are shaped by these globalising influences.

The Global Context of Health

Depending upon how the term *global* is used, there is a sense in which health in the Third World has long had a global dimension. There is an abundant literature which documents the health impacts of colonialism. These range from the direct effects of conquest and wars, the dissemination and spread of new diseases and epidemics, and the health impacts of the slave trade to the indirect effects of a colonial legacy in the form of a distorted distribution of resources, the dominance of Western medicine, and the undermining of traditional communities and systems of healing (Doyal 1979).

Although the legacy of this period continues to cast shadows over the contemporary health context, today's global context presents a far more complicated scenario.

[. . .]

Global developmental processes today are working to create environments which for a majority of people present major challenges to health. The growth of poverty and the risks to health from industrial hazards and pesticide contamination are but two areas of concern. Alongside these are the ideologies of consumerism and individualism, which have increasingly become a way of life for growing numbers of people around the globe. The complex ways in which these are inserted into local cultures and their impact on social relationships and identities are not easy to grasp. As old and new cultures blend and mix, traditional forms of social relationships, social supports, and patterns of sexual activity can be undermined or transformed and new lifestyles forged which can have uncertain implications for health. Feeding into this is the growing influence of Western medicine—which, combining as it increasingly does with aspects of traditional therapeutic practices and the market power of global pharmaceutical transnational corporations (TNCs), creates its own problems of inappropriate prescribing and drug misuse and abuse.

Policies and funding for health are also caught up in a variety of global processes and the activities and conflicting interests of a growing number of multilateral agencies, such as the World Bank, the World Health Organisation (WHO), bilateral donor aid agencies, and TNCs in the drug, food, and alcohol industries. As well as these, there are the increasing numbers of international and national nongovernmental organisations (NGOs), consumer groups, and social movements, all of which are active in attempting to shape the policy agenda (Walt 1994). In this sense, health and health

policies have become highly contested, and these conflicts are increasingly played out at an international level through a variety of strategies and vocabularies which are not easy to penetrate.

[. . .]

Health and Development Policies

Throughout the 1950s and 1960s, policies for health as well as for development were largely based on the assumption that what had worked for the West was also best for the other two-thirds of the world population. Western-style economic development, supplemented by Western-style biomedically based health care services, was assumed eventually to bring about an amelioration of the health problems of all. This, however, has not been realised. While health gains in terms of reduced mortality rates and increased life expectancy were made, these gains were highly uneven, with large disparities between countries and groups (Gray 1993). The failure of growth to trickle down, persistent poverty, and growing inequalities in the distribution of resources forced a rethink both in the development field and in international health policy.

[. . .]

The development strategies of the global agencies such as the World Bank and the International Labour Organisation (ILO) changed in the direction of advocating policies for redistribution and meeting basic needs. Parallel to this came a reorientation of WHO policy away from the traditional high-tech, hospital-based approach which had characterised its policies for health in the developing world up to the 1970s. Catering as it largely did to the health needs of the urban-based middle classes, this approach was now considered inappropriate for meeting the health needs of the poorer populations. A more equitably based system of health care, which focused on meeting the basic health needs of populations in rural areas in particular, was advocated. This was known as the Primary Care Approach and sought to combine basic and accessible health services with the promotion of clean water supplies, sanitation, and access to nutritional supplies (WHO 1978).

However, the development context within which Primary Care policies were to be implemented had by now moved on and development strategies had again changed. A combination of rising interest rates, falling commodity prices, and rising indebtedness of Third World countries ushered in the World Bank/IMF's new neoliberal development paradigm. As part of this strategy, structural adjustment policies (SAPs) were put in place in many countries which created major constraints on the implementation of WHO policies and exacerbated the already severe health problems which prevailed.

SAPs involved the removal of price controls, cuts in subsidies, and rising food prices, which worked to undermine food security and the nutritional status of large numbers of waged labourers in rural and especially urban areas. This, combined with labour market deregulation (which worked to depress incomes and employment opportunities), meant that many households were unable to meet minimum food needs (Cornia *et al.* 1987). Cuts in state expenditure also put severe pressure

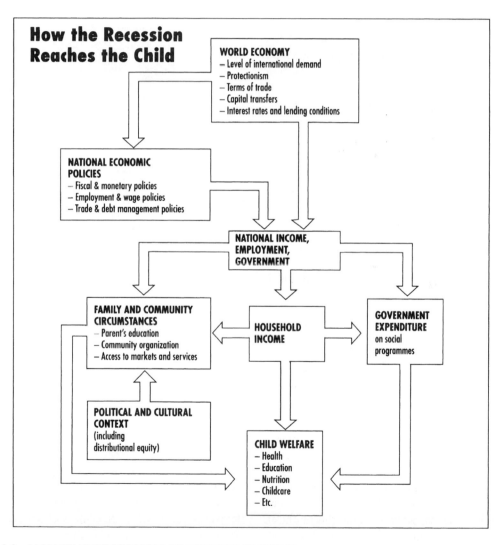

FIGURE 1.6   HOW THE RECESSION REACHES THE CHILD

FIGURE I.7 DEFAULT ISN'T OURS

on health budgets—with resulting shortages of personnel, essential drugs, and medical supplies, a decline in child immunisation programmes, and the introduction of user charges (Asthana in Phillips and Verhasselt 1994).

In all, these policies have created serious adverse conditions for health. Whatever the long-term prospects for structurally adjusting countries, the short-term effects on the living standards of the poorer populations have resulted in a slowing down or worsening of health status in the regions most severely hit—such as sub-Saharan Africa, parts of Latin America, and the Middle East, where a deterioration in the nutritional status of children, increased incidence of infectious disease, and raised infant and maternal mortality rates are reported (UNICEF 1995; Cornia *et al.* 1987).

Running alongside and compounding these problems have been the displacement of populations, violence, and civil unrest, which these dislocations have contributed to and which create their own physical and psychological threats to health. It is clear that prospects for health are now more than ever before complicated and constrained by the operation of development processes which to a large extent fall outside the control of local states and communities. Policies and mobilisations for health must therefore increasingly engage with multilateral development agencies such as the World Bank/IMF and their major funders.

[. . .]

Expanding Industrial Activity

At the same time we can see how industrial activity is speeded up by intense competition within the global market economy and the activities of TNCs create altered patterns of work and new hazards for health. The weak position of many countries within the global economic order puts pressure on governments to create favourable environments for TNCs and to an increasing extent for local investors. This, combined with developing countries' lack of experience and resources for the management and regulation of heavy industry, often results in a relaxation or absence of environmental controls, presenting serious health risks for workers and their families. These risks are found in unsafe plant design and production processes, lax safety standards, and exposure of workers to hazardous materials and chemicals that are often banned or restricted in the developed countries (Cooper Weil *et al.* 1990). It is estimated, for example, that a manufacturing worker in Pakistan is approximately eight times more likely to die in an accident on the job than a worker in France (World Bank 1995).

In many countries, including those recently caught up in the rapid scramble for development, such as the Philippines, Thailand, Indonesia, and China, workers (especially women) work long hours for low levels of pay, often in cramped and poorly ventilated conditions. In Jakarta, for example, where many of the global names in sports shoe manufacture such as Reebok and Nike are to be found, we read of young women earning 16 pence (approx. 22¢) an hour and working in 90-degree heat. Work is contracted out by the TNCs, who pass responsibility for terms and conditions to national governments. A workday can stretch to 18 hours, and free trade unions are illegal (*Guardian* 3 December 1996).

Mechanisation and Chemicalisation of Agriculture

Other hazards are presented by the mechanisation and chemicalisation of agriculture as Western technologies and techniques are transported around the world through the activities of giant agribusinesses. There are a variety of health problems linked to irrigation schemes and resettlement of populations which are beyond the scope of this chapter (see Cooper Weil *et al.* 1990). Pesticides are, however, one important area where there is a growing concern about their misuse and abuse. The pesticide market is truly global and dominated by a small number of transnational corporations; the top 10 companies control 73 percent of the world market (Dinham 1993). Imports of pesticides to developing countries have shown a continuous increase over the past decade and a half. This is encouraged by pressure from the IMF to increase cash crops for export in order to service their debts.

Widespread use and abuse (though not adequately monitored) pose increasing problems of pesticide poisoning, pest resistance, environmental contamination, and pesticide residues in food (Cooper Weil *et al.* 1990). The World Health Organisation estimates that more than 1 million workers across Latin America alone are poisoned every year and 10,000 die from exposure to chemicals (World Bank 1995). Aerial spraying carries particular hazards not only for operators but also for people and crops in nontarget areas. For example, local practices of drying foodstuffs such as couscous, spices, meat, and fish on the roofs expose food to aerial spray drift. Health and safety issues are accentuated in these countries by a lack of hazard awareness on the part of both health professionals and users, a lack of regulatory authorities, and problems surrounding labelling, language, and high levels of illiteracy among the local population. Adequate washing facilities and protective clothing are unavailable and problems of disposal are exacerbated where contaminated drums are frequently reused for storing water and foodstuffs (Dinham 1993).

Health and the Urban Context

Other problems for health are thrown up by the rapid rates of urbanisation now being witnessed across the

Third World. These are creating new and uncertain conditions which can have many health implications. Within the new urban environments, cultures blend and mix and social relationships are made and remade within the global context of modern cities. Individualistic values come to challenge, modify, or replace the more traditional normative controls on identities and behaviours as migrants move from rural to urban areas and adapt to urban ways of life. International tourism and global media networks feed into this process, mediating and constructing new identities and realities.

This new social environment is conducive to altered patterns of sexual interaction, which have particular significance for the development and spread of HIV/AIDS and other sexually transmitted diseases that present major challenges to health in the modern Third World. In some cities in sub-Saharan Africa, it is estimated that as many as one in three adults are infected with HIV (UNICEF 1994). As the traditional parameters governing sexual relationships are dismantled or weakened, more liberalised sexual behaviours can mean greater numbers and variety of casual sexual contacts and hence greater vulnerability to infection. A number of factors feed into this, such as the growth of commercial sex and patterns of circular migration as separated partners move between rural and urban areas, thereby increasing the risks of infection transmission.

Underpinning and greatly aggravating these problems is the growth of poverty in urban areas, which contributes to weakened resistance and greater vulnerability to infection. In some cities, it is estimated the poor can constitute up to 60 percent of the population. They are typically housed in urban slums and squatter settlements (Harpham in Phillips and Verhasselt 1994). This presents major threats to health in the form of overcrowding, contaminated water supplies, and inadequate sanitation. These factors, combined with high levels of malnutrition, create major threats to health and life with high infant mortality rates from infectious diseases, particularly diarrhoea and respiratory infections (Harpham 1995).

Less researched but recognised as a growing health issue is mental health (World Bank 1993). Although major problems are implicated in how mental health problems are conceptualised in different cultures and reliable data is patchy, conditions known in the devel-

oped world to be associated with poor mental health status are abundantly prevalent in the urban environments of many countries. Among these are the social dislocation of migration, displacement from the labour force, erosion of the social supports of the rural family and community, poverty, stress, and high levels of violence. What research exists points to mixed anxiety/depression disorders as the most common presenting mental health problems, with the highest prevalence among women (Harpham 1995).

However, no easy generalisations based on Western models of mental health or illness can be made without much greater understanding of the local historic and symbolic orders within which mental health concepts and problems are constructed and articulated.

[. . .]

Concepts of health and prescriptions for health are therefore not ideas which can be transported uncritically across cultural boundaries. As Western ideas and technologies of health are increasingly available around the globe, there is a need for greater understanding of how they are mediated by local sociocultural circumstances. The globalised nature of Western medicine and how it is appropriated at a local level provide an interesting example in this respect.

[. . .]

Women's Health Issues

Women's movements and women's health issues are a telling example of the problems and prospects which confront those seeking to influence policy in a more equitable direction. Women's status and women's health are now major issues on the international policy agendas of the major developmental and health agencies. Pressure from the international women's movement and grassroots campaigns, as well as the recognition by the development establishment of the potential contribution of women to the "development" effort, has meant that no serious policy for health or development can any longer ignore a woman or gender dimension. Grassroots campaigns around development and women's health are now a major political reality, especially in Third World countries, and international collaboration has continued to grow since the 1975/85 U.N. Decade for the Advancement of Women. (For an overview of the important health issues related to women in the Third World, see Smyke 1991; WHO 1995.)

However, although all groups, including the major donors, claim to prioritise women's interests, there are many different perspectives and strategies deployed both nationally and internationally in addressing them. Cleeves Mosse identifies two broad tendencies. On the one hand are the more needs-based welfarist approaches most favoured by the major donors and national governments, which attempt to couple improving the status of women through education and income generation with provision for mother and child health and family planning.

On the other hand are the more radical and feminist-based approaches, which locate women's health issues within the broader context of unequal gender relations and see the necessity for a more bottom-up grassroots approach of empowering women. Such approaches are less likely to gain more than a rhetorical helping hand from governments or major donors (Cleeves Mosse 1993).

These positions and the conflicts which they engender are often glimpsed at international conferences, where they become caught up in a variety of political and cultural conflicts which cut across gender divisions and work to reconstitute them in often contradictory and uncertain ways. This was seen in the U.N. Cairo Conference on Population 1994 and the Beijing World Conference on Women 1995, where a discourse of needs versus rights, especially around reproduction and sexuality, became entangled in the global ideologies of the Vatican and Islam (Petchesky 1995; *Independent* 5 September 1994).

There is, however, no doubt that women's movements have been and continue to be a major force in instilling a gender awareness into the policies and practices of agencies in the fields of development and health at both international and local levels and in the mobilisation of women around these issues. The major campaigns mounted around contraceptive issues and the challenges to the ideology of population control are notable examples of the critical role played by women as arbiters of women's health (Hartman 1987).

It is nevertheless unclear how far working through official bodies such as the U.N. agencies or local states can amount to fundamental challenges to entrenched gender interests and the many technological, political,

and religious forces which go to shape policy in this area. The issue of reproductive health, for example, highlights the many conflicts and compromises which gender issues throw up and the uneasy alliances which are often forged among a variety of conflicting interests.

Reproductive Health Issues

Women's reproductive health is a major health issue for the poorer countries, not least because of continuing high rates of maternal mortality—especially in South Asia and Africa, where a woman is at least 100 times more likely to die in a single pregnancy than a woman from the developed world (Doyal 1995).

While it would appear that major progress has been made within the international policy community in transforming the discourses which frame the issue of reproductive health, outcomes in terms of policy implementation are a great deal more uncertain.

Over the last decade or so, policies in this area have been redefined and remade as pressure from women's groups, combined with policy failure in the area of maternal health, worked to push thinking beyond previously narrow concerns with family planning and mother and child health. These programmes, in which women were targeted largely in their capacities as bearers and rearers of children, have come to be modified or superseded by strategies which claim to locate maternal health within a broader woman-centred approach. Women's needs across the lifespan and in their productive as well as reproductive roles need to be addressed (Sweetman 1994).

Major discursive transformations have taken place, particularly at the level of the international women's movement, where reproductive health has come to be defined in terms of reproductive rights, the empowerment of women, and gender equality. Interestingly, too, population and family planning groups, who have come under increasing pressure from the Vatican and fundamentalist groups, also seem to have shifted their position and in forging alliances with women's NGOs have come to embrace the new vocabulary of women's rights. How these latest conference proceedings work themselves through is another matter, and certainly there are women's groups both North and South who are wary of such alliances and see the new discourse as nothing more than population control with a feminist face (Petchesky 1995).

It is notable that for some time the major development agencies, such as the World Bank and population groups, have deployed a status of women discourse in their analysis and programmes for development and population control. As research in the 1970s and 1980s came to link development, population, and the status of women, these agencies came to recast their programmes in line with improving the status of women. Thus for the World Bank, "enhancing the status of women is of critical importance in strengthening the demand for smaller families" (World Bank 1986, quoted in Sweetman 1994). And, as Hartman demonstrates, antipoverty programmes, education, and income-generation projects have been promoted by population agencies, running alongside family planning programmes (Hartman 1987).

Richter's (1996) account of the recent and ongoing struggles surrounding immunological birth-control methods (antifertility vaccines) demonstrates the immense versatility and subtlety of agencies such as The Population Council and others engaged in this research in their attempts to co-opt or marginalise opposition from women's groups, from discrediting their objections as unscientific and questioning their representativeness to framing contraceptive research in terms of enhancing women's choice. There is also the fine line women's movements must thread between the interests of the church and prolife groups and the interests of women in many countries who lack access to any form of safe contraception (Richter 1996). All of this works to create potential cleavages and opportunities for the co-option of a woman-centred agenda.

✍Action at a Local Level

Changing vocabularies and policy formulation at the international levels notwithstanding, it is a great deal more difficult to assess their impact at a local level, where a variety of officially sanctioned initiatives and informal women's projects are to be found. Thus, expanded women's health programmes that emanate from the WHO and the World Bank and seek to integrate family planning with a broader range of services

have certainly been put in place in many areas, and there are a variety of more informal community-based women's health projects which are clearly based on feminist principles (Sweetman 1994; Doyal 1995).

However, many of the more formally based programmes have been criticised for being no more than add-on initiatives to existing programmes, such as screening and counselling, within the context of the same personnel and often the same clinics. Wider issues such as those identified above, as well as the material and cultural constraints which shape women's health chances, do not appear to be addressed in any significant sense.

There are also concerns about the high profile accorded to family planning within some of these programmes. Smyth, for example, argues that in the case of Indonesia's Safe Motherhood Campaign (a WHO/World Bank initiative) resources are disproportionately allocated in favour of family planning activities (Smyth in Sweetman 1994). There is clearly a need for a great deal more in-depth research in this area in order to clarify how these different interests work to shape policy at both the international and national levels. There can be no doubt but that the major players identified, such as population groups and donor aid and research agencies, form a powerful coalition of interests with both the financial and technical resources to potentially coopt their opposition. Women's groups have, however, shown a marked resilience in maintaining a critical scrutiny of policies and research in this area and in ensuring that women's interests are kept on the international policy agenda.

✍Conclusion

While clearly all the health problems of the poorer Third World cannot be explained away as a result of globalisation, it is nevertheless the case that health is intimately caught up in this process. Global processes which are shaping the development process are also both directly and indirectly shaping prospects for health. We have seen how current development strategies are working to create environments of poverty and health risks for large numbers of people. Means of livelihood and ways of life are being transformed as new production techniques, increasing urbanisation, and cultures of modernity are inserted into traditional settings, creating new hazards and uncertainties for health.

At the same time, the ability to affect decision making in the procurement and allocation of resources for health appears to be increasingly displaced from local and national communities and has come to be concentrated in the hands of supranational bodies, such as United Nations agencies and the variety of technical and commercial interests which patrol the international policy arena. The roles of the World Bank, donor aid agencies, and drug TNCs are a case in point. How far opposition groups active at international levels can be effective in challenging these dominant interests is highly problematic. There is no doubt that the globalisation process has created new sites of resistance and has brought together a variety of overlapping spheres of interest in the areas of health, development, environmental, and women's groups. Local, regional, and international networks have been created as communications technology and international travel have made contact and coordination a great deal more accessible. Global media networks have also worked to create a greater general awareness of and receptivity to Third World issues.

However, as demonstrated above, the dangers of dilution and co-option by dominant interests are an ever-present threat, given the heterogenous nature of this opposition. This is compounded by the fact that global–local links, essential for effective mobilisation, are also often difficult to forge and get caught up in contradictions emanating from the particularistic interests of religion, ethnicity, class, and gender. Without effective mobilisation of communities, radical international agendas are no more than fine rhetoric. Prospects for health therefore depend upon overcoming these obstacles and building alliances which can effectively challenge current policies in both development and health.

REFERENCES

The Black Report and The Health Divide (1980), in P. Townsend and N. Davidson (eds). *Inequalities in Health.* London: Penguin.

Cleeves Mosse, J. (1993). *Half the World, Half a Chance,* Oxford: Oxfam.

Cooper Weil, D., A. Alicbusan, J. Wilson, M. Reich, and D. Bradley. (1990). *The Impact of Development Policies on Health,* Geneva: WHO.

Cornia, G., R. Jolly, and F. Stewart. (1987). *Adjustment with a Human Face.* Oxford: Oxford University Press.

Dinham, B. (1993). *The Pesticide Hazard,* London: Zed.

Doyal, L. (1979). *The Political Economy of Health,* London: Pluto.

——— (1995). *What Makes Women Sick,* London: Macmillan.

Gray, A. (1993). *World Health and Disease,* Milton Keynes: Open University Press.

Harpham, T. (ed.). (1995). *Urbanization and Mental Health in Developing Countries,* New York: Avebury.

Hartman, B. (1987). *Reproductive Rights and Wrongs: The Global Politics of Population Control and Contraceptive Choice,* New York: Harper & Row.

McKeown, T. (1976). *The Modern Rise of Populations,* London: Edward Arnold.

Petchesky, R. (1995). "From Population Control to Reproductive Rights." *Reproductive Health Rights* 6, November.

Phillips, D., and R. Verhasselt. (1994). *Health and Development,* London: Routledge.

Richter, J. (1996). *Vaccination against Pregnancy: Miracle or Menace,* London: Zed.

Smyke, P. (1991). *Women and Health,* London: Zed.

Sweetman, C. (ed.). (1994). *Population and Reproductive Rights,* Oxford: Oxfam.

Szreter, S. (1988). "The Importance of Social Intervention in Britain's Mortality Decline," in B. Davey, A. Gray, and J. Seale (eds) (1995) *Health and Disease,* Milton Keynes: Open University Press.

UNICEF. (1994). *The State of the World's Children,* New York: UNICEF.

——— (1995). *The State of the World's Children,* New York: UNICEF.

Walt, J. (1994). *Health Policy,* London: Zed.

World Bank. (1993). *World Development Report: Investing in Health,* Oxford: Oxford University Press.

——— (1995). *World Development Report: Workers in an Integrating World,* Oxford: Oxford University Press.

World Health Organisation. (1978). "Alma Ata 1978," in *Primary Health Care: Health for All,* Series No. 1, Geneva: WHO.

The Women's Health Movement in the United States
JUDY NORSIGIAN

Judy Norsigian describes the history of feminist organizing for women's health care delivery and education in the United States during the "second wave" (the feminist movement of the 1960s and after).

‒◦ Introduction

The Women's Health Movement (WHM) in the United States had its origins in the late 1960s, when women's groups, health and medical providers, and others organized a nationwide effort to legalize abortion. Many of these groups subsequently took up other health issues. Some established women-controlled health centers, some produced women's health publications[1] and educational materials, and others carried out a number of women's health advocacy projects, often with the goal of changing public policies affecting women's health.[2]

Nationally, the WHM found a unified voice with the establishment of the Washington, D.C.-based National Women's Health Network in 1976. The Network emphasized federal health policy, which, up to that point, had had little or no feminist consumer input; collaborated with progressive health and medical professionals; and increased contact with members of the media. The Network is now a powerful and credible presence among members of Congress, administrators in key federal agencies, and other important policymakers and has had, for example, major input in the decisions by the Food and Drug Administration (FDA) to label various drugs and devices used by women.

Judy Norsigian, "The Women's Health Movement in the United States," in *Man-Made Medicine: Women's Health, Public Policy, and Reform,* Kary L. Moss, ed. Durham: Duke University Press, 1996: 79–85, 93.

Early groups in the WHM were primarily white and middle class in their composition and orientation, although they sometimes addressed the concerns of poorer women and women of color. During the 1980s, many women of color created both local and national organizations[3] to focus more intensively on their priority issues. Women with disabilities, older women, overweight women, and lesbians also organized to form new groups,[4] as well as to raise specific issues within existing women's health groups. This growing diversity of individuals and organizations generated new tensions and conflicting analyses of the same problems, although the general environment has been one where many values and goals are held in common. Differential access to financial resources has at times caused resentment, making it more difficult for many to participate in cooperative ventures.

During the last decade, the WHM has been trying to influence the national health care reform debate. Whether *all* women's health and medical needs will be better met under a new national health plan remains to be seen.

[. . .]

‒◦ The Women's Health Movement during the 1970s and 1980s

Much of the activity of the early WHM focused on basic education and sharing of information and experiences about health and sexuality, often in a small group setting. *Our Bodies, Ourselves,* for example, which became one of the most popular books about women's health, emerged out of an unmet need to demystify medical care and redefine and reclaim female sexuality. The first edition, a 112-page newsprint book published by the New England Free Press in late 1970, re-sulted from meetings and informal "courses" organized by women who met at a women's liberation conference in the spring of 1969. The phenomenal success of this "underground" publication (over 250,000 copies were sold, mainly by word of mouth, until commercial publication in 1973) demonstrated women's profound need for clear, comprehensive information about their bodies as well as about health and medical care.

Collective ignorance about the most elemental aspects of anatomy, physiology, and reproduction, coupled with the growing anger of many women about frequent mistreatment by a mostly white, privileged, and male medical profession, helped to spark numerous initiatives, from self-help groups to women-controlled health centers. Women taught one another how to perform cervical self-examinations, shared information about self-help treatments for vaginal infections, established advocacy groups that sought to make medical institutions and professionals more responsive to their needs, joined local health planning boards, and even became involved in the training of medical students (for example, the teaching of pelvic exams).[5]

Critiques of medicine as an institution of social control over women[6] emerged alongside analyses exposing problems such as racism, classism, sexism, ageism, ableism, and homophobia. Women also protested the emphasis on pathology and treatment versus prevention. Some argued that this led to the overmedicalization of women's lives, which turned normal events such as childbearing and menopause into necessarily disabling conditions requiring routine medical intervention.

As part of the solution to these myriad problems, women's health advocates sought to increase the decision-making power of women at all levels by working to place women in policymaking positions in medical institutions, educational settings, legislatures and local governing bodies, and relevant governmental agencies. Medical schools have seen little improvement over the past two decades, but there have been more female legislators and hospital administrators, two female Surgeons General,[7] and the first female director at the National Institutes of Health.[8] Even President Clinton's major effort to bring about health care reform in the early 1990s was headed by a woman—Hillary Rodham Clinton. Having women in influential positions does not necessarily change health and medical institutions, especially when powerful corporate interests are at stake, but it has lent legitimacy to raising the special concerns of women.

Many women's health activists have argued that the language of the WHM has been co-opted by larger institutions that remain generally unresponsive to women's needs. They argue that most women directly affected by particular problems still do not have an adequate voice in the organizations and institutions dealing with those problems.

Activists urge that initiatives and programs designed to address particular problems—such as high infant mortality rates or high rates of HIV infection among women in a given community—involve women from that community, including women experiencing these very problems. At a conference on women's health research sponsored by the National Institutes of Health, activists succeeded in garnering support for a recommendation that committees reviewing breast cancer research proposals include lay women who themselves have or have had breast cancer.[9] Programs or policies that foster "empowerment," a term often used to describe this kind of involvement in problem solving, are still few and far between, especially in low-income communities and communities of color.

In addition to particular health issues such as contraception, abortion, cancer, gynecological problems, childbearing, and menopause, the WHM has recognized other factors central to overall health and well-being: safer, cleaner, less stressful living and working environments; adequate food and housing for all; reduced violence against women, recognizing that such violence contributes substantially to women's health and medical problems; and a national health program that would guarantee everyone access to needed care.[10] Making sure that the many links among these issues are repeatedly articulated remains a high priority.

Accomplishments of the Women's Health Movement

The successes have been many and varied. In the early 1970s, lack of information about birth-control pills[11] and a growing awareness among women about problems associated with their use led to organized protests, including disruption of special hearings in Congress conducted by Senator Gaylord Nelson. Fortuitously, Barbara Seaman, author of *The Doctor's Case against the Pill,* and Alice Wolfson met at the Nelson hearings; several years later they cofounded the National Women's Health Network with Dr. Mary Howell, Belita Cowan, and Phyllis Chesler.

One important result of women's efforts to obtain more and better information about oral contraceptives (as well as other drugs) was the introduction of the Patient Package Insert (PPI) program by the FDA. The PPI, a very detailed summary of known problems and contraindications associated with a particular drug, provided women with important information, albeit in a dense, difficult-to-read format. Although a planned expansion of this program to other widely used drugs was subsequently eliminated during the Reagan administration, the Clinton administration resumed the program.[12]

A related struggle involved the provision of PPIs for so-called estrogen-replacement-therapy hormones. Not long after PPIs appeared for estrogen products, the Pharmaceutical Manufacturers Association (PMA), joined by the American College of Obstetricians and Gynecologists (ACOG), sued the FDA in an effort to block the distribution of PPIs for estrogen products. In response, four women's and consumer organizations, led by the National Women's Health Network (NWHN), entered the case as codefendants and filed an amicus brief cogently arguing for the right to such basic information. And we won. PPIs for estrogen products were retained.

Although difficult to prove, it is likely that pressure from the WHM played a significant role in increasing the number of nurse practitioners who provide primary care services for women. Many women's health activists believe that the greater likelihood of being cared for by a nurse practitioner or nurse-midwife often has improved the quality of care experienced by many women.[13]

Sterilization abuse, a long-standing problem for poor women in the United States, became the focus of a government inquiry after activists, journalists, and community organizations documented and publicized the degree to which certain women, especially women of color and Native American women, were sterilized

without informed consent.[14] This happened in a variety of ways: some women agreed to be sterilized without fully understanding what it meant, especially when information was given in terminology they did not understand; others were told that their public welfare benefits would be denied unless they agreed to sterilization; and some were told that the procedure was reversible, when, of course, that was not true.

Special hearings[15] resulted in regulations designed to curb the incidence of abuse among federally funded sterilizations. These regulations included a 30-day waiting period, the provision of information in a language clearly understood by the woman, and prohibition of the use of hysterectomy solely for the purpose of sterilization. Though far from a perfect solution, these regulations have been somewhat effective.

Ironically, with the exception of a handful of states in the United States, low-income women who are on Medicaid can obtain a federally funded sterilization but *not* a federally funded abortion. This limitation has led some women to "choose" sterilization because they have so few options. As the WHM continues to emphasize, without access to *all* reproductive health services, there can be no real choice in matters of childbearing.

During the 1970s, women-controlled health centers emerged as an alternative to the conventional delivery of health and medical care. Many were organized in a nonhierarchical fashion, with physicians having little or no policymaking roles. Most offered self-help groups that taught cervical self-exams, abortion services that were often the only ones in the region, and support groups for dealing with experiences such as premenstrual problems, infertility, and menopause. They also pioneered a more thorough, client-centered approach to informed consent. Because of these women-controlled health centers, abortion services became firmly entrenched as outpatient health services. In 1992 only 7 percent of abortions were performed in hospitals, whereas in 1973 more than half of all abortions had been performed in hospitals.[16] This assured that first-trimester abortions in this country would be appropriately demedicalized. (In contrast, European countries have adhered to a more medical, hospital-based approach.)

Unfortunately, relatively few of these centers have survived, especially in the face of competition from imitative facilities run by hospitals.[17] Some continue to offer an important model of how to provide responsive care in a politically conscious fashion. Several produce outstanding newsletters that are distributed nationally.

As early as the mid-1970s, the WHM addressed controversies surrounding breast cancer. For many years the standard practice of American doctors, upon doing a breast biopsy and finding malignant tissue, was to proceed immediately with a mastectomy. Several years of hard work during the 1970s, especially on the part of activist and journalist Rose Kushner, who has since died from the disease, resulted in a landmark recommendation by the National Cancer Institute that in most cases breast biopsies should be performed as part of a two-step procedure. The panel advised that a diagnostic biopsy specimen be studied with permanent histologic sections before various treatment options are discussed. This represented an important step forward in the treatment of breast cancer and also increased general awareness of the importance of nonsurgical treatments.

In the early 1980s, the WHM publicized the early results of clinical trials as, for example, in instances where lumpectomies represented an improved approach over more radical forms of surgery. Activists also challenged the overuse and misuse of chemotherapy.[18] By the late 1980s, WHM activists and other women with breast cancer founded the first of many grassroots women's cancer groups that challenged the failure of the breast cancer establishment to adequately

address causation and prevention of breast cancer.[19] In the early 1990s, many of these groups formed the National Breast Cancer Coalition, which has continued to press for laywomen's involvement in breast cancer policy-setting at all levels.[20]

Conclusion

As the WHM moves into the next century, the ability to build broad coalitions will, to a large extent, determine the political effectiveness of women's health care advocates. The emergence of "single-issue" organizations, such as the Endometriosis Association and the Interstitial Cystitis Association, may make it harder to keep the broader feminist context in focus. The WHM's success in influencing national health care reform will depend upon effective collaboration and networking among many diverse organizations.

Although the WHM has had a significant impact on the consciousness of many, most medical institutions remain largely unchanged. Many of the inequities that stirred feminists to action in the early 1970s continue to exist. Poverty, the single most important factor affecting health and well-being, continues to affect a growing percentage of the population. Violence persists as a major cause of disability and death among women. Amid worsening statistics, it will take patience, stubborn persistence, and a good sense of humor to sustain a movement that has had much to be proud of.

NOTES

1. For example, see *HealthRight* (New York: Women's Health Forum, 1974–1979), *WomenWise* (Concord, N.H.: New Hampshire Feminist Health Center), and the *Santa Cruz [Calif.] Women's Health Center Newsletter* (Santa Cruz: Santa Cruz Women's Health Center).

2. For an extended discussion of what has happened to many of these groups, see "Women's Health Movement Organizations: Two Decades of Struggle and Change," a report by Sandra Morgen and Alice Julier, 1991. Copies available from Sandra Morgen, Center for the Study of Women in Society, Prince Lucien Campbell Hall, University of Oregon, Eugene, OR 97403.

3. For example, these organizations include the National Black Women's Health Project (Atlanta, Ga.), the National Latina Health Organization (Oakland, Calif.), the Native American Health Education Resource Center (Lake Andes, S.D.), and the National Women of Color Reproductive Health Coalition.

4. For example, the Project on Women and Disability (Boston, Mass.), Lyon-Martin Women's Health Center (San Francisco, Calif.), and *Radiance: A Publication for Large Women* (Oakland, Calif.: Radiance Enterprises).

5. See Susan Bell, "Political Gynecology: Gynecological Imperialism and the Politics of Self-Help," *Science for the People* II, no. 5 (1979): 8–14.

6. See Gena Corea's classic book *The Hidden Malpractice: How American Medicine Mistreats Women* (New York: Harper & Row, 1985) and Diana Scully's *Men Who Control Women's Health, supra* note 12.

7. Dr. Antonia Novello and Dr. Joycelyn Elders, who was forced to resign in late 1994 because of her outspokenness on the importance of sexuality education and access to contraception for teens.

8. Dr. Bernadine Healey, who left her position in the summer of 1993.

9. See "Breast Cancer: A National Strategy/A Report to the Nation," by the President's Cancer Panel/Special Commission on Breast Cancer, NIH, October 1993, p. 3. This same subject arose earlier at the Workshop on Opportunities for Research on Women's Health, sponsored by the Office of Research on Women's Health, September 1991, Huntsville, Md.

10. Currently, the United States and South Africa remain the only industrialized countries without such programs, a scandal that this country continues to tolerate.

11. At that time, birth-control pills contained much more estrogen (and carried greater risks) than the current low-dose estrogen pill.

12. See "The Phoenix Rises: Patient Package Inserts Reborn," *Network News* [newsletter of the National Women's Health Network], 19, no. 6 (November/December, 1994): 4.

13. Cynthia Pearson, Program Director, National Women's Health Network, personal communication, February 1995.

14. Allan Chase, "American Indian Women Not Fully Informed, FAO Study Finds," *Medical Tribune,* August 10, 1977, 1, 6; Allan Chase, "Passing the Word on Sterilization 1933–1977," *Medical Tribune,* September 21, 1977, p. 1.

15. The hearings were held before the Department of Health, Education and Welfare during 1978; a federal hearing was conducted on January 17, 1978, and accompanied by numerous regional hearings.

16. Stanley K. Henshaw and Jennifer Van Vort, "Abortion Services in the United States, 1991 and 1992," *Family Planning Perspectives* 26, no. 3 (May/June 1994): 112.

17. Interestingly, in a country like Australia, where services are largely state supported, public funding has ensured the continued existence of women's health centers. Women in Melbourne even succeeded in obtaining approximately $400,000 from the Victorian government to start a women's health information center. The women's health movement in Australia is in many respects stronger than its American counterpart because of its ability to influence government expenditures and create a more stable financial base for women-directed services and advocacy.

18. See Susan Rennie, "Breast Cancer: The Latest Conference Results," *Network News* 10, no. 6 (November/December 1985): 3.

19. See Susan Ferraro, "The Anguished Politics of Breast Cancer," *New York Times Magazine,* August 15, 1993, 25; Monte Paulsen, "The Profits of Misery/Breast Cancer and the Environment: How the Chemical Industry Profits from an Epidemic It May Be Causing," *Detroit Metro Times,* May 19–25, 1993, 12; "The Politics of Breast Cancer," *Ms.,* May/June 1993, 37–60.

20. See "The Phoenix Rises: Patient Package Inserts Reborn," *Network News* [newsletter of the National Women's Health Network], 19, no. 6 (November/December 1994): 4.

More than Mothers and Whores: Redefining the AIDS Prevention Needs of Women

KATHRYN CAROVANO

Although women are at high risk for HIV/AIDS, the needs of poor women have not been addressed until recently. Patriarchal attitudes and underreporting constitute major threats to women and children in the age of HIV/AIDS.

Women are increasingly at risk for AIDS. At the root of this risk is women's relative lack of control over their bodies and their lives. Those women with least control, generally poor women of color, are at greatest risk in both developed and developing countries. To date, AIDS prevention programs have ignored most women, focusing almost exclusively on women in the sex industry and, more recently, prenatal women. We urgently need prevention programs for women that view women as more than "mothers and whores" and recognize that AIDS poses a real risk to many of us, programs that are sensitive to the complex realities of women's lives and offer realistic alternatives that will allow women to protect themselves from HIV infection.

In the spring of 1989, while I was working in Lima, Peru, a group of feminist women organized a meeting so that I could talk with them about women and AIDS. We talked a lot about the risks to women and about what they thought could be done, and we got into a discussion of options: the condom and nonpenetrative sex. Frescia, a health educator there, told me this story:

> We had just finished a health promotion program with a group of women and we asked them to fill

out an evaluation form. One of the women who was very good during the training was taking a long time to finish the questionnaire, so I asked her if she was having trouble with it. She told me that she was having a hard time reading it, so I asked her if maybe she needed to use glasses. She said yes, that she had had her eyes tested 10 years ago, and the doctor had prescribed glasses for her. She had bought a pair but lost them a few months later. To explain why she had never gotten a new pair she said, "My husband told me that I was so stupid that he would never buy me another pair of glasses." So just imagine this woman asking her husband to use a condom or consider having nonpenetrative sex.

Around the world, women are at increasing risk for AIDS. At the root of this risk is women's lack of control over their bodies and their lives. As Herbert Daniel[1], a writer and activist living with AIDS in Brazil, has pointed out, "Like every other epidemic,

This article was prepared with funds provided by the Academy for Educational Development, Inc., as Prime Contractor to the U.S. Agency for International Development under Prime Contract Number DPE-5972-Z-00-7070-00 for the AIDSCOM Project.

An earlier version of this article was presented at the International Conference on the Implications of AIDS for Mothers and Children, Paris, France, November 29, 1989.

Kathryn Carovano, "More than Mothers and Whores: Redefining the AIDS Prevention Needs of Women," *International Journal of Health Services,* Vol 21.1 (1991): 131–35.

International Journal of Health Services, Volume 21, Number 1, pages 131–42, 1991. © 1991, Baywood Publishing Co., Inc.

AIDS develops in the cracks and crevasses of society's inequalities. We cannot face the epidemic if we try to hide the contradictions and conflicts which it exposes."

As the AIDS epidemic continues to unfold, we are being forced to confront once again one of society's more glaring inequalities—the inequality of the sexes. The relative lack of control by women in relation to men, particularly in the context of sexual relations, places them at increasing risk for AIDS. Those women with the least control, generally poor women of color, are those who face the greatest risk. In order to develop effective AIDS prevention programs, we must confront the challenges that this "crack" exposes and develop programs that give women control over their sexuality and over their own lives. A first step toward developing prevention programs for women is to recognize that women are primarily at risk for AIDS because they are sexually active and that their sexual activity goes beyond the simplified realms of sex for procreation or sex for money. Sex for some is for pleasure. And for many women, sex is simply part of survival.

Throughout the world, women's sexual identities have long been defined on the basis of their reproductive capacity and, to a lesser degree, their involvement in commercial sex. Motherhood legitimizes a woman's sexuality—and very often her life—while prostitution provides women with a means of survival, though with a heavy stigma. Women in many societies have traditionally been identified sexually as either mothers or whores, "good girls" or "bad girls." In examining current AIDS prevention efforts for women, one finds that this dichotomy dominates and is being utilized as a framework to identify the risks posed to and by women. Many societies regard the sensuous, sexual woman as "bad" and, in essence, only "bad girls" are perceived to be at risk for AIDS. "Good girls" in contrast, are viewed as asexual or their sexuality is relegated to the socially sanctioned realm of sex for procreation, which is seen as unrelated to HIV transmission. Both "mother" and "prostitute" are definitions for women that are based on their relationships to others; "As women we are so often defined by who leans on us. Being needed names us"[2]. In the context of AIDS, these definitions reflect the needs of men and children, and it is in their relationship to the HIV-infected woman that she becomes a concern or threat.

The focus on these particular identities, "mother" and "prostitute," among the many that define women, leads one easily to the hypothesis that efforts to prevent AIDS among women have been the result not of a concern for women, but rather a concern that is primarily about protecting the health of men and children.

The impact of this thinking is reflected by the fact that to date, most AIDS prevention programs for women have been designed exclusively to reach women in the sex industry. Women engaged in prostitution have been identified as one of the principal "reservoirs" for HIV and, as such, a "risk group" that threatens the "general population." Faced with increasing numbers of children at risk for AIDS as a result of rising infection rates among women, new programs are also being formulated to target prenatal women. Unfortunately, those women—and they are most of us—who do not fall into one of these limited spheres are being largely ignored by program planners and implementing agencies working in AIDS prevention. Not surprisingly, the numbers of AIDS cases reported among women continue to grow at alarming rates.

The Epidemiology of AIDS among Women

According to the World Health Organization, of the estimated 600,000 people who developed AIDS in the 1980s, over 150,000 were women. During the next two years, 500,000 more people will develop AIDS and of these, 200,000 are expected to be women. In other words, more women are expected to become ill with AIDS during 1990 and 1991 than developed AIDS during the last decade.[3]

These figures are alarming as they stand, yet the actual number of women who have died or are living with AIDS is undoubtedly far greater even than these numbers convey. Underreporting of AIDS cases is a recognized problem throughout the developing world, and underreporting of cases among women is a problem everywhere. Problems of reporting cases among women result from factors as varied as women's lack of access to health care, the exclusion of "female diseases" in the diagnostic criteria for AIDS, and the persistent attitude among many physicians that "good girls don't get AIDS." Despite these problems, data still show that women around the world are being diagnosed with AIDS in ever-increasing numbers and most of them are poor women of color, whether they are living in Newark, Bangkok, Nairobi, or Rio de Janeiro.

In the United States, the proportion of the total AIDS cases occurring among women rose from 7 percent of cases reported before 1985 to 11 percent of cases reported during the first half of 1989.[4] In Frankfurt, West Germany, the percentage of HIV-infected patients who are women rose from 4 percent in 1984 to 25 percent in 1988.[5] Throughout much of sub-Saharan Africa, women represent 50 percent or more of AIDS cases, and similar ratios have been reported in some parts of the English-speaking Caribbean. Studies conducted among pregnant women have revealed seroprevalence rates of 10.5 percent in Port au Prince, Haiti, and 24 percent in Kampala, Uganda. In Latin America and Asia, women currently make up a small but growing percentage of reported cases. The growth of pediatric AIDS cases reveals the ripple effect of HIV infection in women; according to James Grant[6], Director General of UNICEF, over 90 percent of pediatric AIDS cases are the result of perinatal transmission. AIDS accounts for up to one-third of all deaths to children in some African cities, and in some parts of New York City, one of every 100 babies is born with HIV infection.[7] UNICEF has projected that the average infant mortality rate in 10 East and Central African countries will rise from a current rate of 164 deaths per 1,000 to 185 per 1,000 by the year 2000; prior to the introduction of HIV, these rates had been projected to fall to 130 per 1000 during the next decade. In addition, UNICEF has estimated that in these countries, as many as 5 million children will have lost their parents to AIDS by the end of the decade.[6] A survey conducted in 1989 in the Rakai district of Uganda—the region hardest hit by AIDS—found that 23,351 children had already lost one or both parents, the majority of them to AIDS.[8]

These alarming statistics indicate the need to develop AIDS prevention programs that provide information and sexual empowerment to all sexually active women. The remainder of this article will look at the risks that AIDS poses to specific segments of the population of women, beginning with young, adolescent women.

Adolescent Women

If knowledge were power, then adolescent women would probably be among the least powerful—and in fact they are when it comes to their ability to protect themselves against HIV infection.

The guiding philosophy in dealing with adolescent sexuality in many cultures is "if you don't talk about sex they won't do it." This logic, however, is critically flawed. Adolescents are sexual beings at varying stages of self-awareness and understanding. Many of them do and will continue to engage in sexual intercourse despite lack of access to any accurate information about sex. Unfortunately, if you do not talk to them, they will almost undoubtedly also engage in "unsafe sex." Sex can and does occur without much understanding; "safe" sex requires an ability to distinguish between risky and nonrisky sexual activities *and* an ability to choose safer sex.

Whether or not you talk about it, teens clearly are having sex. Many women—and most men—have their first sexual relations prior to marriage, usually during their teens, and most often those first encounters are unprotected. Research in family planning has revealed that the quality of reproductive health information is generally low among adolescents. This is a reflection in part of the lack of social acceptance of providing sex education and contraceptive services to teens in many countries. In the developing world, contraceptive services are often available only to married women, and in some situations, only to women who have already borne one or more children.[9]

In most of the world's countries, births to women under 20 represent a significant proportion of all births; in Swaziland a study conducted in 1985 reported that over 30 percent of children were born to women between 15 and 19 years of age.[10] According to evidence from the World Fertility Survey, the average fertility rate for women aged 15 to 19 in developing countries is 8.7 percent of the global total. High levels of adolescent pregnancy and teenage abortions reported in Japan,[12] Nigeria,[13] and Baltimore, Maryland,[14] reflect the reality of high levels of sexual activity and low levels of correct contraceptive use among adolescents.

Given the sexual practices of teens, the threat of AIDS cannot be ignored. In 1989 in the United States,

26.3 percent ($n = 4,306$) of the AIDS cases reported among females occurred among women between 20 and 29 years of age.[15] Given the long incubation period for AIDS, the majority of these women may very well have been infected during adolescence. A survey conducted in 1988 in a New York City shelter found that 18 percent of the girls in the study tested positive for HIV antibody.[16] In some African cities where infection rates among sexually active adults have reached 30 to 40 percent, the risk of exposure through sexual contact is extremely high. Young women tend to have their first sexual encounter later than their male peers, hence even their first contact could place them at risk for HIV. In Uganda, older men are reportedly looking to young school girls instead of prostitutes for "AIDS-free sex".[17]

AIDS prevention programs for adolescent women and girls, in school, while increasingly common in developed countries, are still extremely rare in the developing world. The need for such programs is critical, though given the very early school dropout rates of many girls in developing countries, school-based programs alone are not enough. On average, 44 percent of never-married women in the developing world have received no formal education and of those who have, only 7 percent have 10 or more years of schooling (11, p. 217). Out-of-school programs will be critical in reaching young minority women in many developed countries as well.

Adolescent women, like everyone else, need to be given information that offers them choices and is based on an understanding of their sexual behavior. Studies of adolescents who have received sex education have shown that they are not likely to engage in sex any sooner or any more frequently than their uninformed peers, but they are more likely to use contraceptives.[18] Sex education and AIDS information are not aphrodisiacs but rather basic tools for adolescent health and survival. To deny adolescents access is to leave them powerless and at high risk for HIV.

REFERENCES

1. Daniel, H. *Vida antes da Morte/Life before Death,* p. 37. Escritorio e Tipografia Jaboti Ltda, Rio de Janeiro, Brazil, 1989.
2. Moskowitz, F. *A Leak in the Heart: Tales from a Woman's Life,* p. 99. David R. Godine, Boston, 1985.
3. Mann, J. Women, Mothers, Children and the Global AIDS Strategy. Paper presented at the International Conference on the Implications of AIDS for Mothers and Children, Paris, November 27, 1989.
4. "Current Trends: First 100,000 Cases of AIDS—United States." *MMWR* 38: 561–63, 1989.
5. Staszewski, S. Epidemiology of HIV Infection in Women from Frankfurt Area. Poster presented at the Fifth International Conference on AIDS, Montreal, June 7, 1989.
6. Grant, J. UNICEF's Present Policy and New Approaches. Paper presented at the International Conference on the Implications of AIDS for Mothers and Children, Paris, November 27, 1989.
7. New York State Department of Health. *Status Report: IIIV Seroprevalence Study.* Albany, N.Y., July 1988.
8. U.S. Department of State. Pediatric AIDS Prevention under FY 90 Child Survival FRA. Unclassified Cable. American Embassy, Kampala, Uganda, December 5, 1989.
9. Germain, A., and Ordway, J. *Population Control and Women's Health: Balancing the Scales,* pp. 1–15. International Women's Health Coalition, Washington, D.C., June 1989.
10. Gule, G. Z. *Youth Education and Services for Health and Family Life: Situation Analysis in Swaziland,* p. 28. International Planned Parenthood Federation, Africa Region, July 1985.
11. United Nations. *Fertility Behavior in the Context of Development: Evidence from the World Fertility Survey.* New York, 1987.
12. Hayashi, K. "Adolescent Sexual Activities and Fertility in Japan." *Bull. Inst. Public Health* 32(2–4): 88–94, 1983.
13. Nichols, D., et al. "Sexual Behavior, Contraceptive Practice and Reproductive Health among Nigerian Adolescents." *Stud. Fam. Plann.* 17:110–116, 1986.
14. Governor's Task Force on Teen Pregnancy. *A Call to Action: Final Report, Governor's Task Force on Teen Pregnancy, State of Maryland,* p. 56. Annapolis, September 1985.
15. Centers for Disease Control. "AIDS Cases by Sex, Age at Diagnosis, and Race Ethnicity, Reported through June 1998, United States." In *HIV/AIDS among Racial and Ethnic Populations,* p. 3. Atlanta, June 1989.
16. Foley, M. J. "Women Health Policymakers: Interview with Dr. Mathilde Krim." *The Network News* (National Women's Health Network) 13(6):52, 1988.
17. Ojulu, E. "Ugandan Prostitutes Are Now Wiser." *New African,* September, 1988, p. 34.
18. "Youth in the 1980s: Social and Health Concerns." *Popul. Rep [M]* 12: M349–M388, 1985.

Norplant Information Sheet
NATIONAL LATINA HEALTH ORGANIZATION

This sheet has been used as a tool for community education to raise awareness regarding population control and reproductive freedom.

The National Latina Health Organization (NLHO) is committed to work toward the goal of bilingual access to quality health care and the empowerment of Latinas through culturally sensitive educational programs, health advocacy, outreach, research, and the development of public policy.

The NLHO would like to break some myths and set the record straight. . . . Latinas do believe in reproductive rights, do use birth control, do get abortions, and do believe passionately that women should be able to make their own reproductive decisions without any political, social, or religious interference. An 84-year-old Mexican Catholic woman sums it up very neatly: "If women don't have that (right), what do they have?"

Norplant . . . is it the answer to a woman's prayers? Or is it a form of social control that will be used to control the reproduction of particular groups of women? Is it a safe form of birth control?

The National Latina Health Organization is very concerned with its safety. The NLHO does not feel that there has been sufficient research done. We are not convinced that 20 years of research is enough to give us information on long-term effects and generational

National Latina Health Organization, "Norplant Information Sheet," in *Women's Health: Readings on Social, Economic, and Political Issues* (2nd ed), Nancy Worcester and Marianne H. Whatley, eds. Dubuque, Iowa: Kendall/Hunt Publishing Company, 1996: 274–76.

effects. No research or testing has been conducted on women under 18 years of age, so we don't know the short- or long-term effects on them. Food and Drug Administration (FDA) requirements and criteria and the FDA seal of approval do not guarantee the complete safety of Norplant. We are still living with the results of the Dalkon shield, Depo-Provera, and silicone breast implants.

We are concerned that actual and possible side effects and the degree of their seriousness have been down played by many health practitioners. Irregular bleeding occurs in 80% of all women. This can mean bleeding two weeks out of the month or not having periods at all. We are concerned that irregular bleeding, an early symptom of uterine cancer, is not being dealt with. Once women are implanted, how will they know whether the irregular bleeding is due to Norplant or an actual symptom of cancer? There is no set protocol on how soon a woman should be examined after Norplant insertion. Will those women who do not have access to regular health care but have been implanted with Norplant have the regular exams that they need?

Side effects also include headaches, mood changes, and acne. The so-called experts are saying that women with high blood pressure and smokers don't have any special concerns. But the Office of Family Planning Policy Statement Guidelines of California and the Wyeth "Norplant System Patient Labeling" make a point of this. To quote, "Women who use the oral contraceptives should not smoke as it greatly increases the risk of serious adverse effects on the heart and blood vessels; therefore, it is likely that it may be a problem with Norplant use." There is no consensus in the medical field that side effects and conditions that are specific to estrogen-based oral contraceptives need not be considered with Norplant.

We are concerned with how quickly Norplant and funding were made available in all 50 states and the District of Columbia—so quickly that there wasn't adequate or language-appropriate information available so women could truly be able to make an informed decision. In February of 1992, the state of California made $5 million dollars available to provide Norplant to women eligible for the Office of Family Planning and Medi-Cal services. How much of this money is being used to target and inform specific or particular groups of women, i.e., women on welfare, Immigrant women, or women of color? This has never been done before for any other type of birth control. Hundreds of health personnel have been trained to implant Norplant, but they have not all been trained to remove it.

We are not being paranoid when we question the ethics of Norplant. We have been victims of selective reproductive control before. The forced sterilization of Latinas and other women of color was blatant and widespread until the class action suit against U.S.C.-Los Angeles County Medical Center in 1975. Approximately 12 Chicanas had undergone forced sterilization, in some instances without their knowledge. One of the results of this case is that sterilization consent forms are now multilingual. Yet these abuses continue to happen, sometimes in very subtle ways . . . doctors will not give all information necessary so women can make their own decisions; or they will give their "medical opinion" for what they think is "best."

The overt and covert coercion of the "Norping" of women is our biggest concern. When women go to their clinics for birth control, is Norplant the only birth-control method available at their clinic? Is it low cost or free? Are other forms of birth control equally available, equally recommended, and equally funded? Are appointments for other forms of birth control difficult to schedule? Once Norplant is implanted, will there be trained personnel available to remove it at the end of five years? If a woman wants it removed before the fifth year, will it be difficult to schedule an appointment for its removal? Will her request be granted? Will she be encouraged to keep it in another few months? Will it be removed regardless of whether she can afford the removal fee that can be as high as $300?

Obviously this is the real issue. Norplant is NOT WOMAN CONTROLLED. So whose control is it under?

What are most alarming about Norplant are the immediate potential for and actual abuse. Norplant was approved by the FDA in late December 1990. By January 5, 1991, Judge Broadman in Visalia, California, ordered a woman to have Norplant implanted as a condition of her probation. Seven states have introduced legislative bills involving Norplant since then. One type links the use of Norplant and public assistance benefits, either by providing financial incentives to encourage women who receive financial assistance to use Norplant or by requiring Norplant use as a condition for receiving public assistance. The second mandates that women convicted of particular crimes, usually child abuse, child neglect, or drug use, be required to have Norplant implanted. Assemblyman Murry in the 56th District of California attempted to pass a bill that linked AFDC benefits to Norplant. Fortunately this bill no longer exists in any recognizable form because of the NLHO involvement at the state level.

We are hearing from Latinas that they are being pressured into using Norplant rather than other contraceptives. We know that some clinics have Spanish-language Norplant pamphlets in their waiting rooms, but none in English. We know that Native American women on reservations are being "Norped." On a reservation in Montana, a large majority of the young teens have been "Norped," yet nowhere on the reservation are there condoms available. A woman from another state came to an Oakland clinic during the summer of 1992 to have Norplant removed after a judge in her home state had ordered her implanted. The clinic did not remove the Norplant until it had called a meeting of its medical board. Why wasn't it removed on demand?

We know that there are very unethical practices being used when health providers are trained to implant Norplant. A woman in Southern California complained that after she was recruited to have Norplant implanted free of charge, her calls were not returned when she requested that Norplant be removed because of the side effects. When her call was finally returned, she was told that it would cost her $300 to have it removed. We alerted "Street Stories," a television program in New York that was preparing a story on Norplant. With the permission of the young woman, a

"Street Stories" reporter contacted the clinic. The clinic providers were very upset and couldn't understand why the young woman thought she could not have it removed. Why must we go through these extraordinary efforts?

The Baltimore School is now making Norplant available through its school clinic. It is extremely important to note that the Norplant "consent forms" state that the removal of Norplant may not be available through its clinic and that one may have to go to another clinic for removal at the individual's own expense. In addition, when the Health Department Director and the clinic director were questioned about the sex education that was provided for their students, they admitted that students only get a few hours of sex education during their entire junior high and high school career.

A clinic provider (who wishes to remain anonymous) in Savannah, Georgia, claims that young adolescent women are being encouraged to accept Norplant. The Norplant "consent form" states that if the individual wants it removed, she will have to go to a local hospital for the procedure, and that it is up to the hospital to decide whether it will be removed or not.

Clinics in South Dakota are adopting the policy of not removing Norplant unless it is "medically indicated." A woman cannot have it removed simply because she requests it for whatever reason. If side effects are intolerable to her, it is still up to the provider to decide whether it should be removed.

A social worker in New Jersey has counseled a young mother who cut the Norplant out of her own arm because her clinic providers refused to remove it.

After having Norplant implanted, a young black adolescent in Atlanta complained about irregular bleeding to her provider. The provider prescribed oral contraceptives to regulate her menstrual cycle. Now this young woman has two systemic hormonal contraceptives coursing through her body.

A clinic in San Francisco at first refused to accept young Asian women in their clinic because they were prostitutes. They were told that it did not accept "their kind of people," that it served middle-class white women. Once an advocate intervened so that the women could be taken care of, the clinic provider kept encouraging the use of Norplant and would not offer another method.

These are the stories we are hearing; there are hundreds more untold stories that have not reached us yet. The women of Color Coalition for Reproductive Health Rights, along with other organizations, have been meeting with David Kessler, Commissioner of the FDA, his staff, and Patsy Fleming and Dennis Hayashi of Donna Shalala's office (the Department of Health, Education, and Welfare) to discuss our deep concerns regarding the abuse of Norplant. We must keep telling these stories and advocating for and intervening for women that have no other recourse.

The National Latina Health Organization believes that women should have all reproductive options available . . . culturally relevant quality health care and information; education about sexuality; alternative forms of woman-controlled birth control that are safe and affordable; prenatal care so that we can have healthy babies; fertility services; safe and legal abortions; and freedom from reproductive abuses. The NLHO also believes that all forms of birth control should be developed with the purpose of giving safe, affordable choices to women of all ages so that they can control their own reproductive lives. This is not an unreasonable expectation. It is a very sane and logical expectation.

The Egyptian Women's Health Book Collective
NADIA FARAH

Nadia Farah discusses how strategies for women's health education that may work in one situation may not be as effective or appropriate in another. In this example, she describes the efforts of a group of Egyptian women to adapt the well-known guide written in the United States, Our Bodies, Ourselves, *to take into consideration the priorities of Egyptian women.*

The publication of the Boston Women's Health Book Collective's famous and controversial book *Our Bodies, Ourselves* (1976) created wide repercussions and charted a way for women all over the world to gain personal control, through the possession of objective and necessary information, over their own bodies, health status, and lives.

A group of interested Egyptian women started to meet in May 1985 with the idea of finding ways to spread the message of the book to Egyptian and Arab women. They agreed to form a collective to produce a similar book in Arabic.

The process started by recruiting a coordinator. The coordinator set three rules for the choice of the collective members: first, members should come from different disciplines and share a deep commitment to women's rights; second, they should reflect different social classes, in order to offset the middle-class bias of most professional women; and third, they should encompass different age brackets.

Formation

The original group was made up of 22 women. An initial meeting in the Suez Canal city of Ismailia set the

Nadia Farah, "The Egyptian Women's Health Book Collective," *Middle East Report,* Vol. 21.6 (Nov/Dec 1991): 16–7, 25.

agenda for the collective. The major decisions taken in Ismailia guided the work of the collective over the next five years and are still operative. These decisions entailed the following:

- It was important to write a book in Arabic, by women and for women, to provide correct and objective information on women's bodies and health. A review of books available in Arabic revealed that they were either highly technical, and therefore unintelligible to most women, or trivial and condescending.
- Our purpose was to produce an original book, taking into consideration the Egyptian and Arab cultural context and emphasizing prominent problems of women in the Arab world. An early idea of simply translating the American edition was rejected because it is couched in a cultural context alien to most Egyptian and Arab women and it reflects the priorities of American women. While women's issues are international, the specific problems and priorities differ from one area to another.
- The Egyptian book should be written from the perspective of women and in a friendly and accessible style. It should emphasize the provision of objective information in order to respect the freedom of women readers to formulate their own decisions.
- All decisions about the book's content, format, illustrations, publication, and distribution should be made collectively and democratically.
- Finally, the collective decided on a broad outline of the contents and divided the book into two main parts. The first part adopted a life-cycle approach to women's health from childhood to after menopause; the second part dealt with particular issues such as work, nutrition, violence, traditional health care, and social and psychological pressures on women.

Dynamics

While the collective process was arduous and time consuming, it was very rewarding. Topics were assigned to the collective members, and each chapter was written by at least two members. All collective members then read each chapter, and criticisms or other ideas were incorporated into later versions in order to insure the collective nature of the text. Some members who were very sensitive to criticism or could not abide by the collective's ideas preferred to leave the collective. While it was hard to see some appreciated members abandon the process, the collective stuck by its initial decision of collaborative writing.

The subjects to be covered by the book stirred some heated debates. Some of the most controversial issues were female circumcision, violence against women, lesbianism, and the right of patients to question methods and procedures of medical treatment.

In many Western feminist health books that discuss Middle Eastern or Muslim women, the entire issue of women's health is reduced to that of female circumcision. An understandable reaction to this attitude was an aversion by Arab women to discuss the issue at all. After many discussions, the members of the collective agreed to present the issue of circumcision in a way that explained the cultural context allowing the continuation of the practice and that offered objective information on the drawbacks of the practice to women readers.

The issue of lesbianism was another topic of heated debate. Western books on women and health seem to offer positive views of lesbianism, regarding it as a way for female liberation. In the Egyptian and Arab cultural context, simply writing about lesbianism might have threatened the whole book with censure from the religious authorities. Our research revealed that lesbianism is a very minor issue in Egypt and not one of the main priorities of Egyptian women for the moment. Therefore, the collective decided to drop the issue of lesbianism from its current edition.

A divisive issue that received a lot of attention from the collective members was the issue of rape. Many women, even among the collective, thought that women themselves are responsible for rape. It took many sessions and a self-education process to convince all members of the collective that rape is not a sexual crime but a crime of violence. Other members were skeptical of suggesting that violence against women is perpetrated solely by males against females, so we supplemented the chapter on violence with a discussion of violence by women against other women.

The last area of wide discussion and controversy was the right of patients to question medical treatment. The collective had insisted from the beginning on the right of women to ask for a second opinion when the matter was a grave one and involved dangerous treatment or surgery. Medical professionals who are members of the collective objected strongly to this attitude, claiming that the doctor knows best. After many discussions and debates, the collective insisted on the right of women patients to question medical treatment if there is any doubt in their mind. The book encourages women to exercise their free right to question any medical treatment and to seek another opinion in grave cases, or whenever they feel they need a second opinion.

The collective met regularly for two years to discuss fully every chapter of the book. By mid-1987, the collective held a seminar to discuss the first draft. Outside consultants and professionals were invited to critique the material, and their comments were taken seriously in rewriting the first draft.

The collective also hired a technical expert to work on the illustrations, which varied from medical graphs to photos and cartoons. After the completion of the illustrations, two chapters of the book were pretested. A sample of 100 women, from all age groups and most urban social classes, reviewed these two chapters. The comments were very positive and encouraging. However, the interviewees objected to the use of cartoons, and we decided to drop these from the book.

After we took into consideration different responses from the experts and the public, a final draft was ready by the end of 1988. The collective then decided to pretest the whole manuscript again to make sure that the book responded to the concerns of Egyptian women. The second pretest revealed the enthusiasm of women for such a book. One woman wrote to say that, for the first time, she felt that women had a voice and that they were speaking to her concerns and problems.

✑Publication

After a lengthy process of searching for a suitable publisher, the collective finally decided on a woman-owned publishing firm. The publisher, while enthusiastic, was a bit hesitant about the public reception of the book. The book finally appeared in early 1991, and the collective held a public seminar to discuss the book in May 1991. The book was received enthusiastically, especially by different women's groups, and members of the collective are constantly invited to discuss the book with different groups. The publisher's qualms about sales were completely put to rest.

In one of the meetings to discuss the book with a group of Palestinian women, one young woman confronted me. She expressed her agony at being illiterate and therefore being deprived of reading such a book.

She then asked if the collective could put the information on cassette tapes so it could be accessible to illiterate women.

The collective is now pursuing this idea, and a project is under way to reissue the book in separate pamphlets that can be used in literacy classes in conjunction with cassette tapes of the material in each pamphlet. We are hopeful that this process can also help in eradicating illiteracy, which plagues over 60 percent of Arab women.

For the moment, the collective is receiving from various Arab women's groups requests to buy the book. Some women have written to ask for help in forming sister organizations in other Arab countries. We hope that the message of the book will spread in the whole of the Arab world and will start a larger movement for the improvement of women's rights in the Arab world.

Reading F

Reproductive Health
LOIS M. SMITH AND ALFRED PADULA

Lois Smith and Alfred Padula discuss Cuban medicine's "high-tech" approach to the state of women's health care during the Castro era. While many feminists in the Western world hesitated to endorse the use of advanced and new technologies in health care organizing, the Cuban government pursued an aggressive strategy to address maternal and women's health. Smith and Padula argue that, while this approach had many benefits, it failed to take into account entrenched patriarchal attitudes toward women's sexuality.

Lois M. Smith and Alfred Padula, "Reproductive Health," in *Sex and Revolution: Women in Socialist Cuba,* New York: Oxford University Press, 1996: 78–81.

✑New Birth Technologies

The "technification" of birth, which was rejected by some feminist critics of Western health care systems, was enthusiastically pursued in Cuba. By 1975, Cuban hospitals were routinely using estrogen measurers, ultrasound, and fetal monitors.

In the 1980s research in genetic diseases, study of infertility, and an improvement in prenatal diagnoses were the focus of the maternal health system.[1] A wide range of prenatal testing was offered, including diagnosis of hemophilia A and B, toxoplasmosis, and the alphafeto protein series. All women between the sixteenth and nineteenth week of pregnancy were to be tested for fetal development and advised of the implications of continuing a problematic pregnancy. Abortions were performed through the sixth month, and the aborted fetuses were used for research on congenital defects. A final test for infant allergies would be performed upon birth, with blood taken from the umbilical cord. In 1987, tests done on approximately 90 percent of the island's more than 200,000 pregnant women identified about 1,000 defects.[2]

Prenatal testing raised difficult ethical issues. Should a fetus with a congenital disease that meant agony for the child and the parents and great expense for the state be aborted? Fidel Castro was sure that every mother would like to know the condition of the fetus and have the option of terminating the pregnancy:

> I don't want to get into matters of religious dogma on this topic. In my opinion this has nothing to do with religion. It has to do with the most elementary common sense and human compassion, because we've seen the tragedy this means to the family.[3]

Cuban officials insisted that they would not pressure women to terminate problem pregnancies, however. In 1986 the president of the Cuban Obstetric-Gynecological Association, Dr. Ada Ovies, indicated that while medical personnel would point out all the difficulties of raising a child with a particular deformity, women would never be forced to terminate their pregnancy. In 1987 Castro stated that "of course, nobody is compelled to undergo an abortion."[4]

Still, some women seemed to be uncomfortable with Cuban medicine's high-tech approach. In 1988 the Mariana Grajales Hospital in Santa Clara lost its title as a model medical facility because of complaints that doctors "had forgotten that the modern equipment was there to back them up, not to represent them."[5]

The treatment of infertility in Cuba has also advanced, and attitudes have changed, if slowly. In 1966, men were reminded that, despite the popular belief that women were responsible for infertility, one-third of infertility cases involved problems with the male. In addition, men were chided for being hesitant to submit to the simplest test while women, anxious to conceive, bravely endured a wide range of uncomfortable procedures.[6]

In 1989 Cuban research showed that one in ten couples was experiencing difficulty in conceiving. The most common causes proved to be low sperm count, abortion-related obstructions, and pelvic inflammation due to IUDs. Each of the patients treated for infertility cost the Cuban state some 200 pesos, primarily for medicines to stimulate ovulation.[7] Fertility counseling was available to patients aged 20 to 40. To be accepted for treatment, a couple had to have been having a stable sexual relationship for two to three years. Sometimes exercises, special diets, and vitamin supplements were prescribed to help with conception, and fertility drugs were also used.[8]

In December 1986 Baby Luis, Cuba's first test-tube baby, was born in Havana. The mother, an office worker, had had an abortion at age 14 which left her fallopian tubes permanently blocked. By June 1989 four babies had been born in Cuba as a result of in vitro fertilization, and there were currently four more in vitro pregnancies in progress; 260 women between the ages of 20 and 35 were enrolled in the program.

The expansion, modernization, and democratization of the Cuban health care system which occurred after 1959 was a boon for Cuban women. By 1992 virtually all Cuban women had access to regular, free, and relatively high-quality medical care. Life expectancy had been greatly extended. Infectious and communicable diseases (except certain sexually transmitted diseases) had been significantly reduced. Pregnancy, birth, and infancy were now rarely life-threatening events.

The benefits offered by the Cuban health system were an important source of support for the regime, consistently cited by the Cuban public as one of the greatest achievements of the revolution. Women, in turn, were reminded that the revolution had women's best interests in mind and that the socialist system could best ensure that their needs were met. To underscore this message, government authorities often informed women of the inadequacies and high costs of health care in capitalist countries.

The revolution made a major effort to modernize the entire process of maternity and childbirth through substantial investments in education, research, and technology. It took enormous pride in its low maternal and infant mortality rates, successes that may well be undone by the economic crisis of the 1990s.

While the overall achievements of revolutionary health care are undeniable, certain aspects of Cuban health policy were inconsistent with Cuba's egalitarian goals. For example, in the 1960s Cuban policymakers displayed a fundamental lack of understanding of the importance of abortion as a birth-control option. Only when illegal abortions threatened maternal health statistics, and thus international prestige, did policymakers decide to improve and extend the service. Twenty years passed before abortion was formally legalized.

A number of other dilemmas hampered women's reproductive choices in Cuba. Periodic shortages of birth-control devices occurred throughout the years, not only because of the U.S. economic embargo and the dissolution of the Soviet bloc, but also from inadequate planning by health administrators. There was a lack of clarity regarding the process for diagnosing sexually transmitted diseases in women. Even worse was the apparent misinformation among gynecologists regarding which birth-control devices were appropriate for women at different times in their reproductive life. This lack of knowledge was particularly perplexing given the large number of women practitioners in the medical field.

From the collectivist perspective of the Cuban revolution, it was the rightful business of the community to monitor the activities of pregnant women. This concern for collective good was also behind Cuba's AIDS policy of compulsory quarantine.

Health education played an important role in the new Cuban system. Many traditional notions, particularly regarding the mysteries of women's reproductive cycle, were challenged. At the same time, some traditional cultural assumptions about women's sexuality were reinforced by the revolutionary "scientific" information machine. The manipulation of information reflected the paternalistic mold of the Cuban system. For example, in its eagerness to promote the use of birth-control devices, the health education machine for years remained mum regarding the potential risks of certain contraceptive methods.

The Cuban experience has shown, in fact, that simply providing birth-control materials and information does not automatically change traditional patterns of behavior. Cuban women continued to shun routine contraceptive use. The proliferation of abortion seemed to facilitate its abuse as a means of birth control. And ironically the best-educated Cubans, the youngest, appeared the least aware in their reproductive choices—or lack of them. Further research is needed into why this is so.

The health system came to rival the military as the most prestigious institution in Cuban society. Unlike the military, it was largely staffed by women—doctors, nurses, researchers, practitioners, and volunteers. Although women were underrepresented in leadership posts, this trend was less pronounced in health care than in other sectors. For women, the new health system was arguably the most successful innovation of the Cuban revolution.

NOTES

1. Isolina Triay, "Antes de nacer," *Mujeres,* September 1975, pp. 50–51; Ministry of Public Health, *Programa Nacional de Atención Materno/Infantil;* Isolina Triay, "Imágen transformada," *Mujeres,* December 1983, pp. 40–42.

2. Padula and Smith, interview with Dr. Ada Ovies; José A. de la Osa, "Dar seguridad y calidad a la vida," *Granma,* December 10, 1987, pp. 4–5; id., "Montan técnica para el diagnóstico prenatal . . .," *Granma,* May 6, 1987, p. 1; id., "Ya han nacido en Cuba cuatro bebés in vitro . . .," *Granma,* June 14, 1989, p. 2.

3. Fidel Castro, speech at the opening session of the Cuba 1984 Pediatric Congress (Havana, *Editora Polftica,* 1984), p. 20.

4. Padula and Smith, interview with Ada Ovies; Susana Lee, "Combatividad multiplicada contra lo mal hecho . . .," *Granma,* September 7, 1988, p. 3.

5. Aldo Madruga, "El día que perdimos la bandera de Modelo," *Granma,* September 7, 1988, p. 4.

6. "Doctor díganos cómo explicar, curar or vencer la esterilidad," *Mujeres,* November 1966.

7. De la Osa, "Posible prevenir la hemofilia"; id., "Ya han nacido en Cuba."

8. Rodríguez Domínguez, *Temas de salud,* pp. 28–31.

REFLECTING ON THE SECTION

How do the articles in this section propose that women gain access to education and power over their own health? Women's health depends on the availability of information about women's bodies, on economic and cultural conditions that women live under, and on laws and social forces that limit or enhance women's abilities to make choices about nutrition, reproduction, sexuality, and the like. Maureen Larkin says that women's health in different parts of the world must be understood within the context of a globalized world, where development policies, multinational corporations, the dominance of Western medicine, and local and national health care systems all combine in complex ways. Can you see how some of these factors work in your own locale?

In particular, the politics of the availability of information limits the kinds of choices and decisions that women make about their health. For example, The National Latina Health Organization argues that Norplant or other birth-control methods need to be "woman controlled," by which they mean women need access without coercion to these technologies as well as information about their potential effects. In a similar vein, both Katheryn Carovano and Nadia Farah emphasize the importance of culturally accessible health education, particularly in light of histories of social inequities.

It is also important to understand that access to health care and technology alone does not ensure that women will be able to develop agency and knowledge about their bodies and health issues. What additional factors inhibit reproductive rights and other health care initiatives?

Gendered Identities: Individuals, Communities, Nations, Worlds

If you look at your driver's license or the forms you fill out to enter college or any number of other official documents, what kinds of information do you have to give to identify yourself? Your name, certainly. You also have to provide a home or mailing address, an identification number of some kind, perhaps your parents' names. In some places, if you are married and a woman, you are required to provide your husband's name—although your husband may not be required to provide yours. Your sex and your birthday are almost always required, as is, in the United States, your race. If you do not have a home or mailing address, can your existence be verified? On a passport, you must have a country of origin. Everyone has to have a nationality. How do governments and educational or financial institutions identify you if you lack any of this required information? For example, what if your sex is indeterminate or changing? Information about sex cannot be left blank on either a birth certificate or a passport.

The information on our licenses, passports, and official documents and applications refers to the categories of identity that the modern nation-state considers essential. With this information, we can be recognized and located. We can receive services, pay taxes, cross or be prevented from crossing borders, be drafted into the military, get married or divorced, or be a domestic partner—in other words, be identified. All governments, large and small, local and national, generate and store information about our identities. Without this information, the state cannot recognize you and you may be disenfranchised; that is, you may have few rights and less access to the benefits of citizenship. If the state does not collect this information (as is the case in many parts of the world), then the state does not assume responsibility for your welfare. Thus, identity is a necessary and crucial aspect of the modern world. But how did these categories of identity come about?

In women's studies, we usually focus on either sexed or gendered identities. But these are only one part of the identification process that modern societies generate. Sex and gender identities have arisen along with other categories, among them nationality, race, class, family status, citizenship, and age. Just as in Part One we discussed the ways that a "new" science in the West created categories of difference that produced inequalities, in Part Two we will examine the ways in which political systems in the West became dominant and influenced forms of belonging and identity in the modern period. Identity is always a relationship; that is, identification signals inclusion in a category or group—such as a nation or a family or a race—but it also signals exclusion and difference from others. Our identities are not always voluntary or chosen by us. They may be forced upon us, or we may have severely limited options in describing or fashioning ourselves to fit into available groups or categories. Obviously, for women, identity serves to differentiate them from men first of all, and also from other women. The ways those differences are established and then acted upon take shape in the context of the rise of the modern nation-state and global capitalism.

The nation-state is relatively recent in the history of the world. Although it can seem as if the nation-state has always existed, only a couple of hundred years ago people described their identities and lived under political rule in very different ways. For instance, in the past, people belonged to small clans or groups governed by a single person, who may have been a chief or a king. In some parts of America, tribes saw themselves as sovereign entities governed by collectively designated chiefs rather than by a ruler determined by hereditary lineage or through conquest. People's identities were primarily formed in relation to families, kin groups, or tribes instead of states with mappable boundaries and borders that are patrolled by soldiers.

Feminist scholarship suggests that many of these premodern groups were patriarchal; that is, the authority of the most senior male member governed the activities of the family or kinship group. Although there is evidence of matriarchal and matrilineal forms of authority and power, patriarchy or male dominance was more widespread. Forms of authority under the more dominant religions, such as Christianity, Judaism, Islam, Confucianism, Hinduism, and Buddhism, were all patriarchal. In general, identity was formed through belonging to a kin group and the roles played within the group. For instance, women under Confucian cultures were positioned and identified as daughters, wives, mothers, and so on rather than as a biologically distinct entity. Caste, class, wealth, and ownership of property were also vital in identifying the family or kin group in relation to others.

Although class, caste, family wealth and position, and roles within the family remain important in the modern world, a new kind of identity became increasingly dominant. In the modern world, to be an "individual" with unique characteristics and behavior became more and more a requirement for inclusion in everyday social and political life. This individual, most often figured as a man, claimed the right to move freely in what came to be characterized as public space, which was defined as that which was outside the increasingly privatized sphere of the family. Yet as many feminists have asserted, even in the private sphere, individuality became an important aspect of personality and family dynamics. In many places where more "traditional" notions of the family remained powerful, the pressure to be seen as an individual led to tensions between the generations, gender roles, and private and public spheres. This modern form of individuality produced gendered individuals with different characteristics and expectations for men and women and the roles they were to play in the new nation-states.

The rise of the nation-state occurred along with the growing influence of capitalist industrialization in the West and colonialism and imperialism in the rest of the world. Capitalism brought an emphasis on individual entrepreneurship. For instance, a Robinson Crusoe could be washed ashore on a deserted island with nothing but the clothes on his back and leave many years later with untold wealth. In this much-beloved narrative, hard work leads to riches and to class mobility. Yet, for most people, capitalism did not guarantee improved conditions of living. With industrialization in the West, the rural poor moved to urban spaces in search of a livelihood in the new factories. Factory work was dangerous, hours were unregulated, and wages were low. But since other forms of work had been disrupted, often this was the only way to survive.

In these growing urban areas, men and women found themselves required to identify as individuals because belonging to a kin group was increasingly irrelevant to collecting wages, renting housing, and associating with other people for work or leisure. Names and addresses as forms of identity that we are still familiar with today became useful to the new industrial nation-state as it created armies, voters, taxpayers, census information, and workers. For women, however, the nation-state was also patriarchal in that it identified them primarily through their relationships to fathers and husbands.

Thus, the patriarchal nation-state produces citizens who are gendered. Women and men have different legal rights and privileges, although race, class, and sexuality alter the ways in which different groups of women access these rights and privileges. Throughout most of the history of the nation-state, women were denied the right to vote. While women gained the right to vote in the United States in 1920, many European nations did not follow suit until after World War II. In many of these countries, male property ownership was the key to the right to vote, so poor men were excluded. Groups designated as minorities were denied the privileges of citizenship. Men and women of color in the United States were discriminated against in multiple ways, including the formal and informal suppression of voting rights. Especially for those groups termed "indigenous," such as Native Americans, the denial of citizenship followed the dispossession of their land. Indeed, it can be said that the privileges of full citizenship always come in relation to the denial of these privileges to those believed unequal or unworthy. Gender, race, sexuality, and class are some of the factors that determine whether or not one can be a full citizen in the nation-state. Although the state has treated women differently from men, it is important not to generalize about women. Instead, we must study the complex histories of diverse women's participation in and exclusion from the nation-state.

Although women have had an unequal history as citizens, some groups of women have shown enormous devotion and allegiance to their nation. In modern times, nationalism has come to be an important form of community; sometimes it replaces an allegiance to family or kin group or village as a primary identity. Almost all individuals across the world now belong to a nation-state. While stateless individuals can experience extreme hardship, they may still have very strong feelings of belonging to one nation or another. Consequently, it is important to distinguish nation from state. A state can be seen as the political and bureaucratic institutions, practices, and policies that govern a given territory and population. A nation implies a community of people who are believed to be or believe themselves to be similar or connected by a common identity. This commonality is usually expressed as a religious, racial, or ethnic identity.

For instance, while we can understand the United States as a territorially sovereign state, a national identity is created though actions and statements that reflect beliefs about "American" character or nature as Christian, white, propertied, heterosexual, and masculine. Many scholars of nationalism argue that such beliefs about national character become powerful because they offer an identity and a sense of belonging to a chosen group by excluding many others. Women are often excluded from national belonging—but can become nationalist by excluding others. Nationalism is both a promise and a threat, since it offers an identity only through exclusion.

Nationalism has been important in the modern period because it made possible both colonial conquest and independence. First, it enabled European conquest by using its large national armies and industries in exploration and expansion in the search for new opportunities for profit and wealth. National projects such as colonization gave citizens of a nation-state a feeling of unified purpose and belonging, as well as new routes to prosperity. More and more, this sense of belonging merged with a sense of superiority over those peoples and cultures who were being colonized. For example, "Englishness" was defined by British colonialists as the characteristics of a people who were more civilized, intelligent, and modern and thus entitled to more of the world's resources than any other nation. British writer Rudyard Kipling's notion of the "white man's burden" reflected the efforts of countless European missionary and military projects to "civilize" and Christianize parts of Asia, Africa, and the Americas that were believed to be inhabited by "heathens," "barbarians," and "savages."

For many women in Europe and the United States, there was a similar "white woman's burden" to civilize and liberate oppressed and suffering "sisters" in the colonies. The identity of an "Englishwoman" became a national as well as a gendered attribute that signaled the most superior form of womanhood on the planet. Each colonial power had its own version of these figures of cultural and political superiority. Thus, colonialism produced new forms of belonging to the nation and specified roles that reflected gender, race, and class power relations.

If nationalism promoted colonial expansion and domination, it also created the possibility of freedom and independence. Thus, the second aspect of nationalism is its ability to provide the tools for opposition to oppression. It is ironic that the very system of education and governance that colonial domination imposed led to the rise of a group of people who could use that education to fight for their independence. Though modern concepts of individuality and nation had been foreign to most colonized peoples, they soon became tools for their liberation. This may seem like a contradiction. However, if we understand nationalism as a powerful form of identity in the modern world then we can see how resistance to domination can itself be nationalist. For instance, in their struggle for independence from France, Algerians created a very strong sense of themselves as a separate entity as the indigenous people of the land that had been occupied by a foreign power. In order to counter French nationalism, with its attendant racism and economic exploitation, the Algerian independence movement created a counternationalism in solidarity with all those nations who sought to bring an end to European colonization.

These nationalist movements generated new gender roles and expected behaviors for men and women as individuals who belonged to an autonomous and sovereign nation. Within anticolonial nationalism, women gained a new identity as citizens of the state, which recognized their status as vital members of their communities. But many women then and now have found that the liberatory aspects of nationalism do not extend to their homes and workplaces. Within many forms of nationalism, women serve subordinate and symbolic roles as mothers, daughters, and martyrs.

For instance, the large number of rapes that accompany every war demonstrates that these struggles are often waged over the bodies of women. If motherhood is the highest sign of female participation in the nation, then the violation of that role will be the most symbolic conquest of that nation. For those women who have given up their sons, brothers, and husbands to the nation, this sacrifice constitutes the ultimate martyrdom. Another role available to women in nationalist struggles is that of the traitor, the one who has sexual relations with the "enemy," whether involuntary or voluntary. In both of these roles, women exist only as symbols and possessions of the nation rather than as persons with complex and contradictory perceptions and actions. While many women have accepted this situation, others have called for more debate and analysis of these politics.

Just as "Americans" forged a national identity in their struggle for independence from Britain, many countries have formed national identities through opposing or resisting foreign occupation. However, the kind of belonging and identity that we associate with nationalism is also possible in relation to other kinds of communities and groups. For example, in recent history, we see religious nationalisms (such as Christian or Hindu fundamentalism), queer nationalism (such as the activist group Queer Nation), and racial nationalism (as in the Black Power or La Raza movements in the United States). While these nationalisms are quite different from each other, they are similar in that they are all involved in the work of producing a group identity that is primary and that distinguishes the group from those seen as "Others." These Others are believed to be opposite in behavior, characteristics, and moral worth.

Some scholars and critics have termed these new nationalisms "new social movements." In general, these new social movements do not seek to form a new nation-state per se but may seek rights and benefits from the state based on a unified identity. This identity is usually perceived to be a minority or marginal one because, regardless of population or demographics, the group claims that it has been excluded from the dominant national identity. While new social movements are usually believed to be progressive, many of them demonstrate the same contradictions and limits that we discussed in relation to territorial nationalism. That is, they have a tendency to create gendered roles and other exclusionary divisions within the community and to proceed through separatist identity politics.

Can feminism be called a new social movement? Certainly, many people think so. First of all, feminism produced an identity of "woman" as culturally different from that of "man." It was argued that women had a distinct female essence based on their experience of male oppression throughout time and across cultures. Our discussion of nationalism has shown us that to a great extent women have been put in a subordinate status in relation to men in many cultures in the past and the present. On the other hand, to put all women across time and culture into one group that has a shared essential nature leads to many problems, political and cultural. For example, it keeps us from differentiating among women of different classes, races, sexualities, nations, and religions, to name just a few important characteristics.

Why should we emphasize differences instead of similarities? We believe that feminist analyses of women's lives must keep power differences among women in view—not to separate and exclude women from a dominant community but rather to allow the complex histories and relationships among diverse women to emerge and become part of the discussion. For instance, a given woman's self-identification may be based not solely on gender but also on race or class or sexuality. A women's studies that accounts for these simultaneous and multiple identities and forms of belonging in any given time and location will create more possibilities for truly effective and meaningful social services, policies, and historical or political accounts. It is true that women's studies rose out of feminist social movements, but it is important to keep in mind that there have been many different feminisms. The relationship of feminism to other new social movements has changed and continues to change as well.

One way to grasp the contexts in which different kinds of feminisms arise is to look at the ways new kinds of differences and equalities are produced by such factors as labor migration, global media and entertainment, commerce and finance, and the Internet. A shorthand term for talking about this phenomenon is "globalization." While globalization has existed in one form or another since the beginning of capitalism, the advent of new technologies in the twentieth century led to an intensification of its effects. For example, as multinational corporations (the industries that produce and distribute goods across national boundaries) have increased in number and size since World War II, people have come to feel a greater sense of belonging across national borders. Thus, employees of Sony or Disney who are differentiated by their class and nationality are connected through their work in meaningful ways. Along with the great growth in wealth and the increase in class differences that are part of recent globalization, more and more people are traveling the globe in search of work. As media are increasingly controlled by a small number of multinational corporations, a more standardized and unified world appears to be the norm. As these examples show, what brings people closer together has a flip side. That is, the idea that the world is more connected and therefore smaller has the same flaws we saw at work in the idea of national unity and belonging. What promises to erase differences between people may often produce new inequalities and differences without the possibility of addressing or changing those conditions.

A good example of this predicament can be seen in the social movement of "global feminism," the belief that all women are fundamentally similar everywhere since they are subordinate to men. In this view, common oppressions have common solutions. Thus, working beyond national boundaries through international and transnational organizations such as the United Nations will bring about significant changes in women's lives. While global feminism is responsible for many effective and significant programs, what it does not address is its own history as a social movement that has its roots in colonialism. Since the colonial project included a policy of "civilizing" and modernizing people considered to be "backward" or "barbaric," the belief that white and European women had a special role in the education and development of women in the colonies was widely held. In the nineteenth and early twentieth centuries, these projects proceeded under the auspices of missionary groups or colonial governments. In the second half of the twentieth century, international organizations in cooperation with local governments continued this approach. International aid, human rights, and development projects often included an emphasis on women's poverty or disenfranchisement. In this current era of globalization, the older and newer forms of feminist social movements have combined to bring attention to women's concerns and status around the world. Feminism remains important as a kind of modern identity politics but many feminists, including some global feminists, continue to rely on ideas that emerged from the histories of colonial domination that we have mentioned.

In Part Two, we emphasize the many ways in which identity comes to be gendered in the modern period. We discuss how colonialism and nationalism and, more recently, new social movements create new identities that both link and differentiate men and women. Identities are not inert concepts. They come alive when people use them to make governments, nations, families, races, communities, genders, and more. However, people can choose from only a limited number and range of identities in any given historical moment. Feminism is an important tool in building identity politics, but it needs to be connected to other forms of identity to be most effective. That is why feminism is such a dynamic social movement; it changes with time and place.

Modern Nations and the Individual in the West

Public and Private

JUDITH SQUIRES

Political theorist Judith Squires outlines how ideas of a "public sphere" and "private sphere" shape liberal political theories and government policies. Within liberal theory, civil society is predicated on the freedom of the individual citizen, yet the private realm of "personal life" creates a sphere in which women cannot exercise civic rights and responsibilities. By recognizing how the third term personal functions in the public/private binary, Squires illustrates fundamental power imbalances based on gender in liberal theories of individual freedom.

Liberalism has been constructed around a distinction between the public and private realms. The key significance of this distinction lies, for its liberal advocates, in its perceived role in securing individual freedom. As Judith Shklar notes, liberalism "has only one overriding aim: to secure the political conditions that are nec-

Judith Squires, from *Gender in Political Theory*. Polity Press: Cambridge, 1999: 24–30.

essary for the exercise of personal freedom" (Shklar 1991: 21). These conditions are held to require the clear demarcation of the spheres of the personal and the public. "The limits of coercion begin," argues Shklar, ". . . with a prohibition upon invading the private realm" (Shklar 1991: 24). Freedom is secured by limiting the constraints placed upon the individual. Given this, the line between the public and the private has to be drawn, and "must under no circumstances be ignored or forgotten" (Shklar 1991: 24).

What is meant by the public and the private here is the distinction between the state and civil society. Politics is equated with the public power of the state. Freedom is equated with the absence of constraint imposed by the state—freedom from political power. Civil society is therefore cast as that sphere of life in which individuals are allowed to pursue their own conception of the good in free association with others. Civil society is "private" in the sense that it is not governed by the public power of the state.

Key Terms

liberalism A political and social philosophy that emphasizes the rights and freedoms of individuals. Enlightenment liberalism was the philosophical foundation for the French and American revolutions and is commonly associated with eighteenth- and nineteenth-century thinkers such as John Locke, Mary Wollstonecraft, and John Stuart Mill.

Romantic period Primarily associated with art and literature of the late eighteenth and early nineteenth centuries, Romanticism emphasized emotionality and self-expression. Politically, romanticism reacted against the idea of the individual in favor of communities based on traditional social orders.

social contract The agreement by free individuals to renounce part of their natural freedoms and recognize political authority in order to enter into civil society.

Private does not here imply the personal, intimate, or familial. As Nancy Rosenblum notes: "Private life means life in civil society, not some presocial state of nature or antisocial condition of isolation and detachment" (Rosenblum 1987: 61). A social sphere freed from the constraints of the political will be more vibrant and allow for greater autonomy than will one in which the power of the state extends to all aspects of life. As politics is conceived as the state-based exertion of power over individuals, it becomes a necessary evil, to be limited and constrained such that it guarantees the framework for civil society without eroding its vitality.

However, the apparently binary division between public and private is complicated by the existence of a third sphere, also labeled private—that of personal life. This creates a tripartite, rather than a dual, division of social relations: the state, civil society, and the personal. It is clear that the state is always cast as public. It is equally clear that the personal (when considered within political theory) is cast as private. Confusingly, civil society is cast as private when opposed to the state and public when opposed to the personal. This inevitably makes any discussion of a single public/private dichotomy either partial or confused, or both.

There are, Kymlicka helpfully notes, "in fact two different concepts of the public–private distinction in liberalism: the first, which originated in Locke, is the distinction between the political and the social; the second, which arose with Romantic-influenced liberals, is the distinction between the social and the personal" (Kymlicka 1990: 250). The social/personal distinction arises later than the state/civil society distinction, and in some ways may be viewed as a response to the latter.

[. . .]

Classic liberals had viewed society as the realm in which individuals could act freely. However, it has become increasingly evident that society itself places intense constraints upon individuals, and the pursuit of individual freedom may require the limitation of both state and civil society in order to create space for self-expression. The relations of power which might work to constrain the individual, it has become increasingly clear, are more extensive and pervasive than those captured by the institutional power of the state alone. Recognition of the pressures of social conformity led to a need to distinguish between the social and the personal in order that one might retreat from ordered social life into a sphere of intimacy.

Significantly, neither of these two public/private distinctions explicitly invokes the family: neither characterizes the family as paradigmatically private. Indeed, the family is not necessarily private in the sense implied by either the term *civil society* or the *personal,* and the arguments for each could actually provide grounds to criticize the traditional family. Nonetheless, when the domestic and familial are considered within liberal theory, they are systematically represented as private (Okin 1998: 117). There is then a third form of the public/private distinction at work: that between the public and the domestic. Here the public comprises both the state and civil society and the private is defined institutionally as the relations and activities of domestic life, often assumed to embody the intimacy valued for self-development.

[. . .]

As Pateman has argued, the separation of state and civil society is a distinction within the nonfamilial world. When civil society is labeled private, the family remains forgotten in theoretical discussion (Pateman 1983: 286–87). Had the family been viewed as a part of civil society, liberal theorists would surely have been compelled to oppose its hierarchical form and argue for its organization on the basis of equality and consent, as they did with all other forms of civil cooperation.

[. . .]

Arguments vary as to why the domestic has been neglected in this way. Feminist critiques of the liberal characterization of the public/private distinction are numerous and qualitatively distinct in focus. Criticism is leveled at the premises of liberalism itself (especially its conception of the self), at liberalism's historical origins in social contract theory, and at the historical practice of liberal regimes.

The first critique focuses on the question of subjectivity. Liberalism, it is frequently charged, works with a conception of the subject as an autonomous agent: it assumes people to be equal, unattached, rational individuals. Yet many critics view this claim as an account of a particular, socially specific type of identity formation rather than as a statement of universal human nature.

Recognition of this fact leads to two further insights. The first is that very particular social structures and institutions are needed to shape individuals into this mould; the second is that this conception of subjectivity may not apply equally to everyone. The first insight leads to a concern with the processes of reproduction, nurturance and socialization, the second to an exploration of the extent to which women have been understood as subordinate, dependent, and emotional, and so excluded from the category of "individuals" within liberal theorizing.

The two issues are linked in women's status as primary carers. Neither the process of caring and nurturing nor the status of carers and nurturers is theorized in liberal theory. The concern of feminist theorists is that, as a result of this omission, not only have women been denied the rights and privileges granted to the "rational individuals" of liberal societies, but also a crucial aspect of life, associated with the caring performed by women, has been glossed over.

[. . .]

The sort of thinking and moral reasoning generated by and required within the social relations characteristic of familial life are quite distinct from those generated by and required within the social relations characteristic of public life. The emphasis here is on empathy, relationality, and caring rather than on autonomy, individuality, and justice. Many feminists explore the implications of recognizing the existence of these two distinct forms of moral reasoning, and there is an extensive literature proposing that the balance between the two should be reassessed.

This critique of the public/private distinction, which emerges from a focus on subjectivity, is complemented by a second, which focuses on contract. Here the object of concern is not the rational liberal individual but liberalism's origins in social contract theory.

[. . .]

The most influential theorist here is Pateman. She claims that the social contract that generates liberal politics and establishes the political freedom of individuals simultaneously entails the sexual subordination of women in marriage. The social contract that is required to create both civil society and the state requires a sexual contract to accommodate the patriarchalism that predates liberalism. The liberal social contact therefore represents the reorganization, but not the abolition, of patriarchy.

[. . .]

Patriarchy was relocated into the private domain and reformulated as complementary to civil society. It was not rejected altogether: it was entrenched rather than eradicated. Classic liberal theory assumed the (male-headed) family to be a natural, biologically determined unit. As politics was assumed to apply only to that which was socially constituted, and so amenable to change, relations within the family were deemed apolitical (Pateman 1988).

Liberal states have been able to act in this apparently contradictory manner because of an essential tension within liberal theory. The original contract upon which contemporary liberal theory still rests was, Pateman has claimed, not only a social contract that established freedom but also a sexual contract that perpetuated domination. The contract established men's political right over women through conjugal right. While the contract theorists challenged the paternal rights of fathers, they incorporated into their theories the patriarchal rights of husbands over wives. As a result they created a division not only between the state and civil society but also between the public sphere of civil freedom and the private sphere of the family.

This private sphere is then deemed politically irrelevant, and theorists focus exclusively on the relation between the state and the sphere of civil freedom. Indeed, public and private come to be understood as relating to the state and the sphere of civil freedom respectively, thereby rendering the "private" sphere of the family invisible. Women, Pateman tells us, "are not party to the original contract through which men transform their natural freedom into the security of civil freedom. Women are the subject of the contract" (Pateman 1988: 6). The public realm cannot be understood in isolation from the private realm, and yet there is now a refusal to admit that marital domination is politically significant.

This critique focuses on the way in which the historical origins of liberal theory rely on the incorporation of already existing patriarchal relations that, being excluded from the categories of both civil society and the state, are then rendered invisible. It then becomes possible for contemporary liberal theorists to forget (or overlook) the fact that the "liberal individual" was explicitly argued to be the male head of household by the classic exponents of liberal theory. In this way gender is given a highly specific and structuring role within liberal theory at the same time as liberal theory presents itself as gender-neutral.

There is a third type of critique of the public/private dichotomy as articulated within liberal theory. This focuses on the historical practice of liberal regimes. The charge here is that, notwithstanding the abstract commitment to the importance of a prohibition on state intervention in the private sphere, liberal states have in practice regulated and controlled the family. Not only has this practice been contrary to the fundamental principle of liberalism, it has been adopted in pursuit of a profoundly illiberal end: the perpetuation of patriarchy. This tension, arising from the very formulation of liberalism itself, is the inevitable conclusion of the ambivalent role of the family in relation to the private sphere.

[. . .]

In the light of these three critiques, many feminists have rejected the "public/private" distinction altogether, believing it to be a central mechanism of the oppression of women within liberal states. Determination to highlight the inequality within the family and to challenge its apolitical status led many feminists to reject the liberal "respect for so-called private life" (Jaggar 1983: 199) as simply a mystification of patriarchal power. It was argued that the liberal commitment to equality (if applied to women as well as to men) required a rejection of the other liberal commitment to a public/private distinction.

REFERENCES

Jaggar, Alison. (1983). *Feminist Politics and Human Nature.* Brighton: Harvester.

Kymlicka, Will. (1990). *Contemporary Political Philosophy: An Introduction.* Oxford: Oxford University Press.

Okin, Susan Moller. (1998). "Gender, The Public and the Private." In A. Phillips (ed.), *Feminism and Politics.* Oxford: Oxford University Press, 116–41.

Pateman, Carole. (1983). "Feminist Critiques of the Public/Private Dichotomy." In S. Benn and G. Gaus (eds.), *Public and Private in Social Life.* London: Croom Helm, 281–303.

———. (1988). *The Sexual Contract:* Cambridge: Polity.

Rosenblum, Nancy. (1987). *Another Liberalism: Romanticism and the Reconstruction of Liberal Thought.* Cambridge, MA: Harvard University Press.

Shklar, Judith. (1991). "The Liberalism of Fear." In N. Rosenblum (ed.), *Liberalism and the Moral Life.* Cambridge, MA: Harvard University Press, 21–38.

Excerpt from A Vindication of the Rights of Woman

MARY WOLLSTONECRAFT

Mary Wollstonecraft (1759–97) was an English writer and political philosopher whose work has been of great significance to Western feminism. In her famous piece A Vindication of the Rights of Woman, published in 1792, Wollstonecraft challenged the Enlightenment philosophers such as Jean-Jacques Rousseau to extend the rights of "Man" to all women. Why, she asked, does the foundation of the democratic revolutions sweeping Europe exclude women as individual citizen-subjects when such a practice runs counter to the general philosophy of the Enlightenment itself?

Let us examine this question. Rousseau declares that a woman should never for a moment feel herself independent, that she should be governed by fear to exercise her natural cunning, and made a coquettish slave in order to render her a more alluring object of desire, a sweeter companion to man, whenever he chose to relax himself. He carries the arguments, which he pre-

Reprinted from *A Vindication of the Rights of Woman* by Mary Wollstonecraft, Miriam Brody, ed. London: Penguin Books, 1992: 108–9, 120, 122, 130–31, 132, 133–34.

tends to draw from the indications of nature, still further, and insinuates that truth and fortitude, the cornerstones of all human virtue, should be cultivated with certain restrictions, because, with respect to the female character, obedience is the grand lesson which ought to be impressed with unrelenting rigour.

What nonsense! When will a great man arise with sufficient strength of mind to puff away the fumes which pride and sensuality have thus spread over the subject? If women are by nature inferior to men, their virtue must be the same in quality, if not in degree, or virtue is a relative idea; consequently their conduct should be founded on the same principles, and have the same aim.

Connected with man as daughters, wives, and mothers, their moral character may be estimated by their manner of fulfilling those simple duties; but the end, the grand end, of their exertions should be to unfold their own faculties, and acquire the dignity of conscious virtue. . . .

But avoiding, as I have hitherto done, any direct comparison of the two sexes collectively, or frankly acknowledging the inferiority of woman, according to the present appearance of things, I shall only insist that men have increased that inferiority till women are al-

---

Key Terms

Enlightenment   European philosophical movement of the eighteenth century that celebrated individualism, scientific rationality, and universal human progress.

Jean-Jacques Rousseau   (1712–78) One of the major figures of the French Enlightenment, Rousseau argued that human beings were essentially good and equal in their natural state but were corrupted by industrial society.

most sunk below the standard of rational creatures. Let their faculties have room to unfold, and their virtues to gain strength, and then determine where the whole sex must stand in the intellectual scale. Yet let it be remembered that for a small number of distinguished women I do not ask a place.

It is difficult for us purblind mortals to say to what height human discoveries and improvements may arrive, when the gloom of despotism subsides, which makes us stumble at every step; but, when morality shall be settled on a more solid basis, then, without being gifted with a prophetic spirit, I will venture to predict that woman will be either the friend or slave of man. [. . .]

These may be termed Utopian dreams. Thanks to that Being who impressed them on my soul, and gave me sufficient strength of mind to dare to exert my own reason, till, becoming dependent only on Him for the support of my virtue, I view, with indignation, the mistaken notions that enslave my sex.

I love man as my fellow; but his sceptre, real or usurped, extends not to me, unless the reason of an individual demands my homage; and even then the submission is to reason, and not to man. In fact, the conduct of an accountable being must be regulated by the operations of its own reason; or on what foundation rests the throne of God?

It appears to me necessary to dwell on these obvious truths, because females have been insulated, as it were; and while they have been stripped of the virtues that should clothe humanity, they have been decked with artificial graces that enable them to exercise a short-lived tyranny. Love, in their bosoms, taking place of every nobler passion, their sole ambition is to be fair, to raise emotion instead of inspiring respect; and this ignoble desire, like the servility in absolute monarchies, destroys all strength of character. Liberty is the mother of virtue, and if women be, by their very constitution, slaves, and not allowed to breathe the sharp invigorating air of freedom, they must ever languish like exotics, and be reckoned beautiful flaws in nature. Let it also be remembered, that they are the only flaw.

As to the argument respecting the subjection in which the sex has ever been held, it retorts on man. The many have always been enthralled by the few; and monsters, who scarcely have shown any discernment

of human excellence, have tyrannized over thousands of their fellow-creatures. . . .

I have, probably, had an opportunity of observing more girls in their infancy than J. J. Rousseau. I can recollect my own feelings, and I have looked steadily around me; yet, so far from coinciding with him in opinion respecting the first dawn of the female character, I will venture to affirm, that a girl whose spirits have not been damped by inactivity, or innocence tainted by false shame, will always be a romp, and the doll will never excite attention unless confinement allows her no alternative. Girls and boys, in short, would play harmlessly together, if the distinction of sex was not inculcated long before nature makes any difference. I will go further, and affirm, as an indisputable fact, that most of the women, in the circle of my observation, who have acted like rational creatures, or shown any vigour of intellect, have accidentally been allowed to run wild, as some of the elegant formers of the fair sex would insinuate.

The baneful consequences which flow from inattention to health during infancy and youth, extend further than is supposed—dependence of body naturally produces dependence of mind; and how can she be a good wife or mother, the greater part of whose time is employed to guard against or endure sickness? Nor can it be expected that a woman will resolutely endeavor to strengthen her constitution and abstain from enervating indulgences, if artificial notions of beauty, and false descriptions of sensibility, have been early entangled with her motives of action. Most men are sometimes obliged to bear with bodily inconveniences, and to endure, occasionally, the inclemency of the elements; but genteel women are, literally speaking, slaves to their bodies, and glory in their subjection. . . .

Women are everywhere, in this deplorable state; for, in order to preserve their innocence, as ignorance is courteously termed, truth is hidden from them, and they are made to assume an artificial character before their faculties have acquired any strength. Taught from their infancy that beauty is women's sceptre, the mind shapes itself to the body, and roaming round its gilt cage, only seeks to adore its prison. Men have various employments and pursuits which engage their attention, and give a character to the open mind; but women, confined to one, and having their thoughts constantly directed to the most insignificant part of themselves, seldom extend their views beyond the triumph of the hour. But were their understanding once emancipated from the slavery to which the pride and sensuality of man and their short-sighted desire, like that of dominion in tyrants, of present sway, has subjected them, we should probably read of their weakness with surprise. . . .

Let not men then in the pride of power, use the same arguments that tyrannic kings and venal ministers have used, and fallaciously assert that woman ought to be subjected because she has always been so. But, when man, governed by reasonable laws, enjoys his natural freedom, let him despise woman, if she do not share it with him; and, till that glorious period arrives, in descanting on the folly of the sex, let him not overlook his own.

Women, it is true, obtaining power by unjust means, by practicing or fostering vice, evidently lose the rank which reason would assign them, and they become either abject slaves or capricious tyrants. They lose all simplicity, all dignity of mind, in acquiring power, and act as men are observed to act when they have been exalted by the same means.

It is time to effect a revolution in female manners—time to restore to them their lost dignity—and make them, as a part of the human species, labour by reforming themselves to reform the world. It is time to separate unchangeable morals from local manners. If men be demi-gods, why let us serve them! And if the dignity of the female soul be as disputable as that of animals—if their reason does not afford sufficient light to direct their conduct whilst unerring instinct is denied—they are surely of all creatures the most miserable! and, bent beneath the iron hand of destiny, must submit to be a fair defect in creation. But to justify the ways of Providence respecting them, by pointing out some irrefragable reason for thus making such a large portion of mankind accountable and not accountable, would puzzle the subtilest casuist. . . .

REFERENCES

Kelly, Gary. (1991). "Mary Wollstonecraft." *Dictionary of Literary Biography.* Vol. 104. *British Prose Writers, 1660–1800.* Donald T. Siebert, ed Detroit: Gale Research.

Rousseau, Jean-Jacques. (1969). *Emile ou De l'education.* Paris: Editions Gallimard.

Reading C

Women and Citizenship

JAN JINDY PETTMAN

In this piece, Jan Jindy Pettman argues that while women are relegated to the private realm, their maternal ability to produce male citizens (especially soldiers and workers) is controlled by public interests and the state. For Pettman, women's role in the modern state is characterized by public equality and private inequality.

Women were long excluded from citizenship through the particular and masculinist constructions of politics and the citizen. They were caught between denial and exaggeration—overlooked, or attended to as different (Rhode 1992: 149). Where noticed, women were excluded from full citizenship on the grounds of unsuitability, as not male and not reasonable; as emotional; as sexual, and so disruptive, or dangerous; as having particular family attachments that precluded the disinterested work of citizenship. They were excluded through their construction as dependents, where the notion of citizen included an independent and autonomous person. They were further excluded through the close associations of citizenship with bearing arms and being

Jan Jindy Pettman, from *Worlding Women: A Feminist International Politics,* New York: Routledge, 1996: 17–21.

prepared to kill or die for the state. This militarisation of citizenship (Elshtain 1985: 42) saw women caught in another dichotomy, with men as protectors and women as protected. This further compromised notions of women's independence and of their suitability for the guarding of the state.

There are tensions in women's citizenship, where they have been both excluded and included on the same grounds, as mothers, and the difficulties they face becoming subjects and citizens in their own right (Jones 1990; Braidotti 1992: 184). The maternal is located in the private and the family, away from the political. Yet the maternal is also claimed by the state, to give (the right kinds of women) particular civic duties; to give birth to, bring up, and offer to the state future citizens, soldiers, workers. So France, like other European and settler states in the early decades of this century fearing declining population and "race suicide," awarded medals with ribbons to women with large families. More recently, Ceausescu banned contraception and abortions in an attempt to achieve a Romanian population of 30 million by the year 2000 (Pateman 1992).

Women seeking admission to the club of the state have been trapped in what Carole Pateman calls

Wollstonecraft's dilemma. Mary Wollstonecraft's *Vindication of the Rights of Women,* published in 1792 in the radical excitement of the French Revolution, argued that women, too, should be included in the rights of man. Seeking to extend and ultimately to universalise citizenship, the "equality" argument looks to a politics where gender does not matter. But arguments to include women as citizens often also assert the special work that women do as women. Earlier suffrage and women's rights advocates claimed maternal citizenship, constructing mothering as an essential service to the state, and pointed out that women birthing future citizens did often die "for their country." They also argued for the particular contributions that women could make, as women, to civic politics, valorising womanly virtues of caring, nurturing, and hoping to "humanise" and heal the masculinist politics of competition, greed, and violence.

—◦Getting Equal

Nowadays in most states women are enfranchised and their states declare men and women equal citizens in some form or other. The last century has seen a gradual extension of formal citizenship and political rights. But equal legal rights have not led to equal participation or representation (Phillips 1993). This is of concern only if it matters who represents you. This is not to argue that only women can represent women (though some might). But we should suspect a system of representation that routinely restricts power to a particular group, usually dominant-group middle-aged and older men (Voet 1994: 62).

What is it about citizenship, or about women, that makes it so hard for women to become full citizens? Women's formal rights and, in a number of states, their growing access to some parts of the state raise the possibility of public equality and private inequality (Bock and James 1992: 7). But women are still far short of public equality, despite significant gains in Finland, Norway, and Sweden, for example, where over one-third of elected parliamentarians are women. The double shift is still in place, and women's responsibilities in terms of family, domestic labour, and care undermine the choice, mobility, independence, and energy needed for sustained public presence. Everywhere many women are still de-

pendents of men or states, and conditions may be attached to that. Women in a number of states are caught between formal or constitutional equality declarations and the relegation of issues of women's status and rights to personal or religious law, which makes them family or community property. Women are frequently victims of violence—in their homes and outside them—aimed, often, at keeping women in their place. As long as the state cannot guarantee women's security, and does not seriously attempt to do so, the citizenship bargain whereby (elite) men give up unrestricted freedom in return for personal security holds little reward for women.

How then do we argue women's equal citizenship in the knowledge of many women's dependence (O'Connor 1993) and their continued construction, often, as mothers of citizens rather than as subjects and citizens themselves? A flashpoint here is abortion rights, so densely symbolic of women's claims for control over their own bodies. Some see abortion as *the* basic female civil right, to establish autonomy over body and self, which is especially controversial given the different political, including state, investments in motherhood (Evans 1993: 257; Hoff 1994). While often dismissed as a white, middle-class, western rights claim, most women who die as a result of illegal abortions or who are forced into abortion through lack of contraception or the means to support more children are in poor states or racialised minorities in rich states.

The state's attention to motherhood also gives it an investment in family, charged with reproduction of the community. Different states have long supported or recognised certain kinds of family, and heterosexual sex. This is part of the state disciplining its citizen body, constructing "deviant" forms of sexuality and regarding sexual minorities, and "unruly" women, as a threat and as somehow disloyal (Alexander 1994). These security threats materialise around debates about women—and gay men—in the military.

The complex and at times lethal connections between bodies, sex, difference, and danger also materialise in a body politics that promotes threats and physical attacks against women, gay men, and racialised-minority men. These threats contain or deny their rights and endanger their security. They mark the boundaries of power and belonging and demonstrate the conditions of entry into full citizenship. Women, gay men, and racialised-minority men suffer both from invisibility, where they and their interests are routinely ignored, and from hypervisibility, which places them in danger when they appear in public space. In these circumstances, some people restrict their own movements and claims. They cannot exercise full citizenship rights, even where they are legally entitled to them. Their insecurities demonstrate something that political theory often ignores—that identities are embodied, and bodies are inscribed in ways that are "read" to grant or deny their rights (Grosz 1994). While women and minority men are seen as threatening the body politic, it is the construction and imposition of a dominant or hegemonic body politic that actually endangers them. Women, sex, and bodies are written out of liberal and other masculinist citizenship politics, leaving men and "reason" in possession of the state.

Citizenship debates, then, are about the nature of the political community, about who belongs and who should have what rights. Still, usually, the boundaries of difference and social rights "are determined by specific, hegemonic, maybe universalist but definitely not universal discourses" (Yuval-Davis in Ward et al. 1993: 14). This universalist language disguises both difference and exclusion.

"Equal access is not enough" (Dietz 1989: 2). Strategies for actualising citizenship call for a challenge to the false universalism of liberal democracy, and for the inclusion of those whose current citizenship status is ambiguous or denied. They urge action to address the drastic underrepresentation of women and minorities in politics and power, including through positive action or provision for group representation. These strategies focus on the system as it now is, but also often entail a redefinition of politics to take account of women's experiences and interests (Jones 1993). Some focus, too, on women's own negotiation of identities and processes through which women become bearers of rights, "becoming subjects," self-consciously occupying a citizen identity (Braidotti 1992: 184; Leech 1994: 86).

REFERENCES

Alexander, M. Jacqui. (1994). "Not Just (Any)Body Can Be a Citizen: the Politics of Law, Sexuality and Postcoloniality in Trinidad, Tobago and the Bahamas," *Feminist Review,* no. 48, pp. 5–23.

Bock, Gisela, and James, Susan, eds. (1992). *Beyond Equality and Difference: Citizenship, Feminist Politics and Female Subjectivity,* Routledge, London.

Braidotti, Rosi. (1992). "On the Female Feminist Subject, or: from She-self to She-other" in *Beyond Equality and Difference: Citizenship, Feminist Politics and Female Subjectivity,* G. Bock and S. James, eds. Routledge, London.

Dietz, Mary. (1989). "Context Is All: Feminism and Theories of Citizenship" in *Learning about Women: Gender, Power and Politics,* Conway, S. Bourque, and J. Scott, eds. University of Michigan Press, Ann Arbor.

Elshtain, Jean Bethke. (1985). "Reflections on War and Political Discourse," *Political Theory,* vol. 13, no. 1, pp. 39–57.

Evans, David. (1993). *Sexual Citizenship: The Material Construction of Sexualities,* Routledge, New York.

Grosz, Elizabeth. (1994). *Volatile Bodies: Towards a Corporeal Feminism,* Allen & Unwin, Sydney.

Hoff, Joan. (1994). "Comparative Analysis of Abortion in Ireland, Poland, and the United States," *Women's Studies International Forum,* vol. 17, no. 6. pp. 621–46.

Jones, Kathleen. (1990). "Citizenship in a Woman-Friendly Polity," *Signs,* vol. 15, no. 4, pp. 781–812.

Leech, Marie. (1994). "Women, the State and Citizenship: 'Are Women in the Building or in a Separate Annex?,' " *Australian Feminist Studies,* no. 19, pp. 79–91.

O'Connor, Julia. (1993). "Gender, Class and Citizenship in the Comparative Analysis of Welfare State Regimes," *British Journal of Sociology,* vol. 44, no. 3, pp. 503–18.

Pateman, Carole. (1992). "Equality, Difference, Subordination: The Politics of Motherhood and Women's Citizenship," in *Beyond Equality and Difference: Citizenship, Feminist Politics and Female Subjectivity,* G. Bock and S. James, eds. Routledge, London.

Phillips, Anne. (1993). *Democracy and Difference,* Pennsylvania State University Press, University Park, Pennsylvania.

Rhode, Deborah. (1992). "The Politics of Paradigms: Gender Difference and Gender Disadvantage," in *Beyond Equality and Difference: Citizenship, Feminist Politics and Female Subjectivity,* G. Bock and S. James, eds. Routledge, London.

Voet, Rian. (1994). "Women as Citizens: a Feminist Debate," *Australian Feminist Studies,* no. 19, pp. 61–77.

Ward, Anna et al. (19930. *Women and Citizenship in Europe,* Trentham Books and European Forum of Socialist Feminists, Oakhill.

Reading D

Owning the Self in a Disowned World
PATRICIA J. WILLIAMS

Patricia Williams, a legal scholar who focuses on race and gender issues, challenges the liberal Enlightenment notion of the individual shared by many contemporary feminist thinkers. Williams argues that certain groups of women cannot ever be recognized as individuals or full citizens with rights when the purpose of a state is to uphold racism and patriarchy. In this context, she points out, the strategy of claiming rights as a citizen may not be possible or desirable for certain women.

Recently, in Massachusetts, a woman who suffered a miscarriage in a drunk-driving accident was charged with vehicular homicide when the fetus was delivered stillborn.[1] I suppose this makes sense from the perspective of some litigation model in which mother "versus" fetus is the order of the day, in which the shell of a woman's body is assumed to be at cross-purposes with the heart within. It makes no sense from the perspective of a model in which woman and fetus are one, and in which the home of the body is also the site of sheer torment; it makes no sense from the sad seductive wisdom of self-destruction.

Patricia J. Williams, "Owning the Self in a Disowned World," in *The Alchemy of Race and Rights,* Cambridge: Harvard University Press, 1991: 183–85.

[. . .]

On TV, there is a news snippet about a pregnant inmate in a Missouri prison who is suing the state on behalf of her unborn fetus, claiming that the Thirteenth Amendment prevents imprisonment of the fetus because it has not been tried, charged, and sentenced. The suit is premised on a Missouri antiabortion statute declaring that life begins at conception; the inmate is arguing that such a statute affords a fetus all the rights of personhood. "The fetus should not serve a sentence for the mother," says Michael Box, the Kansas City attorney representing the inmate.[2] Hearing about this case makes my head throb even harder, and my craziness advances several notches. Somewhere at the back of my head I remember having gone crazy before, only a few months ago, over a story about another pregnant woman, this one in Washington, D.C., who was put into prison by a judge to keep her off the streets and out of drug-temptation's way, ostensibly in order to *protect* her fetus.[3] In the litigation that followed, the underlying issue turned out to be similar to the one in the Missouri case: the living conditions for prisoners, whether pregnant or not, but epitomized by the lack of exercise, health care, and nutrition so necessary for prenatal nurture.

My head is throbbing because these cases don't make sense to me. I don't believe that a fetus is a separate person from the moment of conception; how

---

Key Term

Thirteenth Amendment The amendment to the U.S. Constitution that abolished the legal practice of slavery.

176

could it be? It is interconnected, flesh-and-blood-bonded, completely a part of a woman's body. Why try to carve one from the other? Why is there no state interest in not simply providing for but improving the circumstances of the woman, whether pregnant or not? I'm not sure I believe that a child who has left the womb is really a separate person until sometime after the age of two. The entire life force is a social one, a process of grafting onto our surroundings and then growing apart and then grafting again, all in our own time and in all kinds of ways that defy biological timetables alone. (But I have been called extreme in this, and by my own mother, from whom I have not even yet moved fully apart.)

In both of these cases, it seems to me, the Idea of the child (the fetus) becomes more important than the actual Child (who will be reclassified as an adult in the flick of an eye in order to send him back to prison on his own terms), or the actual condition of the woman of whose body the real fetus is a part. In both cases the idea of the child is pitted against the woman; her body, and its need for decent health care, is suppressed in favor of a conceptual entity that is innocent, ideal, and all potential.

It seems only logical, I think while applying a cold compress to my brow, that in the face of a statute like Missouri's, pregnant women would try to assert themselves through their fetuses; that they would attempt to rejoin what has been conceptually pulled asunder. They would of course attempt to assert their own interests through the part of themselves that overlaps with some architecture of the state's interest, in order to recreate a bit of the habitable world within the womb of their protective-destructive prisons.

In bargaining this way, however, pregnant women trade in interests larger than the world of prisoners' rights. In having the fetus declared an other person, in allowing the separation in order to benefit the real mutuality, they enslave themselves to the state. They become partialized, moreover, in the commodification of that bargain, as a prostitute becomes seen only as a "cunt" and as pigs dressed for slaughter become only "hoof," "head," or "hide." Pregnant women become only their fetuses; they disguise and sacrifice the rest of themselves and their interests in deference to the state's willingness to see only a small part of their need. The fetus thus becomes an incorporation of the woman, a business fiction, an uncomfortable tapestry woven from rights-assertion-given-personhood. It is an odd, semiprivate, semipublic undertaking, in which an adversarial relationship is assumed between the public and the private.

What a cycle of absurdity, I think as the melting ice drips down my nose: protecting the fetus from the woman by putting her in jail, then protecting the fetus from jail by asserting the lack of due process accorded the fetus in placing it there. The state's paternalism in these cases is very like the nightmare of another woman I read about, named Melody Baldwin, who injected her baby with her own toxic antidepressant medication in order to protect the infant from the toxin of life's despair: it was a mad person's metaphor of maternalism.[4]

It's all enough to drive a person legally insane (but then of course the person would get Thorazine).

NOTES

1. Christopher Daly, "Woman Charged in Death of Own Fetus in Accident," *Washington Post,* November 25, 1989, p. A4.

2. "Missouri Fetus Unlawfully Jailed, Suit Says," *New York Times,* August 11, 1989, p. B5.

3. Victoria Churchville, "D.C. Judge Jails Woman as Protection for Fetus," *Washington Post,* July 23, 1988, p. 1.

4. "Proposal for Woman's Sterilization Draws Protest," *New York Times,* September 26, 1988, p. 30.

REFLECTING ON THE SECTION

Readings in this section discuss the legal status of individuals, women's historical exclusions from definitions of citizenship in political thought in the West, and the effects of these definitions and exclusions in modern times. What is the relation of rationality to femininity and citizenship in Enlightenment liberal political theory, as it is illustrated in Mary Wollestonecraft's impassioned writing? Jan Jindy Pettman claims that the division between what are called public and private spheres emerges from this Western history of political ideas, in which women are not seen as citizens and thus are relegated to the domestic sphere of the home. In the twentieth century, when women were acknowledged as citizens, there remained what Pettman calls "public equality and private inequality." Women, unlike men, were still unable to move freely between public and private spheres.

Are women still lesser individuals than men? How do differences in race, class, sexuality, religion, and nationality affect women's rights as full citizens? Patricia Williams demonstrates that race and gender govern the ability of women to be seen as autonomous individuals with full rights. She uses the example of two African-American women's legal strategies to gain control over their own bodies to show that such women do not have full rights of citizenship in the law. In fact, she argues that even access to rights may simply allow greater control by a patriarchal and racist state. Can you think of other examples that show that access to rights may not be the only way to remove inequalities?

Gender and the Rise of the Modern State

Women, Gender, and the State

JAN JINDY PETTMAN

Jan Jindy Pettman, a feminist political scientist, asks: What is the political role of women in modern societies? To answer this question, she investigates the idea of the "individual" as a political agent. Are women individuals in the same way that men are? Historically, the individual was conceived to be a male who was free to move about in the public space as well as in the domestic sphere, while women were confined to the domestic sphere alone. In the aftermath of European colonization, for example, this view of the nation-state as having separate spheres did not take into

Jan Jindy Pettman, "Women, Gender, and the State," in *Worlding Women: A Feminist International Politics.* New York: Routledge, 1996: 5–15.

account the many women for whom this separation was not available due to class or race. This view led to unequal status for men and women. Given these limits, Pettman argues that it does provide a useful place to begin to study gender, citizenship, and the individual.

✑ Making the State

Gendered and feminist analyses reveal that the state is in almost all cases male dominated and is in different ways a masculinist construct. It is simply not possible to explain state power without explaining women's systematic exclusion from it (Runyan and Peterson 1991)...

Feminist tracings of early state formation focus on the emergence and consolidation of public political

---

Key Terms

body politic The many parts that, together, make a whole, organic entity of a society.

citizen A member of a state who owes allegiance to the government and is entitled to rights and privileges in return.

individual A single, unique human being in a social group.

individualism The doctrine that the interests of the autonomous, unique individual ought to be paramount.

patriarchy Power system organized around male authority.

polis Greek city-state; used as model of citizen democracy in Enlightenment and modern philosophy.

socialist state Modern state in which private property is almost eliminated in favor of common ownership and welfare state social programs.

transnational In contrast to international, transnational refers to movements of goods, bodies, and ideas across national boundaries such that the strict distinctions among nations become altered or more flexible.

welfare state Modern state in which the government takes responsibility for the health and welfare of its citizens through social programs.

power and the centralisation of authority, which simultaneously (though in different forms in different times and places) displaced autonomous kin communities and constituted a separate domestic or private sphere that came to be associated with women and the feminine. Myths of the origins of Greek city-states inform western political theory.

The transition to institutionalised forms of domination and control was gendered. The Athenian polis marks the emergence of the (free) male citizen and the construction of public space as male. Politics involved performance and appearance in the public space. In the private space of the home, women, children, and slaves lived and worked to provide for the physical and emotional needs of men thus freed to go about their public and citizen duties.

In many non-western political economies, too, there was a long historical process of state formation, through which patriarchal norms became so extensive and entrenched as to become invisible (Lerner in Silverblatt 1988: 445). Gradually and unevenly, states developed over the period 3100 to 600 B.C. in the ancient Near East. In Asia, for example in China, patriarchal states also developed. In many places regional or local authorities were rather less centralised or formalised, while in other places autonomous kin communities remained the basis of political and social order, at least until colonisation disrupted local power relations.

The modern state system dates from the Treaty of Westphalia in 1648, marking the end of the European religious wars. European state forms were imposed through wars and globally through colonisation. European settler states emerged in the late eighteenth and early nineteenth century in the Americas, and later in Australia, New Zealand, and South Africa, for example. The modern state was globalised through decolonisation after World War II, so that now almost everyone lives in an internationally recognised sovereign state.

Under colonisation, European state-making processes were reproduced in other parts of the world, through the consolidation of centralised government and power. Colonised elites mobilised against foreign control but rarely against the introduced forms of political authority, seeking to take over the state rather than to remove it. Beginning in colonial rule and often intensifying since decolonisation, state-making included the conceding of local political power and resources to the state by some men, in return for men's increased control over their families (Charlton et al. 1989: 180). These processes strengthened the public/private divide and increasingly subordinated women within the private—though the location and meaning of this divide were never fixed or uncontested.

States are historical and contingent. They are ongoing projects and a lot of work goes into keeping them going. State-making is a process that is neither inevitable nor unilinear. States themselves, or those who control and administer them, define boundaries of belonging and authority. The state itself becomes a player in politics; it plays in its own interests.

Gendered States

Classical western political thinkers, such as Plato and Aristotle, and those theorising the development and meaning of the modern state system, such as Hobbes and Locke, didn't ignore gender in the ways that contemporary theorists often do. Instead they incorporated notions of difference, of biology or culture, as reasons for excluding women from the political. Carole Pateman's retelling of the myth of origin (1988) sees the overthrow of the despotic fathers through a fraternal contract establishing the political rule of (elite) men and the gender rule of men as a group over women as a group. This contract did not simply overlook women but was constituted on the basis of their exclusion. It established men's sex right to women's bodies and labour and was a contract of citizenship, a political fraternity or brotherhood. Not all men were admitted to public power, but all men were admitted to sex right, to women's unpaid labour, sexual services, and reproductive powers—to women's bodies.

The enlightenment's man turns out, indeed, to be a man. The state subject becomes an individual male—citizen, soldier, worker—a reasonable man. Women are not only different, but constructed in relation to men, and given inferior value. This gender dichotomy includes men as active, women as passive; men as heads of households and breadwinners, and women as their dependents (Peterson and Runyan 1993).

Men move from public to private and back again. They are in positions of authority over unequals in the domestic sphere and recognised as individuals and citizens in the public sphere (or elite men are). Women are contained and constrained in the home and in their sexed bodies. Because public space is male, and women are seen as belonging in the private, women appearing in public space appear "out of place." "The 'body politic' is masculinised, and a conflict is set up between female bodies and public space" (Jones 1984: 78). There is a complex, shifting, and contested association of women with the domestic, but also with sexuality and danger, which makes women especially vulnerable to attack if they are seen as beyond protection, or out of control (Afshar 1987).

[. . .]

Through the work of many a male political theorist, the public/political of the individual citizen takes on the characteristics of the masculine, associating manhood with ruling. Independence is a quality of the political man, disconnected, impartial, unlike the private female, who is connected, dependent, nurturing, or—alternatively—unruly, sexual, disorderly. In either case, she needs to be under the protection/control of a man (to protect her—or to protect the polis/the man from her?). The relegation of women away from the public sphere facilitates the definition of the political as that where the female and femininity are absent, and constitutes the male citizen and masculine authority.

[. . .]

⌒Women and the State

Feminists theorising the state and women's relations with it frequently focus on the welfare state in the west, the effects of transition to a market economy in Eastern Europe, and on women and development in "the third world." Even within states, generalisations about women and the state are difficult.

"The state" is an abstraction that refers to a set of relations, practices, and institutions. States are not monolithic, uniform, or unitary. Each state consists of a variety of sites, institutions, operations, and functions, ranging in western states, for example, through warfare, policing, welfare, and state funding for community organisations. States try to maintain conditions for capital accumulation and manage productive relations and the labour market. States also attempt to contain different groups' claims in the face of political mobilisation, including claims by those who seek to escape from state power or to renegotiate their relations with the state.

Western liberal democratic states are interventionist states (Yearman 1990). They are highly bureaucratised, with a huge information-gathering capacity, and a reach that affects almost everyone in every aspect of life (Sassoon 1987). They are male states, in terms of those who "man" them, although, especially in the Scandinavian states, there are significant numbers of women in higher positions. The state is still largely masculinist, in its assumption of (elite) male interests and characteristics as the norm, though in some states there is now a feminist presence, often marginalised and contained. What the state does is heavily gendered. The state is "the main organiser of the power relations of gender" (Connell 1990: 520) through its legislation and policies and the ways it is implicated in the construction of the public/private.

The impact of state action and inaction is gendered, affecting men as a group and women as a group differently. Even within any one state, it is very difficult to generalise "an entire range of relationships between groups of women in particular locations and a variety of state policies, agencies, and processes" (Randall 1987: 14). But we can say that women as a group are more dependent on the state than men. Much of the provisioning that is directed at women as women or as mothers comes as a result of long decades of struggle. There is a very complex politics here, as women's organisations and feminists direct demands at the state for more services or protection, while many are profoundly suspicious of the state and its implication in the reproduction of unequal gender relations.

Different feminists conceive of the state and of women's actual and potential relations with it differently. While the labels that emerged from experiences with western states are now often inadequate even in the west, we can identify tendencies or associations (Humm 1992). Liberal or equality feminists seek to end state-directed or sanctioned discrimination against women and urge state action for women's equal rights. The state is dominated by men, but increasing women's access and power can alleviate gender inequalities. Socialist feminists see the state as propagating dominant class as well as gender interests, and often race and ethnic interests as well. They are therefore more ambivalent toward the state and the possibilities of using the state for feminist goals. While seeking state transformation, many also recognise the need to engage with the state in defence of women's practical gender interests now (Molyneux 1985). Radical feminists who prioritise women's oppression and see the male state as part of that oppression are often hostile to any further intrusion of the state into women's lives; yet many also urge state action in defence of women's rights. Feminist commentators remark upon the ironies of appealing to a masculinist state for protection against the violence of individual men (Brown 1992; Alvarez 1990).

Individual feminists also find themselves taking up different positions in relation to the state at different times. This reflects the complexity of women's different relations with the state (Pettman, 1992a). States' construction of women as mothers, for example, helps constitute women's unpaid work, an enormous subsidy to the state and to employers. States have long resisted any responsibility for women's security from male violence and become complicit by not taking violence against women seriously. As well, it is often agents of the state, especially police and military, who are major abusers of women's rights. At the same time, state legislation and provision can make a profound difference to women's survival and choices.

Often, women are treated by the state in ways officially ungendered, as citizens or workers; and yet we know that women's experiences of citizenship and the labour market are radically different from men's. Women also organise and approach the state as claimants and as political activists, where they may or may not constitute themselves as women. They are often dependents of the state, as the vast majority of old-age pensioners or single supporting mothers, for example. Many women are also state workers—in a gendered division of labour—mainly in teaching, nursing, social work, or helping, service, and clerical roles. They are rarely in positions of policy or power. Women's work compensates for states' inadequate or inappropriate services and makes invisible adjustments, in the face of economic crises and cutbacks, in family and community care. Women also mediate between the state and other family members. The state depends for its survival on the labour of women, as obligatory unpaid service. "To eliminate this exploitation would be to bring the whole system into crisis" (Cavarero 1992: 44). No understanding of the state is possible without interrogating its own gender politics, and its gendered effects.

Or is this the western state? States differ radically from each other. There is now much material on states and significant writings on the gender of states. While still preponderantly on western states, there are now numerous studies on, and often by, women in third-world states, and minority women in western states (Afshar 1987; Parpart and Staudt 1989; Charlton et al. 1989; Kandiyoti 1991a; Moghadam 1994a).

The shape and frame of women's relations with different states vary widely, although women everywhere are overwhelmingly responsible for reproductive, domestic, and caring work, within a sexual division of labour that constructs certain kinds of work as women's work. All states are engaged in the construction of the public/private divide. Those with the capacity to do so intervene in the private, to regulate gender relations among other things. But the boundaries and the particular ideologies around the private vary, between states and within them over time.

The growth of the welfare state in the west and the provision of particular kinds of support to women, especially to mothers, has been characterised as a shift from private to public patriarchy. The state replaces individual men, though still with conditions for its "protection," including, often, the surveillance of women's sexual relations. Women in the United Kingdom and the United States have been described as client–citizens (Jones 1988: 25), in a dichotomy that sees men treated as workers and women as mothers, despite the large numbers of women who are both. In the Scandinavian countries, women are constructed more as citizen–workers, winning rights such as child care and maternity leave as supports for this role. This rather different relationship between women and the state leads one writer to describe herself as a "state-friendly feminist in search of the women-friendly state and as part of the rather optimistic, pragmatic, social-demo-cratic tradition of Scandinavian welfare state analysis" (Hernes 1988: 188; see also Siim 1994).

Maxine Molyneux (1989), analysing socialist states before the fall, noted the ways in which their policies toward women were conditioned by international fac-tors. States as diverse as those of Eastern Europe, the Soviet Union, China, Cuba, and Vietnam were officially committed to equality for women and men and treated both primarily as workers. These policies reflected the prioritising of class oppression and also Soviet domi-nance in post-World War II Eastern Europe, leading to the imposition of a Soviet model. Talk of feminism and women's organisations from the late 1970s stemmed partly from transnational and international processes, including the rise of third-world and national-liberation feminists who were also socialists. Meetings of differ-ent women through the U.N. Decade for Women, prompting the collection of extensive information on women's lives, documented the double shift in socialist countries, too.

Dramatic changes in the organisation of state power and productive relations, and in some cases changing state borders in the wake of Soviet collapse, have had mixed results for women. In Poland, for example, the rise of Solidarity and the renewed influence of the Catholic Church have limited women's earlier rights to abortion. Understandings about who is a citizen and who should have what rights, and reorganisation of produc-tive relations in transition to market economies, all have profound effects on different women (*Feminist Review* 1991; Ward 1993; Einhorn 1993). Women's social rights are under attack, as are workers' rights generally in the face of growing unemployment and the radical removal of the socialist right to work. But pressure to push women back into the home also reflects the costs of women's rights as workers, which made women more expensive, rather than cheaper, workers (Moghadam 1995). One result is a reassertion of the private sphere and the worker/mother dichotomy in ideologies of housewifisation, familiar elsewhere. Dramatic too is the drop in the numbers and visibility of women in many ex-socialist states' politics and the difficulties of talking about feminist goals where official gender equality is identified with the now discredited former regimes. At the same time, the lifting of institutionalised repression and, in places, political terror enables a proliferation in women's groups and organisations and growing contacts across the old iron curtain.

Generalising about the many states outside Europe and North America is a dangerous affair, though the in-corporation of "the rest of the world" into a European and later western-dominated international structure was carried into its contemporary mode through de-colonisation along colonially imposed borders. The impact of colonial power and the spread of capitalist productive relations on indigenous and precolonial po-litical forms varied widely. Both precolonial and colo-nial forms of authority were gendered, and both colonial and anticolonial organisation often explicitly aligned with or opposed particular gendered practices, especially concerning the status of women.

[. . .]

In most cases since independence, third-world states have become increasingly centralised and bureaucra-tised and increasingly important in women's lives (Af-shar 1987). Almost all states have been concerned to control women's sexuality and fertility, and "the status of women" often signals priorities in state- and nation-building projects. Difficulties in generalising about women's relations with states is demonstrated by the variety of experiences of women in Muslim-majority states. The position of women in these states cannot be understood apart from the political projects of contem-porary states and their struggles to legitimise their au-thority relations (Kandiyoti 1991a). These may take the form of secularising states, as in Turkey, Egypt, and earlier Iran, or the consolidation of communal control over women, as in Pakistan and post-1979 Iran. In each, different women respond differently.

[. . .]

Despite the variety of state projects and women's responses to them, we can make some generalisations about women and the state that appear to be universal.

- Much state discourse renders women invisible, as if citizens and workers are gender-neutral, or assuming they are men.
- All state policies affect women, often in different ways from the ways they affect men. Women's experiences

of citizenship, the labour market, and state violence are different from men's. Only through feminist analysis or a "gender-sensitive lens" (Peterson and Runyan 1993) do these differences and therefore the full meaning of these institutions become clear.

- All states rely on women's unpaid domestic and reproductive labour. No state could seriously attempt equality in work, or to pay fairly for women's work, without profound transformation of all social and power relations. The domestication of women means naturalising women's work as a labour of love, and so perpetuates the "double load" and the containment of women.

- Many states exclude women from state rights as private or dependent, or as communal property. Women have great difficulties in becoming state subjects and citizens. State legislation regarding marriage, divorce, legitimacy of children, and the status of women profoundly affects women's rights and their access to resources and choices.

- States often attend to women as women, and especially as mothers. Despite historical, cultural, and national specificity, there are remarkable similarities in the construction of women as mothers, and of motherhood as of political concern to states.

- Especially since 1975, states have developed women's sections, desks, and policies. The U.N. Decade for Women placed women's issues on the international agenda and generated a huge amount of information that documented women's inequality internationally. Since then, international networks of feminists and women's nongovernmental organisations (NGOs) have created a language around women's oppression or subordination and have asserted the profoundly gendered nature of all politics, within and between states. Now more than 140 states have "women's machinery" in bureaucracy and government (Lycklama a Nijeholt 1991). Most states still translate women's issues into welfare issues and contain women as a category or special-needs group, rather than analysing the gendered impact of state policies and the impact of gender power on people's lives. Some states have incorporated feminist inputs into policymaking, creating "femocrats" whose relations with other feminists are not always easy (Watson 1990; Alvarez 1990). Elsewhere, "state feminists" appointed to run state policies of gender equity may have few relations with feminists or women's organisations outside the bureaucracy.

- While states treat women differently from men, states also treat different women differently, as citizens or not, or as members of dominant or minority groups, for example. Nira Yuval-Davis and Floya Anthias (1989) suggest a framework for understanding the relations of women/nation/state internationally, in terms of how states attend to women, for example, as biological reproducers of citizens and workers of the state; as reproducers of the boundaries of national and ethnic groups; as culture carriers, responsible for socialising children and transmitting culture; as signifiers of national and ethnic differences; and as contributors to national and state struggles.

So not all citizens, and not all women, experience the state in the same ways. Differences within states push us to ask: Who does the state represent internationally? Who does it speak for? Who is not represented by the state?

REFERENCES

Afshar, Haleh, ed. (1987). *Women, State and Ideology—Studies from Africa and Asia,* State University of New York Press, Albany.

Alvarez, Sonia. (1990). "Contradictions of a Women's Space in a Male-Dominated State: The Political Role of Commissions on the Status of Women in Postauthoritarian Brazil," in *Women, In-*ternational Development and Politics: The Bureaucratic Mire, K. Staudt, ed. Temple University Press, Philadelphia.

Brown, Wendy. (1992). "Finding the Man in the State," *Feminist Studies,* vol. 18, no. 1, pp. 7–34.

Cavarero, Adriana. (1992). "Equality and Sexual Difference: Amnesia in Political Thought," in *Beyond Equality and Difference: Citizenship, Feminist Politics and Female Subjectivity,* G. Bock and S. James, eds. Routledge, London.

Charlton, Sue Ellen, Jana Everett, and Kathleen Staudt, eds. (1989). *Women, the State, and Development,* State University of New York Press, Albany.

Connell, R. W. (1990). "The State, Gender and Sexual Politics: Theory and Appraisal," *Theory and Society,* vol. 19, no. 5, pp. 507–44.

Einhorn, Barbara. (1993). *Cinderella Goes to Market: Citizenship, Gender and the Women's Movement,* Verso, London.

Feminist Review. (1991). Special issue on Shifting Territories: Feminisms and Europe, no. 39.

Hernes, Helga. (1988). "The Welfare State Citizenship of Scandinavian Women," in *The Political Interests of Gender: Developing Theory and Research with a Feminist Face,* K. Jones and A. Jénasdéttir, eds. Sage, London.

Humm, Maggie, ed. (1992). *Feminisms: A Reader,* Harvester Wheatsheaf, New York.

Jones, Kathleen. (1984). "Dividing the Ranks: Women and the Draft," *Women and Politics,* vol. 4, pp. 75–88.

Jones, Kathleen. (1988). "Towards a Revision of Politics," in *The Political Interests of Gender: Developing Theory and Research with a Feminist Face,* K. Jones and A. Jénasdéttir, eds. Sage, London.

Kandiyoti, Deniz, ed. (1991). *Women, Islam and the State,* Macmillan, London.

Lycklamà Nijeholt, Geertje, ed. (1991). *Towards Women's Strategies in the 1990s,* Macmillan, London.

Moghadam, Valentine, ed. (1994). *Gender and National Identity: Women and Politics in Muslim Societies,* Zed Books, London.

Moghadam, Valentine. (1995). "Women, Revolution and National Identity in the Middle East," in *The Women and International Development Annual,* vol. 4, R. Gallin and A. Ferguson, eds. Westview, Boulder, Colo.

Molyneux, Maxine. (1985). "Mobilisation without Emancipation? Women's Interests, the State and Revolution in Nicaragua," *Feminist Studies* vol. 11, no. 2, pp. 227–54.

Molyneux, Maxine. (1989). "Some International Influences on Policy-Making: Marxism, Feminism and the 'Women Question' in Existing Socialism," *Millennium,* vol. 18, no. 2, pp. 255–63.

Parpart, Jane, and Kathleen Staudt, eds. (1989). *Women and the State in Africa,* Lynne Rienner, Boulder.

Pateman, Carole. (1988). *The Sexual Contract,* Basil Blackwell, Oxford.

Peterson, V. Spike, and Anne Sisson Runyan, eds. (1993). *Global Gender Issues,* University of Minnesota Press, Minneapolis.

Pettman, Jan. (1992). *Living in the Margins: Racism, Sexism and Feminism in Australia,* Allen & Unwin, Sydney.

Randall, Vicky. (1987). *Women and Politics: International Perspectives,* 2nd ed., Macmillan, London.

Runyan, Anne Sisson, and V. Spike Peterson. (1991). "The Radical Future of Realism—Feminist Subversions of International Relations Theory," *Alternatives,* vol. 16, pp. 67–106.

Sassoon, Anne S., ed. (1987). *Women and the State,* Hutchinson, London.

Siim, Birte. (1994). "Gender, Power and Citizenship," International Political Science Association congress paper, Berlin.

Silverblatt, Irene. (1988). "Women in States," *Annual Review of Anthropology* vol. 17, pp. 427–60.

Ward, Kathryn. (1993). "Reconceptualizing World System Theory to Include Women," in *Theory of Gender/Feminism on Theory,* Paula England, ed. Walter de Gruyler, New York.

Watson, Sophie, ed. (1990). *Playing the State, Australian Feminist Interventions,* Allen & Unwin, Sydney.

Yeatman, Anna. (1990). *Bureaucrats, Technocrats, Femocrats: Essays on the Contemporary Australian State,* Allen & Unwin, Sydney.

Yuval-Davis, Nira, and Floya Anthias, eds. (1989). *Woman-Nation-State,* Macmillan, London.

Reading B

Power and the State

JEFFREY WEEKS

Historian Jeffrey Weeks argues that the study of sexuality in relation to gender, race, ethnicity, and class aids our understanding of domination and subordination by the modern state. Just as the modern nation-state produces tensions between public and private that influence ideas of gender difference, the same dynamics affect the way that sexual difference is produced.

Issues of sexuality are at the heart of the whole workings of power in modern society. "The state," broadly defined, clearly has a crucial role to play here. Through

Jeffrey Weeks, "Sexuality and History Revisited," in *State, Private Life and Political Change,* Lynn Jamieson and Helen Corr, eds. New York: St. Martin's Press, 1999: 40–44.

its role in determining legislation and the legal process it constitutes the categories of the permissible and the impermissible, the pure and the obscene. Through its symbiosis with the forces of moral regulation (from the churches to the medical profession) it can shape the climate of sexual opinion. Through its organisation of health and welfare it can help to determine the patterns of marriage, childbearing, child-rearing, and so on.

Of course, the actual practice of the state varies enormously, depending on a variety of historical factors and contingencies. A would-be theocracy like modern Iran can make adultery a criminal offence, with draconian penalties. An ostensibly secular state might formally eschew a direct role in moral regulation (though all the evidence suggests that it is easier to make the

---

Key Terms

class A group sharing the same economic or social status.

Michel Foucault (1926–84) French historian and philosopher. Foucault studied the rise of institutions such as prisons, hospitals, and asylums, as well as the emergence of specific practices of sexuality and gender in relation to the ascendancy of the middle class in Europe. He is known for bringing the term "discourse" into common scholarly usage to mean the dominant and powerful ways of thinking that are assumed to be common knowledge rather than historical constructions.

moral regulation Ideology based on moral precepts that are instituted by schools, families, media, religious institutions, and government.

sexual difference Term used to refer to the division between male and female based on biological differences. Also used as a foundational concept in feminist psychoanalytic theories—in contrast to the term *gender,* which can imply subject positions in addition to male and female.

sexuality Human behavior classified or interpreted in many different ways: erotics, libido, heterosexual/homosexual, reproduction, desire, and so on.

theocracy Government run by religious establishments or priests.

declaration of disinterest than to carry it out when faced by the host of pressures to which the modern state is heir). The state can shape through its prohibitions and punishments. It can also organise and regulate through its positive will and injunctions, and influence through its omissions and contradictions.

But however critical the role of the state, both in the abstract and in real historical situations, it would be wrong to see its functions as either predetermined or necessarily decisive. One of the key achievements of the new sexual history is that it has helped us to understand the mechanisms through which sexuality is organised and produced in and through a host of different social practices. And in this complex process a variety of often interlocking power relationships are at play.

Take, for example, the question of gender and sexual difference. Various feminist writers have argued forcibly that the elaboration of sexual difference has been central to the subordination of women, with sexuality not only reflecting but being constitutive in the construction and maintenance of the power relationship between men and women. Sexuality is fundamentally gendered.

On the one hand, this can lead to an argument that all hitherto existing definitions of female sexuality (at least in recorded history) are male definitions, so that the category of sexuality itself is fundamentally corrupted by male power and the actual practices of "masculinity" (Rich 1984; Coveney et al. 1984; Dworkin 1987). On the other, the perception of the symbiosis between definitions of gender and of sexuality can lead to careful analyses of the play of definition and self-definition, power and resistance (e.g., Coward 1984). In other words, it becomes a sensitising device which allows us to explore the complexities of practices—theoretical as well as social and political—which have given rise to the relations of domination and subordination that characterise the world of gender.

This has enabled Laqueur, for example, to argue that "the political, economic, and cultural transformations of the eighteenth century created the context in which the articulation of radical differences between the sexes became culturally imperative" (Laqueur 1987, p. 35). The hierarchical model that held sway from ancient times interpreted the female body as an inferior and inverted version of the male, but stressed nevertheless the generative role of female sexual pleasure. The breakdown of this model, in political as well as medical debates, and its replacement by a reproductive model which stressed the radical opposition of male and female sexualities, the woman's automatic reproductive cycle, and her lack of sexual feeling, was a critical moment in the reshaping of gender relations.

It did not arise straightforwardly from scientific advance. Nor was it the product of a singular effort at social control by and through the state. The emergent discourse about sexual difference allowed a range of separate, and often contradictory, social and political responses to emerge. But this new perception of female sexuality and reproductive biology has been absolutely central to modern social and political discourse. Its effects can be discerned in a vast range of political practices, from the legal regulation of prostitution to the social security structures of the Welfare State (Weeks 1989).

If gender is a key variable in the organisation of sexuality, class is another. Class differences in sexual regulation are scarcely unique to the modern world. In the slave societies of the ancient world, moral standards varied enormously with social status. But in the modern world, class definitions of appropriate sexual behaviour have been sharply demarcated. It has, in fact, been argued by Foucault (1979) that the very idea of sexuality is an essentially bourgeois one, which developed as an aspect of the self-definition of the class against the decadent morals of the aristocracy and the rampant immorality of the lower classes in the course of the eighteenth and nineteenth centuries. It was a colonising system of beliefs which sought to remould society in its own emerging image.

Undoubtedly, the respectable standards of family and domestic life, with its increased demarcation between male and female roles, a growing ideological distinction between private and public life, and a marked concern with moral and hygienic policing of nonmarital, nonheterosexual sexuality, were increasingly the norm by which all behaviour was judged (Davidoff and Hall 1987).

This does not mean, of course, that all or even most behaviour conformed to these norms, or that the state acted in a uniform way to institutionalise acceptable forms of behaviour. There is a great deal of evidence that the sexual lives of the working class remained highly resistant to middle-class mores (Weeks 1989). What one can say with confidence is that the complex sexual and moral patterns that exist in the twentieth century are the product of social struggles in which class played an important part.

Not surprisingly, the imagery of class has become a key element in sexual fantasy (Davidoff 1983; Marcus 1967). At the same time, the impact of formal regulation of sexual behaviour through the law and social policy is inevitably coloured by class-bound assumptions. In the 1860s and 1870s the Contagious Diseases Acts, ostensibly directed against prostitutes, were perceived to be aimed at working-class womanhood in general. This fuelled the feminist and labour opposition to them and helped to shape the new sexual regime that followed their repeal in the 1880s (Walkowitz 1980). More recently, it is impossible to understand the significance of the liberal sexual reforms of the 1960s in Britain without relating them to the re-formation of social boundaries, including, crucially, those of class (Weeks 1989). Class does not determine sexual behaviour, but it provides one of the major lenses through which sexuality is organised and regulated.

Categorisations by class intersect with those of ethnicity and race. Eurocentric concepts of correct sexual behaviour have helped to shape centuries of response to the non-European world. So in the evolutionary model of sexuality dominant until the early twentieth century, the black person was classed as lower down the evolutionary scale, closer to nature than the European. This view has survived even in the culturally relativist work of twentieth-century anthropologists, who in their eagerness to portray the lyrical delights of other cultures take for granted that this is because the natives are somehow more "natural" than modern "civilised" peoples (Coward 1983).

One of the most abiding myths is that of the insatiability of the sexual needs of non-European peoples and the threat they pose to the purity of the white races. This has been constitutive of real effects in shaping sexual codes. A fear of black male sexuality was integral to slave society in the American South and has continued to shape public stereotypes to the present. In South Africa, fear of intermarriage and miscegenation is at the heart of apartheid legislation. In Britain, immigration policy is shot through with a dense network of assumptions where race, sex, and gender are inextricably linked.

As European societies become more ethnically and racially diverse, so dominant racial assumptions shape responses to manifest cultural differences, in family patterns, gender relations and sexual assumptions (Amos and Parmar 1984). Sexuality here, as elsewhere, becomes a battleground for competing notions of what constitutes proper behaviour.

The boundaries of race, gender, and class, as of other social divisions like age or disability I could have discussed, inevitably overlap. They are not clear-cut categories. The essential point is that sexuality is constructed and reconstructed through a complex series of interlocking practices, all of which involve relations of power—and of challenges to that power. In this dialectic of power and resistance, definition and self-definition, the formal bodies of the state inevitably play a crucial part. The state can organise the terrain of sexual struggle through its patterns of legal regulation, its political interventions, and social policies. But the state is itself a locale of struggle over the meaning of sexuality: its impact can be highly contradictory as its different organs adopt conflicting policies. There is no functional fit between state intention and sexual regulation. On the contrary, the historian of sexuality must stand amazed at the unintended consequences of state action: laws designed to outlaw homosexuality which encourage it; injunctions to parents to bring forth children for the greater good of the community which are followed by a drop in the birth rate; and attempts to limit childbirth (for the greater good . . .) which lead to an exponential increase in live births.

The major lesson we can draw from all this is that there is no simple way to understand the social organisation of sexuality. Instead of seeing sexuality as a unified whole, we have to recognise that there are various forms of sexuality, that there are in fact many sexualities: class sexualities and gendered sexualities, racially specific sexualities and sexualities of struggle and choice. The historian of sexuality must try to understand these, both in their distinctiveness and in their complex interactions.

REFERENCES

Amos, V., and P. Parmar. (1984). "Challenging Imperial Feminism," *Feminist Review,* No. 17, July 1984.

Boswell, J. (1980). *Christianity, Social Tolerance and Homosexuality* (University of Chicago Press).

Boswell, J. (1983). "Revolutions, Universals, Categories," *Salmagundi,* No. 58/59.

Bouhdiba, A. (1985). *Sexuality in Islam* (London: Routledge & Kegan Paul).

Bray, A. (1982). *Homosexuality in Renaissance England* (London: GMP).

Bullough, V. (1976). "Sex in History: A Virgin Field," *Sex, Society and History* (New York: Science History Publications).

Cameron, D., and E. Frazer. (1987). *The Lust to Kill* (Cambridge: Polity).

Caplan, P. (1987). *The Cultural Construction of Sexuality* (London: Tavistock).

Coveney, L. et al. (1984). *The Sexuality Papers* (London: Hutchinson).

Coward, R. (1983). *Patriarchal Precedents* (London: Routledge & Kegan Paul).

Coward, R. (1984). *Female Desire* (London: Paladin).

Davidoff, L. (1983). "Class and Gender in Victorian England," in Newton et al. (1983).

Davidoff, L., and C. Hall. (1987). *Family Fortunes* (London: Hutchinson).

Dworkin, A. (1987). *Intercourse* (London: Arrow).

Foucault, M. (1979). *History of Sexuality: Vol 1, An Introduction* (London: Allen Lane).

Foucault, M. (1987). *History of Sexuality: Vol 2, The Use of Pleasure* (London: Viking).

Foucault, M. (1988). *History of Sexuality: Vol 3, Care of the Self* (London: Viking).

Franklin, S., and J. Stacey. (1988). "Dyketactics in Difficult Times. A Review of the 'Homosexuality, Which Homosexuality?' Conference," *Feminist Review,* No. 29, Summer.

Freedman, E. B. et al. (1985). *The Lesbian Issue* (University of Chicago Press).

Gagnon, J., and W. Simon. (1974). *Sexual Conduct* (London: Hutchinson).

Gallagher, C., and T. Laqueur. (eds) (1987). *The Making of the Modern Body* (University of California Press).

Gay, P. (1984). *The Bourgeois Experience: Vol 1, Education of the Senses* (Oxford University Press).

Gay, P. (1986). *The Bourgeois Experience: Vol 2, The Tender Passion* (Oxford University Press).

Howells, K. (ed.) (1984). *Sexual Diversity* (Oxford: Basil Blackwell).

HWH. (1987). Papers of the "History, Which History?" conference. Free University of Amsterdam, December.

Katz, J. (1976). *Gay American History* (New York: Thomas Crowell).

Laqueur, T. (1987). "Orgasm, Generation, and the Politics of Reproductive Biology," in Gallagher and Laqueur (1987).

London Feminist History Group. (1983). *The Sexual Dynamics of History* (London: Pluto).

McIntosh, M. (1968). "The Homosexual Role," in Plummer (1981).

Malinowski, B. (1963). *Sex, Culture and Myth* (London: Hart-Davis).

Marcus, S. (1967). *The Other Victorians* (London: Weidenfeld & Nicholson).

Mort, F. (1987). *Dangerous Sexualities* (London: Routledge & Kegan Paul).

Newton, J. L. et al. (1983). *Sex and Class in Women's History* (London: Routledge & Kegan Paul).

Padgug, R. A. (1979). "Sexual Matters," *Radical History Review,* No. 20, Spring/Summer.

Petchesky, R. P. (1986). *Abortion and Women's Choice* (London: Verso).

Plummer, K. (1975). *Sexual Stigma* (London: Routledge & Kegan Paul).

Plummer, K. (1981). *The Making of the Modern Homosexual* (London: Hutchinson).

Plummer, K. (1984). "Sexual Diversity," in Howells (ed.) (1984).

Rich, A. (1984). "Compulsory Heterosexuality and Lesbian Experience," in Snitow et al. (1984).

Rubin, G. (1984). "Thinking Sex" in Vance (ed.) (1984).

Smith-Rosenberg, C. (1975). "The Female World of Love and Ritual," in Smith-Rosenberg (1986).

Smith-Rosenberg, C. (1986). *Disorderly Conduct* (Oxford University Press).

Snitow, A. et al. (1984). *Desire. The Politics of Sexuality* (London: Virago).

Stone, L. (1977). *The Family, Sex and Marriage* (London: Weidenfeld & Nicolson).

Taylor, B. (1983). *Eve and the New Jerusalem* (London: Virago).

Thewelcit, K. (1987, 1990). *Male Fantasies,* Vols. 1 and 2 (Cambridge: Polity).

Thompson, E. P. (1968). *The Making of the English Working Class,* (Harmondsworth: Penguin).

Vance, C. (ed.) (1984). *Pleasure and Danger* (London: Routledge & Kegan Paul).

Vance, C. (1987). "Social Construction Theory," in HWH (1987).

Walkowitz, J. (1980). *Prostitution and Victorian Society* (Oxford University Press).

Walvin, J. (1987). *Victorian Values* (London: André Deutsch).

Weeks, J. (1977). *Coming Out* (London: Quartet).

Weeks, J. (1985). *Sexuality and Its Discontents* (London: Routledge & Kegan Paul).

Weeks, J. (1986). *Sexuality* (London: Tavistock).

Weeks, J. (1989). *Sex, Politics and Society* (2nd ed) (London: Routledge & Kegan Paul).

Competing Agenda: Feminists, Islam, and the State in Nineteenth- and Twentieth-Century Egypt

MARGOT BADRAN

Feminist historian Margot Badran describes the role of the state in modern Egypt as a contradictory one. By creating opportunities for women's education, the state took women away from their family's exclusive control. They became torn between their roles as citizens and as members of religious communities. To resolve this tension, the state reinforced a new version of the public/private split by relegating the supervision and regulation of women's roles in the family to religious law. Badran's work shows us a different public/private split from that described by Pettman, since each nation-state has diverse and distinct constituencies and interests groups.

Margot Badran, "Competing Agenda: Feminists, Islam and the State in Nineteenth- and Twentieth-Century Egypt," in Deniz Kandiyoti, ed. *Women, Islam and the State.* Philadelphia: Temple University Press, 1991: 201–7.

From the second quarter of the nineteenth century, the state in Egypt tried to draw women into the economic and technological transformations under way. As a consequence it began to wrest women away from the more exclusive control of the family, threatening the authority and domination of men over their women.[1] Earlier in the century, after freeing Egypt from direct Ottoman rule, the new ruler, Muhammad 'Ali, while consolidating his power, had placed the Islamic establishment centred at Al Azhar under the control of the state. The former broad purview of the religious establishment was eroded piecemeal in the drive toward secularisation of education and law. The only exception to this was the sphere of personal status laws. For women this created an awkward dichotomy between their role as citizens of the nation-state (*watan*) and as members of the religious community (*umma*). In a division that was never precise, the state increasingly came to influence their

---

Key Terms

feminist consciousness Awareness of the oppression of women as a group and the creation of feminist strategies to overcome that oppression.

harem Term used to refer to the area of a household in which women are secluded.

Islamic modernism In the aftermath of European colonialism, the movement to synthesize Western thought and practices with Islamic religious beliefs.

Ottoman Empire The large Turkish state, founded in the thirteenth century. It extended into Asia, Europe, and Africa at the height of its powers in the sixteenth century.

personal status laws Laws governing matters related to the family, informed by religious doctrine.

public roles, leaving to religion the regulation of their private or family roles. The structural contradictions and tensions this created have to this day never been fully resolved.[2]

While promoting new social roles for women, the state could not afford unduly to alienate patriarchal interests and has therefore made various accommodations and alliances. Whatever their competing interests, the state and religious forces have retained patriarchal forms of control over women. It is this patriarchal dimension that feminists have identified and confronted and for which they have been variously attacked, contained, or suppressed by state authorities and Islamists alike. However, in Egypt there has been sufficient space—albeit more frequently taken than granted—within state and society for women to speak out as feminists and activists. Moreover, the authorities have at times deliberately encouraged women's initiatives for their own purposes.

The earliest articulation of women's feminist consciousness, first discernable in occasional published writings—poetry, essays, and tales—by the 1860s and 1870s, preceded colonial occupation and the rise of nationalism.[3] It was more widely expressed from the 1890s with the rise of women's journalism and salon debates. This new awareness (not yet called feminist; in fact the term *feminism* was not used in Egypt until the early 1920s) was based on an increased sensitivity to the everyday constraints imposed upon women by a patriarchal society. Muslim, Christian, and Jew alike shared this sensitivity, and they projected an understanding, implicit or explicit, that these constraints were not solely religiously based as they had been made to believe. Furthermore, from the rise of feminism in Egypt to the present, its advocates across the spectrum from left to right have consistently used Islam, as well as nationalism, as legitimising discourses. In this chapter, feminism is broadly construed to include an understanding that women have suffered forms of subordination or oppression because of their sex, and an advocacy of ways to overcome them to achieve better lives for women, and for men, within the family and society. I am using a definition of feminism broad enough to be all-inclusive without intending to suggest a monolithic feminism. I indicate divergences

within this larger framework while keeping the primary focus on the interplay among three major discourses, those of feminists, Islamists, and the state.[4]

[. . .]

The Modern State-Building and Colonial Periods: Nineteenth Century to 1922

During the nineteenth century, especially in the later decades, new contenders appeared in the shaping and control of discourse in general, and particularly discourses on women. With the broadening of opportunities for education and the rise of women's feminist consciousness, women who had previously been the objects of prescriptive pronouncements began to challenge patriarchal domination.

The expanding modern state promoted new educational and work opportunities for women, especially in health and teaching, but incurred resistance from families. In the early nineteenth century, for example, Egyptians did not initially allow their daughters to attend the new state midwifery school (Ethopian slaves were recruited as the first students).[5] In 1836, Muhammad 'Ali appointed a Council for Public Education to look into creating a state system of education for girls, but it was found impossible to implement. Later, however, during the rule of Isma'il, one of his wives sponsored the first state school for girls, which opened in 1873, serving the daughters of high officials and white slaves from elite households. Meanwhile, encouraged by the state, Shaikh Ahmad Rifa'i Al Tahtawi and 'Ali Pasha Mubarak published books in 1869 and 1875 advocating education for women, using Islamic justifications from the Quran and *Hadith*.[6] It was not easy, however, to draw women out of the realm controlled by the family.

Feminist discourse first emerged in the writings of women of privilege and education who lived in the secluded world of the urban harem.[7] Women gained new exposure through expanded education and widening contacts within the female world. They made comparisons between their own lives and those of women and men of other social and national backgrounds. Through their new education women also gained deeper knowledge of their religion. Some urban middle- and upper-class women began to contest the Islamic justification for their seclusion, *hijab* (meaning then the veiling of both face and body), and related controls over their lives.[8] In 1892, Zainab Al Fawwaz protested in *Al Nil* magazine, "We have not seen any of the divinely ordered systems of law, or any law from among the corpus of (Islamic) religious law ruling that woman is to be prohibited from involvement in the occupations of men."[9] When Hind Naufal founded the journal *Al Fatah* (The Young Woman) in the same year, inaugurating a women's press in Egypt, women found a new forum for discussing and spreading their nascent feminism.[10]

This emergent feminism was grounded, and legitimised, in the framework of Islamic modernism expounded toward the end of the century by Shaikh Muhammad 'Abduh, a distinguished teacher and scholar from Al Azhar. 'Abduh turned a revolutionary corner when he proposed that believers, by which he meant the learned, could go straight to the sources of religion, principally the Quran and the *Hadith*, for guidance in the conduct of everday life.[11] Through *ijtihad*, or independent inquiry into the sources of religion, 'Abduh demonstrated that one could be both Muslim and modern and that indeed not all traditional practice was in keeping with Islam. In dealing with gender issues, 'Abduh confronted the problem of patriarchal excesses committed in the name of Islam. He especially decried male abuses of the institutions of divorce and polygamy.[12]

The opening out encouraged by *ijtihad* had a number of consequences. While Muslim women's earliest feminist writing may not have been immediately inspired by Islamic modernism, it was not long before it developed within this framework. The progressive discourse of Muslim men was, however, from the start situated within Islamic modernism. It was generated by men of the upper educated strata mainly new secular intellectuals, often men of law,[13] Later, toward the middle of the twentieth century, *ijtihad* would also be evoked by men and women of the lower middle class to create a populist, conservative Islamist discourse (the method—that is, *ijtihad*—rather than the content was inspired by Islamic modernism). Thus two marginalised groups, women and the lower middle class, entered into the debate.

[. . .]

Early in the twentieth century, women's feminist writing became more visible and reached a wider mainstream audience when Malak Hifni Nasif, known by her pen name, Bahithat Al Badiya (Scarcher in the Desert), began publishing essays in *Al Jarida,* the paper of the progressive nationalist party, *Al Umma.* These essays and her speeches were published by the party press in 1910 in a book called *Al Nisa'iyyat* (which can be translated as Feminine or Feminist Pieces, in the absence of a specific term for "feminist" in Arabic). Women's feminism was becoming more explicit and was increasingly expressed within a nationalist idiom reflecting and fueling the growing nationalist movement in Egypt.

Another principal producer of feminist ideas at this period was Nabawiyya Musa, who later published her essays in a book entitled *Al mar'a wa al 'amal* (*The Woman and Work* 1920). These two women were both from the middle class: Bahithat Al Bad'iya from the upper and Nabawiyya Musa from the more modest stratum. They were among the first graduates of the Saniyya Teachers School, established in 1889, and both became teachers. In 1907, Musa was the first Egyptian woman to sit for the baccalaureate examination, and the last until after independence; the colonial authorities, with their policy of training men for practical administration, were not prepared to subsidize women's secondary education. Meanwhile, these two young women carried on consciousness raising through their public lectures to strictly female audiences composed mainly of upper-class women and at special classes for women at the new Egyptian University (which soon were stopped and the money saved was used to send three men on study missions abroad).[14]

In 1911, Bahithat Al Badiya became a pioneer in feminist activism when she sent demands to the Egyptian National Congress for women's education and rights to employment and women's rights to participate in congregational worship in mosques.[15] While they were claiming women's rights to public space, feminists like Bahithat Al Badiya and Huda Sha'rawi early in the century actually opposed the unveiling of the face that male feminists advocated. As a tactical move, they wanted women to gain more education and to reclaim public space before they unveiled. While for progressive men unveiling had a key ideological and symbolic value, for women unveiling was a practical matter that they themselves would have to undertake, with the attendant risks of taunts and assaults on their reputations.[16]

The nationalists of the *Umma* Party, led by Ahmad Lutfy Al Sayyid and other men of the upper class, supported feminism, while those of the *Watani* Party, mainly men of more modest middle-class origins, headed by Mustafa Kamil, were antagonistic toward women's emancipation, which they saw as an undermining Western influence. Unlike the *Umma* Party, which advocated a more secular society, the *Watani* party favoured an Islamic society supporting the notion of a caliphate. It was within these respective frameworks that men as nationalists situated their views on women's place and roles and their own attitudes towards feminism.[17]

During the national revolution from 1919 to 1922, the first priority for Egyptian feminists and nationalists of both sexes was independence. To a large extent, feminist and nationalist positions temporarily united in favour of the common cause. The extent and harshness of colonial oppression were underscored when upper-class women, mobilised by feminist and nationalist leaders among them, left the seclusion of their harems to demonstrate, and when poor women also filled the streets in more spontaneous protest. Members of the Wafdist Women's Central Committee (WWCC), created in 1920 as the women's section of the nationalist party, the *Wafd,* insisted on fully participating in decision making, not just in auxiliary activities. In the midst of the revolution, these women at times took public feminist stands. In 1920, for example, when the male nationalist leadership did not consult the WWCC on the independence proposal they were circulating, the women publicly announced their objections.[18] Yet during colonial occupation, a feminism that called for greater female participation in society was upheld by progressive male nationalists and generally tolerated by others. Moreover, during the ferment of revolution, male nationalists enthusiastically welcomed women's militancy.

During colonial occupation, women's feminism was not connected with a public, organised, movement; it was the articulation of a broad new philosophy. Men's profeminism likewise expressed a philosophical position, and at the time was seemingly more radical than women's, for example in calling for an end to face veiling. Men's feminist rhetoric, however, reached a climax during occupation.

[. . .]

In the late nineteenth and early twentieth century, polemics were started that have plagued feminist and Islamist positions ever since and have had political reverberations in official discourse. These concern definitions of culture, authenticity, identity, and modernity—and their implications for women's roles, around which a battle of legitimacy has raged. The debate has continued right up to the final decade of the twentieth century, as have the state's efforts to control competing discourses and to appropriate elements useful to itself.

NOTES

1. See Margot Badran, "Huda Sha'rawi and the Liberation of the Egyptian Woman," Oxford PhD thesis, 1977, and "The Origins of Feminism in Egypt," and Judith Tucker, *Women in Nineteenth Century Egypt* (Cambridge: Cambridge University Press, 1985).

2. On this dichotomy, see Nawal El Saadawi, "The Political Challenges Facing Arab Women at the End of the 20th Century," pp. 8–26, and Fatima Mernissi, "Democracy as Moral Disintegration: The Contradiction between Religious Belief and Citizenship as a Manifestation of the Ahistoricity of the Arab Identity," pp. 36–43 in Nahid Toubia (ed.), *Women of the Arab World* (London: Zed, 1988).

3. See Margot Badran and Miriam Cooke (eds), *Opening the Gates: A Century of Arab Feminist Writing.* (London: Virago, and Bloomington & Indianapolis: University of Indiana Press, 1990).

4. Badran, "Over a Century of Feminism in Egypt," pp. 15–34. See Margot Badran, "Independent Women: Over a Century of Feminism in Egypt," *Old Boundaries, New Frontiers,* forthcoming, pp. 15–34.

5. See Laverne Kuhnke, "The 'Doctoress' on a Donkey: Women Health Officers in Nineteenth Century Egypt," *Clio Medica,* 9 (1974) no. 3, pp. 193–205.

6. The books are, respectively: *Tariq al hija wa al tamrin 'ala qawa' id al lugha al 'arabiyya (The Way to Spell and Practise the Rules of the Arabic Language)*, 1869, and *Al Murshid al amin lil banat wa al banin (The Faithful Guide for Girls and Boys)*, 1875.

7. See, for example, selections by Warda al Yaziji, Aisha Taimuriyya, and Zainab Fawwaz in Badran and Cooke, *Opening the Gates*.

8. On the *hijab* in nineteenth-century Egypt, see Qasim Amin, *Tahrir al mar'a* (The Liberation of the Woman) (Cairo, 1899). Bahithat Badiya has written on the changing modes of *hijab* in early twentieth-century Egypt. She generally favoured retaining the face veil for the time being for pragmatic reasons but was aware this was not required by Islam. On the subject see, for example, her "Mabadi Al Nis'ai," in Majd al Din Hifni Nasif (ed.), *Ta'thir Bahithat al Badiya Malak Hifni Nasif 1886–1918 (The Heritage of Bahithat al Badiya Malak Hifni Nasif)* (Cairo, 1962) pp. 318–20. On the historical and contemporary context of *hijab*, see Valerie J. Hoffman-Ladd, "Polemics on the Modesty and Segregation of Women in Contemporary Egypt," *International Journal of Middle East Studies*, 19 (1978) pp. 23–50. For various interpretations in general of *hijab*, see Mostafa Hashem Sherif, "What Is Hijab?" *The Muslim World* (July/October 1978, nos. 3–4, pp. 151–63).

9. Zainab Al Fawwaz, "Fair and Equal Treatment," *Al Nil* no. 151 (18, dhu al hujja, 1892) trans. Marilyn Booth, in Badran and Cooke, *Opening the Gates*.

10. The early years of the women's Arabic press in Egypt are the subject of a dissertation by Beth Baron presented to the University of California at Los Angeles in 1988.

11. See Albert Hourani, *Arabic Thought in the Liberal Age* (Cambridge: Cambridge University Press, 1983) pp. 130–63.

12. See 'Abd Al Razek, "L'Influence de la femme dans la vie de Chiekh Mohamed Abdue," *L'Egyptienne* (August 1928) pp. 2–7. Abudh's writings include: "Hajjat Al Insan lil Zawaj," "Fatwa fi Ta'adud Al Zaujat," and "Hukum Ta'adud Al Zaujat," in Muhammad 'Imara, *Al'amal al kamila li Muhammad 'Abduh (The Complete Works of Muhammad 'Abduh)* (Cairo, c. 1971), pp. 49–54, 111–18, and 127–35.

13. See Juan Ricardo Cole, "Feminism, Class, and Islam in Turn-of-the-Century Egypt," *International Journal of Middle East Studies*, 13, (1981) pp. 397–407, and Thomas Philipp, "Feminism and Nationalist Politics in Egypt," in L. Beck and N. Keddie (eds), *Women in the Muslim World* (Cambridge, Mass.: Harvard University Press, 1978).

14. On the public lectures, see *Huda Shaarawi, Harem Years: The Memoirs of an Egyptian Feminist* (London: Virago, 1986) pp. 92–93. Writings and speeches of Bahithat Al Badiya and Nabawiyya Musa are found, among other places, in their respective books: *Al Nisa'iyyat* (trans. as either *Women's* or *Feminist Pieces*) (Cairo: Al Jarida Press, 1910) and *Al Mar'a wa al 'amal (Woman and Work)* (Cairo: 1920). Donald Reid communicated to me the information related here concerning the closing of the women's section and the new use of the funds saved.

15. See Majd Al Din Hifni Nasif, *Ta'thir*

16. See Margot Badran, "From Consciousness to Activism: Feminist Politics in Early 20th Century Egypt," unpublished paper.

17. See Philipp, "Feminism and Nationalist Politics in Egypt," and Cole, "Feminism, Class, and Islam in Turn-of-the-Century Egypt."

18. Badran, "Dual Liberation."

Reading D

"White Slavery," Citizenship, and Nationality in Argentina

DONNA J. GUY

Historian Donna Guy describes the morality campaign conducted by Europeans in the mid-nineteenth century to limit prostitution by regulating and overseeing women's migration. European women who worked as prostitutes outside of their own country became sensationally characterized as "white slaves" and were the subject of heated public debate. Feeling it was necessary to demonstrate its enlightened and moral superiority to Europeans, the Argentine state extended citizenship rights to all women, including those emigrés working as prostitutes. Thus, women in Argentina obtained civil rights only when their situation was compared to women in European countries rather than through their own organizing or their role as equal political actors. It is important to note that by terming these women "white slaves," public opinion ignored the racist enslavement of other groups of women.

Donna J. Guy, "'White Slavery,' Citizenship, and Nationality in Argentina," in Andrew Parker, Mary Russo, Davis Sommer, and Patricia Yaeger, eds. *Nationalisms and Sexualities*. NY: Routledge, 1992: 201–6, 214.

. . . Before the twentieth century only a few republics granted citizens' rights to women. Women generally were denied such rights even though the nation depended on their participation in various ways. Floya Anthias and Nira Yuval-Davis have identified some of these basic roles women have played in the formation of the nation. Women, they argue, not only give birth to future members of national groups but also reproduce the ideological constructs of the nation by transmitting its culture to new generations. Women serve, moreover, as a "focus and symbol in ideological discourse used in the construction, reproduction, and transformation of ethnic/national categories." And finally, women help defend the nation by participating in its political, economic, and social struggles.[1]

Key Terms

postcolonial A term used to refer to the period following formal European colonization. It can also imply the continuing influence and power of the former colonizers on the economies and cultures of independent or decolonized states.

sovereign nation A self-governing, independent nation-state.

white slavery Prostitution rings that transported mainly European women to other countries based on a form of indentured servitude and sometimes involuntary labor. The specter of "white slavery" was used in the nineteenth century as a scare tactic by conservative politicians and religious groups in Europe and North America.

Despite this variety of reproductive and civic roles typically assigned to women, their participation in national life has often been severely limited. Women can be most useful to the nation as passive wards who require the state's protection. Under certain circumstances they may even be called upon to protect, or rather to demand the protection of, their sexuality as a patriotic gesture. As Christine Obbo commented:

> Women's security is often the last frontier men have to defend when all the other battles against colonialism and imperialism are lost. Human societies always portray their women as more virtuous than women of other groups and therefore in need of protection. Never mind that each society also coerces women to be "good women" through imposing a number of sanctions against "bad women."[2]

Women who emigrated and sometimes married beyond the geographic boundaries of the modern nation-state were expected—regardless of their social or economic status—to maintain the honor of their nation by safeguarding their sexual virtue. If these women were placed in a situation where their honor was threatened, the nation's honor would be compromised as well: patriots felt compelled to defend their female citizens, even if their citizenship and virtue had first to be constructed in order to be defended.

The issue of "bad women" triggered the discourse on female nationality and citizenship as thousands of women left their European homelands from the 1870s onward in search of a better life in the Americas, South Africa, and other parts of Europe. From the last quarter of the nineteenth century until the outbreak of World War II, modern European nations carved out empires, fought to preserve national interests, and sought innovative ways to construct national identity. As male legislators and military leaders devised strategies to manifest national strength, the condition of their women living abroad, whether as respectable wives or as socially marginal prostitutes, affected the rights and inherent restrictions of citizenship beyond national frontiers, as if nationality were an inviolable identity. These "loose" emigrant women would play a major role in defining European citizenship and national responsibility.

Almost as soon as women began to arrive in great numbers at foreign ports, troubling stories appeared about European females in legally sanctioned bordellos in colonial or postcolonial cities. For many Europeans, it was inconceivable that their female compatriots would willingly submit to sexual commerce with foreign, racially varied men. In one way or another these women must have been trapped and victimized. So European women in foreign bordellos were construed as "white slaves" rather than common prostitutes, and the campaign to rescue them became a glorious battle pitting civilization at home against barbarism beyond. In this way "bad women" were rehabilitated to become "good women" as their homelands rushed to defend their imputed, nationally inalienable virtue.

[. . .]

But the rescue efforts were hampered by the modern—yet seemingly premodern—definition of female citizenship in Europe, which owed more to paternal rights in the family than to the paternalism of the state. Children inherited their national identity not only because of where they were born, but also through their father's citizenship. And a married woman's citizenship was determined by that of her husband, not by her parents or place of birth. Female nationals who married foreigners encountered another type of problem: they lost their citizenship and could not be protected by their homelands. Instead they were subjected to the laws and customs of their husband's nation. The situation became even more critical if women were divorced, abandoned, or abused by their husbands, because being husbandless meant being stateless. Even women who married foreigners and remained at home lost their citizenship in most European countries where foreigners were allowed to follow the civil codes of their own homelands.[3]

Thus, when nations were partitioned or conquered, or parents were divorced, both women and children found themselves just as stateless as if they had actually emigrated. Protecting children as well as married women was an opportunity to construct new definitions of citizenship as corollaries to the paternalist state. But of course it was not the plight of married women living abroad that first prompted European diplomats and politicians to contemplate the protection of female citizens as a function of national honor, a need that invested the home country with international authority. The rights of married women were paradoxically defined in an a fortiori manner only after the rights of whores had been posited.

[. . .]

Throughout this process of definition the sexuality of both the prostitute and the married woman generated anxious debate. This was especially so in the case of Argentina, where female citizenship was being defined in terms of sexuality and where a centralized and intrusive state needed to assume civic and moral authority to bolster its political legitimacy.

European nations had many reasons to both fear and admire Argentine laws that focused upon prostitutes and wives. As women whose sexual practices and relationships represented each other's antithesis, these two groups jointly defined the parameters of female citizenship in modern Argentina. Prostitutes determined the limits of socially acceptable female sexual behavior so that self-identified female prostitutes lost the right to move freely within cities, work without medical inspection, and live wherever they pleased. In contrast, wives, by law and religion sworn to remain sexually faithful, enjoyed all those privileges taken from prostitutes, though they still suffered other civil restrictions. Until 1926, married female Argentines could not keep the money they earned nor work without permission of their spouse. Nor could they assume parental authority over their children. Yet despite these differences, after 1926 the combined civil rights of females born in Argentina enabled their nation to boast the most inclusive nonpolitical female citizenship laws found among pre-World War II modern nation-states.

[. . .]

Argentina, one of these newly sovereign nations, imagined its community not only by identifying as citizens all males born in Argentine territory, but also by granting the same rights and privileges, according to its 1853 Constitution, to women born in Argentina. Even foreign-born residents were granted most citizenship privileges except military service. This meant that Argentine and foreign-born women might be restricted in some of their activities, but most Argentine women could obtain passports or other identity documents that reaffirmed their Argentine citizenship.[4]

Traditionally, citizenship has been conceived as a political right which often reflects unequal access to power in societies that differentiate male and female roles. The mere possession of the right to vote, hold office, and serve in the military—all male prerogatives until recently—may tend to obscure, however, other important rights women have possessed as citizens within the nation-state, which include the ability to marry, work, own property, and make a will. The Argentine 1853 Constitution, indeed, guaranteed these civil rights to all inhabitants, although subsequent local, civil, and commercial codes placed limitations on prostitutes, minors, and married women. Discussions concerning the negation of constitutional rights for females, however, became important only after European women began to migrate in significant numbers to Argentina, which by the 1880s had become an extremely attractive destination for both women and men.

Inexpensive ocean passages and high wages for agricultural labor (mostly male), as well as a rapidly growing capital city, prompted Europeans to seek their fortunes there. Thousands of poor European women emigrated between 1870 and 1914 in search of work and marriage partners, and they were treated in the same way that the nation dealt with its own countrywomen. Their ability to work, particularly in medically supervised municipal bordellos opened in 1875 to control venereal disease, and their freedom to marry foreign men led to stories of "white slavery"—the international traffic in women and children for purposes of sexual exploitation—and prompted international concern about the plight of European women reputedly forced into a life of vice in Argentina.

Many civil libertarians in Argentina questioned the legality of depriving women, even sexually dangerous ones, of basic civil rights such as the freedom of movement and work. In response, a French physician resident in Argentina, Dr. Benjamin Dupont, wrote *Pornografía de Buenos Aires* in 1879 to defend the existing system. He argued that it was in fact legal to restrict the civil liberties of prostitutes because they "violate fundamental social laws, therefore they cannot expect the freedom that society assures all its members." Dupont, whose native land created the system of medically supervised prostitution in the early nineteenth century, provided little comfort to those back home who organized to keep French women out of foreign bordellos.[5]

The passage of laws to legalize prostitution in Buenos Aires coincided with the formation of a European moral reform association whose aim was diametrically opposed: to close down state-licensed bordellos within and outside Europe. The group called itself "The British, Continental and General Federation for the Abolition of the Government Regulation of Prostitution." Led by the British feminist Josephine Butler, the federation set out to combat the injustice of state-supported prostitution, where women, but not their customers, were subjected to medical exams and special restrictions. Relatively unsuccessful at prohibiting bordellos in Europe, this group, as well as subsequent organizations, soon identified South American countries, especially Argentina, as morally and politically offensive because European women became "sexual slaves" there.[6]

The campaign to extirpate "white slavery" is usually viewed as one component of the social purity campaigns that swept Europe and North America by the turn of the century. Other factors, such as "the changing role of women, domestic and international migrations, and rapid urban and industrial growth,"[7] have also been identified as issues that fed the often hysterical cries to save white slaves entrapped abroad. This concern of European nations to protect their citizens, even the most marginal, must also be kept in focus. After all, at a time of great international jockeying for strength, what nation could afford to allow foreigners to exploit its countrywomen? Where did national duty or citizenship end?

For countries like Argentina, however, the debate over married women's citizenship served an important purpose. It enabled a postcolonial nation to rehabilitate its international reputation as a haven for white slavery and transform it into a pioneer in progressive citizenship legislation. Allied with its Latin American neighbors, Argentina and other adherents of the Pan American Union showed more powerful imperialist nations that national identity could be constructed in ways that enabled newly independent nation-states to protect their women at home and abroad more effectively than could the empires that originally had conquered and colonized them. In this way Argentina managed to redefine itself from recalcitrant pariah to a vanguard model of married women's rights and modern nationality.

NOTES

1. Floya Anthias and Nira Yuval-Davis, "Introduction," in Yuval-Davis and Anthias, eds., *Women, Nation, State* (London: Macmillan Press, Ltd., 1989), p. 7.

2. Christine Obbo, "Sexuality and Economic Domination in Uganda," in ibid., p. 85.

3. A comparative analysis of citizenship laws in Europe and Latin America, particularly in regard to female citizenship can be found in *Encyclopedia Jurídica Omeba* (Buenos Aires: Bibliográfica Omeba, 1964), xx, pp. 36–37.

4. Benedict Anderson. *Imagined Communities: Reflections on the Origin and Spread of Nationalism* (London: Verso, 1983), pp. 15, 52.

5. Dr. Benjamin Dupont, *Pornografía de Buenos Aires. De la necesidad' imprescindible de un dispensario de salubridad y de una oficina de costumbres para reglamentar y reprimir la prostitución* (Buenos Aires: Imprenta de Pablo E. Coni, 1879), pp. 12–13. It was fortunate for Dupont that the French antiwhite-slavery movement was relatively weak. See Steven C. Hause and Anne R. Kenney, *Women's Suffrage and Social Politics in the French Third Republic* (Princeton: Princeton University Press, 1984), p. 257.

6. Edward J. Bristow, *Vice and Vigilance: Purity Movements in Britain since 1700* (Dublin: Gill and MacMillan: Rowman and Littlefield, 1977), p. 78.

7. Ibid., p. 175.

REFLECTING ON THE SECTION

The articles in this section challenge assumptions that statehood is a purely public construction, in contrast to domestic or private institutions of family life, gender, and sexuality. Pettman points out that not only is this model patriarchal but it is also widespread—it has become the norm across the world. However, Margot Badran's excerpt reveals that the public/private divide is not the same the world over. In Egypt, for instance, the creation of two kinds of legal systems, one based on religious laws and one on civil laws, led to new kinds of public and private divides based on gender and nationalism.

Weeks explains that it is not only gender but also sexuality that leads to disempowerment of individuals within a nation-state. Women, Pettman argues, serve state interests through supplying labor that the state requires to protect itself and to support the economy including sexual services. Badran and Guy discuss past uses of women as symbols for nation formation and nationalism. How are women used as symbols of state power today? How does this symbolic use of women regulate their identities and behaviors?

New Social Movements and Identity Politics

Concepts of Identity and Difference
KATHRYN WOODWARD

Feminist cultural critic Kathryn Woodward defines new social movements as those that cut across the conventional democratic politics, which have been organized around class and region. These new social movements construct identities as marginalized or oppressed groups seeking a political voice. In making such claims, many social movements propose an identity that is unchanging and primordial. Yet, Woodward points out, identities change according to historical time period and location.

"New social movements" emerged in the West in the 1960s and especially after 1968, with its peak of student unrest, peace and antiwar activism, especially anti-Vietnam war campaigns and civil rights struggles.

Kathryn Woodward, "Concepts of Identity and Difference," in *Identity and Difference,* Kathryn Woodward, ed. London: Sage, 1997: 24–28.

They challenged the establishment and its bureaucratic hierarchies and were mostly hostile to the "revisionist" and "Stalinist" policies of the Soviet bloc, as well as to the limitations of western liberal politics. Traditional political class allegiances were questioned by movements which cut across these divisions and appealed to the particular identities of their supporters. For example, feminism appealed to women, the black civil rights movement to black people, and sexual politics to lesbian and gay people. Identity politics developed and defined these social movements through a deeper concern for identity: what it means, how it is produced and contested. Identity politics involve claiming one's identity as a member of an oppressed or marginalized group as a political point of departure, and thus identity becomes a major factor in political mobilization. Such politics involve celebration of a group's uniqueness as well as analysis of its particular oppression.

Key Terms

civil rights movement The term used in the United States to refer to the social movement for racial equality and equal rights.

Greenham Common Peace Camps Beginning in 1981, a group of women camped outside a U.S. Air Force base in Greenham Common, England, to protest development of a missile site.

identity politics Standpoint for claims made by oppressed or marginalized groups; drawing on one's identity to mobilize political action.

new social movements Some people refer to the civil rights, student, women's, gay and lesbian, and indigenous people's political movements from the 1960s to the present as "new social movements" to distinguish them from the worker-based movements of socialist and communist politics earlier in the modern period.

Soviet bloc The nations and states aligned with the Soviet Union from World War II until its demise in 1991.

Stalinist Doctrine linked to the rule of Joseph Stalin (1879–1953), head of the Soviet Union between 1924 and 1953. Known for his tactics of political repression and terror.

However, identity can be appealed to in two very different ways within what has come to be called the movements of "identity politics."

On the one hand, the celebration of the group's uniqueness, which is the basis of its political solidarity, can be translated into essentialist claims. For example, some elements of the women's movement have argued for separatism from men based on women's identity and unique qualities which men per se cannot possess. There are, of course different ways of understanding and defining that "uniqueness." It may involve appeals to biologically given features of identity; for example, the claim that women's biological role as mothers makes them inherently more caring and peaceful. Or it can be based on appeals to history and kinship; for example, where women seek to establish an exclusive women's history or "herstory" (Daly 1979) which men have repressed, and to reclaim a unique women's culture—through a claim to something about the position of women which has remained fixed and unchanged by that history and which applies equally to all women as a kind of transhistorical truth (Jeffreys 1985).

Essentialist aspects of identity politics can be illustrated by the views of some of the supporters of the Greenham Common Peace Camps. Some supporters of the Greenham Common campaign against Cruise missiles claimed to represent the essentially female characteristics of nurturing and pacifism. Others criticized this as "deference to the social construction of woman as maternal principle, which through their feminism they attempt to challenge" (Delmar 1986: 12). Similarly, in order to challenge hostile claims that homosexuality is abnormal or immoral there have been assertions, more recently backed by appeals to scientific discourses, that the gay identity is "given" in that it is biologically determined.

On the other hand, some of the "new social movements," including the women's movement, have adopted a nonessentialist position regarding identity. They have stressed that identities are fluid, having different elements which can be reconstructed in new cultural conditions, and that they are not fixed essences locked into differences which are permanent for all time (Weeks 1994). Some members of new social movements have claimed the right to construct and take responsibility for their own identities. For example, black

women have fought for the recognition of their agenda within feminism and have resisted the assumptions of a women's movement based on one category of "woman" where that category is seen as white (Aziz 1992).

Some elements in these movements have challenged two particular notions of the fixity of identity. The first is based on socioeconomic class and what has been called "class reductionism" where, following the Marxist analysis of the base/superstructure relationship, social relations are seen as reducible to the material basis of society. It is thus claimed that gender positions can be 'read off' from social class positions. While this analysis has the appeal of relative simplicity and of highlighting the importance of material economic factors as key determinants of social positions, the social changes which have been taking place call this view into question. Economic changes such as the decline of heavy manufacturing industries and the changing structure of the labour market undermine the very definition of the working class based largely on male, full-time, industrial workers. Identities based on "race," gender, sexuality, and disability, for example, cut across class affiliations. The recognition of the complexity of social divisions by identity politics, where race, ethnicity, and gender have offset class, has drawn attention to other social divisions, suggesting that it is no longer sufficient to argue that identities can be deduced from one's class position (especially when that class position itself is shifting) or that how identities are represented has little impact on those identities. As Kobena Mercer argues: 'In political terms, identities are in crisis because traditional structures of membership and belonging inscribed in relations of class, party, and nation-state have been called into question' (Mercer 1992: 424). Politics is about recruiting subjects through the process of forming identities—the sovereign consumer, the patriotic citizen—and through new social movements putting on to the agenda identities which have not been recognized and have been "hidden from history" (Rowbotham 1973) or have occupied spaces on the margins of society.

The second challenge of some of the new social movements has been to question the essentialism of identity and its fixity as "natural," that is, as a biological category. Identity politics is ". . . not a struggle between natural subjects. It is a struggle for the very articulation of identity, in which the possibilities re-main open for political values which can validate both diversity and solidarity" (Weeks 1994: 12). Weeks ar-gues that one of the major contributions of identity pol-itics has been to construct a politics of difference which subverts the stability of biological categories and the construction of opposites. He argues that new social movements historicized experience, stressing differences between marginalized groups as an alter-native to the "universality" of oppression.

REFERENCES

Aziz, R. (1992). "Feminism and the Challenge of Racism: Deviance or Difference," in H. Crowley and S. Himmelweit, (eds.), *Knowing Women,* Cambridge, Polity/The Open University.

Daly, M. (1979). *Gyn/Ecology: The Metaethics of Radical Feminism,* London, The Women's Press.

Delmar, R. (1986). "What Is Feminism?," in J. Mitchell and A. Oakley, *What Is Feminism?,* Oxford, Basil Blackwell.

Jeffreys, S. (1985). *The Spinster and Her Enemies: Feminism and Sexuality 1880–1930,* London, Pandora Press.

Mercer, K. (1992). "'1968' Periodising Postmodern Politics and Identity," in L. Grossberg, C. Nelson, and P. Treichler, (eds.), *Cultural Studies,* London, Routledge.

Rowbotham, S. (1973). *Hidden from History: Three Hundred Years of Women's Oppression and the Fight against It,* London, Pluto.

Weeks, J. (1994). *The Lesser Evil and the Greater Good: The Theory and Politics of Social Diversity,* London, Rivers Oram Press.

Feminism and the Question of Class
ALEXANDRA KOLLONTAI

Alexandra Kollontai (1872–1952) was one of the fore-most feminist members of the Bolshevik Party in Russia and worked to implement feminist social welfare ideas in the Communist government under Lenin. She was, nonetheless, an outspoken critic of what she called "bourgeois feminism." In this piece, written in 1909, Kollontai argued that class- and gender-based oppression made the experiences of working-class women very different from those of middle-class and wealthy women. In many ways, Kollontai's writings foreshadow more recent criticisms of the notion of "woman" as an identity politics based solely on similarities among women.

Leaving it to the bourgeois scholars to absorb themselves in discussion of the question of the superiority of one sex over the other, or in the weighing of brains and the comparing of the psychological structure of men and women, the followers of historical materialism fully accept the natural specificities of each sex and demand

"Feminism and the Question of Class." From "The Social Basis of the Woman Question," in *The Selected Writings of Alexandra Kollantai,* trans. Alix Holt. London: Allison and Busby, 1977: 58–62.

only that each person, whether man or woman, has a real opportunity for the fullest and freest self-determination and the widest scope for the development and application of all natural inclinations. The followers of historical materialism reject the existence of a special woman question separate from the general social question of our day. Specific economic factors were behind the subordination of women; natural qualities have been a *secondary* factor in this process. Only the complete disappearance of these factors, only the evolution of those forces which at some point in the past gave rise to the subjection of women, is able in a fundamental way to influence and change their social position. In other words, women can become truly free and equal only in a world organized along new social and productive lines.

[. . .]

The Struggle for Economic Independence

First of all we must ask ourselves whether a single united women's movement is possible in a society based on class contradictions. The fact that the women who take part in the liberation movement do not represent one homogeneous mass is clear to every unbiased observer.

Key Terms

Bolshevism One of the main socialist parties in Russia from 1903–1918, founded by Vladimir Lenin, it was the instigator and organizer of the Russian October Socialist Revolution in 1917.
historical materialism A philosophical approach to history associated with Marxism; the argument that there is a material basis for the process of change through a conscious recognition of class struggle.
the woman question The debate over the role of women in the modern state.

The women's world is divided, just as is the world of men, into two camps; the interests and aspirations of one group of women bring it close to the bourgeois class, while the other group has close connections with the proletariat, and its claims for liberation encompass a full solution to the woman question. Thus although both camps follow the general slogan of the "liberation of women," their aims and interests are different. Each of the groups unconsciously takes its starting point from the interests of its own class, which gives a specific class colouring to the targets and tasks it sets itself. . . .

The proletarian women's final aim does not, of course, prevent them from desiring to improve their status even within the framework of the current bourgeois system, but the realization of these desires is constantly hindered by obstacles that derive from the very nature of capitalism. A woman can possess equal rights and be truly free only in a world of socialized labour, of harmony and justice. The feminists are unwilling and incapable of understanding this; it seems to them that when equality is formally accepted by the letter of the law they will be able to win a comfortable place for themselves in the old world of oppression, enslavement, and bondage, of tears and hardship. And this is true up to a certain point. For the majority of women of the proletariat, equal rights with men would mean only an equal share in inequality, but for the "chosen few," for the bourgeois women, it would indeed open doors to new and unprecedented rights and privileges that until now have been enjoyed by men of the bourgeois class alone. But each new concession won by the bourgeois woman would give her yet another weapon for the exploitation of her younger sister and would go on increasing the division between the women of the two opposite social camps. Their interests would be more sharply in conflict, their aspirations more obviously in contradiction. . . .

The woman question assumed importance for women of the bourgeois classes approximately in the middle of the nineteenth century—a considerable time after the proletarian women had arrived in the labour arena. Under the impact of the monstrous successes of capitalism, the middle classes of the population were hit by waves of need. The economic changes had rendered the financial situation of the petty and middle bourgeoisie unstable, and the bourgeois women were faced with a dilemma of menacing proportions; either accept poverty or achieve the right to work. Wives and daughters of these social groups began to knock at the doors of the universities, the art salons, the editorial houses, the offices, flooding to the professions that were open to them. The desire of bourgeois women to gain access to science and the higher benefits of culture was not the result of a sudden, maturing need but stemmed from that same question of "daily bread."

The women of the bourgeoisie met, from the very first, with stiff resistance from men. A stubborn battle was waged between the professional men, attached to their "cosy little jobs," and the women who were novices in the matter of earning their daily bread. This struggle gave rise to "feminism"—the attempt of bourgeois women to stand together and pit their common strength against the enemy, against men. As they entered the labour arena, these women proudly referred to themselves as the "vanguard of the women's movement." They forgot that in this matter of winning economic independence they were, as in other fields, traveling in the footsteps of their younger sisters and reaping the fruits of the efforts of their blistered hands.

Is it then really possible to talk of the feminists pioneering the road to women's work, when in every country hundreds of thousands of proletarian women had flooded the factories and workshops, taking over one branch of industry after another, before the bourgeois women's movement was ever born? Only thanks to the fact that the labour of women workers had received recognition on the world market were the bourgeois women able to occupy the independent position in society in which the feminists take so much pride.

[. . .]

Mapping the Margins: Intersectionality, Identity Politics, and Violence against Women of Color

KIMBERLÉ CRENSHAW

New social movements have led to many debates about what constitutes identity. Legal scholar Kimberlé Crenshaw believes that the concept of a generalized "essential" gender identity does not address differences among women based on race or culture. She proposes the idea of "intersectional" identities to acknowledge the complexity of belonging simultaneously to several groups.

Over the last two decades, women have organized against the almost routine violence that shapes their lives.[1] Drawing from the strength of shared experience, women have recognized that the political demands of millions speak more powerfully than the pleas of a few isolated voices. This politicization in turn has transformed the way we understand violence against women. For example, battering and rape, once seen as private (family matters) and aberrational (errant sexual aggression), are now largely recognized as

Kimberlé Crenshaw, "Mapping the Margins: Intersectionality, Identity Politics, and Violence against Women of Color," in *Stanford Law Review,* vol. 43, July 1991: 1241–52, 1262–65.

part of a broad-scale system of domination that affects women as a class.[2] This process of recognizing as social and systemic what was formerly perceived as isolated and individual has also characterized the identity politics of African-Americans, other people of color, and gays and lesbians, among others. For all these groups, identity-based politics has been a source of strength, community, and intellectual development.

The embrace of identity politics, however, has been in tension with dominant conceptions of social justice. Race, gender, and other identity categories are most often treated in mainstream liberal discourse as vestiges of bias or domination—that is, as intrinsically negative frameworks in which social power works to exclude or marginalize those who are different. According to this understanding, our liberatory objective should be to empty such categories of any social significance. Yet implicit in certain strands of feminist and racial liberation movements, for example, is the view that the social power in delineating difference need not be the power of domination; it can instead be the source of social empowerment and reconstruction.

Key Terms

intersectionality The necessity of recognizing the many strands that make up identity; for example, the ways in which sexism and racism are intertwined in the identities of women of color.

woman of color The term used since the early 1980s to refer to women in the United States who have been identified as nonwhite or non-European.

The problem with identity politics is not that it fails to transcend difference, as some critics charge, but rather the opposite—that it frequently conflates or ignores intragroup differences. In the context of violence against women, this elision of difference in identity politics is problematic, fundamentally because the violence that many women experience is often shaped by other dimensions of their identities, such as race and class. Moreover, ignoring difference *within* groups contributes to tension *among* groups, another problem of identity politics that bears on efforts to politicize violence against women, Feminist efforts to politicize experiences of women and antiracist efforts to politicize experiences of people of color have frequently proceeded as though the issues and experiences they each detail occur on mutually exclusive terrains. Although racism and sexism readily intersect in the lives of real people, they seldom do in feminist and antiracist practices. And so, when the practices expound identity as woman or person of color as an either/or proposition, they relegate the identity of women of color to a location that resists telling.

My objective in this essay is to advance the telling of that location by exploring the race and gender dimensions of violence against women of color.[3] Contemporary feminist and antiracist discourses have failed to consider intersectional identities, such as women of color.[4] Focusing on male violence against women through battering, I consider how the experiences of women of color are frequently the product of intersecting patterns of racism and sexism, and how these experiences tend not to be represented within the discourses of either feminism or antiracism. Because of their intersectional identity as both women *and* of color within discourses that are shaped to respond to one *or* the other, women of color are marginalized within both.

[. . .]

I observed the dynamics of structural intersectionality during a brief field study of battered women's shelters located in minority communities in Los Angeles.[5] In most cases, the physical assault that leads women to these shelters is merely the most immediate manifestation of the subordination they experience. Many women who seek protection are unemployed or underemployed, and a good number of them are poor.

Shelters serving these women cannot afford to address only the violence inflicted by the batterer; they must also confront the other multilayered and routinized forms of domination that often converge in these women's lives, hindering their ability to create alternatives to the abusive relationships that brought them to shelters in the first place. Many women of color, for example, are burdened by poverty, child care responsibilities, and the lack of job skills.[6] These burdens, largely the consequence of gender and class oppression, are then compounded by the racially discriminatory employment and housing practices women of color often face,[7] as well as by the disproportionately high unemployment among people of color that makes battered women of color less able to depend on the support of friends and relatives for temporary shelter.[8]

Where systems of race, gender, and class domination converge, as they do in the experiences of battered women of color, intervention strategies based solely on the experiences of women who do not share the same class or race backgrounds will be of limited help to women who because of race and class face different obstacles.[9] Such was the case in 1990 when Congress amended the marriage fraud provisions of the Immigration and Nationality Act to protect immigrant women who were battered or exposed to extreme cruelty by the United States citizens or permanent residents these women immigrated to the United States to marry. Under the marriage fraud provisions of the Act, a person who immigrated to the United States to marry a United States citizen or permanent resident had to remain "properly" married for two years before even applying for permanent resident status,[10] at which time applications for the immigrant's permanent status were required of both spouses.[11] Predictably, under these circumstances, many immigrant women were reluctant to leave even the most abusive of partners for fear of being deported.[12] When faced with the choice between protection from their batterers and protection against deportation, many immigrant women chose the latter.

Reports of the tragic consequences of this double subordination put pressure on Congress to include in the Immigration Act of 1990 a provision amending the marriage fraud rules to allow for an explicit waiver for hardship caused by domestic violence.[13] Yet many immigrant women, particularly immigrant women of color, have remained vulnerable to battering because they are unable to meet the conditions established for a waiver. The evidence required to support a waiver "can include, but is not limited to, reports and affidavits from police, medical personnel, psychologists, school officials, and social service agencies." For many immigrant women, limited access to these resources can make it difficult to obtain the evidence needed for a waiver. And cultural barriers often further discourage immigrant women from reporting or escaping battering situations. Tina Shum, a family counselor at a social service agency, points out, "This law sounds so easy to apply, but there are cultural complications in the Asian community that make even these requirements difficult. . . . Just to find the opportunity and courage to call us is an accomplishment for many." The typical immigrant spouse, she suggests, may live "[i]n an extended family where several generations live together, there may be no privacy on the telephone, no opportunity to leave the house, and no understanding of public phones." As a consequence, many immigrant women are wholly dependent on their husbands as their link to the world outside their homes.

Immigrant women are also vulnerable to spousal violence because so many of them depend on their husbands for information regarding their legal status.[14] Many women who are now permanent residents continue to suffer abuse under threats of deportation by their husbands. Even if the threats are unfounded, women who have no independent access to information will still be intimidated by such threats. And even though the domestic violence waiver focuses on immigrant women whose husbands are United States citizens or permanent residents, there are countless women married to undocumented workers (or who are themselves undocumented) who suffer in silence for fear that the security of their entire families will be jeopardized should they seek help or otherwise call attention to themselves.[15]

Language barriers present another structural problem that often limits opportunities of non-English-speaking women to take advantage of existing support services. Such barriers not only limit access to information about shelters but also limit access to the security

shelters provide. Some shelters turn non-English-speaking women away for lack of bilingual personnel and resources.

These examples illustrate how patterns of subordination intersect in women's experience of domestic violence. Intersectional subordination need not be intentionally produced; in fact, it is frequently the consequence of the imposition of one burden that interacts with preexisting vulnerabilities to create yet another dimension of disempowerment. In the case of the marriage fraud provisions of the Immigration and Nationality Act, the imposition of a policy specifically designed to burden one class—immigrant spouses seeking permanent resident status—exacerbated the disempowerment of those already subordinated by other structures of domination. By failing to take into account the vulnerability of immigrant spouses to domestic violence, Congress positioned these women to absorb the simultaneous impact of its anti-immigration policy and their spouses' abuse.

The enactment of the domestic violence waiver of the marriage fraud provisions similarly illustrates how modest attempts to respond to certain problems can be ineffective when the intersectional location of women of color is not considered in fashioning the remedy. Cultural identity and class affect the likelihood that a battered spouse could take advantage of the waiver. Although the waiver is formally available to all women, the terms of the waiver make it inaccessible to some. Immigrant women who are socially, culturally, or economically privileged are more likely to be able to marshall the resources needed to satisfy the waiver requirements. Those immigrant women least able to take advantage of the waiver—women who are socially or economically the most marginal—are most likely to be women of color.

[. . .]

Political Intersectionality

The concept of political intersectionality highlights the fact that women of color are situated within at least two subordinated groups that frequently pursue conflicting political agendas. The need to split one's political energies between two sometimes opposing groups is a dimension of intersectional disempowerment that men of color and white women seldom confront. Indeed, their specific raced *and* gendered experiences, although intersectional, often define as well as confine the interests of the entire group. For example, racism as experienced by people of color who are of a particular gender—male—tends to determine the parameters of antiracist strategies, just as sexism as experienced by women who are of a particular race—white—tends to ground the women's movement. The problem is not simply that both discourses fail women of color by not acknowledging the "additional" issue of race or of patriarchy but that the discourses are often inadequate even to the discrete tasks of articulating the full dimensions of racism and sexism. Because women of color experience racism in ways not always the same as those experienced by men of color and sexism in ways not always parallel to experiences of white women, antiracism and feminism are limited, even on their own terms.

[. . .]

—Race and Domestic Violence Support Services

Women working in the field of domestic violence have sometimes reproduced the subordination and marginalization of women of color by adopting policies, priorities, or strategies of empowerment that either elide or wholly disregard the particular intersectional needs of women of color. While gender, race, and class intersect to create the particular context in which women of color experience violence, certain choices made by "allies" can reproduce intersectional subordination within the very resistance strategies designed to respond to the problem.

This problem is starkly illustrated by the inaccessibility of domestic violence support services to many non-English-speaking women. In a letter written to the deputy commissioner of the New York State Department of Social Services, Diana Campos, Director of Human Services for Programas de Ocupaciones y Desarrollo Económico Real, Inc. (PODER), detailed the case of a Latina in crisis who was repeatedly denied accomodation at a shelter because she could not prove

that she was English-proficient. The woman had fled her home with her teenage son, believing her husband's threats to kill them both. She called the domestic violence hotline administered by PODER seeking shelter for herself and her son. Because most shelters would not accommodate the woman with her son, they were forced to live on the streets for two days. The hotline counselor was finally able to find an agency that would take both the mother and the son, but when the counselor told the intake coordinator at the shelter that the woman spoke limited English, the coordinator told her that they could not take anyone who was not English-proficient. When the woman in crisis called back and was told of the shelter's "rule," she replied that she could understand English if spoken to her slowly. As Campos explains, Mildred, the hotline counselor, told Wendy, the intake coordinator

that the woman said that she could communicate a little in English. Wendy told Mildred that they could not provide services to this woman because they have house rules that the woman must agree to follow. Mildred asked her, "What if the woman agrees to follow your rules? Will you still not take her?" Wendy responded that all of the women at the shelter are required to attend [a] support group and they would not be able to have her in the group if she could not communicate. Mildred mentioned the severity of this woman's case. She told Wendy that the woman had been wandering the streets at night while her husband is home, and she had been mugged twice. She also reiterated the fact that this woman was in danger of being killed by either her husband or a mugger. Mildred expressed that the woman's safety was a priority at this point, and that once in a safe place, receiving counseling in a support group could be dealt with.[16]

The intake coordinator restated the shelter's policy of taking only English-speaking women and stated further that the woman would have to call the shelter herself for screening. If the woman could communicate with them in English, she might be accepted. When the woman called the PODER hotline later that day, she was in such a state of fear that the hotline counselor who had been working with her had difficulty understanding her in Spanish.[17] Campos directly intervened at this point, calling the executive director of the shelter. A counselor called back from the shelter. As Campos reports,

> Marie [the counselor] told me that they did not want to take the woman in the shelter because they felt that the woman would feel isolated. I explained that the son agreed to translate for his mother during the intake process. Furthermore, that we would assist them in locating a Spanish-speaking battered women's advocate to assist in counseling her. Marie stated that utilizing the son was not an acceptable means of communication for them, *since it further victimized the victim*. In addition, she stated that they had similar experiences with women who were non-English-speaking, and that the women eventually just left because they were not able to communicate with anyone. I expressed my extreme concern for her safety and reiterated that we would assist them in providing her with the necessary services until we could get her placed someplace where they had bilingual staff.[18]

After several more calls, the shelter finally agreed to take the woman. The woman called once more during the negotiation; however, after a plan was in place, the woman never called back. Said Campos, "After so many calls, we are now left to wonder if she is alive and well, and if she will ever have enough faith in our ability to help her to call us again the next time she is in crisis."[19]

Despite this woman's desperate need, she was unable to receive the protection afforded English-speaking women, due to the shelter's rigid commitment to exclusionary policies. Perhaps even more troubling than the shelter's lack of bilingual resources was its refusal to allow a friend or relative to translate for the woman. This story illustrates the absurdity of a feminist approach that would make the ability to attend a support group without a translator a more significant consideration in the distribution of resources than the risk of physical harm

on the street. The point is not that the shelter's image of empowerment is empty, but rather that it was imposed without regard to the disempowering consequences for women who didn't match the kind of client the shelter's administrators imagined. And thus they failed to accomplish the basic priority of the shelter movement—to get the woman out of danger.

Here the woman in crisis was made to bear the burden of the shelter's refusal to anticipate and provide for the needs of non-English-speaking women. Said Campos, "It is unfair to impose more stress on victims by placing them in the position of having to demonstrate their proficiency in English in order to receive services that are readily available to other battered women.[20] The problem is not easily dismissed as one of well-intentioned ignorance. The specific issue of monolingualism and the monistic view of women's experience that set the stage for this tragedy were not new issues in New York. Indeed, several women of color reported that they had repeatedly struggled with the New York State Coalition Against Domestic Violence over language exclusion and other practices that marginalized the interests of women of color.[21] Yet despite repeated lobbying, the Coalition did not act to incorporate the specific needs of nonwhite women into its central organizing vision.

[. . .]

The struggle over which differences matter and which do not is neither an abstract nor an insignificant debate among women. Indeed, these conflicts are about more than difference as such; they raise critical issues of power. The problem is not simply that women who dominate the antiviolence movement are different from women of color but that they frequently have power to determine, through either material or rhetorical resources, whether the intersectional differences of women of color will be incorporated at all into the basic formulation of policy. Thus, the struggle over incorporating these differences is not a petty or superficial conflict about who gets to sit at the head of the table. In the context of violence, it is sometimes a deadly serious matter of who will survive—and who will not.[22]

NOTES

1. Feminist academics and activists have played a central role in forwarding an ideological and institutional challenge to the practices that condone and perpetuate violence against women. See generally Susan Brownmiller, *Against Our Will: Men, Women and Rape* (1975); Lorenne M. G. Clark and Debra J. Lewis, *Rape: The Price of Coercive Sexuality* (1977); R. Emerson Dobash and Russell Dobash, *Violence against Wives: A Case against the Patriarchy* (1979); Nancy Gager and Cathleen Schurr, *Sexual Assault: Confronting Rape in America* (1976); Diana E. H. Russell, *The Politics of Rape: The Victims Perspective* (1974); Elizabeth Anne Stanko, *Intimate Intrusions: Women's Experience of Male Violence* (1985); Lenore E. Walker, *Terrifying Love: Why Battered Women Kill and How Society Responds* (1989); Lenore E. Walker, *The Battered Woman Syndrome* (1984); Lenore E. Walker, *The Battered Woman* (1979).

2. See, e.g., Susan Schechter, *Women and Male Violence: The Visions and Struggles of the Battered Women's Movement* (1982) (arguing that battering is a means of maintaining women's subordinate position); S. Brownmiller, supra note 1 (arguing that rape is a patriarchal practice that subordinates women to men); Elizabeth Schneider, "The Violence of Privacy," 23 *Connecticut Law Review* 973, 974 (1991) (discussing how "concepts of privacy permit, encourage, and reinforce violence against women"); Susan Estrich, "Rape," 95 *Yale Law Journal* 1087 (1986) (analyzing rape law as one illustration of sexism in criminal law); see also Catharine A. MacKinnon, *Sexual Harassment of Working Women: A Case of Sex Discrimination* 143–213 (1979) (arguing that sexual harassment should be redefined as sexual discrimination actionable under Title VII rather than viewed as misplaced sexuality in the workplace).

3. This article arises out of and is inspired by two emerging scholarly discourses. The first is critical race theory. For a cross-section of what is now a substantial body of literature, see Patricia J. Williams, *The Alchemy of Race and Rights* (1991); Robin D. Barnes, "Race Consciousness: The Thematic Content of Racial Distinctiveness in Critical Race Scholarship," 103 *Harvard Law Review* 1864 (1990); John O. Calmore, "Critical Race Theory, Archie Shepp, and Fire Music: Securing an Authentic Intellectual Life in a Multicultural World," 65 *Southern California Law Review* 2129 (1992); Anthony E. Cook, "Beyond Critical Legal Studies: The Reconstructive Theology of Dr. Martin Luther King," 103 *Harvard Law Review* 985 (1990); Kimberlé Williams Crenshaw, "Race, Reform and Retrenchment: Transformation and Legitimation in Antidiscrimination Law," 101 *Harvard Law Review* 1331 (1988); A second, less formally linked body of legal scholarship investigates the connections between race and gender. See, e.g., Regina Austin, "Sapphire Bound!," 1989 *Wisconsin Law Review* 539; Crenshaw, supra; Angela P. Harris, "Race and Essentialism in Feminist Legal Theory," 42 *Stanford Law Review* 581 (1990); Marlee Kline, "Race, Racism and Feminist Legal Theory," 12 *Harvard Women's Law Journal* 115 (1989); Dorothy E. Roberts, "Punishing Drug Addicts Who Have Babies: Women of Color, Equality and the Right of Privacy," 104 *Harvard Law Review* 1419 (1991); Cathy Scarborough, "Conceptu-

alizing Black Women's Employment Experiences," 98 *Yale Law Journal* 1457 (1989) (student author); Peggie R. Smith, "Separate Identities: Black Women, Work and Title VII," 14 *Harvard Women's Law Journal* 21 (1991); Judy Scales-Trent, "Black Women and the Constitution: Finding Our Place, Asserting Our Rights," 24 *Harvard C.R.-C.L.L. Review* 9 (1989).

4. Although the objective of this article is to describe the intersectional location of women of color and their marginalization within dominant resistance discourses, I do not mean to imply that the disempowerment of women of color is singularly or even primarily caused by feminist and antiracist theorists or activists. Indeed, I hope to dispell any such simplistic interpretations by capturing, at least in part, the way that prevailing structures of domination shape various discourses of resistance.

5. During my research in Los Angeles, California, I visited Jenessee Battered Women's Shelter, the only shelter in the Western states primarily serving Black women, and Everywoman's Shelter, which primarily serves Asian women. I also visited Estelle Chueng at the Asian Pacific Law Foundation, and I spoke with a representative of La Casa, a shelter in the predominantly Latino community of East L.A.

6. One researcher has noted, in reference to a survey taken of battered women's shelters, that "many Caucasian women were probably excluded from the sample, since they are more likely to have available resources that enable them to avoid going to a shelter. Many shelters admit only women with few or no resources or alternatives." Mildred Daley Pagelow, *Woman-Battering: Victims and Their Experiences* 97 (1981). On the other hand, many middle- and upper-class women are financially dependent on their husbands and thus experience a diminution in their standard of living when they leave their husbands.

7. Together they make securing even the most basic necessities beyond the reach of many. Indeed, one shelter provider reported that nearly 85 percent of her clients returned to the battering relationships, largely because of difficulties in finding employment and housing. African Americans are more segregated than any other racial group, and this segregation exists across class lines.

8. More specifically, African Americans suffer from high unemployment rates, low incomes, and high poverty rates. [. . .] The economic situation of minority women is, expectedly, worse than that of their male counterparts. Black women, who earn a median of $7,875 a year, make considerably less than Black men, who earn a median income of $12,609 a year, and white women, who earn a median income of $9,812 a year. [. . .] Latino households also earn considerably less than white households. In 1988, the median income of Latino households was $20,359 and for white households, $28,340—a difference of almost $8,000. *Hispanic Americans: A Statistical Sourcebook* 149 (1991).

9. For a discussion of the different needs of Black women who are battered, see Beth Richie, "Battered Black Women: A Challenge for the Black Community," *Black Scholar,* Mar./Apr. 1985, at 40.

10. The Marriage Fraud Amendments provide that an alien spouse "shall be considered, at the time of obtaining the status of an alien lawfully admitted for permanent residence, to have obtained such status on a conditional basis subject to the provisions of this section." An alien spouse with permanent resident status under this conditional basis may have her status terminated if the Attorney General finds that the marriage was "improper," or if she fails to file a petition or fails to appear at the personal interview.

11. The Marriage Fraud Amendments provided that for the conditional resident status to be removed, "the alien spouse and the petitioning spouse (if not deceased) jointly must submit to the Attorney General . . . a petition which requests the removal of such conditional basis and which states, under penalty of perjury, the facts and information." The Amendments provided for a waiver, at the Attorney General's discretion, if the alien spouse was able to demonstrate that deportation would result in extreme hardship, or that the qualifying marriage was terminated for good cause.

12. Immigration activists have pointed out that "[t]he 1986 Immigration Reform Act and the Immigration Marriage Fraud Amendment have combined to give the spouse applying for permanent residence a powerful tool to control his partner." Jorge Banales, "Abuse among Immigrants; As Their Numbers Grow So Does the Need for Services," *Washington Post,* Oct. 16, 1990.

13. Immigration Act of 1990, Pub. L. No. 101–649, 104 Stat. 4978. The Act, introduced by Representative Louise Slaughter (D-N.Y.), provides that a battered spouse who has conditional permanent resident status can be granted a waiver for failure to meet the requirements if she can show that "the marriage was entered into in good faith and that after the marriage the alien spouse was battered by or was subjected to extreme mental cruelty by the U.S. citizen or permanent resident spouse."

14. A citizen or permanent resident spouse can exercise power over an alien spouse by threatening not to file a petition for perma-nent residency. If he fails to file a petition for permanent residency, the alien spouse continues to be undocumented and is considered to be in the country illegally. These constraints often restrict an alien spouse from leaving.

15. Incidents of sexual abuse of undocumented women abound. Marta Rivera, director of the Hostos College Center for Women's and Immigrant's Rights, tells of how a 19-year-old Dominican woman had "arrived shaken . . . after her boss raped her in the women's restroom at work." The woman told Rivera that "70 to 80 percent of the workers [in a Brooklyn garment factory] were undocumented, and they all accepted sex as part of the job. . . . She said a 13-year-old girl had been raped there a short while before her, and the family sent her back to the Dominican Republic." Vivian Walt, "Immigrant Abuse: Nowhere to Hide; Women Fear Deportation, Experts Say," *Newsday,* Dec. 2, 1990, at 8.

16. Letter of Diana M. Campos, Director of Human Services, PODER, to Joseph Semidei, Deputy Commissioner, New York State Department of Social Services (Mar. 26, 1992) [hereinafter PODER Letter].

17. The woman had been slipping back into her home during the day when her husband was at work. She remained in a heightened state of anxiety because he was returning shortly and she would be forced to go back out into the streets for yet another night.

18. PODER Letter, supra note 16 (emphasis added).

19. Id.

20. Id.

21. Roundtable Discussion on Racism and the Domestic Violence Movement (April 2, 1992) (transcript on file with the *Stanford Law Review*).

22. Said Campos, "It would be a shame that in New York state a battered woman's life or death were dependent upon her English language skills." PODER Letter, supra note 16.

Reflections on Diversity among Chicanas[1]

PATRICIA ZAVELLA

Anthropologist Patricia Zavella argues that feminist studies should pay attention to multiple social locations rather than construct authentic, singular identities. She questions the overgeneralization of the term Chicana since many differences of ethnicity, class, and region are collapsed or erased within the term. Zavella calls for investigations of ethnicity, gender, and class that do not essentialize the categories of oppression.

Second-wave feminists have been attempting to create a scholarship and conduct research in ways that no longer "privilege" the concerns of white, middle-class, or heterosexual women or take their experiences as the norm.[2] This agenda has often been born from struggle with those women seen as "other." Women of color

Zavella, Patricia. "Reflections on Diversity among Chicanas,"[1] *Frontiers* XII, no. 2, 1991: 73–81.

have argued that race, class, and gender—including sexuality—are experienced simultaneously, and to use only a gender analysis for understanding women's lived experience is reductionist and replicates the silencing and social oppression that women of color experience daily.[3] The response by those feminist theorists who see women's common, biologically based experiences as the basis for the construction of theory has often been to include women's "many voices." Highly influenced by French feminist theory, this view sees that women from diverse class, ethnic, or racial groups have very different perspectives on so-called universal feminine experiences, and the project within feminist studies is to document, listen to, validate those voices. This viewpoint has produced somewhat of a quandary: on the one hand, we have an understanding of the great complexity of all women's experiences and know that there is variation among

Key Terms

French feminist theory A term coined in the United States in the late 1970s and early 1980s to refer to a diverse group of French feminist writers who were influenced by the theoretical approaches of psychoanalytic philosopher Jacques Lacan as well as the poststructuralist and deconstructionist theorists Jacques Derrida, Roland Barthes, and Michel Foucault, among others. Some of the feminist writers included in this rubric are Julia Kristeva, Hélène Cixous, and Monique Wittig.

mestiza A Spanish word for "mixed." Chicana feminists have reinvested the word with an identity politics for living in border zones of North America.

other Stemming from German philosopher G. W. F. Hegel's (1770–1851) concept of dialectical opposites (one concept inevitably generates its opposite), the term has come to be used to refer to the position of marginality and oppression created by the subject (who has power and agency). For example, if man is subject, woman is the "other"; if Europeans are subjects, native or indigenous people are "other."

women on the basis of race, ethnicity, class, sexual preference, age, and abilities. Yet simply recognizing the richness of diversity can lead to an atheoretical pluralism where diversity seems overwhelming and it is difficult to discern the basis of commonality and difference among women. Moreover, expanding the feminist canon to include other women can sometimes replicate stereotypes about internal similarities within the category of women being integrated. I believe we need to reflect on how women within a particular group vary from one another and to research women's lives in ways that identify the sources of diversity without resorting to mechanistic conclusions that class, race, or gender (and I include sexuality within a gender analysis) alone gives rise to differences. That is, we should analyze how race, class, and gender are socially constructed yet not essentialize any of the categories of oppression.

Further, I believe we must begin our analysis with the historically specific structural conditions constraining women's experiences. We can then link these conditions to the varieties of ways in which women respond to and construct subjective representations of their experiences. This suggestion helps us to avoid the problematic assumption of much recent feminist scholarship: beginning with historical material conditions rather than with "experience" embeds "women's diversity" as a theoretical priority and frees us from the artifical task of deriving diversity from prior commonality. In a sense, then, feminists of color are challenging one of the basic assumptions in women's studies—the notion that feminist theory should be grounded in women's experience in which there are commonalities. Instead, we ask that the structure in which women's experiences are framed become the primary analytical locus, which may generate profound differences between white women and women of color, and among Chicanas or women of Mexican origin in particular.

The diversity among Chicanas can initially be seen by the terms of ethnic identification we have claimed for ourselves. When referring to ourselves within a white context, we often prefer more generic terms, like *Las Mujeres* or the combination *Chicana/Latina,* in opposition to *Hispanic,* which is often seen as inappropriate because of its conservative political connotations. When speaking among ourselves, we highlight and celebrate all of the nuances of identity—we are *Chicanas, Mexicanas, Mexican Americans, Spanish Americans, Tejanas, Hispanas, Mestizas, Indias,* or *Latinas*—and the terms of identification vary according to the context. This complexity of identification reflects the conundrum many Chicanas experience: on the one hand, together we are seen by others as a single social category, often Hispanic women. Yet the term *Hispanic,* imposed by the census bureau, is seen as inappropriate by many women, who prefer to identify themselves in oppositional political terms. As Chicanas, we have common issues and experiences with other women of color in the United States and therefore often feel a strong sense of affinity with their struggles. On the other hand, we are a very diverse group of women, with different histories, regional settlement patterns, particular cultural practices, sexual preferences, and occasionally radically different political outlooks, and our solidarity as Chicanas can be undermined by these differences among us.

[. . .]

To begin formulating a framework on diversity among Chicanas, it is important to first deconstruct the stereotypic thinking that often comes to mind among outsiders. Stereotypes sometimes have a grain of truth but mask gross generalizations or ignorance of the diversity not only among but within different groups of women of color. Some of these stereotypes include the assumption that Chicanas all speak Spanish or that we have such a rich culture—when our culture has been repressed. Other assumptions that I've heard include that Chicanas have such loving, big families; in fact, like other groups, Chicanas experience familial breakdown and abuse toward women.

Probably one of the most insidious stereotypes regarding Chicanas is the notion that culture is determinant of behavior. Because Chicanas are racially distinct and have Spanish language as an ethnic signifier, we seem obviously culturally different from white North Americans. This often leads to the assumption that there is a coherent Chicano culture heritage: that the values, norms, customs, rituals, symbols, and material items (such as women's religious altars) form part of a "tradition" that all Chicanos are socialized into. Moreover, this thinking goes, Chicanos mechanistically base their behavior and decisions on these traditional norms.

[. . .]

A way to move beyond stereotypic views and reconstruct how Chicanas have common experiences is through a historical perspective. History helps us to understand how particular stereotypes became hegemonic, and how Chicanas have become marginalized and invisible in the popular, political, and scholarly discourses.

[. . .]

Attention to history, though it does point out the sources of common experiences, also begins our exploration of diversity among Chicanas. History helps us understand the regional settlement patterns of different groups of Chicanas who were then replenished through waves of migration: women of Mexican descent originally settled in South Texas, northern New Mexico, and California in the Southwest, and later migrant streams created settlements in the Midwest, Northwest Coast, and, more recently, on the East Coast. Other recent Latin-American immigrant women have settled in large cities—San Francisco; Los Angeles; New York; Washington, D.C.; Miami—so that Chicano communities are becoming more heterogeneous. Settlement and migration history also helps us to understand the interethnic relations—both conflictual and cooperative—between groups of Chicanos. For example, in California researchers have found that Mexican immigrants who settled here in previous waves of migration have established economic "niches," in particular industries or occupations, and then felt threatened by compatriots who migrated more recently.[4]

Closely related to settlement patterns is the notion of culture-region, a geographic and sociopolitical area where historical processes—including isolation, waves of industrialization, urbanization, and discrimination toward racialized others—have segregated racial/ethnic groups and enabled historical actors to construct particular terms of ethnic identification in opposition to the dominant society.[5] The notion of culture-region helps highlight the particular racial mixtures that occurred—the mestizas from the unions of Spanish men and Indian women in the Southwest, the African and Spanish mixtures near the Caribbean—and helps us to understand the contours of cultural syncretism: Women from the gulf region show Puerto Rican, Cuban, and African influences, whereas Chicanas from desert regions demonstrate more indigenous influences. There are also regional differences regarding the preferred terms of ethnic identification among women: *Chicana* in California, *Mexican American* or *Mexicana* in Texas, *Spanish American* in New Mexico, although there is a good deal of mixing of terms as well.[6]

One implication of culture-region is that generation is important: whether women are of the first generation (that is, born in Mexico) or of subsequent generations born in the United States or are recent immigrants has implications for language use, cultural knowledge, and the process of identification. A Chicana's generation affects whether she feels a sense of identification and solidarity with other Chicanas, whether she feels marginalized, or whether she feels as if she is more "American" than Chicana.

Beyond historical settlement patterns, this framework attends to important internal differences within Chicano populations. Class is clearly an important demarcation: the overwhelming majority of Chicanos are of working-class origins, although with the recent economic crisis in Mexico, a few more middle-class and professional women are migrating to the United States. These women often have higher median incomes and higher educational levels, in contrast to those women who have migrated from rural, underdeveloped areas of Mexico. The class status of Chicanas can take on insidious overtones: foreign-born Chicanas from elite, upper-class backgrounds clearly have very different life chances than those from the working class yet are often categorized as Hispanic and inflate the Affirmative Action statistics about the presence of underrepresented minorities. Class is often a source of tension among Chicanas, coinciding with political disagreements.

Racial physical features are also important: whether women have fair or dark skin and hair; Indian, African, or European features; or some combination thereof bears upon how Chicanas are treated and how they reflect upon their racial/ethnic status. Although some change is occurring regarding the preferred body image, our society still values images of women who are white—and blond in particular—and who have European features. Research shows that women who have dark skin, especially with indigenous features, face the worst treatment from society at large. Individuals within Chicano communities may reflect this devaluation, or even internalize it, so that physical features are often noted and evaluated: Skin color in particular is commented on, with *las güeras* (light-skinned ones) being appreciated and *las prietas* (dark-skinned ones) being admonished and devalued. In contrast to white ethnic women, it is impossible for most Mexican women to "blend in," to opt out of their racial/ethnic status and pass for white. Thus we see examples all the time of U.S. citizens being mistaken for undocumented immigrants and being deported because of the color of their skin.

Sexuality is also a significant demarcation of social location. Whether women establish lesbian, heterosexual, or bisexual relationships is central to their identity and experience. Within our heterosexist society, Chicana lesbians and bisexuals, particularly those of working-class origin, face extreme marginalization from both the dominant and Chicano society. Paraphrasing Cherríe Moraga, being queer and of color is "as rude as women can get."[7] Sexuality, then, forms the basis of, and identity in which, community building is necessary against physical assaults and for survival. Sexual preference has generated political disagreements and conflict among lesbian, bisexual, and heterosexual Chicanas, and some lesbians are creating what Emma Perez calls a lesbian "uninvited discourse" with a separate *lengua y sitio* (language and space).[8]

These aspects of social location—class, gender, race/ethnicity, and sexual preference—all are indications of social inequality and reflect power relations in which Chicanas are often relatively powerless. Yet specifying women's social locations also means taking into consideration various ethnic or cultural attributes that create "borders" over which women cross in their daily lives. These attributes include nativity—whether Chicanas were born in the United States (and, if so, what generation) or in Mexico, and whether immigrants arrived as children and were socialized in the United States or received their education, socialization, and sense of identity in rural villages or urban centers of Mexico. Language use is critical and closely related to nativity. If Chicanas are born in the United States, particularly if they are reared in integrated communities, they are more likely to speak mainly English and without a Spanish accent, whereas Chicanas reared in Mexico or in segregated barrios in the United States are likely to be bilingual (predominantly Spanish) speakers or have Spanish-heavy accents when speaking in English. Whether one was reared in the barrios or grew up isolated from other Chicanos has great implications for cultural knowledge and sense of self. Religion is also significant. The majority of Chicanas come from a Roman Catholic heritage in which religious rituals and practices are often the center of women's social activities and are forms of social control of women's sexuality. Finally, women's sexuality, in particular, but other activities as well are controlled through Chicano cultural forms involving the polar opposites of macho male, aggressive sexual license and passive female chastity.

[. . .]

I believe that we should construct feminist studies that reflect the myriad of social locations among Chicanas, which specify relationships—both personal and structural—that sustain them. I believe that this is the starting point for understanding the social and cultural symbolic representations and consciousness that women express through literature, art, and daily activity.

NOTES

1. This is a revised version of "Divergent Histories, Common Bonds: Chicanas/Latinas in the United States," keynote talk presented at the Instituto de las Mujeros, Project on Incorporating Feminist Scholarship Concerning Gender and Cultural Diversity into the Curriculum, Metropolitan State University, St. Paul, MN, 19 February 1990. Thanks to Louise Lamphere and the anonymous reviewers of *Frontiers* for their helpful comments.

2. For a critique of this perspective and examples of more historically grounded feminist studies, see Micaela di Leonardo, ed., *Gender at the Crossroads of Knowledge: Feminist Anthropology in*

the Postmodern Era (Berkeley: University of California Press, 1991); Faye Ginsburg and Anna Lowenhaupt Tsing, eds., *Uncertain Terms: Negotiating Gender in American Culture* (Boston: Beacon Press, 1990); Sandra Morgen, ed., *Gender and Anthropology: Critical Reviews for Research and Teaching* (Washington, D.C.: American Anthropological Association, 1989).

3. See Gloria Anzaldúa, ed., *Making Face, Making Soul: Haciendo Caras* (San Francisco: aunt lute foundation, 1990); bell books, *Feminist Theory from Margin to Center* (Boston: South End Press, 1984); Aida Hurtado, "Relating to Privilege: Seduction and Rejection in the Subordination of White Women and Women of Color," *Signs* 14 (4, 1989); Gloria Joseph, "The Incomplete Menage à Trois: Marxism, Feminism, and Racism," in *Women and Revolution: A Discussion of the Unhappy Marriage of Marxism and Feminism,* ed. Lydia Sargent (Boston: South End Press, 1981); Amy Swerdlow and Hanna Lessinger, eds., *Class, Race, and Sex: The Dynamics of Control* (Boston: G. K. Hall, 1983).

4. Wayne A. Cornelius, Richard Mines, Leo R. Chavez, and Jorge G. Castro, *Mexican Immigrants in Southern California: A Summary of Current Knowledge* (San Diego: University of California, Center for U.S.–Mexican Studies, Research Report Series 40, 1982).

5. Ernesto Galarza sketches out some Chicano culture-regions. See "Mexicans in the Southwest: A Culture in Process," in *Plural Society in the Southwest,* Edward H. Spicer and Raymond H. Thompson, eds. (New York: Interbook, 1972).

6. For literature on the process of ethnic identification for Chicanos as a whole, see John A. García, "Yo Soy Mexicano . . . : Self-Identity and Sociodemographic Correlates," *Social Science Quarterly* 62 (1, 1981), 88–98; Ramón Gutierrez, "Unraveling America's Hispanic Past: Internal Stratification and Class Boundaries," in *Proceedings of the All-UC Invitational Conference on the Comparative Study of Race, Ethnicity, Gender and Class,* Sucheng Chan ed. (Santa Cruz: University of California, 1987); Susan E, Keefe and Amado M. Padilla, *Chicano Ethnicity* (Albuquerque: University of New Mexico Press, 1987); José E. Limon, "The Folk Performance of Chicano and the Cultural Limits of Political Ideology," in *"And Other Neighborly Names"; Social Process and Cultural Image in Texas Folklore,* Richard Bauman and Roger D. Abrahams eds. (Austin: University of Texas Press, 1981); Joseph V. Metzgar, "The Ethnic Sensitivity of Spanish New Mexicans: A Survey and Analysis," *New Mexico Historical Review* 49 (1, 1974), 49–73. For discussion of how race/ethnicity and gender are intertwined in ethnic identification, see Anzaldúa, *Borderlands/La Frontera;* Cherríe Moraga, *Loving in the War Years, lo que nunca pasó por sus labios* (Boston: South End Press, 1983); Maxine Baca Zinn, "Gender and Ethnic Identity among Chicanas," *Frontiers* 5 (2, Summer 1981), 18–24.

7. Moraga, *Loving in the War Years.*

8. Emma Perez, "Speaking from the Margin: Uninvited Discourse on Sexuality and Power," in Beatriz Pesquera and Adela De La Torre, eds., *Building with Our Hands: Issues in Chicana Studies* (Berkeley: University of California Press, forthcoming). For other works on Chicana/Latina lesbians, see Norma Alarcón, Ana Castillo, and Cherríe Moraga, eds., *The Sexuality of Latinas,* special issue of *Third Woman* (1989); Juanita Ramos, ed., *Compañeras: Latina Lesbians (An Anthology)* (New York: Latina Lesbian History Project, 1987).

Making It Perfectly Queer

LISA DUGGAN

Lisa Duggan studies U.S. lesbian and gay culture, sexual politics, and the history of gender and sexuality. In this essay, written in 1992, she examines the political,

cultural, and critical implications of using the term queer for lesbian and gay politics and identity. She argues that queer had political and cultural possibilities in the 1990s beyond the liberal identity politics that "lesbian and gay" had held from the beginnings of the modern gay rights movement.

Lisa Duggan, "Making it Perfectly Queer," in *Socialist Review* 22.1, 1992: 11, 13–22, 26–31.

Key Terms

ACT UP (AIDS Coalition to Unleash Power): An activist group formed in the 1980s in response to the U.S. government's refusal to acknowledge the AIDS/HIV crisis or to facilitate the treatment of people with AIDS/HIV.

homophile The term that homosexual activists in the Unites States in the 1950s and 1960s created in order to emphasize the element of love *(-phile)* over sex acts *(-sexual)*. Homophile groups encouraged gays, lesbians, and bisexuals to present themselves conservatively in dress and demeanor in order to win over straight society. Radical in the 1950s and 1960s for asserting the civil rights of gays and lesbians, homophile organizations were criticized by the 1970s gay liberationist groups for timidity and assimilation.

liberalism Stemming from eighteenth-century liberal philosophers such as John Stuart Mill and Mary Wollstonecraft, liberalism rests on the ideas of individual rights and responsibilities to the state and the goal of political equality for all people. (see Part Two, Section One, of this text). Liberal advocates for civil rights are most interested in reforming existing structures of the state rather than dismantling them.

militant nationalism Militant nationalism implies a commitment to working to overthrow existing hierarchies and structures of power. Militant nationalists may advocate physical violence or may violate fundamental rules of society by speaking the unspoken or refusing to participate in structures of government or cultural practices that they consider discriminatory or demeaning.

Queer Nation A loosely organized political action group active in urban centers in the 1990s. Associated with militant nationalist activities such as outing, Queer Nation advocated creating queer statements in public spaces through wearing T-shirts with explicit queer images and holding public demonstrations of same-sex love such as "kiss-ins."

situational homosexuality/heterosexuality The theory that under special circumstances people who are "naturally" heterosexual or homosexual will have sexual relations that defy their "true" sexual orientation. Prison and same-sex schools are frequently cited as locations of situational homosexuality.

During the past few years, the new designation "queer" has emerged from within lesbian, gay, and bisexual politics and theory. "Queer Nation" and "Queer Theory," now widely familiar locations for activists and academics, are more than just new labels for old boxes. They carry with them the promise of new meanings, new ways of thinking and acting politically—a promise sometimes realized, sometimes not. In this essay I want to elucidate and advocate this new potential within politics and theory.

[. . .]

Appeals to Liberalism

For nearly 50 years now, lesbian and gay organizations have worked to forge a politically active and effective lesbian and gay "minority" group, and to claim the liberal "rights" of privacy and formal equality on its behalf. As a rhetorical strategy, this positioning has aimed to align lesbian and gay populations with racial, ethnic, and religious minority groups and women in a quest for full economic, political, and cultural participation in U.S. life. This rhetorical move, when successful, opens up avenues of political and legal recourse forged by the civil rights and feminist movements to lesbian and gay action: support for group-specific antidiscrimination statutes, participation in political coalitions to design, pass, and enforce broad civil rights provisions; application to the courts for equal protection under various constitutional provisions; organization to elect and pressure public officials, lobbying of media organizations for fair and equitable representation, etc. [. . .] [And] of course, this strategy has never occupied the field of gay politics unopposed. Challenges to it have appeared from the overlapping yet distinguishable positions of militant nationalism and radical constructionism. In the 1990s, both of these positions appear to be gaining ground.

The Call to Militant Nationalism

[. . .]

"Outing" is a political tactic inaugurated by New York City's now defunct gay weekly newspaper *Outweek* (though the term for it was coined by *Time*), and associated most closely with the paper's "lifestyle" columnist, Michelangelo Signorile. As a practice, it is an extension of the early gay liberationist appeal to lesbians and gay men to "come out of the closet," reveal their hidden lives, and reject the fear and stigma attached to their identities. In "outing," this appeal is transformed from an invitation into a command. Journalists and activists expose "closeted" lesbians or gay men in public life, especially those deemed hypocritical in their approach to gay issues. Their goal is to end the secrecy and hypocrisy surrounding homosexuality, to challenge the notion that gay life is somehow shameful, and to show the world that many widely admired and respected men and women are gay.

Both "outing" and *Outweek* sprang from the efflorescence of militance surrounding the rhetoric and politics of ACT UP and its spinoff, Queer Nation. Many of these new gay militants reject the liberal value of privacy and the appeal to tolerance which dominate the agendas of more mainstream gay organizations. Instead, they emphasize publicity and self-assertion; confrontation and direct action top their list of tactical options; the rhetoric of difference replaces the more assimilationist liberal emphasis on similarity to other groups.

But the challenge that the new politics poses to the liberal strategy is not only the challenge of militance—the familiar counterposing of anger to civility, of flamboyance to respectability, often symbolized through "style"—but also the challenge of nationalism.[1]

Nationalisms have a long history in gay and lesbian politics and culture. From turn-of-the-century German homosexual emancipationist Magnus Hirschfeld to contemporary radical feminist philosopher Mary Daly, the "nation" and its interests have been defined in varying ways. With no geographical base or kinship ties to provide boundaries, gay and lesbian nationalists have offered biological characteristics (as in the "Third Sex"), or shared experience (whether of sexual desire or gender solidarity) as common ground. Of these various nationalisms, two broadly distinguishable competing forms have appeared and reappeared since the mid-nineteenth century: 1) the ethnic model of a fixed minority of both sexes defined by biology and/or the experience of desire (most often estimated at 10 percent)[2] and 2) the single-sex union of gender loyalists, the no-fixed-percentage model associated with lesbian separatism (theoretically, all women could belong to the Lesbian Nation).[3]

The ethnic model also underpins the liberal strategy, of course. The argument for "rights" is made on behalf of a relatively fixed minority constituency. It becomes the basis for a more militant nationalism when the "ethnic" group is represented as monolithic, its interests primary and utterly clear to a political vanguard. The example of "outing" serves as an illustration of this brand of gay politics. Outers generally not only believe in the existence of a gay nation, but are confident of their ability to identify its members and of their authority to do so. They have no doubts about definitions or boundaries and do not hesitate to override the welfare and autonomy of individuals "in the national interest."[4]

Outers present their version of gay nationalism as radical, but like other nationalisms its political implications are complex and often actually reactionary. These new nationalists define the nation and its interests as unitary; they suppress internal difference and political conflict.

[. . .]

—Whose Identity?

Both the liberal assimilationist and the militant nationalist strands of gay politics posit gay identity as a unitary, unproblematic given—the political project revolves around its public articulation. But for people with multiple "marked" identities, the political project begins at the level of the very problematic construction of identities and their relation to different communities and different political projects. In Audre Lorde's much-quoted words: "It was a while before we came to realize that our place was the very house of difference rather than the security of any one particular difference."[5]

[. . .]

The charge I want to make here against both the liberal and nationalist strategies, but especially against the latter, is this: *Any* gay politics based on the primacy of sexual identity defined as unitary and "essential," residing clearly, intelligibly, and unalterably in the body or psyche, and fixing desire in a gendered direction, ultimately represents the view from the subject position "twentieth-century Western white gay male."

[. . .]

From the first appearance of the homosexual/ heterosexual polarity just over 100 years ago, "essentialist" theories, both homophilic and homophobic, have had to account for the observed malleability of sexual desire. Each theoretical assertion of the fixity of desire has had attached to it a residual category—a catchall explanation for those formations of pleasure that defy the proffered euologies. In Havelock Ellis's scheme, flexible "acquired" sexual inversion accompanied the more permanent "congenital" type. In the lexicon of contemporary sociology, "situational" homosexuality occurs among "heterosexual" persons under special circumstances—in prisons or other single-sex institutions, for example ("Situational" heterosexuality is seldom discussed.)[6] In each theoretical paradigm, the "essential" nature and truth of the homo/hetero dyad are shored up with a rhetoric of authenticity. The "real" is distinguished from the "copy," the "true inverts" from those merely susceptible to seduction.

Such constructionist branches on the tree of essentialism grew up on their own during the heady days of early gay liberation. Drawing on the more constructionist versions of psychoanalytic theories of sexuality, visionaries painted a utopia in which everyone was potentially polymorphously sexual with everyone else.[7] During the 1970s, lesbian feminists outlined a somewhat more ambivalent position, with a sharper political edge. They aggressively denaturalized heterosexuality and presented it as a central apparatus in the perpetuation of patriarchy. But these same women often presented lesbianism as the naturalized alternative. When Alix Dobkin sang that "Any Woman Can Be a Lesbian," the implication was that any woman not suffering from false consciousness *would* be.[8]

[. . .]

—Defining a Queer Community

The notion of a "queer community" can work somewhat differently. It is often used to construct a collectivity no longer defined solely by the gender of its members' sexual partners. This new community is unified only by a shared dissent from the dominant organization of sex and gender. But not every individual or group that adopts the name "queer" means to invoke these altered boundaries. Many members of Queer Nation, a highly decentralized militant organization, use the term "queer" only as a synonym for lesbian or gay. Queer Nation, for some, is quite simply a gay nationalist organization. For others, the "queer" nation is a newly defined political entity, better able to cross boundaries and construct more fluid identities. In many other instances, various contradictory definitions coexist—in a single group, or in an individual's mind. This ambivalent mixture is illustrated in a series of interviews with Queer Nation activists published in *OUT/LOOK:*

MIGUEL GUTIERREZ: Queerness means nonassimilationist to me.

REBECCA HENSLER: A lot of what the "queer generation" is arguing for is the same stuff that was being fought for by gay liberation.

ALEXANDER CHEE: The operant dream is of a community united in diversity, queerly ourselves. . . . [The facilitators] took great care to explain that everyone was welcome under the word *queer.*

LAURA THOMAS: I don't see the queer movement as being organized to do anything beyond issues of anti-assimilation and being who we want to be.

ADELE MORRISON: Queer is not an "instead of," it's an "inclusive of." . . . It's like the whole issue of "people of color".[9]

[. . .]

Or, as former *Outweek* editor Gabriel Rotello explained to a *New York Times* reporter,

When you're trying to describe the community, and you have to list gays, lesbians, bisexuals, drag queens, transsexuals (post-op and pre), it gets unwieldy. Queer says it all.[10]

In addition to the appearance of organizations for "bisexuals" and "queers," the boundaries of community have also been altered by a new elasticity in the meanings of "lesbian" and "gay." When Pat Califia announced that sex between lesbians and gay men is "gay sex," and *Outweek* published a cover story on "Lesbians Who Sleep with Men," the notion of a fixed sexual identity determined by a firmly gendered desire began to slip quietly away.[11]

NOTES

This essay was first presented at the University of Illinois at Champaign-Urbana's Unit for Criticism and Interpretive Theory Colloquium in April 1991, then at the Fifth Annual Lesbian and Gay Studies Conference at Rutgers University in November 1991. I would like to thank Alan Hance and Lee Furey for their comments in Urbana, and Kathleen McHugh, Carole Vance, Cindy Patton, Jeff Escoffier, Jonathan Ned Katz, and especially Nan D. Hunter, for their invaluable contributions to my thinking. I would also like to thank Gayle Rubin and Larry Gross for providing me with copies of important but obscure articles from their voluminous files, and the *SR* Bay Area collective for their helpful editorial suggestions.

1. The ideas in this discussion of gay nationalism were generated in conversations with Jenny Terry, Jackie Urla, and Jeff Escoffier. It was Urla who first suggested to me that certain strains in gay politics could be considered nationalist discourses.

2. For a description and defense of the "ethnic model," see Steven Epstein, "Gay Politics, Ethnic Identity: The Limits of Social Constructionism," *Socialist Review,* vol. 17, no. 3/4 (May/August 1987).

3. For an account of a 1970s incarnation of this form of nationalism—based on gender rather than sexuality per se—see Charlotte Bunch, "Learning from Lesbian Separatism," in her *Passionate Politics: Feminist Theory in Action* (New York: St. Martin's Press, 1987).

4. See, for example, Michelangelo Signorile, "Gossip Watch," *Outweek,* April 18, 1990, pp. 55–57. For an extended discussion of these issues, see Steve Beery et al., "Smashing the Closet: The Pros and Cons of Outing," *Outweek,* May 16, 1990, pp. 40–53. The many opinions expressed in this issue indicate that not all editors of *Outweek* agreed with Signorile—though the editor-in-chief, Gabriel Rotello, was in complete agreement.

5. Audre Lorde, *Zami: A New Spelling of My Name* (Watertown, MA: Persephone Press, 1982), p. 226.

6. For discussions of the emergence of the homosexual/heterosexual dyad and its representations in various medical-scientific discourses, see Jeffrey Weeks, *Coming Out: Homosexual Politics in Britain from the Nineteenth Century to the Present*

(London: Quartet Books, 1977) and his *Sex, Politics and Society: The Regulation of Sexuality since 1800* (London: Longman, 1981). See also Jonathan Katz, "The Invention of the Homosexual, 1880–1950," in his *Gay/Lesbian Almanac* (New York: Harper & Row, 1983), pp. 137–74.

7. See Dennis Altman, *Homosexual Oppression and Liberation* (New York: Avon Books, 1971), especially Chapter 3. "Liberation: Toward the Polymorphous Whole."

8. Alix Dobkin, "Any Woman Can Be a Lesbian," from the album *Lavender Jane Loves Women.* The best-known example of this move—the denaturalization of heterosexuality and the naturalization of lesbianism—is Adrienne Rich, "Compulsory Heterosexuality and Lesbian Existence," reprinted in *Powers of Desire: The Politics of Sexuality,* A. Snitow, C. Stansell, and S. Thompson, eds. (New York: Monthly Review Press, 1983), pp. 177–205. It is important to note that male-dominated gay politics has seldom supported a critique of the convention of heterosexuality for most people (the 90 percent or

so seen as "naturally" heterosexual) Lesbian feminists *always* regarded heterosexuality as an oppressive institution, which any woman (potentially all women) might escape through lesbianism.

9. Birth of a Queer Nation," *OUT/LOOK: National Lesbian and Gay Quarterly,* no. 11 (Winter 1991), pp. 14–23. The interviews and articles in this special section were collected from New York and San Francisco, though there are other groups all over the country. My account of Queer Nation is drawn from my own (limited) knowledge of the New York and Chicago groups and from articles and interviews in the gay and lesbian press. Because Queer Nation has no central "organization," I'm not attempting to describe it exhaustively; I am pointing to several tendencies and possibilities within it.

10. " 'Gay' Fades as Militants Pick 'Queer,' " *The New York Times,* April 6, 1991.

11. Pat Califia, "Gay Men, Lesbians and Sex: Doing It Together," *The Advocate,* July 7, 1983, pp. 24–27; Jorjet Harper, "Lesbians Who Sleep with Men," *Outweek,* February 11, 1990, pp. 46–52.

REFLECTING ON THE SECTION

The rise of the modern state and of nationalisms highlighted differences among and different treatments of people based on ethnicity, class, race, nation, and gender identity. New social movements formed in response to such inequalities. The readings in this section emphasize the uses and difficulties of identity politics as strategies for empowering those individuals and groups that have been marginalized by nation-states. Strategies of opposition mobilized by new social movements rely on a variety of identity politics, including essentialized, intersectional, and multiple identities.

What are some of the advantages of identity politics for political organizing? What are the traps of identity? Must identity be essentialized in order to be useful politically? Consider the importance of language for cultural and political organizing: what are the consequences of using *queer* over *lesbian* or *Chicana* over *Hispanic?* What kinds of cultural and political organizing are the authors in this section calling for? Finally, what kinds of feminism do these authors model for us by embracing, transforming, or rejecting identity politics?

Communities and Nations

We, the People

PETER BURKE

Identity politics often draw upon belonging to a community as a basis for political and cultural recognition. In feminism, it is often assumed that women belong to one community based on gender. Where does the notion of community come from and what is its relationship to the nation-state in the modern period? Historian Peter Burke describes the rise of collective identities such as "the people" during the transition from feudalism to capitalism.

In many parts of the world, collective identities have been formed or reformed in the course of resistance to the West. In Latin America in the nineteenth century, for example, there was a long and intense conflict between Westernizing elites, who attempted to reform their countries along foreign lines, and those who fought to preserve their traditional local cultures from modernization. In this case the conflict between centre and periphery and the conflict between dominant and

Peter Burke, "We, the People: Popular Culture and Popular Identity in Modern Europe," in Scott Lash and Jonathan Friedman, eds. *Modernity and Identity* (Oxford: Blackwell, 1992): 298–301.

subordinate classes virtually merged into one (Burns 1980).

However, "identities of resistance" of this kind existed in the West itself. In East and Central Europe in the nineteenth century, the situation was not unlike the Latin American one, with a wide gap, indeed a sharp conflict, between the elites, who generally identified themselves with the "West," and the peasants, who still saw their own villages as the centre of the universe (Hofer 1984; Fel and Hofer 1969). This conflict led to the peasants becoming conscious of themselves as peasants, and on occasion, as in Croatia and Hungary, joining political parties founded to promote their interests.

In Europe generally, one of the most important identities of resistance was and is that of "the people" in the exclusive sense, the people as opposed to the ruling class. It is not difficult to find examples, from the late Middle Ages onward, of the ruling class using the term "the people" to refer to the remainder of the population, to describe them as ignorant, superstitious, disorderly, and so on. The problem is rather to discover whether, or more exactly when and where, this remainder of the population identified themselves as "the people" or the "working class."

Key Terms

center/periphery A concept (best known in relation to the work of Immanuel Wallerstein) that divides the world into two sectors: the center (metropolitan, wealthy, former and current colonial powers) and the periphery (the colonized or "underdeveloped" areas of the world).

class consciousness Awareness of belonging to a social or economic class, especially in relation to strategies of resistance based on class solidarity.
popular culture The term for "culture from below"; that is, the non-elite forms of entertainment and media.

Much has been written on the rise of class consciousness in nineteenth-century Europe. One of the major contributions to the subject is Edward Thompson's famous book *The Making of the English Working Class,* first published in 1963. Thompson's study is a pioneering piece of history from below. It sets out, in its author's words, "to rescue the poor stockinger, the Luddite cropper, the 'obsolete' hand-loom weaver . . . from the enormous condescension of posterity." It tries to reconstruct their experiences, their culture—their religion (Methodism or millenarianism), their reading (chapbooks and almanacs), the ethos expressed in their rituals of "mutuality," and so on. Its central theme is that of modernity and identity, in the sense that it argues that "In the years between 1780 and 1832 most English working people came to feel an identity of interests as between themselves, and as against their rulers and employers" (Thompson 1963: 11–12).

This sense of belonging to the people, well-documented in England and France in the 1830s and 1840s, was not altogether new. The term "people," in opposition to that of the privileged classes, was common enough in political discourse in the age of the French Revolution, from Tom Paine to the Comte de Volney (1791: ch. 15) and of course Rousseau. It can occasionally be found still earlier (Morgan 1988).

[. . .]

However, there are good reasons for identifying the years around 1800 as a turning point in many parts of Europe. It was at about this time that ordinary people seem to have become aware of what we call "popular culture" as *their* culture, in the course of resisting what they regarded as attempts by the privileged classes to take this culture from them.

In 1500, the popular culture of songs, tales, festivals, and so on was still popular in the inclusive sense, open to all, like the tavern and the piazza where so many performances took place. It was everyone's culture, although certain elites had cultures of their own to which access was restricted (via grammar schools, universities, seminaries, noble academies, etc.). However, in the course of the early modern period, as what Norbert Elias calls the "civilizing process" affected their behaviour more and more deeply, the European elites gradually withdrew from participation in popular culture for the same reasons that led them to try to reform it. They came to see it as dirty, barbarous, irrational, uncivilized, everything which they thought their own culture was not. They tried to distance themselves from it in the literal, spatial sense as well as the metaphorical, psychological one. Hence the elites abandoned street festivals to ordinary people or watched them from a safe distance, from a balcony, perhaps, rather than taking part in them. They celebrated carnival in their own houses, instead of going down to the marketplace. One sign of this social "apartheid" in mid-nineteenth-century England was the division of public houses into compartments, the middle-class "private bar" or "saloon bar" being separated from the working-class public bar (Girouard 1975: 57ff.). In the eighteenth and nineteenth centuries European elites spoke less and less dialect, and they stopped listening to, or reading, certain kinds of story, leaving these "folk-tales" to their children and to the common people (a significant equation). By the early nineteenth century, the cultural distance between elites and people had widened to such a degree that it was possible for European intellectuals to discover popular culture as something exotic and enthralling (Burke 1978: 270ff.).

REFERENCES

Burke, P. (1978). *Popular Culture in Early Modern Europe.* London: Temple Smith.

Burns, E. Bradford. (1980). *The Poverty of Progress: Latin America in the Nineteenth Century.* Berkeley: University of California Press.

Fel, E., and T. Hofer. (1969). *Proper Peasants.* Chicago: University of Chicago Press.

Girouard, M. (1975). *Victorian Pubs.* London: Studio Vista.

Hofer, T. (1984). "The Perception of Tradition in European Ethnology," *Journal of Folklore Research,* 21, 133–47.

Morgan, E. (1988). *Inventing the People.* New York: Norton.

Thompson, E. P. (1963). *The Making of the English Working Class.* London: Gollancz.

Volney, C. (1791). *Les Ruines, ou méditations sur les révolutions des empires.* Paris: Desenne.

COMMUNITY

RAYMOND WILLIAMS

Community has been in the language since C14, from fw *comuneté,* oF, *communitatem,* L—community of relations or feelings, from rw *communis,* L—COMMON (q.v.). It became established in English in a range of senses: (i) the commons or common people, as distinguished from those of rank (C14–C17); (ii) a state or organized society, in its later uses relatively small (C14–); (iii) the people of a district (C18–); (iv) the quality of holding something in common, as in **community of interests, community of goods** (C16–); (v) a sense of common identity and characteristics (C16–). It will be seen that senses (i) to (iii) indicate actual social groups, senses (iv) and (v) a particular quality of relationship (as in *communitas*). From C17 there are signs of the distinction which became especially important from C19, in which **community** was felt to be more immediate than SOCIETY (q.v.), although it must be remembered that *society* itself had this more immediate sense until C18, and *civil society* (see CIVILIZATION) was, like *society* and *community* in these uses, originally an attempt to distinguish the body of direct relationships from the organized establishment of *realm* or *state*. From C19 the sense of immediacy or locality was strongly developed in the context of larger and more complex industrial societies. **Community** was the word normally chosen for experiments in an alternative kind of group living. It is still so used and has been joined, in a more limited sense, by **commune** (the French *commune*—the smallest administrative division—and the German *Gemeinde*—a civil and ecclesiastical division. These had interacted with each other and with **community,** and also passed into socialist thought (especially *commune*) and into sociology (especially *Gemeinde*) to express particular kinds of social relations).

[. . .]

A comparable distinction is evident in mC20 uses of **community.** In some uses this has been given a polemical edge, as in **community politics,** which is distinct not only from *national politics* but from formal *local politics* and normally involves various kinds of direct action and direct local organization, "working directly with people," as which it is distinct from "service to the **community,**" which has an older sense of voluntary work supplementary to official provision or paid service.

The complexity of **community** thus relates to the difficult interaction between the tendencies originally distinguished in the historical development: on the one hand the sense of direct common concern; on the other hand the materialization of various forms of common organization, which may or may not adequately express this. **Community** can be the warmly persuasive word to describe an existing set of relationships, or the warmly persuasive word to describe an alternative set of relationships. What is most important, perhaps, is that unlike all other terms of social organization (*state, nation, society,* etc.), it seems never to be used unfavourably and never to be given any positive opposing or distinguishing term.

Raymond Williams, *Keywords,* New York, Oxford University Press, 1983, 75–76.

Reading B

Nationalism and Masculinity
CYNTHIA ENLOE

One of the most powerful forms of community and identity is the nation. Belonging to a nation is a necessary and involuntary act in modern societies. Cynthia Enloe argues that nationalism is often based on patriarchal practices, constructing women as possessions and men as protectors. Thus, as women participate in nationalist struggles, they find themselves in a contradictory position. They are members of a nation and yet they have largely symbolic and subordinate roles.

A *nation* is a collection of people who have come to believe that, they have been shaped by a common past and are destined to share a common future. That belief

Cynthia Enloe, *Bananas, Beaches, and Bases: Making Feminist Sense of International Politics* Berkeley, University of California Press, 1990: 45–46, 52–59.

is usually nurtured by a common language and a sense of otherness from groups around them. Nationalism is a commitment to fostering those beliefs and promoting policies which permit the nation to control its own destiny. Colonialism is especially fertile ground for nationalist ideas because it gives an otherwise divided people such a potent shared experience of foreign domination. But not all nationalists respect other communities' need for feelings of self-worth and control. Some nationalists have been the victims of racism and colonialism; others have been the perpetrators of racism and colonialism.

Today nationalism still thrives, despite the waning of classic colonialism, because foreign influence works in new ways to give peoples a sense that they do not control their own fates. Where once the British, Dutch, French, or American colonial administration was a rallying point for nationalists, today the interventions of

Key Terms

civilizing mission The cultural rationale for colonization; the claim that colonialism's goal was to turn primitive and uncivilized societies into progressive and modern ones.

intifadah Beginning in 1987, the spontaneous uprising of Palestinians against Israeli occupation of the West Bank in Gaza.

Orient/Orientalism The Orient is an imaginary region described by European historians and travelers since the eighteenth century. While the region is generally believed to comprise the Middle East and parts of Asia, the term also came to mark the idea of the East as "other" to the West.

Orientalism is the academic knowledge created to describe and detail the "Orient."

purdah The practice of separate living quarters for women.

refugee A person who has been forcibly displaced from his or her country of nationality and who seeks asylum in another country.

veil The head covering used by certain classes and groups of women in Asia, Africa, and the Middle East. In Western feminism, the "veil" has become a symbol of women's oppression under Islamic fundamentalism.

foreign corporations, bankers, and armies mobilize nationalist energies. Nationalism also remains a powerful political force because so many of the countries which won independence from colonial rule in fact include within their borders more than one national community. Thus, while nationalism is alive and well among those Canadians who feel as though their very identities are on the verge of being blotted out by the behemoth to the south, it is also shaping relations *between* Canadians; since the 1960s French-Canadians have tried to develop nationalist strategies to stave off absorption by dominant Anglo-Canada. Nationalist ideas, therefore, are informing people's relationships with their neighbors—and the larger world—in industrialized as well as agrarian societies. Nationalism is a driving force in the political lives of men and women in countries as different as Ethiopia, South Africa, South Korea, Britain, Ireland, and the Soviet Union.

Nationalist movements have transformed the landscape of international politics. If a state is a vertical creature of authority, a nation is a horizontal creature of identity. The most stable political system, it is now thought, is one in which state power rests on a bed of national identity: a "nation-state." Most governments nowadays assert that they rule in nation-states. The reality is less simple. State officials frequently lay claim to nationally rooted legitimacy because those who cannot stand on wobbly political ground. Without a national foundation to legitimize their power, officials' demands lack credibility in the eyes of their counterparts around the international bargaining table.[1]

One becomes a nationalist when one begins to recognize shared public pasts and futures. But most women's past experiences and strategies for the future are not made the basis of the nationalism they are urged to support. Yet, as Algerian feminists warn, it is a very risky enterprise for women to criticize a movement claiming to represent their own nation or the regime that exercises authority in the name of that nation. Living as a nationalist feminist is one of the most difficult political projects in today's world. Developing nationalist feminist politics is not made easier by the fact that, as we will see below, so many women in colonizing countries supported the policies nationalist movements have organized to reverse. The seriousness

of patriarchal discrimination can seem diluted when women as well as men have participated in the outsiders' conquest.

◦ Nationalism and the Veil

No practice has been more heatedly debated among nationalists than the veil: should a Muslim woman demonstrate her commitment to the nationalist cause by wearing a veil—or by throwing off the veil? Men and women in Algeria, Egypt, Iran, Turkey, and Malaysia have lined up on both sides of this controversy. Colonial officials and men and women from the colonizing societies have also exercised moral and coercive pressure to tilt the argument one way or the other, usually toward rejecting the veil. The more colonialists have promoted the antiveil movement in the name of Western civilization, the harder it has been for Muslim women in the colonized (or neocolonized) country to control the argument. For if colonial male administrators and progressive European women take prominent public stances against the veil, and if they do so without a genuine alliance with local women, as is usually the case, they ensure that rejection of the veil will be taken as compliance with colonial rule. In Algeria, French administrators saw removing the veil as part of France's "civilizing mission." Egyptian feminists in the 1920s and 1930s had more success in controlling the debate, but they too risked being tarred with the antinationalist brush when they stepped out in public unveiled. Those antiveil women who came from the local upper classes, as many did, were only partly protected from ridicule by their privileged status.[2]

European women in Egypt usually expressed strong opinions about the veil. They saw it as emblematic of Muslim women's seclusion, and linked it to the harem. Many of the European women who wrote about the veil did so not primarily out of genuine curiosity about the lives and thoughts of Egyptian women, but because it allowed them to feel sanguine about their own condition as European women: 'By thinking of themselves as all powerful and free *vis-à-vis* Egyptian women, Western women could avoid confronting their own powerlessness and gender oppression at home.'[3] All too often, European women who traveled to Egypt and stayed on as teachers, governesses, and sometimes wives of Egyptian men were notably reluctant to explain why it was that they felt so much freer in the "Orient."

For their part, Egyptian women organizing and writing as feminists in the early twentieth century were frequently more exercised by European women's stereotypical attitudes than they were by Egyptian men's protection of male privilege. They felt compelled to defend Islam in the face of racist Orientalism. They objected to portrayals of Islamic society as incapable of dynamism and reform and to writings that pictured all Arab women as mindless members of the harem, preoccupied with petty domestic rivalries rather than with the artistic and political affairs of their times. They were pressed into this defensive position not only by European women's myopia, but by their need to preserve their alliances with Egyptian nationalist men. Under British colonial rule, some Egyptian men reached positions of considerable influence, positions not open to Egyptian women. In order to protect Egyptian women from some of the most oppressive consequences of British policy, Egyptian feminists needed elite Egyptian men to intervene on their behalf. "Because men were faithful allies during the early phases of the struggle for women's rights, paternalist strategies for change acquired a certain degree of legitimacy."[4] Focusing on European women's misrepresentations and being pressed into defending Islam in response not only kept these practical alliances between local men and women alive; they also allowed male privilege to seep deep into the Egyptian nationalist movement.

What is striking about these past and present arguments over whether a veiled woman is strengthening her nation or betraying it is that they are so important to men in their communities. One is hard-pressed to think of an equally heated debate in any national community about men's attire—or diet or linguistic style—in which women have had so predominant a role to play. Sikh men's wearing of the customary turban is important to Sikh communal solidarity; Sikh men in India and Britain have had to fight for the right to wear their turbans (for instance, as bus conductors in Britain). Yet one doesn't see Sikh women acting as the chief proponents or enforcers of this male ethnic prac-

tice. Rather, men in many communities appear to assign such ideological weight to the outward attire and sexual purity of women in the community because they see women as 1) the community's—or the nation's—most valuable *possessions;* 2) the principal *vehicles* for transmitting the whole nation's values from one generation to the next; 3) *bearers* of the community's future generations—crudely, nationalist wombs; 4) the members of the community most *vulnerable* to defilement and exploitation by oppressive alien rulers; and 5) most susceptible to *assimilation* and co-option by insidious outsiders. All of these presumptions have made women's behavior important in the eyes of nationalist men. But these ideas have not necessarily ensured that women themselves would be taken seriously as active creators of the nation's newly assertive politics. Nor have these ideas guaranteed that male privilege would be effectively challenged in the new state derived from that nation.[5]

Patriarchy Inside the Movement

Arguments about the proper role of women in the nationalist struggle and in the future nation-state have occurred in virtually every nationalist movement since the eighteenth century precisely because these five assumptions have had such potency for people trying to redraw political boundaries.

The American Revolution against British colonial rule should stand as a warning. So should the French Revolution, fought against an indigenous monarchy in the name of the newly self-conscious nation. During and after both nationalist revolutions the concept of "citizenship" provided the terrain on which gendered struggles were fought between nationalist women and nationalist men. French and American women lost those postrevolutionary contests. Changes in relations between women and men necessitated by the exigencies of nationalist warfare did not survive once the new nation-state was established.[6]

Women within the oppressed national communities have often been split over how to connect their emerging sense of national identity and participation with their emerging political identities as women. For instance, women in Jaffna, Sri Lanka, formed a study group in the late 1980s, in the midst of a civil war, in order to work out together how their oppression as women is related to their oppression as Tamils in a Singhalese-dominated state. Some women had become politically conscious because the Tamil nationalist movement made them aware that their status as Tamils affected their chances of educational and economic opportunities in Sri Lanka. It was only after this initial politicization through nationalism that they became aware that women and men were being made to play quite different roles in the escalating violence between Tamil guerrillas, the government's military, and the occupying Indian army. The changes wrought by ethnic mobilization and spiraling violence prompted these Tamil women to come together in a study group. There is no guarantee that their examination of women's conditions in Tamil and Sri Lankan societies will make them feel more comfortable with the nationalist movement as it is currently structured and directed. Participation in the women's study group could make them less willing to be the stalwarts of refugee camps or the symbols of outsiders' victimization. Their discussions might even prompt some of the women to see feminists in the Singhalese community as potential allies.[7]

Yet it isn't always obvious that surrendering the role of cultural transmitter or rejecting male protection will enhance a woman's daily security, reduce her burdens. Women in many communities trying to assert their sense of national identity find that coming into an emergent nationalist movement *through* the accepted feminine roles of bearer of the community's memory and children is empowering. Being praised by men in the nationalist movement for bearing more children and raising them well doesn't always feel like being patronized or marginalized.

But a woman who begins to go out of her home in the evening to attend nationalist meetings in the name of securing a better future for her children may meet strong resistance from her husband. Her husband may accuse her of neglecting her home duties, having a sexual liaison, making him look a fool in the eyes of other men, who may taunt him for not being able to control his wife. He never imagined that supporting the nationalist movement would entail losing control of his family. He may even beat her to stop her from attending such meetings.

Such experiences have raised wife battering to the status of a political issue for women in some nationalist movements. When they became involved in nationalist activities they may not have imagined that critiques of foreign rule, foreign bases, or foreign investment would lead to critiques of relations between husbands and wives. In fact, many women became involved *as* good wives and good mothers. It was only later that they concluded that they would have to overcome male resistance in their homes and neighborhoods if they were to be able to participate fully in the movement. A Filipino nationalist active in resisting her government's alliances with foreign bankers, corporations, and militaries describes a new step in nationalist organizing:

> We have a forum, we call it the women's soiré, where we invite women who are involved in the movement and also encourage them to bring their husbands . . . One evening our topic was "Feminism and Marriage—Do They Mix?" We went into a discussion of the family and some even questioned the value of the family because of the oppression of females that emanates from the family. Then some of the men started airing their grievances, such as that since their wives joined this movement they are no longer attending to the needs of the children . . . It was a very healthy exchange, and it was a very different kind of dialog because it was a group dialog, not just between husbands and wives.[8]

Women active in nationalist movements in the Philippines, Ireland, South Africa, Canada, Sri Lanka, Mexico and Nicaragua have begun to analyze how the "home" and the "international system" are integrally tied to one another. In doing so they are far ahead of those women in industrialized countries who have scarcely glimpsed those political connections. The process that ties them together is not just globalized consumer advertising, it is domestic relations between women and men. If women, they argue, are kept in marginalized roles by men as lovers, fathers, or husbands, the chances of halting foreign-financed invasion, ending an unfair military bases treaty, or holding accountable a multinational employer will be slim. In this sense, foreign base commanders and entrepreneurs may depend on domestic violence as much as they do on alliances with men in the local elite.[9]

On the other hand, it can be very difficult for women to raise these sorts of issues inside a nationalist movement that is under siege. The more imminent and coercive the threat posed by an outside power—a foreign force or the local government's police—the more successful men in the community are likely to be in persuading women to keep quiet, to swallow their grievances and their analyses. When a nationalist movement becomes militarized, either on its leaders' initiative or in reaction to external intimidation, male privilege in the community usually becomes more entrenched.

When, on top of this, foreign governments become involved to defend an ethnic group from attack by an alien-backed power and thereby legitimize their involvement, male privilege gains a foreign ally. This appears to be what happened in Afghanistan. The United States government and its allies cast the war in Afghanistan in classic Cold War terms: the Soviet Union invaded a neighboring country, propping up a puppet regime which lacked a popular base; the anti-regime insurgents represented the real nation, and their brave resistance deserved the Free World's moral and military support. This picture becomes murky, however, when one looks at the situation from the vantage point of Afghan women. The cause for which the insurgent muhjahidin fought was a traditional rural clan way of life that is unambiguously patriarchal. One of the policies the Soviet-backed government in Kabul pursued that so alienated male clan leaders was expanding economic and educational opportunities for Afghanistan's women. While there is little evidence that the Soviet-backed Kabul regime enjoyed wide public legitimacy, outside observers report that its tenure proved beneficial to those mainly urban women who have been able to take advantage of the government's policy. In its hostile foreign policy toward the Khomeini regime in Iran, the U.S. government had been eager to use that regime's harsh repression of women to justify its opposition; but this concern for women conveniently slipped off the policy stage when U.S. officials designed their response to the civil war in Afghanistan.[10]

The militarization of Afghanistan has proved disastrous for women in the rural clan communities waging war. They have been subjected to bombing and exile. The refugee camps over the border in Pakistan had radically different meanings for women and men. For young men the refugee camp was a staging area for guerrilla campaigns across the border; they came to the camps to recoup from battle, to see their wives and children. For the women, "camp life is so sad . . . they cry from morning to night," according to Sadia Ansari, one of the few Afghan women fortunate enough to have a teaching job in the United Nations-run schools. The women's husbands and fathers enforced the seclusion of their women far more strictly in the camps than they did in Afghanistan itself. Here they believed the risk was greater that their women would be seen by men outside the safe boundaries of the family. Whereas back in their villages women had field work, cooking, and housework to do, in the camps they have no legitimate reason to leave their mud huts. Girls are kept out of the U.N. schools by protective fathers. In March 1988 the total enrollment in U.N. schools stood at 104,600 boys and 7,800 girls. "The women are like birds in a cage," admitted one guerrilla commander.[11] This civil war has been fought in a way that has militarized purdah. It has threatened men's control over women and so intensified men's determination to police the behavior of women.

Military mobilization, it is true, may make it necessary for men to permit women to acquire new skills and take on new responsibilities. This has been one of the motivations for the Kabul government to increase opportunities of paid work for women citizens. Journalists visiting rebel camps in the Southern Sahara and Eritrea also report that the women in those nationalist movements have used wartime's premium on their contributions to substantially widen women's sphere of public and private participation.[12] But simultaneously, militarization puts a premium on communal unity in the name of national survival, a priority which can silence women critical of patriarchal practices and attitudes; in so doing, nationalist militarization can privilege men.

If both pressures occur at the same time, a gendered tension will develop within the national community. This could produce a radically new definition of "the nation." Still, it is not assured. In the Palestinian communities in Lebanon and the occupied territories of Israel, there is evidence of such two-sided pressures emanating from escalating militarization. On the one hand, militarization is providing young Palestinian men with new opportunities to prove their manhood, often in defiance not only of Israeli men's authority but also of what many perceive as their fathers' outworn authority. On the other hand, "women are bearing the brunt of the *intifadah,*" as one Palestinian told a reporter in 1988. The Israeli government's use of soldiers to enforce strict curfews and to arrest an estimated 6,000 Palestinian men has raised women's household chores to the stature of national imperatives: "They have to watch the money, make all the family chores, bake their own bread, grow vegetables, take care of chickens and goats. These traditional roles are more important now." Najwa Jardali, a Palestinian woman long active in a movement to provide day care and health clinics for women in the occupied territories, warned Western women not to imagine that day care is simply a women's issue. With militarization, it has become a national concern: "Most Western feminists wouldn't regard kindergarten as important . . . but for us it's very important. The military government doesn't allow us kindergartens in schools, and day care enables women to get involved in other activities." Proof of day care centers' national importance is the Israeli military's efforts to harass the women teachers and close them down.[13]

The popular image of the Palestinian nation until now has been the young male street fighter of the Palestine Liberation Organization. With his checkered scarf, rock in hand, defiant and alert, he has stood for an entire nation. Palestinian women remained in the shadows. They were the protected, or the unprotected. But in 1988 Palestinian women began holding their own marches in the occupied territories to protest against the Israeli government's "Iron Fist" policy. They defied heavily armed soldiers with chants of "We are people, we are women. Never are we subdued. Never do we feel self-pity." The community's leadership committee, the Unified National Command of the Intifadah, began addressing women's as well as men's concerns in its bulletins. The nature of Israeli military policy compelled Palestinians to develop a new way of organizing, one reliant less on outside help and more on small neighborhood committees, less susceptible to police and military disruption. In this type of organization, especially with so many men and boys jailed after the more visible stone-throwing confrontations, women began to come into their own as political actors. Women on the neighborhood committees went from house to house recruiting more members—"collecting money and food for the besieged, asking people knowledgeable about health care to provide health services, urging participation in demonstrations."[14] Will such militarizing pressures lead to an enduring reordering of femininity and masculinity within the Palestinian nation?

NOTES

1. Cynthia H. Enloe, *Ethnic Conflict and Political Development,* Lanham, MD, University Press of America, 1986; Cynthia H. Enloe, *Ethnic Soldiers: State Security in Divided Societies,* London, Penguin, 1980.

2. Marie-Aimée Hélie-Lucas in Isaksson, op. cit. Cynthia Nelson and Akram Khater, 'al-Harakah al-Nisa'eyya: the Women's Movement and Political Participation in Modern Egypt', *Women's Studies International Forum,* vol. 11, no. 5, 1988; Selma Botman, 'The Experience of Women in the Egyptian Communist Movement, 1939–1954', *Women's Studies International Forum,* vol. 11, no. 2, 1988; Sarah Graham-Brown, op. cit.; Margot Bardon, 'Dual Libera-

tion: Feminism and Nationalism in Egypt, 1870–1925', *Feminist Issues,* vol. 8, no. 1, Spring, 1988; Huda Shaarawi, *Harem Years: The Memories of an Egyptian Feminist,* London, Virago, 1986; Mervat Hatem, 'The Politics of Sexuality and Gender in Segregated Patriarchal Systems: the Case of Eighteenth and Nineteenth Century Egypt', *Feminist Studies,* vol. 12, no. 2, Summer, 1986; Elizabeth Sanasarian, *The Women's Rights Movement in Iran,* New York, Praeger, 1983.

3. Mervat Hatem, 'Through Each Other's Eyes: Egyptian, Levantine-Egyptian and European Women's Images of Themselves and of Each Other, 1862–1920', *Women's Studies International Forum,* 12, no. 2, 1989.

4. Ibid.

5. For further discussion of these tensions, see Nira Yuval-Davis and Floya Anthias, editors, *Woman-Nation-State,* London, Macmillan, 1989; Floya Anthias, Nira Yuval-Davis and Harriet Cain, *Resistance and Control: Racism and 'The Community'*, London and New York, Routledge, 1989.

6. Linda K. Kerber, *Women of the Republic: Intellect and Ideology in Revolutionary America,* Chapel Hill, NC, University of North Carolina Press, 1980; Mary G. Dietz, 'Context is All: Feminism and Theories of Citizenship', *Daedalus,* Fall, 1987, pp. 1–24; Sian Reynolds, 'Marianne's Citizens? Women, the Republic and Universal Suffrage in France', in Sian Reynolds, editor, *Women, the State and Revolution,* Amherst, MA, University of Massachusetts Press, 1987.

7. 'A Letter from the Women's Study Circle of Jaffna', *Women's Studies International Forum,* vol. 12, no. 1, 1989. This point was confirmed by Anita Nesiah, a Sri Lankan feminist, in her lecture, Clark University, Worcester, MA, November 7, 1988.

8. 'Philippine Women Say Repression is Worsening', *Listen Real Loud,* American Friends Service Committee, Philadelphia, vol. 9, no. 1, 1988, p. 7.

9. For instance, Sylvia, 'Nicaragua: Working Women in a Women's Brigade', *Off Our Backs,* June, 1988, pp. 12–13; Ailbhe Smyth, guest editor, special issue on 'Feminism in Ireland', *Women's Studies International Forum,* vol. 11, no. 4, 1988; Eileen Fairweather, Roissin McDonough and Melanie McFaryean, *Only the Rivers Run Free—Northern Ireland: The Women's War,* London, Pluto Press, 1984; Ailbhe Smyth, Pauline Jackson, Caroline McCamley, Ann Speed, 'States of Emergence', *Trouble and Strife,* no. 14, Autumn, 1988, pp. 46–52; The Clio Collective, *Quebec Women: A History,* Toronto, Women's Press, 1987; Stephanie Urdang, *And Still They Dance: Women, War and the Struggle for Change in Mozambique,* New York, Monthly Review Press, 1989.

10. Henry Kamm, 'Afghan Peace Could Herald War of Sexes', *New York Times,* December 12, 1988.

11. Henry Kamm, 'Afghanistan Refugee Women Suffering from Isolation Under Islamic Custom', *New York Times,* March 27, 1988; Donatella Lorch, 'An Afghan Exile, Her School and Hopes for the Future', *New York Times,* June 12, 1988; Doris Lessing, *The Wind Blows Away Our Words,* New York, Vintage Books, 1987, pp. 77–80.

12. Laura Cumming, 'Forgotten Struggle for the Western Sahara', *New Statesman,* May 20, 1988, pp. 14–15.

13. Curtis Wilkie, 'Roles Change for Palestinian Women', *Boston Globe,* May 17, 1988.

14. Ellen Cantarow, 'Palestinian Women Resisting Occupation', *Sojourner,* April, 1988, p. 19. See also Beata Lipman, *Israel - The Embattled Land: Jewish and Palestinian Women Talk about Their Lives,* London and Winchester, MA, Pandora Press, 1988; Hamida Kazi, 'Palestinian Women and the National Liberation Movement', in Mageda Salman, et al., *Women in the Middle East,* London, Zed Books, 1987.

Women of Conformity: The Work of Shimada Yoshiko
HAGIWARA HIROKO

Cultural historian Hagiwara Hiroko describes the intersection of motherhood and militarism in the modern nation-state. She addresses how Japanese women's participation in nationalist and patriotic activities during the Second World War made them complicit with their country's imperial projects. Hagiwara examines the work of Japanese-born multimedia artist Shimada Yoshiko (born 1965). Drawing on diverse images and media, Yoshiko, who now works in Berlin, explores the cult of motherhood, nationalism, and militarism during this period of history.

—Images of Japanese Women

Shimada's etchings are quite minimalist. She uses old newspaper photos and postcards published in the 1930s and 1940s without adding complex arrangements. She simply quotes old materials to mount on prints and makes them recite real, hidden or new meanings that were unseen at the time of their production.

The series of prints *Past Imperfect* (1993) manifests her critical view of Japan's modern history, with an

Hagiwara Hiroko, "Women of Conformity: The Work of Shimada Yoshiko," in Griselda Pollock, ed. *Generations and Geographies in the Visual Arts* (London: Routledge, 1996): 254–58.

emphasis on the image of women and their experiences. *Three Women* (Figure II.1) is a reproduction of an old touristic postcard. The images of three Japanese women wearing kimono and the traditional hairdo playfully take the pose of "see no evil, speak no evil, hear no evil." The postcard was produced as a light-hearted souvenir. But with the passage of time, which has provided a change of social context, the pose of the women can be now seen as symbolic of restrictions once imposed on women.

FIGURE II.1 SHIMADA YOSHIKO, *THREE WOMEN*, 1993, ETCHING, 15 × 22.5 CM

Key Terms

comfort women Women, mostly Korean and Filipina, who were forced to serve as prostitutes to Japanese soldiers during Japan's rise as an imperial power in Asia in the twentieth century.

family-state A term that refers to the patriarchal ideology of nation as family.
Joseph Goebbels (1897–1945) Minister of Propaganda for the Nazi regime in Germany.

The ideological functions of established images of women pervading the media are also revealed in many other pieces by the artist. Hara Setsuko, a Japanese film star, best known as the gentle widow in Ozu's *Tokyo Story,* appears in a still of *Die Tochter des Samurai.* [. . .] This propaganda film was jointly produced by Germany and Japan in the 1940s. Another photo, which is juxtaposed with it, is a snapshot of Hara and Goebbels. It is not widely known that Hara featured in many government propaganda films during the war. The artist's concern here is to betray people's fantasized image of Hara, the icon of postwar democratic Japan.

The next piece, *Before and After,* also uses a pair of images of Hara and effectively reveals the fact that the iconic image was a made-up one (Figure II.2). The picture of Hara on the left, which is taken from a still of a wartime film, is of a devoted working mother who would whip up war sentiment. The one on the right is a photo taken after the war. She is smiling, with her hair permed which was condemned as antinationalist luxury in wartime, and, blazoned above her is the slogan of democratization. The image of one woman was used to encourage the prowar nationalist attitude and the antiwar democratic posture. The image of women was something to be manipulated and consistently regarded as being essential for social control.

FIGURE II.2   SHIMADA YOSHIKO, *HARA SETSUKO, BEFORE AND AFTER,* **1993, ETCHING, 30 × 45 CM**

Women's Willing Support of War

Shimada's constant concern is that Japanese women's willing and aggressive participation in the colonialist war should be made visible. She is also anxious to shed light on the cult of motherhood, thanks to which women could be positive about their femininity and, at the same time, could be negative about other ways of living.

A series of prints, *White Aprons,* visually reveals women's virtue in wartime (Figure II.3). The *kappogi,*

FIGURE II.3   SHIMADA YOSHIKO, *WHITE APRONS, TRIPTYCH,* 1993, ETCHING, 45 × 73 CM

the white apron to be worn over a kimono, was adopted as a uniform of the National Defense Women's Organization, the aim of which was to aid and comfort Japanese soldiers and their families. The organization was founded in 1932 and its major activity was to send off soldiers and serve them tea at the port and the station. Thanks to an overalls-type white apron, any woman could participate in the activity without bothering about what to wear. But the most significant function of the apron was to make any member into the mother of any soldier.

The old photos Shimada uses are all startling. The photos in *White Aprons, Triptych* could have been taken in the 1930s and early 1940s. A housewife is cooking in the kitchen, members of the women's organization are sending off soldiers, and women with pistols are learning to shoot. A picture of domesticity is juxtaposed with pictures of Japanese women behaving aggressively. They are all in white aprons. Since the white apron was a symbol of motherly care, and the chastity and asexuality of a housewife, it functioned as a useful tool to encourage ordinary housewives to go out of the home and participate in a social activity. Until then, ordinary housewives had not been expected to be active in public. Before Japanese women gained the suffrage in 1945, they had no legal standing, no chance to get higher education, and no way to be independent individuals who could move freely in a social sphere. Being a mother and housewife was the only acceptable social status for women. As long as they were wearing a white apron, women were allowed to be openly active.

The photo of aproned women holding pistols is repeated in the centrepiece of *Shooting Lesson II* (Figure II.4). They could be colonists in Manchukuo, which was founded in 1932 in the guise of an independent state and was virtually controlled by the Guandong Army, Japan's field army in Manchuria. Wives of colonists are learning to shoot under the guidance of soldiers. Japanese colonists, many of whom were migrants from impoverished farming villages in Japan, took over local people's land to cultivate. Since they were often attacked by anti-Japanese guerrillas, they formed a self-defence civilian force. Even women learned to shoot in order to defend their land and family from "rebellious natives" or "local barbarians." Aprons, which could not have been practically needed for shooting lessons, were needed as a sign to cover up a gap between femininity and armed action.

At each corner of the print, there is a portrait of a Korean comfort woman who was forced to serve frontline Japanese soldiers sexually. The piece shows the contrasting situations of the women. The four military comfort women at the corners are victimized and swayed by events beyond their control, while the four

FIGURE II.4   SHIMADA YOSHIKO, *SHOOTING LESSON II,* **1993, ETCHING, 45 × 60 CM**

aproned women in the centrepiece are learning to be aggressors. The visual images here are all quotes but Shimada's arrangement is successful in showing the different experiences of women. No, "different experiences of women" is euphemistic. Rather, I should say that the differences that women experienced were not simply a matter of possible variants over which each woman exercised some choice. Rather, these differences reflect the hierarchically differentiated social positions of women in the mutual and conflicting determinations of gender, class, and nationality.

[. . .]

The cult of motherhood has both encouraged and suppressed the Japanese women's movement. In wartime the cultist craze of motherhood enabled women to be aggressors. But motherhood was the only channel for women's skills. . . . Women were actually encouraged to reproduce boys, who would be soldiers.

[. . .]

From ordinary women to the empress, from a bombed victim to the Madonna, women were praised as mothers, not as individuals. Women were encouraged to be the National Mother, who would support the family and the state. The cult of motherhood was part of the nationalist ideology, which would sustain that illusory unity, the streadfast and foremost family-state, Japan.

Reading D

The First Ku Klux Klan

KATHLEEN M. BLEE

In another example of complicity between women and nation, historian Kathleen M. Blee's study of women in the Ku Klux Klan in the United States shows how white supremacy offered some women a route to racial power based on gender identity. Blee explains that the Klan posed white women as potential victims of rape by nonwhite and non-Christian men. During the first KKK under Reconstruction, "white womanhood" not only operated as a symbol of the nation among members of the Klan but also became a significant political issue in the country at large. Later, during the Klan resurgence of the 1920s, some newly enfranchised white women organized the Women's Ku Klux Klan (WKKK), combining concerns over racial superiority with such "women's issues" as temperance and female sexual virtue.

From the beginning, the rituals and organized terrorism of the first KKK were based on symbols of violent white masculinity and vulnerable white femininity. When the KKK was organized in Tennessee immediately after the Civil War, it summoned defeated sons of the Confederacy to defend the principles of white su-

Kathleen M. Blee, *Women of the Klan : Racism and Gender in the 1920s,* Berkeley: University of California, 1991: 12–16, 24, 39–41.

premacy against interference by Northerners and retaliation by freed black slaves. As it grew from a prankish club of dejected soldiers to a loosely knit and highly secret vigilante terrorist network in the defeated Southern states, the Klan continued to merge ideas of sexual menace with those of racial and political danger.[1]

During the late 1860s the Klan spread its reign of terror throughout Southern and border states. Gangs of Klansmen threatened, flogged, and murdered countless black and white women and men. But the Klan's violence was not arbitrary. It applied terror to bolster the crumbling foundations of Southern supremacy against political inroads by blacks, Republicans, and Northern whites. Schoolteachers, revenue collectors, election officials, and Republican officeholders—those most involved with dismantling parts of the racial state—as well as all black persons were the most common targets of Klan terror.[2] The KKK was particularly expert in the use of sexual violence and brutality. Klan mobs humiliated white Southern Republicans ("scalawags") by sexually abusing them. Klansmen routinely raped and sexually tortured women, especially black women, during "kluxing" raids on their households. Widely reported acts of lynching, torture, and sexual mutilation intimidated Klan opponents and terrorized its enemies.[3]

The secrecy and juvenile rituals of the early KKK borrowed heavily from the long tradition of male frater-

---

Key Terms

antebellum/postbellum Before and after the Civil War (1861–65) in the United States.
Anti-Semitism Prejudice against Jews.

Knights of Columbus Fraternal organization founded in 1882 in the United States; it is now the largest lay organization in the Catholic Church.

nal societies. Men bound themselves to one another through allegiances of race, gender, and a shared desire to preserve the racial state of the South in the face of military defeat. Even the Klan's name, derived from the Greek *kuklos* (circle), reinforced its quest for white male commonality across divisions of social class and local status.[4] Although the Klan's politics would become fervently anti-Catholic over time, the first Klan created a culture whose costumes and secret ritual mimicked the symbolism and ritual of the male-based hierarchy of the Roman Catholic church. It barred white women (and all nonwhites) from membership, just as the Southern polity did. If the abuse and exclusion of blacks reinforced an ethos of racial power, strength, and invulnerability among the fraternity of white Klansmen so, too, the exclusion of white women served to celebrate and solidify the masculinity of racial politics.[5]

Although women did not participate openly in the actions of the first KKK, the idea of "white womanhood" was a crucial rallying point for postbellum Klan violence. Klansmen insisted that white women benefited from the Southern racial state, even as strict gender hierarchies within white society ensured that women would not be consulted on this matter. In an appearance in 1871 before the U.S. Senate, Nathan Bedford Forrest, the first Grand Wizard, argued that the Klan was needed because Southern whites faced great insecurity. He pointed dramatically at a situation in which "ladies were ravished by some of these negroes, who were tried and put in the penitentiary, but were turned out in a few days afterward."[6]

This theme of imperiled Southern white womanhood echoed throughout writings by the first KKK and its apologists. White women, especially widows living alone on isolated plantations, were highly visible symbols through which the Klan could rouse public fears that blacks' retaliation against their former white masters would be exacted upon white daughters, wives, and mothers. Without the Klan, white men were powerless to assist white women who faced frightful sexual violations by newly freed black men:

> We note the smile of helpless masculinity give but feebly assuring answer to its mate's frown of distressful inquiry, as the sullen roll of the drum and the beastly roar of the savage rasp the chords of

racial instinct. As we watch the noble countenance of modest, innocent Southern maidenhood pale into death-defying scorn, as she contemplates the hellish design of the black brute in human form.[7]

Women were symbols for the first KKK in another way. The feared assault on white women not only threatened white men's sexual prerogatives but symbolized the rape of the Southern racial state in the Reconstruction era as well. In *Hooded Americanism,* David Chalmers notes the double meaning of white womanhood for white men in the antebellum and immediate postbellum South:

> [White womanhood] not only stood at the core of his sense of property and chivalry, she represented the heart of his culture. By the fact that she was not accessible to the Negro, she marked the ultimate line of difference between white and black . . . it was impossible to assault either the Southern woman or the South without having implicitly levied carnal attacks on the other.[8]

The complexity of gender and sexual symbolism in the first Klan shows also in the propaganda circulated among and by Klansmen. Klansmen saw the abolition of slavery both as the loss of sexual access to black women and as the potential loss of exclusive sexual access to white women. An enfranchised black man, the Klan insisted, "considered freedom synonymous with equality and his greatest ambition was to marry a white wife." Klan propaganda steadfastly portrayed women as passive sexual acquisitions of men and insisted that black men used physical coercion to wrest sexual favors (and even marriage vows) from white female victims. Underlying this message, however, was the concern that, given free choice among male sexual partners, at least some white women might choose black men. As a threat to the racial and sexual privileges of white men in the postbellum South, black husbands nearly equaled black rapists of white women.[9]

All histories of the first Klan emphasize that the success of the Klan depended on images of rape and miscegenation between white women and black men. Accounts that lack a feminist-informed analysis, however, miss some of the political significance of references to actual and symbolic rape and miscegenation. In *The Fiery Cross,* for example, Wyn Craig Wade argues that slavery corrupted sexual relations between white men and white women. Placed on a pedestal in antebellum Southern society, white women became "like statues in bed," as Wade remarks, sexually inaccessible to white men. In response white men turned to powerless black female slaves, to "release the passion they were unable to experience with their wives." As the Confederacy crumbled, white men feared that black men would retaliate in like manner by sexually assaulting now vulnerable white mothers, daughters, sisters, and wives.[10]

The interpretation of rape and miscegenation given in *The Fiery Cross*—one shared by most histories of the Klan—presents images of interracial sexuality in the postbellum South as a battle among groups of men divided along racial, class, and regional lines. As men struggled to preserve or challenge a racial caste system, all women were reduced to a common function as political symbols—symbols of racial privilege or subordination, regional self-determination or subjugation. This interpretation superposes hierarchies of gender on the greater cleavages of race and class in Southern society.

A feminist analysis differently interprets the images of rape, gender, and sexuality in the first Klan. Modern feminist scholarship considers rape to be foremost an issue of power, not sexual desire. The Klan's call to defend white women against rape by black men signified a relation of power between men and women as well as between white and black men. On one level, the Klan's emphasis on the rape threat that white women faced was a message about the sexual violation of women by men. Underlying this level, however, was a deeper threat to white men's sexual privileges.

[. . .]

Rape was a volatile issue in both antebellum and postbellum Southern society divided by race and gender. The racial state of the slave South, like the racialist state that followed the Civil War, was built on a foundation that dictated a hierarchical division of male and female, as well as white and black. It kept white women within a role that was exalted in prose but sharply divided from and inferior to the privileged social role of white men. White men monopolized rights to property and the franchise and dictated the rules by which their wives, children, slaves, servants, and hired labor would live. Social privileges were formed along overlapping hierarchies of race, gender, and social class. Political, economic, and social power were reserved for white men, especially propertied white men.[11]

Within this context of hierarchies in Southern society we must imagine the mobilizing power of interracial sexual issues for the Ku Klux Klan. The Klan avowed horror of miscegenation but practiced it, as did antebellum white plantation masters, as a tactic of terror. Too, the Klan characterized rape equally as a metaphor for Southern white male disempowerment and as an atrocity committed against women. We cannot reduce this complex symbolic layering of race, sexuality, and gender in the language and the political practice of the Ku Klux Klan to a collective manifestation of psychosexual frustration, repression, and fear by white Southern men. Rather, we must analyze the massive social movement of the first KKK in the context of longstanding cleavages underlying Southern society.[12]

In these hierarchies of Reconstruction-era Southern states, black men were a threat to white men's sexual access to women (both black and white). Sexual torture and emasculation of black men by mobs of Klansmen validated the claim that masculinity ("real manhood") was the exclusive prerogative of white men. The rape of black women by white Klansmen represented the Klan's symbolic emasculation of black men through violating "their" women, while affirming the use of male sexuality as a weapon of power against women.[13] Southern women, white and black, occupied a symbolic terrain on which white men defended their racial privileges. The symbols of white female vulnerability and white masculine potency took power equally from beliefs in masculine and in white supremacy.

[. . .]

As early as 1922 the *Fiery Cross,* a Klan newspaper, published letters to the editor from women protesting their exclusion from the Klan.[14] Although there is no way to validate the authenticity of these letters (which may in fact have been written by Klansmen), they indicate how Klan leaders envisioned women's place in the "Invisible Empire." The letters compared—unfavorably—women's new right to vote with their continuing exclusion from the Klan. In pioneer days, one author wrote, men justly excluded women from many endeavors in order to protect them from physical harm.

In these "new days of freedom," however, such reasons no longer applied. Now women wanted to "stand alongside our men and help with the protecting" rather than be "patted on the head and told not to worry." In another letter, signed the "unhappy wife," a woman complained about her marriage to a Klansman. Her husband left her at home with the children, without just cause, while he attended meetings. Why should white native-born Protestant women be excluded from the Klan, she protested, along with such inferior groups as the "Knights of Columbus, Jews or negroes"?[15]

[. . .]

From the beginning, there were indications that leaders of the fledgling women's Klan saw the role of Klanswomen in a different light than did their would-be mentors in the men's Klan. A recruiting notice for Klanswomen noted that men no longer have "exclusive dominion" in society. Whether working in the home as a housewife or working in the business world, the ad suggested, a woman should put her efforts behind a movement for 100 percent American womanhood by joining the WKKK.[16] Markwell herself saw great possibilities for the Klan to further the interests of women as women, in addition to their racial and political interests. She noted that women's interest in politics, once latent, had been piqued by the Nineteenth Amendment granting women the vote. Women now saw it as their duty to work "in the maintenance of that amendment."[17]

[. . .]

But if many of the WKKK's basic principles followed existing doctrines of the men's Klan, women and men did not always have a common perception of the problems that required Klan action. Klansmen of the 1920s denounced interracial marriage for its destructive genetic outcomes; their Klan forefathers fought interracial sexuality to maintain white men's sexual access to white and black women. Klanswomen, however, saw a different danger in miscegenation: the destruction of white marriages by untrustworthy white men who "betray their own kind."

[. . .]

Klanswomen embraced the KKK's racist, anti-Catholic, and anti-Semitic agenda and symbols of American womanhood but they used these to argue as well for equality for white Protestant women.[18]

[. . .]

At times the women's Klan sought to portray itself as an organization of social work and social welfare. One national WKKK speaker announced that she left social work for the "broader field of Klankraft" because of the Klan's effectiveness in promoting morality and public welfare. Many chapters claimed to collect food and money for the needy, although these donations typically went to Klan families, often to families of Klan members arrested for rioting and vigilante activities. A powerful Florida WKKK chapter operated a free day nursery, charging that Catholic teachers had ruined the local public schools.[19]

[. . .]

Another activity of many WKKK locals was the crusade against liquor and vice. WKKK chapters worked to "clean up" a motion picture industry in which they claimed Jewish owners spewed a steady diet of immoral sex onto the screen. Other chapters fought against liquor, as evidenced by the case of Myrtle Cook, a Klanswoman and president of the Vinton, Iowa, Women's Christian Temperance Union (WCTU), who was assassinated for documenting the names of suspected bootleggers. In death, Cook was eulogized by Klanswomen and WCTU members alike; all business in Vinton was suspended for the two hours of the funeral.[20]

[. . .]

Klanswomen tended not to be involved in physical violence and rioting, but there were exceptions. In the aftermath of a 1924 Klan riot in Wilkinsburg, Pennsylvania, Mamie H. Bittner, a 39-year-old mother of three children and member of the Homestead, Pennsylvania, WKKK testified that she, along with thousands of other Klanswomen paraded through town, carrying heavy maple riot clubs. Morover, Bittner claimed that the WKKK was teaching its members to murder and kill in the interest of the Klan.[21]

The activities of the women's Klan were shaped largely by the existing political agenda of the men's Klan. It is not accurate, however, to portray the WKKK as a dependent auxiliary of the men's order. Klanswomen created a distinctive ideology and political agenda that infused the Klan's racist and nativist goals with ideas of equality between white Protestant women and men. The ideology and politics of Klanswomen and Klansmen were not identical, though at many points they were compatible. But women and men of the Klan movement sometimes found themselves in contention as women changed from symbols to actors in the Klan.

The difference between the women's and men's Klan grew from an underlying message in the symbol of white womanhood. By using gender and female sexual virtue as prime political symbols, the Klan shaped its identity through intensely masculinist themes, as an organization of real men. Clearly, this was an effective recruitment strategy for the first Klan. But in the 1920s, as both financial and political expediency and significant changes in women's political roles prompted the Klan to accept female members, an identity based on symbols of masculine exclusivity and supremacy became problematic. In addition, if Klansmen understood that defending white womanhood meant safeguarding white Protestant supremacy and male supremacy, many women heard the message differently. The WKKK embraced ideas of racial and religious privilege but rejected the message of white female vulnerability. In its place Klanswomen substituted support for women's rights and a challenge to white men's political and economic domination.

NOTES

1. Walter L. Fleming, "The Prescript of the Ku Klux Klan," *Southern Historical Association* 7 (September 1903): 327–48; David Annan, "The Ku Klux Klan," in *Secret Societies,* Norman MacKenzie, ed. (Holt, Rinehart and Winston, 1967); Mecklin, *The Ku Klux Klan.*

2. Joint Select Committee on the Condition of Affairs in the Late Insurrectionary States, *Affairs in the Late Insurrectionary States,* 42d Cong., 2d sess., 1872 (reprint, Arno Press, 1969); Seymour Martin Lipset, "An Anatomy of the Klan," *Commentary* 40 (October 1965): 74–83; Frank Tannenbaum, "The Ku Klux Klan: Its Social Origin in the South," *Century Magazine* 105 (April 1923): 873–83; Wyn Craig Wade, *The Fiery Cross,* NY: Simon and Schuster, 1987 pp. 31–80.

3. Jacquelyn Dowd Hall, " 'The Mind that Burns in Each Body': Women, Rape, and Racial Violence," in *Powers of Desire: The Politics of Sexuality,* Ann Snitow, Christine Stansell, and Sharon Thompson eds. Monthly Review Press, 1983); Wade, *The Fiery Cross,* 54–79; Frank Tannenbaum, *Darker Phases of the South* (Negro Universities Press, 1924), 33–34. The Klan's unintended advertisement of sex parallels that of the social purity movement of the late nineteenth and early twentieth centuries, as described by David Pivar, *Purity Crusade* (Greenwood Press, 1973), and also the moral reform movement of the mid-nineteenth century, analyzed by Carroll Smith-Rosenberg, *Disorderly Conduct: Visions of Gender in Victorian America* (Oxford University Press, 1986), 109–28.

4. Despite the common stereotype of the first Klan as composed primarily of lower-class Southern whites, men in the professions and business were active also (Wade, *The Fiery Cross,* 31–80; David Bennett, *The Party of Fear: From Nativist Movements to The New Right in American History* [University of North Carolina Press, 1988]).

5. Jacquelyn Dowd Hall, *Revolt against Chivalry: Jesse Daniel Ames and the Women's Campaign against Lynching* (Columbia University Press, 1979); Jacquelyn Dowd Hall, " 'A Truly Subversive Affair': Women against Lynching in the Twentieth-Century South," in *Women of America: A History,* Carol Berkin and Mary Beth Norton, eds. (Houghton Mifflin, 1979); Elizabeth Fox-Genovese, *Within the Plantation Household: Black and White Women of the Old South* (University of North Carolina Press, 1988), esp. 37–70; see also Laurence Alan Baughman, *Southern Rape Complex: A Hundred-Year Psychosis* (Pendulum, 1966), 176–77.

6. Annan, "Ku Klux Klan."

7. Fleming, "Prescript," 10; see also Winfield Jones, *Knights of the Ku Klux Klan* (Tocsin, 1941), 98. Annie Cooper Burton, president of a chapter of the United Daughters of the Confederacy, wrote *The Ku Klux Klan* (Warren T. Potter, 1916) with thanks to the Klan and included an interview with Captain H. W. Head, former Klan Grand Cyclops of Nashville. Peter Stearns suggests that the nineteenth-century creation of an ideology of white female vulnerability was in part a response to the changing image of manhood in an industrial society. Peter N. Stearns, *Be a Man!,* New York: Holmes and Meier, 1979.

8. Baughman, *Southern Rape Complex,* 176–77; David M. Chalmers, *Hooded Americanism,* Durham: Duke University Press, 1987, 21.

9. S. E. F. Rose, *The Ku Klux Klan or the Invisible Empire* (L. Graham 1914), 17.

10. Wade, *The Fiery Cross,* 20.

11. Fox-Genovese, *Plantation Household,* esp. 37–99.

12. This analysis assumes that collective frustration and structural positions cannot explain the development of social movements, in the absence of shared resources and a common worldview. See Sara Evans, *Personal Politics,* N. Y. Vintage, 1980 and Charles Tilly, *From Mobilization to Revolution* (Addison-Wesley, 1973).

13. Hall, " 'The Mind' "; see also Tannenbaum, *Darker Phases,* 31–33.

14. At its peak, the Klan published or influenced over 150 periodicals (Wade, *The Fiery Cross,* 175). A list of 24 Klan weekly papers is in the May 9, 1923, edition of the *Imperial Night-Hawk* (7). The Klan press was always embroiled in the power plays of Klan leaders. Evans wanted to destroy all Klan papers except his *Fellowship Forum.* At one time, Evans tried to establish a KKK Bureau of Education and Publication in Washington, D.C., which would publish the *Fiery Cross* (then controlled by Stephenson); he was not successful. These conflicts caused constant turmoil in the Klan press, with smaller publications forced out, state editions of the *Fiery Cross* promoted, then discontinued, and the names of the publications constantly changing. Details of this struggle are in Edgar Allen Booth, *The Mad Mullah of America* (Boyd Ellison Publications, 1927).

15. *Fiery Cross,* Dec. 8, 1922, 1; Feb. 2, 1923, 3.

16. *Fiery Cross,* Mar. 9, 1923, 8; also June 29, 1923, 4.

17. *Arkansas Gazette,* Oct. 7, 1923, 12.

18. WKKK, *Women of America!;* WKKK, *Constitution and Laws,* 6–7; WKKK, *Kreed;* WKKK, *Ideals,* 2–3, 4–5; *Imperial Night-Hawk,* June 20, 1923, 8; May 14, 1924, 7; advertisement in *Dawn,* Aug. 11, 1923, 2.

19. *Fellowship Forum,* Sept. 19, 1925, 6; July 5, 1924; Mar. 3, 1926, 6. The anonymous speaker is identified only as a "Klan female speaker." January 1925 issues of the *Fellowship Forum* have other examples of such self-promotion, as does that of May 1, 1926, 7; see also Chalmers, *Hooded Americanism.*

20. *Arkansas Gazette,* Sept. 8, 1925, 1; *Fiery Cross,* Mar. 30, 1923, 5; *Fellowship Forum,* Jan. 24, 1925, 6; *New York Times,* Sept. 9, 1925, 1; Sept. 19, 1925, 20; Sept. 11, 1925, 5.

21. Testimony of Mamie H. Bittner in U.S. District Court for the Western District of Pennsylvania, *Knights of the Ku Klux Klan, Plaintiff, v. Rev. John F. Strayer et al., Defendants,* 1928 (Equity 1897 in National Archives—Philadelphia Branch; William M. Likins, *The Trail of the Serpent* (n.p., 1928), 64–67.

REFLECTING ON THE SECTION

What is the relationship among citizenship, nationalism, and community? How do women participate—as symbols, as activists—in community formation and nationalism? What are the differing consequences for women of various political, social, economic, and racial positions within powerful nationalist ideologies? How can identities of resistance, traditionally based on class or race rather than gender, be useful and/or limiting to women of different economic classes? Enloe, Hiroko, and Blee all present specific case histories of women's relation to nationalism and the nation-state.

Each reading also illustrates how ideas of private and public spheres are used to control women and to construct gendered group identities. What roles do women play in national politics and community building in these three examples? How do various groups of men and/or nationalist groups use the concept of femininity and the bodies of women to produce national cultures? What are the roles of disenfranchised and dominant groups of women in these situations? Can women use nationalism to improve the conditions of women in particular nations or communities? What are the potential risks and benefits of such a "nationalist feminism"?

Feminist Organizing across Borders

The International First Wave

LEILA J. RUPP

Although women have had a very contradictory rela-tionship to the nation-state in the modern period, they have also organized across national boundaries. Many women's international alliances have organized around opposition to war. According to historian Leila Rupp, the so-called first wave of the international women's movement emerged at the end of the nineteenth century as an antiwar and antinationalist coalition.

[W]omen have been protesting their exclusion from the elite task of "imagining the nation" and simul-taneously demonstrating that historical acts of imagination, translated into oppressive and violent social systems, have material consequences which must be resisted and transformed through acts of

Leila J. Rupp, *Worlds of Women: The Making of an Interna-tional Women's Movement,* Princeton: Princeton University Press, 3–4, 14, 34, 47–48.

political will into very different systems, which may or may not need nations to support them.

(Aibhe Smyth, 1995)[1]

It is hard to imagine, in the last years of the twentieth century, the women of warring countries crossing en-emy lines, gathering to try to end bloodshed and bring about peace. Yet this, in broad strokes, is what women from Europe and North America did in 1915. The Con-gress of Women, bravely convened in The Hague dur-ing the first year of the Great War, is probably the most celebrated (and was at the time also the most reviled) expression of women's internationalism, but it is neither the beginning nor the end of the story. Women from far-flung countries came together in transnational women's organizations and constructed an international collec-tive identity. Divided by nationality and often fiercely loyal to different organizations, women committed to internationalism forged bonds not only despite but in

Key Terms

first-wave feminism The term commonly used to refer to the nineteenth and early twentieth century European and North American mobilization to gain voting rights and open the professions to women.
second-wave feminism The term commonly used to refer to the emergence in the late 1960s and early 1970s in Europe and North America of a "new social movement" dedicated to raising consciousness about sexism and patriarchy, legalizing abortion and birth control, attaining equal rights in political and economic realms, and

gaining sexual "liberation." Limited by a universalizing definition of *woman* that excluded the concerns of many women of color, working-class women, and lesbians, as well as the points of view of those outside of Europe or North America, the term can be used historically in some specific contexts.
world system The world divided into centers and peripheries for better analysis of colonialism and its aftermath; associated with the work of Immanuel Wallerstein.

fact through conflict over nearly every aspect of organizing. By understanding how they did this and how the dynamics of mobilizing interacted with the economic, political, and social changes that swept across the twentieth-century world, we can contemplate the limitations and possibilities of internationalism.

I focus here on what I believe can be considered the first wave of an international women's movement because I believe that its history is instructive for understanding the very different—but connected—story of the second wave. The Second World War, which nearly severed international connections among women, marked the end of the first wave and the lull before the swell of the second. The emergence of a bipolar world out of the ashes of the war, the spread of national liberation movements throughout the formerly colonized countries, and the emergence and resurgence of national women's movements around the globe in the 1960s and 1970s profoundly transformed the context for an international women's movement. Transnational interaction jumped out of the well-worn transatlantic tracks. Adding to the gatherings of pre-existing and emergent organizations, the United Nations–sponsored Decade for Women conferences and their accompanying nongovernmental gatherings met in Mexico City in 1975, Copenhagen in 1980, and Nairobi in 1985.[2] The latest chapter in this story unfolded at the Beijing conference in 1995.

[. . .]

Three major bodies, open (at least technically) to all constituencies of women from every corner of the globe, held center stage. These were the International Council of Women, the first surviving general group, founded in 1888; the International Alliance of Women, originally the International Woman Suffrage Alliance, an offshoot of the Council that was officially established in 1904; and the Women's International League for Peace and Freedom, which grew from the International Congress of Women at The Hague that met in the midst of the wrenching Great War in 1915. A multitude of regionally organized bodies, groups composed of particular constituencies of women, and single-issue organizations sprang up around these three, especially in the years between the wars, and the whole universe of transnational women's organizations interacted in a variety of ways, especially through coalitions comprising delegates from the different groups.

Early International Connections

The roots of the international women's movement can be traced to a variety of connections forged across national borders, creating what social movement scholars call a "pre-existing communications network" for the international women's movement.[3] Women travelers, migrants, missionaries, and writers—of books, newspaper articles, and letters sent off across the lines that divided nations—made contacts that prepared the way for more formalized interactions.[4] A variety of movements, including abolitionism, socialism, peace, temperance, and moral reform, called women's attention to the cross-national character of their causes and brought together women from different nations in mixed-gender meetings. The World Anti-Slavery Convention held in London in 1840, which refused to seat women delegates elected by their home societies, has gone down in history as the spark that ignited the U.S. women's rights movement. But it and similar meetings also set the precedent for the formation of the international women's organizations.

With the first stirrings of organized feminism in the United States and Europe, international connections among women solidified.[5] Works such as Mary Wollstonecraft's *Vindication of the Rights of Woman* (1792), translated into French and German, had already roused women on both sides of the Atlantic, suggesting that feminist analyses and demands might transcend national contexts. Radical women activists across Europe and in the United States stirred to each others' proclamations and translated each others' words. The transnational development of a feminist ideology led to formalized contacts among women—committed to womens' rights rather than some other cause—at conferences unattached to any permanent body. The first international women's congress, the Congrès international de droit des femmes, convened in Paris in 1878 in connection with the World Exposition.[6] All of this activity laid the groundwork for the founding of international women's organizations, which institutionalized and perpetuated the impulse to work on behalf of women on the international stage.

[. . .]

These three major international women's groups—with related origins but different natures and trajectories—

cooperated and competed with a host of other bodies. Reaching out across the borders of their nations, women came together as socialists; as advocates of single issues, such as equal rights; as members of occupational categories; as adherents of different religious traditions; and as inhabitants of different regions of the world.[7] Some of these multinational bodies interacted on a regular basis with the Council, Alliance, and League, while others kept their distance. In coming together internationally, women marched in step with a whole range of constituencies who founded transnational groups; the establishment of such groups began in the latter half of the nineteenth century and reached a crescendo between the wars.[8] Despite the crippling global depression, the intensification of nationalism embodied both in fascism and in the communist shift to "socialism in one country," and in what seems in retrospect the inexorable march toward war in the 1930s, the years between the world wars represented the high tide of internationalism.

[. . .]

The building of the international women's movement was, then, a process that lurched slowly into motion in the late nineteenth century, gathered steam at the end of the First World War, and nearly screeched to a halt in 1939, although the existing transnational groups reconstituted themselves in the late 1940s in a world transformed by bipolar rivalry and accelerated decolonization. In reflecting on the trajectory of the movement, one feels an insistent tugging at one's sleeve. "But the international women's movement seems to have flourished just when the national movements of Europe and the United States slid into decline," a small voice whispers.

In fact, the pattern of growth of the international women's movement challenges what has become a nearly hegemonic model of "first wave" and "second wave," which is based on the rise of women's movements in the Euro-American arena in the late nineteenth century, their ebbing after the First World War, and their resurgence in the 1970s. For if we pay attention to the world system beyond the industrialized core nations, we see instead choppy seas, with women's movements emerging in countries newly free or struggling for political or economic independence in the 1920s.[9] And we can witness the international women's movement cresting in the interwar period, with new organizations springing up and existing bodies adding sections in Asia, Latin America, and even Africa.

The three major groups, despite their differences, all began with national sections in Europe or the "neo-Europes," areas of similar climate where European settler colonies succeeded.[10] The First World War undermined European control of the world system and both stimulated the growth of national women's movements in formerly dependent or colonized countries and also encouraged attempts by international women's organizations to expand their reach. Nevertheless, the patterns of interaction among the whole range of transnational groups mirrored the dominance of European or European-settled, Christian, capitalist nations in the world system. It was within this context that members of the international women's organizations came together across their countries' borders and, through both conflict and cooperation, constructed a collective identity as feminist internationalists.

NOTES

1. Smyth 1995 is writing here of Irish women.

2. On the Decade for Women, see Boulding 1977; Cagatay, Grown, and Santiago 1986; Miles 1996.

3. See, for example, Luard 1966; Huntington 1973; Keohane and Nye 1973; D. Armstrong 1982; Diehl 1989; Murphy 1994; Ishay 1995; Long 1996. Recently feminist international relations theory

has challenged the field of political science: see Enloe 1990; Foot 1990; Grant and Newland 1991; Peterson 1992; Sylvester 1994; Whitworth 1994. Tyrrell 1991a calls for greater attention to transnational history, including a history of organizations. Existing work on transnational organizations includes Lyons 1963; Joll 1974; van der Lindon 1987; Milner 1990; Cooper 1991; Riesenberger 1992; Strikwerda 1993; Berkowitz 1993; Herren 1993; Hoberman 1995; Hutchinson 1996.

    4. Rupp 1992.

    5. On this point, see Bulbeck 1988.

    6. Benedict Anderson 1991 (1st ed. 1983). The literature on nationalism is, of course, extensive and has long recognized that there is no universal basis for nationalism; recent works include Isaacs 1975; J. Armstrong 1982; Gellner 1983; Chatterjee 1993 (first published 1986); Jayawardena 1986; A. Smith 1986; Greenfeld 1992; Pfaff 1993.

    7. On different kinds of organizations and various schemes of classification, see C. Miller 1992 and Boy 1936.

    8. See C. Miller 1992 and Skjelsbaek 1971.

    9. See, for example, Jayawardena 1986; Basu and Ray 1990; Hahner 1990; Johnson-Odim 1991; Stoner 1991; Badran 1995.

    10. The term "neo-Europes" comes from Crosby 1987.

REFERENCES

Anderson, Benedict. (1991). *Imagined Communities: Reflections on the Origin and Spread of Nationalism*. Rev. ed. London: Verso.

Armstrong, David. (1982). *The Rise of the International Organisation: A Short History*. London: Macmillan.

Armstrong, John A. (1982). *Nations before Nationalism*. Chapel Hill: University of North Carolina Press.

Badran, Margot. (1995). *Feminists, Islam, and Nation: Gender and the Making of Modern Egypt*. Princeton: Princeton University.

Basu, Aparna, and Bharati Ray. (1990). *Women's Struggle: A History of the All-India Women's Conference, 1927–1990*. New Delhi: Manohar.

Berkowitz, Michael. (1993). *Zionist Culture and Western European Jewry before the First World War*. New York: Cambridge University Press.

Boulding, Elise. (1977). *Women in the 20th Century World*. New York: Halsted.

Boy, Magdeline. (1936). *Les Associations Internationales Féminines*. Thesis, Faculty of Law, University of Lyon. Lyon: Paquet.

Bulbeck, Chilla. (1988). *One World Women's Movement*. London: Pluto.

Cagatay, Nilüfer, Caren Grown, and Aida Santiago. (1986). "The Nairobi Women's Conference: Toward a Global Feminism?" *Feminist Studies* 12: 401–12.

Chatterjee, Partha. (1993). *Nationalist Thought and the Colonial World: A Derivative Discourse*. 1986. Reprint, Minneapolis: University of Minnesota Press.

Cooper, Sandi E. (1991). *Patriotic Pacifism: Waging War on War in Europe, 1815–1914*. New York: Oxford University Press.

Crosby, Alfred. (1987). *Ecological Imperialism*. New York: Cambridge University Press.

Diehl, Paul F. (1989). *The Politics of International Organizations: Patterns and Insights*. Chicago: Dorsey.

Enloe, Cynthia. (1990). *Bananas, Beaches, and Bases: Making Feminist Sense of International Politics*. Berkeley: University of California Press.

Foot, Rosemary. (1990). "Where Are the Women? The Gender Dimension in the Study of International Relations." *Diplomatic History* 14: 615–22.

Gellner, Ernest. (1983). *Nations and Nationalism*. Oxford: Blackwell.

Grant, Rebecca, and Kathleen Newland, eds. (1991). *Gender and International Relations*. Buckingham: Open University Press.

Greenfeld, Liah. (1992). *Nationalism: Five Roads to Modernity*. Cambridge, Mass.: Harvard University Press.

Hahner, June E. (1990). *Emancipating the Female Sex: The Struggle for Women's Rights in Brazil, 1850–1940*. Durham: Duke University Press.

Herren, Madeleine. (1993). *Internationale Sozialpolitik vor dem Ersten Weltkrieg: Die Anfänge europäischer Kooperation aus der Sicht Frankreichs*. Berlin: Duncker and Humblot.

Hoberman, John. (1995). "Toward a Theory of Olympic Internationalism." *Journal of Sport History* 22: 1–37.

Huntington, Samuel P. (1973). "Transnational Organizations in World Politics." *World Politics* 25:333–68.

Hutchinson, John F. (1996). *Champions of Charity: War and the Rise of the Red Cross*. Boulder, Colo.: Westview.

Isaacs, Harold R. (1975). *Idols of the Tribe: Group Identity and Political Change*. Cambridge, Mass.: Harvard University Press.

Ishay, Micheline R. (1995). *Internationalism and Its Betrayal*. Contradictions of Modernity, Craig Calhoun, ed. vol. 2. Minneapolis: University of Minnesota Press.

Jayawardena, Kumari. (1986). *Feminism and Nationalism in the Third World*. London: Zed.

Johnson-Odim, Cheryl. (1991). "Common Themes, Different Contexts: Third World Women and Feminism." In *Third World Women and the Politics of Feminism*, Chandra Talpade Mohanty, Ann Russo, and Lourdes Torres, eds. 314–27. Bloomington: Indiana University Press.

Joll, James. (1974). *The Second International, 1889–1914*. Rev. ed. London: Routledge and Kegan Paul.

Keohane, Robert O., and Joseph S. Nye, Jr., eds. (1973). *Transnational Relations and World Politics*. Cambridge, Mass.: Harvard University Press.

Long, David. (1996). *Towards a New Liberal Internationalism: The International Theory of J. A. Hobson*. New York: Cambridge University Press.

Luard, Evan, ed. (1966). *The Evolution of International Organizations*. New York: Frederick A. Praeger.

Lyons, F. S. L. (1963). *Internationalism in Europe, 1815–1914*. Leyden: A. W. Sythoff.

Miles, Angela. (1996). *Integrative Feminisms: Building Global Visions, 1960s–1990s*. New York: Routledge.

Miller, Carol. (1991). "Women in International Relations? The Debate in Interwar Britain." In *Gender and International Relations*, Rebecca Grant and Kathleen Newland, eds. 64–82. Buckingham: Open University Press.

Miller, Carol. (1992). "Lobbying the League: Women's International Organizations and the League of Nations." PhD. diss., Oxford University.

Milner, Susan. (1990). *The Dilemmas of Internationalism: French Syndicalism and the International Labour Movement, 1900–1914*. New York: Berg.

Murphy, Craig N. (1994). *International Organization and Industrial Change: Global Governance since 1850*. New York: Oxford University Press.

Peterson, V. Spike. (1992). *Gendered States: Feminist (Re) Visions of International Relations Theory*. Boulder, Colo.: Lynne Rienner.

Pfaff, William. (1993). *The Wrath of Nations: Civilization and the Furies of Nationalism*. New York: Simon and Schuster.

Riesenberger, Dieter. (1992). *Für humanität in Krieg und Frieden: Das Internationale Rote Kreuz, 1863–1977*. Göttingen: Vandenhoeck und Reprecht.

Rupp, Leila J. (1989). "Feminism and the Sexual Revolution in the Early Twentieth Century: The Case of Doris Stevens." *Feminist Studies* 15: 289–309.

Rupp, Leila J. (1992). "Eleanor Flexner's *Century of Struggle*: Women's history and the women's movement." *NWSA Journal* 4, p. 157–69.

Skjelsbaek, Kjell. (1971). "The Growth of International Nongovernmental Organization in the 20th Century." *International Organization* 25:420–42.

Smith, Anthony D. (1986). *The Ethnic Origins of Nations*. New York: Basil Blackwell.

Smyth, Ailbhe. (1995). "Paying Our Disrespects to the Bloody States We're In: Women, Violence, Culture, and the State." *Journal of Women's History*, vol. 6, no. 4-7, no. 1: 190–215.

Stoner, K. Lynn. (1991). *From the House to the Streets: The Cuban Woman's Movement for Legal Reform, 1898–1940*. Durham: Duke University Press.

Strikwerda, Carl. (1993). "The Troubled Origins of European Economic Integration: International Iron and Steel and Labor Migration in the Era of World War I." *American Historical Review* 98: 1106–29.

Sylvester, Christine. (1994). *Feminist Theory and International Relations in a Postmodern Era*. New York: Cambridge University Press.

Tyrrell, Ian. (1991a). "American Exceptionalism in an Age of International History." *American Historical Review* 96:1031–55.

Van der Lindon, W. H. (1987). *The International Peace Movement, 1815–1874*. Amsterdam: Tilleul.

Whitworth, Sandra. (1994). *Feminism and International Relations: Towards a Political Economy of Gender in Interstate and Non-Governmental Institutions*. New York: St. Martin's.

Reading B

A Program for Voting Women
CRYSTAL EASTMAN

Crystal Eastman (1881–1927) was a labor lawyer, suffragist, and socialist who drafted the first workers' compensation law in the United States. This pamphlet was written in March 1918, in the depths of World War I and only months after women won the right to vote in New York State (although it would be two more years until all U.S. women gained this right). Here, Eastman describes her work for the International Committee of Women for Permanent Peace and makes a case for a North American Woman's Peace Party based on international connections between women.

Why a *Woman's* Peace Party?, I am often asked. Is peace any more a concern of women than of men? Is it not of universal human concern? For a feminist—one who believes in breaking down sex barriers so that women and men can work and play and build the world together—it is not an easy question to answer. Yet the answer, when I finally worked it out in my own mind, convinced me that we should be proud and glad, even as feminists, to work for the Woman's Peace Party.

To begin with, there is a great and unique tradition behind our movement which would be lost if we merged

Crystal Eastman, *On Women and Revolution.* Blanche Wiesen Cook, ed. Oxford, Oxford University Press, 1978: 266–67.

our Woman's Peace Party in the general revolutionary international movement of the time. Do not forget that it was women who gathered at The Hague, a thousand strong, in the early months of the war, women from all the great belligerent and neutral countries, who conferred there together in friendship and sorrow and sanity while the mad war raged around them. Their great conference, despite its soundness and constructive statesmanship, failed of its purpose, failed of its hope. But from the beginning of the war down to the Russo-German armistice there was no world step of such daring and directness, nor of such honest, unfaltering international spirit and purpose, as the organization of the International Committee of Women for Permanent Peace at The Hague in April, 1915. This Committee has branches in 22 countries. The Woman's Peace Party is the American section of the Committee, and our party, organized February 1 and 2, is the New York State Branch.

When the great peace conference comes, a Congress of Women made up of groups from these 22 countries will meet in the same city to demand that the deliberate intelligent organization of the world for lasting peace shall be the outcome of that conference.

These established international connections make it important to keep this a woman's movement.

But there is an added reason. We women of New York State, politically speaking, have just been born.

Key Term

universal disarmament The ending of war and dismantling of military arsenals worldwide, in every nation.

We have been born into a world at war, and this fact cannot fail to color greatly the whole field of our political thinking and to determine largely the emphasis of our political action. What we hope, then, to accomplish by keeping our movement distinct is to bring thousands upon thousands of women—women of the international mind—to dedicate their new political power, not to local reforms or personal ambitions, not to discovering the difference between the Democratic and Republican parties, but to *ridding the world of war.*

For this great purpose we have an immediate, practical program. We shall organize by congressional districts and throw all our spirit and enthusiasm and the political strength of our organization to the support of those candidates who stand for our international program. If the candidate is a Socialist, all right. If the candidate here and there is a woman, so much the better.

To be concrete, we shall go before each candidate in each district of this state with the following definite propositions:

As a candidate for the Congress, which will be in session while the problems incident to the settlement of the war are before the world, *we ask you to indorse the following proposals:*

A democratic league of all nations, based upon: Free seas,—Free markets,—Universal disarmament,— The right of peoples to determine their own destiny.

The development of an international parliament and tribunal as the governing bodies of such a league.

Daylight diplomacy, with democratic control of foreign policy.

Legislation whereby American delegates to the end-of-the-war conference shall be elected directly by the people.

Furthermore, that America's championship of the principle of reduced armaments may appeal to the rest of the world as disinterested and sincere, *we ask you to oppose* legislation committing this country to the adoption of universal compulsory military training.

As the candidate stands or falls by this test, so he will win or lose our support; and we believe that by next fall our support will be something to be reckoned with. There are thousands of radical women in this state, whose energies, whose passion for humanity, have been released by the suffrage victory of last November. Among them are experienced workers, speakers, organizers, writers. Every day more of these women leaders come forward and reveal themselves as eager, thinking internationalists. They are caught and held by the intellectual content of our program and its great world purpose. They will work with us, and I may say seriously that we expect to measure the effects of our campaign in the character of New York State's representatives in the next United States Congress.

Thus we shall play a part in building the new world that is to come—a great part; for, unless the peoples rise up and rid themselves of this old intolerable burden of war, they cannot progress far toward liberty.

CRYSTAL EASTMAN, Chairman,
Woman's Peace Party of New York State,
March 1918.   *70 Fifth Avenue.*

Whither Feminism?

MAMPHELA RAMPHELE

Mamphela Ramphele, trained as a physician and an anthropologist, was active in the struggle against apartheid in South Africa and was Vice Chancellor of the University of Cape Town. Ramphele describes South African women's struggles against war and authoritarian white supremacist rule as the foundation of a "transnational" women's studies. She calls for a focus on both differences and solidarities, not only among different groups of women but also between women and men.

I speak as one whose career and life experience have been shaped by political criticism within the Black Conciousness Movement (BCM) in the 1970s, and within feminist consciousness. These two streams of consciousness occurred at different times but coalesced into a life force more than a decade ago, which translated into greater understanding of power relations as intertwined—the everyday in the public and private sphere and how that shapes the long-term quality of social relations that transcend categories and yet take them into account. Such an understanding is crucial to transitional politics toward greater equity within a democratic framework.

Mamphela Ramphele, "Whither Feminism?," in Joan W. Scott, Cora Kaplan, Debra Keates, eds. *Transitions, Environments, Translations: Feminisms in International Politics,* New York: Routledge, 1997: 334–38.

[. . .]

Transnational solidarities of feminists must seek alliances with others to become effective agents of transformation of global politics.

I would like to make the following propositions:

1. We need to define a vision of gender equity that recognizes the diversity of its meanings across the globe. Equality between men and women or even between women in different circumstances may be iniquitous. We need to problematize equality and develop an equity framework that enables us and our various societies to address the needs of people—men and women—in an equitable way, bearing in mind the differential impact of race, class, age, and other constraints on power relations.

2. We can no longer ignore the oppression of men by patriarchy, in the same way that in South Africa one could not ignore the oppression of whites by apartheid. The violence embedded in the definition of "manhood" across cultures is at the heart of the violence of patriarchy, mentally, emotionally, and physically (e.g., male initiation rites, military conscription, and socialization, all of which deny the feminine in men).

It is not enough for us as women to offer a disclaimer about our conspiracy of silence around war—both private

---

Key Terms

affirmative action programs Programs to redress past discriminations through preferential treatments of disadvantaged groups.

gender equity Attainment of equality with males in legal, political, and economic spheres, a goal of feminism.

and public—which our husbands, brothers, sons, and other men have to submit to in the name of higher ideals, e.g., the liberation struggle in South Africa or the disciplining of Saddam Hussein in Iraq by United States Marines. Our silence in the war talk that distinguishes "the men" from "the mice" is as culpable as the noise of the war talk itself. The role—passive or active—that women play in this definition of what it is to be a "man" is crucial. We need to theorize this and understand anew what Carolyn Heilbrun meant when she said that "men need women to be unambiguously women for them to be real men."[1] To what extent is women's role as "harmonizer" part of the culture of silence doing violence to young boys who are desperately searching for a new masculinity? The corollary is true about young women—to what extent have feminists given their own daughters mixed messages about what it means to be a woman?

3. We need to articulate a vision of transition from authoritarian rule that offers a different approach to human relations and social power structures from those informed by patriarchal ones. Simply joining cabinets, Parliament, or the military in the name of equality is not going to lead to transformation of these structures of power. We need to infuse a new ethics and morality into the institutional cultures of these structures and insist on the centrality of people in all public and private affairs.

Replacing men with women in positions of power through affirmative action programs is not enough for a transformative politics. We need a new approach that humanizes social relations. We need to develop an equity framework for social relations that promotes development of human potential of all, and a change in the institutional culture to promote a more human-centered development process. In the same way that essentializing, totalizing views of race, class, age, and sexual orientation are not helpful, so too focusing only on "feminists" is unlikely to translate into transformative policies.

[. . .]

The history of feminism in the United States is instructive in this regard. A sophisticated feminist critique and consciousness are not enough to transform social relations. The record of women's advances in the United States is impressive in some ways, but not in others. For example, how have the numerous and excellent women's studies programs in the United States contributed to, or failed to contribute to, the transformation of the academy from its male-dominated cultural orientation and practices, which are oppressive of the Other: youth, blacks, and women? What have been the areas of success and failure? What factors have promoted transformative politics in major institutions, and how replicable are these to other institutions?

It seems to me that to deal with them adequately we need to look beyond feminist theory and policy and examine the theories of power and the impact of the definition of "gender" and gender policies and power relations in general. The problematic of gender politics involves both men and women, and this requires a theoretical framework that goes beyond just understanding "women" in their various configurations as defined by race, age, class, sexual orientation, and geographical location.

The insistence of some women on defining themselves as mothers, wives, party political activists, workers, or family people is an indicator of their embracing their environments as they present themselves to them in reality. It is a reality that any feminist movement interested in transition from authoritarian patriarchal rule should take serious account of it, instead of dismissing it as antifeminism and right-wing rhetoric.

If we are to make headway toward transcending the limitations of feminism in the past, we have to confront the unanswered questions posed above.

NOTE

1. Carolyn Heilbrun, *Writing a Woman's Life* (Toronto: Penguin, 1988).

Reading D

Controlled or Autonomous: Identity and the Experience of the Network, Women Living under Muslim Laws

FARIDA SHAHEED

Addressing the problem of religious nationalism that has brought new patriarchies into power in Islamic states, sociologist Farida Shaheed describes the group "Women Living under Muslim Laws," who organize against fundamentalist religious doctrine. Even though the practice of Islam may differ from nation to nation, the use of religion for political and patriarchal ends remains widespread. Thus, Shaheed claims, women have to organize collectively without losing sight of their differences.

The International network Women Living under Muslim Laws (WLUML) was initially formed in response to several incidents urgently requiring action in 1984, all of which related to Islam, laws, and women. In Algeria, three feminists were arrested and jailed without trial, then kept incommunicado for seven months. Their

Farida Shaheed, "Controlled or Autonomous: Identity and the Experience of the Network, Women Living under Muslim Laws," *Signs: Journal of Women in Culture and Society* 1994: vol. 19, no. 4, 997–1,019. © 1994 by Farida Shaheed.

crime was having discussed with other women the government's proposal to introduce a new set of laws on the family (Code de la Famille) that severely reduced women's rights in this field. In India, a Muslim woman filed a petition to the Supreme Court arguing that the application of religious minority law denied her rights otherwise guaranteed all citizens under the Constitution of India. In Abu Dhabi, for the alleged crime of adultery a pregnant woman was sentenced to be stoned to death two months after giving birth. In Europe, the Mothers of Algiers (a group formed by women divorced from Algerian men) were seeking access to or custody of their children.[1] Excepting the condemned woman, on whose behalf others initiated action, those concerned in each incident asked for international support. Starting as an action committee, WLUML coalesced into a network between 1984 and 1986, when it formulated its first Plan of Action.

Geographically scattered, these first incidents were symptomatic of the much wider problem confronting women in the Muslim world, who increasingly find that, in the tussle for political pre-eminence, political

---

Key Terms

customary laws Laws emerging from custom rather than legislation.

minority religious laws Laws based on religion that apply specifically to minority groups; for example, in areas relating to family and domestic

life, many countries have different legal codes for different religious groups.

secular Those aspects of society that are not overtly organized through religion.

forces (in and out of office) are increasingly formulating legal, social, or administrative measures justified by reference to Islam that militate against women's autonomy and self-actualization.

To understand the logic underpinning WLUML's creation and in order to assess the possible impact of its actions and strategies, it is essential to first locate women in the complex web of Islam, law, and society in the Muslim world and to clarify some basic issues in this respect. First, the essential components of patriarchal structure in Muslim societies do not differ from those enumerated by non-Muslim feminists, and, like elsewhere, women's subordination occurs at multiple levels (kinship structures, state-building projects, anti-imperialist and populist ideologies, and national and international policies). Nor should women be viewed as passive victims, as "they are fully fledged social actors, bearing the full set of contradictions implied by their class, racial, and ethnic locations as well as gender" (Kandiyoti 1989, 8)[2]—all being factors that in turn moderate women's interaction with both the state and religion.

Second, the idea of one homogeneous Muslim world is an illusion and, in fact (as Deniz Kandiyoti puts it),

So-called Islamic societies embody widely differing histories of state and class formation. The relationships between state and religion have correspondingly varied as they have evolved. . . . [But] all have had to grapple with the problems of establishing "modern" nation-states. This meant forging of citizenship, and finding new legitimizing ideologies and power bases. . . . Most Muslim states have failed to generate ideologies capable of coping realistically with social change. This and their histories of dependence vis-à-vis the West have led them to rely on Islam not only as the sole coherent ideology at their disposal but also as a symbol of their cultural identity and integrity. [1989, 5]

Third, when identity is transformed into a set of beliefs and behavioral patterns ordering community life, existing socioeconomic and political structures play a major role in shaping the transformation. Consequently, while it is frequently claimed that any given state, society, or community is Islamic, it is in fact not *Islamic* (i.e., that which is ordained) but *Muslim* (i.e.,

of those who adhere to Islam) and reflects the assimilation of Islam into prevailing structures, systems, and practices—hence the many significantly different varieties of Muslim societies that exist today. And, finally, the diversity of Muslim societies and the differing realities of women within them have produced a plethora of feminist responses in the political arena that range from the exclusively secular to the exclusively theological, with many permutations in between.

[. . .]

⌐ Formation of the Network

It is against this backdrop that the network Women Living under Muslim Laws was created to break women's isolation and to provide linkages and support to all women whose lives may be affected by Muslim laws.

[. . .]

The formulation of the network's name is an acknowledgment of both the complexity and diversity of women's realities in the Muslim world. A less obvious concern that went into the choice of name is that women affected by Muslim laws may not be Muslim, either by virtue of having a different religion or by virtue of having chosen another marker of political or personal identity. The emphasis in the title and in the group is therefore on the women themselves and their situations and not on the specific politicoreligious option they may exercise. As a network, WLUML therefore extends to women living in countries where Islam is the state religion as well as those from Muslim communities ruled by religious minority laws, to women in secular states where a rapidly expanding political presence of Islam increasingly provokes a demand for minority religious law, as well as to women in migrant Muslim communities in Europe, the Americas, and Australasia, and further includes non-Muslim women who may have Muslim laws applied to them directly or through their children.

Propelled by concrete, on-the-ground issues rather than the outcome of merely theoretical discourse, WLUML's objectives are to create and reinforce linkages between women and women's groups within Muslim communities, to increase their knowledge about both their common and diverse situations, and to strengthen their struggles by creating the means and channels needed to support their efforts internationally from within and outside the Muslim world. In essence, the purpose of WLUML is to increase the autonomy of women affected by Muslim laws by encouraging them to analyze and reformulate the identity imposed on them through the application of Muslim laws, and by so doing to assume greater control over their lives. The WLUML aims to achieve this by building a network of mutual solidarity and information flow; by facilitating interaction and contact between women from Muslim countries and communities, on the one hand, and between them and progressive and feminist groups at large, on the other; by promoting the exposure of women from one geographical area to another in and outside the Muslim world; and by undertaking common projects identified by and executed through network participants. The WLUML's initial Plan of Action clearly states that "its purpose is simply to facilitate access to information and to each other. Its existence therefore depends on our links and not on the specific activities undertaken or positions held by any group or individual involved in this process" (1986, 1).

Women Living under Muslim Laws believes that the seeming helplessness of a majority of women in the Muslim world in effectively mobilizing against and overcoming adverse laws and customs stems not only from their being economically and politically less powerful but also from their erroneous belief that the only existence possible for a Muslim woman that allows her to maintain her identity—however that may be defined—is the one delineated for her in her own national context. In fact, the common presumption both within and outside the Muslim world that there exists one homogeneous Muslim world is a fallacy. Interaction between women from different Muslim societies proves that, while some similarities may stretch across cultures, classes, sects, schools, and continents, the diversities are at least equally striking. The different realities of women living under Muslim laws, according to WLUML, "range from being strictly closeted, isolated and voiceless within four walls, subjected to public floggings and condemned to death for presumed adultery (which is considered a crime against the state) and forcibly given in marriage as a child, to situations where women have a far greater degree of freedom of movement and interaction, the right to work, to partici-

pate in public affairs and also exercise a far greater control over their own lives" (1986, 5).

Dreaming of an alternative reality is not simply a matter of inspiration but, to a large extent, depends on accessing information on the sources of law and *customary practices* and on the political and social forces that determine women's current reality. Beyond this is the need to belong to a social collectivity. As mentioned above, the fear of being cut off from one's collective identity militates against women challenging "Muslim laws." Therefore, taking initiative against such laws is facilitated if women can be sure of the support of another collectivity that functions as an alternative reference group and, by so doing, may also help women redefine the parameters of their current reference group(s). In this, contacts and links with women from other parts of the Muslim world—whose very existence speaks of the multiplicity of women's realities within the Muslim context—provide an important source of inspiration. Likewise, information on the diversity of existing laws within the Muslim world gives material shape to alternatives. Both encourage women to dream of different realities— the first step in changing the present one.

In contrast, an inability to unravel the various strands of an apparently inseparable but actually composite identity presented in the name of Islam serves to silence and immobilize women. This silence is deepened by women's isolation in specific environments and their lack of knowledge about their official legal rights—both in terms of Muslim personal laws and/or civil codes and of the source of these laws. Most women remain ignorant of even the basic disparities between customary laws applied to them and the official version of Muslim laws. Action is likewise impeded by women's negligible access to information enabling them to challenge the validity of either type of law, including information about the strategies and struggles of other women in the Muslim world and the discussions and debates that flow from these.

Then there is the political use of Islam. In most of the Muslim world Islam has been used by those in power and those out of it, more often by right-wing elements than progressive forces but inevitably in a bid for political power: for consolidating support or legitimizing force (Mumtaz and Shaheed 1987, 1). This practice is so widespread as to provoke one feminist to conclude that "not only have the sacred texts always been manipulated, but manipulation of them is a structural characteristic of the practice of power in Muslim societies" (Mernissi 1992, 8–9). For women living under Muslim laws, one of the dangers is that politicoreligious groups find it convenient to cite so-called Islamic laws already being applied in different Muslim countries in support of their own demands for more stringent, essentially undemocratic or discriminatory "Islamic" laws. For their part, when women can cite examples of positive legislation or their demands are supported from within the Muslim world (though not necessarily from within a religious framework), their effectiveness is strengthened.

Women Living under Muslim Laws posits that it is only when women start assuming the right to define for themselves the parameters of their own identity and stop accepting unconditionally and without question what is presented to them as the "correct" religion, the "correct" culture, or the "correct" national identity that they will be able effectively to challenge the corpus of laws imposed on them. The WLUML is convinced that while controlling women through identity has multiple ramifications—in which religion, nationality, ethnicity, and class all come into play—"depriving [women] of even dreaming of a different reality is one of the most debilitating forms of oppression [they] face" (WLUML 1986, 7). It is the vision of a different reality that propels the reformulation of the present one, and it is here, in opening the doors to a multiplicity of possible alternatives, that the WLUML network hopes to make its most important contribution.

REFERENCES

Kandiyoti, Deniz. (1989). "Women and Islam: What Are the Missing Terms?" *Dossier 5/6* (Grabels), December 1988/May 1989, 5–9.

Mernissi, Fatima. (1992). *The Veil and the Male Elite: A Feminist Interpretation of Women's Rights in Islam,* Mary Jo Lakeland, trans. New York: Addison-Wesley.

Mumtaz, Khawar, and Farida Shaheed. (1987). *Two Steps Forward, One Step Back? Women of Pakistan.* London: Zed Books.

Shaheed, Farida. (1986). "The Cultural Articulation of Patriarchy: Legal Systems, Islam and the Women in Pakistan." *South Asia Bulletin* 6(1): 38–44.

WLUML. (1986). *Plan of Action (Aramon).*

NOTES

1. In Algeria, the three feminists were released; however, the new Family Code was enacted in 1984, negatively affecting women. In India, the Muslim Women (Protection of the Rights on Divorce) Act 1986 allowed Muslim minority law to supersede the Constitutional provisions, depriving Muslim women of rights enjoyed by others. In Abu Dhabi, after a strong international campaign of numerous groups, the woman was repatriated to her own country, Sri Lanka. After several years, the governments of Algeria and France signed a treaty providing for visiting rights to divorced mothers of Algerian children.

2. For a more complete discussion on the subject of the cultural articulation of patriarchy, see Shaheed 1986; on the complexities of the situation, see Kandiyoti 1989.

Reading E

Belgrade Feminists 1992: Separation, Guilt, and Identity Crisis

LEPA MLADJENOVIC AND VERA LITRICIN

Antiwar activists Lepa Mladjenovic and Vera Litricin argue that feminists organizing across ethnic and national boundaries must critique the nationalist and state-sponsored violence that has splintered the former Yugoslavia.

Writing this paper about the feminist activities and our lives during the past couple of years, here we are, the three of us in the kitchen thinking about the most horrible facts about our lives, the war. Two million people have already been moved from their homes: many injured; many dead. A couple of million more have no food, no heat, nor much hope to hold on to. And we are aware that citizens around us do not want to know that winter will kill thousands more people: that soldiers and other men will rape thousands more women: that rape is not a nationalist but a gender issue. One of us is nervous on and off, the other cannot even hear s, e, r, or b (i.e., Serb) in one place without being angry—it's high time women should get out on the streets and scream.

Lepa Mladjenovic and Vera Litricin, "Belgrade Feminists 1992: Separation, Guilt, and Identity Crisis," transcribed by Tanya Renne, *Feminist Review* 45, Autumn 1993: 113–19.

For the 40 years of our past, the ideology of the equality of the genders so well known to the entire Eastern bloc has masked the reality of everyday life for women. Still, a semi-autonomous women's association, the Anti-Fascist Front of Women, was formed during World War II (1942) and many of our mothers were active in it. In 1953 it evolved into the Union of Women's Associations and included approximately 2,000 small women's units all over Yugoslavia. In 1961 these women's organizations were abolished and the Party formed "The Conference for the Social Activities of Women," which was hierarchically organized and governmentally divided.

The history of Yugoslav postwar feminism started with Belgrade's International Feminists' Meeting in 1978, which was the turning point for the rise of women's groups. From 1980 on, two "Women and Society" groups were formed, first in Zagreb and then in Belgrade. The Belgrade group provided an open forum for discussing women's issues. But in 1986 women decided to call the group "feminist," create "women-only space" and start activities and meetings on a regular basis. At this time The Conference for the Social Activities of Women was accusing the group of being an "enemy of the state," "procapitalist," and "pro-western."

Key Term

Eastern bloc The countries of eastern Europe that were in alliance with the Soviet Union.

Activities of the group included action research on the streets of Belgrade concerning violence, solidarity, and housework; workshops and public discussions on topics such as mothers and daughters, guilt, violence, abortion, sexuality, working rights for women, psychiatry, the medical system, and cinema. From the beginning the group has been without any institutional, financial, or any other state support and therefore has worked completely independently.

At that time there was a great deal of cooperation with feminists in Ljubljana and Zagreb, the result of which was the first feminist meeting of Yugoslav feminists in Ljubljana in 1987, when the "Network of Yugoslav Feminists" was formed. Three similar meetings were held following this, in Zagreb, Belgrade, and the last in Ljubljana in May of 1991.

In the summer of 1991, Yugoslavia disintegrated.

In April 1992, the so-called Third Yugoslavia was formed with a new constitution that, among other things, eliminated Article 191 (included in the Constitution of 1974) about Free Parenthood. The article protected "the human right to decide about the birth of one's own children." And now, its absence introduces the possibility of reducing access to abortion and reproductive rights.

In 1990 the feminist group Women and Society disbanded and multiplied in several other women's groups. The first of them was the SOS Hotline for Women and Children Victims of Violence, established 8 March 1990, and the second, the Women's Lobby. That summer, in response to the first "free" elections, women from different non-nationalist parties formed the Women's Lobby in order to put pressure on political parties running for election. Then in the autumn of the same year the Women's Party—ZEST—was born, with the aim of improving the quality of women's lives in every respect. In fact, it was formed with the intention of utilizing political campaigns for promoting consciousness about women's issues.

On 8 March 1991, the Women's Parliament was formed as a response to a presence of only 1.6 percent women in the Serbian parliament (the lowest percentage in Europe). The purpose of the Women's Parliament was to observe and respond to all new laws that discriminated against women.

On 9 October 1991, Women in Black against War appeared on the streets in Belgrade in protest against the war in Croatia (later in Bosnia) and were afterwards joined by women in Pancevo.

On 8 March 1992, after a year of preparation, a women's studies group was formed to discuss feminist knowledge. The subjects include women's perspectives on patriarchy, philosophy, lesbianism, family, socialism, and literature, among others. The course is outside the university, free and open to all women.

The lesbian and gay lobby, Arkadia, was founded in the winter of 1990 to work on the social visibility of lesbians and homosexuals. The group has organized public discussion; some activists have written a few articles. But student and youth institutions refused to offer space for the group meetings and a few times even refused the proposal for public discussion.

We would now like to give details of some actions of the Women's Lobby and Women's Parliament which we consider important.

One of the first actions of the Women's Lobby was a "Minimal Programme of Women's Demands" addressed to parties and movements. The demands concerned the field of work and unemployment, sexist education, reproductive rights, violence against women, health care and the change of certain laws concerning women. The final demands were for a Ministry of Women, a refuge for women and children victims of violence, the inclusion of a certain percentage of women in parliament and the parties themselves, the decriminalization of prostitution, the recognition of rape in marriage as a crime, and mandatory child support for all children of divorce.

In September 1990 the Lobby issued an open letter to the public reacting to one of the leaders (Bulatovic) of the opposition nationalist party "Serbian movement of Renovation" who urged Serbian women to "reproduce the greater Serbian nation." Among other things the letter said, "One supposes that young Serbian fetuses will be immediately baptized, conditioned to hate and lead the war against the many Enemies of the Serbian nation."

Just before the elections, on 5 December 1990, the Women's Lobby issued an appeal to the public that reads as follows: "Don't vote for the Socialist Party of

Serbia . . . don't vote for their leader, Slobodan Milo-sevic . . . don't vote for nationalist, Serbo-chauvinistic parties (SRS, SPO, SNO, etc.) . . . vote for the candi-dates of the civil democratic parties."

At the beginning of 1991, a joint demand for the creation of a Ministry of Women was handed to the Serb parliament signed by the Women's Lobby, the Women's Parliament, and the Feminist Group.

One of the most important actions of ZEST was in organizing housewives in a few communities in Bel-grade and giving public space to their voices.

Other protests included:

- a petition regarding the Resolution of Population Politics in Serbia and a law concerning family plan-ning (June 1990)
- a protest against the representation of women in the 1990 census (in which women were instructed to give their husband or father's name only)
- an appeal for the demilitarization of Yugoslavia (Au-gust 1990)
- support of the Mothers' Peace Initiative in Serbia and Croatia (August 1990)
- a protest against new textbooks based on nationalist, patriarchal, and sexist values (December 1990)
- a protest of discrimination against lesbians and gay men in derogatory political discourse (August 1991)
- a protest against the sexist behaviour of the members of the Serb parliament (1991–92)
- a protest against the document "Warning," issued in the Serbian Academy of Science and approved by the leading party programme. Eight men who signed it condemn the high birth rate of Albanians, Mus-lims, and Gypsies as being "deviant from rational human reproduction" (1992)
- critiques of the sexist language used in the inde-pendent media (1992)

A few other appeals have been made together with Women in Black, in which it was made clear that the feminist groups of Belgrade believe that the Serbian regime is responsible for violence, war, and the ab-sence of civil democracy and civil society.

Women in Black consists of a very small number of women who have been coming out into the streets for a year now. Even though their number is small, their vigil is important in maintaining the pressure and pres-ence of women against war in the streets of Belgrade. They symbolize women's condition in war: as refugees, as those who care for the refugees, as moth-ers and sisters of the dead, as those raped and forced into prostitution. In their appeals they point to the pa-triarchal and sexist essence of nationalism and war. Women in Black have become part of international women's peace initiatives in Italy, Germany, Belgium, and Great Britain. In their international meetings in Venice and Novia Sad, they opened a new space for consciousness-raising on specific themes—such as women and fatherland, national and gender identity, women and the embargo—as well as providing an op-portunity to experience the globality of sisterhood.

The SOS Hotline for Women and Children Victims of Violence is run by about 30 women, and in the past two and half years more than 150 women volunteered and responded to more than 3,500 calls. Women who call testified that 80 percent of the perpetrators were ei-ther husbands, ex-husbands, sons, brothers, or fathers. They also stated that in 30 percent of the cases they suffered severe injuries and that in 60 percent of the cases the violence has lasted more than 10 years. The work of SOS has proved well-known facts about male violence against women, but in the last year new types of war-related violence have appeared.

- Death threats increased from 30 percent to 55 per-cent of all calls.
- The percentage of guns among violent men doubled.
- Veterans of the war turned violent against their wives and mothers for the first time (machine guns under the pillow, rape of wives, constant mental abuse, se-vere injuries).
- Violence in interethnic marriage increased.
- The post-TV news violence syndrome appeared. Men were violent against their wives after being ex-posed to nationalist propaganda. The wives in these cases are of every nationality.

As a general conclusion, SOS proves that the war has led to an increase in all types of male violence against women. Beyond that, within the family men are using nationalist hatred as an instrument of violence against women.

—The New Issues That Belgrade Feminists Have Faced Since the Beginning of the War

Separation

When the war started, nationalist hatred increased drastically and the Serbian government began to produce propaganda and the notion of the Enemy. All of a sudden Slovenians became an enemy, then Croats, then Muslims, then Americans, Albanians, and so on. Deep conflicts emerged in families, in workplaces, and women began to separate on that basis. Completely new questions appeared in women's groups. Can a feminist be a nationalist chauvinist? Can a pacifist be a nationalist? Is a weapon an instrument of defence? Should the groups take clear attitudes toward nationalist questions (and therefore the war) and in that way lose some women? Should the groups avoid the issue of nationalism altogether? Should the women merely sit down and confront their beliefs about it and see what happens?

Apart from Women in Black and Women's Lobby, where the non-nationalist statement is clear, all the other groups had many problems. The most difficult situation, and the most often avoided, was a confrontation. Every time the nationalist question came up (usually by itself) there was no way to overcome the fact that a lot of women were being hurt. Women suffered but usually did not change their attitudes. There was a great deal of silence and crisis.

For example, the Women's Party was eventually not able to continue. The conflicts over nationalism were far too strong in dividing women and there was no way to go on. They decided to "freeze" their activities until the war was over and then see.

SOS Hotline had many problems as well. Despite the fact that the SOS group had a deliberately nonnationalist policy from the beginning, some volunteers were unable to keep their nationalist feelings out of their SOS work. Several attempts were made to reconcile the opposing viewpoints; after that some of the women left and some of them stayed and remained silent.

So, nationalism made some women split within themselves. It also caused painful scars to Zagreb–Beograd feminist relationships. Nationalism brought in new discriminatory population policies. The reduction of available abortion is already true for Croatia and on the way in Serbia. Here we find ourselves in the unfamiliar process of the legitimation of hatred against women increasing daily. These new nation-states function over women's bodies. They need their national bodies and women to reproduce them. They are fed with hate and therefore with the separation of women. They are based on violence against Others, but everyone is a potential Other. Neither the "sacred nationality" nor the "sacred gender" is a guarantee anymore. Nationalist policy brought in the war, the death, the war rapes, the refugees, and then the punishment of the ordinary people with an economic embargo.

Guilt

Not all the feminists in Belgrade feel guilt about the ongoing war. They either do not feel guilt because they have anarchist orientations or because they have separatist tendencies. Some of the women do feel guilt, and it's a guilt for what the government they haven't voted for has done in their names. The others feel guilt for the fact that innocent women are dying and being raped and they can do little or nothing about it. We came to a conclusion that some of this guilt can be stimulating but too much of it can overwhelm you and make you feel helpless. Moreover, the absence of guilt does not mean the absence of responsibility.

How can I speak to a friend in Sarajevo?
Just because I have electricity and food and she has not makes the gap sometimes unbearable to overcome, and what am I to do? Can peace activities lessen my feelings of guilt? Does my presence at opposition (chauvinist and male-oriented) demonstrations against Milosevic reduce my feelings of helplessness? If I tell her that I care and that I think of her and that my dreams are full of fear, will that help her? If I tell her that we stand here in black on the corner every week— and people spit on us, saying that we are "the bloody traitors of the Serbian nation" and "idle whores of Tudjman and Izetbegovic"—if I tell her all this, will she

say I am a fool, that she risks her life every moment? If I publish an essay in which I express hatred of the war killers and rapist of all sides, and in which her suffering becomes the essay's pulse and a value beyond telling, will that help at all? And if I say we've been in Italy, Germany, and France and women are sending their love and support from all around the world, will she even blink? If her windows are broken, if a litre of water costs 20 dinar, and her hair has gone white and her cheeks sunken. Seven months later she is speechless, awaiting the winter that could wipe them all out.

Identity

Many women in Belgrade have no ethnic identity problems; they always felt Serb. Others are able to feel "positively Serb" as pacifists and feminists. Some of us, though a small group, cannot identify with the "Serbian nation." Before, we were "Yugoslavs" and therefore never really identified with Serbs at all. At this point, when we are forced to take a Serbian nationality as our own, we see that there is nothing, nothing at all that can attract feminists to accept it as their own national identity. The "Serbian nation," as the present government creates it, certainly has nothing in common with a "Women's nation." Our Yugoslav post-Second-World-War feminist movement has never done anything in the name of this, their Serbian nation.

In addition, some of us believed in some of the socialist ideas that were legitimated by former Communist governments; relative social equality, free education, free health care and access to abortion, inexpensive housing and cultural events. (We have always believed that class differences literally kill some people, especially women.) But we are facing the fact that the realization of our beliefs has come to an end. So for those of us who are not Serbians yet, who are not Yugoslavs anymore, and who feel the lot of women's rights with the fall of Communism, there is a lot of identity work to be done. Women-identified women have a strong basis of identity to begin that work.

We know that to overthrow the present government we have to vote for another one that will be against us, and we must take that responsibility; we know that if we are to manifest our disobedience toward the war and be noticed, we have to stand in the opposition's street crowds and feel awful among sexist, royalist speeches and songs; we know that if we stand on the streets as small women's groups against war we expose ourselves to insults, but we still do that and feel brave; we know that if we are to deny the concept of national identity there is nothing else they'll allow us to stand for in exchange; we know that white men are urged to die courageously for their nation. Raped, murdered women will never be considered brave, except by us; we know that if we are to say aloud who we are and what we want there will be no historically accepted political patterns for our experience or our language. And yet here we are.

Reading F

Welfare, Rights, and the Disability Movement

LINA ABU-HABIB

Lina Abu-Habib, an advocate for disability rights in the Middle East, argues that women with disabilities must organize since disability combined with gender leads to increased oppression for women. This new social movement is globalizing rapidly, incorporating identity politics strategies from feminism and the human rights movement.

> *Just as men assume that they know what women want, so nondisabled assume that they know what disabled people want.* (Hannaford 1985)

Worldwide, men and women with disabilities have relatively better life-chances today than a decade or more ago. For one thing, disability has come out into the open. Disabled persons have fought the practice of incarceration in residential homes and hospitals, "treatment" which was legitimate not only in the Middle East but also in the Western world (Finkelstein 1991).

There is a sense among the able-bodied that disabled people need their protection. Concern with the welfare of disabled people is seen as "charitable." Yet

Lina Abu-Habib, "Welfare, Rights, and the Disability Movement," in *Gender and Disability: Women's Experiences in the Middle East,* Oxfam, 1997: 3–8.

these breakthroughs can only partially be attributed to a change of heart on the part of the able-bodied decision makers at national and international levels. As Lambert puts it, "my survival at every level depends on maintaining good relationships with able-bodied people" (Lambert 1989: 39).

Achievements and successes in advocacy work on disability can be attributed in large measure to the efforts and perseverance of groups of disabled people. The disability movement is, in many countries of the Middle East, proactive, strong, and involved in advocacy on the rights of the disabled. Disabled activists from various parts of the Middle East have become more vocal on essential issues such as rights for disabled persons, representation, and full integration and independence. Fifteen years ago, such initiatives were in their infancy. Even now, such successes remain small-scale in comparison to the need and are possible only when lobbying groups have gained strength and negotiating power, and receive the goodwill and cooperation of the public.

If certain policy changes have in fact occurred, changes in discriminatory perceptions, attitudes, and behaviour have been far slower. Ensuring rights for the disabled does not in itself affect the prevailing patriarchal system, and therefore is not threatening. In addi-

---

Key Term

Prepcoms Preparatory planning meetings in different cities for the Fourth United Nations Conference on Women, held in Beijing in 1995.

tion, politicians can always postpone commitments by using the all-too-common excuses of financial constraints, conflicting priorities, and the fact that isolation and discrimination can be attributed only to mere ignorance.

Thus, the strong message from the nondisabled world remains that the lives of disabled persons are not necessarily worth living. Both men and women with disabilities are made to feel "different"; they fail to conform to a traditionally and socially agreed norm of beauty and strength. Pity, condescension, embarrassment, or a mixture of the three are the reactions men and women who have a disability most commonly encounter from nondisabled people. Many activists believe that disabled people are in some senses considered by able-bodied people—both women and men—to be less than human (Morris 1993).

During the summer of 1993, there was a major Israeli military offensive in South Lebanon which caused hundreds of casualties and massive exodus and displacement. The Lebanese Sitting Handicapped Association (LSHA), along with other local NGOs, was involved in relief and emergency work. LSHA was surveying damages suffered by disabled persons and their families, as well as cases of new injuries. On arriving in the village of Kfarroumane, they asked as usual for the cooperation of the villagers in surveying the houses. Knowing that LSHA is an association of disabled persons, a woman approached them and told them that she knew of a next-door neighbour who had a disabled daughter, now a teenager. However, she had not seen her for a long time, and certainly not after the military offensive. She was concerned because their house had been directly hit by a mortar shell. On entering the half-destroyed house, LSHA volunteers discovered the girl inside, injured and in a pitiful state. An investigation revealed that when the family fled the village, her father refused to take her, leaving her under fire and perhaps hoping that she would be killed, and this would be "God's wish." He also told LSHA volunteers that he had preferred to save their cow because she is more useful to them than their disabled daughter. When LSHA wanted to take the girl to a nearby hospital for her wound to be treated, her father categorically refused. "What for?" he asked "So that I start paying for her?" LSHA had to ask for the assistance of the local gendarmerie to take the girl to the hospital.

Women and the Disability Movement

Where disabled lobby groups have been active in advocating changes in discriminatory laws, emphasis has not tended to be placed on rendering this work gender-sensitive. Although lobbying for rights, services, education, and employment for disabled people in general is of utmost importance and long overdue, such work is of very limited use to disabled women if they suffer discrimination differently and more deeply on grounds of their sex.

Disabled women in different contexts have complained that rehabilitation programmes appear to have been designed to suit disabled men's aspiration for recovering their masculinity and sexuality, while the needs and aspirations of disabled women are often ignored (Begum 1992, Morris 1993).

The leadership of the disability movement is to a large extent still dominated by disabled men, who may consider their own experience as the norm. In the case of Lebanon, the country of which I have most personal knowledge, only one of the current disabled associations is presided over by a woman (personal communication 1996). However, she acceded to the post by appointment and following the prolonged sickness of the former male president. At the time of writing this book, there are no disabled women leading or presiding over associations of disabled persons in any other Middle Eastern country.

The disability movement in the Middle East has yet to herald the specific issues pertinent to disabled women on its agenda. Even now, major international disability events which have direct implications for policymaking, such as the September 1996 conference on disability convened by the International Labor Organization in Sana'a, Yemen, have little input from people who see gender as a central concern for women who are disabled.

Just as statistics on women assume able-bodied status, statistics on disabled people frequently fail to disaggregate by sex the people being studied. Nevertheless, empirical evidence shows beyond doubt that disabled women have had less access than disabled men to the potential benefits that may be gained from national governments and nongovernmental organisations set up to address the practical and strategic needs of disabled people.

—Disabled Women in the Feminist Movement

If the marginalisation of women within the disability movement is being to some extent addressed and rectified, disabled women remain absent from the leadership and agenda of the women's movement, in the Middle East and beyond. For the past 30 years, since International Women's Year in 1975, the women's movement has struggled to place women's rights and needs in development squarely on the international agenda.

According to the last *Human Development Report* (UNDP 1995), there have recently been a number of concrete, albeit limited, changes for the better in the lives of women in the Middle East, which is the regional context of the case studies in this book.

The report states that more women have access to basic services such as health and education (UNDP 1995), yet women's strategic interests have yet to be met: women will have to wait longer for full inclusion and better representation in political life. But the main point in respect of the concerns of this book is that there is no evidence that disabled women have benefited either practically or strategically, on equal terms with able-bodied women, from this advancement. How could such evidence exist, when most official statistics and research on women ignore this aspect of social difference?

I attended the Beijing Preparatory Meeting in Amman in November 1994, and by the end of the NGO meeting, I had given up trying to locate a disabled woman among the 800 or so participants. This was surprising, because hardly a month before this meeting, a prepreparatory meeting was convened in the same city, especially for women with disabilities, to discuss strategies to ensure that their perspectives were included in the Beijing process, and in particular at the subsequent Prepcom meeting.

A similar chain of events occurred at other regional Prepcoms for Beijing: for example, in the Prepcom meeting held in Dakar during that same period, disabled women participants strongly criticised the conference organisers in Senegal for failing to expect and accommodate women with disabilities. According to the participants, none of their major requirements to allow their full participation in the Dakar Prepcom were met: from accessible toilets to transport which was suitable for the use of disabled people.

In parallel with questions asked in the women's movement, the question of representation of one group by another—seen in the feminist movement, and in international development bodies—also arises in the context of disability and gender. It takes outspoken, eloquent disabled feminists to be able to infiltrate the women's movement and put forward the disability agenda. Before leaving to attend the U.N. IV Conference in Beijing, Miriam, a young woman who uses a wheelchair, visited one of the pioneers of the women's movement of Lebanon to inquire about the attitude of her association vis-à-vis women with disabilities. Taken by surprise with an unexpected question, the activist replied "er . . . dear, well we're thinking of you all the time. . . " (personal communication, 1996).

The fact that the representation of disabled women by others is problematic has been apparent even at forums which are intended to discuss their concerns. For example, a seminar on the role of the family in integrating disabled women into society run by ESCWA (United Nations Economic and Social Commission for Western Asia) in Amman, Jordan, in October 1994, and a Conference on Blind Women held by the World Blind Union in Amman in 1995, were both described by many of the participants as events lacking any significant participation of disabled women; the fact that there was virtually no disabled presence meant that there was a consequent lack of focus and clarity on possible strategies for follow-up.

Whatever the difficulties involved in disabled women's participation, the Fourth U.N. Conference on Women, held in Beijing in 1995, witnessed the highest number of disabled women participants to date—200 in total (although the representation from the Middle East was fewer than 10 women). This was the first time there had ever been an organised representation of disabled women at an international women's conference. While the conference itself was poorly prepared to receive disabled women and communicate with them effectively, disabled women themselves were well-organised and demanded that they be listened to. This event showed the importance of the presence and representation of disabled women in events where policy decisions can often be taken on behalf of disabled women *in absentia.*

Beijing was a landmark for disabled women, who refused to be relegated to a category of "women with special needs." Their struggle to be heard as individuals in their own right, and on equal terms with able-bodied women, was reminiscent of the earlier days of the women's movement where women were fighting for equal rights and the right to be heard.

Apart from the personal experience of being disabled themselves, women may experience the issue from another perspective, in their role as primary carers for children and other family members and within the community. This issue, too, is pertinent to the wider concerns of the women's movement. For many years now, feminists have emphasised the value of the work of caring and questioned the fact that much of this work remains invisible to national and international planners and policymakers, in development agencies as well as governments.

In the Middle East, as elsewhere, mothers of disabled children are in most instances the sole caregivers and nurturers at home, a role they have to fulfill in addition to the already backbreaking household chores and other productive functions (Begum, N. 1992). As carers, women have to spend the rest of their lives at home, nursing the disabled child, and caring for the family as a whole, with no possibility of any improvement later in life. Again, planners have failed to consider this important aspect of disability, and the fact that women carers will forever be unable to care for and invest in themselves. Caring for the disabled will have to be added to the list of other unrecognised and unpaid tasks that women have to perform. As if this were not enough, in the Middle East context, mothers are invariably blamed, shamed, and stigmatised for the birth of a disabled child.

REFERENCES

Begum, N. (1992). "Disabled Women and the Feminist Agenda," in *Feminist Review.*

Finkelstein, V. (1991). "Disability: An Administrative Challenge," in Oliver, M. (ed.) *Social Work: Disabled People and Disabling Environment,* Kingsley: London.

Hannaford, S. (1985). *Living Outside Inside,* Canterbury Press: Berkeley, California.

Lambert, A. (1989). "Disability and Violence," in *Sinister Wisdom.*

Morris, I. (1993). *Pride against Prejudice,* Women's Press: London.

Morris, I. (ed.) (1989). *Able Lives,* Women's Press: London.

Sen, A. K. (1990). "Gender and Cooperation Conflicts," in Tinker I *Persistent Inequalities,* Oxford University Press: Oxford.

Sherr, B. (1992). "We Are Who We Are: Feminism and Disability," in *Ms.,* November.

UNDP (1995). *Human Development Report 1995,* Oxford University Press: Oxford.

REFLECTING ON THE SECTION

Women are often asked to put national, ethnic, racial, or class identity before gender, especially in historical moments of crisis. Yet the readings in Part Two demonstrate the connection of gender to these other social divisions. According to Leila Rupp, the "first wave" of the international women's movement emerged at the end of the nineteenth century as an antiwar and antinationalist coalition. Writing almost a year after the United States entered World War I, socialist feminist Crystal Eastman describes her work in the International Committee of Women for Permanent Peace and makes the case for a North American Women's Peace Party.

More recently, Mamphele Ramphele describes South African women's struggles against war and white supremacist rule as the foundation for a "transnational women's studies." Lepa Mladjenovic and Vera Litricin argue that feminist organizing across ethnic and national boundaries must critique the nationalist violence that has splintered the former country of Yugoslavia. These writers, along with Farida Shaheed and Lina Abu-Habib, suggest that cross-border coalitions work against nationalisms and fundamentalisms. What are some of the problems and the advantages of these cross-border feminist coalitions?

PART THREE

Representations, Cultures, Media, and Markets

Have you seen any good movies lately? In any social occasion, at a party or having coffee with a friend, we ask this kind of question without thinking very much about it. Yet it's a worthwhile question. For many people, a "good" movie is one that transports them away from daily life. Movies, like other forms of entertainment such as television, music, art, theater, and literature, provide people with a break from stress or work. Even talking about entertainment can be relaxing. So how do we talk about movies or television shows? Very often we describe the plot or the characters or stars who we enjoyed and admired. We might talk about the special effects, the photography, the music. What else is there to discuss? In women's studies there seem to be a million things to talk about when we consider media and visual communication! In Part Three we present some of the ways movies, television, the Internet, the arts, and culture in general can be approached from feminist perspectives.

We will use the term *representation* to address the ideas and images that pervade the media and forms of communication and culture, written and visual. The notion of representation allows us to think about how art, media, and communication create meanings in specific times and places. Thus, *representation* stands for how we understand, think about, or make meanings about something or someone. How a word or concept may lead us to learn or understand an idea is crucial, since these meanings may also shift with time or place. For instance, when we see an advertisement for a car, how do we know for whom the ad is intended? We understand its intention from the words used to describe the car, its color and style, the overall graphic design, the kinds of figures used in the image, and so on. When we look at an ad, we decode its language without thinking too much about it. In women's studies we turn that almost unconscious process into an awareness of the ways the images and words give us information about gender and culture.

Are we reading too much into things that should be simple and taken for granted or are just for entertainment? If we believe that culture does not simply appear out of nowhere, then we have to take an interest in the ways that power and politics produce these cultural forms. Every day we are faced by events that tell us that culture is a political matter. For example, in recent years, various social movements have launched protests about the way their group or identity is portrayed in the media. In the United States and elsewhere, social movements have created organizations that evaluate their representation in the media and also work to create positive images for themselves. Feminists everywhere question negative or stereotypical images of various kinds and offer alternatives to them.

If these representations do not appear out of nowhere, where do they come from? That is, we need to think about how these aspects of culture are produced, circulated, and consumed. By "production" we mean the way that art and media are created and manufactured; how they are made by people and companies in specific places and in particular times. For instance, a book is written by an author, who may be funded in many different ways, who has an identity such as a novelist or a technical writer, and who needs an agent or an editor to publish the book. The book itself will need to be printed, marketed, and distributed. This set of activities is called *circulation*. Circulation leads to another important aspect of representation—consumption. By *consumption* we mean the ways in which the book is bought and interpreted by various readers. This set of practices—production, circulation, and consumption—underlies any work of art or media. Does it spoil our enjoyment to consider these aspects?

In women's studies it is important to talk about representation for several reasons. The first reason is that knowledge is power. The knowledge that is available to us is at the heart of our culture; that is, everything we can know and think. If that knowledge is biased or incomplete or dated, our ability to act in the world and think meaningfully will be compromised severely. Yet it is impossible to know everything about a particular topic. Rather than seeking to master all knowledge, we ask, what is the history of knowledge or information that we obtain from our culture? Is it sufficient for our current goals and needs? Is it biased in any way? Where do images and ideas come from? Thinking about representation leads us to ask these questions and others, especially in regard to gender and global politics.

Second, since women are often depicted in art and media in ways that reflect the kinds of politics and history we have discussed in Parts One and Two of this book, women's studies has focused on what can be called "images of women." Since all images have both politics and histories, it is important to understand that images are neither natural nor inevitable. For example, the Disney movie *Pocahontas* relies on a pervasive stereotype of Native American women as both sexually available and traitorous: a dual stereotype. In the Disney movie, this story is repeated and updated in a visually glossy and beautifully packaged format that attracts viewers of all ages and backgrounds around the world. In women's studies, we learn to place a film like *Pocahontas* in a historical context to understand the political reasons for portraying native women in such a manner, as well as the patterns of representation that have created new versions of a stereotype.

Third, women are not just the object of media industries. They also participate in multiple ways, ranging from writers, actors, artists, directors, and producers to workers at the many jobs that are invisible to viewers and consumers. These workers include the people who manufacture goods that are used in media such as film and TV or in art. They also include the people who are involved in supporting the white-collar media workers: nannies, food preparers and servers, chauffeurs, janitors and more. In the current phase of globalization, many of these jobs are sent "offshore" (to low-paid workers in the Third World) or staffed by people who have migrated from other countries or rural areas in search of work. If we consider all of these activities and kinds of work, we can see that many women are integral to what is called "cultural production." Since women have historically been more likely to be the service and support workers rather than the creators and manufacturers, they have also been less likely to profit from media and art industries. While we can always point to exceptional cases, for the most part one's gender (along with many other aspects such as race, class, sexuality, religion, and nationality) affects the types of work and recognition that one can obtain. Thus, gender is part of the division of labor that makes products of many kinds available in culture industries.

A fourth point to consider concerns consumption and gender. In this part of the book, we will learn about the role women have played as consumers and how that role has influenced representations of women. In the United States, for instance, as industrialization led to greater speeds in printing and in the transportation of goods, including printed matter, new kinds of media appeared. Magazines, tabloid newspapers, and later radio and television created unique opportunities to sell products and create new needs and desires. Middle-class women in industrial societies were positioned to become the model for the ideal consumer. Even in a globalized world, middle-class, First World women remain the paramount symbol of consumption. In women's studies we can approach the subject of shopping and consumption as one that includes globalized divisions of labor, histories of advertising, and the cultures of beauty and fashion that offer pleasure as well as domination. It is common knowledge that women are portrayed in the popular media in stereotypical and unrealistic ways. The superslim Barbie-like figure pervades mass media, yet we know that such a body is almost impossible to realize. The billion-dollar diet, cosmetic, and fashion industries have capitalized on the creation of a desire for such a body and related fashions in clothing and appearance. For decades, beauty pageants all over the world have sought out women with specific physical characteristics, ignoring cultural differences in beauty standards for both men and women.

Fifth, how does a new social movement such as feminism create alternative kinds of media and representations? In women's studies the debate around alternative representations has been a long and heated one. Is it sufficient to replace a negative stereotype with a positive image? Who decides what is "bad" or "good" or "negative" or "positive"—and for whom? Who decides whether a representation is pornographic or artistic? Does it matter whether or not the artist or writer or producer is a woman? For many feminists, the biological sex of the creator does not ensure that the representation works against dominant stereotypes. On the other hand, given the masculinist nature of most mainstream art and media, it might matter a great deal. In the first part of the book we presented materials that argued that biology, too, has a history. In this part of the book, we can draw on that insight to see how representations of male and female are part of that history. So when we ask if it matters whether the writer or the artist is a female, we are asking how gender came to matter in a specific craft, profession, or industry, not simply whether or not a representation is linked to an essential identity. The question of "good" or "bad" images is always connected to larger contexts of power in a world where most women have less access to technologies that enable representation.

Since access to technology is a crucial issue for feminists, literacy is an important tool for the empowerment of poor women across the world. Without literacy and education, they may be unable to own property, follow a profession, or participate in electoral politics. In this regard, the accepted versions of biological differences that have led to gender formation have had drastic effects, ranging from the underrepresentation of women in all forms of public life to extreme impoverishment. Historically, only a few elite women were literate. The emergence of the printing press created new ways for people to obtain information, news, and ideas. When printing was mechanized, books became part of mass culture rather than only of elite culture. Increased literacy led to availability of books and newspapers directed at both elite and non-elite audiences. As more kinds of media became available and affordable, women's participation in public life increased. Thus literacy remains a crucial issue, since women cannot be citizens or modern individuals if they do not have access to information.

If feminist alternative media are not necessarily produced only by women and alternative media are not simply all media produced by women, then what does the term mean? In some contexts, media produced by groups of women are alternative when they critique dominant practices that place women in subordinate positions. For instance, many individuals and organizations who work on women's issues use the Internet, a creative use of a dominant technology. There are many groups that organize around media such as radio, cinema, TV, video, and the Internet to produce fresh perspectives and new information. For example, an Internet search using the phrase "Asian women" may lead to a preponderance of sites offering sexually explicit images or ads for contacts and arranged marriages. In this context, feminist websites that present other views and information can be considered an alternative. To take another example, radio is one of the primary means of communication all around the world. Since radio takes relatively fewer resources to set up than many other media, it has been used by many groups who need to present their viewpoints.

Although the issue of alternate media is crucial to us in women's studies, we should be careful to not romanticize it. Once we discover the pervasiveness of negative images of women, we find it natural to seek the alternative to this situation. However, replacing the negative with the positive may not be sufficient, nor is it useful in every situation. For example, if we say that the dominant representation of women on TV in India is as submissive housewives, then is the positive alternative the woman with the career? Certainly, the woman with the career could also have a home life where she is still responsible for most of the housework. The career might still lead to lower wages and an exploitative situation. Or it might be possible to see differences among housewives depending on many factors, such as class, caste, religion, and region. Looking only at "roles" can leave out many important issues. There is also much to be learned from life experiences that may not be seen as successful or ideal. The concept of the positive role model can be a superficial one, since the role hides the more complex life of an individual.

When we study representation, we want to discuss more than positive versus negative images. We need also to consider the ways in which these images are produced—not simply by individuals but also by communities, industries, cultures, and technologies. One of the debates that informs our understanding of these issues concerns the difference between 'high" (elite) and "low" (mass) culture. High culture, it is argued, includes music, painting, sculpture, and the forms of art and literature that are produced for artistic or noncommercial reasons. In fact, one definition of the term *culture* is high culture; that is, to be cultured means to be elite. Low culture is openly commercial and does not get judged or valued in the same way as artistic work. Yet the division between high and low culture is not necessarily a firm one. Many artists and writers move back and forth between these two realms, depending on their circumstances. In addition, it can be argued that few areas of social life can be firmly or clearly separated from commerce or economic considerations. The fact that high culture does not aim to appeal to as *wide an audience* as low culture doesn't mean it has nothing to do with money.

Since women, for the most part, have been excluded from recognition in the arena of elite culture, we should not be surprised that much of so-called mass culture is directed to female consumers or to non-elite groups. Soap operas, romance novels, talk shows, gossip magazines, and popular music have engaged either female audiences or audiences who also belong to more marginal groups. In women's studies, we look at the participation of women in both elite and mass cultures in order to understand the ways art and entertainment are separate but intertwined.

Another key debate in the area of feminist scholarship on representation focuses on the concept of aesthetics, which refers to the appreciation of the beautiful. Aesthetics underlies the system of value in the art world and has been shaped by considerations of ideal or beautiful forms. But what can we make of the fact that many of the objects and artworks created by women have not been judged to be either beautiful or art? Pottery, quiltmaking, embroidery, dressmaking, and cooking, for example, have been marginalized as domestic crafts. In particular, the objects created by women outside the West have been viewed as "primitive" or as anthropological artifacts. In these examples, we see that the designation of art can shift. Sometimes a work can be judged to be merely useful, or a piece of folk art, or even valueless. At other times, the same object may become valuable, deemed to be of aesthetic interest and part of elite culture. The feminist study of art history and literature has helped us understand the ways that women's creative work has moved into and out of the system of value established by the institutions of elite culture.

Given the range of feminist interests in culture and representation, in Part Three of this book we do not focus on either mass culture or elite culture alone. Instead, we focus on the relationships among forms of communication, gender, and power. This relationship is a foundational one; that is, it gives us the tools to understand that the forms of subordination and power that influence gender are culturally specific. It also inspires us to understand the many different ways that feminists challenge dominant representations of gender. Learning to critique representations does not have to lead to dismissing all the familiar forms of media, culture, and entertainment that have given us pleasure. Rather, we can find new kinds of enjoyment in our ability to engage and work critically with these forms.

Ways of Seeing: Representational Practices

Excerpts from Ways of Seeing

JOHN BERGER

John Berger, art critic and cultural historian, made an important contribution to the way in which people think about art and images when he created a television series for the British Broadcasting Company in the early 1970s. He presented what was then a radically different way to view the history of Western art from a viewpoint that addressed issues of patriarchy and class difference. In this excerpt from the book based on the series, Berger tells us why it is important for us to take images, whether popular or elite, very seriously and how the way they convey meaning (their method of representation) differs from the written word.

Seeing comes before words. The child looks and recognizes before it can speak.

But there is also another sense in which seeing comes before words. It is seeing which establishes our place in the surrounding world; we explain that world with words, but words can never undo the fact that we

John Berger, *Ways of Seeing,* Harmondsworth, England: Penguin Books, 1972: 7–11, 16–17, 45–47, 63–64.

are surrounded by it. The relation between what we see and what we know is never settled. Each evening we *see* the sun set. We *know* that the earth is turning away from it. Yet the knowledge, the explanation, never quite fits the sight.

[. . .]

The way we see things is affected by what we know or what we believe. In the Middle Ages, when men believed in the physical existence of Hell, the sight of fire must have meant something different from what it means today. Nevertheless, their idea of Hell owed a lot to the sight of fire consuming and the ashes remaining—as well as to their experience of the pain of burns.

When in love, the sight of the beloved has a completeness which no words and no embrace can match: a completeness which only the act of making love can temporarily accommodate.

Yet this seeing which comes before words, and can never be quite covered by them, is not a question of mechanically reacting to stimuli. (It can be thought of in this way only if one isolates the small part of the process which concerns the eye's retina.) We see only

---

Key Terms

cultural mystification The concealing of historical truth by ideologies.

perspective A method used to represent a three-dimensional object on a flat surface, as in a painting. Used in European art since the sixteenth century, this method involves shortening receding objects in reference to one converging viewpoint.

Renaissance This term, which means "rebirth," refers to the period in Europe following the Middle Ages, which was characterized by an interest in the values and culture of "classical" Greece and Rome.

representation There are two common ways in which this term is used; 1) an image or likeness of a thing, and 2) in politics, when one person speaks on behalf of a group of constituents.

what we look at. To look is an act of choice. As a result of this act, what we see is brought within our reach—though not necessarily within arm's reach. To touch something is to situate oneself in relation to it. (Close your eyes, move round the room and notice how the faculty of touch is like a static, limited form of sight.) We never look at just one thing; we are always looking at the relation between things and ourselves. Our vision is continually active, continually moving, continually holding things in a circle around itself, constituting what is present to us as we are.

Soon after we can see, we are aware that we can also be seen. The eye of the other combines with our own eye to make it fully credible that we are part of the visible world.

If we accept that we can see that hill over there, we propose that from that hill we can be seen. The reciprocal nature of vision is more fundamental than that of spoken dialog. And often dialog is an attempt to verbalize this—an attempt to explain how, either metaphorically or literally, "you see things." and an attempt to discover how "he sees things."

In the sense in which we use the word in this book, all images are man-made.

An image is a sight which has been recreated or reproduced. It is an appearance, or a set of appearances, which has been detached from the place and time in which it first made its appearance and preserved—for a few moments or a few centuries. Every image embodies a way of seeing. Even a photograph. For photographs are not, as is often assumed, a mechanical record. Every time we look at a photograph, we are aware, however slightly, of the photographer selecting that sight from an infinity of possible sights. This is true even in the most casual family snapshot. The photographer's way of seeing is reflected in his choice of subject. The painter's way of seeing is reconstituted by the marks he makes on the canvas or paper. Yet, although every image embodies a way of seeing, our perception or appreciation of an image depends also upon our own way of seeing. (It may be, for example, that Sheila is one figure among 20; but for our own reasons she is the one we have eyes for.)

Images were first made to conjure up the appearance of something that was absent. Gradually it became evident that an image could outlast what it represented; it then showed how something or some-body had once looked—and thus by implication how the subject had once been seen by other people. Later still the specific vision of the image maker was also recognized as part of the record. An image became a record of how *X* had seen *Y*. This was the result of an increasing consciousness of individuality, accompanying an increasing awareness of history. It would be rash to try to date this last development precisely. But certainly in Europe such consciousness has existed since the beginning of the Renaissance.

No other kind of relic or text from the past can offer such a direct testimony about the world which surrounded other people at other times. In this respect, images are more precise and richer than literature. To say this is not to deny the expressive or imaginative quality of art, treating it as mere documentary evidence; the more imaginative the work, the more profoundly it allows us to share the artist's experience of the visible.

Yet when an image is presented as a work of art, the way people look at it is affected by a whole series of learned assumptions about art, assumptions concerning:

Beauty
Truth
Genius
Civilization
Form
Status
Taste, etc.

Many of these assumptions no longer accord with the world as it is. (The world-as-it-is is more than pure objective fact; it includes consciousness.) Out of true with the present, these assumptions obscure the past. They mystify rather than clarify. The past is never there waiting to be discovered, to be recognized for exactly what it is. History always constitutes the relation between a present and its past. Consequently, fear of the present leads to mystification of the past. The past is not for living in; it is a well of conclusions from which we draw in order to act. Cultural mystification of the past entails a double loss. Works of art are made unnecessarily remote. And the past offers us fewer conclusions to complete in action.

When we "see" a landscape, we situate ourselves in it. If we "saw" the art of the past, we would situate ourselves in history. When we are prevented from seeing it, we are being deprived of the history which belongs to us. Who benefits from this deprivation? In the end, the art of the past is being mystified because a privileged minority is striving to invent a history which can retrospectively justify the role of the ruling classes, and such a justification can no longer make sense in modern terms. And so, inevitably, it mystifies.

Today we see the art of the past as nobody saw it before. We actually perceive it in a different way.

This difference can be illustrated in terms of what was thought of as perspective. The convention of perspective, which is unique to European art and which was first established in the early Renaissance, centres everything on the eye of the beholder. It is like a beam from a lighthouse—only instead of light travelling outwards, appearances travel in. The conventions called those appearances *reality*. Perspective makes the single eye the centre of the visible world. Everything converges onto the eye as to the vanishing point of infinity. The visible world is arranged for the spectator as the universe was once thought to be arranged for God.

According to the convention of perspective, there is no visual reciprocity. There is no need for God to situate himself in relation to others: he is himself the situation. The inherent contradiction in perspective was that it structured all images of reality to address a single spectator who, unlike God, could be in only one place at a time

[. . .]

According to usage and conventions which are at last being questioned but have by no means been over-

come, the social presence of a woman is different in kind from that of a man. A man's presence is dependent upon the promise of power which he embodies. If the promise is large and credible, his presence is striking. If it is small or incredible, he is found to have little presence. The promised power may be moral, physical, temperamental, economic, social, sexual—but its object is always exterior to the man. A man's presence suggests what he is capable of doing to you or for you. His presence may be fabricated, in the sense that he pretends to be capable of what he is not. But the pretence is always toward a power which he exercises on others.

By contrast, a woman's presence expresses her own attitude to herself and defines what can and cannot be done to her. Her presence is manifest in her gestures, voice, opinions, expressions, clothes, chosen surroundings, taste—indeed there is nothing she can do which does not contribute to her presence. Presence for a woman is so intrinsic to her person that men tend to think of it as an almost physical emanation, a kind of heat or smell or aura.

To be born a woman has been to be born, within an allotted and confined space, into the keeping of men. The social presence of women has developed as a result of their ingenuity in living under such tutelage within such a limited space. But this has been at the cost of a woman's self being split into two. A woman must continually watch herself. She is almost continually accompanied by her own image of herself. While she is walking across a room or while she is weeping at the death of her father, she can scarcely avoid envisaging herself walking or weeping. From earliest childhood she has been taught and persuaded to survey herself continually.

And so she comes to consider the *surveyor* and the *surveyed* within her as the two constituent yet always distinct elements of her identity as a woman.

She has to survey everything she is and everything she does because how she appears to others, and ultimately how she appears to men, is of crucial importance for what is normally thought of as the success of her life. Her own sense of being in herself is supplanted by a sense of being appreciated as herself by *another*.

Men survey women before treating them. Consequently, how a woman appears to a man can determine how she will be treated. To acquire some control over this process, women must contain it and interiorize it.

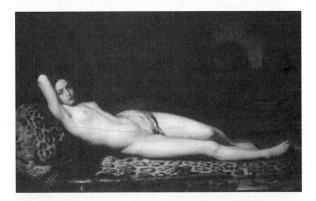

FIGURE III.1   *RECLINING BACCHANTE BY TRUTAT*

FIGURE III.2 *THE VENUS OF URBINO* BY TITIAN (C. 1487–1576)

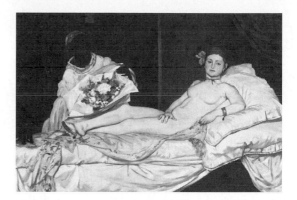

FIGURE III.3 *OLYMPIA* BY MANET (1832–83)

That part of a woman's self which is the surveyor treats the part which is the surveyed so as to demonstrate to others how her whole self would like to be treated. And this exemplary treatment of herself by herself constitutes her presence. Every woman's presence regulates what is and is not "permissible" within her presence. Every one of her actions—whatever its direct purpose or motivation—is also read as an indication of how she would like to be treated. If a woman throws a glass on the floor, this is an example of how she treats her own emotion of anger and so of how she would wish it to be treated by others. If a man does the same, his action is read only as an expression of his anger. If a woman makes a good joke, this is an example of how she treats the joker in herself and accordingly of how she as a joker-woman would like to be treated by others. Only a man can make a good joke for its own sake.

One might simplify this by saying: *men act* and *women appear*. Men look at women. Women watch themselves being looked at. This determines not only most relations between men and women but also the relation of women to themselves. The surveyor of woman in herself is male, the surveyed female. Thus she turns herself into an object—and most particularly an object of vision: a sight.

[. . .]

In the art form of the European nude, the painters and spectator-owners were usually men and the persons treated as objects usually women. This unequal relationship is so deeply embedded in our culture that it still structures the consciousness of many women.

They do to themselves what men do to them. They survey, like men, their own femininity.

In modern art the category of the nude has become less important. Artists themselves began to question it. In this, as in many other respects, Manet represented a turning point. If one compares his *Olympia* with Titian's original, one sees a woman, cast in the traditional role, beginning to question that role, somewhat defiantly.

The ideal was broken. But there was little to replace it except the "realism" of the prostitute—who became the quintessential woman of early avant-garde twentieth-century painting (Toulouse-Lautrec, Picasso, Rouault, German Expressionism, etc.). In academic painting the tradition continued.

Today the attitudes and values which informed that tradition are expressed through other, more widely diffused media—advertising, journalism, television.

But the essential way of seeing women, the essential use to which their images are put, has not changed. Women are depicted in a quite different way from men—not because the feminine is different from the masculine, but because the "ideal" spectator is always assumed to be male and the image of the woman is designed to flatter him. If you have any doubt that this is so, make the following experiment. Choose from this book an image of a traditional nude. Transform the woman into a man, either in your mind's eye or by drawing on the reproduction. Then notice the violence which that transformation does. Not to the image, but to the assumptions of a likely viewer.

Making Things Mean: Cultural Representation in Objects

CATHERINE KING

Feminist art critic Catherine King explores the ways in which gendered meaning is conveyed through representation. King argues that a broad definition of art is needed to view the participation and points of view of women. This approach calls for a revaluation of women's activities and ways of seeing.

Cultural representation states notions of gender difference in a variety of ways. Although the most obvious kinds of representation entail words and visual images, I want to begin by drawing attention to other powerful ways in which ideas of the feminine are transmitted. For gender is expressed in the rules about who is allowed to make all the things that surround us daily, about the values assigned to women's making, and the way women are supposed to respond to artifacts. Just as the gendering of everyday speech relates to representations of the feminine in literary terms, so the gendering of everyday objects and arts underpins the representation of femininity in the "Fine Arts." To consider the positions women have been pushed into, and how they might be able to refuse them, it is important to define

Catherine King, "Making Things Mean: Cultural Representation in Objects," in *Imagining Women: Cultural Representations and Gender,* Frances Bonner et al. eds. London: Polity Press, 1992: 15–20.

art in very broad terms, and to stress the potential openness of art's boundaries and partitions.

Art-making is the skilled production of more or less lasting objects and visual images. The emphasis is strong on the physically tangible, and on sight (as well as scent and flavour). The skills of painting and sculpture, as well as cookery, ceramics, weaving of all diversities, metalwork and woodcarving, can be considered arts. We can include the dressing, adornment, and shaping of the human body since we use these things to state ourselves. If we include our bodies, we can surely include the forming of the landscape, or gardening. These kinds of making continue into and are part of what we call technology, which is appropriate, since *techné* is Greek for skill or *art*. Definitions shift as skilled makers invent new arts. For instance, women have been interested in using the powers of performance art entailing actors, props, and costumes. This is a little like drama, but it stresses the visual and physical more than words, because it has been made by artists. Yet we could imagine it shifting *more* toward drama. The American artist Jenny Holzer has made art which consists of sentences engraved on large slabs of stone. (One reads, "Men don't protect you any more.") This could be "literature," except that the epigraph is physically monumental, and the heavy stone validates the words in a way in which a page or voice could not do. Again,

---

Key Term

binary Two opposite terms in which one may be subordinated to the other; for example, the binaries of male/female, modern/tradition, mind/body.

women have used video to good effect, and, rightly, this suggests the links with the media of film and television.

These boundaries are fluid and there are continual contests for hierarchies of value within this group. Women are seeking free movement through such categories, the revaluation of our making of things, and the treatment of all these skills as equal. We can point to such masculine-led shifts in the past as valuable precedents for how flexible these systems are. I refer to three important regroupings of the arts: first, when specialists in the making of figurative images (painters and sculptors) were, in the sixteenth century, prised away from decorative arts like embroidery or utilitarian arts (such as armourers) to create the category of "Fine Arts," along with architecture; and second, the slightly later groupings of arts linked with mechanized manufacture to create technology, as distinct from "craft" and "art," third, most recently, "Design" has been created to form a category allowing Fine Art skills to "style" both manufactured and crafts goods to be commodified more successfully (thus joining "technology," "craft," and "Fine Art" for commercial gain).

One of the key ways in which gender is represented culturally is through the segregation to women of certain kinds of art-making which are seen as both feminine and inferior. Lace making is done by women and considered to represent the delicacy and decorativeness of the feminine. This can be contrasted with net making, which entails the same skills but is exclusively masculine and signifies the adventure of men, killing for food, beyond the home. Often a skill is gendered only in so far as, if it is done in the home, it is a feminine craft, while if it is paid employment outside the home, it is an art for men (this applies to knitting, dressmaking and cookery, for example). Or if women work alongside men, in paid employment outside the home, as the Birmingham chainmakers did, an "important" gender difference must be created here, in that women make slightly smaller and lighter chains (Bailey 1990: 75–78). In the so-called Fine Arts, women are more likely to paint than sculpt (because of the "unfeminine" heaviness of the material for sculpture) and if they design buildings they will be steered into house, school, or hospital work. Within such categories, women must be placed at the least valued end of the ladder: in craft, not painting; or once in painting, they

must paint less prestigious kinds of subjects, like the flower pieces and portraits, or landscapes, made by women in the nineteenth century, rather than producing the highest allegorical and narrative art. Again, women are likely to dabble in all these arts, as accomplishments, while a man will follow an important career in his profession as painter, sculptor, filmmaker, photographer, or architect.

Most obviously, male control over the representation of gender difference in producing things, and the notion of female inferiority, is effected through the powers of unions and masters in the workplace, such that, for example, women are employed in certain categories, like the surface decoration of pottery, but not the throwing or casting of pots (*so* heavy and messy). In this way, women can be represented to others as decorative, and these meanings can be re-presented to the next generation.

Representation of gender difference is also effected through male control over human reproduction, such that women are represented as the main carers of the family of "man" and are made dependents of men. Women are associated with making things in the home and are supposed to gain satisfaction from making things "freely" and without professional training. Men have the power to make women's effortful and painful birth of children characteristic of a delicate and decorative femininity and the power to make our making of things in the home private, amateur, and secondary to paid work done outside the home. The so-called discourses of the home, of paid work and of human reproduction (that is, ways of valuing and defining the activities included in the scope of, say, "home"), are all linked to similar "discourses" in law, medicine, education, leisure, and entertainment, to announce that women's making of things is less important than and different from men's. In this way, masculine control of institutions, from the family to the state (which is visible, and somewhat vulnerable to being re-formed), is based on vast ideological foundations that seem much more difficult to move.

Important also is the masculine control of the forms of knowledge and values which link notions of gender difference, and the supposed relative weakness of women, to a cluster of binary concepts used to "make sense of" the world. Such couples as: public versus private; nature versus culture; body versus mind; reason versus emotion, have formed dualities in which women always take the characteristics of the subordinate, dependent "partner," which is made to appear opposite. This characterizing of women as body, emotion, nature, and private has been used to place women's art-making in connection with the home, the family, and our supposedly caring duties. This dualistic thinking has also extended into binaries used in the evaluation of art (such as decorative or functional; ornamental or structural; original or imitative; form or colour, and so on), which can be added to the basic dichotomies to create evaluations of women making things regarded as emotional, sensuous, colourful, ornamental, derivative and decorative.

Western masculine investment in this system of ideas is intense, but it can be shown that its rigidity ignores the way the "dichotomies" can be thought of as equal partners (as in "body *and* mind," or "public *and* private") and that other characteristics can be placed usefully with them, like "reason *and* emotion *and* imagination" (perhaps to describe a visual image), or "functional *and* decorative *and* structural" (perhaps to describe a building). The either/or system, which underpins the categorization of women and men as opposites, could be demolished to create a structure which would be subtly discriminating about our world and allow diverse distinctions of people. The binary system can be seen to achieve self-definition for the man at the expense of the negative concept "opposed" to his apparent primary quality (of public importance and capacities, of reason, culture, and the powers of the mind). Similar categorizations have been shown to operate to create the fictions of racial differences. In both cases, there is a privileged position, apparently independent of, but actually secured by, the subordinate position of the "other."

REFERENCE

Bailey, C. (1990). "Black Country Working Women," *Oral History* (The Crafts), no. 18, 75–78.

Reading C

Feminist Art Practices
ROZSIKA PARKER

Feminist art critic Rozsika Parker reviews three art exhibits that took place in 1980 in London. Her review highlights the history of women's activism around their inclusion and participation in the art world. Explaining that feminist artists do not merely provide positive images of women as a response to patriarchal ways of seeing, Parker tells us that they also use diverse approaches and mediums to show how representations of women are produced in contemporary culture.

In 1974 no public gallery in London would accept an exhibition of 26 women conceptual artists. In 1980 the ICA housed three major feminist exhibitions, a women's film season, a series of panel discussions, and a weekend conference, "Questions on Women's Art," involving artists from all these shows as well as those

Rozsika Parker, "Feminist Art Practices in 'Women's Images of Men,' 'About Time,' and 'Issue,' " *Art Monthly* 43 (1981): 16–19.

from the related venture "Eight Artists: Women: 1980" at the Acme Gallery.

Why the shift? It cannot be viewed as a token gesture, a way of accommodating feminist demands before the door is closed behind us again. A complex set of factors determined the events at the ICA. At one level they signified the great change of consciousness brought about by the women's liberation movement since the early 1970s. For example, though public critical response to the shows continued to negate and contain feminist art practices, no one outrightly dismissed the shows.

But most importantly, the shows were the result of diverse strategies by feminist artists. Since 1974 they have continued to campaign for equal access to art-world structures, while simultaneously organising alternative exhibition spaces and producing small magazines. And women working within the system—in art schools, galleries, universities, art centres, and regional arts associations—have purposefully supported

---

Key Terms

experience Knowledge derived from daily life through personal observation. The emphasis on experience adopted by many feminists in the 1970s and 1980s critiqued knowledge produced by male institutions.

figurative art The use of a likeness or image of something (especially the human body) rather than an abstract idea in art and painting.

ICA Institute of Contemporary Art, in London, United Kingdom.

performance art Experimental and theatrical performance and spectacle that by its ephemeral nature goes against the idea of works of art as permanent and timeless objects. This kind of art originated in the Futurist movement of the early twentieth century.

women's liberation movement A term used in European and North American contexts to refer to the 1970s version of the feminist movement; part of the second wave.

women's endeavours, while independent networks of women artists' groups have developed throughout the country. Panel discussions, feminist conferences, and workshops have repeatedly addressed the issue, 'What is feminist art?'

The answer produced by the ICA shows was, "It doesn't exist." Instead we were presented with a multiplicity of feminist art practices, deliberately intervening in the main currents and institutions of contemporary art practice—or equally deliberately raising questions about them. The achievement of feminists over the last decade has been not only to break the silence on women's specific experience, but to question the basic assumptions about art and the artist that have worked to establish the dominance of white, male, middle-class art. I want to look at some of the strategies that emerged at the ICA shows and identify a few of the approaches developed so far, their problems and potential.

"Women's Images of Men" was primarily concerned with transformation at the level of content. The organisers advertised widely for work, asking "Women, how do you see men?" From the submissions they selected a show of narrative painting, sculpture, drawing, and photography. Figurative work, they believed, would be above all accessible: "To reach beyond, but including, the women's movement and the usual visitors to galleries" was one of their major aims.

The show aspired to make visible the invisible; to confront women's oppression by revealing hitherto repressed or censored aspects of our lives.

It demoted men from standing unproblematically for mankind; presented through women's eyes, men can no longer be Man. The women returned the gaze that is usually turned upon them and refused to be objectified. It was a subversive act. In Lisa Tickner's words, "How threatening, how disruptive, to return the scrutiny; to attempt at least to stay author of one's own look; coolly to appraise the male not just in himself, but as bearer, rather than maker, of significance."

The makers of significance hurriedly marshalled their forces and made out the show to be simply women making spectacles of themselves. The organisers deliberately sought publicity in order to draw a wide audience. Therefore, it is important to examine

critical response to the show; moreover, the genuine lack of understanding and/or profound anxiety with which the show was received is in itself illuminating.

Work providing a far-ranging appraisal of women's experience of a patriarchal society was viewed entirely mistakenly as a querulous demand for role reversal. This was partly due to the fact that since the nineteenth century the figurative tradition has been dominated by the female nude. Visitors may thus have expected to find ranks of naked men. The few penises on show multiplied in anxious minds—and debate descended to the level of a numbers game.

Although misread and misrecognised as a demand for role reversal—something all feminists entirely reject—the show was provocative and popular. Indeed, it broke all previous attendance records at the ICA. And many women, including me, found that the work provided absorbing evidence of patterns in the way women have seen men.

The reception of the exhibition indicates why some feminists consider that introducing a novel content is in itself insufficient. For example, somewhat bitter experiences have shown feminists that so-called positive images of women, though an important means of consciousness raising among women, have not been able to radically challenge the narrow meanings and connotations of "woman" in art. Because meanings depend on how the art is seen, from what ideological position it is received, the most decisively feminist image of a woman can be recuperated as body, as nature, as object for male possession. Therefore, some feminist artists turned to radical art practices other than the traditional fine arts of paintings, sculpture, and photography. Some are exploring performance art and video to investigate novel ways of presenting women's experience. They are not attempting the impossible—the creation of a new language untouched by existing expectations—but rather to show how representations of women are reproduced in our culture.

"To unlock the power of imagery, to decode its mystery, to make the impossibly evocative also a moment of dissection and comprehension." That is the aim of feminist performance art, wrote Sally Potter in the catalog for "About Time: Video, Performance and Installation by 21 Women Artists."

The selectors requested work which "indicated the artist's awareness of a woman's particular experience within patriarchy." So this too was a theme show, but less tightly defined, and interesting because of its stress on particular media. New media are not essential for feminist art practice, but they do offer possibilities for working directly with the artist–audience relationship and exposing multiple, complex, overlapping meanings within the same piece—useful for feminists determined to challenge the certainties of our society.

Most work went beyond presenting women's experience within patriarchy to show how that experience is constructed; through the mass media, the family, education, advertising, consumerism, fashion, domestic labour, and styles of art. Within installations, mixed media were juxtaposed to powerful effect. The artist's intention or personal experience was conveyed on tape, in a text, or in person and juxtaposed to photographs, slides, objects, drawings, or video—which interacted with her words, sometimes revealing the power of media to transform meanings, or indicating contradictions and conflicts between a woman's subjective experience and the cultural expectations and definitions within which she works.

It is dangerous, though, to generalise about the diverse work contained in "About Time" and even more dubious to attempt to sum up the different approaches contained within the performances. Feminist performance today is, I think, determined by two developments within the recent history of feminism. First, a growing understanding of the role of audiences in producing meanings makes performance art appealing in that it can allow an artist to engage directly with her audience; second, feminists have always placed importance on collective work. Initially feminist performances invariably involved several performance artists—a device for questioning the notion of artist as isolated, purely self-expressive, exceptional being. Today, however, the emphasis is more on collaboration between individual artists and audience, not in the sense of direct audience participation, but in that audiences are rarely allowed to simply "appreciate" the work. Offered elliptical fragments of sounds and images, we had to draw out connections and form meanings, within a framework nevertheless carefully

determined by the artist, calculated to raise issues about women in a partriachal society.

One of the problems facing feminist performance artists is the tradition of female performers as spectacle for an audience. How, asked Sally Potter in the catalog, can women avoid appearing simply as objects on display, positioned always in relation to male desire: "Women performance artists who use their own bodies as the instrument of their work constantly hover on the knife edge of the possibility of joining the spectacle of women." A variety of methods were employed to focus the audiences' attention from the artist as object to the subject of her work. The artist herself was distanced though video, lighting and recorded voice. She rarely, if ever, engaged directly with the audience; she worked with her back to the audience, sometimes altogether "off stage," leaving the audience with a curious assemblage of objects—the traces of her presence.

The drawback to all performance art—the number of people who can manage to see the work—is particularly acute for women who are fighting institutional discrimination. Installations relating to the performances were on show in the gallery, but the problem was exacerbated by the brevity of the exhibition. It lasted only 10 days and there was a different performance every evening.

The next show, "Issue," unlike the others (which were selected by participants), was put together by the American critic Lucy Lippard. The exhibition was conceived of from an overtly political perspective. It demonstrates "the contributions of feminist art to the full panorama of socialchange art."

All of the artists in 'Issue' challenged the idea that art is ever simply a visual experience. They raised questions about how art can be used to produce knowledge of structures of power. The practices and media they employed were those most appropriate to each artist's objectives and her intended audience. There was no pure painting, sculpture, or photography.

Lucy Lippard described the feminist art in "Issue" as "moving out into the world, placing so-called women's issues in a broader perspective and/or utilizing mass production techniques to convey its messages about global traumas such as racism, imperialism, nuclear war, starvation, and inflation to a broader audience."

The issues examined in "Issue" were shown not simply to be either the result of capitalism or of patriarchy but of their intersection. After an exhibition like "Issue," overtly political art which excludes a critique of partriarchy will, I think, appear incomplete.

[. . .]

The varied approaches in the exhibitions, underlines the point I made initially—there is no feminist art, but a multiplicity of practices, ever developing, and undoubtedly pushed forward by the events at the ICA.

WOMEN AND ART HISTORY

GRISELDA POLLOCK

We started from the premise that women had always been involved in the production of art, but that our culture would not admit it. The question to be answered is: *Why is this so?* Why has it been necessary for art history to create an image of the history of past art as an exclusive record of masculine achievement? We discovered that it was only in the twentieth century, with the establishment of art history as an institutionalized academic discipline, that most art history systematically obliterated women artists from the record. While most books do not refer at all to women artists, those that do make reference do it only in order to remind us how inferior and insignificant women artists actually are. Our conclusion was therefore unexpected. Although women artists are treated by modern art history negatively—that is, ignored, omitted, or when mentioned at all, derogated—women artists and the art they produced nonetheless play a structural role in the discourse of art history. In fact, to discover the history of women and art at all means accounting for the way art history is written. To expose its underlying assumptions, its prejudices and silences, is to reveal that the negative way in which women artists are recorded and dismissed is nevertheless crucial to the concepts of art and artists created by art history. The initial task of feminist art history is therefore a critique of art history itself.

Griselda Pollock, *Vision and Difference: Femininity, Feminism, and the History of Art,* New York: Routledge, 1988: 23–24.

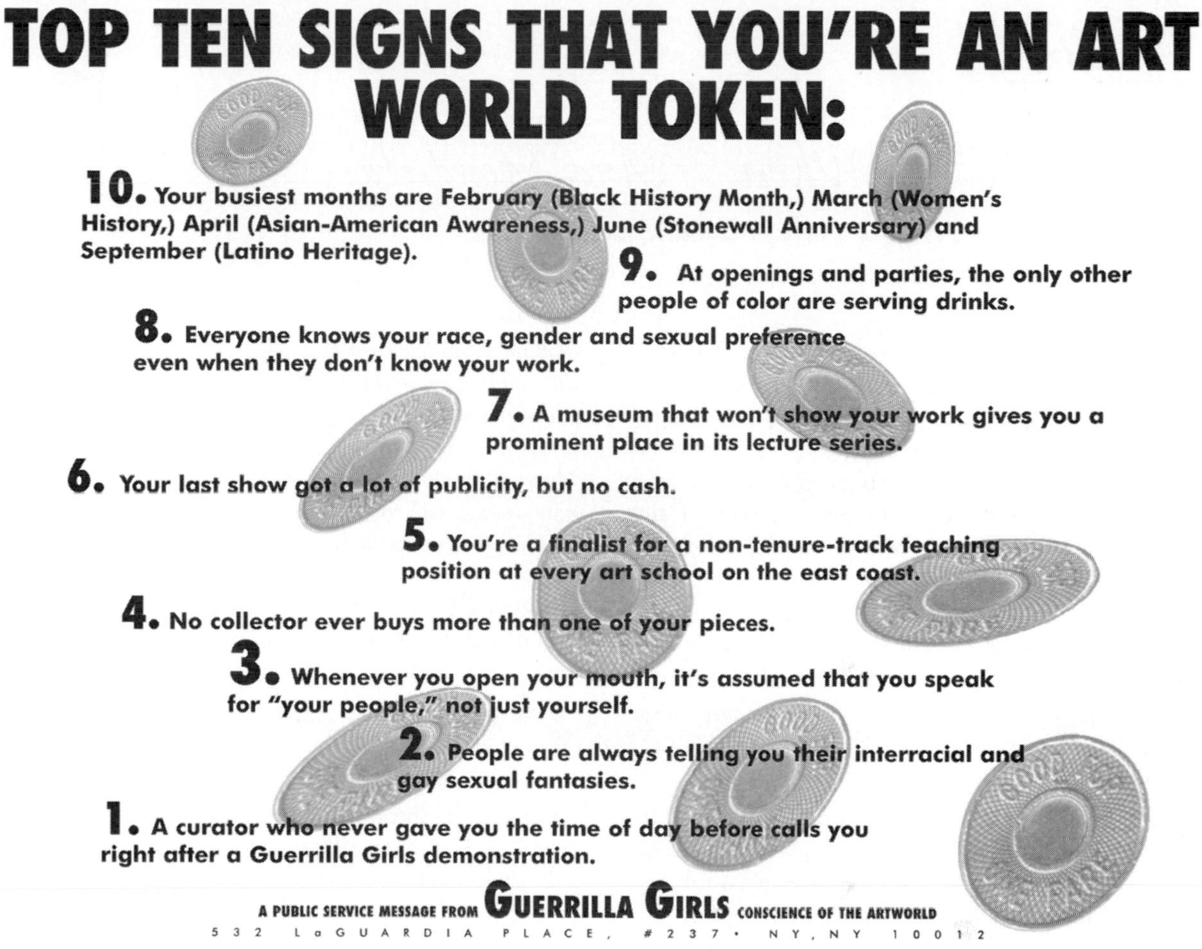

TOP TEN SIGNS THAT YOU'RE AN ART WORLD TOKEN:

10. Your busiest months are February (Black History Month,) March (Women's History,) April (Asian-American Awareness,) June (Stonewall Anniversary) and September (Latino Heritage).

9. At openings and parties, the only other people of color are serving drinks.

8. Everyone knows your race, gender and sexual preference even when they don't know your work.

7. A museum that won't show your work gives you a prominent place in its lecture series.

6. Your last show got a lot of publicity, but no cash.

5. You're a finalist for a non-tenure-track teaching position at every art school on the east coast.

4. No collector ever buys more than one of your pieces.

3. Whenever you open your mouth, it's assumed that you speak for "your people," not just yourself.

2. People are always telling you their interracial and gay sexual fantasies.

1. A curator who never gave you the time of day before calls you right after a Guerrilla Girls demonstration.

A PUBLIC SERVICE MESSAGE FROM **GUERRILLA GIRLS** CONSCIENCE OF THE ARTWORLD
532 LaGUARDIA PLACE, #237 · NY,NY 10012

FIGURE III.4 TOP TEN SIGNS. "THINGS ARE IMPROVING A LITTLE FOR WOMEN AND ARTISTS OF COLOR. JUST A LITTLE. THIS POSTER WAS CREATED TO HELP US HANDLE OUR NEW ROLE." GUERRILLA GIRLS 1995

Where Is Ana Mendieta?

JANE BLOCKER

Art historian Jane Blocker poses an important question for feminists about the absence of women in art history through her study of the late artist Ana Mendieta. Mendieta was a Cuban-born artist who worked in numerous media, always investigating the relationship between female bodies and natural elements. Using materials such as earth, sand, water, and wood, as well as bones and her own body, Mendieta's work suggests the changing nature of identities and meaning. Blocker's study focuses in part on the obstacles and limits faced by women artists even as the examples of Mendieta's work demonstrate the profound effect of new social movements based on gender and racial identity on the world of art.

Jane Blocker, *Where Is Ana Mendieta? Identity, Performativity, Exile,* Durham, NC: Duke University Press, 1999: 1–4.

In June 1992, on the day the new Guggenheim Museum in SoHo opened its inaugural exhibition, 500 protesters

---

Key Terms

marked/unmarked A designation for subjects or objects; "unmarked" categories (to which Mendieta belongs) are often the targets of discrimination or are placed outside the boundaries of the norm, while "marked" categories (within which Andre can be placed) are assumed to be generic, general, and universal.

minimalism Art movement that began in the late 1950s and remained influential through the 1970s. Minimalism required the most simple design, often used repetition, and left very little "sign" of artistry.

postmodern A cultural movement, first identified in art, architecture, and music in the late 1960s and later in the humanities and social sciences, that questions the focus on progress and originality. In the arts, this movement led to a rejection of the idea of newness and individual genius in favor of inquiring into methods and styles of the past. In the humanities and social sciences, postmodern approaches led to questioning the dominant narratives produced in the West and to decentering the powerful centers of knowledge and culture.

poststructuralism A school of thought that emerged in the 1970s as a response to the universal systems proposed by an earlier movement, structuralism. Structuralism's universalizing classifications of human society and culture influenced the modern disciplines of sociology, anthropology, and other social sciences, as well as studies of poetics and other humanities approaches. The proponents of poststructuralism argued that there is no one structural system that can apply universally in every place and time and that the very effort to explain everything in the terms of one dominant point of view can lead to the suppression or invisibility of important differences. Both structuralism and poststructuralism have been the subject of debates in women's studies, especially in terms of essentialist versus socially constructed approaches.

gathered in front of the museum, a small group among them holding a banner that said, "Carl Andre is in the Guggenheim. Where is Ana Mendieta? ¿Donde está Ana Mendieta?".[1] In addition to this gathering outside the museum, some protesters managed to get into its invitation-only gala and drop copies of a photograph of Mendieta's face onto Andre's floor sculptures. Some of the demonstrators wore T-shirts with this photograph printed on the back.[2] The demonstration was organized primarily by the Women's Action Coalition because the museum's exhibition featured only one female artist with four white male artists and because Carl Andre, Ana Mendieta's accused killer, was among them.[3]

Ana Mendieta was born in Havana in 1948, was forced into exile in the United States in 1961, married minimalist sculptor Carl Andre in 1985, and died tragically later that year. Andre's defense attorneys claimed that she fell or jumped from his 34th-story apartment in Manhattan; the prosecution said that he pushed her. Although he was acquitted of her murder in February 1988, there were many who still believed at the time of this protest that he was guilty.[4] The protest staged in front of the Guggenheim was a response to a variety of injustices: not just the exclusion of women from an art museum, but their persistent absence from a wide range of domains of power; not just the marginalization of people of color, symbolized by Ana Mendieta, but the seeming institutional sanction of a judicial verdict that pronounced Andre innocent of having killed her.

The question on the banner held up by the protesters—"Where is Ana Mendieta?"—is rhetorical; that is, it asks for but does not really want an answer. The one literal answer—that she is dead and her ashes buried in Cedar Rapids, Iowa—is painfully dissatisfying. By asking where she is, the demonstrators are really asking where she is not. Location and dis-location are laminated, mutually sustaining, sometimes indistinguishable sources of power. Thus, the strength of the question lies in the fact that it makes palpable, indeed, demands a space for, Mendieta's incoherence and illegibility within the terms of the exhibition. It performatively reproduces her absence and makes her an elusive and powerful figure. No one asks, "Where is Carl Andre?" because it is presumed that we know all too well. Andre is in the Guggenheim, which is to say that he is securely established in gender, racial, aesthetic, and institutional

traditions. His identity is reduced to a simple tautology that makes him nakedly legible, lays bare his privilege. He is (to use Peggy Phelan's twist on Simone de Beauvoir) "marked," while Mendieta remains "unmarked."[5]

The powerful indeterminacy of this question makes it interesting to me. In asking it, one simultaneously demands and forecloses an answer. Therefore, by asking the question, the protesters have neatly summarized the central paradox of writing about this artist. With it, they effectively articulate the common perception that, despite nearly 25 years of critical success and worldwide exposure, Mendieta is missing. The catalog edited by Gloria Moure that accompanied Mendieta's recent one-woman exhibition in Spain gives voice to the pervasive (if problematic) desire to find her. It makes the strong claim that the exhibition "*rescues from oblivion* a body of work that deserves the recognition of public and critics alike."[6]

To what degree can Mendieta, about whom scores of reviews, articles, and catalogs have been written, whose work has been shown in over 100 exhibitions around the world, be in need of such rescue? To what degree is she in peril of being forgotten?

The answer is complex. Certainly, the monstrous way in which she died and the sense of raw injustice that persists as a result of it suggest that no amount of celebrity, exposure, critical acclaim, or financial success is enough. Remembrance is a process, not a task to be completed; it is carried out through constant repetition and renewal. To be satisfied that Mendieta has been sufficiently memorialized is to admit, finally, that she is gone. "Where?" serves as a living reminder rather than a stone marker for that loss.

It is not simply out of mourning, however, that the sense of Mendieta's dis-location persists. The SoHo protest made it clear that she is tied up with a great many things whose regular disappearance from the art world is mystifying, shocking, and enervating. It was very difficult to believe that, in 1992, after 20 years of feminist art, after the advent of poststructural critiques of power, after the pluralization of media and the politicization of message, the Guggenheim could so unapologetically set forth its myopic vision of modern art. It was thus hardly surprising when five years later, in January 1997, *Artnews* published a list of "the 50 most powerful people in the art world," which included

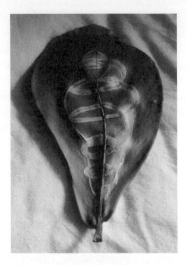

FIGURE III.5   ANA MENDIETA, UNTITLED, 1982–84. DRAWING ON LEAF, 6 INCHES. COURTESY OF THE ESTATE OF ANA MENDIETA AND GALERIE LELONG, NEW YORK.

only six women and one nonwhite man.[7] The politics of backlash remind feminists that gender equality is neither simple nor final. The successful visibility of

any female artist in this context must be met with skeptical questions: For whose benefit is this success, and for how long? In an era of such political insecurity, "Where?" can be a powerful weapon against a world map, hastily redrawn in light of new postmodern "discoveries," in which *feminism* and *multiculturalism* are officially approved tourist attractions.

Ana Mendieta's short life, aesthetic choices, gender, ethnicity, and politics have contributed to her absence from a variety of discursive sites. I am drawn to the question "Where is Ana Mendieta?" not only because it interrogates her absence, but also because it reveals the willful refusal to appear as an act of transgression. Mendieta has been a victim of normative mapping that, by gerrymandering or simple elimination, has made her unrepresentable. As a consequence, however, she has also escaped to some degree the limitations of these territorial disputes. The question is thus useful because it points to Mendieta as a subject produced discursively by questions of location. By asking "Where?" and being unable definitively to provide an answer, this question places Mendieta in motion, thwarting the logic of fixed categories, yet making space for alternative identifications.

NOTES

1. This protest was organized by the Women's Action Coalition (WAC), a women's group formed in 1991 after the Anita Hill hearings in Washington. At the time of this demonstration, the group numbered about 1,500 nationally and consisted largely of white women. A faction within that group was actually responsible for that part of the protest that included the banner, T-shirts, and photocopies. This group included Raquel Mendieta, Josely Carvalho, Juan Sanchez, Mañuel Pardo, Joey Silverman, and Lucy Lippard, among others. According to Raquel Mendieta, the specific invocation of Ana Mendieta and Carl Andre by her group was not sanctioned by the larger organization because it feared alienating art-world leaders loyal to or associated with Andre. For information on WAC, see Catherine S. Manegold, "No More Nice Girls," *New York Times,* 12 July 1992, pp. 25, 31. For information on the protest, see Elizabeth Hess, "Born Again," *Village Voice,* 7 July 1992, p. 38.

2. Hess, "Born Again," p. 38.

3. For a detailed account of the circumstances of Mendieta's death and the subsequent trial of Carl Andre, see Robert Katz, *Naked by the Window: The Fatal Marriage of Carl Andre and Ana Mendieta* (New York: Atlantic Monthly Press, 1990).

4. The suspicions were reignited during the trial of O. J. Simpson, who was similarly accused and later acquitted of murdering his wife. Witness the 1995 Guerrilla Girls poster featuring pictures of both men and the caption "What do these men have in common?"

5. See Peggy Phelan, *Unmarked: The Politics of Performance* (New York: Routledge, 1993).

6. Gloria Moure, ed., *Ana Mendieta* (Barcelona: Fundació Antoni Tàpies; Santiago de Compostela: Centro Galego de Arte Contemporánea, 1997), frontispiece (emphasis added).

7. Ann Landi, "The Fifty Most Powerful People in the Art World," *Artnews,* January 1997, pp. 90–97.

REFLECTING ON THE SECTION

John Berger tells us that the way we see things is strongly determined by what we know or believe. The selections in this section pose the question, then, in what way art can be seen to be gendered? Or rather, are there gendered ways of seeing? If John Berger and Rozsika Parker believe that meanings depend on how art is viewed and received, Catherine King and the Guerrilla Girls, an activist group of performance artists, argue that the making of art is heavily influenced by legacies of social and political struggles. As Jane Blocker points out, women artists remain excluded from the canon of genius and achievement.

The authors in this section each strive to change our perception of art's production, consumption, and reception: What changes are they advocating? Parker suggests that "art can be used to produce knowledge of structures of power." What does she mean by this? Do you agree? If so, how does art do this? Consider the images presented in this section and other art that you have encountered.

Artistic Production and Reception

Prologue
JUDITH FRYER DAVIDOV

The media technologies developed from the nineteenth century to the present have led to new modes of representation of gender. Each kind of technology has its own history and its own way of conveying information and ideas. For example, Judith Fryer Davidov discusses the history of photography and the ideological use of photographs in specific time periods. Writing about one famous photograph taken in 1936 in the middle of the Great Depression in the United States, Davidov traces the ways the photo takes on different meanings depending on the contexts in which it is shown.

All stories are discontinuous and are based on a tacit agreement about what is not said, about what connects the discontinuities. . . . The discontinuities of the story and the tacit agreement underlying them fuse teller, listener, and protagonists into an amal-

Judith Fryer Davidov, *Women's Camera Work: Self/Body/ Other in American Visual Culture* Durham, NC: Duke University Press, 1998: 3–6.

gam. An amalgam which I would call the story's reflecting subject. . . . If this sounds unnecessarily complicated, it is worth remembering for a moment the childhood experience of being told a story. . . . You were listening. You were in the story. You were in the words of the storyteller. You were no longer your single self; you were, thanks to the story, everyone it concerned.

John Berger, Another Way of Telling[1]

Reading photographs—visual records of time past—is a way of constructing versions of history. Interpretation includes assigning categories of meaning ("art," "document") to images, ordering them into sequences of other pictures and words, and from these pieces creating a narrative—which might be based upon chronology (a linear mode of perception) or differently grounded in circularity, indirection, and play, as memory and imagination, ideology and cultural context direct. Narrative patterns are potentially as multiple and as changeable as readers of images.[2]

Key Terms

Black Panthers Founded in 1966 by Bobby Seale and Huey Newton in Oakland, California, the Black Panther party became one of the primary arms of the Black Power movement, the new social movement that advocated a nationalist agenda for African Americans.

Farm Security Administration A program in the U.S. Department of Agriculture formed in 1937 out of the Resettlement Administration, which granted

low-cost loans and other forms of assistance for poor farmers and sharecroppers hardest hit by the Great Depression that began in 1929. The administration hired photographers, sociologists, and historians to record the government efforts to alleviate poverty. It also continued to address rural poverty and initiated projects to develop and improve farmland and farming.

Photographs invite an especially broad range of responses because of their widespread accessibility and use, from art museum to billboard, from police report to family snapshot album. A good example of the way in which responses to images alter over time and of the varied cultural work that photographs do is Dorothea Lange's well-known *Migrant Mother* (Figure III.6). When Lange took this picture in 1936 in a Nipomo, California, migrant workers' camp, she was on assignment for the Resettlement Administration (later the Farm Security Administration), hired to "document" the living conditions of homeless families pouring into California in a futile search for work. Roy Stryker, head of the RA's Historical Section, would later call this one, of the set of photographs Lange made that day, "the ultimate, . . . *the* picture of Farm Security."[3] But it was two other pictures in the series that generated immediate and dramatic results. Within days after the photos were made, the *San Francisco News* carried these two images in a story that reported the heroic role of the photographer—"Ragged, ill, emaciated by hunger, 2,500 men, women, and children are rescued after weeks of suffering by the chance visit of a government photographer to a pea-pickers' camp in San Luis Obispo County"—and the news that the federal government was rushing 20,000 pounds of food to feed the hungry migrants.[4] In September 1936, *Survey Graphic* (the journal that had published so many of Lewis Hine's child labor photographs) reprinted the soon-to-be-famous image along with other Lange photos and a report by sociologist Paul Taylor on the work of the RA. In the same year, *U.S. Camera* invited Lange to include *Migrant Mother* in its show of outstanding photographs. Recognizing the importance of this new context, she demanded both control over the printmaking and that the print be signed.[5] Its first gallery showing, at the Museum of Modern Art (MoMA) in the new photography department's first exhibit, firmly stamped *Migrant Mother* as art. In 1962 art critic George Elliott, in attempting to account for the response to this work, would call it an "anti-Madonna and Child" and attribute its power to "the viewer's . . . understanding [of] the profounder, the humanly universal, results of . . . poverty"; by 1966, in his introductory essay for the catalog of the Lange Retrospective at the Museum of Modern Art, he would acknowledge its wide acceptance "as a work of art with its own message rather than its maker's; . . . a

FIGURE III.6   DOROTHEA LANGE, *MIGRANT MOTHER*, 1936. U.S. FARM SECURITY ADMINISTRATION COLLECTION, PRINTS AND PHOTOGRAPHS DIVISION, LIBRARY OF CONGRESS, NO. USF3+2T01-9058.

great, perfect, anonymous image [that] is a trick of grace."[6]

This photograph would go on to have a life beyond both the FSA files in the Library of Congress and the MoMA holdings. *Popular Photography* reproduced the image in 1960 along with Lange's account—a story about an exchange between an anonymous photographer in a hurry and an anonymous suffering woman that presents the making of the image as a two-way transaction. As she headed home on a rainy day from a long assignment, passing a sign saying "Pea-Pickers Camp," something made her turn around and backtrack 20 miles. "I drove into that wet and soggy camp and parked my car like a homing pigeon," she recalled:

I saw and approached the hungry and desperate mother, as if drawn by magnet. I do not remember how I explained my presence or my camera to her, but I do remember she asked me no questions. I made five exposures, working closer and closer from the same direction. I did not ask her name or her history. She told me her age, that she was 32. She said that they had been living on frozen vegetables from the surrounding fields, and birds that the children killed. She had just sold the tires from her car to buy food. There she sat in that lean-to tent with her children huddled around her, and seemed to know that my pictures might help her, and so she helped me. There was a sort of equality about it.[7]

In later years, Lange would complain that the Library of Congress never reproduced *Migrant Mother* the same way twice, despite the guide print she supplied. Indeed, as the image became a kind of icon, assimilated into vernacular culture, it never was reproduced the same way twice. Margery Mann, in a 1970 *Popular Photography* story on Lange, recalled passing "the display window of an artist who would paint your portrait from your photograph, and amidst his samples, the glorified girls and the 30-year-old, slyly smiling Bette Davis and the muscle men, sat *Migrant Mother,* big as life, and blue and yellow and lilac." Closer to its original purpose, a Spanish Civil War artist would make a closely copied lithograph of the mother alone, entitled "The Spanish Mother, Terror of 1938." In 1964 the Latin American magazine *Bohemia* reproduced an artist's rendering of the photograph on its cover, turning the head of one child to show its face (Figure III. 7). And in 1973 the Black Panthers' newsletter ran in full page an artist's version of the photograph that gave black features to the faces and the hair, adding the caption, "Poverty is a crime, and our people are the victims" (Figure III. 8). None of these credited Lange as the author of the image.[8]

Migrant Mother, then, is not only a visual representation of "our" history but a picture with a 60-year history of use and appropriation. An all-inclusive icon—mother and child—it is also a locus for different stories, for alternative histories that have to do with class and race. In fact, the power of this image to convey both sameness and difference, not only in 1936 but in 1964 and 1973, suggests that its meanings have been and are constructed by powerful responses to it. Yet this is also Dorothea Lange's image—the work of a

FIGURE III.7   "DIA DE LAS MADRES," *BOHEMIA VENEZOLANA* **(MAY 10, 1964), OAKLAND MUSEUM.**

FIGURE III.8   MALIK, "POVERTY IS A CRIME," *BLACK PANTHERS' NEWSLETTER* **9, NO. 8 (DEC. 7, 1972), BACK COVER. SPECIAL COLLECTIONS, ALDERMAN LIBRARY, UNIVERSITY OF VIRGINIA. © 1972 BY HUEY P. NEWTON.**

photographer who would claim her own physical and historical "outsidedness" as a source of special affinity for her suffering subjects. Her own "otherness," which made it possible for her to understand others' stories, was also the source for her claim to agency: to be a Photographer, a History Maker, a Storyteller. The question that interests me here is this strategy of claiming agency for oneself by representing otherness, particularly when it is practiced by women photographers emerging from a tradition (into which they at first tried to place themselves) of the history of art that had consistently represented *them* as other.

NOTES

1. John Berger and Jean Mohr, *Another Way of Telling* (New York: Pantheon, 1982), pp. 285–86.

2. John Berger and Jean Mohr demonstrate this in *Another Way of Telling*. Mohr asks nine people to respond to five of his photographs and records nine separate stories for each image, each different from his own conception of "what was happening" (pp. 41–57). "Memory, based upon the visual, is freer than reason" (p. 133), Berger writes. "Memory is a field where different times coexist" (p. 280).

3. Roy Emerson Stryker and Nancy Wood, *In This Proud Land: America, 1935–1943, As Seen in the FSA Photographs* (Greenwich, Conn.: New York Graphic Society, 1974), p. 19. Lange recalled making five photographs, but she actually made six, all of which are reproduced in Lawrence W. Levine, "The Historian and the Icon: Photography and the History of the American People in the 1930s and 1940s," in Carl Fleischhauer and Beverly W. Brannan, eds., *Documenting America: 1935–1943* (Berkeley and Los Angeles: University of California Press, 1988), pp. 16–17.

4. *San Francisco News,* March 10, 1936, cited in Milton Meltzer, *Dorothea Lange: A Photographer's Life* (New York: Farrar, Straus, Giroux, 1978), pp. 133–34.

5. "Please, mister," she wrote to Stryker's assistant Edwin Locke, in charge of the Washington lab, "this show is the most important photographic show we have. It tours the country. It tours Europe. I couldn't afford to show prints unsigned which I have not even *seen.* I'll send the negatives right back." Dorothea Lange to Edwin Locke, Sept. 10, 1936. Cited in Meltzer, *Dorothea Lange,* p. 134.

6. George P. Elliott, "Things of This World," *Commentary* (December 1962):542; *Dorothea Lange,* exhibit catalog, with an introduction by George P. Elliott (New York: Museum of Modern Art, 1966), p. 7.

7. Dorothea Lange, "The Assignment I'll Never Forget: Migrant Mother," *Popular Photography* 46, no. 2 (February 1960):42–43, 126.

8. Margery Mann, "Dorothea Lange," *Popular Photography* 66, no. 3 (March 1970):84.

Karen Alexander: Video Worker

MICA NAVA

Feminist cultural critic Mica Nava interviews Karen Alexander about her work with video in London in the 1980s. Alexander describes how she became involved in using video not only as an "art form" but as a tool for education, training, and political awareness.

MICA NAVA: When did you start working with video?

KAREN ALEXANDER: I made my first tape when I was a second-year student at Goldsmiths. It was a documentary called *Contradictions in Housing,* about the gentrification of the Lots Road area of Chelsea; it tried to look at housing history and different perspectives in housing policy. During my research I had a lot of help from the local tenants' association. In my final year I decided to make a tape about the Asian Community Action Group. Instead of just saying, "these people are really suffering, that's why they set up this group," I focused on one woman who worked

Mica Nava, "Karen Alexander: Video Worker," *Feminist Review* 18, 1984: 28–34.

there and showed her in different settings and taking on different roles, such as Asian expert in a TV interview or militant picket outside the Home Office. I tried to show her as a person who was brought up in this country, who negotiated both Western and Asian cultures and who was using knowledge gained from the former to benefit the latter. I wanted to avoid the cliché of showing an Asian woman trapped between two cultures and unable to cope. But it wasn't a radical tape really; it was just a college project. It didn't change the situation or the politics of the group, though it got them interested in using video.

MICA NAVA: Tell me about the work which is done at the Albany Video unit.

KAREN ALEXANDER: The video work at the Albany tends to fall into four main areas: distribution, production, education, and training. The unit runs a distribution library with about 20 different tapes made either by us or by similar community groups. They range from *The Irish in Britain* to *Us,* a tape made by and about physically and men-

---

Key Terms

Channel 4 British public television channel for education, information, and entertainment.

gentrification Beginning in the 1960s in Europe and the United States, affluent people reversed the trend of moving from the cities to the distant suburbs and began to establish themselves in very poor city neighborhoods, buying property cheaply and changing the character of the neighborhood as well as the financial base. The end result of

gentrification is the displacement of poor people to outlying areas or worse neighborhoods.

Goldsmiths College Part of the University of London, Goldsmiths College focuses on adult education with special emphasis on creative, social, and cultural processes.

mixed media Several different kinds of media in one work.

tally handicapped people. In production we work with groups and either produce tapes for them or enable them to produce their own tapes. By "education" I mean sensitizing youth and community workers and groups to the possibilities of video technology as a resource, especially as a discussion initiator about different or difficult issues such as racism, sexism, and sexual prejudice. As far as training goes, this may consist of running courses for groups or for youth and community workers who are interested in using video in a constructive and imaginative way. Most recently, my work there has been concerned with fundraising and preparing for another woman worker to join the project. I have also been involved—though not as much as I would have liked—with a group of black women youth and community workers who are producing a mixed-media package for use with black girls in youth clubs.

MICA NAVA: Have you done much video work with girls and young women?

KAREN ALEXANDER: Yes, but it's always quite complicated. You can't just barge into a room and say, "OK, I'm a video worker and the best thing in your life you can do is produce a videotape." For example, I worked with a group of young mothers—they were all black—in a youth club in Lewisham, and I went there and talked to them for weeks before they felt they had enough confidence to make a tape. In the end they decided to make one about the attitudes they found really annoying when they told people they were pregnant. They made the situation quite comic: they took on the roles of their parents, their boyfriends, and the doctors, and really exaggerated them. At the same time they were learning how to use the equipment, and then they edited the tape. The whole process took a long time and some of them got bored after a while, but they didn't have much time—only two hours a week—because of the problem of finding someone to look after the children. I think the experience was useful because before that they wouldn't ever have imagined themselves learning to use video equipment and producing a tape. They probably thought, "Black women don't use video, it's not for me." When I work with women's

groups, especially black women's groups, they always ask me how I got involved and say it's good to see a black woman doing such things. On the other hand, they are really suspicious of people who come from places like the Albany because they think that they are all do-gooders or lefties, or worse still, communists. I think that being a black person gave me one less hurdle to get over when working with groups like that.

MICA NAVA: So do you think that the process of making the tape actually changed the way those young women thought about things?

KAREN ALEXANDER: I think it may have changed the way they view the media. When you go into a group with a videocassette recorder, camera, microphone, and lights, they go, 'Do we need all this for just a little videotape?' Then you can start talking about the way TV programmes are put together and you get them to think about when and where on television they see such things as lights, mikes, and cameras. This sort of low-key questioning can happen while they are constructing shots; for example, you can suggest that they use a head-on shot rather than the one they are mimicking from TV; you can point to the types of people who have full mid-shots facing the camera and to the authority that is invested in what those people have to say. It's not thrusting theory down their throats, but trying to make them question the things they look at. Another example of this kind of approach occurs when people I am working with don't like the colour of their skin on the video that we produce. Our equipment isn't very sophisticated, of course, but then we start talking about how even on television black people don't appear as black as they should, their colour just doesn't look right. All this leads to a discussion about television technology and how the cameras are set up to give a perfect picture against a test card which consists of a white woman with brown hair; and so you start to talk about the construction of a technology which is often portrayed as neutral, as offering a window on the world.

Another interesting example of this kind happened when I was working with a group of sixth-form girls. They had decided that they wanted to make a tape about what they didn't like at school, but then at one point they suddenly stopped and said, "Look, we can't do this, it's not fair because there aren't any white girls here to say what they think, it wouldn't be balanced if they didn't put their view." So I just asked when the last time was that they had seen a black woman on television saying what she thought about anything. Then they thought for a bit and said, "I suppose you're right," and carried on. Those are the kinds of points that come up all the time when you're working with groups, and if you think about how to answer them you can put over quite a lot of information. It's important to my work to point out the whole constructive nature of the medium I'm working with and to relate it to representations of black women; in this way I think I can help to create a consciousness about power and control. But it's also important that the women in the groups I work with gain confidence, learn some skills and feel they are capable of producing something. The thing about video is that it's so immediate, and it's relatively simple.

MICA NAVA: Apart from your work at Albany Video, you are also involved in the Pictures of Women collective. How did that project get off the ground?

KAREN ALEXANDER: Late in 1981, four women, three of whom had been at Goldsmiths' College, started to meet to talk about setting up a multi-media production group. Our project was to produce visual material by and for women. In order to do this we needed money. At the time that we were meeting, Channel 4 was just setting up and putting out feelers for innovative programmes. During the same period certain issues around female sexuality were being pinpointed for study, and we thought it was essential to look at common-sense assumptions in this area and offer a feminist analysis. We also wanted to use the medium of television in an exciting way. All this constituted enough difference in Channel 4's eyes to get a commission; it was also a time when they were actively looking for applications from ethnic minorities and women. So a lot of our success in getting finance had to do with being in the right place at the right time. I think that if we wanted to do the same thing today, we

wouldn't be able to; there is no longer the money or the goodwill around for groups such as ours. Channel 4 took a risk when it commissioned the *Sexuality* series from us because we hadn't done anything for broadcast television before. I learned a lot by working on the series, it's been invaluable in that respect. Perhaps that knowledge and those skills can be passed on to other women to help them produce things as well.

MICA NAVA: What are you doing with POW at the moment?

KAREN ALEXANDER: We all do one day a week in the POW office. At present I am doing a lot of liaison work, which entails going out with the tapes to do presentations to women's groups or trade unions about the issues dealt with in the programmes. It's important that the tapes have a life after broadcast and are used by interested groups. We want to get some money now so that we can compile short tapes, consisting of chunks from each of the programmes, which can be used to initiate discussion.

MICA NAVA: What kinds of responses have you had to the POW programmes?

KAREN ALEXANDER: We have recently had a very interesting invitation. We have been asked to go to a women's prison by the education officer there, in order to run a weekend course for prisoners around the themes brought up in the POW series. I am really looking forward to that. Overall it's fascinating to see the diversity of response to the programmes. For example, some of my male relatives and their friends asked me about the sexual harassment one. It was at a party shortly after the programme had gone out, and somebody said, "I hear you have been involved in this women's lib series, I watched the one on sexual harassment at work." Then they all discussed whether they agreed with it or didn't agree and commented on the things they did or didn't like about particular programmes. I've been amazed at the number of black men that I've spoken to who watched at least one and were interested enough to talk about the issues which were raised. At a friend's house, a guy recognized me from the programmes and started to talk to me about the one on pornography; I thought he was going to say he didn't know what all the fuss was about, or something like that. Instead he told me that it had really made him think about the issues. He said that he and the man he worked with had looked at pornography and he was now asking himself, "Why are we like that?" It was quite interesting getting feedback like that from men.

MICA NAVA: Independent film and video work is enormously constrained by the funding that is available. What, ideally, would you like your next project to be?

KAREN ALEXANDER: One of the things I would like to do is to make a film. I've put in an application for finance to the Greater London Arts Association (GLAA) with a friend of mine, another black woman. We want to do something about black women and the reflections we experience of ourselves. We want to examine how we view ourselves and what sort of cultural representations of black women are offered up to us to consume. To accompany the visuals we hope to get verbal reflections from black women about the experience of being in a society which continually negates or assimilates our existence. We want to do a film rather than a video because of the quality of the image and because we would like to make something which could go out as a short with a longer independent film.

MICA NAVA: Have you got any other plans?

KAREN ALEXANDER: In about a year's time I'd like to do a video about my mother and my aunt. I am always interviewing people about their lives, and yet I don't know very much about their history—and to a certain extent their history is my history. I keep telling my mother that I'm going to do a tape with her and she says, "Any time you're ready." I'm really looking forward to that. A while ago I did a short interview with her for a seminar I was giving for a Black Women and Representation course organized by the women in Sankofa (a recently formed black film and video group) and some other black women. What was interesting was the answer I got when I asked my mother about the films she liked. She said her favourite was perhaps *Gone with The Wind;* I told her that many people objected to the way in which black people were portrayed in it, and she

said that she would agree with that. I also asked her which bit had the most impact for her and she said, "The bit I'll always remember is when Scarlett O'Hara holds up the red dust and says 'I'll never be hungry again, as God is my witness I'll never be hungry again.'" The way she said it conveyed a whole experience of poverty which I'd never known because I was born here and not in Guyana. It was an indication of the wealth of experience that she hadn't let come to the surface about things which are very important to her. It's also interesting talking to my mother about the types of women she identified with when she was young. They were all white women, but they were all women like Joan Crawford—very strong women. She's seen *Mildred Pierce* again and again. When my mother lived in Guyana, she would go to the cinema once or twice a week.

MICA NAVA: I wonder if you would like to say anything about your political commitment as a black person and as a woman. Has this double commitment ever been contradictory or difficult to reconcile?

KAREN ALEXANDER: At the time that I left Goldsmiths I didn't know of any black women producing things on video, so I joined Albany Video, a white group which had a history of working with women's groups and black groups. While I was at Goldsmiths I tended to work with women, so in a way it was a natural progression to involve myself with women and women's groups when I left—groups of white women. POW was an example of this. Members of the black community, or rather certain black men, sometimes asked me why I worked on those programmes with all those white women; in effect they were saying that I should be putting my skills to work for black people. During my first year as a video worker at the Albany I felt very confused. I'd get black groups phoning up and women's groups phoning up and I just couldn't do everything; I was being pulled in two directions and I felt equally committed to working in both areas. I was meant to be just a video worker, but because of my sex and colour I felt I was like an extra resource, which was sometimes uncomfortable in spite of the fact that I thought it was important to be visible, to show that black women were getting involved in film and video production.

But more recently the situation has improved. There is a growing participation of black women in the independent sector, and I feel that I am part of that movement. Three black film and video workshops have recently been established. They are Ceddo, Sankofa, and Retake—all mixed groups. The funding they receive comes from a mixture of sources: GLAA, The British Film Institute, Channel 4, and the Greater London Council. So recently there has been a dramatic increase in the number of black women involved in a sec-tor where previously we were conspicuous by our absence. There are also more black women who have done film, media, or communications courses at college and who like me are very interested in looking at questions of black women and representation. So overall I now feel that my allegiances lie with the up-and-coming black independent sector in general and towards black women in particular—towards making tapes and films about ourselves and our struggles.

Reading C

Female Pleasures and Perversions in the Silent and Early Sound Cinema

ANDREA WEISS

Feminist film historian Andrea Weiss discusses the history of cinema in relation to the emergence of lesbian identity in the West. Pointing to the cinema's major role in representing women as objects of desire, Weiss argues that lesbian desire is shaped by the way in which homosexuality and lesbianism are portrayed.

Lesbians and the cinema made their first appearance in the western world at the same historical moment. Of course, it may be argued, lesbians can be traced back to Sappho of ancient Greece, but the modern phenomenon of a woman whose identity (rather than merely behavior) is homosexual emerged in western Europe and the United States only in the decades closing the nineteenth and opening the twentieth centuries.[1] The twin birth of modern lesbian identity and the motion picture in this

Andrea Weiss, "Female Pleasures and Perversions in the Silent and Early Sound Cinema," *Vampires and Violets: Lesbians in Film,* Harmondsworth, England: Penguin Books, 1992: 7–11.

fin de siècle era has meant that their subsequent developments have been irrevocably linked.

It is an odd claim, because so many other major social changes were also occurring in this period. Complex processes of industrialization, urbanization, the transformation to consumer-oriented society, all fundamentally altered people's perceptions of themselves and the world around them. So it seems misleading to single out these two social "inventions" as having a special relationship.

[. . .]

Nonetheless, the cinema historically has played a major role in shaping the contours of lesbian desire and community. And conversely, lesbianism has had a major impact on the cinema (primarily through the threat it poses to patriarchal culture), influencing the way cinema represents women, represses and co-opts lesbianism, and is unrelentingly obsessed with heterosexual romance.

The idea that a woman's identity might involve sexual desire for another woman was greatly popularized at the turn of the century by the rather disturbing theories of a number of male "experts" on female sexuality. British sexologist Havelock Ellis, in particular, scrutinized traditional women's friendships and labeled some of them socially dangerous and sexually perverted. [Unlike his predecessor, the Austrian neurologist Krafft-Ebing, whose theories were based on women who rejected the feminine social role and exhibited male physiological traits,] Ellis insisted that most lesbians were virtually indistinguishable from (although less attractive than) "normal" women, and herein lay their danger. Not a genetic anomaly or helpless victim (as Ellis sympathetically believed male homosexuals to be), the female homosexual, as man's sexual rival, was instead "a woman on the make, sexually and racially dangerous."[2]

To Havelock Ellis and many of his contemporaries it seemed that the lesbian population was increasing along with (and because of) the expansion of women's public roles in the turn of the century. As an acquired rather than congenital condition, female homosexuality was "the result of the [female] college environments," unwholesome places which bred pathological attachments between women.[3] It was of course no coincidence that Ellis levelled his attack against the new women's colleges, not only all-female environments but ones which offered the possibility for intellectual growth, self-fulfillment, a career, and financial autonomy from men. Ellis's position found support among American and British physicians and educators; medical journals reported that "female boarding schools and colleges are the great breeding grounds of artificial [acquired] homosexuality."[4] By 1910 in England and the United States, Ellis's ideas had moved from the pages of scientific tracts to those of literary and political journals, which began to use charges of lesbianism as a way of discrediting women's institutions and of launching a campaign against the New Woman.

The relationship between the history of ideas and their manifestation in popular culture is rarely (if ever) simple or direct. In this case, Ellis's preoccupation with all-female environments was taken up, popularized, and significantly refocused in several European and American films of the late 1920s and early 30s. Where Ellis saw danger, these films—especially two by female directors—imagined pleasure. *Mädchen in Uniform* (Leontine Sagan, Germany, 1931), *Club de Femmes* (Jacques Deval, France, 1936), and *The Wild Party* (Dorothy Arzner, United States, 1929) all focus on the joys rather than the perils of all-girl living; any potential danger is posed by an outside threat rather than by the women's attachments per se.

These films, set in women's schools, established a veritable genre that appears throughout movie history, continuing with the several remakes of *Mädchen in Uniform,* [including a 1957 technicolor version with Romy Schneider and Lily Palmer, and the Mexican version *Muchachas en Uniforme* (1950). Two films in this genre which retain *Mädchen in Uniform's* female eroticism but abandon its radical feminist politic are *Olivia*

Key Terms

acquired homosexuality The belief that homosexual orientation is due to circumstances such as same-sex environments, poor parenting, or sexual abuse.

censorship The act of suppressing or eradicating the group or individual's speech or actions that someone else finds objectionable.

congenital homosexuality The belief that some people are born with same-sex preference.

heterosexual romance The way in which modern Western culture constructs the story of sexuality as a romance between a man and a woman such that it appears to be natural and inevitable.

sexology The late-nineteenth-century, European study and classification of sexual behaviors, identities, and relations based on biological explanations; prominent sexologists included Richard von Kraft-Ebing and Havelock Ellis.

subculture A sociological term used to refer to a smaller group that lives in a distinctive way within the parameters of a larger group or society.

Weimar Republic Founded in the city of Weimar, Germany, in 1919, this liberal, democratic government encouraged progressive public culture before it was crushed by the rise of national socialism (the Nazi party).

(Jacqueline Audry, France, 1951), based on the autobiographical novel of English girls' boarding-school life by Dorothy Strachey Bussy, and *Theresa and Isabel* (Radley Metzger, France, 1968), the soft-core porn depiction of Catholic schoolgirl affection, featuring a memorable sex scene in the church pews.] The lesbian vampire skin-flick *Lust for a Vampire* (Jimmy Sangster, England, 1971), also exploits the setting of that hotbed of lesbian sexuality, the girls' boarding school. Less sentimental, more vicious female relationships can be found in a somewhat different all-female environment also favored by the cinema: lesbianism is a prime "horror" ingredient in women's prison movies, from *Caged* (John Cromwell, United States, 1950), to *Scrubbers* (Mai Zetterling, Sweden, 1983).

The classic, unparalleled girls' boarding-school film is the original *Mädchen in Uniform.* This early sound film was suppressed by the Nazis and virtually disappeared from film archives; the few prints to be found outside of Germany were assigned misleading or minimal subtitles that diffused the passion between the "mädchen." If remembered at all, it was only as an anti-Fascist film (which it also was) until feminists in the early and mid-1970s rediscovered it and established its significance as a lesbian film. Shown in a circuit of women's film festivals during the 1970s, it was once again, as it had been in the early 1930s, embraced by lesbian viewers who were thrilled to see such a strong proclamation of erotic desire between women.

Much critical writing has also focused on this film, of which B. Ruby Rich's article "From Repressive Tolerance to Erotic Liberation" gives the most in-depth analysis of the relationship between lesbian eroticism and political repression, and between the film itself and the circumstances surrounding its production. Rich places the film in the context of Germany's short-lived Weimar Republic, which witnessed a proliferation of gay and lesbian bars and journals and flourishing movements for women's rights and homosexual emancipation. In 1928, when 20-year-old American actress Louise Brooks came to Berlin to film *Pandora's Box,* she found, to her delight, "The nightclub Eldorado displayed an enticing line of homosexuals dressed as women [while] at the Maly, there was a choice of feminine or collar-and-tie lesbians."[5] This subculture was familiar as well to *Mädchen's* director Leontine Sagan, who was then a popular figure in Berlin's wild theater

scene, and to the Berlin-based playwright Christa Winsloe, on whose play the film was based, and her lover, American journalist Dorothy Thompson.

While *Mädchen in Uniform* does take an anti-Fascist stance, the lesbian relations of the film are not merely a metaphor for the struggle against Fascism but are also, as Rich has argued, central to an understanding of this "first truly radical lesbian film."[6] The symbols of Fascism and patriarchy (the forbidding iron staircase, the sound of a bugle in the distance, the school principal whose function and image as "phallic woman" embody these ideologies) are placed in juxtaposition with the unspoken, contained lesbian sexuality of the girls, which ultimately triumphs into full expression by the film's end.

As the prevalence of these symbols suggests, what is unusual about this boarding-school film is its militaristic, authoritarian, absolutely nonfeminine atmosphere; it stands in for the girls' absent Prussian officer fathers, literally the absent patriarchy, rather than a loving female-defined space. The film's opening montage, as Rich points out, "establishes an exterior world of military preparedness, steeples and archways, bugle calls, and the marching rhythm of soldiery."[7] The symbolic forces of danger point to the world outside of the school, and not to the relationships between the girls within, as Havelock Ellis would have it. Erotic attachments between students develop in spite of rather than because of this environment. Instead, the school nurtures a particular relationship with erotic overtones between student and teacher; as Rich has insightfully described it, the adored teacher Fräulein von Bernburg (Dorothea Wieck) functions as an agent of repressive tolerance for such feelings: "If the girls focus their sexual desires upon her, where the desires can never be realized, then the danger of such desires being refocused on each other (where they could be realized) is averted."[8]

But this precarious balance is broken by a public speech by Manuela (Hertha Thiele), a young student who announces her love for Fräulein von Bernburg and precipitates a crisis that resolves favorably for her, von Bernburg, and all the schoolgirls. The school principal immediately recognizes Manuela's subversive action as a "scandal." As Rich explains,

Despite the generally permissive setting, it is this act of pronouncement which constitutes the transgression of the school's most rigid social codes. It is the naming of what may well be known, this claiming of what is felt by speaking its name publicly that is expressly forbidden.[9]

The school principal was not the only one to find the spoken expression of lesbian desire scandalous. The American censors denied the film a license until certain cuts were made and subtitles deleted so as to obscure the passion between Manuela and Fräulein von Bernburg. While the theme of lesbianism persisted despite the mutilations, its political meaning was successfully defused. One change eliminated the line spoken by Fräulein von Bernburg in defense of Manuela: "What

you call sins, Principal, I call the great spirit of love, which has thousands of forms." Film historian Vito Russo has written, "This deletion, a political act, effectively removed any defense of such emotions and thereby perverted the intent of both [writer] Winsloe and [director] Sagan."[10]

Although the censorship efforts in the United States would not go into full force until 1934, this early example of *Mädchen in Uniform* in 1931 set the tone for the next 30 years: lesbianism would be tolerated as subtext but any spoken pronouncement of desire, like Manuela's for Fräulein von Bernburg, was "expressly forbidden."

[. . .]

NOTES

1. This 20 year period between 1890 and 1910 has been considered by some historians as something of a watershed in the area of sexual theory, out of which the modern concepts of homosexuality and lesbianism were formed. In this time the "science" of sexology emerged and gained legitimacy, benefiting from the strengthening in status and authority of the medical profession, to which sexology attached itself. As science asserted the pleasures of order and regulation, sexology stepped in to evaluate, regulate, control, and construct new categories of sexual identity. In the process, a new conceptual alignment came into being: a line was now drawn between normal and natural sexuality on the one hand, deviant and unnatural on the other. Where previous distinctions between reproductive or nonreproductive sex placed emphasis on the sex act itself, normal or deviant came to describe the identity of the individual engaging in the act. Focusing on the male homosexual, Michel Foucault succinctly described this shift, "The sodomite had been a temporary aberration; the homosexual was now a species." (*The History of Sex,* vol. I)

A number of feminist historians, including Smith-Rosenberg, have argued that the sexologists, and especially Havelock Ellis, were responsible for shattering the nineteenth-century Victorian homosocial female world by pathologizing women's romantic friendships. Other historians such as John D'Emilio and Estelle Freedman disagree about the importance of the sexologists, claiming that they were responding to real changes in the social organization of same-sex eroticism." But whether or not the sexologists created or merely responded to social phenomena, or whether they actually closed down or perhaps unwittingly opened up the possibilities for female sexual and emotional experience at the end of the nineteenth century, through their medical definitions sexologists did describe and popularize, if not create, the modern homosexual and lesbian. Their so-

cial categorization, aimed at regulation and control, contributed to the development of what we now consider homosexual identity.

On the role of Havelock Ellis in pathologizing women's friendships, see Carroll Smith-Rosenberg, "The New Woman as Androgyne: Social Disorder and Gender Crisis, 1870–1936," in *Disorderly Conduct* (New York: Oxford University Press, 1985), p. 267. For a more functional view, see John D'Emilio and Estelle Freedman, *Intimate Matters* (New York: Harper & Row, 1988), p. 226.

2. Havelock Ellis, Appendix B, "The School-Friendships of Girls," *Studies in the Psychology of Sex,* vol. 2 (New York: Random House, 1936), p. 374.

3. R. W. Shufeldt, "Dr. Havelock Ellis on Sexual Inversion," *Pacific Medical Journal* XLV (1902), pp. 199–207, cited in Smith-Rosenberg p. 280.

4. Much as during the "lavender menace" scare of the early 1970s, feminists joined their homophobic attackers rather than be discredited by them. One feminist publication ran a series of essays, entitled "Spinsters in the Making: the College Woman," warning against female colleges and the pathological attachments they encouraged between women. See "Spinsters in the Making. Type I — The College Woman," the *Freewoman* (28 December, 1911), p. 66.

5. Louise Brooks, *Lulu in Hollywood* (New York: Alfred A. Knopf, 1982), p. 97.

6. B. Ruby Rich, "From Repressive Tolerance to Erotic Liberation," *Jump Cut,* 24/25 (March 1981), p. 44.

7. Rich, "Repressive Tolerance," p. 44.

8. Ibid. p. 45.

9. Ibid. p. 46.

10. Vito Russo, *The Celluloid Closet* (New York: Harper & Row, 1981), p. 58.

Yearnings

JIANYING ZHA

Cultural critic Jianying Zha describes the introduction of a new TV series in China in 1990. "Yearning" became extremely popular, running on all major television stations in China, using a melodramatic plot revolving around the romance and tragedy of class mixing. The response to the series is an example of the power of the TV viewer in a country that has only recently offered televisions for general sale. Viewers of "Yearning" came away with new versions of gender relations that reflected both older patriarchal ideals from the Cultural Revolutions and new ones from a growing consumer society.

Teacher Bei is a buxom, 63-year-old retired elementary school teacher who lives in a prefabricated apartment in the east side of Beijing. I call her "Teacher Bei" instead of "Aunt Bei," as Chinese normally call

Jianying Zha, *China Pop,* New York: The New Press, 1995: 25–28.

somebody her age, because of a warning from the friend who introduced us: It is very important, he said, to make her feel that she belongs to the educated class and is someone with culture. Teacher Bei was so pleased by our visit and got to talking so much that she skipped her nap and made a big pot of tea. She made us a delicious lunch in her spotless, drab living room, but she herself only nibbled. "I haven't had such a good time since '*Yearning,*'" she admitted.

She says she has always been prone to depression. She has a history of breakdowns—the first one when she was 25 and married off against her will. Maybe this is why she always finds the gloom of Beijing's harsh winters so difficult. Last year, though, she didn't mind the winter because "*Yearning*" was on television just about every night. Two stations were showing it on different evenings, and she watched them both. "A good show gets better the second time," she says. She would shop, clean, wash, cook, and do what she could for her-

Key Terms

Cultural Revolution The mass campaign in China between 1966 and 1969 to renew revolutionary fervor and adherence to Communist party ideologies of proletarianism. So-called "bourgeois" elements were rooted out of cultural and bureaucratic circles by the army and the revolutionary Red Guards, leading to social disorder, violent removals, exile, and widespread intimidation.

Mao Tse-Tung (1893–1976) The first chairman of the People's Republic of China (in 1949), Mao influenced national and international politics until

his death. He was the son of peasants, a union organizer, one of the original members of the Chinese Communist Party, and the founder of the Red Army.

Tiananmen Square A student-initiated occupation of a major plaza in Beijing in 1989. The students were protesting official corruption and the denial of certain political freedoms. When armed forces moved in to remove the protests, world media circulated images of the violent repression that powerfully influenced public opinion and exerted pressure on the Chinese government.

self and her husband (which was not that much at all), then get ready for the evening. She has two sons, both married, living away. They drop by only once in a while. "They are good children, as filial and respectful as anybody's, but they're always busy and have their own families to worry about now," Teacher Bei tells me stoically, not wanting to complain about what is obvious in her old age: the boredom, the emptiness, the marriage that never would have lasted were it not for the children.

Her husband, old Tang, is a railway engineer, half deaf from an accident but still working part-time. They have long lived in separate rooms; nowadays they hardly talk to each other. But in the months when "*Yearning*" was on, their household was almost conjugal. Every evening at 6:30, Tang would arrive from work and find dinner ready on a tray and his wife settled into a puffy lounge chair in front of the television, ready for "*Yearning*." He would join her, sitting doggedly through the show, his eyes fixed on the screen even though half of the dialog was lost on him. "It was bliss," Teacher Bei admits, sounding wistful. "Why can't they make a show like that more often? I guess it must be hard to come up with a story so complicated and gripping."

"*Yearning*" was a 50-part Chinese television serial, in a genre that the Chinese television people call "indoor drama" because it is mostly shot with studio-made indoor scenes. The Chinese title, "*Kewang*," literally means "a desire like thirst." Desire is a central theme of the show, which covers the lives of two Beijing families during the years of the Cultural Revolution and the 80s reforms. In normal times, according to normal social customs in China, they are not the kind of families who would care much to mix or socialize with one another: the Lius are simple workers living in a traditional courtyard house, whereas the Wangs are sophisticated intellectuals living in a modern apartment. However, the Cultural Revolution struck a heavy blow to the Wang family's fortunes, creating a chance for their son, a forlorn, sappy, soft young man of the type the Chinese call a "Little White Face," to meet the daughter of the Liu family. Of course, they get married, not out of love so much as a desire for the qualities of the opposite class: he for the simplicities of a heart of gold, she for the charm of being "cultured." From there on, despite the omnipresent Chairman Mao portraits on the walls of both homes, the Cultural Revolution

and larger political events remain a blurry, underexamined background. Instead, the show focuses on daily family life and various romantic relationships.

At the heart of the story is Huifang, daughter of the Liu family, whose saintly presence quietly dominates and holds the moral high ground above the clatter of worldly events. Also central to the drama is a little girl whom the Liu family accidentally picks up: Huifang raises her through all manner of hardship, only to find out that she is the baby abandoned by the Wang family. Huifang is forever patient, kind, and giving—what Americans would call a goody-goody—yet she has the worst luck in the world. By the end of the show, she is divorced from her ungrateful husband, hit by a car, paralyzed and bedridden, and has to give back the adopted daughter so dear to her. In the true spirit of a long, drawn-out melodrama, "*Yearning*" entices its viewers with a fairly convoluted plot, conveniently linked by unlikely twists and turns, a good dose of tearjerking scenes, and a large gallery of characters from a broad spectrum of life.

There was little advertising for "*Yearning*" when it first aired in Nanjing in November 1990. The first few episodes attracted little attention, but by the end of the month just about anybody who cared anything about what's happening in China knew that the country was in for a " '*Yearning*' craze." By January 1991, all the major television stations had picked up the show. The number of stations quickly climbed to over 100, and the reception rate was unusually high. In the greater Beijing area, for instance, the rating was 27 percent, surpassing all previous foreign hits. In Yanshan, an oil and chemical industrial town with a population of over 100,000 the audience share was a stunning 98 percent.

Thousands of letters and phone calls flooded the stations daily. Demands were made with a good deal of fervor: people wanted "*Yearning*" on their television every night, and as many episodes as possible. Those who missed the earlier portion begged for a replay. Startled networks responded quickly. The time slot for the show increased, and reruns began even before the first run had ended—which helped to fan the flames and give the show more publicity. In some heavily populated cities such as Nanjing and Wuhan, the streets were deserted whenever "*Yearning*" was on. A department store in Hubei province broke its sales record:

over 1,500 television sets were sold while "*Yearning*" was on the air. In Wuhan, a scheduled power cut occurred in the middle of one episode; instead of sitting in the dark or going to bed as they had always done, an angry crowd surrounded the power plant and put so much pressure on the mayor that he ordered the power back on immediately.

People talked about "*Yearning*" everywhere—in the crowded commuter buses, on the streets, in the factories, offices, stores, and at family dinner tables. You could hear people humming the show's theme music in the narrow, deep lanes of Beijing and Nanjing. The audio track was packaged quickly into 18 cassette versions, all of which sold like hotcakes. By the time the crew took its promotion tour for the show around the country, the main actors were already household names and were mobbed by huge crowds everywhere. In some instances, their arrival caused monumental traffic jams, de facto strikes, and work stoppages.

According to one report, the cast received such a spectacular welcome in Nanjing that the only other comparable turnout in the history of the city was when Chairman Mao first visited there decades ago. Fans waved banners and posters; some wept openly in front of the main actress, who had become, for them, a symbol of the virtuous victim; some even threatened to beat up the main actor, the embodiment of the selfish villain. Male viewers said that they yearned for a wife like Huifang; female viewers said that she was like a lovely sister to them. Everybody said that "*Yearning*" had brought out the best in them and made them understand better what it meant to be Chinese and how deeply rooted they all were in the Chinese values of family and human relations—and how all of this made them yearn for "*Yearning*" every night.

The press also jumped in. All sorts of stories about the series were rushed into print in every possible form: behind-the-scenes reports, on-the-spot interviews, profiles, special columns, analytical essays, letters from the audience, statements from the writers and actors. For months, the promotions raged on fantastically, heating up a public already gripped by the show. Amid the flood of literature on "*Yearning*," a 300-page book topped all others: from collecting the pieces to editing, laying it out, printing, and binding, the entire book was processed in 16 days. And how could a title like *The Shock Waves of Yearning,* with a glossy cover photo of the demurely smiling star, fail to stop the heart of a "*Yearning*" fan browsing at a bookstall?

Such excitement had not stirred in China since Tiananmen.

[. . .]

REFLECTING ON THE SECTION

This section examines the role of gender in the production and reception of photography, video, T.V.'s, and film. Davidov discusses how Dorothea Lange's *Migrant Mother* photograph was transformed through various uses in publications and exhibits. Do you think that these modifications of the original image undercut Lange's authority as the creator of the photograph? What politics influence our perception of the woman and children depicted in the photograph? What happens when women get behind the camera? Karen Alexander believes that black women and girls can be empowered by working with video and producing videos of their own.

Focusing on consumption and reception, Weiss and Zha argue that viewers are not completely passive but may find various levels of empowerment and understanding. Is Teacher Bei's life improved by the soap opera "Yearning"? Is her pleasure feminist? What can the history of censorship and recent lesbian analyses of *Mädchen in Uniform* teach us about the power of representations in feminist thought? Can we approach images as neither all positive or negative but as complicated by any number of viewpoints and desires? Can you think of examples?

Gender and Literacy: The Rise of Print and Media Cultures

The Bribe of Frankenstein

STUART EWEN AND ELIZABETH EWEN

Cultural historians Stuart Ewen and Elizabeth Ewen summarize the changes brought about by the invention of the printing press, especially the availability of information and knowledge to a larger section of the population than the wealthy elites. The connection between knowledge and power that is evident in this history can be linked to the struggles of women to gain the education and skills to read and write.

Stuart Ewen and Elizabeth Ewen, "The Bribe of Frankenstein," in *Channels of Desire: Mass Images and the Shaping of American Consciousness,* Minneapolis: University of Minnesota Press, 1992: 3–7.

For more than 500 years, the growth of capitalism has depended on the ability to manage and distribute standardized know-how and information. "Mass communication" is not an isolated phenomenon of twentieth-century capitalism, sustaining and reorganizing a society *previously* defined by the rise of factory production and discipline and by the development of heavy machinery. For capitalism, mechanical production, and image making have long shared the same quilt. Though the rise of machinery, utilizing interchangeable parts and proliferating standardized goods, preceded the development of modern communications technology, it was the technology of communications that, within Europe by the mid-fifteenth century, of-

Key Terms

autocracy Government by one who has unlimited power.

capitalism The predominant economic system since the Industrial Revolution in eighteenth-century Europe, based on private ownership of property and on private enterprise. Hallmarks of capitalism include individualism, competition, supply and demand, and the profit motive.

exegesis The explanation or critical interpretation of a written text.

feudalism The Western European political and social system based on the agricultural labor of serfs (peasants who owed allegiance to and were under the rule of a regional lord). Feudalism emerged from the end of Charlemagne's empire in the late ninth century A.D. and ended only with the transition to capitalism and urban industrialism, a process stretching across several centuries.

heretic One who dissents from accepted belief or religious dogma.

Johann Gutenberg (1395–1468) With the printing of his 1454 Bible, Gutenberg inaugurated the age of mechanical printing. Thanks to his invention, mass production of books and other printed materials became possible.

mass communication The system of media and information distribution and transmission on a national and then global scale; also associated with the increasingly popular and entertainment focus of contemporary media.

vernacular The common or native language.

fered the prototype for the machine age, for the era of factory industrialism. The first printing presses were ensembles of skills and tools from an artisan tradition. Scribal skills and papers, combined with artisan punches and a modified wine press, produced a mechanism that permanently altered social definitions of work and production. This mechanism—the *printing press*—was the first mass-production machine, and by the late fifteenth century it represented the most dramatic contrast available between the localized, erratic tempo of customary life and the worldly promise of capitalist enterprise. Not only were early printshops capitalist operations; some were factories. By 1480, less than 40 years after Gutenberg's initial enterprise, the Koberger Press in Nuremberg employed 100 men, operating 24 presses.[1]

To a large extent, the history of printing coincides with the history of an emergent world commerce; they were often intertwined. It is no coincidence that the first printer in the English language, William Caxton, was also the leading English wool merchant (*mercer*) at Bruges, Belgium. Printing enabled commerce to develop a more universal and consistent language, appropriate to mobile, contractual transactions. Printing could standardize texts and disseminate information and imagery in ways impossible within the constraints and imprecisions of the traditional scribal culture. Printing was a tool of revolution by which world commercial networks could be established and maintained, by which a mobile economy could be underwritten and secured.[2] Herbert Schiller has noted that in today's world, the integration of capitalism is ensured by the maintenance of a world information order.[3] Already by the sixteenth century, the printed word was, to a large extent, the connective tissue of what Immanuel Wallerstein has termed "the modern world system."[4]

Yet the machinery of print was not, from its inception, the whole or implicit monopoly of an unfolding world commerce. The power to reproduce and spread ideas and information served a variety of social forces and possibilities. Print was also a revolutionary, democratic tool, central in the unraveling of old, feudal seats of authority and power. The spread of knowledge and literacy that came in the wake of printing reached far and wide. Beyond its service in the development of commercial enterprise, print raised the possibility of a transportable popular discourse, explosive in the context of feudalism.

Throughout most of feudal Europe, the written word had been a monopoly of the church. Books were rare and costly, handwritten slowly and individually by scribes. Within such a world, literacy was unusual, limited to those clerics who had access to scribal texts. In addition, texts were for the most part written in Latin. While the clergy could read and understand them, they were indecipherable to those limited to vernacular tongues. This monopoly over the word gave the clergy enormous power, for they reserved the right to interpret what others could not read or understand. This power was particularly significant in the reading of the Bible.

The Bible was the word of God, the universal law, but its interpretation was left to those privileged few who could read it. Within the context of feudal Catholicism, biblical interpretation tended to underwrite the immense social, political, landholding power of the church. Exegesis underwrote structures of hierarchy and authority. Vast chasms between the material abundance of church and nobility and the scarcity experienced by peasants were represented as the immutable order of things. Salvation came from obedience to that order. According to the predominant clerical reading of the Bible, social inequity was the way of God. The sufferings of the poor were humankind's payment for original sin. Those who sat comfortably at the heights of social power did so, it was asserted, as a divine right; they were agents of God.

While feudal power was often held and defended by the sword, it was justified by the word. The monopoly over the *word,* over literacy, and over the ability to interpret what was read was the fundamental aspect of rule.

Even before printing developed in the mid-fifteenth century, there were some radical challenges to this structure. If exclusive access to the word of God was used to justify the position and privilege of an often-profligate clergy, attempts to break that monopoly stood at the heart of social revolt. In England, John Wycliffe and the Lollards (literally, "Babblers") moved against the monopoly over the word in the early fourteenth century. Preparing a vernacular translation of the Bible, and consequently breaking the Latin cipher of the church, Wycliffe went throughout the countryside, reading the Bible aloud in the *vernacular.* Whereas the church limited access and interpretation to a clerical elite, Wycliffe and the Lollards sought to spread access to the Bible among people customarily banned from the power of interpretation. The results were explosive. With the word of God in the hands of the people, church hegemony and practices came under simultaneous attack. Implicitly democratic, the Lollard movement undermined church possession of the word and its interpretation. The spread of literature, the opening up of arenas of interpretation, cut deep into the traditional fabric of power. Denounced by Pope Gregory XI and later condemned by a synod in England, Wycliffe was branded a heretic, his writings and translation banned.

Printing made this democratic impulse behind Wycliffe's heresy all the more realizable. Within less than 100 years of Gutenberg's first printed Bible, vernacular translations were widespread throughout Europe. In addition, a wide variety of literature began to appear in the vernacular, not only accessible to more and more people, but able to be interpreted in terms of those people's experience and perspective.

For increasingly mobile sectors of the European population—not just merchants, but also artisans, low-level civil servants, and rural and an emerging urban poor—the demand for printed, vernacular literature plowed into the static, entrenched soil of the feudal order. The spread of vernacular literature, and of literacy, enabled individuals to spread knowledge and ideas, to interpret the world in their own terms. Alongside commercial networks of printed materials, a radical vernacular tradition began to emerge. The reproducible and transportable capacities of print offered vast possibilities of popular knowledge and expression. Written knowledge, once the exclusive domain of elites, now might reach and permeate populations held down by ignorance. The power to speak through the printing press provided the link between literacy and struggle. Beyond serving as a tool of mercantilism, print was a tool of emancipation; much of the early history of printed materials is that of a vernacular literature of protest and revolt, of popular sentiment and activity. In addition to a commercial intelligence, printing expanded access to democratic ideas, notions of individual and natural rights.

Literacy and access to the printed word were cardinal elements in the overturning of social systems predicated on popular ignorance. For centuries following the development of the printing press, access to the word was an essential demand among people attempting to break the chains of autocracy.

NOTES

1. Elizabeth Eisenstein, "Some Conjectures about the Impact of Printing on Western Society and Thought: A Preliminary Report," *Journal of Modern History* 40 (March 1968), pp. 1–56. Further study along these lines led to the appearance of a major, two-volume study by the same author; see Elizabeth Eisenstein, *The Printing Press as an Agent of Change: Communications and Cultural Transformation in Early-Modern Europe* (Cambridge, England, 1979). See also Lucien Febvre, *The Coming of the Book* (London, 1977); Frederick Hamilton, *A Brief History of Printing in England* (Chicago, 1918); Agnes Allen, *The Story of the Book* (New York, 1967); Marshall McLuhan, *The Gutenberg Galaxy* (New York, 1962); S. H. Steinberg, *Five Hundred Years of Printing* (Harmondsworth, England, 1955). For some provocative thoughts on printing, set within the framework of a more general contemporary essay, see George Gerbner, "Television: The New State Religion?" *Etc.,* (June 1977), pp. 145–50.

2. See Dan Schiller, *Objectivity and the News: The Public and the Rise of Commercial Journalism* (Philadelphia, 1981), for a valuable contribution shedding light on nineteenth-century American developments.

3. Herbert I. Schiller, *Mass Communications and American Empire* (New York, 1969). Also by this author, *The Mind Managers* (Boston, 1973); and *Communication and Cultural Domination* (White Plains, New York, 1976). Schiller's work, widely read internationally, provides the best rundown currently available on the U.S. information structure.

4. See Immanuel Wallerstein, *The Modern World System* (I), (New York, 1975).

The Sixth Composition
RASSUNDARI DEVI

Rassundari Devi, who was born in 1810 in Bengal, India, published her autobiography, entitled Amar Jiban (My Life), in 1876. As the first autobiography to be written in Bengali (the language of Bengal), this remarkable text employs prose style that is extremely vivid and clear. It describes Devi's life from her childhood to her marriage, focusing on the daily hardships and struggles of women of her time. This excerpt shows us the difficulty Devi faced in learning to read and how she deferred learning to write. Overall, we see her great determination to expand the boundaries of her life through literacy.

I was so immersed in the sea of housework that I was not conscious of what I was going through day and night. After some time the desire to learn how to read properly grew very strong in me. I was angry with myself for wanting to read books. Girls did not read. How could I? What a peculiar situation I had placed myself in. What was I to do? This was one of the bad aspects of the old system. The other aspects were not so bad. People used to despise women of learning. How un-

Rassundari Devi, "The Sixth Composition," translated by Enakshi Chatterjee. Susie Tharu and K. Lalita, eds., *Women Writing in India: 600 B.C. to the Present* Vol. I, New York: The Feminist Press, 1991: 199–202.

fortunate those women were, they said. They were no better than animals. But it is no use blaming others. Our fate is our own. In fact, older women used to show a great deal of displeasure if they saw a piece of paper in the hands of a woman. So that ruled out my chances of getting any education. But somehow I could not accept this. I was very keen to learn the alphabet. When I was a child I used to sit in the schoolroom and listen to the chanting of the students. Could I remember any of that? By and by I recalled the 30 letters with all their vowel combinations. I could recognize the letters but was still not able to write them. What was I to do? Actually one cannot learn without a teacher. Besides, I was a woman, and a married one at that, and was not supposed to talk to anyone. If anyone spoke a harsh word to me I would die of shame. That was the fear that kept me from talking to anyone. My only hope was God and my constant prayer was, "Dear God, I can only learn to read and write if you teach me. Who else is there to be my teacher?" Days passed in this manner.

One day I dreamt that I was reading the *Chaitanya Bhagavata*. When I woke up I felt enthralled. I closed my eyes to go over the scene. It seemed that I was already in possession of something precious. My body and my mind swelled with satisfaction. It was so strange! I had never seen the book, yet I had been reading it in my

Key Term

Chaitanya Bhagavata Written by Sri Locana Dasa Thakura, the *Chaitanya Bhagavata* was a book of verses written in devotion to the Hindu deity, Krishna. It suggested, in the Vaishnava tradition, an immediate and simultaneous love between the deity and disciple, a love that bypassed the power of the priests.

dream. For an illiterate person like me, it would have been absolutely impossible to read such a difficult book. Anyhow I was pleased that I was able to perform this impossible feat at least in a dream. My life was blessed! God had at last listened to my constant appeals and had given me the ability to read in my dream. Thank you, dear God. You have made me so happy. He had given me what I had wanted so much, and I was happy.

Our home contained several books. Perhaps the *Chaitanya Bhagavata* is one of them, I thought to myself. But what did it matter to me after all? An illiterate woman like me wouldn't even recognize the book. So I prayed to God again, saying, "You are the friend of the poor; allow me to recognize the book. You must let me have that book. You are the only one whom I can approach." That was how I prayed to God silently.

How strange are the ways of God and the effects of his kindness! He heard my prayers and set out to grant me my wish. My eldest son was then eight. I was working in the kitchen one day when my husband came in and said to him, "Bipin, I am leaving my *Chaitanya Bhagavata* here. Please bring it over when I ask you to." Saying that, he put the book down there and went back to the outer house.

I listened from the kitchen. No words can express the delight I felt when I heard his words. I was filled with happiness and rushed to the spot to find the book there. Pleased with myself, I said to God, "You have granted my wish," and I picked the book up. In those days books were made differently. There were illustrated wooden frames to hold the sheets. Since I did not know how to read, I tried to remember the illustrations.

When the book was brought into the room, I detached one sheet and hid it. But I was afraid lest it were found. That would be a disgrace. I might even be rebuked. It was not easy to face criticism or rebuke. I was very sensitive about those things. Those days were not like present ones. We were completely under the control of men. And I was particularly nervous. I was at a loss with that sheet. Where should I keep it so that nobody would find it? But if they did, what would they say? Finally I decided to put it in some place where I would be present most of the time and nobody else was likely to go. The *khori** in the kitchen was the only hiding place I could think of. Housework kept me busy the whole day. There was no time even to look at it. In the evening the cooking continued until it was very late. By the time I was free, the children had awakened. Some demanded to be taken to the toilet, some were hungry, some wanted to be picked up, some started crying, so I had to attend to their demands. Then I felt sleepy myself—so where was the time for my education? I did not see any way out. No one could learn without the help of a teacher. There were some letters that I could recognize, but I wasn't able to write them. How can one be literate without being able to write? So how was I to read that sheet? I thought and thought about it but could not find a way out. Besides, the danger of being seen was very much there.

Gradually I began to lose hope, but I prayed to God constantly, "Please, God, teach me how to read. If you don't, who else will?" That was my constant prayer. Sometimes I used to think that I would never succeed. Even if I tried hard and somebody was willing to teach me, where was the time? It was useless. I'd never learn. The very next moment I thought, of course I will. God has given me hope. He can never disappoint me. Encouraged, I kept that sheet to myself. But I had no time to look at it. I kept the sheet in my left hand while I did the cooking and glanced at it through the sari, which was drawn over my face. But a mere glance was not enough, because I could not identify the letters.

I decided to steal one of the palm leaves on which my eldest son used to practice his handwriting. One look at the leaf, another at the sheet, a comparison with the letters I already knew, and, finally, a verification with the speech of others—that was the process I adopted for some time. Furtively I would take out the sheet and put it back promptly before anybody could see it.

Wasn't it a matter to be regretted, that I had to go through all this humiliation just because I was a woman? Shut up like a thief, even trying to learn was considered an offense. It is such a pleasure to see the women today enjoying so much freedom. These days parents of a single girl child take so much care to educate her. But we had to struggle so much just for that. The little that I have learned is only because God did me the favor.

---

*The *khori* is an elevated bamboo platform, used as a storage space in East Bengali (now Bangladeshi) village kitchens.

Actually, the man who was my master happened to be a likable person. But it is difficult to ignore or reject accepted customs and practices. That was why I had to undergo all that misery. Anyway, it is no use crying over spilled milk. In those days people considered the education of women to be wrong. Even now we come across some who are enemies of education. The very word excites their displeasure. Actually, they were not really to blame; it was a time that was very precious. If you compare that period with the present you find many changes—beyond count. If the people of the earlier generation were here to witness all these changes, they would have died of disgust and shame. But whatever God directs seems to be for the good. The heavy dress of the women in those days, the heavy jewelry, the conch-shell bangles, and large vermilion dots used to look very nice. Of course not all clothes were like that.

But I have no reason to complain. God has looked after me well and I spent my time with a happy heart. Suffice it to say that whatever he does is for the best. As a child I used to sit with the other children in the primary school. This proved to be useful when I compared the letters of the palm leaf and sheet of the book with the memory of the alphabet I had. All through the day I went on doing this in my mind. After a great deal of time and with great effort I somehow managed to stumble through the *Chaitanya Bhagavata*. Books were not printed in those days. The handwriting was difficult to decipher. Oh, the trouble I had to take to read. In spite of all that, I did not learn to write. One needs a lot of things if one is to write: paper, pen, ink, ink pot, and so on. You have to set everything before you. And I was a woman, the daughter-in-law of the family. I was not supposed to read or write. It was generally accepted as a grave offense. And if they saw me with all the writing paraphernalia, what would they say? I was always afraid of criticism. So I gave up the idea of writing and concentrated on reading. I never thought I would be able to read. It seemed an impossible task in my situation. The little that I have learned was possible because God guided me. I was deeply engrossed in whatever I could read and the idea of writing did not cross my mind.

Reading C

Literacy: Liberation or Lip Service?

PAT DEAN

Pat Dean was the director of the Adult Literacy Organization of Zimbabwe, Africa, in the mid-1980s when she wrote this piece on the value of education and literacy for women. Zimbabwe, formerly the white settler state of Rhodesia, faced serious challenges to educate the black residents, who had been severely disadvantaged under the former government. The new government had to educate adults as well as children, since an estimated 70 percent of the population was illiterate or semiliterate in 1980, when independence was won. The government focused on adult literacy as a way to foster a socialist society.

United Nations estimates of illiteracy indicate that at present there are 814 million illiterates in the world. The majority of these are in the developing countries and approximately 62 percent are women.

A recent estimate of illiteracy in Zimbabwe showed that at least 40 percent of Zimbabwean adults are illiterate, while 15 percent are semiliterate. If we accept the U.N. estimate that 62 percent of these are women, it can be supposed that there are at least 1.2 million illiterate and semiliterate adult Zimbabwean women.

The major reasons for the existence of illiteracy in Zimbabwe are historical and political. "Free, compulsory primary education for all" was never a policy of the Rhodesian regime. And although primary schooling is now free in Zimbabwe, we would have to make it compulsory in the future to ensure that illiteracy will not remain a problem into the next century.

The reason there are more illiterate women than men may relate to cultural values: parents may not have viewed the education of their daughters as equal in value to the education of their sons. The dropout rates in the primary schools have been far higher for girls than for boys, suggesting a lack of support for girls' education. And it should also be noted that a girl who does manage to become literate in primary school, but does not have reason to use her literacy skills during her normal life, will gradually lose them.

People say that illiteracy is not a problem because people can live, have children, and earn an income without being literate. This may be true, but it is the quality of life that is important. Illiteracy is a strong contributing factor to women's poor self-image and lack of social status, as well as poor family health conditions and limited income-earning capacity. In general, an illiterate woman does not see herself as a strong resource, nor does she make the best use of the resources available to improve her situation.

Many of the reasons that women give for wanting to be literate show a limited perception of the problem. Many say that they want a better life or to be able

Pat Dean, "Literacy: Liberation or Lip Service?" *Connexions* 21, Summer 1986: 18–19.

Key Term

literacy The skill to read and write.

to read bus destinations and street signs. Others want to read and write letters. However, as they become literate, women change their expression of their personal goals.

As soon as they can read and write, they are eager to use these new skills to increase their income, to participate in community activities, and to take part in health, agriculture, and other educational programmes. Perhaps their initial motivation to become literate is vague, but there is no doubt that most women are extremely conscious of their need to learn. Literacy for Zimbabwean women is not only a need but a basic human right.

The illiterate woman cannot share, as her educated sister may, in financial decision making at home. She is not only ignorant of issues but unable to plan expenditure; she becomes a victim in her home, condemned to a minor role. As a wife, homemaker, and mother, her illiteracy affects the lives of her husband and children. She cannot read educational material on home economics, nutrition, child care, or preventive healthcare. She stays away—or is excluded—from women's clubs, and so loses further opportunities to come into contact with new ideas.

Outside the home, however capable she is, no matter what her leadership abilities are, she cannot fulfill any political decision-making role which requires literacy and numeracy. We must consider the significance of this on Zimbabwean development.

Women who are the breadwinners in the family suffer financially for their illiteracy. It is essential that every woman have income-earning skills which will protect her and her family in the event of misfortune. Current women's skills seem to be vegetable growing and selling and the making and selling of handicrafts. This is not enough.

If women were trained to buy goods in bulk, work in cooperatives, supply major markets, and so on, they would be more economically self-sufficient. It is clear that any attempt to help women become competent in these areas would be difficult if the women are illiterate.

Our 1.2 million illiterate and semiliterate women need literacy education relevant to their needs to enable them to play a full role in family, community, and national life. Literacy would improve the quality of family life and the education of children and make women economically self-sufficient.

Literacy: No Panacea for Women's Problems

M. S. MLAHLEKI

In a response to Pat Dean, educator and philosopher M. S. Mlahleki takes issue with the kind of well-meaning but narrow view of literacy that promotes reading and writing skills alone. Mlahleki asks whether literacy per se can solve social problems, especially for women. The article points out that literacy carries with it values that are never neutral and that may often transmit the cultural priorities of dominant groups, such as the former colonizers.

The article by Pat Dean is very important and informative in that it comes at a time when efforts are being made to liberate our people from psychological problems emanating from years of colonial rule. As director of the Adult Literacy Organisation of Zimbabwe, she has noted that more than a million women in Zimbabwe cannot improve their personal lives and self-image because they are illiterate. However, it is

M. S. Mlahleki, "Literacy: No Panacea for Women's Problems," *Connexions* 21, Summer 1986: 19–20.

arguable whether literacy skills on their own are a necessary or sufficient precondition for the development of wise people, capable of rational decision making. Pat Dean's literacy programmes will not necessarily be able to develop new women who will, like their educated sisters, contribute to Zimbabwe's progress.

It is necessary to be clear as to the meaning of literacy. For practical purposes, literacy is the mere ability to read and write—nothing more, nothing less. Once we move beyond that level we are entering the domain of education, which is not the object of the current discussion. So, a literate person is not necessarily an educated person, but rather a person with the minimum tools to enable him [sic] to do clerical duties of one sort or another. When we talk of a community of literate people, we are talking of a community of clerks not necessarily having practical skills to contribute to socioeconomic development.

Indeed, an educational system designed to enable people merely to read and write has prompted young school leavers to move to the urban areas from their ru-

Key Terms

development The modernization projects promoted in the so-called developing countries after the end of formal colonialism. The hallmarks of development include the loan programs and policies of international and national organizations such as the World Bank, the United Nations, and the governments. These loans were intended to increase industrialization, mechanize agriculture, and develop education and health infrastructures. Development approaches have been critiqued for being "neocolonial," culturally insensitive, and environmentally destructive.

false consciousness This Marxist term refers to the effects of bourgeois ideology on working-class people as they learn to believe in values and ideas that work against their own class interest.

ral homes with the belief that their literacy skills will be positively rewarded in the cities. These youngsters have turned away from agriculture and have rushed to the already flooded job markets in the cities. This is the dilemma facing literacy experts in developing capitalist countries.

While Pat Dean assumes that an illiterate woman will have a "poor self-image," "lack status," etc., it is clear that she is expressing values inherent in the specific social framework within which she is working. We could ask her to explain what she would consider as a "good" self-image or "status" which a literate woman should have. She will probably argue that a woman with a good self-image and status would have no problems knowing what to do: she would automatically wisely plan family expenditure, participate in community activities, contribute to health care, agriculture, and educational programmes. This wisdom to make a progressive contribution to society, it may be argued, is a result of new literacy skills.

When Pat Dean claims that illiteracy is an inhibiting factor for development, she is in fact saying that there is a desirable set of values needed to contribute to the development of Zimbabwe. Whether these values are brought about by literacy remains to be seen. What this boils down to is that there is no such thing as value-free or neutral literacy programmes.

All literacy programmes are designed to develop a certain type of person depending on whether the social environment in which that person works is capitalist or socialist. In a capitalist society literacy programmes will be designed to develop capitalist values, and in a socialist society the programmes will be designed to achieve socialist values.

Development itself is thus never neutral or value free—it has a class character. What sort of development does our country want? Is our development to be brought about by "clerks" or is it to be brought about by the peasants and proletariat?

I would disagree with the notion that the ability to perceive oneself as a "strong resource" or to make the "best use of other resources" would be improved merely by the ability to read or write. We have many literate young men in the streets of Harare, Bulawayo, Gweru, and Mutare who do not see themselves as strong resources in any sense. What is needed is not literacy per se but sociopolitical and ideological direction so that the people realise that they are a "strong resource," or that they can make the best use of available resources for the development of their communities and themselves.

Moreover, I would not want to argue that decision-making skills are a logical product of literacy, as we have so many literate people who are unable to plan expenditure wisely. However, you cannot hope to plan expenditure when you do not have any expenditure to plan. A poor peasant will obviously decide what she needs according to the problems that confront her and the resources available to her. The question of wise spending will thus be determined by the nature of one's income, needs, and priorities within the value framework of a specific social system.

Literacy alone cannot transcend the value framework and power relations in any particular society. The question "why be literate?" can hardly be adequately answered without relating it to the question "what kind of society do we want?"

Whether the society we want is capitalist or socialist, literacy and education will be determined by those values. Any attempt to ignore the nature of literacy (or indeed education) under the pretence that there is such a thing as a value-free or neutral literacy programme is to do a disservice to our revolution, which seeks to free the people from a false consciousness so that we may achieve socialist and societal values and attitudes. It is more than illiteracy that prevents over one million illiterate women in Zimbabwe from improving their self-images and their lives.

Reading E

World Media

WILLIAM WRESCH

Cultural critic William Wresch argues that the global-ization of media industries does not mean that every-one sees or hears the same thing around the world. Rather, he says, people receive different kinds of infor-mation in various parts of the world due to both eco-nomic and cultural factors. Although countries like United States are able to exert a great deal of influence through the production and export of TV entertainment and news programs, movies, and other media, Wresch points to the complexities of this situation. People show over and over again that they may receive First World media products in ways that are unintended and unexpected. All of this leads us to consider what kinds of information are generated about women and gender issues in an international framework and who pro-duces and consumes this information.

William Wresch, "World Media," in *Disconnected: Haves and Haves-nots in the Information Age,* New Brunswick, NJ: Rutgers University Press, 1996: 23–24, 33–38.

"Baywatch" is more embarrassment than entertainment for people there [in rural areas]. The nudity, the physical contact . . . .

—*NAHUM GORELICK,*
Namibian Broadcast Company

It's a Tuesday night in Africa. You happen to live in a capital city with all the perks—electricity and a televi-sion signal. So you come home from a hard day at the office and switch on the tube. Here is your evening lineup for Windhoek, Namibia:

5:00	"Sesame Street"
6:00	"Casper and Friends"
6:30	"The Rich Also Cry"
7:00	"Zoom"
7:30	"Growing Pains"

Key Terms

cultural imperialism The idea that the culture of one dominant country completely overwhelms or erases the culture of another that is less powerful.
guerrilla warfare Warfare conducted by small bands of troops, usually behind enemy lines, through unpredictable stealth tactics rather than open maneuvers with standing troops and armaments.

Reuters/AP Major news agencies that gather and distribute news to newspapers, periodicals, and broadcasters. Reuters is a European organization founded in 1851 in London. AP (the Associated Press) was founded in 1892 as the Associated Press of Illinois.
right-wing groups Organizations with extremely conservative political views.

8:00	News
8:30	"Tropical Heat"
9:25	"Parliamentary Report"
9:30	"Talking Point"
10:30	Sports

Cable subscribers could supplement that lineup with "Goof Troop," "Scooby Doo," "The Flintstones," and "Garfield and Friends" as well as "The Wonder Years," "The Simpsons," and the movie *Don't Tell Mama the Babysitter's Dead*. What a great way to spend an evening. A mongoose frolicking in the backyard, kudu steaks on the grill, and American reruns on the tube.

Some version of this evening is occurring all around the world. In Hanoi, "Charlie's Angels" now airs six times a week (Huckshorn 1995). In the Crimea 500 Russians demonstrated for a return to Russian-language dubbing of "Santa Barbara," complaining that the new Ukrainian-language version was totally unacceptable: "It's like a friend you've known for years suddenly changing her voice" (Meek 1995). American television appears nearly everywhere.

In one sense, what is on the world's TV screens or in the papers may not seem to matter. After all, we now have electronic mail and new computer systems. Public media seem like quaint artifacts of the past. But they are very much a force of the present. While popular descriptions of life in the information age seem to dwell on state-of-the-art computer systems and communication links, it is clear that much, if not most, of the information people have comes from nothing fancier than television screens and daily newspapers. It is here that information starts, and too frequently it is here that information ends.

—Newspapers

For many people, television and movies may be nice, but newspapers are where the *real* information is. Well, maybe. It is certainly true that newspapers are a major source of information. But just how important are they? Consider one extreme example. Ethiopia sells one newspaper each day for every 1,000 people in the country. Twice as many people watch TV (two per 1,000). Almost 200 times as many Ethiopians get their news over the radio. Think this is an exception that holds only in the developing world? How about the United States? Only one person in four reads a daily paper. Four out of five have televisions, and the average American owns 2.1 radios (U.S. Census 1993).

Newspapers are certainly an important information source, but they suffer two problems: quantity and quality. Let's begin with some of the quantity issues.

Quantity

Here are newspaper circulation figures for some countries around the world (per 1,000 population) (U.S. Census 1993). As you can see, the range is quite dramatic:

Country	Newspaper Circulation
Algeria	51
Bulgaria	451
Cuba	124
Ethiopia	1
Hong Kong	632
India	26
Israel	261
Japan	587
Kenya	15
Mexico	127
Norway	614
Soviet Union	482
United Kikngdom	395
United States	250
Zimbabwe	21

The United States is somewhere in the middle of the pack. The world's great newspaper readers seem to be the people of Hong Kong, Japan, and Scandinavia. On the other hand, the developing world reads even less than Americans. Part of this is a question of literacy, part of it a matter of money. Newspapers can be expensive, often far more as a percentage of a daily wage than they would be in the United States. Newspapers are not the medium of the poor.

Quality

If newspapers lag behind television and radio in circulation, they at least have the advantage of quality, don't they? Well, maybe not. Besides the fact that many stories around the world can't be covered because of censors or danger to reporters, there are two other factors that are shaping the quality of news: cost and international news flow.

Cost   Reporters don't come cheap. One vision of reporting is that it is now a high-tech enterprise with reporters working computers and phones and working with huge databases, cranking out stories without effort. But even at the leading papers where technology is available, the computer work has to be followed up. Too often this means sitting in endless meetings, or waiting to talk to people, or phoning again and again. The result is that even in the best of times under the best of circumstances, reporters aren't very productive. If we were to use an industrial metaphor, while TV production may be at the pinnacle of the industrial/information enterprise, news reporters are essentially still hunters and gatherers. They handcraft each story, producing about as much each day as the average basket weaver or wood carver. They survive from a different age.

Their handcrafting does not come cheap. Neither do paper, printing presses, and all the other associated costs of newspaper production. The results became obvious in the United States in 1995 with the closure of *New York Newsday,* the *Houston Post,* and the *Baltimore Evening Sun.* Add to that 800 layoffs at the *Los Angeles Times* and you get a sense for how desperate the times have become (Kurtz 1995).

What is less obvious is the impact of these financial pressures on the quality of the news. In its fight for circulation, the *Miami Herald* has said it will concentrate on the nine subjects reader surveys indicate are most popular—national and world news are not among the nine. The *Buffalo News* has moved to a front-page format focusing on three main stories. Recent leads have been O. J. Simpson remarriage rumors and coverage of the Dagwood Bumstead comic strip. A local radio ad asserts, "You can get the facts without straining your brain." How lucky for Buffalo.

More subtle is the financial impact on the news mix. Consider these costs from a small-town daily in middle America. Reporters' salaries begin at $20,000. Fifteen reporters are needed to cover local news, sports, and photography. Quick multiplication shows minimum costs of $300,000 per year for local news. Meanwhile, national and international news is coming in off the wire. Cost? For the Associated Press, $800 a week, for *New York Times,* $500 per month. That totals $47,600 ($41,600 plus $6,000), or roughly the cost of two local reporters. So the big cost is local news. Small wonder that larger chains can buy up local papers, cut the local reporters, go with wire-service news, and expect a 20 percent return on their investment (Glennon 1994).

The result is sensationalism and recycled wire-service news. In some cases it is recycled sensationalism—the O.J. story of the day appearing in paper after paper in city after city. Putting out a newspaper with real news in it may never have been harder. To quote one editor, "There's a real spiritual self-doubt that I don't remember experiencing before" (Kurtz 1995: D1).

International News Flow   Every few years the subject of information flow comes up, usually accompanied by accusations of cultural imperialism. The United Nations Educational, Scientific, and Cultural Organization (UNESCO) already had one publication in 1953 calling attention to the prominence of industrialized nations in the world's news flow, and by the late 1970s there were several efforts at analysis under way, most notably Sean MacBride's commission, which produced *Many Voices, One World* (1980), a detailed analysis of information movement around the world. All of this led to calls for a New World Information and Communications Order (NWICO) with increased information rights for developing nations. The United States objected to many of the proposals in NWICO and eventually pulled out of UNESCO entirely, partially as a result of this opposition. With support for NWICO slipping, many of its proposals were dropped, but it did lead to a number of regional news agencies, such as

CANA (Caribbean News Agency), PANA (Pan African News Agency), and IPS (Inter-Press Service). These regional news services were intended to break the hold of international news groups such as Reuters and AP. The new regionals have been uneven in their success, but they are still around today.

Has talk of a new world order in information changed the way news flows today? Studies can point to a few places where regional news has a larger place than in the past, but generally not much has changed. International news traffic is still dominated by Reuters and AP, and the flow is still from the industrialized world to the developing world—from rich to poor. They print far more news about the United States than we print about them.

It is usually the representatives of the developing world who complain about this news flow, concerned about how invisible they are to the rest of the world—getting news coverage only for famines, flood, or genocide—but the flow is not good for the United States and other rich nations either. For one thing, since little news flows to us with any regularity, we know little about the world. Disasters like Rwanda seem to spring at us out of nowhere, when actually the massacres there had been building for months. But a little guerrilla warfare, a little political infighting, a few dozen machete deaths, none were enough to warrant space in American papers. There was no news until tens of thousands were dying. It is as though we are always walking in halfway through a play and are then asked to make brilliant decisions about how the play should end.

Meanwhile, the information that flows from the United States to the rest of the world may not always be the information we would like to share. Consider the famous Bobbitt penis trial. As the trial played out in the United States, the *Citizen,* a daily paper in Johannesburg, South Africa, was giving the penis trial daily coverage—at a time when South Africa was just months from its first democratic elections and at a time when the country was in the midst of de facto civil war. True, the trial was on page three, with page one describing Nelson Mandela's concerns over civil war, an armed standoff at an Afrikaner radio station, and an agreement by *Mandela and De Klerk* on reestablishing legitimate local government. Page two was used for continuations of page one news. But the penis trial was

the biggest story on page three, with a four-column head and over 20 column inches of text. Below the trial story was an article on the arraignment of five terrorists who had fired into a Cape Town tavern (only a two-column head). Only on subsequent pages do we learn about two young people killed in feuds between ANC factions, the daring rescue of a pilot who had crashed in a small plane, the funding of a Zulu march on Pretoria that left 15 dead, and the handover of a major South African port to Namibia. Again, this was not a slow news period, yet an American sex trial was given a major position—both space and placement in priority over a number of serious South African stories.

What is one to think of all this? At first blush it appears the dominant information of the information age is who is pregnant by whom on "The Bold and the Beautiful" and which sex crimes are being committed in which American suburbs. Or maybe all this proves is that America's role in the information age is to provide comic relief.

What could possibly explain the world's fascination with American sex crimes? Having seen endless stories about crazy Americans popping up in one African newspaper after another, I once asked an editor, "Don't you have any crazy people in Africa? Why only cover the crazy people in my country?" His response was that Africa had plenty of crazy people of its own, but: "If I want to cover them, I have to send out a reporter, he's gone all day, when he gets back I have to rewrite everything he's written, and even then I can't be sure he's gotten the names right or quoted correctly so we won't be sued. Meanwhile, sitting across the room from me the Teletype keeps pounding out story after story, all accurately researched and correctly spelled. I can just slip out today's 'Crazy American' story and have 10 or 12 column inches filled in five minutes" (Lush 1994).

In one sense we are back to economics—it is cheaper to get news off the wire than to get original news. In another sense we are looking at quality—American reporters spell better than African reporters. Either way, what appears to be an international plot for "cultural imperialism" is really daily decisions made by editors around the world. Stories about Americans, crazy or otherwise, are easy to get.

The result of these factors is newspapers that are less than anyone would like. Local news seems to be slowly disappearing under financial pressure. News flow seems to be all in one direction, and the news that flows seems more suited for the *National Enquirer* than the *New York Times*. The news in newspapers seems to be less than anyone would like and is declining in quality and quantity.

✎ Radio

Radio is the Rodney Dangerfield of information sources. No one gives it much respect. That is a mistake. The United States may have 2.1 radios for every person in the country, but we are not the only nation with more radios than people. That list includes Australia, Canada, Denmark, the Netherlands, South Korea, and the United Kingdom. Even in the developing world radios are a common commodity. Consider these figures (per 1,000 people) (U.S. Census 1993:856):

Country	Number of Radios
Algeria	233
Bolivia	599
Cuba	345
Ghana	266
Mexico	243
Nigeria	172
South Africa	326

Only in desperately poor countries such as Bangladesh and India does the ownership of radios fall below 100 per 1,000 people, and even in those countries, radio ownership is far more common than ownership of newspapers or televisions. Radio appears to be the one communication medium that is uniformly available around the world.

Radio also tends to be local. Programming does not need to be imported. There may be some music from the United States (country western is very popular in southern Africa), but local music makes it onto the radio as well, as does lots of talk.

Talk can be disastrous. Much of the tragedy of Rwanda can be traced to a radio station that broadcast calls for genocide and then urged people to flee the country. Its lies may be responsible for hundreds of thousands of deaths. Smaller crises have been caused in South Africa when right-wing groups put an illegal radio station on the air and issued calls for armed rebellion. Other problems seem to be occurring in the United States as a few stations have moved from conservative talk to slanderous talk.

But radio talk can also be an amazing forum for average citizens. Namibia has two shows that provide an excellent model of what radio can be. Each morning from 9:00 to 10:00 the public radio station airs "The Chat Show." People call in with complaints. Sometimes it is a business that has bothered the callers, but often it is concerns about the police or government ministries. To an American ear the calls are decidedly calm. There are few grand complaints about "the system." Callers make specific complaints about experiences they have had, and do it fairly quietly. They relate their stories slowly and in detail. Announcers don't rush people and seldom interject their own feelings one way or another. After a person has said all he or she has to say, the announcer tries to sum up and then moves on to the next caller. It all seems far less shrill than American radio (but sometimes more tedious).

From 10 A.M. to 1 P.M. there are periods of music and interview shows with experts on one thing or another. At 1:00 the action starts again. This is the time for "Feedback." Sandra Williams of NBC has spent the three-hour interval from 10 to 1 calling government agencies or private businesses to get their reactions to comments made during the morning. Getting reactions is often quite simple—it turns out many of the ministers listen to the morning show. She records their responses and prepares to put them on the air at 1:00. When "Feedback" begins, Williams plays a tape of the original complaint, unedited and often lengthy. Then she plays the response. On occasion she will ask a question for clarification, but usually she and her colleagues are silent, letting the caller and the minister have center stage.

In rural Namibia the radio serves a more unusual role. There are no phones, there is no mail to speak of. If you want to get hold of a person, how do you do it? You call the local radio station. For no charge you can have the station announce that Johannes should see his aunt, she needs him. Johannes may not be listening, but enough of his neighbors are that he will get the message by the end of the day. The same system is used by government bodies. When the University of Namibia branch office in Oshikati needs to talk to a student who is taking a correspondence course, it will call the local station and have it announce, "Teofilus Shicongo, your biology textbook has come in." They have never had a student not get the message. Even in the poorest, most rural places in the world, radio works.

REFERENCES

Glennon, G. (1994). Sales Manager, Journal Printing Company. Interview by author Stevens Point, Wisconsin, August.

Huckshorn, K. (1995). "TV Invasion." *Milwaukee Journal Sentinel,* 24 September, p. 10A.

Kurtz, H. (1995). "Newspaper Industry Going through a Rough Year." *Milwaukee Journal Sentinel,* 5 November, pp. 1D, 4D.

Lush, D. (1994). President, Media Institute of Southern Africa. Interview by author. Windhoek, Namibia, March.

Meek, J. (1995). "Dubbing of American Soap into Ukrainian Enrages Crimea." *Milwaukee Journal Sentinel,* 24 September, p. 10A.

U.S. Bureau of the Census. (1990). *100 Years of Data Processing: The Punchcard Century.* Washington, D.C.

____. (1993). *Statistical Abstracts of the United States.* Washington, D.C.

REFLECTING ON THE SECTION

Ewen and Ewen write that "the power to reproduce and spread ideas and information served a variety of social forces and possibilities." What are some technological, educational, economic, and social forces that might be necessary to "reproduce and spread ideas"? How does power (cultural, political, religious, or economic, for example) influence the spread of ideas? What are the ramifications of the ways ideas are spread (via print, radio, or spoken word, for example)? What are women's particular relationships to the spread of ideas through print media (books, newspapers, magazines)?

How do globalization and other economic considerations affect the kinds of information available in a particular location? What technologies and identities influence our access to information? For example, how is literacy linked to participation in democratic politics and public life? What kinds of literacy facilitate various kinds of political change? Devi overcomes severe obstacles to gain access to a religious text. Others have sought literacy to oppose colonial rule or slavery or to establish themselves as individuals and citizens. How does a reliance on print in modern culture disenfranchise certain segments of the population?

Representing Women in Colonial Contexts

Woman Is an Island: Femininity and Colonization

JUDITH WILLIAMSON

Feminist cultural critic Judith Williamson, shows us how to analyze advertisements to see not only how women are depicted differently from men but how non-white and non-Western women are portrayed as "Other." Within Western industrial capitalism, non-white and non-Western women come to represent the seemingly "lost," simpler, more natural way of life that people fear is no longer available to them. Williamson argues that as capitalist societies destroy any cultures different from them, they simultaneously require images of difference to make their own power structures acceptable and even normal.

Our current standard of living derives in part from the incredibly cheap labor exploited by multinational companies in "developing countries," which produce many of our consumer goods on wages that would be unacceptable to us, and from the control of markets internationally. Western banks make enormous loans, at enormous interest, to impoverished Eastern bloc countries. Economically, we need the Other, even as politically we seek to eliminate it.

Judith Williamson. "Woman Is an Island: Femininity and Colonization," in *Studies in Entertainment,* Tania Modleski, ed. Bloomington, IN: Indiana University Press, 1986: 111–13, 116–18.

So, with colonial economies as with the family, capitalism feeds on different value systems and takes control of them, while nourishing their symbolic differences from itself. The "natural" and "exotic," the mystery of foreign places and people, appear both as separate from our own culture and as its most exciting product: *Discover The Tropical Secret For Softer Skin.* Travel and holiday advertising offers us the rest of the world in commodity form, always represented as completely different from the fast pace of Western "culture," yet apparently easily packaged by it nonetheless.

[. . .]

The travel images of "colorful customs," of exotic cultures, of people apparently more "natural" than ourselves but at the same time expressing our own "naturalness" for us—all these images of "otherness" have as their referent an actual Otherness which was and is still being systematically destroyed, first by European and then by American capital. Yet it is the *idea* of "natural" and "basic" cultures which seems to guarantee the permanence (and, ironically, the universality) of capitalist culture. It is the value system of our own society that we "read off" other societies; we seek to naturalize our own power structures in the mirror of "natural" life as pictured outside capitalism.

[. . .]

Key Term

commodity form A commodity can be defined as a thing produced for exchange or sale. The Marxist concept of commodity argues that it is not only the thing that the worker produces that can be bought and sold, it is also the labor itself that becomes commodified and therefore something that can be purchased.

FIGURE III.9   POND'S CREAM AND COCOA BUTTER

In Figure III.9, Pond's cream and cocoa butter is less coy about unveiling its tropical mystery: "For centuries, the women of the South Sea Islands have been envied for their soft skin." The Other is pictured less ambiguously, and its capture proclaimed more triumphantly. In showing an actual (albeit very "white"-looking) South Seas woman the control of difference is more complete, and we are placed not between two worlds, but in control of both: "Now your skin can have the best of both worlds." The product has brought the Other together with the known, and the timeless into modernity. "For centuries" and "for generations" the secret has been kept, but now the "traditional South Seas recipe" is combined with "modern, well-tried moisturizers." In this way the tradition of a different culture appears as the modern achievement of our own.

But just as the commodity which expresses another's value loses its own identity in the process, so those "primitives"—women and foreigners—who are

so valuable in reflecting capitalism's view of itself are robbed of their own meanings and speech, indeed are reduced to the function of commodities. We are the culture that knows no "other," and yet can offer myriad others, all of which seem to reflect, as if they were merely surfaces, our own supposed natural and universal qualities. To have something "different" captive in our midst reassures us of the liberality of our own system and provides a way of re-presenting real difference in tamed form.

The fashion for tans shows most clearly of all the necessity of difference in producing meaning and also reveals how the relation of ideological phenomena to production is frequently central to their meaning. [. . .] When the nature of most people's productive work, outdoors, made a suntan the norm for working people, a pale skin was much prized, a mark of luxury: not just a symbol but an indexical sign of leisure time, a measure of distance from the masses' way of life. Now, however, a deep suntan stands for exactly the same things—leisure, wealth, and distance—for it must involve *not* being at work for the majority of people, and therefore suggests having the wealth for both leisure and travel.

In fact, an ad for Ambre Solaire offers you self-tanning lotion that doesn't require hours in the sun; however, the fake tan it produces has a meaning only because it *does* suggest time in the sun, leisure, and so on. [This ad (not reproduced here due to copyright restrictions imposed by Ambre Solaire's parent company, L'Oreal) consists of a shapely pair of tanned, trim female legs. In front of these lovely legs, text proclaims, "Isn't it nice to be brown when everyone else is white." Underneath the text, beside the legs, is a large bottle of self-tanning lotion.] It is typical within ideology that the method of the product, the self-tanning, actually denies what it means, which is "real suntan"—making the inaccessible accessible, while simultaneously boasting that it is uniquely hard to obtain. In theory, anyone and everyone should buy fake-tan lotion and get a tan, yet the tan still represents difference, as the caption shows.

There is another kind of difference which this provocative caption completely ignores. "Isn't it nice to be brown when everyone else is white?" Yes, but only if you were white to start with. The racism of a white colonial society *isn't* very nice.

FIGURE III.10   HAWAIIAN TROPIC

The woman-in-sea-with-garland image in Figure III.10 is the typical representation of the exotic; conversely, femininity is represented by the "woman of the islands": half-naked, dark-haired, tanned. Yet her features make her equally likely to be a white American or European woman who has *acquired* the "natural tan of the islands." It is striking that the deep-tan advertising genre, and the exotic "southern" images, never use either African-looking models or politically contentious places: in this ad "the islands" are obviously Hawaii, but in general there are many imaginary "islands" in make-up, suntan, and perfume ads which serve to represent an "other" place and culture without actually having to recognize any real other country and its culture. The "desert island" is the ideal location for the "other"; it is more easily colonized than an entire continent,[*] and picturing the colony as female makes it so much more conquerable and receptive.

Of course, when the caption offers its product "to all skin types for a safe, dark, natural tan" it doesn't really mean a "natural tan." If one were naturally dark, of course, one would be black—a contingency not anticipated by the ad, which clearly does *not* address "all skin types" but, like almost all public imagery, assumes its audience to be white.

[*]The early capitalist pioneer Robinson Crusoe did well in this respect.

Reading B

Excerpts from Reading National Geographic

CATHERINE A. LUTZ AND JANE L. COLLINS

Feminist anthropologists Catherine A. Lutz and Jane L. Collins describe the influence of magazines such as

Catherine A. Lutz and Jane L. Collins, *Reading National Geographic,* Chicago: University of Chicago Press, 1993: 4–6, 166–68, 172–75.

the National Geographic in circulating representations of non-Western cultures to the American public. While the magazine marketed itself as providing scientific information, Lutz and Collins say, it provided stereotypic ideas about people in other countries. In these excerpts, they show us how such stereotypic im-

Key Terms

Africanism Like Orientalism, Africanism approached the representation of Africa from a Eurocentric perspective to create homogenized images of Africa as "primitive" and "savage."

Frankfurt School In 1923, members of the Institute of Social Research in Frankfurt, Germany, set up the first Marxist research center devoted to the study of culture, society, and politics. Frankfurt School philosophy critiques twentieth-century capitalism and the problems and possibilities of mass culture in Western societies. Prominent members included Theodor Adorno, Max Horkheimer, Walter Benjamin, and Erich Fromm. With the rise of Nazism, many of the Frankfurt School researchers went to the United States and established the institute at Columbia University.

Hottentot Venus/Sarah Bartmann (Saartje Bartman) A South African woman whose birth name is unknown and who was given the Dutch/English name Saartje Bartman/Sarah Bartmann. She was brought to Europe, where she was displayed as a curiosity under the label "the Hottentot Venus" for several years until her death in 1816. The Dutch explorers had named the Bushmen of Southern Africa "hottentots," and a mythology developed about their supposedly "primitive"

characteristics. Bartmann was promoted by her captors as an example of this group. Her physique intrigued anatomist George Cuvier (1769–1832), who made an extensive study of her measurements. Portions of Bartmann's body were preserved after her death in the French Museum of Natural History. In recent years, Bartmann has been remembered by feminists and cultural race scholars as a particularly tragic figure in early colonial racism in the creation of a masculinist science.

Life/Look *Life* magazine was started in 1936 by Henry Luce, the influential publisher of *Time* magazine. *Life* was a large-format, weekly publication modeled after the newest French and German magazines, which pioneered new technologies in printing photographs. In 1937 *Look* magazine began publication and continued the emphasis on photojournalism. Both magazines deeply influenced North American culture, especially in the 1960s. They ceased publication in 1972 (although *Life* has been republished since then).

surrealism An art movement founded in 1924 in Paris by André Breton, linked to earlier modernist literary trends as well as to the work of Sigmund Freud. Surrealist artists represented the imagination as it appeared in dreams and in the unconscious.

ages of nonwhite and non-Western men and women served to create, by contrast, the ideals of white North American femininity and masculinity.

Whose Representations? Power and Geographic Knowledge

To understand how people are acculturated to a particular set of views about the third world, one should look first to television, film, and mass circulation photographs in magazines and textbooks for their content and their effect on readers. Images have been important in the cultural construction of ethnic/racial difference from the earliest periods of European contact with others (Bucher 1981; B. Smith 1985), but never more so than now, when people give more time to television news than to newspapers, when newspapers have less text and more images than in the past, and when Hollywood films (often with ethnic or racial subthemes) have become more spectacular and more widely and frequently viewed than ever before. Other examples include the immense popularity of the picture magazines *Life* and *Look* in mid-century and of the *National Geographic,* whose subscription rate grew from 2 million to 10 million subscribers from the mid-1950s through the 1980s.

[. . .]

The National Geographic Society, which produces *National Geographic* magazine, is a powerful institution. Located in Washington, D.C., it cultivates ties to government officials and corporate interests. It justifies its self-image as a national institution on the basis of its reputation for purveying important scientific knowledge about "the world and all that is in it" and for safeguarding important American values and traditions. The latter include an informed or knowledgeable citizenry, particularly in an epoch in which many have been devoted to the idea of America's global responsibilities. In fact, however, *National Geographic* magazine is no forum for the free exchange of ideas about or from the third world. It is a glossy, stylized presentation of a highly limited number of themes and types of images. As such, it is clearly located within what theorists of the Frankfurt School called mass culture— materials created and disseminated by powerful inter-

ests for the consumption of the working classes. In categorizing the magazine as mass culture, we are not counterposing popular ideas about the non-Western world to a more legitimate set of high cultural or elite ideas. We are pointing to the nature of its photographs as mass-produced images sold to a reading (viewing) public.

Since the writings of the Frankfurt School in the 1930s and 1940s, the term *mass culture* has been used to refer to the commercial production of art and entertainment by powerful culture industries. The reputation of the *National Geographic* as a vehicle for scientific information makes it less obviously a member of this set of cultural products, but examination of its connection to prevalent and historically specific ideas will make clear the relevance of the concept of mass culture for an understanding of its relationship to power and culture.

Far from representing the voices and tastes of the popular classes, or even registering their desires, mass culture was seen by Frankfurt theorists as degenerate and manipulative. To the extent that people accepted and participated in the products of mass culture, they were duped and misled, encouraged to develop a false understanding of their situation in a capitalist society. For adherents of such a view, mass culture represented production *for* the masses by dominant classes, while popular culture referred to the remnants of autonomous culture produced by working-class communities.

[. . .]

More fine-grained analyses of culture industries have been concerned to specify which classes, or fragments of classes, use the industries to express their perspective, who the proposed audience is, and who responds. We argue that while the messages contained in *National Geographic* photos are highly specific in terms of the worldview they encode—that of the white, educated middle class—they speak to, and draw into their vision, a far larger group, extending from highly educated professionals and managers through white-collar clericals and technicians into the working class and lower ranks of the service sector. The magazine claims to articulate a *national* vision, addressing the concerns and curiosity of all U.S. citizens.

[. . .]

The Women of the World

National Geographic's photographs of the women of the world tell a story about the women of the United States in the post-World War II period. It is to issues of gender in white American readers' lives, such as debates over women's sexuality or whether women doing paid labor can mother their children adequately, that the pictures refer as much as to the lives of third-world women.

[. . .]

Research on the visual representation of women makes clear that female images are abundant in some domains (advertising) and virtually absent in others (photojournalism of political subjects). The invisibility extends much further for women of color. In popular images as well as the dominant white imagination, as Hull, Scott, and Smith (1982) have so eloquently told us, "All the women are white, all the blacks are men," and black women are simply invisible. The photographs of *National Geographic* are indispensable because it is one of the very few popular venues trafficking in large numbers of images of black women. While the photographs tell a story about cultural ideals of femininity, the narrative threads of gender and race are tightly bound up with each other. In the world at large, race and gender are clearly not separate systems, as Trinh (1989), Moore (1988), Sacks (1989), and others have reminded us.

[. . .]

As with American women in popular culture, third-world women are portrayed less frequently than men: one-quarter of the pictures we looked at focus primarily on women.[1] The situation has traditionally not been much different in the anthropological literature covering the non-Western world, and it may be amplified in both genres where the focus is on cultural differences or exoticism.

Women and Their Breasts

The "nude" woman sits, stands, or lounges at the salient center of *National Geographic* photography of the non-Western world. Until the phenomenal growth of mass-circulation pornography in the 1960s, the magazine was known as the only mass-culture venue where Americans could see women's breasts. Part of the folklore of Euramerican men, stories about secret perusals of the magazine emerged time after time in our conversations with male *National Geographic* readers. People vary in how they portray the personal or cultural meaning, or both, of this nakedness, some noting it was an aid to masturbation, others claiming it failed to have the erotic quality they expected. When white men tell these stories about covertly viewing black women's bodies, they are clearly not recounting a story about a simple encounter with the facts of human anatomy or customs; they are (perhaps unsuspectingly) confessing a highly charged—but socially approved—experience in this dangerous territory of projected, forbidden desire and guilt.

[. . .]

The racial distribution of female nudity in the magazine conforms, in pernicious ways, to Euramerican myths about black women's sexuality. Lack of modesty in dress places black women closer to nature. Given the pervasive tendency to interpret skin color as a marker of evolutionary progress, it is assumed that white women have acquired modesty along with other characteristics of civilization. Black women remain backward on this scale, not conscious of the embarrassment they should feel at their nakedness (Gilman 1985: 114–15, 193). Their very ease unclothed stigmatizes them.

In addition, black women have been portrayed in Western art and science as both exuberant and excessive in their sexuality. While their excess intrigues, it is also read as pathological and dangerous. In the texts produced within white culture, Haraway (1989: 154) writes, "Colored women densely code sex, animal, dark, dangerous, fecund, pathological." Thus for the French surrealists of the 1930s, the exotic, unencumbered sexuality of non-Western peoples—and African women in particular—represented an implicit criticism of the repression and constraint of European sexuality. The Africanism of the 1930s, like an earlier Orientalism, evidenced both a longing for—and fear of—the characteristics attributed to non-Western peoples (Clifford 1988: 61). The sexuality of black women that so entertained French artists and musicians in cafés and cabarets, however, had fueled earlier popular and scientific preoccupation with the Hottentot Venus and other pathologized renditions of black women's bodies and desires (Gilman 1985).

The *Geographic*'s distinctive brand of cultural relativism, however, meant that this aspect of black sexuality would be less written in by the institution than read in by readers, particularly in comparison with other visual venues, such as Hollywood movies. Alloula (1986) gives the example of the sexualized early twentieth-century "harem" postcards of North African women. His thesis is that the veil fascinates a Western audience because it is read as a no-trespass message, and it is experienced by outside men as frustrating and attractive for this reason. It became an object of Western quest from a sense of the need to penetrate beyond it through, simultaneously, the light of photography, the reason of enlightened social change, the knowledge of science, and the desire of the flesh (compare Fanon 1965). One can also see the distinctive *Geographic* style in comparison with *Life* photography of non-Western women. We can see the stronger cultural viewpoint on race at work in a 1956 *Life* article on "other women," which ran next to an article on American women of various regions of the country. The two articles read as a kind of beauty pageant, with all the photographs emphasizing the sitter's appearance, sexuality, and passivity. Ultimately, the magazine's editors judged American women the better-looking set (many captions also noted the "natural," "healthy," wholesome—nonperverted?—quality of the American women), but the adjectives they used to caption the non-Western women described their sense of the more passive and sexually explicit stance of the other women. So they are variously praised for their "fragility," "great softness," "grace," "langorous" qualities, and eagerness "to please"; "the sensuous quality often seen in women of the tropics" was found in one Malayan woman. The hypersexual but passive woman here replicates the one found by many Westerners in their imaginary African travels throughout the last century (Hammond and Jablow 1977). In the *Life* article, all of the non-Western women except the one Chinese "working girl" (and many of the American women),

touch themselves, their clothes, or fans in the usual pose for characterizing female self-involvement (Goffman 1979).

If *National Geographic* trades on the sexuality of black women, it is less comfortable with that of black men. Men coded black were far more likely than those coded white to appear bare-chested in the pages of the magazine—often in poses that drew attention to musculature and strength. The *National Geographic* has apparently tried to include pictures of "handsome young men" (Abramson 1987: 143). For American readers, male muscles take the place analogous to female breasts as signs of gendered sexuality (Canaan 1984). Many pictures visually or through their captions draw attention to the rippling muscles of photographed men. A picture of a man from the Nuba mountains in the Sudan (November 1966: 699) fills the page, primarily with his torso rather than face or full body, accentuating his strongly defined musculature. The caption highlights his brawn and implicitly suggests that this physicality is at the expense of intelligence: "Muscles like iron, his leather arm amulet worn as insurance against disaster, a champion wrestler exudes confidence. In his world, a man's strength and agility count for much, and at festivals he earns the plaudits of his peers. But modern civilization—a force beyond his comprehension—threatens his primitive way of life."

Like the nude and its role in Western high art painting (Hess and Nochlin 1972; Betterton 1987; Nead 1990), nudity in *Geographic* photographs has had a potential sexual, even pornographic, interpretation. Such interpretations would obviously threaten the magazine's legitimacy and sales, achieved through its self-definition as a serious, relatively highbrow family magazine. Pornography represents just the opposite values: "disposability, trash," the deviant, the unrespectable, the low class (Nead 1990: 325). Like fine art, science attempts to frame the nude female body as devoid of pornographic attributes. While art aestheticizes it, science dissects, fragments, and otherwise desexualizes it. The *National Geographic* nude has at times done both of these contradictory things.

NOTE

1. This proportion is based on those photos in which adults of identifiable gender are shown (*n* = 510). Another 11 percent show women and men together in roughly equal numbers, leaving 65 percent of the photos depicting mainly men.

REFERENCES

Abramson, Howard S. (1987). *National Geographic: Behind America's Lens on the World.* New York: Crown.

Alloula, Malek. (1986). *The Colonial Harem.* Minneapolis: University of Minnesota Press.

Betterton, Rosemary, ed. (1987). *Looking On: Images of Femininity in the Visual Arts and Media.* London: Pandora.

Bucher, Bernadette. (1981). *Icon and Conquest: A Structural Analysis of the Illustrations of deBry's Great Voyages,* trans B. M. Gulati. Chicago: University of Chicago Press.

Canaan, Joyce. (1984). Building Muscles and Getting Curves: Gender Differences in Representaitons of the Body and Sexuality among American Teenagers. Paper presented at the annual meeting of the American Anthropological Association, Denver.

Clifford, James. (1988). *The Predicament of Culture: Twentieth-Century Ethnography, Literature, and Art.* Cambridge, MA: Harvard University Press.

Fanon, Frantz. (1965). *A Dying Colonialism.* New York: Grove Press.

Gilman, Sander. (1985). *Difference and Pathology: Stereotypes about Sexuality, Race, and Madness.* Ithaca: Cornell University Press.

Goffman, Erving. (1979). *Gender Advertisements.* New York: Harper & Row.

Hammond, Dorothy, and Alta Jablow. (1977). *The Myth of Africa.* New York: Library of Science.

Haraway, Donna. (1989). *Primate Visions: Gender, Race, and Nature in the World of Modern Science.* New York: Routledge.

Hess, Thomas B., and Linda Nochlin. (1972). *Women as Sex Object: Studies in Erotic Art, 1730–1970.* New York: Newsweek Books.

Hull, Gloria, Patricia Bell Scott, and Barbara Smith. (1982). *All the Women Are White, All the Blacks Are Men, but Some of Us Are Brave: Black Women's Studies.* Old Westbury, NY: Feminist Press.

Moore, Henrietta. (1988). *Feminism and Anthropology.* Cambridge: Cambridge University Press.

Nead, Lynda. (1990). "The Female Nude: Pornography, Art, and Sexuality." *Signs* 15:323–35.

Sacks, Karen. (1989). "Toward a Unified Theory of Class, Race, and Gender." *American Ethnologist* 16:534–50.

Smith, Bernard. (1985). *European Vision and the South Pacific.* 2d ed. New Haven: Yale University Press.

Trinh, Mmh-ha T. (1989). *Woman, Native, Other: Writing Postcoloniality and Feminism.* Bloomington: Indiana University Press.

Feminism and Difference

MARNIA LAZREG

Marnia Lazreg, a feminist sociologist, explores the ways in which women living in a vast geographic region become homogenized into a singular category, "Middle Eastern women" or "Islamic women." Since there are many religions, cultures, nations, ethnicities, classes, and other differences among women in this region, what is the purpose of creating such a general category? Lazreg discusses the history of the Western,

Lazreg, Marnia, "Feminism and Difference," *Conflicts in Feminism.* Marianne Hirsch and Evelyn Fox Keller, eds. New York: Routledge, 1990: 330–32.

Eurocentric attitudes toward Islam and people different from Christian Europe that have been responsible for this biased framework.

Difference, in general, whether cultural, ethnic, or racial, has been a stumbling block for Western social science from its very inception. Nineteenth-century European ethnology and anthropology were established precisely to study different peoples and their institutions. However, regardless of the conceptual, theoretical, and methodological inadequacies and uncertainties in the works of many classical anthropolo-

Key Terms

Bronislaw Malinowski (1884–1942) Polish-born anthropologist who founded the "functionalism" approach to studying culture, arguing that cultures must be studied according to their unique internal characteristics and dynamics.

cultural universals Commonalities among cultures.

Emile Durkheim (1858–1917) French sociologist who is considered by many to be the founder of modern sociology. Durkheim followed the positivist approach of empirical research methods and argued that common values create social bonds.

ethnology Scientific study of the origin and early development of human culture; a branch of cultural anthropology.

Europocentrism/Eurocentrism Putting Europe in the center of knowledge.

gynocentric Putting women in the center of knowledge; a term used by second-wave cultural feminists (see also Lazreg, fn 4).

Marcel Mauss (1872–1950) French sociologist and anthropologist (nephew of Emile Durkheim), best known for his research into "gift exchange."

Oedipus complex Believed by psychoanalysts to be a developmental stage in the male child from ages three to five characterized by intense love for the mother and hostility toward the father. Named by psychoanalyst Sigmund Freud after the myth of Oedipus, the Greek royal son who was unable to avoid the fate conveyed by an oracle that he would one day marry his mother and kill his father.

ontological Based upon being or existence; a philosophical approach drawing on the metaphysics of the nature of being.

gists and ethnologists, their interest in "difference" was a function of their desire to understand their own institutions better. This was the case with Emile Durkheim's work on religion, Marcel Mauss on exchange, and Bronislaw Malinowski on the Oedipus complex, to cite only a few. Although I do not wish to absolve Western anthropology of its Europocentrism, it showed, at least in its inception, some awareness of a common denominator between people of different cultures, a *human* bond. The notion of "cultural universals" and that of the "human mind," however problematic, are expressions of such a common link between various peoples.

Contemporary academic feminism appears to have forgotten this part of its intellectual heritage. Of course, counterposing feminist scholarship to social science may appear senseless. Aren't female social scientists part of the same society and intellectual milieu as males? Indeed they are. But academic feminists have generally denounced conventional social science for its biases regarding women in both its theory and its practice. Specifically, they have shown that it has reduced women to one dimension of their lives (such as reproduction and housework) and failed to conceptualize their status in society as historically evolving. Academic feminism, therefore, has brought a breath of fresh air into social science discourse on women and held out the promise of a more even-handed, less biased practice. It is surprising, then, when one sees that women in Algeria (or in any other part of the Third World) are dealt with precisely in the ways with which academic feminists do not wish to be dealt.

Women in Algeria are subsumed under the less-than-neutral label of "Islamic women" or "Arab women" or "Middle Eastern women." Because language produces the reality it names, "Islamic women" must by necessity be made to conform to the configuration of meanings associated with the concept of Islam. The label affirms what ought to be seen as problematical. Whether the "Islamic women" are truly devout or whether the societies in which they live are theocracies are questions that the label glosses over.

The one-sidedness of this discourse on difference becomes grotesque if we reverse the terms and suggest, for example, that women in contemporary Europe and North America should be studied as Christian women!

Similarly, the label "Middle Eastern women," when counterposed with the label "European women," reveals its unwarranted generality. The Middle East is a geographical area covering no less than 20 countries (if it is confined to the "Arab" East) that display a few similarities and many differences. Feminists study women in Victorian England or under the French Revolution; few would dare subsume French or English women under an all-encompassing label of "European women" or Caucasian women, as substantive categories of thought. Yet a book on Egyptian women was subtitled "Women in the Arab World."[1] Michel Foucault may have been right when he asserted that "knowledge is not made for understanding; it is made for cutting."[2]

There is a great continuity in the U.S. feminist treatment of difference within gender, whether the difference is within or outside of U.S. society. In each case an attribute, whether physical (race or color) or cultural (religion or ethnicity), is used in an ontological sense. There is, however, an added feature to feminist modes of representing women from the Middle East and North Africa, and these modes reflect the dynamics of global politics. The political attitudes of "center" states are mirrored in feminist attitudes toward women from "peripheral" states. Elly Bulkin rightly notes that "women's lives and women's oppression cannot be considered outside the bounds of regional conflicts." She points out that Arab women are represented as being so different that they are deemed unable to understand or develop any form of feminism. When Arab women speak for themselves they are accused of being "pawns of Arab men."[3] The implication is that an Arab woman cannot be a feminist (whatever the term means) prior to disassociating herself from Arab men and the culture that supports them! In the end, global politics joins hands with prejudice, thereby closing a Western gynocentric circle based on misapprehended difference.[4]

The political bias in these representations of difference is best illustrated by the search of many feminists for the sensational and the uncouth. This search for the disreputable, which reinforces the notion of difference as objectified otherness, is often carried out with the help of Middle Eastern and North African women themselves. Feminism has provided a forum for these women to express themselves and on occasion for them to vent their anger at their societies. The exercise of freedom of expression often has a dizzying effect and sometimes leads to personal confession in the guise of social criticism. Individual women from the Middle East and North Africa appear on the feminist stage as representatives of the millions of women in their own societies. To what extent they do violence to the women they claim authority to write and speak about is a question that is seldom raised.

NOTES

1. See Nawal Saadawi, *The Hidden Face of Eve: Women in the Arab World* (Boston: Beacon Press, 1980).

2. Michel Foucault, *Language, Counter-Memory, Practice,* D.B. Bouchard, ed. (Ithaca: Cornell University Press, 1977), 154.

3. Elly Bulkin, "Semite vs. Semite/Feminist vs. Feminist," in *Yours in Struggle: Three Feminist Perspectives on Anti-Seminism and Racism,* Elly Bulkin, Minnie Bruce Pratt, and Barbara Smith, eds. (Brooklyn: Long Haul Press, 1984), 167, 168.

4. I am using the term "gynocentric," as suggested by Elizabeth Weed, associate director of the Pembroke Center, Brown University, to refer to the situation whereby some women as a group exercise discursive power over other women whom they exclude from their frame of reference.

Excerpt from Images of Women: The Portrayal of Women in Photography of the Middle East

SARAH GRAHAM-BROWN

Sarah Graham-Brown, a historian of photography in the Middle East, describes how information about women in that region was seen through the lens of nineteenth-century European colonization. Western travelers drew on their cultural and racial biases to produce descriptions and histories that highlighted European superiority. Western women were quite active in this process, measuring women they met against their own values and ideas. A good example of this Eurocentric knowledge can be found in the descriptions of female segregation or seclusion found in affluent households in the Middle East, North Africa, and parts of Asia. Western outrage over such "harems" sensationalized these domestic arrangements and created harmful images of the women who lived in them that continue to exert influence even today.

—Women on Women

The images of Middle Eastern women which emerged from the West were not solely the creation of men. By

Sarah Graham-Brown, *Images of Women: The Portrayal of Women in the Photography of the Middle East, 1860–1950*, London: Quartet Books, 1988: 18–23, 71–74.

the end of the nineteenth century, numbers of Western women had visited the Middle East, or lived there as the wives of the growing population of Western officials, doctors, engineers, and businessmen. Women also made up a large proportion of the missionary workers who came from Europe and the United States as teachers and medical assistants. This was one of the few vocations open to women from modest backgrounds who wanted to work and to have some degree of independence. Finally there was a small group of independent women who spent time in the Middle East as travelers, anthropologists, doctors and even, in a few rare cases, political advisers.

Women from all these groups contributed to the body of Western literature and imagery on the Middle East, but there is little evidence that gender alone distinguished their views from those of men, except in one respect: the fact that they had many more opportunities to observe the daily lives of Middle Eastern women, even those who lived in seclusion. However, what use they made of these opportunities varied very much from person to person.

Like their male counterparts, most women who left records of their impressions of the Middle East used their own culture as a yardstick by which to judge what

---

Key Term

missionary women Primarily Christian women who accompanied their husbands or other male family members to convert non-Christian populations around the world.

they saw. However, their conclusions were frequently influenced by the way they perceived women's role in their own societies. Since the late nineteenth and early twentieth centuries were times of considerable debate about the image and status of women in Britain, Western Europe and the United States, the position they took on the issues of emancipation and women's sexual and social freedom was likely to affect their reactions to the problems of women in the Middle East.

Among independent women travelers, the desire to escape the constraints and limitations of life in their own societies was often a motive for launching out into unknown regions. Like men, they did not want to conform to the norms of their own society; however, their motives related more often to intellectual and social constraints than to a yearning for sexual freedom. For talented, energetic women, outlets at home were few and far between, and if they had the money and initiative, travel appeared as an escape from all these forms of frustration. Among the most outstanding examples of women travelers motivated by a desire to escape these shackles were Gertrude Bell and Isabelle Eberhardt.

Gertrude Bell, the daughter of a well-to-do and indulgent family, spent a good part of her adult life in the Middle East. Nevertheless, she showed very little interest in the lives of women. In her books and photographs women appeared from time to time, but they remained peripheral to her main interest in politics and public affairs, which she considered the domain of men. As a Western traveler, she seems to have been accepted in most circumstances as a kind of surrogate man. As a highly intelligent and independent woman who had made the most of her privileged background to enter into male domains in her own society as well as in the Middle East, she had scant patience with what she perceived as the narrower worlds of women and their problems. She even went so far as to campaign briefly against the suffragist movement in Britain.

Another legendary figure among women travelers was Isabelle Eberhardt who, like many other travelers, used the Middle East (in this case Algeria) as a place of escape from the tensions caused by the stifling conventions of bourgeois Europe. Eberhardt was able to play out a role which fitted her own apparently ambivalent sexuality, sometimes as a surrogate man moving in nomadic society, sometimes as the woman who was the lover of an Algerian soldier. She also did not appear to have had any great interest in indigenous women. Some of her writings suggested that she regarded Algerian women as sad and passive victims of men and of economic circumstances.[1]

Women such as Lady Isabel Burton and Lady Anne Blunt, who mostly traveled with their husbands, did not generally make very much of their encounters with women. In the nomadic societies which interested them most, the women of the community received relatively little space in their narratives. In Isabel Burton's case particularly, even questions of marriage and personal relationships were narrated mainly from the male point of view. In Lady Anne Blunt's account, the exception is her vivid description of the personality of the first wife of Muhammad Ibn Rashid, whose harem she visited in Hail, northern Arabia.

The English writer and traveler Freya Stark, who made many journeys in the Middle East from the 1920s until the 1950s, has left a much more detailed record, in her writings and photographs, of her contacts with women. She was certainly much more willing to spend time in women's company and though her comments were sometimes tinged with condescension, she could also be perceptive and humorous. But Stark also shared the common nostalgia of travelers of this era for the "old ways," which were gradually fading as Western influence grew. At the same time, like Gertrude Bell, she seems to have been basically in favour of Britain's imperial role, though she was critical of the practice of particular colonial administrations.[2]

It was frequently missionary women who painted the blackest picture of Middle Eastern women's lot, while they described the moral elevation of the convert, "redeemed" from ignorance and oppression, in glowing terms. Although their zeal sometimes overrode concerns other than those of bringing women to Christ, many of these missionaries were also dedicated teachers and formed close, if unequal, relationships with women they taught or converted.

Most of the Western women who wrote about the lives and status of Middle Eastern women did so with a consciousness of how these lives compared with their own. Some even went so far as to link explicitly their views on women in the Middle East with those on the status of women in their own societies, although the conclusions they reached varied considerably. One such writer was Lucy Garnett, who spent some eight years in the region and whose two-volume account of the lives of Muslim, Jewish, Kurdish, and Armenian women in Turkey was one of the most detailed written in the nineteenth century. Garnett stressed the diversity of conditions under which Middle Eastern women lived, arguing that segregation and seclusion in the various communities were a matter of "the special social and economic conditions under which they live—some conditions necessitating a rigid seclusion of women and others allowing an extraordinary degree of independence. The subjection of women in the East is, consequently, so far as it exists, the result of such conditions, rather than of legal and religious enactments."

At this point, Garnett shifted her focus to the West where, she argued, the subjection of women had been "chiefly the result of the substitution of the Law of the Christian Church for the later Roman Law, under which women enjoyed greater personal and proprietary privileges than are now claimed by the most advanced champions of 'Women's Rights.' " Thus she argued that neither in the West nor in the East was the subjection of women absolute; but in the West the constraints imposed on women were mainly legal ones, while in the Middle East, they related mainly to custom and socioeconomic conditions. While today this may seem a very simplistic argument, it differed from the conventional wisdom of the time, which tended to posit a sharp dichotomy between Western enlightenment and Eastern tyranny over women. Yet Garnett ends her book (published in the 1890s) on a surprising note, with a polemic against the Suffragist movement and its demand for the political enfranchisement of women in the West. This seems incongruous but perhaps indicates that such women observers were often unable to disentangle their feelings about women's status in their own societies from their assessments of women's condition elsewhere.

But I believe that I am at one with the vast majority of Englishwomen in thinking that the assumptions of the Women Suffragists—the "brutality of men" and the "antagonism of the interests of men and women"—are utterly false; hence, that no political slavery of women exists, and no political enfranchisement is, therefore, required; and hence that Womanhood Suffrage would, quite needlessly, introduce into politics an element altogether incalculable.[3]

From the 1920s onward, when feminists from women's movements within the Middle East began to attend international conferences, Western feminists were made more aware of their needs and demands, which included rights to education and work, improved legal status within the family, and in some cases, women's enfranchisement. Some Western women who visited Turkey after World War I were very impressed by the reforms implemented by Kemal Atatürk, which were regarded at the time as something of a model for the rest of the region. But despite the contacts and personal friendships which developed through encounters between feminists from the different cultures, there was often a lack of understanding of Middle Eastern cultures on the part of Western feminists. Even Margery Corbett Ashby, President of the International Alliance of Women for Suffrage and Equal Citizenship in the 1920s and 1930s, who was considered a staunch friend, particularly by Egyptian feminists, took a somewhat condescending attitude toward Arab women in her private correspondence.[4]

Western feminists were not able to escape entirely from the Eurocentrism of their age, nor even from the imperial perspectives of their own nations. This resulted in a growing political divide between European and Middle Eastern feminists over nationalist resistance to Western imperialism in the region. In the period after World War II this rift was widened by the Arab–Israeli conflict—in which, with a few exceptions, the West has sided with Israel—and by the wave of anticolonial struggles throughout the region, culminating in the Algerian war of independence.

[. . .]

Seclusion and Segregation

The word *harim* in Arabic means a sacred, inviolable place, and it also means the female members of the family. From the same root comes also the word *haram*, which bears a double meaning: forbidden, or sacred and protected. But *haram* or *hurma* was also used in upper- and middle-class Arab society as a respectful form of address to a married woman. In Turkey and Iran the equivalent term was *hanum* or *khanum*. But the most common use of the word *harim* (*haremlik* in Turkish) was to denote the space in the family home reserved for women (commonly spelled *harem*). Among the urban elites of the Arab region, Turkey and Iran, this separation of space was accompanied by the seclusion of the women of the family from the sight of all men except husbands and close relatives.[5]

Segregation of space and control over the visibility of women were forms of patriarchal control which emphasized the need to channel and contain women's sexual power. Some commentators argue that this concept of women's sexual power differs from that which developed in European cultures. The Moroccan sociologist Fatima Mernissi, for example, contends that restrictions placed on women in the Islamic cultures of the Middle East are not based on a view of women's biological inferiority: "On the contrary, the whole system is based on the assumption that women are powerful and dangerous beings. All sexual institutions (polygamy, repudiation, sexual segregation, etc.) can be perceived as a strategy for containing their power."[6]

This view of women as possessing powerful, even uncontrollable sexual passions has taken many forms, including popular sayings, myths, and stories. In Morocco, for example, there is a saying that women are *hbel al-shitan* (Satan's leash), implying that they are capable of dragging men away from virtue and also of tying them up (in Arabic this word is also a euphemism for impotence). Thus women who are not kept under strict control appear, in this imagery, as objects of both fear and blame. Their sexuality needs to be channeled into marriage and their visibility controlled to prevent other men from succumbing to their powerful sexual urges. In this view, men's sexuality is less problematic and they are offered numerous socially acceptable ways of indulging their sexual desires.

[. . .]

Rules controlling the visibility of women in public were not, of course, confined to the Middle East. They could be found in other Mediterranean societies and, until the late nineteenth century, in "genteel" society in many parts of Europe. But generally speaking, in the Middle East these rules resulted in a much clearer physical demarcation between male and female society than existed in most European cultures. The boundaries of women's worlds were not, however, set in quite the simple ways suggested by popular Western visions of the harem. Although a high degree of sexual segregation was quite common, strict seclusion of women was practised only by the relatively small proportion of well-to-do urban families in which women did not play an active economic role and could therefore be confined to the home and to the role of childbearers.

In the cities, poorer women would generally veil when they went out in the street and did most of their work at home, but they could not be completely secluded, first because they often had to work to support the family and, second, because their homes were too small to allow for strict seclusion.

[. . .]

But for the majority of people who lived outside the towns and cities, whether as settled peasants or nomads, the need for women to participate in the family labour force made strict seclusion impossible. Patterns of sexual segregation varied greatly from one community and region to another, but seclusion could be practised only among richer families, where women did not need to work.

NOTES

1. See, for example, her story "Fellah," written in 1902 and published in the Egyptian feminist magazine *L'Egyptienne,* 1 September 1925, pp. 242 ff.

2. Gertrude Bell, *The Desert and the Sown* (London: Virago, 1985 rpt). *The Letters of Gertrude Bell,* selected and edited by Lady Bell, 2 vols (London: Ernest Benn, 1927). *Gertrude Bell: From Her*

Personal Papers 1889–1926, Elizabeth Burgoyne, ed. (London: Ernest Benn, 1958/61). Lady Anne Isabella Noel Blunt, *A Pilgrimage to Nejd,* 2 vols (London: Frank Cass & Co, 1968). Lady Isabel Burton, *The Inner Life of Syria, Palestine and the Holy Land: From My Private Journal,* 2 vols (London: H. S. King & Co., 1875). Freya Stark, *Baghdad Sketches* (London: John Murray, 1937); *Seen in Hadramaut* (London: John Murray, 1938); *Letters from Syria* (London: John Murray, 1942). These are just a few of her numerous books on the Middle East.

3. L. M. J. Garnett, The Women of Turkey and Their Folk-lore (London: D. Natt, 1890/91), Vol. II, p. 546.

4. See the private correspondence of Margery Corbett Ashby in the Fawcett Library, London.

5. For a detailed description of life in Turkish palace harems, see N. Penzer, *The Harem* (London: Spring Books, 1965). For a general overview of Western ideas about the harem and its imagery, see Annabelle d'Huart and Nadia Tazi, *Harems* (Paris: Chene/Hachette, 1980).

6. Fatima Mernissi, *Beyond the Veil* (London: Al Saqi Books, 1985), p. 19. For further discussions of women and sexuality in the Middle East, see F. Sabbah, *Women in the Muslim Unconscious* (New York: Pergamon Press, 1984); A. Boudhiba, *Islam and Sexuality* (London: Routledge & Kegan Paul, 1985). For details on *hbel shitan,* see Lawrence Rosen, "The Negotiation of Reality: Male–Female Relations in Sefrou, Morocco," in *Women in the Muslim World,* Lois Beck and Nikki Keddie, eds. (Cambridge, Mass./London: Harvard University Press, 1982), pp. 566–67 and footnote 3, referring to observations by Kenneth Brown.

REFLECTING ON THE SECTION

Colonialism was upheld not only through political and economic means but also through cultural practices; that is, the ability to create and disseminate biased representations and descriptions of colonized societies. Within these representations, descriptions of colonized women served an important purpose. Marnia Lazreg argues that women in the Middle East were exoticized within colonial representation. The region was depicted in a generalized way that erased all differences among people and cultures. What purpose does "difference" serve in colonial and postcolonial culture?

In this context, Judith Williamson writes that "to have something 'different' captive in our midst reassures us [in the West] of the liberality of our own system and provides a way of re-presenting real difference in tamed form." Similarly, Lutz and Collins assert that stories of women "of the world" in *National Geographic* are actuallty commentaries on American women and reflections of a vision of normalcy in the United States. What is "real difference" and how is it tamed? What American anxieties about race, gender, and sexuality are revealed in the ads reproduced by Williamson and in the pages of *National Geographic*?

Consumer Culture and the Business of Advertising

Gender and Consumption
ROBERT BOCOCK

Sociologist Robert Bocock argues that Western consumer culture since the mid-nineteenth century has gendered the figures of consumer and producer. According to this scenario, until the mid-twentieth century, women were seen as the primary consumers while men were seen as the producers of goods and services.

Robert Bocock, *Consumption,* London: Routledge, 1993: 95–108.

Bocock claims that since World War II, men are increasingly visible as consumers.

Women have been seen by social scientists, for example by R. Bowlby (1987), as being especially involved in consumption as a social process. At the end of the nineteenth century, the Paris store Bon Marché opened and made an especial appeal to women in its promotional literature. The diaries which it gave away when

---

Key Terms

consumer/consumption Within industrialized capitalism, the emergence of a particular way of using goods and services led to the rise of consumer society. Among the hallmarks of this society is commercial advertising, which creates needs and wants that can be satisfied by goods produced in the industrial economy. The consumer becomes the primary identity in this society as people define themselves more and more through consumption and ownership.

hailed A term used by followers of Marx such as Louis Althusser, who argue that people come to know or recognize themselves when they are called to (or "hailed" by) ideologies; for example, we understand an ad because we are already a part of the ways of seeing that have been used to create the publicity image and message.

libido Sexual desire.

puritanism The British religious movement in the sixteenth and seventeenth century that sought to reform the excesses of the Church of England in favor of more austere and "pure" forms of worship. Puritans took the side of the parliamentary party during the English Civil War. The early settlers in North America were Puritans, and many aspects of Puritanism—including congregational democratic government, anti-authoritarianism, and suspicion of aesthetics and pleasure—continue to influence the culture of the United States.

the unconscious The part of a person's mind or being that contains repressed thoughts and feelings. The unconscious, according to Freudian psychoanalysis, is not accessible by conscious thought but must be interpreted through signs and symbols contained in dreams or other activities.

use-value Marxist term used to differentiate between the value that is created when an object is exchanged for profit (exchange value) and the value that exists when an object is purely useful and not made for profit or exchange.

it first opened contained detailed instructions about how to reach the new department store by using public transport. Bowlby comments on this as follows:

> That this should have been practically available to the bourgeois lady marks a significant break with the past: department stores were in fact the first public places—other than churches or cathedrals—which were considered respectable for her to visit without a male companion. But this also signalled, at another level, a stepping out from domestic bounds.
>
> (Bowlby 1987: 189)

From the mid-nineteenth century, women had been exhorted to "Go out and buy" in the United States, in Britain and in Germany a little later. But by the last two decades of the nineteenth century, shopping in large department stores had become an important activity outside the household for middle-class women in the main cities of western capitalism.

In this period of modern capitalism, the binary relation of production and consumption was quite strongly gendered: production for men, consumption for women. Production was active, led to men earning money, and provided them with some form of power exercised through newly created trade unions, for instance. Consumption was more passive, involved spending money, and did not lead to any publicly recognisable forms of power. However, consumption involves goods being purchased for their symbolic value, their meaning to the consumer, not just for their material use-value. This aspect of the process gave women some control over the meanings to be associated with consumption. As Judith Williamson (1986) has said: "The conscious chosen meaning in most people's lives comes much more from what they consume than what they produce" (p. 230).

Consumer goods have become a crucial area for the construction of meanings, identities, gender roles, in postmodern capitalism. John Fiske (1989) has argued that: "Commodities are not just objects of economic exchange; they are goods to think with, goods to speak with" (p. 31).

[. . .]

Conceptions of masculinity have changed in the second half of the twentieth century, so that men too are increasingly "hailed" in the mass media, in advertisements particularly, as consumers. Such changes in conceptions of masculinity have been important in developing new consumption patterns among men. Since the end of the 1950s, men in Britain and in much of Western Europe have not been defined or perceived by governments, by businesses, by parents, or by their peers as potential fighters in wars. This contrasted greatly with the situation of those men who had been socialised under the shadow of the two world wars, for in that period masculinity had been defined in terms of being actual or potential members of the fighting forces. This absence of warfare has led to a change in conceptions of masculinity toward the male being defined in his role as a consumer, not as a fighter.

There was another difference, between cultures rather than between generations, which has affected patterns of consumption among men. Whereas in the more catholic cultures of France, Italy, and Spain, for instance, men had been defined traditionally in the culture as discriminating consumers of clothes, perfumes, food, and wines, for example, in Britain, puritanism had been effectively reinforced by wartime shortages and experiences. Men in particular, in contrast to women, were not expected to be discriminating consumers of such things. Women in Britain bought most of their sons' and their husbands' clothes, items for the household, and food for eating in the home—where most consumption of food took place. In Britain, men had a drink in the pub, then went home to eat a meal prepared by their wives or mothers. It was the Latin, catholic cultures in Europe which had a tradition of men eating in restaurants, often before going home to their wives and families. It was some of these traditional patterns of male consumption which began to change in Britain from the early 1950s.

[. . .]

Consumption has become essential to many men's sense of who they are. It has become as significant as work roles, if not more so, for younger men especially. Consumption has entered into the unconscious sense of identity of men and women in the period since the 1950s. It has become a key aspect of recent forms of capitalism and has enabled capitalism's symbols, and the products associated with them, to enter into the desires of the unconscious. The consumption of many goods is now linked with libidinal desires, sometimes in ways which were defined by the culture in the recent past as being perverse (Lyotard 1974). But in this way consumption has made capitalism appear to be legiti-

mate in a more profound way than in other periods of its development (Habermas 1976). It promises the consummation and satisfaction of desires which still may not always speak their name.

REFERENCES

Bowlby, R. (1987). "Modes of Shopping: Mallarme at the Bon Marché," in N. Armstrong and L. Tennenhouse, eds. *The Ideology of Conduct*, pp. 185–205, New York: Methuen.

Fiske, John. (1989). *Reading the Popular,* Boston: Unwin Hyman, Inc.

Habermas, J. (1976). *Legitimation Crisis,* London: Heinemann.

Lyotard, J. F. (1974). *Economie Libidinale,* Paris, Les Editions de Minuit.

Williamson, Judith. (1986). *Consuming Passions: The Dynamics of Popular Culture,* London: Marian Boyars.

Reading B

Urban Women and the Emergence of Shopping
ELAINE S. ABELSON

Social scientist Elaine S. Abelson describes the great changes that occurred in the nineteenth century in the United States when industrialization brought more manufactured goods into the marketplace at prices that more people could afford. Abelson observes that the raised standard of living that accompanied this boom in manufacturing meant increased levels of consumption. The person available to do this shopping, in many middle-class households, was the housewife, for whom shopping led to less drudgery in the home but required new skills and created new needs and desires.

Elaine S. Abelson, *When Ladies Go A-Thieving: Middle-Class Shoplifters in the Victorian Department Store,* New York: Oxford University Press, 1989: 14–15, 18–19, 20–25, 37–40.

What stands out amid the almost compulsive repetitiveness of the written record is the complexity of middle-class domesticity in late Victorian America. Amid timeless routines of keeping house and raising children, new manufacturing technologies and increased levels of industrial production changed the pattern of work in the home and enlarged the activities of the family as a consumer of goods. Many items that had formerly been of home manufacture were, between 1870 and 1880, manufactured elsewhere.[1] While home production did not cease in the post–Civil War period, its nature clearly changed. In the cities, particularly, diverse items of prepared food, ready-made clothing, household tools, and home furnishings appeared in the dry-goods stores and small specialty shops, and the link between these items and the home was the shopping woman.[2] In these decades the department store took its place as a permanent fixture in the commercial center of the larger cities, where it became both the focus of a new consumer ideology and a unique space for middle-class women. Shopping for new commodities in this new urban locale played a major role in the lives of these women, a role that signified opportunity along with status and economic power.

"Middle class" was a designation for growing numbers of urban residents. Not a class in a fixed, traditional sense, and no longer the self-employed artisans, shop-keepers, and gentry of the Republican era, by mid–nineteenth century the middle class was a group in the process of formation: mostly native-born and Protestant, white-collar, salaried, commercial and professional men and their families. There were, however, successive levels within each of these categories, and many marginal people in economically precarious situations feared a social mobility that could go two ways.[3] Not limited to occupation and income, the working definition of this new middle class has a significant cultural component that must include the home and what went in it, residential location, levels and patterns of consumption, child-rearing strategies, and leisure activities.

In those post–Civil War decades, when the ideology of the middle-class home emphasized the independence of the family unit from the stresses of the disordered and rapacious outside world, the woman, who was the theoretical center of this insular unit, was in fact thoroughly engaged in the public domain. Although rarely employed, she spent increasing amounts of time outside her home. It may be legitimately argued that women were acting in public mainly as agents of the family, and while much of their daily routine took place beyond the domestic confines, the domestic was omnipresent and usually took precedence. That may be the case, but it still suggests broad patterns of domestic social life and public activity that are more interesting for their interaction than for their presumed separation.

As *Nation* editor E. L. Godkin observed in 1882, no longer were women sitting tamely at home. Women were now "in the streets, in horse-cars, omnibuses, excursion boats, railroad trains, and hotel corridors."[4] That they were in the dry-goods bazaars as well was evident. In short, "beautifully dressed women" were in public, seeing and being seen, often lending a certain panache by their very presence.[5] Female public life was conducted without the supporting ideology of masculine individualism, but these [women's] diaries demonstrate emphatically just how far social boundaries had expanded for urban, middle-class women.

Home and family provided the background in these meticulously kept diaries, but home was not the private retreat for the women that it was for the men. Quite the opposite. Because home was the female arena, it was also their battleground and workshop, and women sought "recreation and rest elsewhere."[6] Shopping was one such recreation. "A good shop" provided the context for diverse forms of public and even cultural life, yet it was sanctioned by the demands of the private sphere.[7]

Shopping dwarfed all other activities. Women shopped constantly. There is no statistically accurate way to determine how often women shopped in the stores, but diaries indicate it was an ongoing process. In one nine-day period in the spring of 1885, Mrs. Richards "shopped" four times: March 31, April 2, April 4, and

Key Terms

dry goods Goods such as textiles and clothing.
modernity The historical time period that ranges either from the fifteenth century or from the onset of industrialization in the eighteenth century to the present. In Abelson's work, modernity means the society of urban living, characterized by industrialization, consumer culture, and use of technologies. The term is strongly associated with progress and improvement.
social mobility People's ability to move from one social or economic class to another.
trade press Publications whose audience is members of a particular profession or business.

April 8. In May of the same year she mentioned shopping six out of eight days, generally at Macy's. Mrs. Pardee shopped just as often: in May 1893, she noted going downtown to shop both morning and afternoon on the second and again on the third, returning home for lunch on both days. She shopped once more on the eighth and again on the eleventh. When women did not go shopping, they cited often compelling reasons. Alice Stimson invariably mentioned the shopping she either did or should have done in her weekly letters to "My Dear Father" (1893 to 1895). In one such letter she described a meeting of the woman's club, Sorosis, in counterpoint to her usual chores: "It is positively a great refreshment to drop all thought of what we shall eat . . . and where withal we shall be clothed for a brief period and exchange views on every other conceivable subject with a group of very bright women."[8]

For many of these women, the stores provided a use for leisure time that necessitated neither rationalization nor apology. Trade journals promoted the idea that women could find a legitimate occupation in shopping. "When they have a few leisure hours they don't know how to occupy at home," the *Dry Goods Economist* suggested, women could say to themselves, "I guess I'll go down to A's and walk around their store a little. It's always so pleasant in there."[9] Much of the relentless shopping of women like Mrs. Richards did seem to be an attempt to deal with and coherently organize time. The *New York Tribune* captured the meaning of such activity: "To go about and see things, whether one wants them or not, to pick up a bargain here and there, to take a bite at one of the store restaurants, and to return home with stories of lovely things that are being sold. . . ."[10]

Undoubtedly, some women used the department stores to kill time and ease their boredom. "What do these women mean by such aimless shopping?" a woman asked rhetorically in a *New York Times* article on shopping and shoppers. "Why, my dear, it's a cheap entertainment," was the reply.[11] Not idle, despite the pervasive stereotype that men worked and women consumed, many women evidenced, nevertheless, a vague purposelessness. In a culture in which money translated into possessions and time had become a valuable commodity, the contribution of middle-class women was ill defined.[12]

The line between domesticity and female leisure was not clear-cut. The tension between the values embedded in the communal–domestic ideal and the reality of the new "shopping woman participating fully in the commercial world was real, if publicly unacknowledged. More introspective than Harriet Richards, Clara Pardee recognized the balancing act in which she was constantly engaged. After days of sewing on her husband's dressing gown and cutting and fitting her own satin waist, all the while doing a good bit of her own housework, regularly working as her husband's pharmacist/assistant, and repeatedly going downtown to shop, she mused about how much was demanded and how little time she had. "It seems as if I accomplish but little, but days seem so full and business does take a great deal of time."[13] The repeated notation, "Hurried home to sew" was indicative of far more than congested days and the burdens of maintaining her family.[14] It spoke, indirectly, to the frustration and complaints of ennui voiced by many women of this generation, and to the male sense that the women were insufficiently occupied.

[. . .]

These women were not workers in any recognized sense—their labor was publicly invisible—but from the evidence of their diaries, reliance of middle-class women on others to attend to the real work of domesticity has been greatly exaggerated.[15]

[. . .]

The reformulation of housework around new tasks and new levels of sanitation required the full participation of all the females in the house, even with domestic help.[16] In fact, despite the new water and steam technology that became part of the middle-class home after the Civil War, the volume of household labor increased. In her study of housework and household technology, *More Work for Mother* (1983), Ruth Cowan has convincingly argued that some of the work was made easier, but the overall amount of work increased: there was more complex cooking, more laundry, more housecleaning, and quantitatively more clothes per person.[17] For instance, "refined women" were expected to have street and shopping costumes—special clothes, unlike those worn at home, that were subdued and suitable for the eyes of strangers—clothes in which one could present a public face and buy other clothes. Beginning in the

1890s, journals were full of advice about appropriate attire and advised merchants that "the success of every dry goods department depends upon whether or no women can be taught that different costumes must be provided for different occasions."[18]

By the early 1890s, as well, special clothing appeared for the new roles women adopted. The athletic woman, who participated in the growing number of sports available to middle-class women, found accessories and costumes adapted to her needs. Cycling, for example, a symbol of a changing culture as well as a fad, necessitated some modification in women's dress; but suddenly a whole industry revolved around "the wheel." There was a "cyclist corset for all athletic purposes," which came, so the ad said, "in all lengths and 100 different styles."[19] Similarly, there was the bicycle handkerchief in 12 designs for men and women; the bicycle suit, with and without divided skirt; the bicycle shirt, stock, hose, hat, sweater, collar, cap, vest, gaiters, and shoes.

[. . .]

The increasing specialization in the use of clothes, so evident in the late nineteenth century, meant that particular clothes were considered to be right and wrong for more and more occasions. The problem of not wearing the correct attire became one with not knowing how to shop and not understanding how clothes had been transformed into a new symbol of middle-class life.[20] Whether it was the "best and acceptable" dress materials for summer sports costumes, or the appropriate fashion for afternoon tea, the trade journals and the stores worked together to educate the consumer in the minutiae of dress: "The salesmen in the hosiery department," the *Dry Goods Reporter* instructed, "should be coached to urge upon the customer the different varieties which are correct . . . [they should] urge upon the customers the necessity of having variety of hose."[21]

The profound change in consumption patterns was the direct consequence of technological development and market expansion. The links between production and consumption were clear. Needs multiplied because there was more to be had and an increasing standard of living made more things feasible. Social identity was established through the new possibilities of consumption. If we substitute "want" for "need," the nature of

this critical change becomes apparent. People wanted more, wanted variety and costume and decoration, and wants are, by their very nature, both psychological and unlimited.[22]

Notions of what constituted basic necessities gradually expanded on all population levels, of course, but this was particularly true of the growing middle group of white-collar workers and their families.

Although factory-produced clothing held the promise of easing a major burden of domestic life, the stores and trade journals had to overcome a great deal of resistance to such clothing. It was a new idea that touched the very heart of family roles and personal identity. There was also a social basis for the prejudice against ready-made goods. Factory clothing had previously been associated with poverty and war.[23] With the exception of men's shirts and vests, only uniforms and rough-quality garments had been produced under factorylike conditions until after the Civil War.[24] While men's suits and coats were readily available in the early postwar period in men's clothing stores and haberdasheries, only certain items of women's clothing, such as cloaks and shawls, gloves, handkerchiefs, corsets, and a few accessories were ready-made in any great number.[25] Once the techniques for factory production of women's clothes were perfected, however, stores aggressively marketed their new goods, seeking not simply a replacement market but a vastly expanded demand.

The pressure on women to increase their levels of consumption by buying new factory-made clothes was relentless. "New styles just landed," "Ladies' costumes ready-made—all trimmed in the latest styles," "Paris ready-made dresses, very elegant" were common appeals as early as 1875.[26] Immediately identified with European fashion, the new ready-made clothing for women heralded a fundamental change in domestic life. Between the mid-1870s and the first decade of this century, the pages of the daily newspapers and the trade press developed a rationale about clothes and styles that subtly denigrated the woman who sewed at home and made her feel old-fashioned. She was enticed by the lure of rationality and modernity. "You, too, can take advantage of technology," she was assured. Why continue your old and tedious ways when "modern mechanical devices are capable of reproducing even the finest and most delicate designs . . . only experts could tell the difference."[27]

The discourse of consumption had several threads, all seeking to render obsolete home manufacturing, self-sufficiency, and an ethic of restraint. The cheapness of ready-to-wear, particularly children's clothing, was a major appeal. The fatigue of overburdened women was another and was played on in various ways. American attachment to "progress" offered yet another approach in the relentless and successful campaign to sell women on ready-made clothes. Occasionally the themes were interwoven. "Why should a tired woman sew when children's clothes very often are actually cheap?" the *DGE* querried rather ingenuously. "At times mothers would make their children's clothes even when they left their own to the family dressmaker, but with American ideas of progression, we have changed much of that."[28] More up-to-date women bought their garments, easing the "drudgery" in their lives and "saving time sufficient to allow the proper devotion to other domestic duties."[29] Other appeals allotted the time saved to "recreation and amusement."[30] Good mothers were, by implication, progressive mothers who understood that the factory was ready to serve them and their children. Carried a bit farther, this line played on fears of not being a good enough mother. One article, for example, suggested that the manufacturers showed greater concern for children than their own mothers: "These little garments . . . have better and more conscientious work put into them than the average mother will put into a child's dress."[31] Why

should mothers do for their children what manufacturers did better? Mothers were advised to let parental responsibility, freed from the burden of home production, take a new, modern form.

[. . .]

After ready-to-wear became widely available, women visited the stores at increasingly shorter intervals. The department stores had fostered an extravagant demand for clothes. There were more choices, an "endless multiplication of merchandise" amassed all in one place, and shoppers could instantly visualize rapidly changing styles.[32]

Technological innovation and the marketing of new consumer goods worked together to persuade the great majority of women to abandon one tradition and embrace another: to become skilled, modern consumers. As part of a massive reorientation of values, women relinquished traditional skills but gained new ones, along with a degree of flexibility and leisure hitherto unknown.

Women and the new department stores became partners in a profound cultural transformation. Direct production of work in the family and for the family became even more peripheral, and images of satisfaction and plenty became associated with the world outside the home rather than the one within. Before the end of the century, "homemade" had become a term of reproach, while "factory-made" became an encomium.[33] It was a profound and highly significant inversion of values.

NOTES

1. Siegfried Giedion, *Mechanization Takes Command: A Contribution to Anonymous History* (New York: Oxford University Press, 1948).

2. Arthur M. Schlesinger, *The Rise of the City, 1878–1898* (New York: Macmillan, 1933), 132. Schlesinger quotes a *Good Housekeeping* article of 1887 in which a woman, rejoicing at the new prepared foods, says, "Housekeeping is getting to be ready-made as well as clothing"; see also Adna F. Weber, *The Growth of Cities in the Nineteenth Century: A Study in Statistics* (New York: Macmillan, 1899), 219–20.

3. Margaret Gibbons Wilson, *The American Woman in Transition: The Urban Influence, 1870–1920* (Westport: Greenwood, 1979), 9–11, Sinclair Lewis defined the aristocracy of Gopher Prairie as "all persons engaged in a profession, or earning more than twenty-five hundred dollars a year, or possessed of grandparents born in America": Sinclair Lewis, *Main Street* (New York: Harcourt Brace Jovanovich, 1948), 76. Because of the repeated economic crises, one writer noted that "women should be able to work if necessary . . . [it is] a melancholy fact that 'ladies' are at times unexpectedly obliged to support themselves (and even those around

them." See Emma Churchman, *Queen of Home* (Philadelphia: Miller-Megee Co., 1889), 404.

4. E. L. Godkin, "Stewarts," *The Nation* 34 (April 20, 1882), 332; In his *Suburban Sketches,* William Dean Howells describes life on the horse-cars between the suburbs and Boston, the "intimate associations of velvets and patches," and the obvious "contrasts of splendor and shabbiness." Middle-class women shoppers were "strap hangers" as much as anyone else in the "indecently crowded" cars. William Dean Howells, *Suburban Sketches* (Boston: Osgood and Co., 1872), 105–11.

5. Howells, *Suburban Sketches;* Neil Harris, "Museums, Merchandising and Popular Taste: The Struggle for Influence," *Material Culture and the Study of American Life.* Ian Quimby, ed. (Winterthur, 1978), 154.

6. *Appleton's Journal* 51, "A Further Notion or Two About Domestic Bliss" (March 19, 1870), 328–29.

7. Clara Burton Pardee, *Diaries,* 1883–1938 (New-York Historical Society). Harriet Richards (Mrs. George Richards), *Diaries,* 1883–1893, 1900–1901, New-York Historical Society. Ann Douglas, *The Feminization of American Culture* (New York: Avon Books, 1977).

8. Alice Bartlett Stimpson Papers, The New York Historical Society, Folder 3, October 12, 1894. The diaries of Harriet Hanson Robinson also reveal her shopping habits. Living in the suburb of Malden five miles north of Boston, Robinson had access to the city on the Boston & Maine Railroad or on the omnibus line that crossed the river via ferry. Specific shopping expeditions took her to the city approximately 25 times in 1870 and 1871 respectively. She made other trips into Boston for cultural and social events. "I enjoy this running into Boston—it refreshes both body and soul, and relieves the monotony of everyday life," she wrote in 1871. Claudia L. Bushman, *A Good Poor Man's Wife: Being a Chronicle of Harriet Hanson Robinson and Her Family in Nineteenth Century New England* (Hanover: University Press of New England, 1981), 19. I owe this reference to Barbara Balliet. Shopping was obviously not a new activity for many women. See Mrs. John Farrar, *The Young Lady's Friend* (Boston, 1836), cited in Ann Douglas, *Feminization of American Culture,* New York: Avon Books, 1977, 323: "The women visit the dry-goods store every week, perhaps oftener. . . ." *Dry Goods Economist* (Dec. 1, 1894), 69.

9. *Dry Goods Economist* (Sept. 1, 1900), 85.

10. *New York Tribune* (July 21, 1901), (S) 1:4.

11. *New York Times* (Dec. 6, 1885), 4:5.

12. Churchman, *Queen of Home,* 57. Churchman emphasized the importance of labor-saving devices in kitchens. The sense of time was as important for women as for men. "Can women afford to lose time?" she asked. Michael K. Marrus, ed., *The Emergence of Leisure* (New York: Harper & Row, 1974), 94.

13. Pardee, *Diaries,* March 11, 1885.

14. Ibid., April 16, 1898. In their preoccupation with daily accomplishments, women like Clara Pardee had begun to adopt a male model and to see themselves as workers. So common an activity was sewing that diarist Susan Forbes felt it necessary to note a day without it: "I did no sewing today." *Diary,* March 12, 1874; see also Lil-

lie Devereux Blake, *Fettered for Life; or Lord and Master* (New York: Sheldon & Co., 1874), 378.

15. Douglas, *The Feminization of American Culture,* 76.

16. Barbara Ehrenreich and Deirdre English, "The Manufacture of Housework," *Socialist Revolution* 5 (Oct.-Dec. 1975).

17. There is a great deal of evidence about the increasing complexity of household cooking; for instance, the number of cookbooks proliferated after 1870. Jillian Strang, "Recipe for Success: Six Culinary Entrepreneurs, 1870–1900," unpublished paper, *Facing the Future,* Graduate Student Conference on Scholarship on Women, Yale University (April 13, 1985). For a contemporary discussion of the need for "distinct utensils for cooking," see Churchman, *Queen of Home,* 56–57; Ruth Schwartz Cowan, *More Work for Mother: The Ironies of Household Technology from the Open Hearth to the Microwave* (New York: Basic Books, 1983), 62–66, 89, 99.

18. *Dry Goods Economist* (Feb. 21, 1891), 32; (Feb. 18, 1893) 25, editorial; (July 6, 1893), 5; and (March 10, 1900), 28. Cowan, *More Work,* 98; Ehrenreich and English, *Housework,* 7; *Our Manners at Home and Abroad* (Harrisburg: Pennsylvania Publ. Co., 1883), 87–89. Many sources cite the importance of elaborate mourning costume. For mourning ritual and special street attire, see Nathalie Dana, *Young in New York: A Memoir of a Victorian Girlhood* (New York: Doubleday, 1963), 28, 95, 118. Also *Dry Goods Reporter* (Sept. 15, 1900), 47; *San Francisco Chronicle* (Dec. 20, 1896), 15; *Business Woman's Journal* IV (Jan. 1892), 18.

19. *Dry Goods Economist* (Feb. 11, 1893), 13 and (Dec. 19, 1894), 116; *Dry Goods Reporter* (Jan. 22, 1898), 13. What was true for bicycling was also true for ice skating, although to a lesser degree; see *San Francisco Chronicle* (Dec. 6, 1896), 6, "What Eastern Women of Fashion Wear when They Appear in the Rinks." For a discussion of variety and style, albeit in food, see Sidney Mintz, *Sweetness and Power: The Place of Sugar in Modern History* (New York: Penguin Books, 1986).

20. Quentin Bell, *On Human Finery* (New York: A. A. Wynn, 1979); *Dry Goods Reporter* (Oct. 19, 1901), 39.

21. *Dry Goods Economist* (March 28, 1891), 32, (May 30, 1891), 37, and (April 7, 1894), 10; *Dry Goods Reporter* (Sept. 15, 1900), 47 and (March 3, 1906), 23. In December 1897, fashion advertisements in the *Boston Globe* spoke to the specific uses of clothing, e.g., "Street Gown from Paris," ". . . The very latest Gown for Church and Promenade," "Morning Costume from Paris," "House Gown from Paris." *Boston Globe* (Dec. 4–5, 7–9, 1897).

22. Daniel M. Fox, *The Discovery of Abundance: Simon N. Patten and the Transformation of Social Theory* (Ithaca: Cornell University Press, 1967), 109ff. In the same vein, see "The Ethics of Shopping," *Fortnightly Review* LXIII (Jan. 1, 1895), 124–45. See discussion of true and false needs in Herbert Marcuse, *One Dimensional Man: Studies in the Ideology of Advanced Industrial Society* (Boston: Beacon Press, 1964), chap. I; see also Daniel Bell, *The Cultural Contradictions of Capitalism* (New York: Basic Books, 1976), 22; Mintz, *Sweetness and Power,* 58–59.

23. *Dry Goods Reporter* (Sept. 8, 1906), 51; Michael B. Miller, *The Bon Marché: Bourgeois Culture and the Department Store, 1869–1920* (Princeton: Princeton University Press, 1981), 34–35.

24. Christine Stansell, "The Origins of the Sweatshop: Women and Early Industrialization in New York City," in Michael H. Frisch and Daniel J. Walkowitz, eds., *Working-Class America: Essays on Labor, Community and American Society* (Urbana: University of Illinois Press, 1983), 84; Claudia B. Kidwell and Margaret C. Christman, *Suiting Everyone: The Democratization of Clothing in America* (Washington: Smithsonian Institution Press, 1974), 15; Daniel Boorstin, *The Americans: The Democratic Experience* (New York: Vintage Books, 1974), 99–100.

25. Robert Twyman, *A History of Marshall Field & Company, 1852–1906* (Philadelphia: University of Pennsylvania Press, 1954), 45. Dry-goods stores carried few ready-made items before 1865; only cloaks (mantuas), hose, and shawls were generally available. Marshall Field & Co. offered a slightly greater variety after 1871, but the stock was still limited to accessories: gloves, collars, cuffs, and handkerchiefs. Mrs. Caroline Dunstan's diaries suggest the extent to which urban women were engaged in home manufacture. She shopped for shirting muslin, bed sheeting, and toweling, which she and her daughters fashioned into usable products. Handkerchiefs, stockings, gloves, a shawl, an occasional hat and veil, a damask tablecloth, a winter cloak were the types of finished soft goods she was able to purchase in New York City between 1867 and 1870. Caroline A. Dunstan, *Diaries,* 1866–1870 (NYPL). See Lois W. Banner, *American Beauty,* (New York: Alfred A. Knopf, 1983), 28ff; Victor S. Clark, *The History of Manufactures in The United States, II, 1860–1893* (New York: McGraw Hill, 1929), 446, states that the "value of factory-made women's clothing [was] less than 1/2 that of men's in 1890."

26. *New York Daily Tribune* (Oct. 4, 1875), 5: A. T. Stewart advertisement; (Nov. 1, 1875), 6: Lord & Taylor and Arnold Constable advertisements.

27. *Dry Goods Economist* (July 23, 1898), 13; for a discussion of illusion and reality, see Remy G. Saisselin, *Bourgeois and the Bibelot* (New Brunswick: Rutgers University Press, 1984), 126.

28. *Dry Goods Economist* (July 25, 1891), 66.

29. Ibid. (March 9, 1895), 29 and (Oct. 10, 1903), 77.

30. Ibid. (April 23, 1898), 29.

31. *Dry Goods Reporter* (Aug. 4, 1906), 46.

32. Rosalind H. Williams, *Dream Worlds: Mass Consumption in Late 19th Century France* (California, University of California Press, 1982), 15; see Saisselin, *Bourgeois and the Bibelot* 62; *New York Times* (Oct. 4, 1885), 4:1.

33. *Dry Goods Economist* (March 9, 1895), 29 and (Jan. 16, 1897), 67; for a traditional view of homemade items, see *The Business Woman's Journal* I (Nov./Dec. 1889), 176–77.

Reading C

Excerpt from Inarticulate Longings
JENNIFER SCANLON

Women's studies scholar Jennifer Scanlon discusses the influence of the Ladies' Home Journal on consumer culture in the early part of the twentieth century. Scanlon argues that the Journal had a conservative effect because it promoted the idea of individual choice not as a political form of action but solely as a way to perfect consumption habits. This approach created an ideal feminine figure for the "American" nation that emphasized whiteness, middle-class attributes, and a domestic, home-based role.

The *Ladies' Home Journal,* both a medium of popular culture and a business enterprise, promoted for its women readers traditional "woman's values" and full participation in the consumer society. Contradictions naturally followed. It was not an easy task to promote a simple life for women while at the same time promoting the primacy of consumer goods and material desires, nor was it easy to praise women's growing independence from onerous household tasks at the same time that one pleaded with women to limit the boundaries of that independence. Yet another contradiction, which readers themselves occasionally pointed out, was that much of the editorial and advertising content

Jennifer Scanlon, *Inarticulate Longings: The* Ladies' Home Journal, *Gender and the Promises of Consumer Culture,* New York: Routledge, 1995: 4–9.

of the magazine was produced by women who led lives distinctly unlike those they counseled readers to live. Finally, the notion of choice, central to the magazine's message and to the ideology of the larger consumer culture, was often illusory, as the magazine promoted fairly limited roles for women and often ignored or dismissed many of the choices real women faced.

Central to this study is the development of mass or popular culture, which delivered through many vehicles notices of what it meant to be an American. Early analyses of mass culture were hopeful: media participation was deemed a sign of increased literacy and a certain impetus to individuals' greater participation in all elements of the social system. This has not, however, been the case. By its very nature, mass culture has often discouraged rather than encouraged democratic participation. In the case of mainstream magazines, for example, the need for continuity from issue to issue demands a formulaic view of the world. The backdrop for this formula, the ideology of dominant social groups, is a given and, hence, rarely questioned. In many forms of popular culture, the desire for a "mass" appeal negates much discussion of issues that fall outside of the mainstream. The mass appeal also leaves out significant numbers of people, since mass is often associated with race, the white race, and with class, the middle class. For example, literacy gains were enormous in the population at large at the turn of the century, but they were

---

Key Term

target market A specialized group of consumers to which a particular product is marketed.

most significant in the black population, which went from an almost 80 percent illiteracy rate to an almost 80 percent literacy rate.[1] Nevertheless, African-Americans, regardless of their literacy or purchasing power, failed to be considered a target market by the consumer culture that produced the *Ladies' Home Journal* and other popular magazines. An enterprising young man took out a classified advertisement in *Printer's Ink,* the advertising journal, in 1917, in which he called the "10 million Negro-Americans" an "undeveloped volume" for advertising interests. Apparently no one took up his offer, since it was not until 1942 that the first popular periodical for blacks, *Negro Digest,* was founded, and it was not until 1970 that the first mass magazine for black women, *Essence,* reached the newsstands.[2]

In addition to carving out a limited definition of a mass audience, magazines also provide a fairly predictable emotional formula: a balance between the fostering of anxiety that draws readers to seek out advice and the offering of positive messages that encourage them to return the following month. The resulting formula, which worked so well for the *Ladies' Home Journal,* ultimately encouraged inaction rather than action, conformity rather than individual expression, guided rather than self-generated change.[3] In an era in which many different groups of women experimented with definitions of democracy that would include rather than exclude them, the *Journal* suggested that democracy for women meant little more than the choice between one brand of soap and another, one flavor of soup and another.

At the dawn of the twentieth century, women in the United States had no few lifestyles; their varied roles were determined in part by region, race, age, and ethnicity. But by 1930, women's magazines and the consumer culture they offered related the story of a common woman, the "average" woman, the "American" woman. That image obscured the many differences among women and offered instead a promise: if you did not know your neighbor, as people moved from towns to cities and as definitions of community changed, you could tell a lot about her by the brand names she chose.[4] And, in fact, as women's magazines bridged some of the gaps of region and age, if not race and ethnicity, and as the middle class grew, women's lives increasingly became defined by spending power

and habits. The *Ladies' Home Journal* played a significant role in that cultural transformation. This work examines who such definitions of womanhood included, who they left out, and how women both embraced and struggled with the limited definitions of behavior and life the consumer culture offered.

The emergence, tremendous success, and lasting influence of magazines like the *Ladies' Home Journal* and the many magazines of this genre which followed reveals a great deal about the gender issues historians have identified as most significant during the early twentieth century. In a time of tremendous actual and potential societal changes, when middle-class white women faced new opportunities and new challenges in education, in the workforce, and, due to changing technology, in their households, this magazine specifically encouraged them to read rather than act, to conform to middle-class mores rather than seek out new and possibly more revolutionary alternatives. Ironically, the consumer definition of womanhood became dominant at the same time that other essentialist definitions met with conscious and resolute challenges. For example, throughout the nineteenth century, the largest groups of women's rights advocates spoke not of "women's" rights but of "woman's" rights. Secure in their own identity as white, native born, and middle class, these women included in their definition of womanhood only those who looked and acted like them. But by the early twentieth century, several groups of feminists spoke of "women's" rights, recognizing not only the diversity of women but also that through their diversity women had some common goals. They made some political progress operating from this standpoint, as diverse groups, initially organized on the basis of social class, race, or occupation, worked together to achieve women's expanded political participation in general and suffrage in particular.[5] As with the Progressive movement they were a part of, however, divisions of race, class, and ethnicity proved powerful, and few diverse organizations survived into the 1920s.[6]

Internal differences divided groups of women, as did the larger culture, of which women's magazines were just one part. Political in a largely nonpartisan sense, the *Ladies' Home Journal* and other magazines obscured fundamental differences among women in every issue, creating in the consuming woman an amalgam defined and limited by race, class, and ethnicity but promoted now as "average." This "average" woman had certain characteristics: she was, for the most part, married, living what might be called a "his" and "hers" marriage divided by strict gender definitions of work, nurturing, and communication. She was white and native born. A middle-class woman, she resigned her job or career at marriage and preferred spending money to producing goods. Truly modern, she purchased the latest appliances, served her family canned foods, participated in leisure activities. Finally, although she occasionally griped about her husband's lack of attention or her children's selfishness, the "average" woman felt enormous satisfaction with her life.

This *Ladies' Home Journal* prototype increasingly came to define womanhood for the early twentieth century and beyond and for the middle class and beyond. Her limitations would form the composite of women's possibilities, and her activities would shape the vocabulary of gender. Of course, the *Ladies' Home Journal* woman left out as many women as she included. She could not explain the very real gender/generational conflicts faced by older and younger women of the day. She could not explain the women who never married, those who spent their lives with other women, or the African-American, immigrant, or working-class white women whose lives were still defined by work rather than by spending. She did not include the women who found paid work rewarding or those who sought to broaden their political sphere by taking on local, state, or national governments. The composite woman failed all these women by leaving them out of the discussion. Interestingly enough, however, this "average" woman also failed the women who most closely resembled her, since, as this study reveals, even women who most closely fit the bill ultimately failed to have their needs met by the magazine or the consumer culture it promoted.

The *Ladies' Home Journal*'s domestic ideology essentially urged its readership to expand their role as consumers rather than producers, to accept the corporate capitalist model and their home-based role in it. It did this by presenting fragments of opinion—in this case fiction, advertisements, and editorial matter—and then organizing those fragments into a whole which could be called the "consensus" view. These stories, editorial pieces, and advertisements, although seemingly fragmentary and perhaps unrelated, actually worked together to provide this larger, dominant picture. And by offering several elements and distinct points of view, the magazine promoted the idea that there were many choices for women to make, but that the average woman—the middle-class woman with aspirations—was represented by the consensus view. In this way the magazine supported the notion that women benefited by the nation's philosophy of bourgeois individualism; they too had free choice. In this sense, the *Journal* offered images of what readers could be if they wished to conform, what they would reject if they did not. In retrospect, however, the women readers' choices appear clearly delineated rather than open-ended, as the *Journal* essentially encouraged women to internalize norms rather than explore alternatives while they made sense of their changing world.[7]

NOTES

1. James D. Norris, *Advertising and the Transformation of American Society, 1865–1920* (New York: Greenwood Press, 1990), 9.

2. Classified Advertisement, *Printer's Ink* (January 25, 1917), 111. On *Negro Digest,* see John H. Johnson, *Succeeding Against the Odds* (New York: Warner Books, 1989). Johnson, founder of *Negro Digest, Ebony,* and *Jet,* borrowed $500, using his mother's furniture as collateral, to start *Negro Digest.* Following its enormous popularity, he founded *Ebony* in 1942 to give returning black veterans some-

thing to distract them from "the day-to-day combat with racism," 153. On *Essence,* see Ellen McCracken, *Decoding Women's Magazines: From* Mademoiselle *to* Ms. (New York: St. Martin's Press, 1993), 224–26. *Essence* became viable when publisher Jonathan Blount could demonstrate that the readership had disposable income and represented the "young, inquisitive, acquisitive black women" (Blount, quoted in McCracken, 224). At the time that *Essence* was founded, the *Ladies' Home Journal, Good Housekeeping,* and *McCall's* each had over one million readers categorized as minority; *Essence* went after that substantial population (McCracken, 224). *Latina,* targeted toward Latina-American women, was founded in 1982 and is described in McCracken as targeting a monied but neglected group (230). Interestingly, according to Bryan Holme, ed. *The Journal of the Century* (New York: Viking Penguin, 1976), 10, John Mack Carter, editor of the *Ladies' Home Journal* from 1965 to 1973, was the first editor to feature a black model on the cover of a mass magazine. Carter was also editor when a group of feminists staged a sit-in at the *Journal* offices in 1970, protesting the traditional approach of the magazine, particularly its "Can This Marriage Be Saved?" column. See Jean Hunter, "A Daring New Concept: The *Ladies' Home Journal* and Modern Feminism," *NWSA Journal,* Vol. 2, No. 4 (Autumn 1990), 583–602.

3. Richard Ohmann, "Where Did Mass Culture Come From? The Case of Magazines," *Berkshire Review,* 16 (1981), 99; Todd Gitlin, "Prime Time Ideology: The Hegemonic Process in Television Entertainment," *Social Problems,* 26 (Feb. 1979), 251. On the notion of cultural hegemony, see also Raymond Williams, *Marxism and Literature* (New York: Oxford University Press, 1977), and Antonio Gramsci, *Selections from the Prison Notebooks,* Quintin Hoare and Geoffrey Nowell Smith, eds. (New York: International Publishers, 1971). A debate among historians about the value of or methods of studying popular culture can be found in "AHR Forum," Lawrence W. Levine, Robin D. G. Kelley, Natalie Zemon Davis, and T.J. Jackson Lears, *American Historical Review,* Vol. 97, No. 5 (Dec. 1992), 1369–1430. Levine argues that the seeming differences within and among modes of popular culture warrant rather than discount their study: "Indeed, it is the very asymmetry and diversity in popular culture that should convince us that it can be used as an indispensable guide to the thought and attitudes of an asymmetrical and diverse people," (1399).

4. Raymond Williams argues that consumers do judge each other based on the purchases they have made; consumption becomes an important form of communication. Raymond Williams, "Advertising: The Magic System," in his *Problems in Materialism and Culture* (London: Verso Editions and New Left Books, 1980), 185. For a review of theories about the nature of consumption, see Gary Cross, *Time and Money: The Making of a Consumer Culture* (London: Routledge, 1993), 155–64.

5. Nancy Cott, *The Grounds of Modern Feminism* (New Haven: Yale University Press, 1987), 1.

6. On the accomplishments of women in homogeneous organizations and the struggles for cross-race or cross-class cooperation during the Progressive era, see Noralee Frankel and Nancy S. Dye, eds., *Gender, Class, Race, and Reform in the Progressive Era* (Lexington: University Press of Kentucky), 1991. Dye, in the introduction, concludes that "Progressive women's sense of female difference, then, often could not overcome the boundaries of race and class," (7).

7. Stuart Hall, "Culture, the Media and the 'Ideological Effect,'" in *Mass Communication and Society,* James Curran, Michael Gurevitch, and Janet Woollacott, eds. (Beverly Hills, CA: Sage Publications, 1979), 33–339.

Reading D

The Gay Marketing Moment
AMY GLUCKMAN AND BETSY REED

Amy Gluckman is a high-school teacher and member of a collective that publishes a progressive economics magazine. Betsy Reed is a journalist and editor. In this co-authored piece, Gluckman and Reed examine the surge in business interest in gay and lesbian communities as target markets. They question whether this new trend is a sign of progress for the gay liberation movement or a turn toward conservatism.

A cocky k. d. lang revels in Cindy Crawford's feminine attentions on the cover of *Vanity Fair;* the same icon of "lesbian chic" claims the present as her moment on the cover of *New York* magazine; *Newsweek,* among others, declares gayness the latest trend, and straight, white, middle-class readers scratch their heads in wonder: Wow, they look just like us.

Liberation is not the bottom line for many of the interests that have molded such mainstream depictions of lesbians and gay men—money is. Ads for companies like Absolut and Benetton, famous within the gay community for their prescient cultivation of the gay market, shadow images of gay and lesbian style in both the gay and straight media. Corporate America has had a revelation. The profits to be reaped from making gay men and lesbians into a trendsetting consumer group finally outweigh the financial risks of inflaming right-wing hate. "Our demographics are more appealing than those of 80-year-old Christian ladies," says George Slowik, Jr., publisher of the glossy gay and lesbian bimonthly *Out*.

But it is not only corporate America feeding the media frenzy. While mainstream gay magazines like *Out* have appealed to advertisers by accurately boasting of a rich readership, other voices claiming to represent the wider lesbian and gay community have echoed these claims—with less credibility. In order to stimulate interest in the gay market, gay-and-lesbian-run marketing firms have circulated specious data, disregarding whole segments of the gay population in order to make the average incomes of lesbian and gay households appear disproportionately high. "Visibility is what it's all about," says David Ehrlich of Overlooked Opinions, a Chicago-based firm that churns out statistics depicting a wealthy, free-spending, brand-loyal gay and lesbian community.

Lee Badgett of the University of Maryland, who has recently conducted a study comparing the incomes of gay men and lesbians to those of straight men and

Amy Gluckman and Betsy Reed, "The Gay Marketing Moment: Leaving Diversity in the Dust," *Dollars and Sense* 190, November/December 1993: 16–18, 35.

Key Terms

gay liberation A new social movement that most historians date from the Stonewall rebellion in New York City in June 1969. The movement called for a new visibility and civil rights for gays and lesbians.

marketers The profession that specializes in research into consumer activities.

FIGURE III.II

women, contends that these popular assertions of higher-than-average gay and lesbian incomes are way off base. Her findings directly contradict those of Overlooked Opinions and other marketing firms, revealing that gay men earn less—by some measures, nearly one-third less—than their straight counterparts, while lesbians lag slightly behind heterosexual women in earning power.

That is not to deny that a narrow segment of the gay and lesbian community *is* rich—and perhaps even unusually brand loyal, as Absolut has discovered by tracking the impact of its local gay-targeted ads through monitoring buying patterns in gay bars in the region after the ads appear. But marketing firms and members of the media have conflated the buying behavior and class status of readers of gay publications with the characteristics of the community as a whole.

These stereotypes play well with advertisers not only because they make the gay market itself seem potentially lucrative. The growing power of lesbian and gay male consumers to influence, by example, the buying decisions of the (witting or unwitting) straight community has further enhanced their appeal. "We created button-fly jeans—I can't prove it, but I know it," says Ehrlich. Danae Clark, a professor at the University of Pittsburgh, says that "fashion has become a safe way to make lesbians and gay men into trendset-

ters, as it portrays them as hip but fails to represent the political aspects of the community."

The success of advertisers in creating images of gay men and lesbians capable of setting trends for straight consumers has depended at least in part on complementary editorial representation; for ads to have optimum effect, they have to be placed in the right environment. So, wittingly or unwittingly, magazines and other media—both gay and straight—have obliged their advertisers by touching up their snapshots of lesbians and gay men. Just as demographic information pointing to high incomes first captured corporate interest in the gay market, so pictures of apparently wealthy and otherwise nonthreatening gay men and lesbians have earned the acceptance of—and in some cases, the emulation of—an audience of straight consumers. As a result, the real contours of the multicultural, class-stratified gay population are languishing in the closet, while images of white, upper-middle-class lesbians and gay men become increasingly conspicuous.

Advertising trends indicate that corporations are cleaving to such stereotypes. They are placing ads in gay publications, but primarily in glossy mags like *Out* and *The Advocate* that have been cleansed of the objectionable: phone sex ads, "militant" politics, and hardcore leather culture. Meanwhile, radical gay media like *Gay Community News* are biting the dust (though *GCN* is currently trying to make a comeback). Along with Absolut and Benetton, corporations that have taken the lead in advertising in mainstream gay media include Calvin Klein, Philip Morris, Columbia records, Miller beer, Seagram, and Hiram Walker. Others, interested in the gay market but more gun-shy, are sticking to what's known as "gay window advertising." These are the "stealth" ads now all over mainstream straight publications—ads with homoerotic or otherwise gay images that are intended to attract gay consumers without revealing their orientation to straight ones.

[. . .]

Lesbian and gay rights activists are . . . rejoicing in the newfound visibility. After a long war against a homophobia that either ignored gay men and lesbians or blamed them for "deviance" and disease, the proliferation of positive media images represents a limited victory. Cultural acceptability can pave the way for legal civil rights protection for all gay men and lesbians, not just those the straight world likes. And the gay and lesbian community can wield its newly recognized market power wisely, rewarding corporate social responsibility and punishing capitulation to the Right.

But there are risks in projecting a rich, powerful image to get mainstream attention, even beyond the erasure of the community's diversity in media representations. "The radical right has appropriated our numbers," admits Ehrlich. Overlooked Opinions got a request for evidence of the gay community's financial power from the Colorado Attorney General's office, evidence that was used to support the campaign for the antigay ballot initiative Amendment 2.

[. . .]

Overlooked Opinions and other gay and lesbian organizations have responded by insisting that income should have no bearing on the question of civil rights. But by using the hyped demographic figures to court corporations, the same organizations are participating in—and perpetuating—a market system that values lesbians and gay men first and foremost for their incomes. Being valued *as consumers,* rather than as human beings, gay men and lesbians stand to lose their claim to social significance if anything hampers their ability to consume.

[. . .]

It is too early to tell whether concrete, day-to-day political action in the gay community will change as well, coming more into line with the typical politics of groups led by individuals who feel they are faring well under capitalism. But it is already clear that in some important ways, the "gay moment" is more of a hurdle for gay politics than a source of strength.

[. . .]

The problem is not simply that some gay subgroups get to see themselves in a Banana Republic ad while others do not. The absences in the pictures have profound implications for gay politics.

It's tempting to embrace the new recognition ecstatically, and unconditionally; as Andrew Schneider, who wrote *Northern Exposure*'s lesbian episode, told *Vogue,* the network was inundated with letters from lesbians after the show aired. "They were very grateful, like starving people getting a crust of bread," he said. But seizing the gay moment even as it reinforces racial and class hierarchies will allow for limited gains. As the best feminism is sensitive not only to questions of gender, the fight against homophobia will take on its most deeply radical forms only if it is conceived as part of a broader vision of social and economic justice.

REFLECTING ON THE SECTION

Consider the history of women's involvement in consumption in the United States: what were the economic, cultural, and political consequences of the rise of the middle-class woman shopper in the nineteenth century? How did cultural ideas of femininity and masculinity change? Whose interests were served by new technologies in the home and the transition from homemade food and clothes, for example, to mass-produced items? What was the role of marketing and advertising in the emergence of a powerful female consumer?

Given that women of many races, classes, and sexual orientations were either treated as exoticized symbols or erased from representation entirely, how do we understand the role of nationalism in the image of the ideal consumer? Given the arguments of Abelson and Scanlon, do you think that gay consumer groups like those discussed by Gluckman and Reed should continue to seek recognition of gays and lesbians as a desirable target market? Based on the kinds of issues raised in this section, what interpretations can you make of the *Newsweek* cover?

Consumer Beauty Culture: Commodifying the Body

The Body Beautiful
ROSALIND COWARD

Feminist cultural critic Rosalind Coward reminds us that the ideal of female beauty in the West in modern times emphasizes extreme slimness. Coward reads ads and other images to conclude that slimness masks a disgust for flesh, an anxiety about power and competence, and sexual immaturity. Overall, this ideal puts all women, and especially older women, in conflict with their bodies.

There is a definite female outline which is considered the cultural ideal. This "perfect" female body would be between 5 foot 5 and 5 foot 8, long-legged, tanned and vigorous looking, but above all, without a spare inch of flesh. "Brown, slim, lively, and lovely . . . that's how we would all like to see ourselves on holiday. Here are a few tips on achieving this and maintaining it" (*Ideal Home*).

Ever since the sixties, with its key image of Twiggy, there has been a tendency within fashion and beauty writing and imagery toward the idealization of a female body with no fat on it at all. Concern with achieving this "fashionable slimness" has become a routine part of many women's lives; dieting, watching what you eat, feeling guilty about food, and exercising affect most women to a greater or lesser degree.

The ideal outline is the silhouette which is left behind after the abolition of those areas of the body which fashion writing designates "problem areas." First, bottoms:

Rosalind Coward, "The Body Beautiful," in *Female Desires,* New York: Grove Press, 1985: 39–46.

Female behinds—whether sexy and shapely or absolutely enormous—have long been the subject of saucy seaside postcards. But this important structure can make or mar flimsy summer clothes . . . to say nothing of beachwear. If what goes on below your back is no joke to you, join Norma Knox as she looks at ways to smooth down, gently reshape, and generally improve the area between your waist and your knees.

Woman's Own, 24 July 1982

We are encouraged to "beat saddle-bag hips" because pear-shaped buttocks tend to wear badly in middle age if they have lacked exercise or have been constantly flattened in overtight trousers (ibid.). Next we learn of the disadvantages of flabby thighs. We are told to "ride a bike and firm up *slack* calves and *floppy* thighs." Elsewhere we learn of the horrors of loose stomach muscles and their dire consequence, "the potbelly." Bosoms are a little more recalcitrant but even these can be "toned up," which means "your bust's firmness can be improved if the circulation is encouraged" (*Annabel,* December 1980). Finally we should "Take a Long Look at Legs" (*Woman's Own,* 1 May 1982). The "best" are "smooth, flawless, unflabby, and golden". But there is good news, because "legs are leaner . . . thanks to dieting and exercise" (ibid.).

And if all or any of these problem parts continue to cause you trouble, you can always resort to the knife—cosmetic surgery. Women's magazines, beauty books,

---

Key Term

androgynous Having both male and female characteristics.

and beauty advice regularly give out information about this or make it the subject of lighthearted asides: "The only known way to remove surplus body fat (short of an operation) is to consume fewer calories" (John Yudkin). Cosmetic surgery is offered not just for altering the shape of your nose but for cutting away bits of flesh that cling stubbornly to those problem areas.

These exhortations leave us in little doubt that the West has as constricting an ideal of female beauty and behaviour as exists in those non-European societies where clitoridectomy is practised. In the West, the ideal of sexual attractiveness is said to be upheld voluntarily, rather than inflicted by a compulsory operation to change the shape of women's anatomy. But the obsession with one particular shape, everywhere promoted by the media, is no less of a definite statement about expectations for women and their sexuality.

Confronted with the strictness of this cultural ideal, we need to understand the meanings and values attached to this shape. We also need to understand the mechanisms which engage women in a discourse so problematic for us; and we need to know how women actually perceive themselves in relation to this idealized image.

What are the values which Western society attributes to this body shape?

The shape is slim, lacking in "excess fat," which is defined as any flesh which appears not to be muscled and firm, any flesh where you can "pinch an inch," as a current slimming dictum suggests. The only area where flesh is tolerated is around the breasts. The totally *androgynous* style of the sixties has relaxed somewhat—perhaps men couldn't stand the maternal deprivation, when it came to it. But even with breasts, the emphasis is on the "well-rounded" and "firm" in keeping with the bulgeless body.

The most striking aspect of this body is that it is reminiscent of adolescence; the shape is a version of an immature body. This is not because with the increase in the earnings of young people, the fashion industry now has them in mind (though there may be an element of truth in this), because the ideal is not exactly a young girl. Rather, it is an older woman who keeps an adolescent figure.

[. . .]

This valuation of immaturity is confirmed by other practices concerned with rendering the female body

sexually attractive. The practice of shaving under the arms and shaving the legs removes the very evidence that a girl has reached puberty. It is considered attractive that these "unsightly" hairs are removed. Body hair is considered ugly, and beauty advice strongly recommends shaving the body to restore prepubescent smoothness.

[. . .]

It is no coincidence that this sexual ideal is an image which connotes powerlessness. Admittedly, the ideal is not of a demure, classically "feminine" girl, but a vigorous and immature adolescent. Nevertheless, it is not a shape which suggests power or force. It has already been fairly widely documented how women often choose (albeit unconsciously) to remain "fat" because of the power which somehow accrues to them.[1] And it is certainly true that big women can be extremely imposing. A large woman who is not apologizing for her size is certainly not a figure to invite the dominant meanings which our culture attaches to femininity. She is impressive in ways that our culture's notion of the feminine cannot tolerate. Women, in other words, must always be seen as women and not as impressive Persons with definite presence.

The cultural ideal amounts to a taboo on the sexually mature woman.

[. . .]

Perhaps the mechanism most important in maintaining women's concern with this ideal is that it is built on a *disgust* of fat and flesh. It is not just a simple case of an ideal to which some of us are close and others not, which we can take or leave. The ideal says as much about its opposite, because the war with fat and excess flesh is a war conducted in highly emotive language. And this language constructs the meanings and therefore the emotions which surround body image. The most basic point about this is that it is difficult to find a nonpejorative word to describe what after all is the average female shape in a rather sedentary culture. When it comes down to it, "plump," "well-rounded," "full," and so on all sound like euphemisms for fat and therefore carry negative connotations. No one wants to be plump when they could be firm; it would be like choosing to be daft when you could be bright. But perhaps more important is that language pertaining to the female body has constructed a whole regime of representations which can only result in women having a punishing and self-hating relationship with their bodies. First, there is the fragmentation of the body—the body is talked about in terms of different parts, "problem areas," which are referred to in the third person: "flabby thighs . . . they." If the ideal shape has been pared down to a lean outline, bits are bound to stick out or hang down, and these become problem areas. The result is that it becomes possible, indeed likely, for women to think about their bodies in terms of parts, separate areas, as if these parts had some separate life of their own. It means that women are presented with a fragmented sense of the body. This fragmented sense of self is likely to be the foundation for an entirely masochistic or punitive relationship with one's own body. It becomes possible to think about one's body as if it were this thing which followed one about and attached itself unevenly to the ideal outline which lingers beneath. And the dislike of the body has become pathological. The language used expresses absolute disgust with the idea of fat. Fat is like a disease: "if you *suffer* from cellulite . . ." The cures for the disease are even worse. The body has to be hurt, made to suffer for its excess. . . .

It is almost as if women had to punish themselves for existing at all, as if any manifestation of this too, too solid flesh had to be subjected to arcane tortures and expressions of self-loathing.

I have already suggested that one of the reasons behind this self-disgust may be the conflict surrounding the cultural valuation of the sexually immature image. It seems as though women have to punish themselves for growing up, for becoming adults and flaunting their adulthood visibly about their bodies. It is as if women feel that they are too big, occupying too much space, have overgrown their apportioned limits. And a punishment is devised which internalizes the negative values which this society has for such women. It is of course sensual indulgence which is seen as the root cause for

women overspilling their proper space. Women who feel themselves to be overweight also invariably have the feeling that their fatness demonstrates weakness and greed. Being fat is tantamount to walking around with a sandwich board saying, "I can't control my appetite."

[. . .]

The ideal promoted by our culture is pretty scarce in nature; there aren't all that many mature women who can achieve this shape without extreme effort. Only the mass of advertising images, glamour photographs, and so on makes us believe that just about all women have this figure. Yet the ideal is constructed artificially. There are only a very limited number of models who make it to the billboards, and the techniques of photography are all geared toward creating the illusion of this perfect body.

Somewhere along the line, most women know that the image is impossible and corresponds to the wishes of our culture rather than being actually attainable. We remain trapped by the image, though, because our culture generates such a violent dislike of fat, fragmenting our bodies into separate areas, each of them in its own way too big. Paradoxically, though, this fragmentation also saves us from despair. Most women actually maintain an ambiguous relation to the ideal image; it is rarely rejected totally—it pervades fantasies of transforming the self. But at the same time, there's far more narcissistic self-affirmation among women than is sometimes assumed. Because of the fragmentation of the body into separate areas, most women value certain aspects of their bodies: eyes, hair, teeth, smile. This positive self-image has to be maintained against the grain, for the dice are loaded against women liking themselves in this society. But such feelings do lurk there, waiting for their day, forming the basis of the escape route away from the destructive and limiting ideals which are placed on women's bodies.

NOTE

1. See S. Orbach, *Fat Is a Feminist Issue* (Hamlyn, 1979).

Nourishing Ourselves
NANCY WORCESTER

Nancy Worcester, professor of nutrition, points out the importance of a proper diet for the health and work needs of women. Arguing that the subordinate status of women across the world is responsible for their malnutrition, especially in a context of poverty or war, Worcester sees the need for everyone to understand the consequences of food deprivation and eating disorders. Cultural as well as economic phenomena such as food taboos, dieting, ideals of slimness, and conditions of poverty all contribute to the ways gender affects health.

What could be more ironic? Nourishing others is a fundamental part of women's lives, but that very role itself limits the ability of women to take care of their own nutritional needs.

Women are the world's food producers and throughout the world, within a wide range of family units, women have responsibility for purchasing and/or preparing the daily food. Yet, both globally and within families, women are much more likely than men to be malnourished. Nearly universally, wherever there is a shortage of food or a limited supply of quality food, women's diets are inferior to men's quantitatively and qualitatively. Even when food supply is adequate or abundant, women's diets may be nutritionally inferior to men's.

It matters! At some level we all have a feel for how important a good diet is: "We are what we eat." If we feed our bodies the basic nutrients, the healthy body is amazingly clever at being able to take care of itself. An adequate diet is obviously important for *every* man, woman, and child. However, both societally and individually, a terrible mistake is being made when women's diets are inferior to men's.

A woman's diet must be more "nutrient-concentrated" than a man's in order to be nutritionally adequate. Most women require considerably less energy than most men. For example, the U.S. Food and Nutrition Board recommends an intake of 1,600–2,400 Calories per day for women age 23–50, compared to 2,300–2,700 Calories per day for men the same age. A U.S. food consumption survey showed that the average 23-year-old woman consumes only two-thirds as many Calories as the average 23-year-old man, 1,600 compared to 2,400.[1] However, women's requirements for many specific nutrients are identical to or greater than men's. The ramifications for this are most serious for calcium and iron. The U.S. Food and Nutrition Board

Nancy Worcester, "Nourishing Ourselves," *Women's Health: Readings on Social, Economic and Political Issues* (2nd e.), Nancy Worcester and Mariamne H. Whatley, eds. Dubuque, IA: Kendall/Hunt Publishing Company, 1996: 385–87, 389–93.

Key Terms

cognitive development The development of recognition and understanding in a child.
intrauterine Within the uterus.

vegan A person who follows a diet exclusively devoted to fruits, vegetables, and whole grains and avoids meats, dairy, and processed foods of any kind.

recommended daily allowance (RDA)[2] for calcium is the same for men and women. The RDA of 15 milligrams of iron per day for reproductive-aged women is 50 percent higher than the 10 mg RDA for men.

Picture a woman and a man sitting down to consume their daily nutritional needs. The man's pile of food will be 50 percent bigger than the woman's, but in the woman's smaller pile she will need to have the same amount of calcium and 50 percent more iron. Each bite the woman takes must contain 50 percent more calcium and twice as much iron! Put another way, even if a man does not have a particularly nutrient-rich diet, he will probably be able to meet his body's needs and he will even get away with consuming quite a few empty-calorie or low-quality foods, whereas a woman's diet must be of a relatively higher quality. A man's diet can be nutritionally inferior to a woman's and still be adequate for his needs. The world and millions of individuals are paying a high price for the fact that women's diets are often inferior to men's.

—⌒Sex Differential in Food Distribution and Consumption

The trend to feed boys better than girls gets established early in life. In Kashmir, girls are breastfed for only eight to ten months but boys are allowed to suckle for three years or longer.[3] In Arabic Islam, girls are breastfed for only one to one-and-a-half years, while it is common for a boy to be nursed until the age of two or two and a half.[4]

A recent Italian study also showed differences in the patterns of feeding baby boys and girls—girls are breastfed less often and for shorter periods; girls are weaned an average of three months earlier than boys. Additionally, it was observed that boys were more irritable and upset before feeding but went to sleep immediately after feeding. In contrast, the girls were less aggressive in asking for food but settled down less easily after feeding.[5]

Throughout the world, men and boys get feeding priority. In many cases, men literally eat first and women and children get what food is left over, such as in Bangladesh, where the tradition of sequential feeding means adult men are served first, followed by male children, then adult women and female children. Ethiopian women and girls of all classes must prepare two meals, one for the males and a second, often containing no meat or other substantial protein, for the females.[6] Boys' better access to food based on a gender-defined division of labour can get started early in life. For example, in Alor, Indonesia, very young boys are encouraged to do "masculine" work, and food serves as an important incentive and reward for that work. Boys receive "masculine" meals as guests of adult men for whom they have performed some service. In contrast, young girls do less valued work like weeding and get a lower-quality vegetable lunch.[7]

In whatever way a particular society works it out, there is a nearly universal pattern of men getting fed more and better. Most women recognize this pattern and can identify ways in which they feed their children and their partners better than themselves. Although this may mean nothing more serious than taking the burnt slice of toast or the least attractive piece of dessert for oneself, in times of shortage this pattern means that women are the most likely to be malnourished.

[. . .]

Studies in both Britain and the United States have shown that poor parents go without food in order to leave enough food for their children. A British survey found that children were generally better and more regularly fed than their parents. "Only" 15 percent of the children had fewer than three meals during the previous 24 hours, in contrast to 75 percent of the parents having had fewer than three meals (50 percent having had two meals and 25 percent having had only one meal) in the 24-hour period.[8] A 1983 New York study interviewed people at various sites, including emergency feeding centers, food stamp offices, health centers, and community centers. When asked, "Do your children eat and sometimes you're unable to?," over one-third of all respondents answered yes and 70 percent of the parents interviewed at the emergency feeding sites said yes.[9] (These studies did not look for different impacts on mothers and fathers.)

[. . .]

Efforts specifically designed to improve women's diets are not successful if programmes are not planned around the recognition that women feed their families before they feed themselves and that men tend to get the high-status foods. For example, a very ambitious $86 million (U.S. dollars) World Food Programme (WFP) project set up to improve the nutrition of pregnant and nursing mothers and their young children in Pakistan has had practically no nutritional impact. The major problem with the programme was that food was rationed so that each woman would receive an individual dietary supplement of 850 Calories per day, but, of course, the women shared the extra food with their families. The average family had six people, so one-sixth of the supplement, less than 150 Calories a day, did not make a significant improvement in women's diets.

[. . .]

The differential access to food is often exaggerated by food taboos, which have more impact on women than men. Food habits, including rituals and taboos, are an integral part of defining cultures ("us" versus "others"). Food taboos serve the function of reinforcing social status differences between individuals and social groups and symbolize the place one has in society. Taboos characteristically involve the prohibition of the highest-quality protein foods.

[. . .]

Overall, it seems that most permanent taboos and avoidances have little effect on the nutrition of individuals practicing them because the group's diet will have evolved so that other foods supply the nutrients found in prohibited foods. However, temporary avoidance, particularly at crucial periods of the life cycle, can have grave consequences.

Such limited-duration taboos particularly affect women because they occur at the most nutritionally sensitive periods. For example, hot and cold or yin and yang classifications of food are common throughout the world and are especially important in Latin America and parts of Asia. Although hot and cold and yin and yang are defined differently in diverse cultures, in all cultures practicing these classifications, the balancing concept is closely tied to women's reproductive cycles. So, however menstruation, pregnancy, and lactation get defined, it will be particularly important that women avoid certain "unbalancing" foods during those times. The foods which must be avoided are often foods of high nutritional value. Some Puerto Rican women consider pregnancy to be a hot state, so they avoid hot foods and medications, including vitamin and iron sup-

plements, to prevent babies from being born with a rash or red skin. Bangladeshi women must not eat meat, eggs, fish, or hot curries for several days after childbirth because those foods are believed to cause indigestion. Women are expected to eat only rice, bread, tea, and cumin seed for those nutritionally demanding postpartum days.[10]

There are two more points to consider in looking at the impact of food taboos and avoidance on women's nutrition. First, food taboos, as a cultural construct, are a part of the values of the society which are taught to people as they grow up. People learn those taboos as patterns of behavior which are right, normal, best. Other ways of doing things are viewed as wrong, misguided, or irrational. Understanding and appreciating another culture will require getting to know the food habits and vice versa. Second, sound nutritional practices can, with thought and planning, be developed and reinforced within the context of most existing food patterns.

[. . .]

Our society's fear of fat and obsession with dieting play a role in limiting women's access to optimum nutrition similarly to the way food taboos can affect women's nutrient intake in more traditional cultures. Dieting certainly has more impact on women than men, reinforces social-status differences, and leaves more food for others. As a cultural phenomenon, there can be no denying that women from many parts of the world would find the notion of purposefully restricting food intake to lose weight to be "wrong" or "misguided." Imagine trying to explain the pattern of American college women who intentionally skip meals to save calories for snacking and beer drinking at parties to Western Samoan women who exaggerate the amount they eat on diet surveys because, "The more they could say they had eaten . . ., the more powerful that meant the village was in being able to amass lots of food."[11,12] When we hear that many nine-year-old girls are already on slimming diets, we must recognize dieting to be a part of the values which our society now teaches to young women. Because much dieting is erratic behavior, "a temporary drastic measure just to take off a few pounds" (repeatedly performed!), it is more similar to temporary taboos with the potential for grave consequences than to permanent taboos for which people have learned to compensate. Just as one can eat a nutritionally adequate or even nutritionally superior vegetarian or *vegan* diet if one knows animal products are going to be consciously avoided or unavailable, it is certainly possible to consume nutrient-rich low-calorie or weight-maintenance diets. But that is not how the dieting taboo is usually practiced in this society.

[. . .]

Intergenerational Consequences of Female Malnutrition

[. . .]

The most profound and long-term effect of women's malnutrition is demonstrated by the link between poor maternal height and weight and low-birth-weight babies. Low-birth-weight babies, defined as weighing less than 2,500 grams (five and one-half pounds) at full gestation, have a much higher mortality rate and are more susceptible to illness throughout childhood than normal-weight babies. A Sri Lankan study found an average maternal height of 150 cm (4'9") for low-birth-weight babies and a modal maternal height of 155 cm (5'1") for well-grown babies.[13] Poor maternal height and weight can be a reflection of the mother's own *intrauterine* growth retardation and inadequate childhood nutrition. Healthy diets for *all* potential mothers from preconception through pregnancy can be seen as a high societal priority when one realizes that *it takes at least two generations to eliminate the effect of stunted maternal growth on future generations of women and men.*

Reversing the effect of malnutrition brings new challenges. When a basic nutritionally adequate diet for everyone becomes a national priority, young women with a family history of malnutrition will have access to a healthy diet after their own development has been stunted. In revolutionary China, as a consequence of major improvements in food production and distribution, birth weights rose dramatically within one generation. In order to maximize on its nutritional achievements, China's health services had to be able to cope with an increased rate of complicated deliveries, as there was a generation of small mothers producing relatively large babies.[14]

[. . .]

In Britain, low-birth-weight babies and stillbirths are nearly twice as common in poor families (social classes IV and V) as in wealthier families (classes I and II). In the United States, the infant mortality rate is 30 times higher in low-birth-weight babies than normal-weight babies.[15] Infant mortality rate (IMR = the number of babies per thousand live births who die in the first year of life) is an invaluable tool for comparing the health status of groups because it is a figure which is calculated similarly all over the world and is an excellent reflection of maternal and infant nutrition, as well as general standard of living and access to preventative and curative health care. IMR is 50 percent higher for U.S. whites living in poverty areas than for U.S. whites living in nonpoverty areas and IMR is at least 2.5 times higher in poor than in wealthy families in the United Kingdom. The intersection of poverty and racism is obvious from national (U.S.) figures showing IMR more than twice as high for Black babies as white babies. Blacks in poor areas have a far higher IMR than Blacks in nonpoor areas, although Black IMR is higher than white IMR in both income areas.[16,17]

The potential for change with an improved standard of living, including an emphasis on nutrition and access to health care, is most striking when IMRs are compared for small geographic areas. The Physician Task Force on Hunger in America contrasts the New York City IMRs of 5.8 in the Sunset Park section of Brooklyn with the 25.6 rate for Central Harlem and the Houston, Texas, IMRs of 10.0 in the Sunnyside areas versus 23.5 in the Riverside Health Center community.[18] When we see that two to four times as many babies are dying in one part of town as in another, little guessing is needed to figure out where the poor, malnourished people live in New York City or Houston.

Malnutrition: Cause and Effect on Women's Role in Society

It is women, not men, who are unequally distributing food within the family, giving men and boys more than their share of what is available for the household. Women depriving themselves and their daughters of life-sustaining nourishment is the ultimate example of internalized sexism. Men do not need to discriminate against women or carry out nasty plans to "keep women in their place" if women are sufficiently well socialized to their inferior role that they themselves perpetuate keeping women in inferior roles.

A profoundly intermeshing relationship exists between women's status in society and the responsibility for food production and distribution. Women's responsibility for domestic work, especially food production, is so undervalued that women internalize that low value and starve themselves literally or figuratively. Although millions of women and girls die each year as a result of malnutrition, that number is a mere fraction of the number of women and girls who cannot reach their full potential because of undernutrition and because their responsibilities for feeding others do not leave them food, time, or energy to nourish and nurture themselves.

Women's role as food producers can actually restrict a woman's ability to feed herself and others. How often have we observed a woman who eats practically nothing herself after spending hours preparing a meal for others? How often have we seen a woman so busy serving others that she barely sits down herself? A woman's standards for feeding herself may be totally different from those she holds to for her family. For example, a (London) *Daily Mirror* survey showed that even though mothers of school-age children make sure their children have breakfast, a fifth of mothers do not take time to eat breakfast themselves.[19]

It is exactly the women who face the most demanding food preparation tasks who have the least time and energy for this work. The woman who can afford the latest food processor and microwave may also be able to afford to buy easy-to-cook or partially prepared nutritious foods when she is too busy to cook. The woman who has to work overtime to have money to buy beans may not be able to buy a pressure cooker to reduce cooking time. Before or after a long day, she may have to decide between spending several hours on food preparation and eating less nutritional foods.

In many agricultural communities, it is *because* women have put all their time and energy into growing and harvesting the food that they may not be able to take the final steps, often extremely time and energy consuming, of turning the raw products into an edible form so that they can feed themselves and others.

One report speaks of African women "sitting about hungry with millet in their granaries and relish in the bush" because they were too exhausted to tackle the heavy, three-hour work of preparing the food for eating.[20]

The seasonal nature of agriculture exacerbates this. Peak periods for women's work in the fields are normally at planting, harvesting, and post-harvesting processing times, when the working day can average 15 hours. This coincides with the food supply being scarcest, most expensive, least varied, and least well prepared. As a consequence, it has been noted that in Gambia, pregnant women actually lose weight during the peak agricultural time, and in Thailand, there is a marked increase in miscarriages and an early termination of breast-feeding during the rice planting and harvesting seasons.[21,22]

The relationship between productivity and nutrition works in several ways. Not only does extreme work keep women from feeding themselves, but also undernutrition is clearly a factor limiting women's productivity. Intensity of work, the productive value of work activities selected, and labour time are all dimensions of productivity which have been shown to be affected by nutrition. If women are not able to maximize their productivity, food production is limited; several studies have identified women's labour input as the critical constraint on crop production. Although the value of women's productivity is universally and consistently *not* recognized, any signs of poor performance are definitely used to prolong women's low status.

A wide range of other nutrition problems also has an impact on women's status. As an illustration which has nearly universal ramifications, low-Calorie diets serve as an important example of undernutrition which, for very different reasons, can interfere with women maximizing their potential and limit their role in society in both rich and poor countries and for both rich and poor women. It is well known that low energy intakes restrict work potential and conversely that Calorie supplementation significantly increases work intensity and capacity.[23] The body, of course, has to work equally hard at coping with the limitations of a low-Calorie diet whether that restriction is imposed because of a natural disaster food shortage or the fact that someone "chooses" to diet down to a smaller size. Research from poor countries indicates that the body does have adaptation mechanisms for adjusting to *permanently* restricted food intake, but the body has a particularly chaotic job adjusting to great dietary fluctuations such as erratic food supply or yo-yo dieting.

What price do individuals and society pay for women's undernutrition caused by lifelong dieting?

Hilde Bruch, psychiatrist respected for her ground-breaking work on eating disorders, describes "thin fat people" as people (usually women) who routinely eat less than their bodies require in order to stay at a weight which is artificially low for themselves. Very often these women are tense, irritable, and unable to pursue educational and professional goals as a direct result of their chronic undernutrition. But if they never allowed themselves to eat properly, they do not recognize the signs that these limitations are due to under-eating rather than personal weaknesses. Characteristic signs of malnutrition—fatigue, listlessness, irritability, difficulties in concentration, and chronic depression—often escape correct professional diagnosis because the starved appearance (and especially average weight appearance in someone meant to be heavy) is a matter for praise rather than concern by our fatphobic society. "It has become customary to prescribe tranquilizers for such people; three square meals a day would be more logical treatment, but one that is equally unacceptable to physicians and patients because they share the conviction that being slim is good and healthy in itself."[24]

Is it possible that the relationship to food is sufficiently different between women and men that it helps determine gender differences in how women and men operate in the world? What if our scientific studies which "prove" that men are superior at performing certain tasks are actually measuring men's superior ability to fulfill their nutritional requirements rather than measuring task-performing abilities? How would we even begin to start to think about or "measure" such things?

Claire Etaugh and Patricia Hill have started on some fascinating research to test their theory that gender differences in eating restraint (dieting) influence previously reported gender differences in *cognitive restructuring* tasks. Their initial study found that gender differences were in fact eliminated on one of two tasks when men and women were matched for eating restraint. On the other task, eating-restricted females performed the task more poorly than unrestricted females, thus exaggerating the male–female difference.[25] This work certainly confirms that eating restraint is a factor which must be controlled in any study which attempts to measure gender differences. This research builds on previous work which showed that many differences found between fat and thin people are actually differences between restrained eaters (dieters) and non-restrained eaters (nondieters). Even without further research, we know that some cognitive-restructuring-task gender differences disappear when dieting is controlled for and we know that dieting can result in poorer performance on a range of tests. What more proof do we need that dieting can prevent women from maximizing their potential?

[. . .]

The relationship of girls' undernutrition and girls' not being able to maximize their mental development and educational capabilities obviously has enormous ramifications for what women can contribute to society, what women are expected or encouraged to do, and the recognition they are given for their achievements. We saw how a child's birth weight, and thus "good start in life," was influenced by the mother's height and weight which was affected by the grandmother's nutrition. We now see the vital link among childhood nutrition, female educational opportunities, and child mortality. Although this may be two different ways of looking at similar information, it is also a reminder of how these social and economic factors work together and exaggerate each other.

Consequently, the low value of females can cause the mothers to feed boys better than girls so that boys are less apt to be malnourished and more likely to be capable of benefitting from, and having access to, educational opportunities. Boys will then be far more likely to be the "well-nourished workers to qualify for the higher-paying, higher-status, physically or mentally demanding jobs" than their undernourished sisters. In one generation, in one community, the pattern could be clear-cut—the boys worked to their potential more than the girls and the boys have more status than their sisters. When the sisters have their own children, how equally will they distribute the food, and will they be aware of the unequal distribution if they give more to their sons than their daughters? In the extreme Bangladesh example, women tended to deny unequal distribution except when male child preference was expressed in relation to marked food shortages or in reference to sex differentials with regard to food quality.[26]

Does this extreme but not exaggerated example give us clues to how this process may operate more subtly? Having seen that *cognitive development* is dependent on both adequate nutrition and intellectual stimulation and having seen gender differences disappear (in one test) when men and women were matched for eating restraint, what significance is there in the fact that many nine-year-old girls are now dieting? We know the physical abilities of girls and boys are pretty evenly matched until age 10–12, when social pressure discourages young women from developing their physical potential. We know that many girls excel in maths at an early age but then internalize the "girls aren't good at maths" idea by adolescence. In what ways do these messages which limit young women from maximizing

their potential now get exaggerated by the pressure on them (and their mothers) not to let themselves get fat?

A young woman's nutritional needs are among the highest of her life when she is 11–14 years old: an average 100-pound girl uses up 2,400 Calories a day and needs a very vitamin- and mineral-concentrated diet. This is also one of life's most crucial times for making educational decisions which will influence future choices. If individuals or society wish to improve the role of women in society, this is the worst possible stage for young women to start practicing their lives as "thin fat people"!

NOTES

1. Judith Willis, "The Gender Gap at the Dinner Table," *FDA Consumer,* June 1984, pp. 13–17.

2. 1989 RDA, U.S. Food and Nutrition Board.

3. Mary Roodkowsky, "Underdevelopment Means Double Jeopardy for Women," *Food Monitor,* September/October 1979, pp. 8–10.

4. Lisa Leghorn and Mary Roodkowsky, *Who Really Starve? Women and World Hunger,* New York: Friendship Press 1977, p. 20.

5. Colin Spencer, "Sex, Lies and Fed by Men," *Guardian,* November 4–5, 1989, p. 11.

6. Leghorn and Roodkowsky, op. cit.

7. E. M. Roenberg, "Demographic Effects of Sex Differential Nutrition," in N. W. Jerome, R. F. Kandel, and G. H. Pelto (eds.), *Nutritional Anthropology—Contemporary Approaches to Diet and Culture,* Redgrave Publishing Co. 1980, pp. 181–203.

8. Hilary Graham, *Women, Health and the Family,* Brighton, Sussex: Wheatsheaf Books 1984, pp. 120–35.

9. Ruth Sidel, *Women and Children Last—The Plight of Poor Women in Affluent America,* New York: Viking 1986, p. 149.

10. Paul Fieldhouse, *Food and Nutrition: Customs and Culture,* London: Croom Helm 1986, pp. 41–54.

11. Betsy A. Lehman, "Fighting the Battle of Freshman Fat," *Boston Globe,* September 25, 1989, pp. 23, 25.

12. Joan Price, "Food Fixations and Body Biases—An Anthropologist Analyzes American Attitudes," *Radiance,* Summer 1989, pp. 46–47.

13. Priyani Soysa, "Women and Nutrition," *World Review of Nutrition and Dietetics,* vol. 52, 1987, pp. 11–12.

14. Discussions with Chinese health workers and the All China Women's Federation, March 1978 and March 1983.

15. Physician Task Force on Hunger in America, *Hunger in America—The Growing Epidemic,* Middletown, Connecticut: Wesleyan University Press, 1985.

16. Melanie Tervalon, "Black Women's Reproductive Rights," in Nancy Worcester and Mariamne H. Whatley (eds.). *Women's Health: Readings on Social, Economic and Political Issues,* Dubuque, Iowa: Kendall/Hunt 1988, pp. 136–37.

17. Victor W. Sidel and Ruth Sidel, *A Healthy State—An International Perspective on the Crisis in United States Medical Care,* New York: Pantheon 1977, p. 17.

18. Physician Task Force on Hunger in America, op. cit., p. 109.

19. Charmian Kenner, *No Time for Women—Exploring Women's Health in the 1930s and Today,* London: Pandora, 1985, p. 10.

20. Ester Boserup, *Women's Role in Economic Development,* London: George Allen and Unwin 1970, p. 165, quoted in Barbara Rogers, *The Domestication of Women—Discrimination in Developing Societies,* London: Tavistock 1981, p. 155.

21. Sahni Hamilton, Barry Popkin, and Deborah Spicer, *Women and Nutrition in Third World Countries,* South Hadley, Mass.: Bergin and Garvey Publishers 1984, p. 45.

22. Ellen McLean, "World Agricultural Policy and its Effect on Women's Health," *Health Care for Women International,* vol. 8, 1987, pp. 231–37.

23. Hamilton, Popkin, and Spicer, op. cit.

24. Hilde Bruch, "Thin Fat People" in Jane Rachel Kaplan (ed.), *A Woman's Conflict—The Special Relationship between Women and Food,* Englewood Cliffs, New Jersey: Prentice-Hall 1980, pp. 17–28.

25. Claire Etaugh and Patricia Hall, "Restrained Eating: Mediator of Gender Differences on Cognitive Restructuring Tasks?," *Sex Roles,* vol. 20, nos. 7/8, 1989, pp. 465–71.

26. Lincoln C. Chen, Emdadul Huq, and Stan D'Souza, "Sex Bias in the Family Allocation of Food and Health Care in Rural Bangladesh," *Population and Development Review,* vol. 7, no. 1, March 1981, pp. 55–70.

Reading C

Grotesque Moderne
ROLAND MARCHAND

Cultural historian Roland Marchand discusses the major role that advertisements play in creating the ideal image of the female body. Examining ads from the 1920s and 1930s, Marchand argues that the female figure came to be distorted in particular ways that turned women into decorative objects.

Exactly what "look" women should adopt to play their modern roles was defined less by the close-ups of soap and cosmetic ads than by the stances, silhouettes, and accessories of women in the whole range of social tableau advertisements. The "Fisher Body girl" established the normative image for women in the late 1920s and early 1930s. The creation of illustrator McClelland Barclay, this heroine of the Fisher Body ads was slender,

Roland Marchand, "Grotesque Moderne," *Advertising the American Dream: Making Way for Modernity, 1920–1940*, Berkeley: University of California Press, 1985: 179–85.

youthful, and sophisticated. Her finely etched facial features formed a slightly aloof smile, suggesting demure self-confidence in her obvious social prestige and her understated sexual allure. Attired elegantly, but not exotically, she stood tall and angular, her fingers and toes tapering to sharp points. In her role as a model of the proper feminine look, she gained credit for attracting the attention of women as much as men (Figure III.12).[1]

In one direction, this modal image of modern woman shaded off into that of the housewife and mother. Her outlines were usually softer and slightly more rounded than the Fisher Body girl's. Her posture was less self-consciously canted or accentuated, her neck and limbs slightly shorter (Figure III.13).[2] In the other direction, the divergence from the Fisher Body model moved more abruptly toward striking "high-fashion" extremes, until the "modern woman" approached the status of a geometric abstraction.

Key Terms

Art Deco Design style popular during the 1920s and 1930s, influenced by technology and characterized by sleek, slender forms and straight lines.

Lamarck Relating to a theory of organic evolution holding that environmental changes in animals cause structural changes that are transmitted to their offspring. Named after French naturalist Jean Baptiste Pierre Antoine de Monet, chevalier de Lamarck (1744–1829).

Thorstein Veblen (1857–1929) Economist who was most famous for his book *The Theory of the Leisure Class* (1899), in which he coined the phrase "conspicuous consumption" (excessive consumption of manufactured products by the newly wealthy middle class who have the leisure to consume).

FIGURE III.12

FIGURE III.13

It was in the increasingly abstract portrayals of this high-fashion version of the American woman that advertising men effectively propagated their contention that the "beloved buying sex" must also be the more modern.[3] Men were sometimes depicted in modernistic illustrations. But never did advertising artists distort and reshape men's bodies as they did when they

transformed women into Art Deco figurines. Women in the tableaux, as symbols of modernity, sometimes added more than a foot to their everyday heights and stretched their elongated eyes, fingers, legs, arms, and necks to grotesque proportions. . . . The proportions of some women in the tableaux suggested a height of over nine feet. In deference to the geometric motifs of popularized modern art in the 1920s, women's legs sometimes extended in cantilevers or absolutely straight lines from thigh to toe. Their pointed feet and toes appeared to have emerged fresh from a pencil sharpener. Foot-long fingers similarly tapered into icy stilettos. As for their legs, one advertising writer observed that they were "just as long as the artist cares to make them, and evidently he is paid by the running foot."[4]

Thus the woman of high fashion—and, by implication, all women of high social status—appeared in advertising tableaux as physically distinct from the woman of lower social position. By a Lamarckian process of natural selection, the lady of high class had acquired an elongated neck to accentuate her pearl necklace and her hat, and a body tall enough for the artistic drape of an evening dress. Her sculpted head evoked images of Grecian culture and aristocratic poise; her brittle, tapered appendages conformed to Thorstein Veblen's specifications for the look of conspicuous leisure. So extreme were some of these distortions that a comparison of advertising drawings with contemporary advertising photographs is often startling, even though the photographs themselves were often taken at extreme angles in an effort to approximate the fashionable ideal. Even next to the moderately high-fashion drawings of the retail advertisements, women in the advertising photographs look squat, neckless, and beefy (Figure III.14).[5]

What relationship did the modern woman of these illustrations bear to social realities? Certainly the physical resemblance was meager. Fashion economist Paul Nystrom estimated in 1928 that only 17 percent of all American women were both "slender" and over 5 feet 3 inches in height.[6] The emphasis on youth and slimness, however, did reinforce the notion of women's new freedom of physical activity; and like the cut of women's clothes, the stance of fashion models, and the postures of modern dance, it fostered the image of the woman in actual or impending motion—

FIGURE III.14

the woman on the move.[7] The tubular shapes and angular lines also suggested a rejection of the traditional motherly image. In fact, advertising tableaux that cast women in maternal roles with children usually modified the modern image appreciably, rounding out the figure, bringing the proportions back toward normal, and softening the lines (see Figure III.13). Perhaps significantly, mothers looked like women of more modest social status.

If extreme height and exaggerated "artistic" postures gave the modern woman of the ads a certain claim to elegance and prestige, still she gained stature mainly in comparison to other, nonfashionable women. In relation to men, as Erving Goffman has intriguingly suggested in *Gender Advertisements,* distortions of women's shapes and gestures often convey messages about social subordination. Women, Goffman argues, appear in poses that are more "canted," more exaggerated and grotesque, more off-balance and tentative than those assumed by men. These stances and gestures imply a sense of dependence on the man for stability and balance, a willingness to make oneself into an interesting "object," and a greater vulnerability to the caprices of a dominating emotionality.[8]

Particularly common in the illustrations of the 1920s and 1930s is the contrast, which Goffman noted in the 1960s, between the predominance of a solid, firmly planted stance for men and an unbalanced stance for women. Men in the tableaux usually balanced their weight on both feet. Women placed their weight on one foot while the other leg indulged in a "bashful knee bend" or complemented the supporting leg and foot by posing at an artistic angle. If such off-balance and tentative stances implied, as Goffman argues, a status of dependence and a "foregoing of full effort" to prepare for assertive, self-reliant action, then illustrators of the 1920s and 1930s certainly exaggerated these qualities in depicting the modern woman.[9]

Advertising illustrations thus reinforced the tendency to interpret woman's modernity in a "fashion" sense and to define the status of "decorative object" as one of her natural and appropriate roles. Women took on the contours and angles of their modern art backdrops more decisively than men, suggesting their pliability in the service of art. In some tableaux, women with less distorted shapes and postures still functioned as decorations for the depicted room, as much as did the sculptured art objects or the curtains.[10] Even the distortions of body proportions, which elevated women of fashion and status to awesome heights of eight or nine feet, served more to accentuate their decorative potential than to suggest their commanding presence as new women of broader capacities and responsibilities.

NOTES

1. *Chicago Tribune,* Jan. 15, 1926, picture section, p. 6; *Saturday Evening Post,* Feb. 2, 1929, p. 30; Feb. 16, 1929, p. 32; Mar. 16, 1929, p. 34; May 25, 1929, p. 42; James R. Adams, *Sparks Off My Anvil* (New York, 1958), p. 97. The Fisher Body girl also appeared occasionally in ads for other products. See, for example, *Saturday Evening Post,* May 11, 1929, p. 70; Mar. 16, 1929, pp. 80–81; Mar. 23, 1929, p. 163.

2. *Saturday Evening Post,* June 19, 1926, p. 127; July 27, 1935, p. 25; *American Magazine,* Mar. 1926, p. 117; *McCall's,* July 1928, p. 44; *Ladies' Home Journal,* Sept. 1926, p. 166; Oct. 1926, p. 55.

3. *Printers' Ink Monthly,* Aug. 1926, p. 87; *Printers' Ink,* May 12, 1927, p. 88.

4. *Printers' Ink,* Aug. 25, 1927, p. 18; *Advertising and Selling Fortnightly,* Mar. p. 10, 1926, p. 27; *Printers' Ink Monthly,* Feb. 1929, p. 132. For salient examples of the woman as modern art object, see *American Weekly,* Feb. 20, 1927, p. 24; Apr. 17, 1927, p. 19; *Chicago Tribune,* Dec. 21, 1927, p. 24; Nov. 10, 1926, p. 8; June 28, 1929, p. 17; Oct. 3, 1930, p. 10; *Saturday Evening Post,* Feb. 18, 1928, p. 2; Jan. 5, 1929, pp. 72–73; Mar. 22, 1930, p. 137; *Los Angeles Times,* July 21, 1929, part III, p. 3; Aug. 10, 1930, part III, p. 5; Aug. 13, 1930, part II, p. 8; *True Story,* May 1930, p. 107.

5. For instance, compared with the women in the department store ad on page 24 of the *Chicago Tribune,* June 12, 1929, the woman photographed on the following page appeared to have no neck at all. See also *Saturday Evening Post,* Aug. 6, 1927, p. 142; Dec. 8, 1928, p. 139; Apr. 6, 1929, p. 48; May 4, 1929, p. 217; Sept. 14, 1929, p. 168. A contemporary advertising woman estimated that the camera could only distort a model to appear about one head higher than her real stature, whereas drawings regularly elongated her figure more strikingly (*Advertising and Selling,* Oct. 24, 1935, p. 30).

6. Paul H. Nystrom, *Economics of Fashion* (New York, 1928), p. 466.

7. Elizabeth Kendall, *Where She Danced* (New York, 1979), pp. 208–209; Hollander, *Seeing through Clothes,* (New York, 1978), pp. 339–41.

8. Erving Goffman, *Gender Advertisements* (New York, 1979), pp. 45–47.

9. Ibid., p. 45. For examples of the two common types of gender-specific stances, see *Saturday Evening Post,* Mar. 2, 1929, p. 92; June 22, 1929, pp. 124, 129; June 29, 1929, pp. 4, 36; Aug. 10, 1929, p. 63; Aug. 17, 1929, pp. 60, 176; Aug. 24, 1929, p. 40; *Collier's,* May 26, 1928, p. 49. Arthur William Brown, a prolific illustrator for *Saturday Evening Post* fiction and for advertisements, created a kind of visual formula out of such contrasts in stance. See *Saturday Evening Post,* June 15, 1929, pp. 6–7; Nov. 2, 1929, p. 154; Nov. 15, 1930, pp. 3, 5; Nov. 22, 1930, pp. 16–17, 20.

10. *Chicago Tribune,* Nov. 10, 1926, p. 8; *Saturday Evening Post,* Sept. 11, 1926, p. 186; Nov. 13, 1926, p. 139; July 2, 1927, p. 42; Aug. 13, 1927, p. 78; Feb. 19, 1927, p. 48; June 1, 1929, pp. 114–15.

Reading D

Black Beauty's New Face

ALLISON SAMUELS

Following Coward and Marchand, who give us a background for understanding the contemporary ideal of extreme thinness, Newsweek *journalist Allison Samuels reports on the success of fashion model Alex Wek. Born in Sudan, Wek is seen as exotically beautiful by some observers and as a stereotype of "blackness" by others. This example shows us how a woman's physical attributes can become symbolic of a nation or a race and how "beauty" is intertwined with politics.*

Alek Wek giggles a lot. She giggles at the mere mention of Method Man, her favorite rapper, and she giggles when she talks about sashaying down the runways of New York, Paris, and Milan. And why shouldn't she? At 20, Wek is the hottest face in fashion, keeping heads turning with her flawless ebony skin, tightly cropped hair, and never-ending legs. Cameos in Janet Jackson and Busta Rhymes music videos have even made her a strikingly different-looking presence on MTV. After Wek modeled Cynthia Rowley's spring line two weeks ago, the designer declared that "her happy personality wears the clothes."

"It's all been such a blast—particularly seeing myself on MTV," says Wek in her thick British accent. "It's just been real fun—that's the best I can say." Born into the Dinka tribe in Sudan, Wek escaped the war-torn country with her family when she was 14. After relocating to London, the 5-foot-11 beauty was discovered at an outdoor market two years ago. Since then her African look has begun to redefine what and who is considered beautiful (Figure III.15).

Or has it? Many applaud the fashion industry's departure from the white norm in promoting Wek. She also shatters the accepted look among black top models such as Tyra Banks and Naomi Campbell, who tend to have more European features, lighter skin, and straightened hair. But some African-Americans complain that Wek is a demeaning stereotype of black features: wide nose, full lips, natural hair, and ultradark skin. Ironically, at a time when many African-Americans thirst for African culture, some are suspicious of Wek's fame. Says Jamie Simpson, a Los Angeles hairstylist: "I think they [white Americans] want us to look like her—primitive."

That's self-hatred, says Bethann Hardison, a black manager who handles male supermodel Tyson. "We've been taught that Vanessa Williams is the ideal of black beauty. That's why Alek is absolutely necessary—she forces us to deal with the fact that she is beautiful, as well." Wek knows about the black backlash—her agent's gotten letters criticizing her looks—and she's confused and hurt by it. "I can't understand the fuss," she says. "In my village there is no problem because we all look the same. Here there is so much difference in skin—so much is thought about it, and that's sad."

But Gilles Bensimon, the (white) creative director of *Elle* magazine who put Alek on the cover of this month's issue, says it has resulted in more positive mail than any other cover. "One 12-year-old black girl told us it brought her out of her depression," she says. And that's the response that will make Alek Wek happy again.

Allison Samuels, "Black Beauty's New Face," *Newsweek*, November 24, 1997: 68.

FIGURE III.15

Reading E

Italians Contemplate Beauty in a Caribbean Brow
CELESTINE BOHLEN

New York Times *reporter Celestine Bohlen relates the controversy over the Miss Italy contest in 1996. When Denny Méndez won the title that year, her Caribbean background became a source of racist questioning about her ability to represent the nation of Italy. Méndez's case reveals the way that the feminine ideal is often a national one, especially in the*

Celestine Bohlen, "Italians Contemplate Beauty in a Caribbean Brow," *New York Times*, Tuesday, September 10, 1996.

context of recent immigration patterns, which are changing the cultural and racial makeup of European countries.

ROME Sept. 9—Can a black woman, a Caribbean immigrant who has lived in Italy for four years, be a symbol of Italian female beauty?

If she is Denny Méndez, 18, who was crowned Miss Italy 1996 over the weekend, the answer is yes, although the question is still under heated debate.

"How did a beauty contest turn into a mini-national psychodrama?" the newspaper *La Repubblica* asked this morning, in one of the dozens of commentaries that have used Miss Méndez's victory to analyze racial tolerance in Italy, the relative nature of beauty and, above all, what it means to be Italian.

The controversy began days before the final competition on Saturday. Two members of the Miss Italy jury were suspended for saying that Miss Méndez, as a black woman, could not represent Italian beauty.

One, Alba Parietti, a television announcer who was later reinstated, defended herself against charges of racism, questioning whether China would accept a Miss China without almond-shaped eyes, or if a non-black African could become Miss Senegal.

In what many say was a backlash of sympathy, Miss Méndez swept to victory in the judges' vote on Saturday, buoyed by a third of the call-in vote, which was phoned in by over a million of the 13 million Italians—81 percent of the viewing public—who were watching the pageant live.

Since then, Miss Méndez, a naturalized Italian citizen who moved here from the Dominican Republic when her mother married an Italian, has held her own.

"I know that I don't represent Italian beauty, but they elected me, so what am I supposed to do—refuse?" she told one newspaper.

But at the core of the continuing debate is Italy's changing identity—from a relatively homogenous society (although that too is debatable) to a one that in recent years has accepted a growing population of non-European immigrants.

Even Prime Minister Romano Prodi had a comment on the Miss Italy results. "Italy is changing," he said. "We also have black soccer players, and now this too is a sign."

Officially, there are just under one million foreigners living in Italy, a country with a population of 56 million—although that figure does not include either naturalized Italians like Miss Méndez or the hundreds of thousands of illegal immigrants here. Blacks are a small minority of immigrants, most of whom come from North Africa, Albania, or the Balkans.

Compared with Germany, with its long tradition of "guest workers," or France or Britain, which have a his-

FIGURE III.16   DENNY MÉNDEZ, A DOMINICAN IMMIGRANT, WAS CROWNED MISS ITALY.

tory of taking in immigrants from former colonies, the number of foreign-born in Italy is relatively low. But as commentators have pointed out, Italy, which not long ago was a country of emigrants, is having trouble adapting to the notion that it has become a land of immigrants.

"Italy became a land of immigration without ever deciding to, and, in some cases, without ever wanting to," Guido Bolaffi wrote in *La Repubblica* on Saturday.

Some commentators have suggested that the vote to crown Miss Méndez was an attempt by the Italian judges and viewers to go out of their way to prove to themselves and others that Italy, too, is ready to accept a multi-ethnic identity.

"The contest ended under a sort of blackmail," said Enrico Mentana, a judge who is a producer of one of Italy's main television news programs and who voted for another contestant. "Not to elect Denny would mean looking like a Class-B country."

Mr. Mentana argued that Miss Méndez was neither the most beautiful contestant nor the most beautiful foreign immigrant. "She is exotic," he said, "like the women whom Italians who spend their vacations in Cuba find attractive."

But others have noted that few Italians complained about Fiona May, a British black athlete who won a silver medal competing for Italy in the long jump at the Olympic Games in Atlanta. Nor, they noted, do they challenge George Weah, a black Liberian with a French passport, who plays for the AC Milan soccer team.

Commenting on the furor over the Miss Italy case, Gianni Vattimo, an Italian philosopher, said the test was not over whether Miss Méndez won the Miss Italy title, but over whether she was allowed to compete.

"To dismiss a black soccer player because he is black is racist," he told the leftist newspaper *L'Unità.* "To get annoyed because he plays well is less significant."

Reading F

Ugliness in India over Miss World

BARRY BEARAK

When the Miss World contest was held in Bangalore, India, crowds of protestors disrupted the pageant. As Los Angeles Times reporter Barry Bearak tells us, a range of groups, from right-wing religious fundamentalists to socialist farmers to feminists, came out against the event. Despite their many differences, they all agreed that the Miss World event symbolizes the worst aspects of Western culture—its commodification of women and its exploitation of exotic locales in a search for bigger audiences and market share.

Barry Bearak, "Ugliness in India over Miss World," *San Francisco Chronicle.* Thursday, November 21, 1996: C1.

BANGALORE, INDIA—India's "garden city" may never have been an ideal spot for the Miss World pageant, what with its water shortages, power failures, and the air quality of a bus terminal.

But not even the most dour of pessimists expected mayhem of this sort, with the contest being assailed as a merchandising device for the decadent cultural imperialists of the West.

Fanatical protesters are threatening to immolate themselves in the streets—and one has already done so. Commandos smeared cow dung in public places. And militant farmers have promised to burn down the cricket

Key Terms

British sahibs The colonial rulers in India. "Sahib" means "master."
Hindu nationalism Political movement that draws upon the Hindu religion and traditions as a basis of group identity.
Nehru-era socialism Jawaharlal Nehru (1889–1964) was the first prime minister of India

after independence from Britain in 1947 and served until his death. His policies were marked by alliances with the Soviet Union and a socialist-style economy based on the public ownership of major industries and utilities.

stadium, the very arena where the queen is to be crowned Saturday as 2.5 billion people watch on global television.

Dozens of groups have come out against the extravaganza. Beauty contests make for a strange combination of enemies, and this one has brought together modern feminists and turn-back-the-clock Hindu nationalists, left-wing students and right-wing politicians. Already, the swimsuit competition has been chased out of the country to the more hospitable Seychelle Islands.

"Today, it's Miss World; tomorrow it's electrolysis, liposuction, artificial eyes, and facelifting," said Pramila Nesargi, a right-wing state legislator.

M. D. Nanjundaswamy, the socialist leader of the farmers' group, said: "The degeneracy of the West needs to be corrected, not exported."

Defenders of the pageant—and they enjoy the sympathy of most Indians—find it hard to believe that an event so trivial has provoked such a tumult. What about India's poverty? What about illiteracy? What about official corruption?

But to many, the Miss World contest is symbolic of something far more substantial, for what was once a stream of Western influences has recently become a gush. Embraced by some, deplored by others, change is penetrating India's soul. East is East and West is West, but now the twain have met.

Two great thresholds have been crossed in the 90s, one in the marketplace and the other on the television.

Five years ago, this nation shrugged off the last vestiges of Nehru-era socialism and enacted reforms that welcomed the global economy. Executives of multinationals rushed to India like the British sahibs.

How could they resist? The potential of this market would speed the heartbeat of any merchant. One in every six people on Earth lives in India, and while 730 million of them have little in their pockets, a middle class of an estimated 200 million has rupees to spare for consumer goods.

Television ads tell them what to buy. In 1992, Star TV, owned by unblushing impresario Rupert Murdoch, began to offer its many channels of attractions. Programs include the antic showmanship of pro wrestling, the gyrating flesh of music videos, and the moral teachings of the soap opera "Santa Barbara."

Among current sentiments is the suspicion that India has become a dumping ground for the West's rejects, and the Miss World pageant surely fits the bill. In 1990, after 39 years in London, declining interest forced the contest into a nomadic existence. It has since wandered to Atlanta and Sun City—South Africa's answer to Las Vegas—before making its current stop in Bangalore, a south India metropolis of 6 million with a booming computer industry.

Along the way during this globe-trot, Miss World founders Eric and Julia Morley discovered that what had become passe in the prosperous West was now en-vogue in much of the Third World, where beauty competition is not so burdened by political correctness.

In India, the pageant's main financial backer is Amitabh Bachchan, the actor known as the Big B. Famous for playing the role of the angry young man, he was once the leading heartthrob in this nation's huge film industry. Now 54, he has gone the way of many angry young men before him, starting his own corporation, the entertainment conglomerate Amitabh Bachchan Corp. Ltd.

What the Big B has in mind for Bangalore is its biggest gala ever, with 2,000 technicians, 500 dancers, 88 contestants, and 16 elephants. As the judges sleuth for personality, poise, and perfect measurements, about 20,000 patrons will watch from the outdoor seats of Chinnaswami Stadium. Ticket prices are $55, $400, and $715, steep fare in a nation where the average annual income is $335.

Miss World promoters do not want their pageant confused with the rival Miss Universe affair, which was held last May in Las Vegas. The major distinction, they insist, is that Miss World's motto is "beauty with a purpose," the purpose being charity. About 10 percent of the profit—an estimated $1 million—will go to the Spastics Society of Karnataka (Bangalore's home state).

Bachchan thought this charitable gesture would be enough to subdue any likely opposition—and this may well have been so. But when the sniping began, Karnataka's chief minister, J. H. Patel, inadvertently poured gas on the fire, defending the contest with the words: "If women want to show themselves in the nude, let them [and] let those who want to see, see."

For two months, the controversy has been a staple on India's front pages, delighting several gadflies and small-time politicians whose threats and invective are usually not taken so seriously. "The fury of the mob cannot be controlled," said the newly important conservative legislator Nesargi in her dramatic way.

Nesargi is a member of the Bharatiya Janata Party, which has had political success of late as a guardian of Hindu traditions.

By her understanding of Hinduism, a woman's beauty must be natural, not affected. For example, the three spectacular diamond rings on her fingers are natural—"taken from Mother Earth"—while cosmetics are not. "The West wants all women to look alike, and the only way to do this is with makeup."

Barbie and the World Economy

RONE TEMPEST

Los Angeles Times reporter Rone Tempest describes how Barbie, an American icon of feminine beauty, is really a multinational product. Tempest traces the manufacturing of the Mattel toy to show how the world economy works—that is, how a multinational corporation uses resources and labor from diverse places to keep costs extremely low. This article shows us that just as the feminine ideal of beauty can become a political tool, it can also become profits in a global economy.

BEIJING—A Barbie doll is for sale at the Anaheim Toys "R" Us store in a bright cardboard-and-cellophane box labeled "Made in China." The price is $9.99.

But how much will China make from the sale of the pert fashion doll marketed around the world by Mattel Inc. of El Segundo?

About 35 cents, according to executives in the Asian and American toy industry—mostly in wages paid to 11,000 young peasant women working in two factories across the border from Hong Kong in China's Guangdong province.

"What China is mostly exporting is its cheap labor," said David A. Miller, president of Toy Manufacturers of America in New York.

Rone Tempest, "Barbie and the World Economy," *Los Angeles Times,* Sunday, September 22, 1996, A1, A12.

China's cut of the Barbie doll is important because it touches one of the main political strains between China and the United States today: the growing, lopsided trade deficit in favor of Beijing.

China contends that the U.S. Commerce Department's calculation of the deficit, estimated to reach $36.2 billion by the end of the year, is distorted and unfair. U.S. political leaders view the deficit with alarm, proclaiming it America's next No. 1 trade issue, eclipsing the long-standing wrangle with Japan.

But tracing Barbie's peripatetic, multicountry path from her raw material source in a Saudi Arabian oil field to aisle 12-C of a Southern California toy store raises even bigger questions being debated in business and academic circles:

- How relevant are traditional bilateral trade calculations—a baseball-type scorecard of winners and losers—in an era of increasing globalization of products?
- If such calculations are relevant, should the deficit with China, a developing country where most exports are still labor-intensive "processed products," be placed in the same category as the deficit with Japan, a fully industrialized country that has systematically targeted key American industries?
- In the end, what does the label "Made in China"—or "Made in U.S.A." or "Made in Japan" or "Made in Mexico"—really mean?

Key Term

bilateral deficit The amount of trade deficit one country has in relation to another country.

"The America–China trade issue is a red herring," contends Arjun Appadurai, a professor of cultural anthropology at the University of Chicago who has written extensively about the international flow of commodities. "It fails to take into account a much more complex set of values, of energies, of labor, and of nationalism congealed into a package that carries the emotional label 'Made in China.'"

Appadurai, editor of a pioneering 1986 book, *The Social Life of Things (Commodities in Cultural Perspective),* argues that the traditional model for calculating trade relations is no longer valid.

"The whole issue of bilateral deficits works within a framework that has been in question for some time, both in business and in government," Appadurai said in a telephone interview. "Today's forms of production are elusive and highly flexible. It is very difficult to localize a product like Barbie. But the political side can accommodate only two-player games, played between nation-states."

—Complicated Trade Rules

China gets its estimated share of the "My First Tea Party" Barbie sold in Anaheim from minimal taxes and licensing fees as well as in worker wages. But, because of complicated international trade rules that define a product's point of origin, China is charged with an export value of $2 by the time the doll reaches the United States.

Eventually, after transoceanic shipping, domestic trucking, advertising, and other functions that employ thousands of workers in the United States, the Anaheim Barbie will achieve her full price, resulting in at least a $1 profit per doll for Mattel.

According to the U.S. Customs figures, toys imported from China in 1995 totaled $5.4 billion, about one-sixth of the total deficit figure as calculated by the U.S. government.

Several other countries contributed to the making of the Anaheim Barbie as much as or more than China did. From Saudi Arabia came the oil that, after refining, produces ethylene. Taiwan used the ethylene to produce vinyl plastic pellets that became Barbie's body. Japan supplied her nylon hair. The United States supplied her cardboard packaging. Hong Kong managed everything.

Each country took a cut along the way of the doll's $2 export value, the number used in calculating trade figures (about one-fifth of the eventual retail price). But China was stuck with the bill: In the trade ledgers, Barbie is one of *its* exports.

This fact is increasingly important as China's trade advantage with the United States continues to grow, alarming politicians and pushing the world's richest country and its most populous country into a testy standoff.

U.S. Commerce Department officials recently announced that, according to June figures, for the first time in history China had surpassed Japan as the country with the largest trade imbalance with the United States.

As it has in the past, China immediately cried foul, contending that the U.S. figures failed to take into account the value added to the product in Hong Kong and other way stations.

"The business transaction is so complicated that it involves two or three 'places' in the whole course of processing," Ma Xiaoye, an official in China's Ministry of Trade and Economic Cooperation, wrote in a recent article describing Beijing's position. "Value-added is accumulated in more than two places and combined with transshipment. This has led to great difficulties in determining the origin of goods, and the sizable scale of processing trade has resulted in a serious distortion of trade statistics."

—$25 Billion Misunderstanding

A vast gap divides the U.S. estimate of its trade deficit with China and the calculation of China's Ministry of Trade.

In 1995, the Commerce Department placed the deficit at $33.8 billion in China's favor. China said the deficit was $8.6 billion.

This $25 billion misunderstanding may seem irreconcilable. But China's claim of a lower figure has supporters inside and outside the U.S. government.

"When you go through the analysis," said Miller of the American toy manufacturers association, "the U.S. figure is about double what it should be."

Washington, while sticking to its higher number, appears to recognize that the U.S.–China deficit is different in nature from the U.S.–Japan deficit. In announcing the June figures, Commerce Secretary Mickey Kantor

Toys Are Serious Business for U.S.

Made in China?

That's what the box says. But Barbie is a global product.

U.S. CHINA TRADE
In billions of dollars

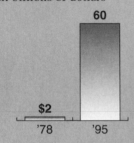

- 60 — '95
- $2 — '78

TRADE DEFICIT FAVORING CHINA
In billions of dollars

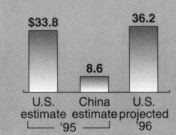

$33.8	8.6	36.2
U.S. estimate	China estimate	U.S. projected
'95	'95	'96

BARBIE COST ANALYSIS

"MY FIRST TEA PARTY" BARBIE
Retail price: **$9.99**

$7.99: shipping, ground transportation, marketing, wholesale, retail, profit

■ *EXPORT VALUE*

$2.00: Value in Hong Kong used to calculate import value in U.S. Breakdown at right.

■ *EXPORT VALUE*

$1.00: Overhead and management **(Hong Kong)**

65¢: Materials **(Taiwan, Japan, U.S., Saudi Arabia, China)**

35¢: Labor **(China)**

KEY SPOTS AND THEIR IMPORTANCE IN BUILDING BARBIE

U.S.: Cardboard packaging, paint pigments, molds

China: Factory space, labor, electricity

Saudi Arabia: Oil

Hong Kong: Assembly, shipping

Japan: Nylon hair

El Segundo: Mattel Inc.

Taiwan: Refines oil into ethylene for plastic pellets for Barbie's body.

Sources: U.S. Commerce Dept., Chinese Ministry of Foreign Trade and Economic Cooperation, Mattel Inc., Hong Kong Toy Council

was careful to avoid the charged rhetoric that sometimes accompanies announcements on trade-related issues.

"This is a deficit that cannot be construed as a U.S.–China deficit," one official acknowledged, "but it has to be viewed in light of its regional components as well."

Nicholas Lardy, an economist and China specialist with the Brookings institution in Washington, contends that both the United States and China err in their trade figures but that the U.S. calculations are off by about 50 percent.

In a recent position paper, the United States–China Business Council, a high-powered lobby dedicated to promoting U.S.–China trade, blamed the trade discrepancy on two main accounting errors: the Commerce Department's failure to factor in the role of Hong Kong as a critical entrepot, or middleman trade port, for both exports from China to the United States and exports from the United States to China.

"These large statistical errors, by both countries, are due to the ever-expanding role of Hong Kong as entrepot in the China trade," the paper contends. And although China is scheduled to revert from British control to mainland China sovereignty next July, the Chinese and American governments have agreed that the trade relationship will remain the same, with Hong Kong considered for trade purposes as if it were a separate country.

In fact, the differences in calculations would not matter much if they did not have an important political dimension in the United States. In recent years, the U.S. government has focused on trade issues, such as the annual renewal of most-favored-nation trading status, as a way of trying to influence China on a range of unrelated issues, including human rights and nuclear proliferation.

Like the bitter ongoing dispute with Japan, the U.S.–China trade clash could be a volatile political issue in years to come.

[. . .]

In a recent appearance on CNN, Ross Perot's running mate or [a third party vice-presidential candidate in the 1992 presidential election] Pat Choate referred to Chinese factory workers as "coolies" who have deprived Americans of jobs.

Giants in Toyland

U.S. figures put the 1995 trade deficit with China at $33.8 billion, about a sixth of which is toy imports. But some say the figure is distorted—Beijing earns only 35 cents on a Barbie whose export value is $2, for example. Here's a look at U.S. toy imports overall.

Taiwan $500 million **6%**

China $5.4 billion **60%**

Japan $1 billion **11%**

Others $2.1 billion **23%**

Source: Toy Manufacturers of America

Such pronouncements are usually based on the assumption that, as the exporting country, China makes more from its products than does the United States. In fact, with transportation, advertising, and other elements that create thousands of jobs in the United States—including Mattel's $1 profit—factored in, most of Barbie's eventual $10 cost is accumulated in the United States.

Mattel's profit alone is three times what China gains from each Barbie.

The contradictions and peculiarities of U.S.–China trade are not limited to the toy industry or its most successful creation, the 37-year-old teenager called Barbie. Similar anomalies exist in a wide range of other products exported by China, including shoes, garments, electronic goods, and small home appliances.

The Chinese government estimates that 75 percent of its products exported to the United States are "processed products," for which most raw materials and components come from other sources.

"For most of these products," said Ma Xiaoye from the Ministry of Foreign Trade, "China contributes almost nothing except the labor."

That labor is provided by workers like 20-year-old Qin Tingzhen, a Sichuan peasant woman who until June toiled for $40 a month making plastic Mighty Morphin Power Ranger action dolls at the Qualidux toy factory in Dongguan in Guangdong province. The wages of China's toy makers range from $30 to $40 a month.

But Barbie, the most profitable toy in history, serves as a familiar and convenient example.

Barbie accounted for $1.4 billion in sales for Mattel in 1995, according to Mattel spokesman Glenn Bozarth. Barbie is sold in 140 countries at a rate of two dolls every second. More than 40 percent of the dolls are sold overseas, primarily in Europe and Japan.

Optimum Locations

Barbie's story begins in the "commodity management" center in the one-story Maple Building in Mattel's El Segundo headquarters on the outskirts of Los Angeles International Airport. That is where Mattel's team of experts on commodity and material prices determine the optimum locations to buy the plastic resins, the cloth, the paper, and other materials.

Mattel declined to provide details of the materials' sourcing and prices.

"We consider the information to be proprietary in nature," Bozarth said.

But Mattel officials consented to provide guidance in certain areas, specifically to the percentage of China's participation in the manufacturing cost and a rough idea of the source country for most materials. Meanwhile, interviews with executives in the Hong Kong and U.S. toy industries provided a fairly detailed Barbie "biography."

According to Mattel, all Barbie dolls are made in four Asian factories, two in China and one each in Indonesia and Malaysia. Barbie has never been made in the United States. The first doll was produced in Japan in 1959, when that country was still struggling with its post-World War II economic recovery.

"The history of these toys is really the history of the growth of the economies of Asia," Bernard Loomis, a former designer and executive with Mattel and several other American toy companies, said in a telephone interview from his home in Palm Beach Gardens, Florida.

After Japan's economy took off, labor costs became too expensive for the production of plastic toys, and the factories were gradually relocated to other areas of East Asia where labor was cheaper.

At one time, Mattel maintained Barbie factories in Taiwan, Hong Kong, and the Philippines. In 1988, after a bitter labor dispute, Mattel closed two Philippine factories that employed 4,000 workers.

The Indonesian Barbie plant, 30 miles from Jakarta in Cikarang, opened in 1992. Another factory opened in Malaysia. Meanwhile, for much the same economic reasons that Japan ceased making Barbies a decade earlier, the doll factories in Taiwan and Hong Kong were shut down and relocated to mainland China.

The two plants in China are the Meitai factory in Dongguan and the Zhongmei toy factory in Nanhai. According to the plant managers, each factory employs about 5,500 workers. The Meitai factory produces both plastic dolls and clothes. The Zhongmei factory makes only the dolls.

Evolution of Regional Economies

Because all Barbie factories are located in eastern and southern Asia, the commodities managers in El Segundo look to Asian countries for most of the materials. The evolution of the region's economies is still tied in some way to the toy business.

At one time, Japan and Taiwan were the world's toy makers. As their economies advanced, they stepped up the evolutionary industrial ladder, replacing the United States and Europe as suppliers of plastic resins. China also makes vinyl plastics, but American and Hong Kong toy companies say they are not yet of sufficiently high quality to be used in their products.

According to Fred Wan, public relations specialist with Formosa Plastics in Taipei, the world's largest producer of polyvinyl chloride plastics used in toys (including Barbie), most of the oil the company uses to make its plastic resins is bought from the Chinese Petroleum Corp., Taiwan's state-owned oil importer.

When supplies of crude oil are not available, Formosa Plastics sometimes gets its liquefied petrochemicals from its $4 billion natural gas polymerization plant in Point Comfort, Texas.

In theory, Wan said, it is possible that the Anaheim Barbie was made from natural gas obtained in Texas or Louisiana. In all likelihood, however, the resins, transported to China via Hong Kong in pellets or "chips," came from the Taiwan oil import monopoly.

According to Ho Li-chun, spokeswoman for the Chinese Petroleum Corp., the biggest share of Taiwan's imported oil—about 32 percent—comes from Saudi Arabia. Other major sources include Oman (10 percent), Kuwait (10 percent), Iran (8 percent), and the United Arab Emirates (7 percent).

Many toy companies get the nylon hair for their dolls from Italy. But, for reasons of quality and history, Mattel obtains Barbie hair from Japan. In addition to the cardboard packaging for the dolls, many of the paint pigments and oils used in decorating them come from the United States.

Only the cotton cloth used in making Barbie's dress comes from China.

According to Hong Kong toy manufacturers, almost all of the machinery and tools, including the plastic mold injection machines used to produce most toys, are imported from Japan, Europe, and the United States. Most of the molds themselves, the most expensive item in toy making, come from the United States (for Barbie), Japan, or Hong Kong.

Virtually all the materials used in making Barbie are shipped through Hong Kong and trucked to the Guangdong factories.

According to the Hong Kong Trade Development Council, about 23,000 trucks make the daily four-hour round trip from Hong Kong harbor. They arrive bearing the raw materials and leave carrying the finished products, already packed in containers ready to load onto ships destined for the world's ports. Los Angeles gets the biggest share.

"In most cases, the only things that China supplies are the factory space, labor, and electricity," said Edmund K. S. Young, executive vice president of Perfekta

Enterprises Ltd., a leading Hong Kong toy maker, and chair of the Hong Kong Toy Council. "China doesn't even get the benefit of the banking, the insurance, or the shipping, because those are all in Hong Kong."

The $2 export value placed on the Barbie doll when it leaves Hong Kong harbor, Young said, breaks down roughly as follows: 35 cents for labor, 65 cents for materials, and $1 for transportation and overhead, including about 10 to 20 cents' profit for the Hong Kong companies that manage the manufacturing process.

Labor Is Critical Aspect

Although the labor component is probably the cheapest aspect of toy making, it is also the most critical. The workers operate the plastic mold injection machines, sew the clothing, and paint the details on the doll. A typical Barbie requires 15 separate paint stations.

This, in turn, requires an enormous, cheap workforce.

In the labor-intensive factories of Guangdong, more than 300,000 people are engaged in making toys for export to the United States and other countries.

During a 1994 visit by a *Times* reporter to the Qualidux toy factory in Dongguan, Hong Kong manager Y. S. Wong offered a profile of the workforce in his factory, where 6,000 women make Power Ranger action dolls and plastic gift toys for American fast-food restaurants.

The typical worker, Wang said, is an unmarried woman between 18 and 23 from Sichuan province who will work at the factory two to five years. Most are the second or third child in a peasant family that had already produced at least one son. In many rural areas of China, peasants are permitted two children, in variance with China's general "one-child" family planning policy.

Most of the young women interviewed on that day in the factory said their goal was to save enough money to return to Sichuan with a dowry. One of them was Qin Tingzhen, a pretty, smiling 18-year-old who wore her hair tied atop her head with a bright pink scarf.

Asked about her job operating a mold injection machine to make a Power Ranger figure, Qin was delighted to learn that her product would eventually make it to the United States.

"I thought it was for Hong Kong," she said, beaming.

BY TOM MEYER/THE CHRONICLE

REFLECTING ON THE SECTION

Globalization has increased the quantity and modified the content of images of women that people see around the world. The dominance of Western commodity or mass culture can influence ideas of beauty globally. Samuels, Bohlen, and Bearak each report on the globalization of beauty: in what ways might nationalism and the symbolic use of women's bodies be important in the newly globalized cultures? Why do you think that Rone Tempest chose Barbie dolls as the example of a globalized commodity? How would an article about another toy be read differently by a U.S. reader? In other words, think about the special qualities of the female body that lend it to conversations about globalization, beauty, and femininity.

What stakes do transnational corporations have in this globalized notion of beauty and femininity? How do they influence our eating and dieting habits? What is the effect of corporate practices on women's health worldwide? How does knowing this history and context affect your body image?

Cyberculture

Feminism for the Incurably Informed

ANNE BALSAMO

Feminist cultural critic Anne Balsamo discusses the rise of computer technologies in relation to the complicated history of women and technology in general. Although women have been integral to office work and skilled in many kinds of technologies, when technologies become attached to higher-paid professions, those jobs are usually filled by men. Balsamo points out that since there is little research on women's creative or educational use of computer technology, there may be important aspects of the relationship between gender and technology that we do not yet fully understand.

My mother was a computer, but she never learned to drive. Grandmother was an order clerk in a predominantly male warehouse; she did all the driving for the family, having learned to drive almost before she learned to speak English; her first car was a 1916 Model T Ford equipped with a self-starter.[1] Both my mother and grandmother worked for Sears and Roebuck in the 1940s; Mother entered orders on a log sheet, Grandmother filled those orders in the ware-

Anne Balsamo, "Feminism for the Incurably Informed," *Flame Wars: The Discourse of Cyberculture,* Mark Dery, ed. Durham, NC: Duke University Press, 1994: 125–26, 143–47.

house.[2] When an opening in payroll came through, my mother enrolled in night school to learn to be a computer. Within two years she received a diploma from the Felt and Tarrant School of Comptometry that certified her to operate a comptometer—one of the widely used electromechanical calculating machines that preceded electronic calculators.[3] She worked at Sears for two more years before she was replaced by a machine.

My sister and I both work for the technostate—it seems only natural. In 1991, my sister was deployed to the borderland between northern Iraq and southwest Turkey as part of the U.S. military's humanitarian effort, called "Operation Provide Comfort," to give medical attention to the Kurdistani refugees exiled during and after the technologically hallucinogenic Gulf War.[4] About the same time, I was deployed to a technological institution to teach gender studies (their term) or feminism (mine). Situated within different histories, biographical as well as cultural, these technological encounters suggest several topics of investigation for feminist studies of science and technology.

These working-class histories will span 100 years before they're finished, and even that is an arbitrary

---

Key Terms

deskilling The downgrading of the skill levels that workers need when their jobs become automated. Deskilling leads to lower wages.

information technology The technologies that process information instead of simply storing and disseminating it. Primarily associated with the advent of computer technology.

technostate The government seen as a technological monolith.

span of time, determined more by the mangling of immigrant names and the near impossibility of extrapolating from today into tomorrow than by any formal sense of narrative closure. I do not want to invoke an experiential framework for the elaboration of this essay; I have no stories to tell here about the subjective experiences of a mother, sister, or grandmother using technology, displaced by it, or even cleaning up after it. Instead, I use these autobiographical notes as a platform upon which to stage a feminist reading of the current (cyber) cultural moment.

[. . .]

Gathering even basic biographical material about the women who participated in traditionally male-dominated technical and professional fields, including the physical and natural sciences, engineering, mathematics, military science, and astronomy, is not an easy project. The historical material that is available illuminates the daunting structural barriers that many women had to overcome in order to pursue their interests and research in scientific and technological fields. The structural barriers ranged from formal prohibitions against women's education to the legal restrictions on women's property rights which caused many women inventors to patent their inventions under their brothers' or husbands' names. In reporting on her analysis of the treatment of gender and women's subjects in the 24-year history of the journal *Technology and Culture*—the journal of the Society for the History of Technology—Joan Rothschild asserts that one of the reasons for the lack of discussion about gender in the historiography of technology is a "literal identification of the male with technology."[5] This association has been seriously challenged by recent feminist studies that seek not only to recover women's contribution to the historical development of different technologies, but also to rethink the history of technology from a feminist perspective. Autumn Stanley, for example, argues that the history of technology omits women in part because of a categorical exclusion of the technology that women were specifically instrumental in developing as not "proper": here she lists food preparation, nursing and infant care, and menstruation technologies.[6] Other feminists investigate social arrangements that reproduce the masculinist identification with technologies that intimately affect women's lives, such as domestic technologies, as well as specific domains that are still dominated by male scientists, engineers, and medical researchers, such as the new reproductive technologies.[7]

As I implied in the opening remarks about my mother's computer employment history, women's relationship to the technology of the workplace has been a troubled one. The expansion of clerical occupations after World War I resulted in the feminization of such occupations; women were preferentially hired over men because they were less expensive to employ. This kept the costs of expansion contained. After World War II, many forms of female office work were subjected to the analysis of scientific management. Tasks were routinized and rationalized; bookkeepers and other office workers became "machine attendants who performed standardized repetitive calculating operations."[8] This repetitive work was the perfect material for automated calculators. Although some labor historians assert that the introduction of electronic calculators and computers occurred during a time of economic expansion, and thus had the effect of actually increasing the number of clerical jobs available for displaced workers, the new jobs were often sex-stratified such that better-paying data-processing positions were staffed by men. I offer this brief outline to point to the fact that women have been involved with the implementation of information technology in U.S. business and industry since at least World War I. This technology had contradictory effects on women's employment: it increased the opportunity for new jobs, but at the same time it downgraded the skill level of office workers who were employed to attend to the new machines.[9] In forming a judgment about the impact of these technologies on women's lives, it is important to remember that it is likely that the women who were displaced from their bookkeeping positions in the 1950s by the introduction of electronic technology did not necessarily experience this as an employment failure. No doubt some of them, like my mother, were eager to get on with the real business of their lives, which was getting married, having children, and raising families.

In the 10 years since the personal computer became widely available as a mass-produced consumer item, it has become an entirely naturalized fixture in the workplace, either at home or at the business office.[10] It is also becoming common to criticize the claims that computers increase office worker productivity—the primary marketing line for the sale of PCs to businesses and industries. Some critics protest that the real impact of computers and word-processing systems has been to increase the quantity of time spent producing documents, while others argue that the computerized office decreases the quality of work life due to physical discomfort and information overload.[11] Sociological studies of the gendered aspects of computer employment focus on the deskilling and displacement of female clerical workers in different industries. While these studies on women as laborers are vital for an understanding of the social and economic impact of computers, there is less research available about women's creative or educational use of information technologies or their role in the history of computing. But there is also a class bias reflected in these investigations due to the fact that, by focusing on women's computer *use* in the workplace, such studies restrict their critical investigation to those women who have access to what remains a costly technology that is out of the reach and the skill level of most women in the United States today. The question of women's employment and computer technology can be asked another way. For example, Les Levidow studies the women who make the tiny silicon chips that serve as the electronic guts for cheap computer gadgets. Both in affluent (until recently) Silicon Valley and in a relatively poor Malaysian state (Penang), the large majority of chip makers are poorly paid immigrant women.[12]

Yet another way to approach the question of women and technological histories, more sensitive to class-related issues, is to ask "Who counts?" This leads to the investigation of both those who determine who counts as instances of what identities and also those who are treated as numbers or cases in the construction of a database. The politics of databases will be a critical agenda item for the 1990s as an increasing number of businesses, services, and state agencies go online. Determining who has access to data, and how to get access to data that is supposedly available to the "public," is a multidimensional project that involves the use of computers, skill at network accessing, and education in locating and negotiating government-supported databases. Even a chief data coordinator with the U.S. Geological Survey asserts that "data markets, data access, and data dissemination are complicated, fuzzy, emotional topics right now." She predicts that "they likely will be the major issues of the decade."[13] Questions of public access and the status of information in the computer age are just now attracting public attention. As Kenneth B. Allen argues, the same technologies that enable us to "create, manipulate, and disseminate information" also, ironically, "threaten to diminish public access to government information." The issue of citizens' rights to information needs to be monitored by computer-savvy citizen advocates. The question is: Where will such advocates come from?[14] Two answers immediately arise: they will be either educated or elected. Feminist scholars and teachers can contribute to both processes by encouraging women students to address information policy issues in their research projects and by supporting women candidates who will serve on the federal and state boards that govern information access.[15]

NOTES

1. In her historical study of the gendering of the automobile, Virginia Scharff reports that the first woman in the United States to get a driver's license was Mrs. John Howell Phillips of Chicago in 1899. See her *Taking the Wheel: Women and the Coming of the Motor Age* (New York, 1991), 25.

2. Jumping 30 years in this abbreviated history leaves several threads hanging. From World War I to the end of World War II, Chicago was the scene of several significant industrial and cultural transformations. Like thousands of other new immigrants, one set of my grandparents emigrated from southern Italy, the other set from Lithuania. Each settled in an ethnic-identified Chicago neighborhood and began working for one of several large corporate employers already dominating Chicago politics and economics: Grandfather Balsamo at International Harvester, Grandmother Martins at Hart, Schaffner and Marx, and Uncle Barnes at the Swift stockyards. See Lisbeth Cohen, *Making a New Deal: Industrial Workers in Chicago,*

1919–1939 (Cambridge, 1990). Cohen's project enacts a cyborgian logic to investigate a historical pattern of recombinant social identity, whereby we can read how mass culture played a significant role in the unification of previously disparate groups.

3. According to Sharon Hartman Strom, "The comptometer, developed by Felt and Tarrant in Chicago, was often more popular than the calculator because it was key driven, lightweight, and inexpensive. . . . Its chief drawback was that it was nonlisting; that is, there was no printed tape which showed each item entered, only a window in which a running total appeared" (70). See Sharon Hartman Strom, " 'Machines Instead of Clerks': Technology and the Feminization of Bookkeeping, 1910–1950," in *Case Studies and Policy Perspectives,* Heidi I. Hartmann, ed. (Washington, DC, 1987), 2: 63–97.

4. Rose Balsamo was one of the 800 troops assigned to the Headquarters Company Fourth Aviation Brigade; she was assistant to the NCO in charge of medical support for the other U.S. troops and Kurdistani refugees.

5. Joan Rothschild, "Introduction," in *Machina Ex Dea: Feminist Perspectives on Technology* (New York, 1983), xviii. In her 1982 review of women and the history of American technology, Judith McGaw identifies Ruth Schwartz Cowan's address to the 1976 meetings of the Society of the History of Technology as a significant founding moment for the feminist study of technology. It was also a *literal* founding moment for the organization of Women in Technological History (WITH). See Judith A. McGaw, "Women and the History of American Technology," *Signs* 7 (1982): 798–828.

6. Autumn Stanley, "Women Hold Up Two-Thirds of the Sky: Notes for a Revised History of Technology," in Rothschild, ed., *Machina Ex Dea,* 5–22. See also Judy Wajcman's discussion of how women are "hidden from histories of technology": *Feminism Confronts Technology* (University Park, PA, 1991). A more popularized treatment of the topic is Ethlie Ann Vare and Greg Ptacek, *Mothers of Invention: From the Bra to the Bomb, Forgotten Women and Their Unforgettable Ideas* (New York, 1987).

7. See especially Cynthia Cockburn, *Machinery of Dominance: Women, Men and Technical Know-How* (London, 1985): Gina Corea, *The Mother Machine: Reproductive Technologies from Artificial Insemination to Artificial Wombs* (New York, 1985); and *Reproductive Technologies: Gender, Motherhood, and Medicine,* Michelle Stanworth, ed. (Minneapolis, 1987).

8. See the chapter "Historical Patterns of Technological Change," in *Computer Chips and Paper Clips: Technology and Women's Employment,* Heidi I. Hartmann, Robert E. Kraut, and Louise A. Tilly, ed. (Washington DC, 1986), 40.

9. Other studies of women and workplace technology include Margery Davis, *Woman's Place Is at the Typewriter: Office Work and Office Workers, 1870–1930* (Philadelphia, 1982); Judith S. McIlwee and J. Gregg Robinson, *Women in Engineering: Gender, Power and Workplace Culture* (Albany, 1992); and *WomanPower: Managing in Times of Demographic Turbulence,* Uma Sekaran and Frederick T. L. Leong, ed. (Newbury Park, 1992).

10. As a more recent contribution to the study of women's relationship to the technology of the workplace, Ruth Perry and Lisa Greber edited a special issue of *Signs,* published in 1990, on the topic of women and computers. The scholarship that they review considers the impact of the computer on women's employment and the structural forces that limit women's access to computer education. See Ruth Perry and Lisa Greber, "Women and Computers: An Introduction," *Signs* 16 (1990): 74–101.

11. See Chap. 5, "Conclusions and Recommendations," in Hartmann, Kraut, and Tilly, eds., *Computer Chips and Paper Clips.*

12. Levidow explores the "price paid for cheap chips" in terms of the harassment and forms of control that Malaysian women endure. See Les Levidow, "Women Who Make the Chips," *Science as Culture* 2 (1991): 103–24. See also Aihwa Ong's ethnographic study, *Spirits of Resistance and Capitalist Discipline: Factory Women in Malaysia* (Albany, 1987).

13. The quotation is from Nancy Tosta, chief of the Branch of Geographic Data Coordination of the National Mapping Division, U.S. Geological Survey in Reston, Virginia ("Who's Got the Data?" *Geo Info Systems* [September 1992]: 24–27). Tosta's prediction is supported by other statements about the U.S. government's efforts to build a Geographic Information System (GIS): a database system whereby "all public information can be referenced by location," the GIS is hailed as "an information integrator." The best use of GIS would be to support the coordination of local, regional, and national organizations—both governmental and private. See Lisa Warnecke, "Building the National GI/GIS Partnership," *Geo Info Systems* (April 1992): 16–23. Managing data, acquiring new data, and safeguarding data integrity are issues of concern for GIS managers. Because of the cost of acquiring new data and safeguarding data integrity, GIS managers sometimes charge a fee for providing information. This process of charging "has thrown [them] into a morass of issues about public records and freedom of information; the value of data, privacy, copyrights, and liability and the roles of public and private sectors in disseminating information." See Nancy Tosta, "Public Access: Right or Privilege?" *Geo Info Systems* (November/December 1991): 20–25.

14. Kenneth B. Allen, "Access to Government Information," *Government Information Quarterly* 9 (1992): 68.

15. Teola P. Hunter, for one, argues that African-American women must seek out potential political candidates who are already "appearing in city council seats, on county commissions, on school boards, in chambers of commerce and on many advisory boards at all levels of government." The key for success that these women hold is their connection to "civil rights groups, education groups, and church groups." Hunter goes on to argue that when "minority women use these contacts and these bonds, they have a support base that is hard to match." See Teola P. Hunter, "A Different View of Progress—Minority Women in Politics," *Journal of State Government* (April/June 1991): 48–52.

Reading B

The Internet and the South: Superhighway or Dirt-Track?
PANOS MEDIA BRIEFING #16

The Panos Institute in London promotes public policy debates in the media concerning developing countries. In this web piece, published in October 1994, the institute warns that new information technologies will create an even greater gap between the wealthy countries of the North and the less wealthy countries of the South. Without the infrastructure that makes networking possible, such as phone lines, many people will be left out of the new global economy. Panos predicts that disparities between rich and poor, as well as between men and women, in the South will increase as this process continues.

Connecting to the Net

There is no precise inventory of Internet users, but the Internet Society estimates that more than 40 million people have access to the Internet and that in mid-1995 there were around 5 million "host" computers connected to the internet worldwide. [2] Some of these have one user, some hundreds; around 70 percent are in the United States. Meanwhile, in April 1994, Viet-

Panos Media Briefing #16, "The Internet and the South: Superhighway or Dirt-Track?," October 1994.

namese academics proudly announced the first 12 connections in the country, offering a few dozen people next-day delivery of text messages only.

Over 110 countries have direct Internet access—with at least one "host" computer in-country; but if other email networks are taken into account, about 168 countries have links with the Net. All Northern countries have direct access to the Net, as do most of Eastern Europe, Latin America, and Southeast Asia.

Parts of Central and South Asia are connected only to email, as is most of Africa—mainly through networks like FIDOnet, a network run almost entirely by hobbyists on the sort of personal home computer which is common in the North. Every night, a FIDO-connected computer contacts two or three neighbours—using normal telephone lines—and exchanges messages with them. A FIDO message may take two or three days to travel from Siberia to the Sudan, but this is the only way for individuals and small organisations to get an electronic message between these places. In these countries, however, it is generally possible to access the Internet by dialing an international number. Several countries, most of them in Africa, are not connected at all.

"Internet access" can mean very different things. Dave Wilson of Rhodes University in South Africa

---

Key Term

G7 conference Since 1975, the heads of state or government of the major industrial countries (France, the United States, Britain, Germany, Japan, and Italy) have met annually to discuss economic and political issues. Canada and the European Community joined the meetings in 1976 and 1977, respectively. In 1994, the G7 and Russia began to meet as the P8 ("Political 8") following each G7 conference.

says, "The difference between high- and low end access can be illustrated by comparing a researcher in the United States who has a fixed link to a [high-speed] multi-megabit-per-second network to a researcher in Africa, who may be connecting at around 200 characters a second over an unstable telephone line." [3] It might take a few seconds, at no measurable cost, for the U.S. researcher to download the contents of a dense journal article (complete with graphs) into his computer—while it would take 10 minutes at international call rates for the African one.

Two countries, Finland and the United States, have more than one Internet host computer per 100 people. In comparison, 49 countries, from China to Cambodia (35 of them in Africa), had fewer than one telephone per 100 people in 1992. India, for instance, has 8 million telephone lines for 900 million people.

In February 1994, South Africa's deputy President Thabo Mbeki pointed out to the G7 conference of wealthy countries that there were more telephone lines in Manhattan, New York, than in the whole of sub-Saharan Africa. "Half of humanity has never made a telephone call," he said. And in many parts of the South, what phone networks exist don't talk to each other. Calls from Dakar in Senegal to Lusaka in Zambia are still routed from Dakar to Banjul, Banjul to London, and London to Lusaka. This colonial pattern of communication means that revenue is drained from Southern telecommunications companies to the North.

At a global level, at least 80 percent of the world's population still lacks the most basic telecommunications. Within countries, urban areas may be better served, but entire rural areas are left out. Leonard Subulwa, Zambia's Minister for the Western Province, points out that to communicate with officials in his constituency, "I have to drive 250 kilometres because the country's telecommunications network does not serve this district." [4]

[. . .]

A Space beyond Reach

Even in cities where there is a working telephone system, most people are excluded from accessing the Internet. David Dion works for the U.N. Food and Agriculture Organization (FAO) in Rome. He spends

the equivalent of U.S. $400 a month on food and U.S. $200 a month on telephone calls, including those his computer makes to the Internet. Harry Surjadi works for *Kompas Morning Daily* newspaper in Jakarta, Indonesia. He estimates that he spends six times more on telephone charges and Internet access than on food.

In real terms, Internet access time is 12 times more expensive for Harry Surjadi and his neighbours than for David Dion. The differential is higher for the computers they need to compose, send, and read messages—although the cost of hardware excludes a high proportion of people in the North. For the 10 percent of Londoners who are unemployed, a new U.S. $1,500 computer would represent about six months' total income. For the 45 percent of Indonesians who are "underemployed," it represents several years' cash income—and prices for imported electronic goods are often much higher in developing countries. The cost of a modem in India is about four times that in the United States—even without taking into account the huge differences in standards of living.

[. . .]

Africa is particularly badly affected. Tariff rates on information technology products are over 40 percent in most African countries, restricting access further in a continent already poor in infrastructure. Many experts also worry about Africa becoming a dumping ground for obsolete technology. At a conference on African Information Technology in the United Kingdom in late 1994, Dr. Adebayo Akinde of the Computer Association of Nigeria suggested a complete ban on importation of hardware systems, advocating the establishment of computer systems manufacturing industries in Africa [11].

—*Superhighway or Superhypeway?*
The Economic Impact of the Internet

One effect of the Internet on the economies of the North is to make possible new forms of economic activity. Some describe these as "postindustrial." They range from "home shopping"—where consumers browse through products on their computers, and order directly from the companies—to the development of new commercial opportunities for information services, such as companies selling news or financial analysis, and for services which make the Internet easier to use. Already, more than 80,000 companies are connected to the Internet. Among them, they have more than 1.4 million Internet hosts, which support many more individual users [12].

Clearly, nations without widespread access cannot join in this economic expansion. For countries of the South, which are already experiencing an "industry gap," the threat of a superimposed "postindustry gap" is looming.

Another effect on the North, however, is to make it possible for corporations to export clerical jobs to developing countries, where labour costs are far cheaper. A bank in New York may find it profitable to fly all the checks its customers write to the Caribbean. There the details can be keyed cheaply into computers and transmitted back to the bank.

Physical access to the Internet is not a problem for these corporations. Around U.S. $10,000 buys equipment to communicate with Inmarsat communications satellites from anywhere on the surface of the earth. Then to transmit one page of text—or the details on 200 checks—costs less than 10 U.S. cents.

Countries with low wage rates and a high level of literacy may stand to gain jobs from the North.

In "Electronic City" outside Bangalore in India, technology companies such as IBM, 3M, Motorola, Sony, and Texas Instruments have set up shop, exploiting the difference in time zones as well as labour costs. "While their European clients sleep," Patrick Donovan wrote in London's *Guardian* newspaper, "workers clear backlogs of programming or wrinkle out technical hitches in electronic circuits on the other side of the world." [13]

The government of Singapore envisages part of its economic future as a "middle office" between Northern corporations and their manufacturing plants in less-developed countries. Its IT2000 initiative for a "wired island" aims to put high-speed communications into every major building within five years.

But this applies only to those low-wage countries which have Internet access. As John Mukela of the Centre for Development Information in Lusaka, Zambia, warns, "Information-based production processes will increasingly elude developing countries and consequently exclude them from advanced manufacturing and world trade—thus further exacerbating their poverty."

The Net Welfare Provider

In the North and South, depending on connections, the Internet has the potential to assist in areas such as health. In western Zambia, for example, doctors working in rural hospitals have access to email. A doctor can get prompt specialist advice from the Lusaka Medical School, and this can save lives.

During the recent Ebola virus outbreak in neighbouring Zaire, Zambia was able to use the Internet to check details about similar cases in the Copperbelt. Doctors can also access a wealth of information on anything from AIDS to clinical and management practices.

"People see the Internet as a luxury," says the deputy health minister, Dr. Katele Kalumba, "but it can save costs as well as lives." Health workers can check the availability of essential drugs and so avoid making unnecessary journeys.

[. . .]

Creating a New Elite—or Bolstering Existing Disparities?

For a number of reasons—primarily cost, but also the need for literacy and technological know-how, and the dominance of English as the Internet language of choice—Internet access is likely to remain the domain of a privileged elite, in developing countries much more so than in the North.

But is this elite merely a carbon copy of the existing wealth disparities? Harry Surjadi of *Kompas Morning Daily* observes, "Not all rich people in Indonesia have any idea of accessing the Internet: only intellectuals are aware . . . [though] the main gap is between the rich and the poor."

Sally Burch, working for Agencia Latino Americana de Informacion in Quito, Ecuador, points to the possibility of the "reinforcement of an informed elite within the country creating a bigger internal information and technology gap . . . [and] greater dependence on Northern information sources and technology."

From Nepal, journalist Kanak Dixit comments: "It's not that this will strengthen a class structure—it's better to make sure that the intellectual elite . . . will get access than that no one does." But intellectual elites remain a very small part of the population—and overwhelmingly, they are men.

"Women are underrepresented both as technicians and as users of most computer networks," says Sally Burch, underlining the existing gender gap in access and use of technology, "and this is particularly true in the South."

Clearly, economic inequality makes it even harder for women than for men to get access in their own right. Biases in education, as well as in access to education, play a part in keeping women out of technology, and Burch supports training women to remedy this.

Training is an essential issue. "People will need to be literate," says John Mukela. "The availability of technology in primary and secondary schools will be paramount. Donor agencies operating in Africa have, I think, recognised the need for enhancing technological awareness. The educational community here recognises the need for some kind of basic computer literacy in schools."

For Amadou Mahtar Ba, of the Pan African News Agency (PANA), in Senegal, training in information technology is also seen as a crucial means of narrowing the North–South information gap—as are giving telecommunications infrastructure development top priority, and adjusting the cost of telecommunications.

[. . .]

REFERENCES

[2] Information from World-Wide Web: http://www.isoc.org

[3] *Democracy in Action,* 28 February 1995

[4] Gemini News feature, UK, 24 February 1995

[11] West Africa, UK, 21–27 November 1994

[12] *The Economist,* UK, Internet survey, 1 July 1995

[13] *The Guardian,* UK, 30 March 1995

Using Information Technology as a Mobilizing Force: The Case of the Tanzania Media Women's Association

FATMA ALLOO

Feminist journalist Fatma Alloo describes the formation and operations of a women's media group in Tanzania. Allo argues that "information is power" and that women's access to producing and distributing information through media and new technologies is vital for the future of Africa.

Africa has been portrayed by the media as poor and powerless. But the media have a role to play in the process of empowerment. The media can enable the people to challenge the powers that be and question the direction they are taking. In Tanzania, women are at the forefront of meeting this challenge. This case study will show the importance of technology in taking control of one's situation. Information technology can be used to destroy the "poor and powerless" myth, and to mobilize a community for empowerment and social change.

—Historical Background

The inception of TAMWA as an association had its seeds in 1979, with a group of women who had just finished journalism school and were beginning work in various mass-media institutions. We became aware that we were working very much individually. This method of work was also reflected in the way women's issues were covered in the mainstream press.

Fatma Alloo, "Using Information Technology as a Mobilizing Force: The Case of the Tanzania Media Women's Association," in *Women Encounter Technology: Changing Patterns of Employment in the Third World,* Swasti Mitter and Sheila Rowbotham, eds. London: Routledge, 1995: 303–13.

We found this situation unsatisfactory and formed ourselves into an informal group to produce radio programmes. The first issue we picked was schoolgirl pregnancies. We produced a total of five programmes on that issue with an in-depth analysis of the social context. These programmes were broadcast and were very popular both in Kiswahili and in English. Listener response was enthusiastic. This encouraged and inspired us to produce another set of programmes on violence against women, beginning with domestic violence. It was never broadcast because most of the mass-media heads were men who refused to see this as an issue. Since they had the decision-making power, we began to become aware of our limitations. Although many of us were demoralized and discouraged, since we had worked so hard on the programmes, the event taught us that we did not have a forum of our own.

Years passed and many of us went our separate ways, but in 1986, after going through many individual trials and tribulations as women, we regrouped and decided to officially launch an association on a formal basis. At that time the association had 13 members (it has since grown to 55, working in television, radio, and newspapers). This kind of urban-based professional women's association is a relatively new phenomenon in Eastern and Southern Africa. Other such associations in the region have been initiated by legal and health professionals (Alloo 1991).

While waiting for registration, which was to come after a year, we did a stage show on International Women's Day in 1987 to demonstrate different forms of media, including both conventional and popular media. The show was highly successful. We made an impact in the community and especially with the heads of mass media, who until then had not understood what we were really about. We felt that, for the first time, an understanding was beginning to emerge in the community.

We were registered in November 1987, and started a newsletter called *Titbits* which we produced for ourselves. *Titbits* covered a wide range of issues and was produced through the initiative of TAMWA members. It became our forum, through which we could express ourselves and respond to a need. Eleven monthly issues of *Titbits* were produced. In the process, various talents were identified. Eventually *Titbits* evolved into *Sauti Ya Siti* which will be described below.

In January 1988 we did a seminar on the "Portrayal of Women in the Media in Tanzania." We chose this topic because we needed to understand our situation first. We also looked into how our language perpetuated the negative portrayal of women. The seminar was attended by about 60 women's groups, who passed a recommendation that we needed a forum in the form of our own magazine. TAMWA met this challenge and in March 1988, just a month later, we launched our magazine, *Sauti Ya Siti—Voice of Woman*—which was also named after one of the first prominent woman communicator in nineteenth-century Zanzibar, Siti Binti Saad. Siti was not only a singer, she communicated for justice.

We now produce this magazine on a quarterly basis, in English and Kiswahili versions. We charge more for the English version, so that it subsidizes the Kiswahili version, which we try to make accessible to the rural population. The literacy rate of Tanzanian women is among the highest for women in sub-Saharan Africa (USAID 1985). *Sauti Ya Siti* now has a circulation of 10,000 copies. The English edition is distributed via bookshops and through subscriptions. The Kiswahili edition requires much more effort. We distribute copies to rural libraries (where each copy is read by an average of 30 persons), schools, ministries, and women's groups (those who belong to our network and friends of TAMWA) and through street children, who sell in the regions and earn a commission. The latter sales system is organized by our focal-point supporters: women who have trained with us in paralegal work, NGO management, and outreach work. We also target hairdressing salons.

Popular education materials are also distributed in this manner. For example, we produce brochures on the laws which affect women's lives, written in a simplified Kiswahili, with visuals and big letters for the new literates in Tanzania. These are disseminated through legal aid clinics in the countryside.

As we continued, we began to explore other forms of action in accordance with our objective to become a vehicle for increasing understanding of our situation as women and educating ourselves on our rights. In May every year we organize a Day of Action on women's health issues. One of the questions we ask of society is: why is it that so many of us continue to die in childbirth, when we have been performing our reproductive role from time immemorial (Sheikh-Hashim 1989), and how long will we continue to be denied our rights in terms of appropriate medical care facilities and human rights? This day mobilizes the community over questions pertinent to our situation as women. The people attending effectively raise these issues in their various workplaces and organizations. We continue to focus these annual events on health, since it is an effective tool for mobilizing women. The process has a multiplier effect in building a gender-sensitized community.

Information Technology and TAMWA

As we continue to work in TAMWA, various needs which relate to information dissemination and development education emerged. Generally, as members initiate new ideas, TAMWA undertakes the development of the viable ones (see Figure III.21).

In producing *Sauti Ya Siti* we felt the need for a Research and Documentation Unit, together with a Reference Library, for material on women. This unit is operational and several basic studies have already been prepared and published by TAMWA, on subjects ranging from sanitation to traditional education. The community involved in the study participates in the evaluation stage.

The growth of TAMWA called for a more rational retrieval, selection, and diffusion system. The need was met by installing a programme called File Maker and creating databases, one for books and another for unpublished documents and reports. In 1994 the collection

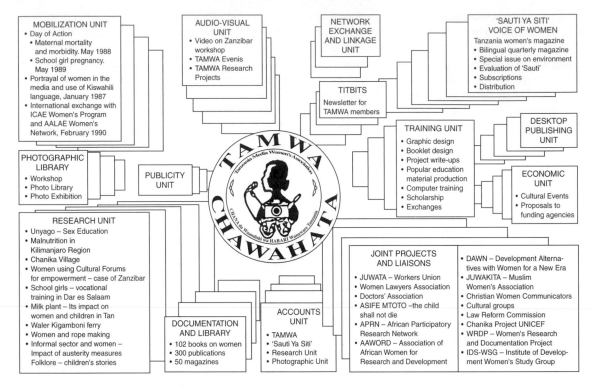

FIGURE III.21   TAMWA ORGANIZATIONAL CHART

included 3,000 books and 2,800 unpublished documents, plus periodicals.

All documents in the library are classified using keywords. Keywords are terms of constant vocabulary for particular ideas or facts which help describe the contents of a document. The keywords used to classify documents in TAMWA have been selected to reflect the theme and subjects dealt with by the Association. We also take trainees from the Tanganyika Library, who help us with needed expertise while getting practical exposure to our Association and becoming gender sensitized.

Our Documentation Unit is having a multiplier effect, as it is popularly used by the community, especially the youth. Gender sensitization through basic research is quite effective in empowering both men and women, and it particularly affects young minds. We also have a close collaboration with the Tanzanian School of Journalism, which trains young journalists. Right now (in 1994) the unit is in the process of be-

coming part and parcel of a nongovernmental organization (NGO) Resource Centre, thus planting the seed of a gender-sensitized NGO community with our documentation unit as a basic source.

Another unit is the Audio-visual Unit, whose programmes are used by Radio Tanzania. At the moment, we feed into existing radio programmes using research conducted by TAMWA members. We have developed a small studio on our premises. The target is to launch a community radio in 1995. The Visual Unit is fully equipped and produces video programmes on the issues which are being researched, to show to women's groups as part of a process of empowerment. So far, we have produced three documentations of women's history, the first one being on Siti Binti Saad. This unit is currently producing programmes for television, which has now been introduced to mainland Tanzania. We have also launched artists and artists' groups in our attempt to support young artists and foster aesthetic values in society.

The Economic Unit is another step toward self-sustainability (see Figure III.22). The goal is for the organization to earn sufficient income to cover its costs. The acquisition of proper office space and the appointment of a full-time administrative secretary have increased these costs. At present most of the funding still comes from donors, with the office costs being met from a 15 percent administrative charge, which is added to every project proposal. To meet the goal of self-sufficiency, entrepreneurship in various forms has found a place in TAMWA. Entrepreneurial activities in 1992 included an alternative fashion show, and the production of African clothing for men and women is now a project. Self-sufficiency is both a financial necessity and, in the long term, a requisite if TAMWA is to have an equal partnership with its counterpart organizations. Reliance on donor funds brings with it the temptation to produce for the sake of satisfying the funders rather than our own constituency, and the risk of losing our freedom to criticize the policies of development agencies. It also commits us to a "project" approach rather than a "process" approach, with all the costs in terms of lack of continuity and failure to build up an institutional memory which that entails.

The Children's Unit has transmitted our heritage through a book of children's songs and games. This material comes with an audiocassette. We believe that instead of growing up singing "London Bridge Is Falling Down," our children should sing our traditional songs, which impart values relevant to us. The Health Unit engages in outreach on AIDS, targeting especially the youth, and engages in debates on reproductive health in order to influence policy decisions at the national level. This is a vibrant unit.

Technology and the Media

Media, for us, encompasses all forms of communication, be it theatre, art, dance, songs, and folklore or the conventional media such as radio, television, and printed media. When TAMWA was formed, we had a specific definition of the media, and we knew that our forum would be a magazine, *Sauti Ya Siti*. Our goal was to produce a magazine of high technical quality. This was a conscious decision on our part as an organization. Information technology was to be used in TAMWA, we said, to change our society's behavioural patterns and attitudes towards women. For those of us within TAMWA, working with this technology would demystify our own concepts of technology vis-à-vis women. We began with desktop publishing. The Canadian Organization for Development Education (CODE) donated a desktop publishing unit and funded the printing of our magazine fully for the first two years. The support was to be reduced in phases, so as to achieve our goal of self-sustainability.

The desktop unit plays a role, not only in producing a high tech, quality magazine, but in beginning to give us an income and making the magazine cost effective. Five years later, TAMWA is producing a magazine, popular education materials (booklets), videos of women's cultural histories, radio programmes, posters, brochures, etc.—all using information technology. Contact has been established with publishers elsewhere in Africa, in India, and with the Women's publisher Kali. Another development is providing feature articles for other publications.

Being in the media ourselves gave us the consciousness that information is power. The "haves" select how much and what kind of information trickles down to the people through the mass media. The development of this kind of media is a project, not a process. There is no participation from the people, and

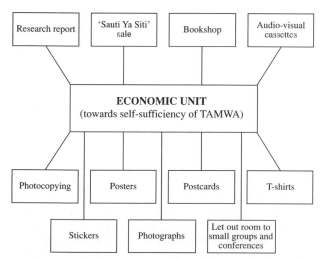

FIGURE III.22   TAMWA ECONOMIC UNIT

these media transmit to the people in a one-way, top-down process. This "beaming down" approach creates dependency and sells us our own images in a distorted way. When we studied the history of conventional media in Tanzania (see, e.g. Alloo 1988), we found that the print and electronic media were indeed introduced by the colonialists and used as an ideological weapon to control our societies. But the traditional popular media, such as folklore, songs, dance, and theatre, could not be controlled by the colonialists, not only because they used the language of the people, but also because the participation of the people was built in (see Mlama and Lihamba 1988).

As for Africa as a whole, the western media tries to sell us distorted images of ourselves. Africa is portrayed as a problematic continent rather than a continent with problems. Those images of wormlike bodies crawling with begging bowls have been powerful in perpetuating the "poor and the powerless" ideology. These projections render us powerless and make us believe there is something wrong with our continent. There are similar generalizing images of Asia, portrayed as not so bad except for their "sex trade and communal violence," and of Latin America, where the "drug trade" is the problem. All of these images are dangerous. They handicap us in our struggle for self-analysis and dehumanize us in the same way as images which sell the woman as a sex symbol—a commodity. The western media act in this way because, so far, the powers that control these media are commodity-oriented. These media are powerful because they have access to information technology which we in Latin America, Africa, Caribbean, Asia, and Pacific (LAA-CAP) countries lack.

A study of cultural development in Zanzibar revealed not only that the traditional media have remained powerful throughout various colonizing periods, but that conventional media were also used powerfully in the independence struggle. Zanzibar, with a population of around half a million, had 21 newspapers before independence. Their voices played an important role in the anticolonial struggles of the Islands (Sheriff 1987).

Throughout Africa, popular media are emerging as a powerful tool of empowerment. It is a form which women identify with and use, and have used in the past, for empowerment. For example, we have our traditional cloth, Kanga, which incorporates written messages in the design (Alley-Hamid 1995). The cloth is worn around the waist. Women wear it to portray feelings towards a spouse, in-law, or friend. This is a powerful medium in a culture of silence. This is paralleled by an awareness in the west of the value of technologies such as audiovisual media in empowering women by creating true images of women and showing the oppression of women in patriarchal systems in a global connection.

TAMWA tries to understand these macrodynamics as it forms strategies for information dissemination at a local level. Lack of access and control of media and information technology exposes us to the dehumanizing portrayal of women. Thus, control of information technology is crucial if we are to transform society through the media.

Until five years ago, Tanzanian government policies restricted the importation and use of these technologies. Thus, Tanzania is very new to information technology. Even now the prices are high and software is quite inaccessible. Technology and infrastructure are the basis of the process of empowerment. We felt that we ourselves would be empowered in mastering technology as a production tool, and we could in turn use it to disseminate information. As women, we saw this as particularly important, since new technology has generally been the domain of men. The technology could also generate income. We have established an effective Publishing Unit based on this fact (see Figure III.23).

The emphasis in our publishing work has been on media images—on achieving the positive media portrayal of women and permitting the voices of the voiceless to be heard. This, we feel, must be effected in a highly professional manner with aesthetically excellent programmes, whether on the air, on video, or in the print media. Professional excellence is important for ourselves, for we must and can produce quality material in spite of the so-called third world syndrome (insinuating technical incompetence). One of the problems of powerlessness is the psychology of feeling inadequate, which leads to sloppy work. TAMWA's experience has shown us that women generally do fear technology and have to be pushed and cajoled to mas-

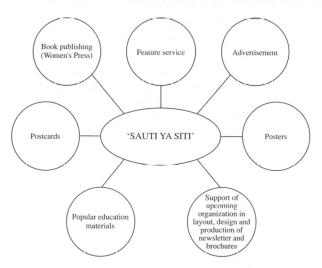

FIGURE III.23   TAMWA PUBLISHING UNIT

ter it or even try it. But once women do take it on, they are unstoppable. The fact that we can produce so-called first world quality in spite of being a so-called third world group has been an empowering process. Besides publications, we do popular education materials, pamphlets, brochures, cards, reports, and more. The income generated is helping the association toward its goal of self-sustainability. We now have an email system, which is an aid in networking and information dissemination.

I would like to mention here that to begin with we had male consultants as our trainers. They have since gone and established their own computer technology companies. Learning from TAMWA's experience as an organization, one of them has even established a glossy colour women's magazine with a more conventional portrayal of women! His example is another reason for us to emphasize the control of technology by women when we mobilize over issues of concern. Images portrayed through information technology are crucial.

Since 1992, TAMWA has focused particularly on the issue of violence against women. A special issue of *Sauti Ya Siti* was produced with desktop publishing, radio programmes were transmitted, and positive images of women were produced, including screen-printed T-shirts and stickers. A national rally during the Day of Action included an art exhibition. On this day, we is-

sued a call over the radio for those who felt concern over the issue to come. Some 50 percent of those who heeded the call were men, and women came on their own initiative from up-country. Out of this initiative, a Crisis Centre was born—the only one of its kind in Tanzania. The centre promotes legal literacy, provides counselling, and fights court cases involving violence against women. It also provides paralegal training, an exposure to and training in information technology, and some training in NGO management to members of up-country women's organizations, who then return to establish community-based centres in rural Tanzania. This kind of development gives us hope and the strength to go on.

Conclusion: TAMWA and Information Technology

As TAMWA grows as an organization, and undertakes a restructuring this year (1994), we are becoming very conscious of information technology. But we continuously ask the question, for whom and to what purpose are we using it? If expertise becomes a status symbol, it is of no use to those whom we wish to empower. If mastering these technologies raises class barriers or leads to a glossier type of publication in a foreign language, this is not progress. If, through the control of information technology, one maintains two-way communication in the language of the people, and women are portrayed in a manner which will create growth and empowerment, then it is to be encouraged.

Another important aspect is the demystification of information technology for that class which needs it the most in order to have their voices heard. To this end we produce booklets which teach, in practical terms, how to produce a newsletter using locally available materials. These booklets are used in participatory methodology workshops with gender perspectives. In these workshops women use the popular media, portraying problems with songs, drums, storytelling, and sung drama. Within these popular media, which have largely been women's domain, women have the "sociological space" to manoeuvre and resist the images of women portrayed in the conventional media. The process itself, combining the appropriation of conventional (i.e. technological) media with the revaluation of popular media, empowers. To bring about positive changes in women's lives, it is necessary to identify forms of expression and mobilization.

Recently, we did a four-day workshop for NGOs, looking at the project proposals in their programmes to assess whether gender sensitization is incorporated. The last day was reserved for media heads, the deci-sion makers in the newspapers and radio. The response was encouraging, and we hope the impact, although slow, will be a steady one. With advanced information technology, TAMWA is beginning to become a sophis-ticated alternative means of providing positive media images. As long as it continues its role of facilitating the voice of the voiceless, it will remain a force.

REFERENCES

Alley-Hamid, M. (1995). *Kanga — A Medium of Communication*, Dar-es-Salaam, TAMWA.

Alloo, Fatma. (1988). "Women and Popular Media," paper presented at the Women's Visions and Movements Conference, University of Ibadan, Nigeria, 27–29 September.

Alloo, Fatma. (1991). "A Regional Profile of Existing Women's NGOs and Networks in Southern and Eastern Africa," (mimeo), Dar es Salaam.

ISIS-WICCE. (1984). *Powerful Images: A Women's Guide to Audio-visual Resources*, Rome, Isis International.

Mlama, P. and A. Lihamba. (1988). *Popular Theatre and Participa-tion in Morogoro Region*, Dar-es-Salaam, TAMWA.

Sheikh-Hashim, L. (1989). *Unyago: Traditional Sex Education*, Dar-es-Salaam.

Sheriff, A. (1987). *Slaves, Spices and Ivory in Zanzibar*, Ohio, Uni-versity of Ohio Press.

TAMWA. (1991). *Origin, Development, Programmes and Prospects of Tanzania Media Women's Association*, annual report.

USAID. (1985). *Women in the World: A Chartbook for Developing Regions*, Washington, United States Agency for International Development, Office of Women in Development.

REFLECTING ON THE SECTION

New media have changed the way that words, ideas, and images travel around the globe over the past few decades. Yet these changes are experienced differently depending on one's economic status, education level, and geographic region. This is especially the case for new computer technologies, which over the last few decades have changed the nature of work and commu-nications as well as economic and cultural exchanges. What are some of the negative consequences for women of these new technologies? Which women in particular experience these effects? How are women using technology for personal, community, economic, educational, or political advantage? What resources do they need?

What is your relationship to new technologies? (How) is this relationship gendered? Think about how cyberculture is used in your local community: Who has access? Where? How? What benefits and/or disad-vantages does it bring to your life and the lives of those around you?

PART FOUR

Gendering Globalization and Displacement

Sometimes it seems as if everyone in the world is on the move. It can appear that few people live out their lives in the places in which they were born. If they do so, we may think that they are unusual or old-fashioned. Since being modern is associated with movement and with speed, living in one place may seem anachronistic. On the other hand, always being on the move is increasingly blamed for many of the problems that mark modern life.

While human beings have always moved around for a variety of reasons, the kind of movement that has come to characterize the modern period began with the rise of capitalism and the expansion of European trade routes and industries. Trade was always a primary reason for travel. Before European dominance, trade routes spanned most of the globe, armies traversed the continents, and people moved in search of better living conditions. What distinguishes this new era of movement under capitalism is its increasing speed and scale, as well as the deepening gap between the haves and have-nots. During this modern period, new kinds of genderings became intertwined with movement. Whether people move or not, whether they participate in travel or immigration, whether they are displaced or refugees, depends on many factors, including gender. In this part of the book, we will explore why gender matters when we consider the central activity of travel, displacement, and migration.

Think about what you learned about modern travel, trade, and exploration in the past. We all learned about the "great" explorers who mapped the continents and established the routes for contemporary trade. They were all men, mostly European or of European origin, and they seemed to be singularly accomplished as leaders and adventurers. Although we've begun to hear about the "native" or local guides who aided the explorers and often ensured the success of their expeditions, the "hero" of the story is always the European male adventurer. The narrative of the male adventurer survives in popular culture, especially in cinema—for example, Indiana Jones or James Bond. We have come to think of this male adventurer as the paramount traveler, overcoming adversity, seeking new scenes and routes, and finding thrills in the adventure of travel.

Where are the women in this mythology? In the standard narratives, women either were waiting to be discovered or rescued or remained at home, waiting for the hero's return. In this scenario, non-European women were either invisible or a dangerous element to be conquered. Non-European males were presented as either fearsome monsters whose irrationality justified their destruction or feminized weaklings who needed masters. Metaphors and phrases like "virgin" land and "penetrating the dark continent" speak to the gendered attitudes found in the adventure story. Since this story ignited the imaginations of many generations of European men, women, and children, it should not surprise us to discover that European women emerged as adventurers in their own right throughout this period. Often following male family members or religious organizations but sometimes traveling under their own auspices, European women took advantage of colonial trade and military activities to carve out their own paths to adventure.

While European women often believed that they were traveling for their own personal reasons or for the welfare of poor women in impoverished regions, their travels facilitated and enabled colonial rule in many ways. For example, in Part One of this book, we read about the work of British women health workers in colonial India, whose work perpetuated British interests in the region. Even missionary women, whose project of conversion to Christianity may not have directly benefited colonial rule, increased European domination over the so-called natives or savages. Female adventurers, just as much as the male adventurers, emerged from their travels with a heightened sense of their own capabilities and of their identities as whites and as Europeans. Two examples of nineteenth-century white British women travelers are Anna Leonowens, who wrote the autobiography that inspired *The King and I,* and Mary Kingsley, who collected scientific specimens in central Africa. Traveling under the sign of the British flag, these female adventurers sought out examples of cultural difference even as they brought with them Victorian values and attitudes. For them and many other such travelers, their identity as British women was shaped and reinforced by their travels outside their country.

Women travelers who were neither white nor European were more common than the historical record may indicate at first glance. While some nonwhite travelers such as Mary Seacole, a trader from Jamaica, sought the protection and power of British national identity, others, such as Pandita Ramabai from India, became symbols of the emerging independence of their nations. Then there are the many women who did not write their own accounts. They traveled as nurses, teachers, migrants, camp followers, prostitutes, traders, wives, daughters, and domestic workers. Many women were coerced or forcibly moved from one region or continent to another. We find evidence of their lives in government records, other travelers' stories, and family histories. Many of these experiences and stories have become the basis for new social movements that formulate identities through the histories of modern displacement and migration. For instance, identities such as African-American in the United States and Black British in the United Kingdom have been formed through dispersal and displacement, bringing about new forms of empowerment and claims for recognition.

It is impossible to discuss travel and displacement in the modern period without considering the history of slavery and indentured labor. If the adventure narrative is the paramount tale of the modern period, then it is also important to consider the other side of the story. That is, capitalism underwrote the exploration that is celebrated in the adventure narrative. That economic system required the forced labor of many groups, including Africans, indigenous people from South and North America, and indentured workers from Asia. The ideology of "race" and racial superiority legitimated the hierarchical structure of forced labor and slavery. Indentured laborers and slaves were less entitled to citizenship and participation in the generic category of the "human." Those seen as "heathens" and "savages" were viewed as expendable and treated as livestock who were valuable only as long as they were useful to their "masters."

Female slaves in North America were valued not only for their manual labor but also for their ability to reproduce more slaves. In this way, even their sexuality was considered a possession of their owners, and their progeny were taken away to be sold if the owner so desired. Such brutal displacements disrupted social groups not only in the regions from which the slaves and laborers were taken but also in the colonies and plantations in the "New World." For many women, this historical legacy remains alive and is a vital part of their identity as women, as members of families, and as citizens of the nation-state in which they live.

As a result of these racial/cultural attitudes and European demand for unrestricted wealth throughout the modern period, indigenous peoples faced genocide. In North America, early colonizers showed little interest in creating a renewable labor force. Their inhumane treatment of native peoples led to millions of deaths. When European settlers arrived in North America, they began a process (which only in-

tensified with the formation of the United States as a nation) to push indigenous peoples out of the regions in which they had lived and into new "reservations." The conquest of the "western frontier" in the
United States generated many tales of adventure in which the hero—who could be a soldier, a cowboy,
a farmer, or a lawman—destroyed indigenous groups—who were always represented as savage threats
to Western civilization.

Countless tales were told in books and newspapers of vulnerable white women who needed to be
rescued from these "savage hordes." While white women moved to the West in search of economic opportunities for themselves and their families, indigenous women became sexual prey for white settler
males. The stereotype of the Indian "squaw" depicted a downtrodden drudge, erasing the long history
of indigenous women's active participation in the governance and social life of their communities. More
recently, a sanitized romantic view of the indigenous woman has appeared in popular culture as represented by Pocahontas and Sacagawea (two women who were associated with powerful white male colonizers and explorers).

These disparate histories of race, class, and gender in the same region have left a legacy of conflicting interests among women and made the category of "woman" a complicated one in the United States
Histories of colonialism and imperialism have created inequalities that make it hard for women to see
each other as holding common interests. Yet when some feminists claim that women around the world
share an identity or that they are "sisters" by virtue of their sex, these histories and their legacies of inequalities are suppressed or forgotten. While many women share similar conditions and situations, they
may also hold drastically different views on how these conditions came about, which ones are most important, and what to do about them.

For instance, the international women's conferences held by the United Nations since the 1970s have
elicited both conflict and agreement. Delegates often clash over nationalism, claims for similarity in the
face of inequalities, distribution of resources, and cultural differences. Very often, the dominance of the
wealthier countries is unacknowledged by their delegates, leading to tensions and misunderstandings.
To find a way to address these differences, feminists need to acknowledge the varying ways in which gender becomes an issue or forms an identity in diverse places and times. Along with cultural and national
differences, histories of colonialism and European domination in the last three centuries have to be taken
into account in international or transnational women's organizing.

Colonialisms in the modern period have also left a legacy of impoverishment and political instability,
a lethal combination for women and children the world over. The numbers of displaced women and children increased steadily throughout the twentieth century and show no signs of abating. War on an unprecedented scale characterized the century, along with the redrawing of borders and the institution of
new political regimes. These events resulted in large-scale displacement of millions of people who became unwanted, stateless, or endangered. The establishment of new national boundaries led to the institution of passports and other documents that regulated and policed departure from one nation-state
and entrance to another.

In response to the disruptions of modern war and the intensification of border policing, refugee
camps were created to house ever-larger numbers of displaced people. Among the population of
refugee camps, women and children predominate. Women who are illiterate, impoverished, or under
threat may have less access to documents and other resources than men, leading to their further disempowerment and endangerment. It is ironic that even though at present women comprise the largest
group of refugees, the official view (in documents of the United Nations) of the refugee is a man fleeing
political persecution.

The common and equally inaccurate perception of the immigrant or migrant also depicts a man. Although people have always moved in search of a livelihood, modern industrial capitalism and war have

changed the nature of migration. Since the nineteenth century, large numbers of people have traveled or resettled in their search for work. Among them have been many women of different ages and from different places. Although migration improves living standards for some women, for others the process robs them of skills and capabilities they might have had in the past. Restrictions based on race, ethnicity, language, religion, class, and national origin continue to place some women at a greater disadvantage in their new homes. Separation from kin groups, friends, and communities can add to the losses experienced by migrant women. Inability to speak the language of a destination country may leave women isolated or functionally illiterate.

In many ways the experience of migration changed enormously through the twentieth century, yet many aspects remain the same today. The legacy of colonialism and racism ensures that some groups are always at a disadvantage, since their impoverishment in the past affects their conditions in the present. For example, Japanese and U.S. imperialism systematically underdeveloped the Philippines over a period of more than a century. Ongoing colonial relationships with various nations have led to societies where a few people are extremely wealthy and a large number are very poor. This is why many Filipinas seek work in countries such as Saudi Arabia, Hong Kong, Japan, Canada, and the United States, most often as nurses, domestic workers, and nannies. The Philippine government depends on the income these women send back to their families. Working conditions vary, but reports indicate that Filipinas' exploitation in terms of hours, wages, and benefits is quite severe. Many Filipinas are extremely overqualified for the work that is available abroad; for example, a woman with a medical degree may find herself working as a nurse or doing child care.

Yet the experience of migration over the last 20 years has changed. Globalization of finance organizations has made it easier to send money more quickly and frequently. Air travel has reduced the amount of time it takes to cross great distances, and telephones keep women in touch with the families they have left at home. There are also more advocacy groups that seek to organize against the isolation and exploitation of women migrant workers. Despite these changes, globalization itself depends on a gendered division of labor in which particular women do certain kinds of work in specific places.

Even if women do not cross continents or oceans to seek work, globalization has changed their lives. The nature of agriculture has changed due to the increasing threat to small, independent farmers from large agribusiness and from development policies that mandate certain products and methods. New industries, such as tourism, have brought new kinds of employment as well as leisure activities. Previously remote or underdeveloped areas have become developed as tourist resorts where women find employment as maids, receptionists, waitresses, sex workers, and other service employees. As industrialization has intensified, environmental degradation has increased dramatically, leading to health hazards and changes in work and household patterns. For example, a woman may have to walk much farther to chop wood for cooking or to get clean water.

The migration of more and more people from the diminishing farm economies to the cities, where some work may be available, has led to the sprawl that characterizes metropolitan areas in the First World as well as the Third. This so-called internal migration provides labor for the kind of production that has become increasingly common in border zones, or EPZs (export processing zones—also known as "free enterprise zones" or maquilladoras, as those on the U.S.–Mexican border are called). In these areas, governments that need foreign capital investment offer special conditions to multinational corporations, such as lower wages, taxes, and environmental standards.

Who is available to work for less? Very often it is young women who find no other employment possibilities, especially close to home, who work on the assembly lines that produce televisions, computers, and clothing. For many women, the opportunity to earn wages and to become more independent can lead to the purchase of more consumer goods and a change in their families' lifestyles. When a teenage girl who had been the least powerful person in the family begins to send home wages, her status and her role change (although not always for the better). These changes in the family are being played out everywhere, although in many different ways.

All of these social, political, and economic shifts change the meanings attached to gender and make for new conditions that need to be studied and discussed in women's studies courses. As we learn about gender in a transnational framework, we come to understand more about the ways that women are responding to current conditions. For example, advocacy groups working in EPZs have fought for and obtained better working conditions and wages. Transnational groups that work on labor, environmental, and human rights issues concerning women lobby the United Nations and other international bodies to change policies and treaties. Feminist critiques of biased representations based on class, race, religion, sexuality, nationality, and other criteria have led to new ways of thinking about and portraying women's issues and identities in a global framework.

Feminist researchers have shown over and over that globalization and development programs have not delivered the improvements in women's lives that were promised. Indeed, in many cases, women's situations have worsened. This research has resulted in critiques of structural adjustment programs— the economic policies required by lenders such as the International Monetary Fund, which force countries to place debt reduction before social welfare. In insisting that women are affected differentially by globalization, feminists have begun to achieve improvements in policies and approaches to poverty and health issues. Attention to women as a group has resulted from these efforts.

The questions of what counts as female and what constitutes the condition of women can be answered in many different ways. In this final part of the book, we suggest that feminist futures will be shaped by an awareness of colonial legacies, the new dominance of transnational culture and economy, new social movements and identities, and the changing nature of national cultures in both the wealthy and the "developing" nations.

Travel and Tourism

On the Beach: Sexism and Tourism

CYNTHIA ENLOE

We begin this part of the book with Cynthia Enloe's discussion of the ways that divisions of labor, representations of masculinity and femininity, and new industries such as tourism entrench the power of patriarchal authority. Since tourism relies upon traditional, dominant ideas about gender, Enloe believes it is an ideal site for understanding the effects of globalization on women.

The Portuguese woman perched on the ladder seems to be enjoying her work. Wearing a colorful dress under several layers of aprons, she is not too busy picking olives to smile at the photographer.

Selecting postcards is one of those seemingly innocent acts that has become fraught with ideological risks. Imagine for a minute that you are a British woman traveling in Portugal. You have saved for this holiday and are thoroughly enjoying the time away from stress and drizzle. But you haven't left your feminist consciousness at home. You think about the lives of the Portuguese women you see. That is one of the

Cynthia Enloe, "On the Beach: Sexism and Tourism, in *"Bananas, Beaches, and Bases: Making Feminist Sense out of International Politics,* Berkeley: University of California Press, 1990: 19–24, 28–32, 40–41.

reasons you search the postcard racks to find pictures of Portuguese women engaged in relatively ordinary occupations—weaving, making pottery, pulling in heavy fishing nets, hoeing fields, or harvesting olives. These are the images of Portuguese women you want to send your friends back home.

Still, you are a bit uneasy when you realize that in the eyes of those Portuguese women you are probably just another northern tourist able to afford leisurely travel outside her own country. They know you don't search for those less picturesque but no less real images of Portuguese women's lives today: women working in the new plastics factories around Porto, marking Portugal's entrance into the European Common Market; women working as chambermaids in hotels, representing the country's dependence on tourism. Such pictures wouldn't mesh with the holiday image you want to share with friends back in damp, chilly Britain.

No matter how good the feminist tourist's intention, the relationship between the British woman on holiday and the working women of Portugal seems to fall short of international sisterhood. But is it exploitation? As uncomfortable as we are when we look at women smiling out from foreign postcards, we might pause before leaping to the conclusion that they are merely one more group of victims under the heel of international

---

Key Terms

British Museum The national museum in London, established in 1753.
ritual fetish An object that is believed to have magical powers and is sometimes used in rituals.

temperance The movement to abstain from or even outlaw alcohol.

capital. Women in many countries are being drawn into unequal relationships with each other as a result of governments' sponsorship of the international tourist industry, some because they have no choice, but others because they are making their own decisions about how to improve their lives. Many women are playing active roles in expanding and shaping the tourist industry—as travel agents, travel writers, flight attendants, craftswomen, chambermaids—even if they don't control it.

Similarly, women who travel are not merely creatures of privilege; nor today are they only from Western societies. They—or their mothers—have often had to fight against confining presumptions of feminine respectability to travel away from home on their own.

The hushed and serious tones typically reserved for discussions of nuclear escalation or spiraling international debt are rarely used in discussions of tourism. Tourism doesn't fit neatly into public preoccupations with military conflict and high finance. Although it is infused with masculine ideas about adventure, pleasure, and the exotic, those are deemed "private" and thus kept off stage in debates about international politics. Yet since World War II, planners, investors and workers in the tourist industry, and tourists themselves, have been weaving unequal patterns that are restructuring international politics. And they depend on women for their success.

By the mid-1980s, the global tourism business employed more people than the oil industry. These employees were servicing an estimated 200 million people who each year pack their bags and pocket their Berlitz phrase books to become international tourists.[1] The numbers continue to rise steadily. The United Nations World Tourism Organization forecasts that by the year 2000, tourism will have become the single most important global economic activity.[2]

The British woman's dilemma in trying to find a postcard expressing sisterhood rather than exploitation suggests that the galloping tourist industry is not necessarily making the world a more equal or harmonious place. Charter flights, time-share beach condominiums, and Himalayan trekking parties each carry with them power as well as pleasure. While tourism's supporters cite increased government revenues and modernizing influences, its critics ask whether tourism's remarkable growth is narrowing or widening the gap between the affluent and the poor. They question whether the foreign currency, new airstrips, and hotels that come with the tourist industry really are adequate compensations for the exacerbation of racial tensions and other problems that so often accompany tourism.[3]

⟶ Footloose and Gendered

Tourism has its own political history, reaching back to the Roman empire. It overlaps with other forms of travel that appear to be less dedicated to pleasure. Government missions, military tours of duty, business trips, scientific explorations, forced migrations— women and men have experienced them differently, in ways that have helped construct today's global tourism industry and the international political system it sustains.

In many societies, being feminine has been defined as sticking close to home. Masculinity, by contrast, has been the passport for travel. Feminist geographers and ethnographers have been amassing evidence revealing that a principal difference between women and men in countless societies has been the licence to travel away from a place thought of as "home."

A woman who travels away from the ideological protection of "home" and without the protection of an acceptable male escort is likely to be tarred with the brush of "unrespectability." She risks losing her honor or being blamed for any harm that befalls her on her travels. One need only think of the lack of sympathy accorded a woman who has been assaulted when trying to hitchhike on her own: "What does she expect, after all?" Some women may unwittingly reinforce the patriarchal link between respectable womanhood and geographic confinement with their own gestures of defiance. A bumper sticker has begun to appear on women's well-traveled vans: "Good girls go to Heaven. Bad girls go everywhere."

By contrast, a man is deemed less than manly until he breaks away from home and strikes out on his own. Some men leave the farm and travel to the city or mining town looking for work. Other men set off hitchhiking with only a knapsack and a good pair of boots. Still others answer the call to "Join the Navy and see the world."

"I cut off my hair and dressed me in a suit of my husband's having had the precaution to quilt the waist-coat to preserve my breasts from hurt which were not large enough to betray my sex and putting on the wig and hat I had prepared I went out and brought me a sil-ver hilted sword and some Holland shirts."[4] So Chris-tian Davies set off in the 1690s to enlist in the British army. If she couldn't travel as a woman, she would dis-guise herself as a man. The stories of Christian and women like her are not unmixed tales of feminist re-bellion, however. While some of the women ran away to sea or enlisted as drummer boys to escape suffocat-ing village life, others claimed they were simply acting as a loyal wife or sweetheart, following their man. If a woman was exposed—while being treated for a battle wound or giving birth—the punishment she received frequently depended on which of these two interpreta-tions was believed by the men who pulled away her disguise.

[. . .]

More recently, women have been lured into joining the military—without a disguise—by thoughts of leav-ing home. Getting away from home, not killing Rus-sians or Vietnamese, is what Peggy Perri, just out of nursing school, had in mind when she and her best friend decided to enlist in the U.S. Army nursing corps in 1967. "Pat and I were both living at home and we were both miserable. I was living at my mother's house. I was unhappy, really unhappy," Peggy recalls. "Pat and I had become nurses with the expectation that we could go anywhere and work. We wanted to go somewhere, and we wanted to do something really dif-ferent." Peggy wasn't a classic "good girl." She chewed gum and liked parties. But she didn't want to surrender her status as a respectable young woman. "We needed to know that there was going to be some kind of structure to hold us up. The military sure prom-ised that. . . . I was infatuated by the idea of going to Vietnam. . . . I really didn't know where I wanted to go. I wanted to go everywhere in the world." She soon got her wish. "I remember we got our orders; my mother took me shopping in every major department store. Pat and I both bought new sets of luggage. Pat's was hot pink! . . . It was January and we would go to all the 'cruise' shops looking for lightweight clothing. I wanted everyone to think I was going on a cruise."[5]

The most famous of the women who set out to travel further than convention allowed without disguise are now referred to as the "Victorian lady travelers." Most of them came from the white middle classes of North America and Europe. They set out upon travels that were supposed to be the preserve of men. They defied the strictures of femininity by choosing parts of the world which whites in the late nineteenth and early twentieth century considered "uncharted," "uncivi-lized." Not for them the chic tourist meccas of Italy and Greece. These Victorian lady travelers wanted *adven-ture*. That meant going to lands just being opened up by imperial armies and capitalist traders.

In their own day these women were viewed with suspicion because they dared to travel such long dis-tances with so little proper male protection. Even if their husbands accompanied them as missionaries or scientists, these women insisted upon the separateness of their own experiences. The fact that most of them were white and chose to travel in continents whose populations were not added to the "exotic" aura sur-rounding their journeys. Space and race, when com-bined, have different implications for women and men, even of the same social class.[6]

Mary Kingsley, Isabella Bird, Alexandra David-Neel, Nina Mazuchelli, Annie Bullock Workman, Nina Benson Hubbard—these women in the nineteenth and early twentieth centuries took for themselves the iden-tities of "adventurer" and "explorer." Both labels were thoroughly masculinized. Masculinity and exploration had been as tightly woven together as masculinity and soldiering. These audacious women challenged that ideological assumption, but they have left us with a bundle of contradictions. While they defied, appar-ently self-consciously, the ban on far-flung travel by "respectable" women, in some respects they seem quite conventional. Some of them rejected female suf-frage. Some refused to acknowledge fully how far their own insistence on the right to adventure undermined not only Victorian notions of femininity but the bond being forged between Western masculinity and West-ern imperialism.

Mary Kingsley is one of the most intriguing lady travelers. Mary's father was an explorer, her brother an adventurer. Mary was born in 1862 and grew up as the twin movements of women's domestication of women and imperial expansion were flowering in Victoria's England. She seemed destined to nurse her invalid mother and to keep the homefires burning for her globe-trotting brother. But Mary had other ideas. In 1892 she set out on the first of several expeditions to Africa. She traveled without male escort and headed for the West African interior. For it was in the continent's interior where "real" adventures were thought to happen. In subsequent years she befriended European male traders plying their business along the coasts and up the rivers of Africa. Her detailed knowledge of African societies' ritual fetishes was even acknowledged by the men of the British Museum.[7]

Mary Kingsley also became one of the most popular speakers on the lively lecture circuit. She drew enthusiastic audiences from all over England to hear about her travels to Africa and her descriptions of lives lived in the newly penetrated areas of Victoria's empire. Many women travelers helped finance their travels by giving public lectures. The lecture circuit may have provided a crucial setting in which the women who stayed at home could become engaged in the British empire. They could take part vicariously in British officials' debates over how best to incorporate African and Asian peoples into that empire by listening to Mary Kingsley describe colonial policies and their consequences for local peoples.

The women lecture-goers are as politically interesting as Mary Kingsley herself. Together, lecturer and audience helped to fashion a British culture of imperialism. The stay-at-home listeners would develop a sense of imperial pride as they heard another woman describe her travels among their empire's more "exotic" peoples. And they could expand their knowledge of the world without risking loss of that feminine respectability which enabled them to feel superior to colonized women. Their imperial curiosity, in turn, helped Mary Kingsley finance her breaking of gendered convention.

[. . .]

—◦ Package Tours for the Respectable Woman

Tourism is as much ideology as physical movement. It is a package of ideas about industrial, bureaucratic

life.[8] It is a set of presumptions about manhood, education, and pleasure.[9]

Tourism has depended on presumptions about masculinity and femininity. Often women have been set up as the quintessence of the exotic. To many men, women are something to be experienced. Women don't have experiences of their own. If the women are of a different culture, the male tourist feels he has entered a region where he can shed civilization's constraints, where he is freed from standards of behavior imposed by respectable women back home.

Thomas Cook perhaps deserves credit for making the world safe for the respectable woman tourist. On an English summer's day in 1841, walking to a temperance meeting, Thomas Cook had the idea of chartering a train for the next meeting so that participants could board a single train, pay a reduced rate, and while traveling to their meeting be treated to "hams, loaves and tea" interspersed with exhortations against the evils of drink. Some 570 people signed up for that first trip.[10]

Initially, Thomas Cook was concerned primarily with working men like himself. He wanted to provide them with a diversion that didn't involve liquor.

[. . .]

Only later did Cook come to realize that package tours might attract working men and their wives and children and eventually women traveling without a male member of the family. By the 1850s, Britain's more adventurous middle-class women were beginning to earn their own income and to think about traveling for pleasure, if not to West Africa, at least to Germany. They still needed to safeguard their respectability in order to stay marriageable and so were looking for a chaperoned tour led by an honorable man. Thomas Cook, temperance advocate, offered precisely such a service.

[. . .]

Today the package tour holiday is a profitable commodity for some of the international economy's most successful companies. In Britain 40 percent of the population cannot afford an annual holiday, but one-third of the upper middle class take two or more holidays a year. There are now 700 tour operators in Britain selling more than 12.5 million package holidays annually, worth £3.1 billion. While most of their customers pick the Mediterranean, British and continental tour companies are nudging clients to travel further afield—to North Africa, North America, and the Caribbean.[11]

Japanese government officials are predicting that foreign travel will be one of that country's major growth industries in the 1990s. Although only 5 percent of Japanese took holidays abroad in 1987, large tourist companies like JTB and Kinki Nippon Tourist Agency have already turned foreign travel into a $16 billion business. One-third of Japanese overseas tourists today travel as part of a package tour. Most notorious are groups of businessmen traveling to South Korea, the Philippines, and Thailand on sex tours. But the country's second-largest tourist market is single working women: 18 percent of all Japanese tourists. Their favored destinations are the shops and beaches of Hong Kong, Hawaii, and California.[12]

The Tourism Formula for Development

From its beginnings, tourism has been a powerful motor for global integration. Even more than other forms of investment, it has symbolized a country's entrance into the world community. Foreign-owned mines, military outposts, and museum explorations have drawn previously "remote" societies into the international system, usually on unequal terms. Tourism entails a more politically potent kind of intimacy. For a tourist isn't expected to be very adventurous or daring, to learn a foreign language or adapt to local custom. Making sense of the strange local currency is about all that is demanded. Perhaps it is for this reason that international technocrats express such satisfaction when a government announces that it plans to promote tourism as one of its major industries. For such a policy implies a willingness to meet the expectations of those foreigners who want political stability, safety, and congeniality when they travel. A government which decides to rely on money from tourism for its development is a government which has decided to be internationally compliant enough that even a woman traveling on her own will be made to feel at home there.

When mass tourism began to overtake elite travel following World War II, most travel occurred within and between North America and Western Europe. By the mid-1970s, 8 percent of all tourists were North Americans and Europeans traveling on holiday to Third World countries. A decade later, 17 percent were.[13] Middle-class Canadians who a decade ago thought of going across the border to Cape Cod or Florida in search of holiday warmth are now as likely to head for the Bahamas. Their French counterparts are as apt to make Tunisia or Morocco rather than Nice their holiday destination. Scandinavians are choosing Sri Lanka or Goa instead of the Costa del Sol.

Third World officials and their European, American, and Japanese bankers have become avid tourism boosters. Tourism is promoted today as an industry that can turn poor countries' very poverty into a magnet for sorely needed foreign currency. For to be a poor society in the late twentieth century is to be "unspoiled." Tourism is being touted as an alternative to the one-commodity dependency inherited from colonial rule. Foreign sun-seekers replace bananas. Hiltons replace sugar mills. Multinational corporations such as Gulf and Western or Castle and Cook convert their large landholdings into resorts or sell them off to developers. By the mid-1980s, tourism had replaced sugar as the Dominican Republic's top foreign-exchange earner. In Jamaica, tourism had outstripped bauxite as the leading earner of foreign exchange. Caribbean development officials are happily reporting that, with more than 10 million visitors a year, the region is outstripping its main tourism rivals, Hawaii and Mexico. But, they add reassuringly, all the new hotel construction isn't turning Caribbean islands into concrete jungles: "Many of the islands are mainly wild and underpopulated, with room for many more hotels and resorts before their appeal is threatened."[14]

In reality, tourism may be creating a new kind of dependency for poor nations. Today tourism represents 40,000 jobs for Tunisia and is the country's biggest foreign-currency earner. Countries such as Puerto Rico, Haiti, Nepal, Gambia, and Mexico have put their development eggs in the tourism basket, spending millions of dollars from public funds to build the sorts of facilities that foreign tourists demand. Officials in these countries hope above all that tourism will get their countries out of debt. The international politics of debt and the international pursuit of pleasure have become tightly knotted together.[15]

[. . .]

The indebted governments that have begun to rely on tourism include those which previously were most dubious about this as a route to genuine development, especially if "development" is to include preservation of national sovereignty. Cuba, Tanzania, North Korea, Vietnam, and Nicaragua all are being governed today by officials who have adopted a friendlier attitude toward tourism. They are being complimented and called "pragmatic" by mainstream international observers because they are putting the reduction of international debt and the earning of foreign currency on the top of their political agenda.[16]

[. . .]

—Conclusion

Tourism is not just about escaping work and drizzle; it is about power, increasingly internationalized power. That tourism is not discussed as seriously by conventional political commentators as oil or weaponry may tell us more about the ideological construction of "seriousness" than about the politics of tourism.

Government and corporate officials have come to depend on international travel for pleasure in several ways. First, over the last 40 years they have come to see tourism as an industry that can help diversify local economies suffering from reliance on one or two products for export. Tourism is embedded in the inequalities of international trade but is often tied to the politics of particular products, such as sugar, bananas, tea, and copper. Second, officials have looked to tourism to provide them with foreign currency, a necessity in the ever more globalized economies of both poor and rich countries. Third, tourism development has been looked upon as a spur to more general social development; the "trickle down" of modern skills, new technology, and improved public services is imagined to follow in the wake of foreign tourists. Fourth, many government of-

ficials have used the expansion of tourism to secure the political loyalty of local élites. For instance, certain hotel licences may win a politician more strategic allies today than a mere civil-service appointment. Finally, many officials have hoped that tourism would raise their nations' international visibility and even prestige.

Many of these hopes have been dashed. Yet tourism continues to be promoted by bankers and development planners as a means of making the international system less unequal, more financially sound, and more politically stable. A lot is riding on sun, surf, and souvenirs.

From the Roman empire to the eighteenth-century European grand tour, the rise of Cooks Tours and Club Med, travel for pleasure and adventure has been profoundly gendered. Without ideas about masculinity and femininity—and the enforcement of both—in the societies of departure and the societies of destination, it would be impossible to sustain the tourism industry and its political agenda in their current form. It is not simply that ideas about pleasure, travel, escape, bedmaking, and sexuality have affected women in rich and poor countries. The very structure of international tourism *needs* patriarchy to survive. Men's capacity to control women's sense of their security and self-worth has been central to the evolution of tourism politics. It is for this reason that actions by feminists—as airline stewardesses, hotel workers, prostitutes, wives of businessmen and organizers of alternative tours for women—should be seen as political, internationally political.

Movements which upset any of the patterns in today's international tourist industry are likely to upset one of the principal pillars of contemporary world power. Such a realization forces one to take a second look at the Portuguese woman on her ladder picking olives, smiling for the postcard photographer. She has the potential for reshaping the international political order. What is behind her smile?

NOTES

1. Paul Fussell, "The Modern Age of Tourism," from Fussell's *Abroad: British Literary Travelling between the Wars,* excerpted in *Utne Reader,* July/August 1987, p. 105.

2. Shelly Attix, "Socially Responsible Travel: How to Prevent the Social and Ecological Damage of Tourism," excerpted from *Building Economic Alternatives,* Spring 1986, in *Utne Reader,* July/August 1987, p. 109.

3. Among the sharpest critiques of tourism's effects on local cultures is Afro-Caribbean writer Jamaica Kincaid's description of postcolonial Antigua: Jamaica Kincaid, *A Small Place,* London, Virago,

1988; New York, Farrar, Straus & Giroux, 1988. Cultural Survival, an organization devoted to research related to the rights of indigenous peoples, has published a special issue of its journal *Cultural Survival Quarterly:* "The Tourist Trap: Who's Getting Caught," vol. 6, no. 3, Summer 1982. A publication monitoring tourism's impact on Third World societies is *Contours: Concern for Tourism,* published by the Ecumenical Coalition on Third World Tourism, 55 m/173–4 Saranom 2 Village, Thanon Nuanchan, Sukhapibanl Road, Klong-gum, Bangkapi, Bangkok 10230, Thailand. In Britain the address for *Contours* is c/o Roger Millman, 70 Dry Hill Road, Park Road, Tonbridge, Kent.

4. From Richard Montague's *The Life and Adventures of Mrs. Christian Davies,* 1740, quoted in Julie Wheelwright, "Amazons and Military Maids," *Women's Studies International Forum,* vol. 10, no. 5, 1987, p. 491. See also Julie Wheelwright, *Amazons and Military Maids,* London and Winchester, Mass., Pandora Press, 1989.

5. Lisa Wenner with Peggy Perri, "Pack Up Your Sorrows: The Oral History of an Army Nurse in Vietnam," typescript, Smith College, Northampton, Mass., 1986, pp. 15–16. A revised version of this oral history will be published in a volume edited by Peggy Perri and Julia Perez, University of Illinois Press, forthcoming.

6. Mary Seacole, a Black Caribbean woman, is an important exception to the otherwise white Victorian lady travelers. For an account of her adventures in the Crimea and Europe, see Ziggi Alexander and Audrey Dewjee, editors, *Wonderful Adventures of Mrs. Seacole in Many Lands,* Bristol, Falling Wall Press, 1984. Two useful guides to the abundant literature written by lady travelers, much of it now in new editions, are Jane Robinson, editor, *A Bibliography of Women Travellers,* Oxford, Oxford University Press, 1989; Marion Tinling, editor, *Woman into the Unknown: A Source Book on Women Explorers and Travelers,* Westport, Conn., Greenwood Press, 1989.

7. Katherine Frank, *A Voyager Out,* New York, Houghton Mifflin, 1986. For a more critical assessment of Mary Kingsley, see Deborah Birkett, "The Invalid at Home, the Samson Abroad," *Women's Review,* London, no. 6, 1987, pp. 18–19. Also see Deborah Birkett, "West Africa's Mary Kingsley," *History Today,* May 1987. Deborah Birkett's biography of Mary Kingsley is forthcoming from Macmillan.

8. Louise Turner and John Ash, *The Golden Hordes: International Tourism and the Pleasure Periphery,* New York, St Martin's Press, 1976, pp. 20–21.

9. Maxine Feifer, *Tourism in History: From Imperial Rome to the Present,* New York, Stern & Day, 1986, pp. 10–11. For more on later European travel, especially by male aristocrats in the seventeenth and eighteenth centuries, see John Tower, "The Grand Tour: A Key Phase in the History of Tourism," *Annals of Tourism Research,* vol. 12, 1985, pp. 297–333; Judith Adler, "Youth on The Road: Reflections on the History of Tramping," *Annals of Tourism Research,* vol. 12, 1985, pp. 337–50; Susan L. Blake, "A Woman's Trek: What Difference Does Gender Make?" in Margaret Strobel and Nupur Chaudhuri, editors, "Western Women and Imperialism," special issue of *Woman's Studies International Forum,* 13 no. 4 1990.

10. The principal source of information on Thomas Cook Tours is the Thomas Cook Archives: Edmund Swinglehurst, archivist, 45 Berkeley Street, London W1. The archives hold the collections of Cook's *Excursionist,* launched in 1855, and *Travellers' Gazette,* which made its debut in 1905.

11. "Across the Class Divide," *The Economist,* January 16, 1988, pp. 47–48; "Europe's Charter Airlines Love the Summer Weather," *The Economist,* August 1, 1987, p. 57.

12. "Japanese Tourism: Broadening the Mind," *The Economist,* May 7, 1988, p. 64; Susan Chira, "It's Official! Vacations Really Aren't UnJapanese," *New York Times,* August 6, 1988.

13. Peter Stalker, "Going Places: Westerners Invade Paradise," *The New Internationalist,* December 1984, excerpted in *Utne Reader,* July/August 1987, p. 104.

14. Joseph Treaster, "Caribbean Savors Tourism Boom," *New York Times,* November 7, 1988. On Gulf + Western's sale of its Dominican Republic sugar lands to Florida's Franjui development company, see Joseph Treaster, "Is There Life After Gulf + Western?," *New York Times,* May 26, 1985. On Japanese tourism earnings, see *New York Times,* September 12, 1987. On Hawaii's sugar-tourism connection, see Walter Cohen, "Hawaii Faces the Pacific," *Pacific Research,* vol. 6, no. 2, January/February, 1975; Noel Kent, *Islands under the Influence,* New York, Monthly Review Press, 1979; Jan H. Mejer, "Capitalist Stages, State Formation and Ethnicity in Hawaii," *National Journal of Sociology,* vol. 1, no. 2, Fall 1987, pp. 173–207.

15. *New York Times,* June 5, 1988; Erlet A. Carter, "Tourism in the Least Developed Countries," *Annals of Tourism Research,* vol. 14, 1987; Linda Richter, *The Politics of Tourism in Asia,* Honolulu, University of Hawaii Press, 1988.

16. In 1988 Fidel Castro announced that Cuba would put into effect policies meant to attract 600,000 foreign tourists by 1992. Although he led a revolution which sought to end the tourist industry's corruption of Cuban society, the fall in the international price of sugar, the country's chief export, left the government with no choice but to pursue the tourism strategy: *New York Times,* September 1, 1988. On Vietnam's tourism policies, see Murray Hiebert, "Enterprise Encouraged to Invigorate the Economy," *Far Eastern Economic Review,* July 23, 1987, p. 31; Barbara Crossette, "Vietnam for Visitors," *New York Times,* September 13, 1987; Melanie Beresford, "Revolution in the Countryside: Report on a Visit to Vietnam," *Journal of Contemporary Asia,* vol. 16, no. 3, 1986, p. 399. On North Korean tourist policy, see Derek Hall, "North Korea Opens to Tourism: A Last Resort," *Inside Asia,* July/August, 1986, pp. 21–22; Nicholas D. Kristof, "North Korea Tourism Signals New Openness," *New York Times,* September 20, 1987. On Nicaragua's still tentative moves to develop tourism, see Stephen Kinzer, "Nicaragua's Ideology of Sun and Surf', *New York Times.* November 23, 1988.

Wonderful Adventures of Mrs. Seacole in Many Lands

MARY SEACOLE

Written in 1857, Wonderful Adventures of Mrs. Seacole in Many Lands *describes the travels of Mary Seacole (1805–81), a Jamaican woman of Scottish and African ancestry. Mary Seacole's contribution to travel literature is an important one and serves as a contrast to the many narratives written by white European and North American women of the nineteenth century. Seacole's combined interests and talents in medicine and trade brought her many opportunities even as she struggled against the prejudices and inequities of her era. In addition to her spirit of adventure and her accomplishments, what is striking in Seacole's narrative*

Mary Seacole, *Wonderful Adventures of Mrs. Seacole in Many Lands,* New York: Oxford University Press, 1988: 1–5, 82–86.

is her allegiance to the British crown and to England. Unlike more contemporary writers from the Caribbean, who protest and struggle against the colonial relationship, in her writing Mary Seacole chose British identity as a route to empowerment.

My Birth and Parentage—Early Tastes and Travels—Marriage, and Widowhood

I was born in the town of Kingston, in the island of Jamaica, some time in the present century. As a female, and a widow, I may be well excused giving the precise date of this important event. But I do not mind confessing that the century and myself were both young together, and that we have grown side by side into age and consequence. I am a Creole, and have good Scotch

---

Key Terms

Battle of Trafalgar On October 21, 1805, the British, led by Nelson, defeated the Spanish and French forces off the coast of Spain at Cape Trafalgar in this decisive battle during the Napoleonic Wars.

caicque A small, lightweight rowing boat used on the Bosphorus in Turkey.

Constantinople The name of Istanbul, Turkey, until 1930. The first city founded at the site was Byzantium in 660 B.C.

creole Person born and naturalized in the Caribbean to parents of European and African descent.

Crimea A peninsula (now part of Ukraine) bounded by the Black Sea, site of the Crimean War (1853–56) between Russia and the allied powers of Turkey, England, France, and Sardinia. The war is remembered for the many casualties at Balaclava and for the innovations in nursing accomplished by Florence Nightingale and others.

Florence Nightingale (1820–1910) English nurse who was one of the founders of modern nursing.

Margery Daw Character in a nursery rhyme.

Ulysses In Greek mythology, the king of Ithaca and husband of Penelope. The hero of Homer's Odyssey, he fought in the Trojan War and wandered for many years before returning home.

blood coursing in my veins. My father was a soldier, of an old Scotch family; and to him I often trace my affection for a camp-life, and my sympathy with what I have heard my friends call "the pomp, pride, and circumstance of glorious war." Many people have also traced to my Scotch blood that energy and activity which are not always found in the Creole race, and which have carried me to so many varied scenes: and perhaps they are right. I have often heard the term "lazy Creole" applied to my countrypeople; but I am sure I do not know what it is to be indolent. All my life long I have followed the impulse which led me to be up and doing; and so far from resting idle anywhere, I have never wanted inclination to rove, nor will powerful enough to find a way to carry out my wishes. That these qualities have led me into many countries, and brought me into some strange and amusing adventures, the reader, if he or she has the patience to get through this book, will see. Some people, indeed, have called me quite a female Ulysses. I believe that they intended it as a compliment; but from my experience of the Greeks, I do not consider it a very flattering one.

It is not my intention to dwell at any length upon the recollections of my childhood. My mother kept a boardinghouse in Kingston, and was, like very many of the Creole women, an admirable doctress; in high repute with the officers of both services, and their wives, who were from time to time stationed at Kingston. It was very natural that I should inherit her tastes; and so I had from early youth a yearning for medical knowledge and practice which has never deserted me. When I was a very young child I was taken by an old lady, who brought me up in her household among her own grandchildren, and who could scarcely have shown me more kindness had I been one of them; indeed, I was so spoiled by my kind patroness that, but for being frequently with my mother, I might very likely have grown up idle and useless. But I saw so much of her, and of her patients, that the ambition to become a doctress early took firm root in my mind; and I was very young when I began to make use of the little knowledge I had acquired from watching my mother, upon a great sufferer—my doll. I have noticed always what actors children are. If you leave one alone in a room, how soon it clears a little stage; and, making an audience out of a few chairs and stools, proceeds to act its

childish griefs and blandishments upon its doll. So I also made good use of my dumb companion and confidante; and whatever disease was most prevalent in Kingston, be sure my poor doll soon contracted it. I have had many medical triumphs in later days, and saved some valuable lives; but I really think that few have given me more real gratification than the rewarding glow of health which my fancy used to picture stealing over my patient's waxen face after long and precarious illness.

Before long it was very natural that I should seek to extend my practice; and so I found other patients in the dogs and cats around me. Many luckless brutes were made to simulate diseases which were raging among their owners, and had forced down their reluctant throats the remedies which I deemed most likely to suit their supposed complaints. And after a time I rose still higher in my ambition; and despairing of finding another human patient, I proceeded to try my simples and essences upon—myself.

When I was about 12 years old I was more frequently at my mother's house, and used to assist her in her duties; very often sharing with her the task of attending upon invalid officers or their wives, who came to her house from the adjacent camp at Up-Park, or the military station at Newcastle.

As I grew into womanhood, I began to indulge that longing to travel which will never leave me while I have health and vigour. I was never weary of tracing upon an old map the route to England; and never followed with my gaze the stately ships homeward bound without longing to be in them, and see the blue hills of Jamaica fade into the distance. At that time it seemed most improbable that these girlish wishes should be gratified; but circumstances, which I need not explain, enabled me to accompany some relatives to England while I was yet a very young woman.

I shall never forget my first impressions of London. Of course, I am not going to bore the reader with them; but they are as vivid now as though the year 18—(I had very nearly let my age slip then) had not been long ago numbered with the past. Strangely enough, some of the most vivid of my recollections are the efforts of the London street-boys to poke fun at my and my companion's complexion. I am only a little brown—a few shades duskier than the brunettes whom you all admire so much; but my companion was very dark, and a fair (if I can apply the term to her) subject for their rude wit. She was hot-tempered, poor thing! and as there were no policemen to awe the boys and turn our servants' heads in those days, our progress through the London streets was sometimes a rather chequered one.

I remained in England, upon the occasion of my first visit, about a year; and then returned to Kingston. Before long I again started for London, bringing with me this time a large stock of West Indian preserves and pickles for sale. After remaining two years here, I again started home; and on the way my life and adventures were very nearly brought to a premature conclusion. Christmas-day had been kept very merrily on board our ship the *Velusia,* and on the following day a fire broke out in the hold. I dare say it would have resisted all the crew's efforts to put it out, had not another ship appeared in sight; upon which the fire quietly allowed itself to be extinguished. Although considerably alarmed, I did not lose my senses; but during the time when the contest between fire and water was doubtful, I entered into an amicable arrangement with the ship's cook, whereby, in consideration of two pounds—which I was not, however, to pay until the crisis arrived—he agreed to lash me on to a large hen-coop.

Before I had been long in Jamaica I started upon other trips, many of them undertaken with a view to gain. Thus I spent some time in New Providence, bringing home with me a large collection of handsome shells and rare shellwork, which created quite a sensation in Kingston, and had a rapid sale; I visited also Hayti and Cuba. But I hasten onward in my narrative.

[. . .]

Voyage to Constantinople—Malta—Gibraltar—Constantinople, and What I Thought of it—Visit to Scutari Hospital—Miss Nightingale

I am not going to risk the danger of wearying the reader with a long account of the voyage to Constantinople, already worn threadbare by book-making tourists. It was a very interesting one, and, as I am a good sailor, I had not even the temporary horrors of sea-sickness to mar it. The weather, although cold, was fine, and the sea good-humouredly calm, and I enjoyed the voyage amazingly. And as day by day we drew nearer to the scene of action, my doubts of success grew less and less, until I had a conviction of the rightness of the step I had taken, which would have carried me buoyantly through any difficulties

On the way, of course, I was called up from my berth at an unreasonable hour to gaze upon the Cape of St. Vincent, and expected to feel duly impressed when the long bay where Trafalgar's fight was won came in view, with the white convent walls on the cliffs above bathed in the early sunlight. I never failed to take an almost childish interest in the signals which passed between the *Hollander* and the fleet of vessels whose sails whitened the track to and from the Crimea, trying to puzzle out the language these children of the ocean spoke in their hurried course, and wondering whether any or what sufficiently important thing *could* happen which would warrant their stopping on their busy way.

We spent a short time at Gibraltar, and you may imagine that I was soon on shore making the best use of the few hours' reprieve granted to the *Hollander's* weary engines. I had an idea that I should do better alone, so I declined all offers of companionship, and selecting a brisk young fellow from the mob of cicerones who offered their services, saw more of the art of fortification in an hour or so than I could understand in as many years. The pleasure was rather fatiguing, and I was not sorry to return to the marketplace, where I stood curiously watching its strange and motley population. While so engaged, I heard for the first time an exclamation which became familiar enough to me afterwards.

"Why, bless my soul, old fellow, if this is not our good old Mother Seacole!" I turned round, and saw two officers whose features, set in a broad frame of Crimean beard, I had some difficulty in recognising. But I soon remembered that they were two of the 48th, who had been often in my house at Kingston. Glad were the kind-hearted fellows, and not a little surprised withal, to meet their old hostess in the marketplace of Gibraltar, bound for the scene of action which they had left invalided; and it was not long before we were talking old times over some wine—Spanish, I suppose, but it was very nasty.

"And you are going to the front, old lady—you, of all people in the world?"

"Why not, my sons?—won't they be glad to have me there?"

"By Jove! Yes, mother," answered one, an Irishman. "It isn't many women—God bless them!—we've had to spoil us out there. But it's not the place even for you, who know what hardship is. You'll never get a roof to cover you at Balaclava, nor on the road either." So they rattled on, telling me of the difficulties that were in store for me. But they could not shake my resolution.

"Do you think I shall be of any use to you when I get there?"

"Surely."

"Then I'll go, were the place a hundred times worse than you describe it. Can't I rig up a hut with the packing-cases, and sleep, if need be, on straw, like Margery Daw?"

So they laughed, and drank success to me, and to our next meeting; for, although they were going home invalided, the brave fellows' hearts were with their companions, for all the hardships they had passed through.

We stopped at Malta also, where, of course, I landed, and stared about me, and submitted to be robbed by the lazy Maltese with all a traveller's resignation. Here, also, I met friends—some medical officers who had known me in Kingston; and one of them, Dr. F____ , lately arrived from Scutari, gave me, when he heard my plans, a letter of introduction to Miss Nightingale, then hard at work, evoking order out of confusion, and bravely resisting the despotism of death, at the hospital of Scutari.

So on, past beautiful islands and shores, until we are steaming against a swift current, and an adverse wind, between two tower-crested promontories of rock, which they tell me stand in Europe and in Asia, and are connected with some pretty tale of love in days long gone by. Ah! Travel where a woman may, in the New World, or the Old, she meets this old, old tale everywhere. It is the one bond of sympathy which I have found existing in three-quarters of the world alike. So on, until the cable rattles over the windlass, as the good ship's anchor plunges down fathoms deep into the blue waters of the Bosphorus—her voyage ended.

I do not think that Constantinople impressed me so much as I had expected; and I thought its streets would match those of Navy Bay not unfairly. The caicques, also, of which I had ample experience—for I spent six days here, wandering about Pera and Stamboul in the daytime and returning to the *Hollander* at nightfall—might be made more safe and commodious for stout ladies, even if the process interfered a little with their ornament. Time and trouble combined have left me with a well-filled-out, portly form—the envy of many an angular Yankee female—and, more than once, it was in no slight danger of becoming too intimately acquainted with the temperature of the Bosphorus. But I will do the Turkish boatmen the justice to say that they were as politely careful of my safety as their astonishment and regard for the well-being of their caicques (which they appear to love as an Arab does his horse, or an Esquimaux his dogs, and for the same reason perhaps) would admit. Somewhat surprised, also, seemed the cunning-eyed Greeks who throng the streets of Pera at the unprotected Creole woman who took Constantinople so coolly (it would require something more to surprise her); while the grave English raised their eyebrows wonderingly, and the more vivacious French shrugged their pliant shoulders into the strangest contortions. I accepted it all as a compliment to a stout female tourist, neatly dressed in a red or yellow dress, a plain shawl of some other colour, and a simple straw wide-awake, with bright red streamers. I flatter myself that I woke up sundry sleepy-eyed Turks, who seemed to think that the great object of life was to avoid showing surprise at anything; while the Turkish women gathered around me, and jabbered about me, in the most flattering manner.

Reading C

Give a Thought to Africa: Black Women Missionaries in Southern Africa

SYLVIA M. JACOBS

Historian Sylvia M. Jacobs brings to our attention a little-known aspect of the history of Christian missions in Africa. Focusing on African-American women missionaries, Jacobs discusses two aspects of how race, gender, and colonialism combined. First, the African-American women knew little about African customs and shared the colonialists' beliefs about a civilizing mission. Yet, second, the racism of the white missionaries and the European colonial authorities led to accusations that the African-American women missionaries were preaching revolt rather than the Christian doctrine.

The late nineteenth and early twentieth centuries witnessed the European partitioning and subsequent colonization of the continent of Africa. A small segment of the African-American community, including journalists, religious and secular leaders, diplomats and politi-

Sylvia M. Jacobs, "Give a Thought to Africa: Black Women Missionaries in Southern Africa," *Western Women and Imperialism: Complicity and Resistance,* Nupur Chaudhuri and Margaret Strobel, eds. Bloomington, IN: Indiana University Press, 1992: 207–11, 221–24.

cians, missionaries, and travelers and visitors, addressed themselves to the issue of the impact of the establishment of European imperialism in Africa. Although they may have viewed the different elements of imperialism (cultural, social, economic, political) in various ways, most middle-class blacks, believing that Africa needed to be "civilized and Christianized," generally concluded that if the interests and welfare of the indigenous African populations were being considered, European activity on the continent would be beneficial. They therefore supported the European imperialists in Africa as long as exploitation was not their only goal. Black American views on the European partitioning of Africa varied only slightly, from tacit approval to partial rejection. This chapter will discuss the response of one African-American group—black American women missionaries—to the European colonization of Africa, and how imperialism, gender, and race limited their roles as missionaries in Africa.

In the nineteenth century, white American and European Protestant church boards began to establish missions in Africa. These churches gave serious consideration to using African-Americans as missionaries on the continent. Thus began many successive attempts

Key Terms

Dark Continent Term nineteenth-century explorers and travelers used to refer to Africa.
Jim Crow Originally a tool used for straightening iron rails on the railroad, the term came to refer to

the many laws that enforced racial segregation in the U.S. South between the end of Reconstruction in 1877 and the beginning of a strong civil rights movement in the 1950s and 1960s.

to appoint blacks to missionary work in their ancestral homeland. The largest number of African-American missionaries sent to Africa went during the late nineteenth and early twentieth centuries. Black American missionaries were affected by the prevailing Western image of Africa as a "Dark Continent" in need of "civilizing." Their relationship with Africa and Africans was both ambivalent and contradictory. On the one hand, these black American missionaries, women and men, believed that Africa needed to be "civilized and Christianized" and that it was their "duty," as descendants of the continent, to assist in that redemption. Race, then, was a factor in their commitment to Africans. But they had to wrestle with their Western orientation and their biases about African culture and society, and thus they initially held Africa and Africans at arm's length.

Although more than half of the American Protestant missionaries who went to Africa during this period were males, they were assisted by their wives, who were designated "assistant missionaries." But even single women sent as missionaries had secondary roles. The mores of the late nineteenth and early twentieth centuries prescribed that women be engaged in "women's work": that meant teaching in day, Sunday, and industrial schools; maintaining orphanages and boarding schools; making house-to-house visitations; and dispensing medical care to women and children.[1]

Between 1880 and 1920 almost 80 African-American women were assigned to or accompanied their husbands as missionaries to Africa. Of that number, 14 went to five southern African countries: Angola and Mozambique, which were under Portuguese colonial rule; and the British colonies of Nyasaland, Southern Rhodesia, and South Africa. They represented six mission-sending societies. But only nine African-American women missionaries are discussed in this essay because there is little information on three of these women, who accompanied their husbands to South Africa—Celia Ann Nelson Gregg (1904–6, 1924–28), Mattie E. Murff (1906–10), and Lucinda Ernestine Thomas East (1909–20)—and the two others served the major portion of their terms of service after 1920—Julia Cele Smith (1918?–48) and Bessie Cherry Fonveille McDowell (1919–37). Were the views of these black female missionaries about European imperialism in Africa any different from their black male or white counterparts'? Were there major differences in the experiences of African-American women missionaries in African mission work? Did these women have to adjust in any way to the European presence on the continent? Because of the nature of available sources, it is not always easy to distinguish the views of black female missionaries from those of black male missionaries. Of the nine women discussed here, only five sent home letters or reports or wrote about their experiences in Africa. What this means is that often we are left with only the writings of black male missionaries. Thus to understand the views of some of these women, we need to look at other things, such as applications, letters to newspapers and magazines, college and university catalogs and histories, and unpublished manuscripts.

The American Board of Commissioners for Foreign Missions (ABCFM) was the first American board to send missionaries to Africa. The ABCFM, one of several Congregational missionary societies, was organized in 1810 and two years later sent out its first foreign missionaries to India. At its 1825 annual meeting, the board voted to open a mission in Africa. In 1834 missionaries set up the first ABCFM mission at Cape Palmas, Liberia. ABCFM missionaries reached Natal in 1835 and subsequently set up the Zulu Mission, the first American-sponsored mission in South Africa.[2]

In 1882, the Reverend William C. Wilcox asked for and received permission from the board to explore the region around Inhambane, located between the cities of Sofala and Lorençalo Marques in the southeastern corner of Mozambique, 500 miles east of the Umzila kingdom and about 600 miles north of Natal on the seacoast. Inhambane was at first a part of the Zulu Mission, but eventually the name East Central African Mission was adopted to designate this area, with the idea that it was only a stopover point from which an advance later would be made into the interior. Though not having received formal permission from the Portuguese government to open the mission, representatives of the ABCFM secured a location a few miles outside the city of Inhambane and employed Africans to begin building mission houses. Several locations around the bay were ultimately occupied, and three

African-Americans—Benjamin Forsyth Ousley, Henrietta Bailey Ousley, and Nancy Jones—pioneered one such station of the East Central African Mission at Inhambane, that of Kambini.[3]

Benjamin Ousley, born a slave of the brother of the Confederate States president, in Davis Bend, Warren County, Mississippi, was the first ordained black missionary of the ABCFM. Ousley earned a BA degree and an MA degree from Fisk University and a BD degree from Oberlin Theological Seminary.[4]

Henrietta Bailey was born to slave parents, Henry and Harriet Bailey, on October 4, 1852, in Washington County, Mississippi, although during the Civil War her family escaped to Knoxville, Illinois. She united with the African Methodist Episcopal (AME) Church in 1875 but was not fully accepted until 1878. Bailey studied at Knoxville High School and Fisk University, and before going to Africa she was employed as a teacher in Corinth, Mississippi. On August 14, 1884, she married Reverend Benjamin Ousley, who was under appointment by the ABCFM to the East Central African Mission. On her application of September 24, 1884, for mission service, in reply to the question "When did you decide to go to the heathen, and what led you to think of the subject?," Henrietta Ousley answered: "It had been brought to notice first by the departure of some missionaries for the West Coast of Africa, then an appeal was made to me personally by a friend to fit myself for a teacher for the Mendi Mission [mission of the American Missionary Association in Sierra Leone], then finally this request of Mr. Ousley's that I would share with him the life of a foreign missionary."[5] Benjamin Ousley apparently had sought a wife when he was commissioned to go to Mozambique. Henrietta Ousley, the first black woman sent out by the ABCFM, served in Mozambique with her husband from 1884 to 1893.

The last of the African-American pioneer missionaries in Mozambique appointed by the ABCFM was Nancy Jones. Jones, the first unmarried black woman commissioned by the American Board, was born in Christian County, near Hopkinsville, Kentucky, in 1860 and during her childhood moved with her family to Memphis, Tennessee. She was baptized at the age of 14 while a student at Lemoyne Institute (now Lemoyne-Owen College), and united with the First Colored Baptist Church of Memphis soon afterwards. Jones also attended Fisk University, graduating from the Normal Department course in 1886. At the same time, she taught in Alpika, Mississippi, commuting to Fisk. Although a Baptist, she applied to the Congregational American Board for a missionary appointment. In her letter of application she stated: "I have wanted to be a Missionary ever since I was 12 years old. . . . I have earnestly prayed to the Lord to teach me my duty, show me just what he would have me do and I received in answer to these petitions an urgent longing for work in a Mission field in Africa." Jones served the board in Mozambique, and later in eastern Rhodesia, from 1888 to 1897. The Ousleys and Jones worked together at Kambini for over five years. Henrietta Ousley and Jones had known one another at Fisk and apparently both had given some thought to their "duty" to assist in the "religious uplift" of Africa before their appointment.[6]

On September 25, 1884, the Ousleys departed from New York to join the East Central African Mission. They arrived at Durban, Natal Colony, South Africa, three weeks later, on November 14, and sailed for Inhambane on November 28, reaching the bay on December 2. Benjamin Ousley and William Wilcox traveled into the interior and Ousley selected the station at Kambini that he and his wife, and later Nancy Jones, eventually occupied. In the 1885 annual report of the East Central African Mission from the Kambini station, Ousley noted that because the Portuguese government in Mozambique was so restrictive of foreigners, missionary activities were limited to religious instruction, and only in those areas surrounding the mission; ABCFM missionaries were forbidden to preach outside these boundaries.[7]

In the Reports of Committees on the Annual Report in 1885, the Committee on Missions in Africa, chaired by James Powell, made the following observation:

> The East Central Mission . . . has been marked the past year by the exploration, selections of new stations, and the reinforcement of the mission by Mr. and Mrs. Ousley, colored graduates of Fisk University, Nashville; Mr. Ousley being also a graduate of Oberlin. We note the possible significance that the lives of these missionaries, trained in the schools of

our denomination at the South, are to play in the future in the evangelization of the Dark Continent.[8]

Obviously, the Committee was reflecting the positive feelings, at that time, of the Congregational Church toward assigning African-Americans as missionaries to Africa.

In 1886, the Ousleys completed their mission compound at Kambini, and having learned to speak the Sheetswa language, opened a school, which numbered about 50 students by the end of the year. Henrietta Ousley's duties, because of her training, included teaching in the mission school. She taught alone in the mornings, but because of a larger number of students, Benjamin Ousley joined her in the afternoon. He spent his mornings studying and translating an English Bible study and a book of catechisms into Sheetswa, the language of the people around the bay of Inhambane. In view of the nature of nineteenth-century mission responsibilities for women, Henrietta Ousley also worked with the children and women of the area. But she found great disappointment in the work, partly because of her own Western biases. In a report to the board, Benjamin Ousley pointed out: "It is sad, but nevertheless true, that woman seems more degraded here, and harder to reach, than man. . . . We often commiserate the degraded condition of these poor women; yet they do not appreciate our pity, or even desire to live different lives. They are satisfied with their present lot."[9]

A few explanations may help to clarify black missionaries' negative views about African women. First was the issue of labor roles. African-American missionaries were distressed over the fact that African women did agricultural work, which these missionaries viewed as "man's work." During slavery, African-American women had been forced to work side by side with male slaves in farming on plantations, and consequently, among African-Americans, female farm labor became an indication of low status. However, in African agricultural societies, women who farmed had a high economic and social status. Second, black American missionaries viewed African women as inferior in African society because of polygamy. Often in African societies polygamy was beneficial to women because they assumed a higher social status as wives and because it resulted in the sharing of "women's

work" among more persons. Because of their own cultural limitations, these missionaries failed to see the social and economic benefits to African women of agricultural work and polygamy. Third, African-American missionaries were disturbed by nudity and sexuality among African women.

[. . .]

It is clear from the applications, speeches, and letters written by these African-American women missionaries before they traveled to southern Africa that they believed that they were assisting in the redemption of the continent. They hoped to transfer Western gender-linked roles and functions to African women and many times they could not understand why African women rejected them and wanted to maintain their traditional way of life. Black American women missionaries often viewed African women's responsibilities and duties in their own societies as foreign, alien, and even unacceptable.

A significant influence in their decision to pursue a missionary career was the colleges that they attended. Of the six women who are known to have received a postsecondary education, four graduated from southern black institutions. These schools promoted the idea that it was the "special mission" of African-Americans to help in the redemption of Africa. Fisk University, a privately controlled liberal arts institution, was founded in 1865 by the American Missionary Association (AMA) and historically has been associated with the Congregational Church. E. M. Cravath, Fisk's first president, was also field secretary of the AMA. Nancy Jones recalled the words on a banner in the dining room at Fisk, "Her Sons and Daughters are ever on the altar," and confessed that she felt that she was included in that number.[10] At Spelman College, a private women's school, students sang a song:

> *Give a thought to Africa,*
> *'Neath the burning sun—*

which typified a spirit prevalent throughout the institution, that of the duty of African-American women to help "Christianize and civilize" their ancestral homeland. The motives of individual women missionaries may have been various, but it is clear that the overriding theme of duty helped to explain why so many

African-Americans volunteered for mission work in Africa. These African-American women who served in southern Africa, like most women missionaries, were trained as teachers, nurses, and deaconesses.

Additionally, African-American women missionaries most times did not fully understand the nature of European imperialism in Africa. Missionaries had the goals of economic, social, educational, and religious development for Africans, but these did not coincide with the main objective of European imperialists in Africa before 1920, which was simply to maintain control in the African colonies, with as little cost as possible to the home governments. European administrators were not concerned about African societal growth. The Ousleys and Jones were critical of the Portuguese government in Mozambique for being restrictive, for not providing for African workers, and for being unfair in its dealings with Africans. Delaney, Cheek, and the Branches in Nyasaland and Fanny Coppin in South Africa reprimanded the British government for its lack of educational opportunities for Africans.

By the end of World War I, the general consensus of European colonialists in Africa, who by that date had occupied all of the continent except for the Republic of Liberia and Ethiopia, was that African-Americans caused too many disruptions to warrant their effective use as missionaries in Africa. Generally, there were no legislative restrictions directed against black American missionaries after 1920, but most European governments began to exclude them based on the belief that the African-American presence caused unrest among Africans and was dangerous to the maintenance of law and order on the continent.

European imperialists accused black missionaries of encouraging political revolts, and colonial governments, believing that they preached revolt rather than religion, discouraged their entry. But in southern Africa, where revolts occurred before 1920—such as the Herero Rebellion in Southwest Africa from 1904 to 1907, the Bambata (Zulu) Rebellion in South Africa in 1906, and the John Chilembwe Uprising in Nyasaland in 1915—African-American missionaries either were not present or did not exert enough influence to stage such uprisings. It is probably true, though, that the presence of educated black American missionaries was a constant reminder to Africans of the opportuni-

ties denied to them in their own land. Furthermore, by 1910 over 150 southern Africans had been educated in American black colleges and universities and exposed to African-American protest.

But other changes occurring in southern Africa and in the United States made the post-World War I world quite different from the prewar one. In southern Africa, Africans began to form political organizations at the end of the nineteenth and beginning of the twentieth centuries. The principal one was the African National Congress (ANC), founded in 1912. In the United States, Booker T. Washington, the conciliatory black leader, died in 1915. A year later, the Jamaican, Marcus Garvey, arrived in the United States with his more militant stance. In 1919 W. E. B. Du Bois called the first Pan-African Congress in Paris, emphasizing the poor conditions under which worldwide blacks lived and calling for unity among this group. The post–World War I period also witnessed an increase in black American self-consciousness with the New Negro movement and the Harlem Renaissance. Additionally, Africans and African-Americans had fought in World War I and returned to their countries after the war with a much more militant outlook. European imperialists, hoping to maintain law and order and develop Africa's resources with little resistance, feared the consequences if these two groups, Africans and African Americans, both with increasing political awareness, were to get together. Europeans feared the rise of Ethiopianism, or the independent African church movement, in southern Africa. In the late nineteenth century, the Ethiopian Church united with the American-based African Methodist Episcopal Church. Colonialists were also frightened by the popularity and spread of the Garvey movement throughout Africa with its "Africa for the Africans" philosophy. Attempting to keep "troublemakers" out of Africa, European governments in Africa concluded that African-American missionaries upset the status quo and were dangerous to the maintenance of law and order in Africa. Therefore, these colonialists discouraged the entry of not only black missionaries, but all black visitors to Africa.[11]

Black American women missionaries faced triple jeopardy. In addition to having to deal with European colonial policy in Africa, African-American women missionaries in southern Africa from 1880 to 1920 also faced sexism and racism from other American and European missionaries. Women were discriminated against as missionary workers. They were viewed by their mission boards and by their male colleagues as second-class missionaries. In this age of imperialism, racism also became a dominant issue in European and American thought. Whether they worked with white missionaries or at segregated mission stations, African-American missionaries were constantly being scrutinized by whites.

Some conclusions can be made about these African-American women missionaries who were stationed in southern Africa from 1880 to 1920. All served in countries—Angola, Mozambique, Nyasaland, Southern Rhodesia, and South Africa—with little or no previous experience with African-American missionaries. In almost all instances these women were among the first black women missionaries in the country (Ousley and Jones were the first in Mozambique, Jones was the first in Southern Rhodesia, Delaney and Branch were the first in Nyasaland, Collins and Drummer were the first in Angola, and Tule and Johns were among the first in South Africa). Five of the nine women were married (three of them wed immediately before they sailed with their husbands to Africa) and four were unmarried. The age when they went to Africa is known for five of the nine women. The average age for four of those was 28 years old. Because Drummer was graduated from college in 1901, she probably also fit into this average. Coppin was 65 years old when she went to South Africa. Only the Branches took children to Africa with them. All of the women appeared to have been ignorant of the situation in Africa before their arrival and not only had to adapt their attitudes to a partial acceptance of the African way of life in order to be effective among them, but also had to take care not to offend the European imperialists. In this age of imperialism and racism, the perceptions and experiences of African-American female and male missionaries in Africa were not dissimilar. With the assumption of Europeans of the "white man's burden" and the rise of Jim Crow in the United States, Africans and African-Americans were treated with the same prejudice. There was really no difference between the exploitation of and discrimination against Africans on the continent and the degradation and oppression of diasporic Africans throughout the world. African-American women missionaries in Africa faced this discrimination, as well as the sexism inherent in this imperialistic age.

NOTES

A version of this article appeared in *Women's Studies International Forum* 13, no. 4 (1990): 381–94; reprinted with the permission of Pergamon Press.

1. For a discussion of African-American views on the establishment of European imperialism in Africa during the late nineteenth and early twentieth centuries, see Sylvia M. Jacobs, *The African Nexus: Black American Perspectives on the European Partitioning of Africa, 1880–1920* (Westport, Conn: Greenwood Press, 1981). See also Sylvia M. Jacobs, "Afro-American Women Missionaries Confront the African Way of Life," in *Women in Africa and the African Diaspora,* Rosalyn Terborg-Penn, Sharon Harley, and Andrea Benton Rushing, eds. (Washington, D.C.: Howard University Press, 1987), p. 122.

2. In *Black Americans and the Missionary Movement in Africa,* Sylvia M. Jacobs, ed. (Westport, Conn.: Greenwood Press, 1982) there is a discussion of the role of African-Americans in the American Protestant mission movement in Africa before 1960. See also Wade Crawford Barclay, *History of Methodist Missions,* vol. 1:

Missionary Motivation and Expansion, 1769–1844 (New York: Board of Missions and Church Extension of the Methodist Church, 1949), pp. 165–66; and William E. Strong, *The Story of the American Board: An Account of the First Hundred Years of the American Board of Commissioners for Foreign Missions* (Boston: Pilgrim Press, 1910), pp. 124–25, 132.

3. Strong, *American Board,* p. 342; *The Missionary Herald, Containing the Proceedings of the American Board of Commissioners for Foreign Missions* 80, Editorial Paragraphs (March 1884): 85, and (October 1884): 383; "Zulu Mission," *Annual Report of the American Board of Commissioners for Foreign Missions,* no. 73 (1883), p. 27; and "East Central African Mission," *Annual Report,* no. 74 (1884), pp. 20–21.

4. American Board of Commissioners for Foreign Missions Papers, Biography File, Benjamin Forsyth Ousley, Houghton Library of Harvard University, Cambridge, Mass. Samuel Miller, who taught in Angola from 1880 to 1884, was the first ABCEFM black missionary.

5. ABCFM Papers, Memoranda Concerning Missionaries, vol. 9, Henrietta Bailey Ousley, Houghton Library of Harvard University, Cambridge, Mass. "Notes for the Month," *Missionary Herald* 80 (Oct. 1884): 406 mentions the marriage of the Ousleys.

6. Strong, *American Board*, pp. 343–44 and Nannie Jones to Mr. E. K. Alden, July 19, 1887 (no. 612), ABCFM Papers, 6, vol. 35, Candidate File, Nancy Jones, Houghton Library of Harvard University, Cambridge, Mass. Nancy Jones's nickname was Nannie.

7. See "Notes for the Month" *Missionary Herald* 80 (Nov. 1884): 465; "Notes for the Month," ibid., vol. 81 (Feb. 1885): 79; and Editorial Paragraphs, ibid., vol. 81 (Apr. 1885): 135. See also "East Central African Mission, Kambini," *Annual Report*, no. 75 (1885), pp. 20–21.

8. "Reports of Committees on the Annual Report: The Committee on Missions in Africa" *Missionary Herald* 81 (Dec. 1885): 508.

9. See *Missionary Herald* 83, "East Central African Mission: A Day At Kambini" (Apr. 1887): 142 and "East Central African Mission: Degradation of Women" (Aug. 1887): 309. See also "East Central African Mission," *Annual Report*, no. 77 (1887), p. 60.

10. Nannie Jones to Mr. E. K. Alden, July 19, 1887 (no. 612), ABCFM Papers, vol. 35, Candidate File, Nancy Jones.

11. Jacobs, ed., *Black Americans and the Missionary Movement in Africa*, pp. 20–22.

Reading E

Female Employment in Puerto Vallarta: A Case Study
SYLVIA CHANT

Feminist geographer Sylvia Chant discusses unequal gender segregation in the tourist industry in Puerto Vallarta, Mexico, in the 1990s. Women are found in the lower-paying jobs, which have the least status and security. The impact of the new employment patterns on gender roles and the structure of the family can be assessed in the experiences of women who find work in the resorts. While their workload and opportunities to work outside the home increase, their subordination in the family remains the same.

Puerto Vallarta is one Mexican resort which does not owe its origins to government initiative, even if the state has participated in various phases of its development since its initial establishment as a tourist destination

Sylvia Chant, "Female Employment in Puerto Vallarta: A Case Study," in *Gender, Work, and Tourism*, M. Thea Sinclair, ed. London: Routledge, 1997: 136–37, 139–43.

some 30 years ago. Originally a small fishing village contained within a predominantly agricultural hinterland, Puerto Vallarta now has a population of around 250,000 and first came to major international attention in the early 1960s when John Huston chose it as the setting for his film of Tenessee Williams' *The Night of the Iguana*. The film starred Richard Burton, who was visited on location by Elizabeth Taylor; this gave the town something of a romantic mystique and enhanced its attraction among North American visitors. Shortly afterward, the Mexican government began intervening to create the necessary infrastructure for tourism expansion, including the building of a major road link to the western Pacific Highway, the construction of an international airport, and the establishment of a major regional planning agency to monitor and oversee development and, in particular, to regulate land occupation (see Chant 1991: Chapter 2, 1992).

From 1970 onwards, demographic growth proceeded at a dramatic pace, averaging about 12 percent per annum during the 1970s and early 1980s. Growth was so impressive that, by the late 1980s, the construction of a major marina development was under way some four miles north of the traditional town centre, with numerous new hotels, restaurants, and commercial establishments springing up along the connecting highway. Most international tourists have traditionally come from the United States and Canada, especially during the dry season from October through to March, with large numbers of national tourists filling in during the rainy period, especially in July and August when Mexican schoolchildren have their long vacation (see Chant 1991: Chapter 2). However, the deteriorating dollar:peso exchange rate and the recession in the United States from the late 1980s onward reduced international demand relative to Puerto Vallarta's expanded capacity with the result that, at the beginning of the 1990s, the town was experiencing something of a crisis. While high-season occupancy of hotel rooms was as much as 100 percent in the mid to late 1980s, by 1992 it was only 60–70 percent. Even low-season occupancy dropped from around 75 percent to only 45 percent over the same period (Chant 1994b). These problems are exacerbated by the fact that foreign and national visitors alike have less money to spend during their stay.

Although the town's population continues to grow, and Puerto Vallarta received at the beginning of the 1990s almost as many visitors by air as in the mid 1980s (around 1.5 million national and foreign visitors per annum), local people face declining opportunities for employment, and the income to be made from independent and/or informal entrepreneurial activity is now drastically reduced (see Chant 1994b for a fuller discussion). This seems to have affected men to a greater extent than women although, while women may have been able to retain their access to work, they are still found in the lower rungs of the local labour market hierarchy. Reasons for the gender-differentiated nature of job losses possibly include the fact that the construction industry, a major employer of men, has been hardest hit by the crisis of overinvestment. In addition, many men are unwilling to accept low-paid jobs which have traditionally been designated as "female."

Looking more closely at gender differences in employment in Puerto Vallarta, a detailed survey by the author in 1986 of low-income households and key local employers[1] revealed that while the three main sectors of tertiary employment in the city—commerce, catering, and hotels—all employed women as well as men, women generally made up a lower proportion of the workforce, were usually in less prestigious positions, earned less money, and had fewer opportunities for upward occupational mobility (see Chant 1991: Chapter 3). [. . .]

This horizontal segregation between the male and female workforce is important for a number of reasons. First, it reflects (and in several respects reinforces) the traditional association of women with reproductive chores such as washing and bed-making and that of men with "heavier" duties, "outside work," or work with a more "public" orientation. Indeed, certain hotel managers claimed that interacting with customers in bars and restaurants was not suitable for women given the connotations surrounding hostessing and its perceived association with prostitution (Chant 1991: 78). A second and related implication of gender segregation in hotel work is that many jobs that males perform are, by virtue of their public nature, likely to reap greater earnings. Although the basic wages of male and female service workers are often comparable (ibid.: 77, Table 3.5), bellboys and porters, drivers, waiters, and barmen tend to be much more directly involved with clients than female chambermaids and laundry workers, with the result that gratuities are often more substantial. Indeed, some male employees receive up to five times as much as their basic wage from tips alone (ibid.: 76–77).

A third consequence of gender segregation in hotel employment and, in particular, the small number of "female" sectors is limited occupational mobility. Unlike men, who often achieve upward mobility by strategic "sideways" moves into other sectors, women are more restricted to waiting for posts to become vacant in their own departments. In turn, female departments tend not to have a wide range of ranks and specializations, which means that women have to wait longer for promotion. To give an example, the only higher-status position to which a chambermaid can aspire is that of *ama de llaves* (housekeeper) (or deputy housekeeper if a department is large enough to sustain two supervisors). Such a move might take 10–15 years to attain, if at all, with most large hotels having one housekeeper for every 20 chambermaids. In contrast, in restaurant work there are possibilities for male kitchen hands to move into the dining area, which in turn has an elaborate range of posts, ranging from commis waiter (a "runner" operating between the kitchen and serving staff), to full waiter, section waiter, wine waiter, chief waiter, and even restaurant supervisor and/or manager. Most men entering at low levels can expect some kind of promotion within a three to four-year period. A related consideration is that it is rare for women to end up supervising a predominantly male section due to the perceived difficulties of men taking orders from women (Chant 1991: Chapter 3).

Having perhaps provided a rather bleak outline of women's involvement in tourism employment in Puerto Vallarta, it is also important to point out that the mere fact that women have *access to work* is itself significant, especially at the household level. Comparative research by the author in two other Mexican cities—the industrial towns of León and Querétaro—in 1986 (see note 1, p. 167), revealed that women's labour-force participation was much higher in Puerto Vallarta (Chant 1991: 136, Table 4.8). This is mainly because tourist resorts are characterized by a large service sector where demand for female labour is high and because of the existence of feminized niches within hotel and restaurant work where women's assumed "domestic" skills' give them an advantage over men (see also Kennedy *et al.* 1978 on the Mexican resort of Ixtapa-Zihauatanejo and Torres, 1994 on Cancun).

One notable outcome of women's greater perceived and actual access to employment in Puerto Vallarta (also documented for other centres in Mexico and Latin America where women have above-average entry to the labour force, such as the U.S.–Mexico border and Puerto Rico (see Fernández-Kelly 1983; Safa 1981), is the high number of female-headed households in the locality. According to the author's survey among low-income households, as many as 19.6 percent of households in Puerto Vallarta are headed by women, compared with only 13.5 per cent in Querétaro and 10.4 per cent in León.[2]

This high proportion of female-headed households in Puerto Vallarta is very much related to employment. On one hand, because tourism offers a range of female job opportunities, lone women, with or without children, who may lack access to the means of survival in other places, are attracted to resort towns. At another level, the scope to earn an independent (and often reasonable and/or guaranteed) income means that there is not the same pressure on women to unite with men or remain with existing partners as in places where they have a less favourable position in the labour market.

[. . .]

At the same time as there would appear to be certain advantages to women accruing from residence (and employment) in Mexican tourist resorts, it is also important to bear in mind that some men cannot seem to cope with their wives' or partners' economic independence and may "retaliate" by either dropping out of work or scaling down their contributions to household income. In addition, some husbands in this position even use their wives' earnings to play cards or to go out drinking with male friends. Another important issue is that women who work outside the home are usually still left with the majority of domestic tasks, to carry out either alone or in conjunction with other household members (generally female kin or daughters).

Whether these patterns will persist will depend on a number of factors. In the wake of the economic crisis which has hit Puerto Vallarta since the beginning of the 1990s, it seems that a greater number of husbands and sons are unemployed, while women have maintained their hold on waged work and indeed in some cases have moved upward in the employment hierarchy in terms of position or earnings (Chant 1994b). If unable to increase their returns from a single job, one way in which women have sustained their earning power is through diversifying their income-generating activities. For example, one 34-year-old mother of two, Fildelina, who in 1986 had been doing hair-cutting on a part-time basis in her own home, by 1992 both converted her front room into a retail outlet and took a job as a domestic servant. Another respondent, Elba, who was a domestic servant in 1986, has since supplemented her income by selling bags of ice from her kitchen fridge (see Chant 1994b). Men, on the other hand, even if unemployed, have tended to keep their sights set on formal employment, rather than diverting their efforts into informal and/or domestic-based income generation. Nor is there much evidence for an upturn in the amount of unpaid work they might do around the home, such as housework and child-minding. This asymmetry in male–female inputs into family life

could conceivably result in further fragmentation of household units if the crisis persists (see Benería 1991). There is also the danger that women's labour-market gains in tourist resorts such as Puerto Vallarta will be canceled out by serious erosion of their time and energy as the burdens of working in and outside the home remain unrelieved by any assistance on the part of men.

NOTES

1. Survey work in Puerto Vallarta in 1986 formed part of a larger project concerned with the analysis of female labour-force participation and its interrelations with household structure, organization, and survival among the poor in three cities with different types of economic base, the others being Querétaro, a modern manufacturing centre, and León, a traditional centre of shoe production. Fieldwork in Puerto Vallarta *per se* involved conducting questionnaire interviews with 92 low-income households, in-depth semistructured discussions with a subsample of 24 respondents, and interviews with 21 employers selected from hotels, restaurants, and the commercial sector (see Chant, 1991: Appendixes 1 and 2 for full details). As noted

earlier in the text, contact has been kept up with several households in low-income communities in each city, with 10 in one Puerto Vallarta settlement (El Caloso) being re-interviewed in 1992 to provide an idea of changes occurring in household livelihood as a result of crisis and restructuring (see Chant, 1994b).

2. The figures for Puerto Vallarta and León relate to the household surveys carried out by the author in 1986 with 92 and 77 households, respectively (see Note 1), and Querétaro in 1982–83, when 244 households were randomly sampled for interview. Household interviews did take place in Querétaro in 1986, but these were with a nonrandom sample of only 20 households (see Chant, 1991).

REFERENCES

Benería, Lourdes. (1991). "Structural Adjustment, the Labour Market and the Household: The Case of Mexico," in Guy Standing and Victor Tokman (eds) *Towards Social Adjustment: Labour Market Issues in Structural Adjustment,* Geneva: ILO, 161–83.

Chant, Sylvia. (1991). *Women and Survival in Mexican Cities: Perspectives on Gender, Labour Markets and Low-income Households,* Manchester. Manchester University Press.

— (1994b). "Women, Work and Household Survival Strategies in Mexico, 1982–1992: Past Trends, Current Tendencies and Future Research," *Bulletin of Latin American Research* 13, 2: 203–33.

Fernández-Kelly, María Patricia. (1983). "Mexican Border Industrialisation, Female Labour Force Participation and Migration," in June Nash and María Patricia Fernández-Kelly (eds) *Women,*

Men and the International Division of Labour, Albany, New York: State University of New York Press. 205–23.

Kennedy, Janet, Antoinette Russin, and Amalfi Martínez. (1978). "The Impact of Tourism Development on Women: A Case Study of Ixtapa-Zihuatanejo, Mexico." Draft report for Tourism Projects Department, Washington: World Bank.

Safa, Helen. (1981). "Runaway Shops and Female Employment: The Search for Cheap Labour," *Signs: Journal of Women in Culture and Society* 7, 2: 418–33.

Torres, Eduardo. (1994). 'Desarrollo Turístico, TLC y Cambio Social en la Frontera Sur de México: EL Caso de Quintana Roo', Anuavio de Estudios Urbanos (UNA-CAD, Mexico, DF).

REFLECTING ON THE SECTION

Because in many cultures, women are associated with the home and domesticity, their relationship to travel is very complex. How does the legacy of nineteenth-century woman explorers and missionaries affect women around the globe today? Enloe states that tourism is about power as well as pleasure. Women travel to empower themselves and to escape difficult or limiting situations at home. Compare the desires, goals, and experiences of African-American woman missionaries to that of Mary Seacole in the nineteenth century. How do these women represent themselves racially and nationally? Enloe and Chant discuss the different positions that women occupy in the travel industry today. How are women transforming ideas of femininity and the domestic sphere through tourism and travel? Conversely, how are women's subjugated positions reinforced by tourism and travel? Can we reconcile these opposing results of women's travel? Should we try?

Forced Relocations and Removals

Excerpt from The World Labor Market: A History of Migration

LYDIA POTTS

Sociologist Lydia Potts offers a theory of migration from the fifteenth century to the present. Potts argues that migration can be understood as "labor power"— the movement of persons, coerced or voluntary, as resources for capitalism's quest for profits. In this market for labor power, racism and sexism are important ideologies that create specific pools of labor.

The World Market for Labour Power— Historical Development, Present-Day Structures, and Developmental Analysis

The world market for labour power in its direct form emerged not as a result of present-day migration, but hundreds of years ago. Living labour power has been transferred in large quantities and over long distances since the end of the fifteenth century.

[. . .] The journey spans the enslavement of the Indians that followed the conquest of America, the vari-ous forms of forced labour and forced migration in Latin America, Asia, and Africa, African slavery, the coolie system used to despatch the people of Asia all over the world, and finally present-day labour migra-tion and the brain drain, the exodus of academics from the developing nations.

Regarded thus, the world market for labour power appears to be a universal structure with a history of several hundred years. In the course of that history, every inhabited continent and almost every society on earth has been drawn into the world market—although with differing, even opposing, functions. For the orig-inal inhabitants of America and Australia and the resi-dents of Asia and Africa this has meant extermination, abduction, and exploitation. For at least part of the white people's world it has meant material wealth.

The system under which the workers of the world are transferred across its surface appear, at first sight, very different. Closer inspection reveals that, to some extent at least, they build on each other and interlink

Key Terms

coolies Indentured laborers taken from Asia to work in other parts of the British empire. A term first used by British colonial authorities.

labor power The value of people's work that produces profits for capitalists. A Marxist term.

fascist Modern totalitarian political movements, usually associated with the European national socialist movements led by Hitler in Germany and Mussolini in Italy, characterized by a hatred for non-Christians and immigrants.

Las Casas Bartolomé de Las Casas, a Spanish priest. In a famous treatise written in 1583, he criticized the Spanish for their cruelty and inhumanity against the Indians.

half-caste A person of mixed race.

metropole An urban center.

both temporally and geographically, that experience of the one form is used to develop new forms, that time and time again, even in the recent past, humankind has reverted to older, apparently obsolete forms. The history of the world market for labour power—as we understand the term—is, of course, not primarily the story of free wage labour; often the worker concerned was neither "free" nor paid a wage. Both in the twentieth century and before, essentially compulsion and force shaped its evolution.

Women play an important part in the labour market. Although in terms of labour migration, slavery, and coolie labour they constituted a minority (as a rule around one-third), they were no less affected by the structures of the world market for labour power than men: their reproductive function and its control have been the subject of particular attention and have attracted various measures during every stage in the market's development. Women have suffered exploitation not only in the productive process, but also in the reproductive process, and this in the most extreme forms imaginable. Moreover, the women left behind in their country of origin have borne the brunt of often forced emigration in very specific ways.

[. . .]

The world market for labour power may be roughly divided into two main historical phases. The first encompassed the emergence and development of the world market for labour power under colonialism; the second began with industrialization and resulted in the direct incorporation into the world market of the capitalist metropole. From then on, labour power acquired abroad was integrated into the productive process not only outside the capitalist societies but also inside them, and it was thus not until labour migration began that foreign labour power first appeared in the metropole.

The world market for labour power in its colonial variant did not disappear when the second phase began. Instead it reached new peaks in the nineteenth and twentieth centuries, and the two phases became closely interwoven.

[. . .]

Between the colonial phase of the world market for labour power and the second phase, which extends into the present day and encompasses the import into the metropole of living labour, there have been a number of developments of a continuous nature. Present-day labour migration and the brain drain, like the slavery and the coolie systems and the fascist system of forced labour, are all methods of importing living labour. The fact that the calculations of profitability used by slave traders as early as the sixteenth century have been further developed since then and are still common is a clear indication of this. The calculation of profitability for the hire of forced labour from Nazi concentration camps is just one extreme illustration of the fact that the inhumanity which underlies the slave traders' calculations is still intensifying.

[. . .]

Ultimately these calculations were forerunners of the markedly economics-oriented, often hugely mathematical cost-benefit analyses that were for a long time commonly used in the study of labour migration.[1]

Racism, Sexism, and the Reproduction of Labour Power

Not only did Europe create the external, material conditions necessary to the exploitation of the colonized peoples, but it also created the corresponding racist ideologies.

Since Las Casas it is the Africans who have been considered particularly suited to working on the plantations and in the mines. The Indians, on the other hand, have been associated with a disastrously high incidence of death. During the Age of Imperialism racist ideologies, which since the Enlightenment have rested upon scientific foundations, were expounded and assimilated in a particularly aggressive manner. The economic motives behind various countries' colonial endeavours were veiled with talk of educational, religious, or some such missions in which the teaching of Africans in particular to work was a central issue. As one German colonialist put it, "First we must create the preconditions under which trade can exert an influence on culture and, in fact, on the cultural development of our natives. This can be done by educating them to work systematically" (cited in Bald et al. 1978 p. 112).

Whereas Africans were regarded as lazy but strong, Chinese coolies were described, not only by the German colonial rulers, as "this diligent, modest, if disagreeable people" (cited in Mamozai 1982, p. 49).

From the very beginning the world market for labour power operated according to racist principles, which permitted the highest degree of exploitation of those at the base of racial hierarchy. Of the American Indians, for example, the Europeans singled out the Caribs as a special group and declared that the members of this group could be enslaved without hesitation. Further examples of hierarchization include the plac ing of American half-castes into a hierarchical sequence, the ban on the enslavement of Indians, and the simultaneous intensification of the enslavement of Africans.

[. . .]

Like racism, the phenomena of sexism, categorization, and discrimination on the grounds of membership in the female sex are also a generally accepted principle on the world market for labour power. At first glance, women play a seemingly rather insignificant part in many of the stages in the development of this market. It was primarily the men in colonized societies who were obliged, directly or indirectly, to carry out forced labour; every cargo of slaves from Africa is said to have contained two-thirds men and only one-third women and children; under the coolie system, women formed only a minority of the workers exported, and labour migration is always portrayed as a male-dominated process.

Nevertheless, the reality of colonialism is that large numbers of women were recruited as forced labour: as bearers, mine workers, gatherers, and servants. The slave-owning societies of the Caribbean and the United States made hardly any distinction between male and female slaves when assigning work. In the United States there was an equal number of enslaved men and women, unlike in the Caribbean, where female slaves were in the minority.

It is difficult to discover the history of women on the world market for labour power from the literature on this subject, for colonized women were of even less interest to the historians of Europe than their men. Such women also had less opportunity to pass on or rediscover their own history.

This is still the case today. The literature on the subject of labour migration, for example, paints a picture dominated by the male or apparently sexless migrant, and women are included at best as dependent relatives. Even in the field of women's studies female migrant workers are not discussed, especially in relation to the formulation of theory.

Yet every form of colonial or capitalist exploitation affected women more intensely than it did men. Exploitation was not restricted to the recruitment of women for colonial production and as servants, but also extended to their sexual and reproductive capacity. This is particularly evident in the case of Indian women when one considers the emergence of the race of half-castes which replaced the original population of America, but it also holds true for African female slaves and the women in Africa, Asia, and Australia who lived through the colonization of their continents (for Africa see Mamozai 1982).

Moreover, as a result of forced and migrant labour, men became unavailable to help produce the means of subsistence, so this burden had to be borne by women, possibly assisted by children and the elderly. Every form of forced and migrant labour, even those that directly affected only men, increased the workload of the women in colonized societies.

Women were thus more important to the world market for labour power as producers and reproducers of labour power than through their incorporation into capitalist commodity production. This in no way meant that they were treated more considerately, for example by being exempted from hard physical labour, but meant above all that their specifically female capabilities were used in the interests of the users of labour power.

Through every stage in the development of the world market for labour power, women have resisted being used in this way. The problems encountered when the United States and the Caribbean attempted to breed slaves are proof enough. Industrial action of the sort where women refuse to bear children has probably been used in all colonized territories and is possible only if women apply knowledge handed down to them through the ages. Indian women, female African slaves in America, and colonized women in Africa. Australia, and the South Seas, as well as female coolies, all resorted to this form of nonacceptance.

The Europeans' desire to gain control over the reproductive capacities of colonized women—until well into the first few decades of the twentieth century, this meant prevailing upon women to bear more children—

manifested itself in the inducements, such as bonuses and privileges, offered to mothers, midwives, overseers, and the like. By making use of the usually relatively small number of women involved in the transfer of labour power (particularly under the coolie system), the colonizers attempted to ensure that the societies to which these women belonged would continue to function as reservoirs and suppliers of labour power.

NOTE

1. Examples include Bahadir's 1978 study of labour migration from Turkey, Lakhoua's detailed calculations for Tunisian labour migration (1976), works by Leuschner (1973), Blitz (1977), Nagel (1979), and others on the employment of foreigners in West Germany, and by Lebon (1978) on France.

REFERENCES

Bahadir, Sefik Alp. (1978). "Volkswirtschaftliche Kosten und Nutzen des Exports von Arbeitskraften." In *Aubenwirtschaft,* 33, 1978/4, pp. 350–54.

Bald, Detlef, P. Heller, V. Hundsdorfer, and J. Paschen. (1978). *Die Liebe zum Imperium: Deutschlands dunkle Vergangenheit in Afrika,* Bremen.

Blitz, Rudolf C. (1977). *A Benefit-Cost Analysis of Foreign Workers in West Germany, 1957–1973.* In *Kyklos,* vol. 30, no. 3, pp. 479–502.

Lakhoua, Mohamed F. (1976). Cost-Benefit Analysis of Exporting Workers: the Tunisian Case, Michigan State University, thesis.

Lebon. (1978). "Les Migrations externes (Approches diverses de quelques aspects significatifs du fait migratoire en France)." In *Revue Francaise des Affaires Sociales,* vol. 32, April/June.

Leuschner, Dieter. (1973). Volkswirtschaftliche Kosten und Ertrage der Beschaftigung auslandischer Arbeitnehmer. In *Zeitschrift fur die gesamte Staatswissenschaft,* vol. 129, no. 4, pp. 702–13.

Mamozai, Martha. (1982). *Herrenmenschen: Frauen im deutschen Kolonialismus,* Hamburg.

Nagel, Gerhard. (1979). *Volkswirtschaftliche Kosten von Wanderungen,* Hanover.

Reading B

Refugee Ship
LORNA DEE CERVANTES

"Autobiagraphy"
HOWARDENA PINDELL

Poet Lorna Dee Cervantes, long active in the American Indian and Chicano movements, published her first book of poetry, Emplumada, *in 1980. In much of her work she has chosen to write in English rather than in Spanish or bilingually, mediating between linguistic and culturally diverse communities. In this poem she describes the loss of homeland and language.*

Refugee Ship

like wet cornstarch
I slide past mi abuelita's *eyes*
bible placed by her side
she removes her glasses
the pudding thickens

mamá *raised me with no language*
I am an orphan to my spanish name
the words are foreign, stumbling on my tongue
I stare at my reflection in the mirror
brown skin, black hair

I feel I am a captive
aboard the refugee ship
a ship that will never dock
a ship that will never dock

Lorna Dee Cervantes. "Refugee Ship," in *Revista Chicano-Riquena* 3.1 (Winter 1975): 20.

FIGURE IV.1   HOWARDENA PINDELL, "AUTOBIOGRAPHY: WATER/ANCESTORS, MIDDLE PASSAGE/FAMILY GHOSTS, 1988, ACRYLIC, TEMPURA, CATTLE MARKERS, OIL STICK, PAPER, POLYMER PHOTO-TRANSFER, AND VINYL TAPE ON SEWN CANVAS, 118″ × 71″. COLLECTION WADSWORTH ATHENEUM, HARTFORD, CONNECTICUT, ELLA GALLUP SUMNER AND MARY CATLIN SUMNER COLLECTION. (PHOTO: JAMES DEE)

This water image from the "Autobiography" series centers on a sewn insertion of the artist's body template, with a whitened self-portrait indirectly influenced by Michael Jackson's "Thriller" makeup. It includes the blank white shape of a slave ship and references to Pindell's own African ancestors and to the abuse of slave women in the United States. There are also allusions to twins (significant in African folklore), because of the frequency of twins on both sides of the artist's family, and perhaps as a metaphor for biculturalism. Lucy Lippard, *Mixed Blessings: New Art in a Multicultural America* (commentary accompanies Plate 1)

444

Reading C

Excerpt from Mankiller: A Chief and Her People
WILMA MANKILLER AND MICHAEL WALLIS

In the excerpt from the autobiography of Chief Wilma Mankiller, we learn that many Native American families have undergone series of displacements and removals. Mankiller's family moved from Georgia to Oklahoma in the nineteenth century as part of the U.S. government policy of termination and relocation. In the 1950s, her family was urged to move again, out of Oklahoma to California as part of another relocation program. Mankiller's account reveals the pain and disorientation caused by such dislocations.

On August 1, 1953, the Eighty-third Congress adopted House Concurrent Resolution 108. This legislation, which withdrew the federal commitment for Indian people, stated in part, "It is the policy of Congress, as rapidly as possible to make Indians within the United States subject to the same laws and entitled to the same privileges and responsibilities as are applicable to other

Wilma Mankiller and Michael Wallis, *Mankiller: A Chief and Her People*, New York: St. Martin's Press, 1993: 67–74.

citizens of the United States, to end their status as wards of the United States, and to grant them all of the rights and prerogatives pertaining to American citizenship."

I have no hesitancy whatever in calling it one of the most valuable and salutary Congressional measures we have had in Indian Affairs in many years.

Commissioner Glenn L. Emmons
In praise of House Concurrent Resolution No. 108

Almost immediately, Utah Senator Arthur V. Watkins, who headed the Senate subcommittee on Indian affairs and was a vigorous proponent of the termination movement, secured the passage of additional legislation to use the policy with specific tribes. Watkins labeled termination as "the Indian freedom program." He and his congressional cronies considered the policy a cure-all for the "Indian problem." Immediately, Congress passed bills seeking termination of

---

Key Terms

Bureau of Indian Affairs (BIA) One of the oldest agencies within the U.S. government, the BIA was part of the War Department until 1849, when it was transferred to the Department of the Interior. That adversarial history was reflected in the BIA's treatment of Indians as it removed them to reservations and tried to control every aspect of their lives. In recent years, the BIA has reversed its termination policies and officially supports Indian self-determination and tribal rights.

Trail of Tears In 1830 Congress passed the "Indian Removal Act," which was signed into law by President Andrew Jackson. In 1838 in Georgia, despite legal appeals, the Cherokee tribe was forced to give up its land and begin the trek to Oklahoma. The trip was made under terrible conditions and at least 4,000 Cherokee died along what came to be known as the Trail of Tears.

various tribes. From 1954 until 1962, Congress imposed the policy on 61 tribes and native communities, effectively cutting them off from federal services and protections. It was not until 1970 that Congress censured this detestable policy, too late for most tribes that had been terminated. However, some of the tribes, including the Menominees of Wisconsin, were successful in regaining federal recognition in the 1970s.

The passage and implementation of termination bills during the 1950s shocked many Indian leaders, who immediately understood that the United States government again intended to destroy tribal governments. Many of them also realized that the government intended to break up native communities and put tribal land on the market by abolishing its status as nontaxable trust land. Native Americans would soon lose control of their land. Termination also meant the imposition of state civil and criminal authority and the loss of state tax exemptions and special tribal programs. Tribes would find it increasingly difficult to remain sovereign.

The United States policy of Indian relocation did not, in fact, get under way until the mid-1950s. Large numbers of Native Americans began to move en masse from reservations and ancestral lands to targeted metropolitan areas in anticipation of receiving job training, education, and a new place to live. By 1955, about 3,000 reservation Indians, mostly from the Southwest, were living in housing developments in Chicago. Many other native people had also made the move to low-rent apartments and public housing in other big cities, including Los Angeles, Detroit, St. Louis, and Seattle.

The following year, my own family experienced the pain of United States government relocation. The year was 1956. It was one month before my eleventh birthday. That was when the time came for our Trail of Tears.

We were not forced to do anything, but that did not matter—not to me. Not when the time came for our family to leave Mankiller Flats. Not when we had to say farewell to the land that had been our family's home for generations, and move far away to a strange place. It was then that I came to know in some small way what it was like for our ancestors when the government troops made them give up their houses and property. It was a time for me to be sad.

Our poverty had prompted the move. In 1955, my father first started talking to Bureau of Indian Affairs officials about the various forms of assistance for Cherokees.

Relocation was a possibility. I recall hearing at that time that the relocation program was being offered as a wonderful opportunity for Indian families to get great jobs, obtain good educations for their kids and, once and for all, leave poverty behind. In truth, the program gave the government the perfect chance to take Indian people away from their culture and their land. The government methods had softened since the nineteenth century, but the end result was the same for native people. Instead of guns and bayonets, the BIA used promotional brochures showing staged photographs of smiling Indians in "happy homes" in the big cities.

Some of the BIA people came to our house. They talked to my father, explaining the particulars of the program. They said the government wanted to "get out of the Indian business," and one of the ways to do that was by helping individuals and families relocate in larger cities. Dad listened to their pitch. The BIA people came out to our place a couple of times. I think Dad initially was opposed to our leaving Oklahoma and our land. As a boy, he had been taken from his home against his will to attend Sequoyah Boarding School. He did not want to leave his community and people again. But he talked it over with some Cherokee friends, and eventually he decided it would be a good idea to move. He must have honestly believed that in a distant city he could provide a better life for his children, with all the modern amenities.

I never liked the idea of our moving away. I can still remember hiding in a bedroom in our house of rough-hewn lumber, listening while my father, mother, and oldest brother talked in the adjoining room about the benefits and drawbacks of relocating our family. We younger children tried to listen through the door. We were terrified. They were talking about possible destinations. They spoke of places we had barely heard of—Chicago, New York, Detroit, Oakland, and San Francisco. California seemed to be their favorite. Finally my parents chose San Francisco because Grandma Sitton, my mother's mom, had moved to California in 1943. A widow when she left Oklahoma, she had remarried and settled in Riverbank, a community in the farm belt about 90 miles east of San Francisco.

None of us little kids could visualize California. We had been as far as Muskogee to go to the fair on a school field trip. We had been to Stilwell and Tahlequah, but that was about it. My world lay within a 10-mile radius of our family house at Mankiller Flats. Dad and my oldest brother had traveled to Colorado to cut broom-corn. My mother had been to Arkansas to see her sister, but no farther than that. My mother was scared about leaving and hated the idea of moving to California. She really opposed it at first, more than anyone else. But finally, knowing she would be living close to her mother, she was convinced to go along with my father, believing that life might be better for us all.

Despite my mother's decision, I still was not ready to leave. Neither was my sister Frances. We asked about the possibility of staying behind with friends, but my folks said we had to go with the others. So then we talked about running away to avoid the move, but we never did that. We kept hoping right up until the day our family left that something would happen—some kind of miracle—and we would stay put and not have to go to San Francisco. We did not have very much materially, but we really did not need much either. We had always managed to get by. From my point of view as a child, I could see no value in leaving our home. If life was not idyllic, at least it was familiar.

Finally, the day arrived in October of 1956 for us to depart for California. That day is branded into my memory. There were nine of us kids then. It was before the last two were born. My oldest sister, Frieda, was attending Sequoyah High School and did not move with us. My folks had sold off everything, including the old car. We all piled in a neighbor's car, and he drove us to Stilwell so we could catch the train headed west to California. As we drove away, I looked at our house, the store, my school. I took last looks. I wanted to remember it all. I tried to memorize the shapes of the trees, the calls of animals and birds from the forest. All of us looked out the windows. We did not want to forget anything.

When we got to Stilwell, Dad took us to a restaurant, and we had bowls of chili. We were not a very happy crew—two adults and eight children leaving everything behind for an unknown place. Just getting aboard the train was terrifying for the smaller children. It was a new experience. We settled in all over the place. Some of the children were more comfortable sleeping on the floor, others stayed on the seats or beneath them. My youngest baby sister was marking the back of a seat with a crayon. We were a wild bunch. We must have looked like a darker version of the Joad family from John Steinbeck's novel *The Grapes of Wrath*.

My mother was still scared about the move. Dad was also worried, but he was excited about the chance for a better life for all of us. As we got settled on the train, he turned to my mother and said, "I don't think I will ever be back until I come home in a coffin." As it turned out, Dad was right. The next time he came home was more than 14 years later, when he was buried in his native land.

As soon as we were all on the train, my sister Frances started to cry. It seemed as if she cried without stopping all the way from Oklahoma to California, although I am sure she did not. The conductor came along and asked her why she was crying. She could not answer him. I cried, too. All of us did. The train headed north. Then we had to change to another train in Kansas City. The trip took two days and two nights. We finally reached California, passing through Riverbank, where my grandmother lived. We kept on going until we stopped in San Francisco.

My folks had vouchers the BIA officials had given them for groceries and rent. But when we arrived, we found that an apartment was not available, so we were put up for two weeks in an old hotel in a notorious district of San Francisco called the Tenderloin. During the night, the neighborhood sparkled with lots of neon lights, flashily dressed prostitutes, and laughter in the streets. But in the morning, we saw broken glass on the streets, people sleeping in doorways, and hard-faced men wandering around. The hotel was not much better than the streets.

The noises of the city, especially at night, were bewildering. We had left behind the sounds of roosters, dogs, coyotes, bobcats, owls, crickets, and other animals moving through the woods. We knew the sounds of nature. Now we heard traffic and other noises that were foreign. The police and ambulance sirens were the worst. That very first night in the big city, we were all huddled under the covers, and we heard sirens outside in the streets. We had never heard sirens before. I thought it was some sort of wild creature screaming. The sirens reminded me of wolves.

My mother seemed sad and confused. When we went to get breakfast for the first time, we were not acquainted with the kinds of food on the menu. Back in Oklahoma, we usually had biscuits and gravy every morning. My mother scanned the menu, and the only item she could find with gravy was a hot roast-beef sandwich. So that is what we all ate for breakfast— beef sandwiches with gravy. My dad left the hotel early every morning to see about obtaining a job and a house—all the things the BIA had promised us. While he was gone, we explored around the hotel. Everything was new to us. For instance, we had never seen neon lights before. No one had bothered to even try to prepare us for city living.

NO DOGS, NO INDIANS.
Popular sign in restaurants, 1950s

One day, my brother Richard and I were standing by the stairway when we saw some people come down the hall and stop. All of a sudden, a box in the wall opened up. People got inside. Then the box closed and the people disappeared! After a minute or two the box suddenly opened again and a new bunch of people came out. Of course, we had never seen an elevator before. All we knew was that we were not about to get inside that box. We used the stairs.

After a couple of weeks, the BIA was finally able to find us a permanent place to live in San Francisco. We left the hotel and moved into a flat in a working-class neighborhood in the old Potrero Hill District. The apartment was quite small and crowded, but it seemed to be the best location for us. The rope factory where my father was able to get a job was not too far away. He was paid the grand sum of $48 a week. There was no way, even then, that a man could support a big family in San Francisco on that salary. That is why my big brother Don also worked in the factory making ropes. He and my father walked to the factory every day and worked long, hard hours. Even with both of them bringing home paychecks, we had a tough time, and our family was growing. My brother James Ray was born while we lived in the Potrero Hill District.

Many Hispanics lived in our neighborhood, and we became good friends with a Mexican family next door named Roybal. They took us under their wing and made our adjustment a pet project. For example, we had never had a telephone before, so the Roybals showed us how one worked. None of us had ever ridden bicycles, so they taught us how to bike and roller-skate.

Still, I did not like living in the city. I especially hated school. The other kids seemed to be way ahead of us in academic and social abilities. We could hold our own in reading because of what our folks had taught us, but the other students were much more advanced at mathematics and language skills. I spent most of the time trying my best to make myself as inconspicuous as possible.

I was placed in the fifth grade, and I immediately noticed that everyone in my class considered me different. When the teacher came to my name during roll call each morning, every single person laughed. Mankiller had not been a strange name back in Adair County, Oklahoma, but it was a very odd name in San Francisco. The other kids also teased me about the way I talked and dressed. It was not that I was so much poorer than the others, but I was definitely from another culture.

My sister Linda and I sat up late every night reading aloud to each other to get rid of our accents. We tried to talk like the other kids at school. We also thought about our old home in Oklahoma. My big sister Frances and I talked about our life back at Mankiller Flats. We tried to remember where a specific tree was located and how everything looked. That helped a little, but I still had many problems trying to make such a major adjustment. We simply were not prepared for the move. As a result, I was never truly comfortable in the schools of California. I had to find comfort and solace elsewhere.

I was not alone in my feelings. I have met many native people from different tribes who were relocated from remote tribal communities. They discovered, as we did, that the "better life" the BIA had promised all of us was, in reality, life in a tough, urban ghetto. Many people were unable to find jobs, and those who did were often offered only marginal employment. I later learned that many native people endured a great deal of poverty, emotional suffering, substance abuse, and poor health because of leaving their homelands, families, and communities. Children seemed to be especially vulnerable without the traditional support of the extended family at home. Urban Indian families banded together, built Indian centers, held picnics and powwows, and tried to form communities in the midst of large urban populations. Yet there was always and forever a persistent longing to go home. "I was as distant from myself as the moon from the earth," is how James Welch, a native writer, described the sense of alienation he experienced in an urban setting.

Reading D

The Refugee
PHIL MARFLEET

Cultural studies scholar Phil Marfleet describes the history of modern displacement, which has created millions of refugees. His discussion highlights the politics of definition and the question of who should be counted as a refugee, as well as the new predicaments that place seekers of asylum in increasingly difficult circumstances.

In the late 1950s, says the United Nations High Commissioner for Refugees (UNHCR), there were some 2 million refugees; by 1995, the organisation estimated that numbers had reached 27 million (UNHCR 1995). Other sources quote far higher numbers: according to Harris, there may be as many as 70 million refugees, with possibly the same number in flight within countries (Harris 1995: 120). To these figures may be added the numbers judged to be "at risk," among whom many are potential refugees. According to a U.S. government study, in 1996 some 42 million people were in extreme physical danger, mainly as the result of regional political conflicts (*Guardian International* 14 April 1996).

These figures provide only the most crude measures: not only is the process of counting often hap-

Phil Marfleet, "The Refugee," *Globalisation and the Third World,* Ray Kiely and Phil Marfleet, eds. London: Routledge, 1998: 70–71.

hazard but the notion of "refugee" is differently constructed among states and transnational bodies. Headline statistics nonetheless give a sense of the unprecedented scale of migration and of the vast numbers of those whose insecurity leads to flight.

Who should be counted? The matter of definition is a battleground (Tuitt 1996: 2). . . . Much rests upon interpretations of the 1951 Geneva Convention Relating to the Status of Refugees. This document and its 1967 Protocol lay down a definition, to be applied specifically to individuals, which turns upon subjective interpretation of the asylum-seeker's experience of persecution. There is no conception of the collective refugee, notwithstanding that the Convention introduces a notion of persecution which implies oppression of whole groups on the basis of their "race, religion, nationality, membership of a social group, or political opinion." . . . The focus upon European concerns, together with disinterest in contemporary forced migration in the Third World, amounted to a "Eurocentric orientation" of the early refugee regime.

Although there is now formal recognition that "refugee-producing" countries are overwhelmingly in the Third World, the Convention has not been modified. Wider definitions, including those adopted by the Organisation of African Unity, incorporate the idea that "every person" threatened by a range of external or internal threats should be offered asylum (Tuitt

Key Terms

refugee asylum Official, legal request for refuge in a new country.

Geneva Convention Treaties signed between 1869 and 1949 in Geneva, Switzerland, that

provide for humane treatment of both civilians and combatants in war.

capital Wealth in the form of money or goods.

1996: 12). But laws based upon the Convention continue to exclude assistance for all involuntarily displaced persons and insist on the principle of "alienage" —that the "legitimate" refugee must, in the words of the Geneva Convention, be "outside the country of his [sic] nationality." Displaced persons who have not crossed national borders cannot be granted refugee status. The overall effect of these legal principles, Hathaway concludes, is that need is defined "in terms which exclude most refugees from the less developed world" (Collinson 1994: 21).

As against these narrow definitions, the notion of "forced migration," of those coerced into flight, is the only approach which encompasses the predicament of most asylum-seekers. Such an idea has long been resisted by Western governments keen to differentiate refugees from other categories of migrants. During the 1950s and 1960s, migrants were usually identified on the basis of crude categories: "economic" migrants, those seeking family reunion, recognised refugees, asylum-seekers, and "illegals." Today migrants are less exceptions to a rule in which stable settled communities are rooted in "place of origin" than part of the process in which capital, information, and ideas do move more freely across national boundaries and in which large numbers of people are both induced and coerced to migrate. Differentiation between "economic" migrants, "refugees," and others becomes meaningful only for those most determined to perpetuate systems of exclusion.

How should we understand the refugee in this context? Traditional notions of "pull" and "push" factors in migration may still be useful. It has often been argued that mass migrations are a result of movement into expanding economies or a function of expectations that migration can provide enhanced "life chances"; this constitutes a pull factor. On the other hand, intolerable conditions in places of origin similarly make for a move, even when conditions elsewhere might be less attractive than hitherto—the push factor. When this approach takes account of political and social as well as economic factors, it has an explanatory value: refugees are those among whom the push factor is absolutely decisive. The refugee is a woman or man with the narrowest range of choice, usually because specific local conditions have made for exclusion. Such conditions may be explicitly "political"—relating to repression of particular parties, organisations, or individuals, ethnic, "racial," or religious groups, or people of a particular sexual orientation. Equally, causal factors may be primarily economic—related to immiseration, landlessness, famine, or environmental collapse. Even the U.S. Department of Labor—not usually identified with refugee causes—comments that "increasingly, both pure refugees and purely economic migrants are ideal constructs rarely found in real life; many among those who routinely meet the refugee definition are clearly fleeing both political oppression and economic dislocation" (Papademetriou 1993: 212–13).

REFERENCES

Collinson, S. (1994). *Europe and International Migration,* London: Pinter.

Harris, N. (1995). *The New Untouchables: Immigration and the New World Order,* London: I. B. Tauris.

Papademetriou, D. (1993). "Confronting the Challenge of Transnational Migration: Domestic and International Responses," in *The Changing Course of International Migration,* Paris: OECD.

Tuitt, P. (1996). *False Images: the Law's Construction of the Refugee,* London: Pluto.

UNHCR. (1995). *The State of the World's Refugees,* Oxford: Oxford University Press.

The Human Rights of Refugees with Special Reference to Muslim Refugee Women

KHADIJA ELMADMAD

Legal scholar Khadija Elmadmad points out that women refugees are a diverse group. Focusing on Muslim women refugees, Elmadmad argues that their specific needs must be understood in the context of variations within the practice of Islam as well as the discrimination and violence directed against Muslims.

The situation facing refugees and other forced migrants is one of the most serious of this century of displacement. Today, we speak of 20 to 23 million refugees and of 24 to 25 million internally displaced persons. It is well known that women and children now represent 80 to 90 percent of these numbers (Jack

Khadija Elmadmad, "The Human Rights of Refugees with Special Reference to Muslim Refugee Women," in *Engendering Forced Migration: Theory and Practice,* Doreen Indra, ed. New York: Berghahn Books, 1999: 261–66.

1996: 11). Few, however, appreciate that the majority of these migrant women and children are Muslim. Not only are the human rights of most of these female Muslim refugees *not* guaranteed, but the very violation of their rights has become a well-institutionalized dimension of war. All four main terms in the title of this chapter ("human rights," "refugees," "women," and "Muslim") have something in common: their conceptual ambiguity and inconsistent usage. This can lead to much practical confusion and to inadequate legal and physical protection for members of this large population. It is important to reflect on this association of terms and to analyze each one individually.

First, international declarations notwithstanding, notions of human rights vary according to ideology, geography, and culture. They can also differ according to which legal instrument has precedence in any given jurisdiction. Indeed, the concept *human rights* reveals all the problems we face in balancing universality and

Key Terms

Berlin Wall At the end of World War II in 1945, the German city of Berlin was divided into a British, American, and French sector and a Soviet sector (which became known as East Berlin). The Berlin Wall, erected in 1961, became a symbol of Cold War animosity and suspicion between East and West. When Communist rule ended in Russia in 1989, the wall in Berlin was pulled down to symbolize the end of the Cold War.

human rights With the United Nations-sponsored Universal Declaration of Human Rights of 1948, the right to life, liberty, equality before law, freedom of movement, religion, association, and nationality became acknowledged as part of international law.

polygyny The practice of one husband having more than one wife. When a woman has more than one husband, it's called *polyandry*. The term *polygamy* encompasses both practices.

specificity. Promising an end to the dominance of overarching "master" ideologies from the West and East, the fall of the Berlin Wall signaled a new era in which human rights could be conceptualized and used in increasingly different ways, as we have seen. This reflects the resurfacing of local and regional interests and beliefs previously muted. Even so, I think it can be said that there is a universal thread running through this diversity. Human rights in a universal sense pertain to the rights that guarantee respect for human life and dignity. These rights are, in turn, grounded in notions of justice, liberty, and equality.

The word *refugee* also has several different meanings: legal, linguistic, sociological, religious, and so forth. There are even several major international definitions that are not consistent with each other: the 1951 United Nations Convention and its 1967 Protocol Relating to the Status of Refugees, the 1969 Organization of African Unity (OAU) Convention, and the 1984 American Cartagena Declaration. Western Europeans monopolized the definitional origins of the concept. Concerned as they were with keeping others out and with making statements about the lack of freedom under communism, the framers of the 1951 Convention used a much more restrictive definition of who is a refugee than, say, the OAU. Again, there is a universal thread running through the legal language: a refugee can be simply defined as someone fleeing persecution and in need of protection because his or her human rights have been, or are at risk of being, violated.

The dangerously global term *woman* has an even wider range of contextual meanings and connotations. It varies dramatically according to national and international law, social group, culture, religion, and situational practice. Generally, a "woman" is, of course, someone of the female sex who has attained majority: one who is no longer a girl-child. However, there is no internationally agreed-upon definition of a child, and no international consensus on the age of majority or on when maturity is reached. The 1989 International Convention on the Rights of the Child does not give a fixed age for the end of childhood.[1] Based upon masculinist ideas of individual responsibility within civil society, inter and intranationally there are differing standards and different ages for majority: civil (commonly 18), penal (often 16), and military (informally

accepted as 15). Therefore, a woman in one place could be a girl elsewhere, and vice versa.

Difference-leveling Western stereotypes notwithstanding, the meaning of *Muslim* varies with the type of Islam adopted. Theologically, Islam is one faith; it is the religion of all Muslims. It is based on five pillars: belief in the Prophet Mohammed, praying in the Islamic way, fasting for one month, giving alms (*azzakat*), and going on pilgrimage to Mecca when possible. However, there are socially and politically different "Islams," and various kinds of Muslims have different interpretations of the Islamic sources and form different sects (Shia and Sunni), schools (Hanafi, Hanbali, Maliki, or Shafii), and political states (secular or nonsecular). Sometimes ethnic and national cultural differences strongly affect Muslim belief and practice even among those practicing what is nominally the same form of Islam. Hence, what is allowed in one Muslim state can be forbidden in another, as in the case of polygyny. We could perhaps stereotypically distinguish these cultural differences in yet another way as "liberal" or Westernized, "conservative," and "fundamentalist" Islam.

Why Pay Greater Attention to the Protection of Muslim Refugee Women?

Today more than ever before, women have become the specific victims of refugee-generating cruelty and injustice. Muslim refugee women, in particular, often face specific persecutions because they are both Muslim and women. Their persecution arises from a range of factors, including the resolve of certain non-Muslim groups and states to destroy or distort Muslim religion, cultures, and traditions. Recall that, as noted above, when we speak of the violation of the human rights of "refugees," the majority of the adult people to whom we refer are Muslim women.

Their Specificity as Women Refugees

Talking about "the" special situation of refugee women, the United Nations High Commissioner for Refugees, Sadako Ogata, has noted that "Refugee women and children bear a disproportional share of the suffering" (Marshall 1995: 4) involved in forced displacement. In fact, refugee women are likely to face gendered violence before, during, and after fleeing their countries of origin. Tragically high numbers of women are victims of "men's wars," and they are the ones who often suffer the most from armed conflicts, even when they take little active part in them. A potent symbol of "our" superiority over "them," rape is a prevalent and persistent threat.[2] As is the case for other refugee women, many Muslim refugee women are forced to flee their places of origin because of fear of reprisal by the state or its agents for the actions or beliefs of a father, brother, or husband. This is yet another way in which violence against women is often used as a means to punish either a particular man or a whole community.

After exile, women often still face violence. While Islam condemns all sexual relations outside of marriage, rape and forced prostitution in refugee camps have become common practice. In addition, the employment opportunities for men and women in asylum countries are often profoundly unequal, both inside and outside camps. Discrimination against refugee women in the type and allotment of most services and development programs is also a common practice in refugee camps. Critically, women also face problems of access to food and services; when men are in charge of distributing assistance, they often forget the weakest people.

Their Specificity as Muslims and Women

Homayra Etemadi, from the Geneva-based international NGO Working Group on Refugee Women, declared in her address to the November 1994 Sharjah Conference on Uprooted Muslim Women that

> Muslim women were facing persecution, massive human rights violations, and armed conflicts in different parts of the world. Those affected were not only Afghans, Azeri, Bosnians, Palestinians, and Somalis, but also the Muslim communities in Cambodia, Kashmir, Mozambique, and the Philippines.
> (*Gulf News* 13 November 1994: 3)

Millions of women from as diverse places as Bosnia, Burma, Azerbaijan, and Palestine have been targeted by non-Muslims for violence. At the same time, Muslims themselves use violence against women and push them, their families, and their communities to flee their countries and to look for security and protection outside their place of origin. Here, different Islamic ways of thinking and behaving have important consequences, as women are often a focal point of pan-Islamic and local controversy. Violence against women is a common way of effectively asserting one faction's perception of the Islamic religion over others. Such struggles can be found in Afghanistan, in Algeria, and even in Egypt.

Such strategies are not unique to Muslim factions, but the prevalence of patriarchy and the rise of Islamic fundamentalism certainly make discrimination against Muslim refugee women more obvious than that against others. Persecution against "deviant" women by fundamentalist groups is, for example, a common means employed to stop the spread of liberal Islam. To illustrate, in Algeria the present civil war is, in part, a war against women. As reported in the Moroccan newspaper *Libération* (16 May 1997), women are killed daily in Morocco if they do not wear the "Islamic veil" or if they do not stay at home. Others are victimized to punish their male relatives. In Iran, the work of the Islamic revolution has, at least in symbolic terms, turned into a "veiling revolution." In Sudan, many refugees are displaced non-Muslims from the south; women among them are unfamiliar with Islamic codes of conduct and yet nevertheless persecuted for their non-respect of Islam. Even though these forms of persecution constitute well-founded reason to be granted asylum, Muslim women are frequently refused asylum. Perhaps it is because of persistent stereotypes of Islam and Muslims. It is my impression that when seeking asylum, Muslim refugee women receive less help and are less often welcomed by their hosts than Muslim men or other refugee women. In some cases, Muslim refugee women are clearly thought to represent a danger to non-Muslim communities and are not granted asylum for fear of Islamic contamination.

[. . .]

In refugee camps, discrimination against Muslim women by Muslim men is obvious everywhere. They suffer particularly from discrimination in education, food distribution, and employment opportunities.

During the November 1994 International Conference on Uprooted Muslim Women, the representative of UNHCR, Mustapha Al Jamali, said:

> In refugee camps Muslim women are subject to violence from their husbands and family members, because men have nothing else to do but fight against their wives and children. This doubles the volume of pain for women particularly.
>
> (*Gulf News* 13 November 1994: 3)

Access to education is particularly problematic. Ideally, education is an obligation for all Muslims, men and women, but practice can be quite different. As a case in point, many Afghan refugee women in Pakistani camps were denied an education.[3] Moreover, those who try to educate girls there often find themselves at risk (Colville 1995: 24; see also Cammack).

Inequalities in the distribution of assistance are exacerbated by patriarchy and fundamentalism. Neither of these is unique to Muslims, but both are prevalent among them. To illustrate, during the Kurdish crisis of 1991, refugees fled to the northern mountains of Iraq, and an internationally organized food distribution program was put in place. UNHCR eventually realized that little food was going to families headed by women, the key reason being that most of the appointed food distributors were men. Much malnutrition, exploitation, and suffering were the result (Marshall 1995: 3)

[. . .]

Displaced Muslim women, of course, have specific needs beyond the distribution of assistance. Those who have undergone rape or other sexual violence need specialized care, too. The nature of many source cultures at least nominally associated with Islam is such that Muslim women are generally viewed as being responsible for what happened to them. They may be punished, humiliated, and eventually rejected by their families. Children conceived in rape are usually not recognized by their community. Very often, violated women receive little formal or informal assistance and either flee their communities, commit suicide, or keep their secret to themselves out of a sense of shame. The scope of this particular problem and its consequences is enormous.

NOTES

1. In fact, Article I of this Convention declares: "For the purpose of the present Convention, a Child means every human being below the age of 18 years *unless, under the law applicable to the child, majority is attained earlier.*"

2. Vietnamese women being raped in front of other refugees was a very common sight for "boat people." Somali women also experienced the same horrific treatment. During interviews I conducted with refugee and displaced women in Sudan in 1992, I observed that some of them could not enter the country without granting sexual favors to the border officers.

3. In Iran, the situation was quite different. There Afghan women refugees could enroll in vocational and training courses.

REFERENCES

Cammack, Diana. (1999). "Gender Relief and Politics During the Afghan War." *Engendering Forced Migration: Theory and Practice,* Doreen Indra, ed. New York: Berghahn Books, 94–123.

Colville, R. (1995). "The Difficulty of Educating Leyla." *Refugees* 100.

Jack, S. (1996.) "Continent in Conflict: African Women Must Play a Vital Role." *New Nation* 8 (Nov.): 11.

Marshall, R. (1995). "Refugees, Feminine Plural." *Refugees: Refugee Women* 2(100): 3–9.

REFLECTING ON THE SECTION

What is the two-phase framework that Lydia Potts offers for thinking about the logics of forced migrations and enslavement? How does it complement the other readings in this section? Cervantes' poem and Pindell's artwork draw connections between past forced migrations and present-day fragmented identities; Mankiller compares the migration of her family in the 1950s to the earlier Trail of Tears; Marfleet juxtaposes the European framework for refugees developed in the 1950s with the realities of refugees in the 1990s. How do these comparisons and connections illuminate the racial, economic, political, and gendered aspects of migration and refugee movements?

Elmadmad writes that "women and children now represent 80 to 90 percent" of refuges and internally displaced persons. Potts argues that "every form of colonial or capitalist exploitation affected women more intensely that it did men." Why do you think that women are often disproportionally dislocated?

Diasporas

From "Routes" to Roots

STUART HALL

Sociologist Stuart Hall argues that it is possible to think about the term diaspora *in two ways: as "closed" and "open." Closed diasporas refer to groups who immigrate but keep their idea of a culture of origin distinct and separate from the culture in which they live. Open diasporas refer to cultures that have changed and mixed over time. In this excerpt, Hall explains that the modern era has given rise to numerous diasporas that represent new kinds of identity.*

The term *diaspora* can, of course, be used in a "closed" way, to describe the attempt of peoples who have, for whatever reason, been dispersed from their "countries of origin," but who maintain links with the past through preserving their traditions intact and seeking eventually to return to the homeland—the true "home" of their culture—from which they have been separated. But there is another way of thinking about diasporas.

Stuart Hall, "From 'Routes' to Roots," in *A Place in the World,* Doreen Massey and Pat Jess, eds. New York: Oxford University Press, 1995: 206–7.

Diaspora also refers to the scattering and dispersal of peoples who will *never* literally be able to return to the places from which they came; who have to make some kind of difficult "settlement" with the new, often oppressive, cultures with which they were forced into contact; and who have succeeded in remaking themselves and fashioning new kinds of cultural identity by, consciously or unconsciously, drawing on more than one cultural repertoire. They are people who belong to more than one world, speak more than one language (literally and metaphorically), inhabit more than one identity, have more than one home; who have learned to negotiate and translate *between* cultures, and who, because they are irrevocably the product of several interlocking histories and cultures, have learned to live with, and indeed to speak from, *difference*. They speak from the "in-between" of different cultures, always unsettling the assumptions of one culture from the perspective of another, and thus finding ways of being both *the same as* and at the same time *different from* the others among whom they live (Bhabha 1994). Of course, such people bear the marks of the particular

---

Key Terms

diaspora Originally used to refer to the dispersal of Jewish people in ancient times and after, the term now signifies the movements of groups of people from an original "home" to many other locations and the networks of affiliation that are formed between these communities.

imagined communities Term coined by cultural historian Benedict Anderson to describe the national identities created through media representations of people in diverse geographical locations.

cultures, languages, histories, and traditions which "formed" them; but they do not occupy these as if they were pure, untouched by other influences, or provide a source of fixed identities to which they could ever fully "return" (Hall 1990, 1992).

[. . .]

They represent new kinds of identities—new ways of "being someone"—in the late-modern world. Although they are characteristic of the cultural strategies adopted by marginalized people in the latest phase of globalization, more and more people in general—not only ex-colonized or marginalized people—are beginning to think of themselves, of their identities and their relationship to culture and to place, in these more "open" ways. It is certainly one of the greatest sources of cultural creativity today—and what much late-modern culture (novels, poems, paintings, images, films, video, and so on) seems to be *about*.

Used in this way, the concept of *diaspora* provides an alternative framework for thinking about "imagined communities." It cuts across the traditional boundaries of the nation-state, provides linkages across the borders of national communities, and highlights connections which intersect—and thus disrupt and unsettle—our hitherto settled conceptions of culture, place, and identity.

REFERENCES

Bhabha, H. (1994). *The Location of Culture,* London, Verso.

Hall, S. (1990). "Cultural Identity and Diaspora" in Rutherford, J. (ed.), *Identity: Community, Culture, Difference,* London; Lawrence and Wishart.

Hall, S. (1992). "Cultural Identity in Question" in Hall, S., D. Held, and T. McGrew (eds.), *Modernity and Its Futures,* Cambridge, Polity Press.

FIGURE IV.2　MARINA GUTIÉRREZ, "BIOGRAPHY," 1988, ACRYLIC ON MASONITE WITH SUSPENDED PAINTED METAL RELIEFS, 48″ × 60″ × 6″.

Biography
Marina Gutiérrez

"Gutiérrez is a NuYorican artist whose works are inspired by Puerto Rican folk arts. She plays with scale, usually to symbolize power relations. She often fragments body parts and uses small cut-out images, which are hung delicately before larger forms, reminiscent of the milagros *(miracles) in Latin Catholicism. In this triple portrait, . . . (t)he subject might be a creation of and by the self, with another self as mediator. Two of the Marinas stare directly at the viewer, regal and confrontational, while the third, hand raised in incantation, seems to invoke the promised miracles, to put the pieces together. The added shapes, each of which has a private meaning for the artist, include a blue eye (a reference to Toni Morrison's book* The Bluest Eye), *which stands for racism, and a business suit—"the embodiment of evil, the real Evil Empire." "I think of myself as being very literal," says Gutiérrez. "My subjects are those of the world which move me . . . life versus death, oppression and hope, political struggle, stories of the simple beauty of life, of earth and humanity. There is always a story, a narrative to be read in the placement and interaction." (quotations from unpublished 1984 statement and unpublished 1989 interview with Moira Roth)." Lucy Lippard,* Mixed Blessings: New Art in a Multicultural America *(commentary accompanies Plate 4).*

Gal . . . You Come from Foreign

CLAUDETTE WILLIAMS

Writer Claudette Williams describes her life before and after immigration. She looks back fondly at her Caribbean childhood and reflects on the struggles with racism she has faced in England.

It often goes unacknowledged that the Black diaspora has survived, resisted, and developed in exploitative hostile environments which threaten physical and psychological destruction. It has been our history and past struggles which have offered us the rejuvenating substance of struggle, to carry our fight forwards. This is just one story; there are many like this to be told. Migration, like slavery, could not and will not silence our voices and kill our spirit.

  This story is part of that tradition. My first 10 years were spent in the small district of Heartease in St Thomas, Jamaica. To my child's mind our district consisted of my family, aunts, uncles, cousins, nieces, and our extended family, all living within the space of over 100 yards, with three or more families sharing the

Claudette Williams, "Gal . . . You Come from Foreign," *Charting the Journey: Writings by Black and Third World Women,* Shabnam Grewal et al., eds. London: Sheba Press, 1988: 145–56.

same yard. This meant that even the poorest of children grew up in a communal environment, with ample space to be adventurous. We grew up knowing and being known by the community of which we were a part, all adults looking after and looking out for each others' children. We grew up knowing our places and having respect for all adults. Knowing that disrespect would result in punishment. For example, passing an adult in the street without acknowledging them, could, when made public to your parents, result in a beating.

  Heartease District stretches two to three miles west from the old Yallahs riverbed to the beautiful foothills of Heartease in the east. In the north it stretches for a mile and a half toward Easington Hills and southward to the sea. During the rainy months, the old Yallahs river floods its banks and provided great excitement for us. When "river com dung" the Kingston to Morant Bay road becomes impassable. The traffic subsequently goes via Easington bridge and then down through Heartease. Despite the danger of the heavy traffic roaring through the only main street, the excitement of seeing buses and lorries in such numbers far outweighed the danger we were warned of constantly.

  Our community was poor, and dependent for work on cultivating absentee landlords' land, or on the few

Key Terms

Black diaspora The dispersion of Africans through slavery and immigration.
Rastas Followers of the Rastafarian religion. Rastafarianism originated in the Caribbean, based on the ideas of Marcus Garvey, who sought to lead a return to Africa.

available local government works projects. Agriculture determined everyone's life chances. Those who worked for a wage worked long, hard hours, and often subsisted by cultivating small family plots. Those without their own plots managed to make a living by selling crops they bought on trust. They picked and marketed whatever crops were in season, such as ackees, mangoes, lime, yams, pears (avocados), pease, sold them at whatever the market price was, and paid the seller in relation to the market price. This kind of relationship often created problems, especially when the market price happened to be much lower than the original agreed price, or when the goods were not sold at all.

A large majority of Heartease women, like my aunt, supported their families as market women. The memories of the few occasions I went to market with my aunt remain sharp and pungent. On market day the entire house would be awake, at what seemed like the middle of the night, to prepare for the 5:00 bus. My aunt would wake us up, and I would make tea, which might be "bush tea" like sericea, lime, or orange leaf boiled and sweetened with condensed milk. (Indian Black tea was something I discovered in England and hated because it tasted so much like herb tea, herb as in medicinal and not very nice.) I would wash and dress quickly and be ready and waiting with our goods outside the gate listening for the market bus. The bus would announce its approach by blowing its horn continuously.

Women would gather at their gates with bundles, bankras, and boxes. The market bus took everything: bunches of bananas, huge bundles of breadfruits, sticks of sugar canes, even livestock. The bus boys would skillfully toss baggages up to each other on top of the bus, and secure them. This often proved to be a point of contention with the market women, who would instruct the boys not to "bust dem bag" or "bruse dem goods," and the bus boys, often young men, gave as good as they got in return. Meanwhile we would be clambering over the gangway to find a seat, or sitting on some makeshift seat, leaving space for the older women. Once on board we would trundle through the darkness with the bus horn honking, and the women would exchange news about their families and discuss the state of the world. The women's voices had to be pitched higher than the horn so that they could be heard. Everyone would be adding to the topic of conversation, and one thing would lead to another. This continued, with the bus stopping and picking up more women and goods and with repeated instructions to the bus boys.

Once we arrived in the market area of Kingston and unloaded, the women would display their goods on the stalls, with regular market women (women who sold in the market six days a week) coming to buy bulk for their own stalls. My aunt, who only occasionally went to market to sell, would nevertheless have a network of regular market women whom she would sell to. Sometimes they would buy most of what came in, so the rest of the day would be spent shopping. Otherwise we would take up our position at the stalls and induce buyers to purchase our goods.

The market was vibrant with greetings, exchanges of news, and bartering. At the same time we kept a sharp lookout for thieves and shoppers who were prepared to put up a hard bargain. The market was huge with individual stalls. Food and meat were in one section, household goods and clothes in another. The atmosphere was alive with odours and sounds. The communality of the market was not instantly apparent, but the women looked out for each other—while maintaining a competitive spirit when it came to getting their goods sold.

By three o'clock we would be packing up, and setting off to Parade—the bus depot. Huge bankras, boxes, and bags would again be packed high on the bus, with anything else from beds to cupboards tied down on top of the bus, and off we went full of sounds, smells, and excitement.

The majority of women in Heartease, during the 50s and 60s, like my aunt were totally dependent on agriculture and marketing of local crops. During the late 60s, four small factories were built in Poor Man's Corner, a mile and a half from Heartease, offering limited employment for the area. The tobaccos, leather, cosmetic, and canning factories provided a limited outlet for local produce. Much of this local development can be credited to Michael Manley's government, which encouraged local people to develop local produce and generate local industries. However these plans were full of contradictions; the local industries were owned by individual local captialists, and during the recession they pulled out of the area.

Another job creation project was government investment in agricultural development, where local crops were researched and successful strains encouraged, and fertilizer and farming advice was accessible to local farmers at a reasonable price.

Older established families in Heartease lived mostly off the main road, with the newer, younger families living off the second road, called the Lane. Around the Lane also lived some East Indian families (descendants of indentured labourers from India) and Rastas, and though we knew of them and were as poor as they were, we lived separate lives.

As we grew up we were warned (without explanation) to keep away from certain men. Twenty years later, I realize that they might have been homosexuals. As children we were taught to keep our distance. While no known situations warranted these warnings, we grew up learning to be cautious of certain men who kept themselves apart, yet remained part of the community.

Until I was 10 the life I knew and remembered was centred around my aunt and our immediate family, my three nieces and my youngest brother. As one of the eldest girls I was expected to do many chores: cook, wash, iron, fetch water from the standpipe down the road, or if the water was cut off (and it often was) collect water from the river. Often I was expected to look after the house and keep an eye on the younger children when my aunt was at the market or out in the fields, collecting crops to take to market. My uncle went to work early in the mornings and returned exhausted late at nights. So although he was present, he was marginal to the everyday household happenings.

Aunt Salna was often out in the fields, planting, weeding, cutting, or collecting crops to take to market. (Twenty years later her routine is much unchanged.) However, my memories of Aunt Salna are both painful and happy. Painful because I suffered whenever anything went wrong in the house. If the meal was late, burnt, or too salty, if the house was in a mess, the floor not polished, the yard not swept, the chickens not fed, or one missing, eaten by dog or mongoose. For a nine-year-old there were always other more exciting things to do than chores. So it was inevitable that things would go wrong. As one of the oldest, all those responsibilities fell on me. It seemed that I was unable to

do anything correctly. I grew up doubting my abilities, and because reprimand would be associated with my colour I simply linked being Black with being unable to do anything correctly. I was the darkest of the children in the household, and colourism featured strongly in Jamaican life. My inability to believe in myself took me many years to recognize and attempt to correct. My happy memories, however, recall people whom I wholeheartedly love, those who combed and plaited my hair lovingly, those who allowed me to be a child, those who granted me the space and freedom to roam, live outside in the open, running in the warm rain, swimming in the fast-rushing rivers and the mysterious blue salty sea. I have memories of the freedom of picking and eating fruits when they were in season, knowing there would always be something else when they came to an end, mangoes, sugar cane, sweetsops, gineps, juneplums, red plums. . . . My relationship with my aunt was offset by my access to others who would console and indulge me in my childish ways. However, the harshness of a peasant life cannot eradicate people's capacity to be creative, to carve out space for laughter and fun, and in so doing allow ourselves the chance to regenerate and struggle onward.

Like many migrants in Britain, my happiest memories of Jamaica override the cruelty of poverty and the hostility of life in Britain. I hold onto the warm memories of belonging. The material poverty of my childhood has taught me many lessons: the value of having plenty (relatively) and the gift of sharing emotionally and physically. These contradict the deprivation theories which would have us believe that the brutality of poverty renders us emotionally bankrupt and noncreative. In fact, it is from these years that I draw much of my motivation and creativity. My childhood experiences provided me with the tools to overcome pain and develop as a whole person.

Growing up in the Heartease community, my contact with white people, though I must have seen them, was minimal. We had our lives and they had theirs. White people were equated with richness and land— they were outside our everyday experiences. We saw landlords like Delisser once or twice a year during the inspection of his property at either planting or reaping time. Other rich (not necessarily white) people who lived closer or had any contact with the people of

Heartease were the headmaster of Yallahs School, and those who farmed a sizable amount of their own land and who could afford to build better, bigger houses than the rest of the community. Not having any contact with white people did not, however, rule out the influences of racist, colonial ideas (still prevalent in Jamaican society) from encroaching on our lives.

Colourism can be described as the fusion of colonial racism with the classism of Jamaican society, resulting in a gradation according to colour, which closely reflects the class system. Eighty-five per cent of the Jamaican population are of African descent and black in skin colour. They occupy the peasant and lower classes; the "fair," "light," "white-skinned" people generally occupy the upper and ruling classes of Jamaican society. Colourism permeates into the consciousness of Jamaicans, with "white skin" or "fair skin" holding the swing (power).

During the Manley government, a programme of nationalism attempted to educate and address the issue of colourism. Manley actively promoted black-skinned Jamaicans into visible positions in banks, public offices, and television. Rastas were also given a high profile: they wore their locks in public offices and on television. The bush jacket also became a national symbol.

My school experience reinforced colourism. It taught me that it was the fair-skinned children who received praise and the teacher's attention, and the Black children who were relegated to the back of the classroom. The lessons of colonialism continued to be reinforced in my life, in my family's attitude, and projected in statements such as, "Gal, a meck you black and stupid so." My blackness became associated with my gender, my mistakes, and my misbehaviour.

So although my immediate contact with white people might have been limited, I had learned the elementary lessons of racism and sexism. It took the Black Power movement of the 60s to help me dismantle some of the damage done to me and many like me.

In 1965 I came to Britain, having no experience of city life, to join my parents in Brixton Hill, London. The transfer provoked a mixture of excitement and fear. What would my parents be like? What was England like?

My brother and I were full of anticipation. Our memories of our parents were dim. We had seen pictures, but what would they be like in the flesh? We had a clearer memory of our mother. She had left Jamaica in 1960, but our dad had left in 1957. In fact, we did not know them as individuals. We only knew that our father and mother were in England.

After an adventurous overnight stop in a New York hotel, with a TV set which did not work, we arrived in London on 6 November, cold and freezing. I recognized my mother immediately as we came through the airport. She looked a lot like me. We hugged and kissed, with shy hellos. I remembered being wrapped in a big warm green cape borrowed from my mum's friend's daughter.

My brother was wrapped in a big brown coat three sizes too big and also borrowed, perhaps because our sizes were unknown, or maybe because finances did not allow for such a purchase. However, they were very welcome.

I had mixed feelings of excitement and bewilderment. I remember thinking: what am I going to call these two new people—mum or mother, father or dad? My bewilderment was solved some days later when on answering my mother, I called her Salna (my aunt's name). "You can call me mother or mum," she offered. I chose mum. That little dilemma was solved. I never asked my parents what they felt when they met us.

In the car coming from the airport, my brother and I were busy commenting on the miles of yellow street lights and dark houses sitting right on the road. Also they were all stuck together. How could people live in such a small space? How were those lights turned on?

The emotional impact of leaving Jamaica was to strike some days later, but for the time being we were excited at reaching England, and finding our parents.

To say we were culture-shocked is irrelevant; but we were definitely cold, and cut loose from all that was familiar. We wanted to go back home. I still possess a strong emotional attachment to the concept of "back home"; England has never emotionally become my home, even though I've lived here some 20 years now.

The cold made the biggest and most lasting impact on my transfer. It snowed on our first day in London (7 November 1965), and after the initial elation and excitement of watching the soft, fluffy snowflakes fall and accumulate, Orvil and I rushed out to play. It did not take long before the sharp, piercing cold reached our inadequately clad hands and feet. The cold that day left them stinging, the pain of which has been repeated many times, reducing me to tears.

Even today when I see an "idyllic" winter scene, it recalls the coldness of 7 November 1965.

A week later Orvil and I started at King's Acre Primary School, London. I was placed in the fourth year and stayed at the school for eight months. The schoolwork was similar to that which I had done in Jamaica in the fourth class of Easington All Age School, which had six classes in all.

The work was not hard. The difficulties came with living and working with white children and a white teacher. I was constantly asked to repeat what I said with, "Pardon? I beg your pardon?" I soon learned that what I was speaking was not considered English. Yet, if I listened hard, I understood what was being said. "Pardon" had its desired effect, so that within a year of leaving Jamaica I had lost my Jamaican speech and soon sounded like the other children in my class. It was only later in secondary school that I rediscovered my Jamaican speech with other newly arrived Jamaican girls.

Another major irritation at primary school was the fact that I knew a lot about Britain and British history, while the English kids were very ignorant about the Caribbean and Jamaica in particular. This lesson I would relearn many times during my adult life. I realized that information was available about other Caribbean islands and the rest of the world. It has been the experience of living in Britain and our struggle against racism which has allowed many Caribbean people to learn about neighbouring islands who shared similar colonial histories with the rest of Europe, and forced us to lose some of those unfounded inter-island rivalries.

The arrival of the Black Panther movement and the Black consciousness era offered me the necessary knowledge and confidence to survive Britain. Black Power taught me to value myself and others like me in a way I had not experienced before. "Black Is Beautiful"and "Be Proud to Be Black" carried their unique message to my heart.

I was presented with a history, people, and struggle of which I was a part; and I found out that there was much beauty and pride in being a Black woman. I was able to recognize the significance of pressing my hair and bleaching my skin. While consciously I did not want to be white, everything I had learned and was surrounded by told me that to be white was "good," but here for the first time in my life were other Black people addressing "me" and my personal doubts and inadequacies. I was being told not to be ashamed or afraid of what and who I am. This profound message nevertheless had its contradictions. We did not all fit the "African Queen, Mother Creation" male-defined image of Black womanhood. However, it did serve a purpose and remains an important and significant symbol of self-definition. An aspect which the Black women's movement was to refine, and to more accurately describe Black woman and Black womanhood.

During the intense political climate of the 70s I was part of the school student movement. As a Black girl I found myself in one of the lowest bands within Dick Sheppard Secondary School London. Band five was where the majority of us were to be found. We were not expected to achieve any great heights academically. By the fourth year we had identified who was in the lowest band, and who was to be found in the top bands, and as such we forged links with each other, forming our own subgroups and isolating the few Black girls to be found in bands two, three, and four. In our groups, which also isolated the few white girls to be found in the lower bands, we shared and supported each other. Our lives were similar. Our parents worked for London Transport, the National Health Service, Fords and British Rail; they worked as nurses, cooks, ticket collectors, guards, and nursing auxiliaries doing shift hours. This meant that as girls we all had to take responsibilities for household chores: cooking, washing, looking after and collecting younger sisters and brothers. Some of us had more responsibilities than others. Some of us had a bad time with our newly reunited families. Some girls had discovered they had families they did not know: older sisters and brothers, or stepfathers they hated. We talked, and laughed, and cried together. We shared those experiences, usually while carrying out self-grooming activities: hair plaiting or cutting, or experimenting with makeup and dress. Through sharing in this way, our feelings of inadequacy and poor self-esteem were exposed, our weaknesses revealed, and our wounds healed. We acted as our own consciousness-raising groups. Black Power allowed us to set our experiences in a context which we could understand, and offered us the strategies to counteract and challenge the racism of our situations.

Academically, I tried very hard in school, only to be told, "Your spellings keep letting you down." Unfortunately for me, I arrived in England at a time when formal spellings and grammar teaching were out of vogue in teaching circles, and this, compounded by the break with my formal Jamaican schooling, resulted in my failure to learn the basis for correct spelling techniques. Teachers would, however, suggest that I read more newspapers and books. This encouragement alongside the influence of the Black consciousness motivated me to explore books. Reading soon became a favourite pastime, while writing remained a painful experience. During my adventures to the public libraries I stumbled across *The Master of Falconhurst, Mandingo,* and *Drum,* that whole series of slave novels. Racist, sexist, and totally eurocentric as they were, they unfolded for me the brutality and painful historical exploitation of slavery. These books made me angry, disgusted, and outraged. How could such barbaric acts be romanticized? Black people were still suffering here in Britain as well as throughout the world. It was during this same period that I also discovered Walter Rodney's *How Europe underdeveloped Africa* and *Africa's Gifts to Europe* by Basil Davidson. These two books redirected my outrage and offered me the substance which Kyle Onstoot could never hope to project in his slave dramas.

These books taught me about European mercantilism, colonialism, about how Europe destroyed a continent and civilizations, plundered wealths and riches, destroyed cities and kingdoms of Africa.

The ultimate injustice happened for me when for my Certificate of Secondary Education (CSE) English oral examination I chose to read a passage from *Africa's Gift to Europe.* The response of my English teacher was, "Yes, it's interesting to know that Africans had achieved all this greatness." I was appalled to discover that all this was common knowledge, yet nothing of this was ever taught or referred to during class activities or the school curriculum in general. Such deception, and the lack of any positive information throughout the school curriculum, propelled me to explore further African writings and literature eagerly. These helped to put the slave trade in context. They located European expansionism, colonialism, and what had happened in those countries when the specific European exploitation had transformed countries.

Through reading such books I was able to understand racism and why it was necessary, and how it functions, and why it needs to be constantly changing in order to be effective. The rise of Black militancy enabled me to translate what I was reading and what I was living into political action both inside and outside of the school.

As Black students we linked with other secondary schools and together we demanded to have a Black perspective introduced to the education we were getting. Such demands brought us into direct conflict with school authorities. At Dick Sheppard, a group of us demanded not only to have Black studies, but to identify the presence and contribution of Black people throughout history, and bring that into the school curriculum, and to be allowed to wear black socks and black tams, the military colours of the Black Panthers. The immediate response of our headmistress was, "Why should you be so angry? Why can't you live together as one happy family?"

The paternalism simply heightened our anger and outrage. We were fast realizing that what we were being denied was our selves, our past, and our future. Through our debating society we allied ourselves with the Black boys from Tulse Hill Comprehensive School London, and strengthened our demands for a curriculum which recognized our presence and acknowledged Black people's past. Tulse Hill boys did manage to gain major curriculum changes within their school. What became very clear to us during our campaigns was that the struggle within schools was making a natural link with events occurring in the outside world, such as the arrest in Brockwell Park of nine young Black school pupils from Tulse Hill, the police raid on the Mangrove restaurant in Notting Hill, London, another arrest and trial of 10 known Black political activists, and the general increased police brutality and harassment of Black people. The Black Panthers were tearing up North America and were being murdered by the U.S. police and assassins alike. Here in Britain, Black people were being politicized, and mobilized more and more. The general political climate of the 70s and my own political awareness propelled me to join and become active in a political organization.

The Black Panthers offered a political education and a practice in organizing, yet they also threw up some serious contradictions. The "brothers" would preach self-love and the beauty of African womanhood while abusing and relegating Black women to the "lesser political business" such as child care, the typing of minutes, and cooking.

Black consciousness enabled me to make the connection between class and racism, and offered the context within which to understand migration from the Caribbean in the numbers and at that particular historical time: why we acquire the worst housing, education and health care, why we are targeted for racial abuse and assaults. We learned that racism and economic exploitation are features of capitalism and necessary for the advancement of British capitalism. However, with political enlightenment came contradictions that became very antagonistic with women's demands for autonomous groups.

The "brothers" took it hard. They saw autonomy as a threat to male leadership and male egos. Gender oppression was reduced to sexuality, and lesbianism became a weapon to deter women from organizing independently.

My involvement in Black women's organizations consolidated further my class, race, and gender politics, and provided the interconnections for my individual situation with that of the oppression and exploitation of people generally, thus strengthening the belief that politics is about struggle, which can never stop because it's also about survival.

"Gal, you come from foreign," so aptly reflects my situation as a migrant to Britain. However, after 20 years outside of Jamaica, on return visits I am perceived very much as a "stranger outsider." To the daily experiences of the people I am indeed a stranger, but I bring with me an understanding which extends beyond my first 10 years of childhood in Heartease.

Dislocated Identities: Reflections of an Arab Jew

ELLA SHOHAT

Feminist film and cultural studies scholar Ella Shohat describes the complexity of diasporic identity. In particular she discusses the difficulties of being both Arab and Jewish in the context of political conflict in the Middle East.

I am an Arab Jew. Or more specifically, an Iraqi Israeli woman living in the United States. Most of my family was born and raised in Baghdad, and now lives in Israel, the United States, England, Holland, and Iraq. When my grandmother arrived in Israel in the early 50s she was convinced that the people she encountered who looked, spoke, and ate so differently, the European Jews, were actually European Christians. Jewish-

Ella Shohat, "Dislocated Identities: Reflections of an Arab Jew," *Emergences* 3/4, Fall 1992: 39–43; and *Movement Research: Performance Journal* 5, Fall/Winter 1992: 8.

ness for her generation was inextricably associated with Middle Easternness. My grandmother, who still lives in Israel and still communicates largely in Arabic, had to be taught to speak of "us" as Jews and "them" as Arabs. For Middle Easterners the operating distinction had always been "Moslem," "Jew," "Christian," not Arab versus Jew. The assumption was that "Arabness" referred to a common shared culture and language, albeit with differences.

Americans are often amazed to discover the existentially nauseating or charmingly exotic possibilities of such a syncretic identity. I recall a well-established colleague who despite my elaborate lessons on the history of Arab Jews still had trouble understanding that I was not a tragic anomaly, the daughter of an Arab (Palestinian) and an Israeli (European Jew). Living in North America makes it even more difficult to communicate that we are Jews and yet entitled to our Mid-

---

Key Terms

Ashkenazi Jews from eastern Europe.

Holocaust (1933–45) The persecution and murder of millions of Jews by the German Nazi government.

Maimonides (1135–1204) Jewish rabbi and philosopher.

mosque Muslim place of worship.

scud attack During the Gulf War in 1991, scud missiles were used extensively and caused civilian deaths.

Sephardi Jews descended from those who were expelled from Spain and Portugal in the fifteenth century or forced to convert during the Spanish Inquisition.

Spanish Inquisition Established in 1478 by Spanish monarchy to punish converted Jews and Muslims, characterized by torture and execution. It was not abolished until 1834.

synagogue Jewish place of worship.

Yiddish Hybrid language formed from Hebrew and German. Spoken originally by northern, central, and eastern European Jews, who carried it with them when they immigrated.

dle Eastern difference. It was precisely the policing of cultural borders in Israel that led some of us to escape into the metropolises of syncretic identities. Yet, in an American context, we face again a hegemony that allows us to narrate only a single Jewish memory: European. For those of us who don't hide our Middle Easternness under one Jewish "We," it becomes tougher and tougher to exist in an American context hostile to the very notion of Easternness.

As an Arab Jew, I am often obliged to explain the "mysteries" of this oxymoronic entity. That we spoke Arabic at home, not Yiddish; that for millennia our cultural creativity, secular and religious, had been largely articulated in Arabic (Maimonides being one of the few intellectuals to "make it" into the consciousness of the West); and that even the most religious of our communities in the Middle East and North Africa never expressed themselves in Yiddish-accented Hebrew prayers, nor did they practice liturgical-gestural norms and sartorial codes favoring the dark colors of centuries-ago Poland. Middle Eastern Jewish women similarly never wore wigs; their hair covers, if worn, consisted of different variations of regional clothing. (In the wake of British and French imperialism, many wore Western-style clothes.) If you go to our synagogues (even in New York), you'll be amazed to hear the winding quarter-tones of our music, which the uninitiated might imagine to be coming from a mosque.

Now that the three cultural topographies that compose my ruptured and dislocated history—the United States, Israel, and Iraq—have been involved in a war, it is crucial to say that we exist. Some of us refuse to dissolve so as to facilitate "neat" national and ethnic divisions. My anxiety and pain during a scud attack on Israel, where most of my family lives, does not cancel out my fear and anguish for the victims of the bombardment of Iraq, where I also have relatives.

But war is the friend of binarisms, leaving little place for complex identities. The Gulf War has intensified a pressure already familiar to the Arab Jewish diaspora in the wake of the Israeli–Arab conflict: a pressure to choose between being a Jew and being an Arab. For our families, who have lived in Mesopotamia since at least the Babylonian exile, who have been Arabized for millennia, and who abruptly found themselves in Israel 40 years ago, to be suddenly forced to

assume a homogeneous European Jewish identity based on experiences in Russia, Poland, and Germany was an exercise in self-devastation. To be a European or an American Jew has hardly been perceived as a contradiction, but to be an Arab Jew has been seen as a kind of logical paradox. This binarism has led many Oriental Jews (our name in Israel referring to our common Middle Eastern countries of origins) to a profound and visceral schizophrenia, since for the first time in our history Arabness and Jewishness were imposed as antonyms.

Intellectual discourse in the West highlights a Judeo-Christian tradition, yet rarely acknowledges the Judeo-Moslem culture of the Middle East, of North Africa, or in pre-Inquisition Spain and European parts of the Ottoman Empire. The Jewish experience in the Moslem world has often been portrayed as an unending nightmare of oppression and humiliation. Although I in no way want to idealize that experience—there were occasional tensions, discriminations, even violence—on the whole, we lived quite comfortably within Moslem societies. Despite George Bush's facile assimilation of Hussein to Hitler, for Jews in the Moslem world there was no equivalent to the Holocaust. In the case of the Inquisition (1492), both Jews and Moslems were the victims of Christian zealotry. Our history simply cannot be discussed in European-Jewish terminology. As Iraqi Jews, while retaining a communal identity, we were generally well-integrated and indigenous to the country, forming an inseparable part of its social and cultural life. Thoroughly Arabized, we used Arabic even in hymns and religious ceremonies. The liberal and secular trends of the twentieth century engendered an even stronger association of Iraqi Jews and Arab culture, which brought Jews into an extremely active role in public and cultural life. Prominent Jewish writers, poets, and scholars played a vital role in Arab culture, distinguishing themselves in Arabic-speaking theatre, in music, as singers, composers, and players of traditional instruments. In Egypt, Syria, Lebanon, Iraq, and Tunisia, Jews became members of legislatures, of municipal councils, of the judiciary, and even occupied high economic positions. (The Finance Minister of Iraq in the 40s was Ishak Sasson, and in Egypt, James Sanua—higher positions, ironically, than those our community has generally achieved within the Jewish state.)

The same historical process that dispossessed Palestinians of their property, lands, and national-political rights, was linked to the dispossession of Middle Eastern and North African Jews of their property, lands, and rootedness in Moslem countries. As refugees, or mass immigrants (depending on one's political perspective), we had to leave everything behind and give up our Iraqi passports. The same process also affected our uprootedness or ambiguous positioning within Israel itself. In Israel we have been systematically discriminated against by institutions which deployed their energies and material resources to the consistent advantage of European Jews and to the consistent disadvantage of Oriental Jews. Even our physiognomies betray us, leading to internalized colonialism or physical misperception. Sephardic Oriental women often dye their dark hair blond, while the men have more than once been arrested or beaten when mistaken for Palestinians. What for Ashkenazi immigrants from Russia and Poland was a social *aliya* (literally "ascent") was for Oriental Sephardic Jews a *yerida* (a "descent").

Stripped of our history, we have been forced by our no-exit situation to repress our collective nostalgia, at least within the public sphere. The pervasive notion of "one people" reunited in their ancient homeland actively dis-authorizes any affectionate memory of life before Israel. We have never been allowed to mourn a trauma which the recent images of destruction of Iraq have only intensified and crystallized for some of us. Our cultural creativity in Arabic, Hebrew, and Aramaic is hardly studied in Israeli schools, and it is becoming difficult to convince our children that we actually did exist there, and that some of us are still there (in Iraq, Morocco, and Yemen).

The notion of "in-gathering from exile" does not allow for a narrative of Jews feeling exiled even in the Promised Land. My parents and grandparents, 30 and 40 years after they left Baghdad, still long for its sights and sounds. Oriental Jews in Israel are enthusiastic consumers of Jordanian, Lebanese, and Egyptian television programs and films, just as our Oriental-Sephardi music is consumed in the Arab world often without being labeled as originating in Israel. (Ofra Haza, of Yemeni background, has been recognized by the Yemenites as continuing a Yemeni cultural tradition.) Back in the days before the horrific bombing of Baghdad, we used to play a bittersweet game of scanning the television to spot changes in the urban topography of Baghdad. But the impossibility of ever going there once led me to contemplate an ironic inversion of the Biblical expression: "By the waters of Zion, where we sat down, and there we wept, when we remembered Babylon."

Reading and watching media images from the Middle East, one is led to believe that there are only Euro-American Jews in Israel and only Moslem Arabs in the rest of the Middle East. In the media, one finds few images of Iraqi, Moroccan, or Ethiopian Israelis, even though we compose the majority of the Jewish population in Israel. Most Israelis interviewed by American reporters tend to be Euro-Israelis, often speaking English with an American accent. The elision was especially striking when the missiles hit Iraqi-Jewish neighborhoods in the south of Tel Aviv (television networks referred to the "working-class neighborhood," the equivalent of calling Harlem a working-class neighborhood, effacing its ethnic/racial cultural identity) and in Ramat Ghan, a city well known for its Iraqi population, popularly nicknamed "Ramat Baghdad." (A local joke had it that the scuds fell there because they smelled the *Amba,* an Iraqi mango pickle.) Furthermore, some Iraqi Jews living in New York, London, and Israel still have relatives in Iraq and even in the Iraqi army. The media showed images of prayers in the mosques, and even in the churches of Baghdad, but there was no reference to prayers in the synagogue of Baghdad.

As an Iraqi Jew I cannot but notice the American media's refusal to value Iraqi life. The crippled animals in the Kuwait Zoo received more sympathetic attention than civilian victims in Iraq. (The *New York Times* recent headline: "War Takes a Devastating Toll at the Kuwait Zoo.") The media much prefer the spectacle of the triumphant progress of Western technology to the peoples and cultures of the Middle East. The case of Arab Jews is just one of many elisions. There is little sense of our community, and even less sense of the diversity of our political perspectives. Oriental-Sephardic peace movements in Israel, the Black Panthers of the 70s and more recently East for Peace and the Oriental Front, and in *Paris Perspectives Judeo-Arabes,* for example, call not only for a just peace for Israelis and Palestinians but also for the cultural, political, and economic integration of Israel into the Middle East. And thus an end to the binarisms of war.

"Arab Noise and Ramadan Nights: Rai, Rap, and Franco-Maghrebi Identity"

JOAN GROSS, DAVID MCMURRAY, AND TED SWEDENBURG

Three anthropologists explore the history and culture of rai, *a popular music form that traveled from Algeria to France and then into the "world music" market. In this excerpt, they discuss the gendered aspects of* rai *in diasporic communities in France to analyze the importance of cultural expressions such as music in the formation of identity.*

In the aftermath of the Berlin Wall's collapse, Western Europe has been forced to rethink its identity. If in the recent past its conception of itself as a haven of democracy and civilization depended—in part—on a contrast to the evils of the Communist Empire, today an idea is being revived of Europe as "Christendom," in contradistinction to "Islam." Only this time, the Islam in

Joan Gross, David McMurray, and Ted Swedenburg, "Arab Noise and Ramadan Nights: Rai, Rap, and Franco-Maghrebi Identity," *Diaspora* 3:1 (Spring 1994): 3–7, 9–11, 17–20, 27–28.

question is not being held back at the frontier (Spain, the Balkans) but has penetrated Europe's very core in the shape of new "minority" populations of Muslim background. Questions about the nature of European identity and the place of Muslim immigrants within it are now among the most contentious on the Continent (Morley and Robins). So acute is European anxiety about "foreigners" that many white Western Europeans increasingly feel that they are living under cultural and economic siege due to the presence of 10 to 12 million "immigrants" (Miller 33).

[. . .]

So severe are French apprehensions about the *immigré* "problem" that during the "*hijab* affair" of 1989, when nine female Franco-Maghrebi students demanded the right to wear Islamic headscarves in the state-run lycées, the media were able to merge together the signifiers "immigrant," "Muslim fundamentalist," and "invasion" into a horrifying specter of an Islamic

Key Terms

banlieu Suburbs outside of French cities.
Berber People of North Africa; language spoken in Algeria and Morocco.
Beur Second-generation North African immigrants in France.
chorba North African lamb stew.
hijab Head covering.
Kabyle Of the Kabylia regions in northern Algeria.

lycées Schools.
Maghrebi A person from the Maghreb region of North Africa.
Provencal From the Provence region of France.
syncretism Combination of different forms of belief or practice.
tajine North African dish.

France, a vision that alarmed a good portion of the French population, left and right (Koulberg).[1]

[. . .]

"Noise and smell"—music and cuisine—are crucial cultural forms of expression, essential vehicles through which North Africans assert, sustain, and re-configure their identities in France. And probably the most well-known type of "Arab noise" heard in the Franco-Maghrebi community is *rai* music, a genre which began to reach audiences in the United States via world music programs in the late 1980s.

[. . .]

Algerian Rai: From Country to Pop

Rai developed during the 1920s, as rural migrants in-corporated their native musical styles into the culture of the growing urban centers of western Algeria, particu-larly the port town of Oran.[2] It was a hybrid blend of ru-ral and cabaret musical genres, invented by and for distillery workers, peasants who had lost their land to European settlers, shepherds, prostitutes, and other members of the poorer classes (Virolle-Souibés, "Le raï entre résistances" 51–52). The permissive atmosphere of Oran proved a congenial one for rai artists, who were able to perform in its extensive network of nightclubs, taverns, and brothels, as well as in more "respectable" settings like wedding celebrations and festivals. Oran's geographic position and its port economy opened it to many cultural influences, affording rai musicians the opportunity to absorb an array of musical styles: fla-menco from Spain and *gnawa* (a popular musical genre performed by Sufi musicians) from nearby Morocco, French cabaret, the music of the Berbers of the region of Kabylia, the rhythms of Arab nomads, and more. Rai artists sang in Orani (*wahrani*), an Arabic dialect rich in French and Spanish borrowings.

[. . .]

As early as the 1930s, rai musicians were reportedly singing about social issues afflicting Arabs of the colony, such as typhus, imprisonment, and poverty, and they were harassed by the colonial police for do-ing so. Likewise, during the independence struggle, rai artists participated in the nationalist glorification of Algeria (Virolle-Souibés, "Ce que chanter"). But the main subjects of rai singers were wine, love, and the problems and pleasures of marginal life, expressions of a rather libertine sensibility. Women singers played a prominent role in rai from the beginning. In addition, unlike those of other Algerian musical genres, rai per-formances were associated with dancing, often in mixed-gender settings (Benkheira 174).

After Algeria won its national independence in 1962, a state-sponsored Islamic reformist chill de-scended over all manifestations of popular culture. In the wake of this official puritanism, drastic restrictions were imposed on public performances by women singers (Virolle-Souibés, "Le raï entre résistances" 54). But the genre was kept alive in the margins, flour-ishing in respectable sex-segregated events like wed-ding parties and in the "disrespectable" demimonde. Young men began to sing rai after women were virtu-ally banned from singing in public.

[. . .]

In 1979, rai began to emerge from the shadows, as the new president, Chadhli Benjedid, loosened moral and economic restraints. In the meantime rai artists had incorporated many more musical influences from Egypt, the Americas, and Europe and had begun per-forming and recording to the backing of trumpets and electric guitars, synthesizers and drum machines. This new sound marked the inauguration of "pop rai," sung by a new generation of singers, the *chabs* (young men) and *chabas* (young women).[3] Cassette sales prolifer-ated, extending rai's audience. Rai, in its pop incarna-tion, now shed its regional limitations. By the early 80s it had become a *national* music for Algerian youth. Its popularity depended not only on its updated sounds but on its reputation as a racy music whose singers treated subjects like sex and alcohol frankly and chal-lenged official puritanism and patriarchal authority within the family. The modernity of rai's musical tex-ture and its social messages won over a new generation of disaffected, often unemployed, youth, who were chafing at traditional social constraints.

[. . .]

Ramadan Nights in the Franco-Maghrebi Diaspora

At the same time that "pop" rai was winning over the youth of Algeria in the early 80s, it was gaining audiences among Maghrebi immigrants in France and their offspring—the Beurs, as the second generation had come to be known. Rai became an important means of cultural expression for a minority struggling to carve out an ethnic identity and a space for itself in an inhospitable, racist environment. It was played widely on the local radio stations that sprang up to serve North African communities throughout France in the early 80s, Radio Beur in Paris being the most prominent among them.

[. . .]

Rai gained greater public visibility during an upsurge of Franco-Arab struggles against racism and as part of the burgeoning Parisian world music scene.[4] SOS-Racisme, a multiethnic, antiracist organization established in 1985 to counter escalating anti-Arab violence and channel the militancy of young Franco-Maghrebis, regularly featured rai at the multicultural concerts it sponsored. Rai also began winning over a white audience sympathetic to the antiracist struggle. Prominent Algerian rai performers started touring in France, while Franco-Maghrebis formed their own local rai groups. From the mid- to late 80s, rai's star was rising in both Algeria and France. By 1990, when Islamist campaigns against rai caused several of its stars (Chab Khaled, Chab Mami, Chaba Fadela, and Chab Sahraoui) to relocate from Algeria to France, Paris became a major rai center, and rai artists began to win an international audience through world music circuits.

[. . .]

—Visions of Gendered Rai

Analysis of rai's significance within the North African diaspora reveals much, not only about the changing valence of religion and tradition in Franco-Maghrebi identity construction, but also of gender, as the following examples illustrate.

Women sat on low cushions along the three walls at one end of the rented room in the banlieue of Avignon. The older women all wore long, empire-waisted, shiny, polyester, Algerian dresses, as did some younger women. Interspersed were young women in slacks and miniskirts, including one in a black strapless minidress. Chairs lined the other side of the room for those who preferred not to sit on the floor. Some

women had flown in from Algeria for the wedding. Others had traveled north from Marseille or south from St. Etienne. Of about 60 women, only five were not of North African origin.

Various rai tapes provided the soundtrack for the festivities. No one seemed to know who was singing or what they were saying. The women said that if I wanted to find an artist's name or the song playing, I should go look at the cassettes, so I walked over to the stereo and picked up a bag loaded with coverless tapes.[5] They looked to be second-generation, dubbed at home. Many contained only minimal or no information.[6] Several Chab Khaled tapes at least were visible. When Khaled's "Didi" came on, many younger women jumped up to dance. The place was hopping until we were all stopped short by a power outage.

The blackout led some women to open the windows onto the courtyard, where the men were gathered. A rai musician named Chab Kader[7] began singing, accompanied by a keyboard synthesizer player. Inside, the dancing started again in earnest: a shimmering crowd of sequins and beads, provencal skirts, satin and linen, bare shoulders and legs. Many older women wore gold marriage belts. The younger ones sported new-wave geometric earrings and miniature colored-plastic pacifiers (the new teenage fashion craze throughout Europe). I was familiar with the dance steps from the time I had spent in northeastern Morocco, but occasionally someone threw in disco steps. Some of the younger girls seemed to be imitating cabaret belly dancers.

After midnight, over bowls of *chorba* and *tajine,* I asked some very chicly dressed lycée girls if they liked the music that was playing. "Not very much," they responded. What did they listen to? "Funk"—African-American. But they supposed that when it was their turn they would have weddings like this one. I tried to imagine James Brown on the tape recorder in such a setting. . . .

Rai seemed to be passé for the under-20 set at the wedding. However, for the 23-year-old bride and her friends, it signified a still strong attachment to Algerian roots. For the older women, rai was merely familiar Arabic music, perhaps not what they would choose, but it got people on the dance floor.

Weddings remain a major site for rai's performance and consumption. Local Beur radio stations in the major cities also allow regular access to rai, played in astonishing mixes of African-American funk, rap, Berber Kabyle music, and sundry world music offerings. Another important space where rai is consumed is in the home in front of the VCR. A number of these videotapes feature chabs (male rai singers) in concert footage, at festivals in Oran or on European tour. Others show chabas and cheikhas not in concert but in staged settings, like the television studio "wedding" performance in which Cheikha Rimitti appears with Cheikha Rabia.[8] Such women's tapes often feature female dancers in "traditional" dress, who perform while the chaba or cheikha sings.

More interesting from the point of view of gender are the new narrative videos, in which the ideal of romantic love is represented visually as well as lyrically. In Anouar's successful video *La Ballade d'Anouar,* teenage dating and the angst of separation from one's lover are acted out. The videos of the famous married couple of rai, Chaba Fadela and Chab Sahraoui, depict the pair involved in exclusive romantic relationships in typically western settings. Such narrative rai videos reject the dominant role parents play in choosing partners for their children, the brother's policing of his sister's movements, and the girl's duties as a servant in the home—the family power relations defining the lives of so many Maghrebi and immigrant girls.

For the outsider, it is hard to understand the liberating, even revolutionary potential that romantic love has in North African and many Franco-Maghrebi families. Young Franco-Maghrebi women who seem completely at ease in French society say they would face tremendous trouble at home if they were spotted sitting with a man in a café. Marrying a non-Muslim would automatically cause a radical break with their families.

Franco-Maghrebi women are still expected to stay primarily in the private realm, according to stereotypical traditional values, while men must live in the public eye. Such codes are even reflected on the covers of rai music cassettes. For instance, a photograph of the chab almost invariably adorns his cassette. Tapes by the chabas, by contrast, frequently portray Algerian scenery or pictures of other women who are more conventionally beautiful than the actual singers of the music inside the package. Rumors circulate about this absence. The very popular, throaty-voiced Chaba

Zahouania, unmarried, was said to be forbidden by her family to appear or give concerts in public. She recorded, one heard, only in studios. Imagination takes flight. What resemblance does Zahouania bear to the exquisitely beautiful, chiffon-draped belly dancer on the cover of her United States release, suggestively titled *Nights without Sleeping* (Island 1990, catalog number ZCM 9831)? New rumor: She does not appear in public because she's a divorcée with four children and does not want her ex-husband's family to argue, on the basis of her public performances, that she is an unfit mother and win custody of the children. Later we find a Chaba Zahouania videotape on the market. She looks to be around 40; she wears modest Western-style clothing and thick, clunky glasses. She performs in front of a television studio set. Is this also a transgression?

Chaba Aicha, who identified herself as the only young unmarried woman to sing rai publicly today, told us that rai is the music of women who have lots of experience in life. Women without husbands have traditionally sung rai to support their children. With her close-cropped hairdo and total rejection of "feminine" clothing, Aicha is one of a kind among chabas. Like Zahouania, she did not want her face to be used on the cover of her cassette, but the recording company insisted.[9] Chaba Fadela also appears on her own cassettes, modestly dressed and accompanied by her husband.

So cheikhas and chabas usually achieve success by entertaining and singing publicly at weddings and festivals, yet often their faces are not used to sell their own music. Sometimes even beautiful young blonds resembling tanned California surfer girls adorn their tapes marketed in France. While Euro-American listeners tend to see this practice as a trick, many Maghrebis see it as a simple means of decoration, not meant to indicate authorship.

In contrast to the photographic modesty of the chabas, Saliha, the Franco-Maghrebi *rappeuse,* poses defiantly on the cover of her cassette, *Unique,* dressed in a black, form-fitting minidress, hands encased in black leather half-gloves.

[. . .]

Rai is one possible line of flight taken by Franco-Maghrebis, a cultural border zone of syncretism and creative interminglings of French and Arab. . . . At once "ethnic" and French, rai is one front in a wider

cultural struggle that—despite racist opposition—is recasting French national identity.

NOTES

1. Koulberg (34) shows that, amid the media onslaught, it was ignored that 48% of French Muslims actually opposed wearing the *hijab*.

2. *Oran* is Wahran in Arabic.

3. These are alternately spelled *cheb* and *cheba*.

4. The lead article by Jean-François Bizot in *Actuel* 92 is an interesting rundown of the world beat scene in Paris at that early date.

5. The "I" in this section is Gross since McMurray and Swedenburg didn't attend this event.

6. The women's total lack of interest in labels and authorship is reminiscent of the same attitude among the label-destroying sound-system disc jockeys of Britain's black music underground of the

early 70s. The disc jockeys thought that "the record could be enjoyed without knowing who it was by or where it was in a chart. Its origins were rendered secondary to the use made of it in the creative rituals of the dance-hall" (Gilroy 167).

7. Not the Chab Kader one hears on U.S. rai releases (*From Oran to Paris*, Shanachie [1990, 64029]) but a local musician who goes by the same name.

8. Older singers are referred to as *cheikh* (male) and *cheikha* (female).

9. Chaba Aicha's first album, *Maman Cherie*, is a 1991 release of Contact Music in Marseilles (CM 790).

REFERENCES

Benkheira, Mohamed Hocine. (1986). "De la musique avant toute chose: Remarques sur le raï." *Peuples méditerranéens* 35–36, 173–77.

Bizot, Jean-François. (1987). "Ces musiciens grandissent la France." *Actuel* June, 145–55.

____. "Sex and Soul in the Maghreb." *The Face* 98 (1988): 86–93.

Gilroy, Paul. (1987). *"There Ain't No Black in the Union Jack": The Cultural Politics of "Race" and Nation*. London: Unwin Hyman.

Koulberg, André. (1991). *L'Affaire du voile islamique: Comment perdre une bataille symbolique*. Marseille: Fenêtre Sur Cour.

Miller, Judith. (1991). "Strangers at the Gate." *New York Times Magazine* 15 Sept., 33–37, 49, 80–81.

Morley, David, and Kevin Robins. (1990). "No Place like *Heimat*: Images of Home(land) in European Culture." *New Formations* 12, 1–21.

Virolle-Souibés, Marie. (1988). "Ce que chanter erray veut dire: Prelude à d'autres couplets." *Cahiers de littérature orale* 23, 177–208.

____. (1989). "Le raï entre résistances et récupération." *Revue d' Études du monde musulman et méditerranéen* 51, 47–62.

REFLECTING ON THE SECTION

Stuart Hall describes diasporic people as those who, through migration, "have succeeded in remaking themselves and fashioning new kinds of cultural identity by, consciously or unconsciously, drawing on more than one cultural repertoire." What produces diasporic communities? How do cultural, racial, and national identities become transformed in diaspora? How does the concept of diaspora complement and/or challenge the American concept of the "melting pot"?

In Section 2, Potts and Elmadmad discussed the feminization of forced relocations and displacements.

Examining the narratives by Williams and Shohat in relation to Gross, McMurray, and Swedenburg's study, consider how gender relations and women's gender identities are transformed in diasporic communities. How does a discussion of gender further extend the description of the complexity of diasporic identities in Shohat's excerpt? Are you reminded of other examples of popular music linked to diasporas from the discussion of rai? How is *diaspora* an important term for transnational women's studies?

Women, Work, and Immigration

Women and Labor Migration
EVELYN NAKANO GLENN

Sociologist Evelyn Nakano Glenn argues that if we look at the migration of women as a distinct set of experiences, a different model of immigration will result. In addition, she points out that a two-tiered labor system has divided migrant workers by race so that the experience of European ethnic groups has been different from that of non-European groups.

Starting in the middle of the nineteenth century, millions of women left their homelands in Europe, Latin America, and Asia to work in the United States. Later in the century black women began migrating from the rural South to seek livelihoods in the cities of the North and South. These women were an integral, yet often unnoticed, part of a migrant stream responding to the call for cheap and willing labor in various parts of the country. They migrated initially to find work but over time became settlers, establishing families and building communities in their new surroundings.

Women came alone or, more often, as part of families, as wives and daughters. Whether single or married, they found their lot difficult. Recruited as "cheap hands," migrant fathers and husbands rarely earned a family wage. Moreover, many migrant families had destitute kin at home to support. In this context, women's labor was essential for survival. Most of these women were accustomed to toiling in the household, and they continued to do so in the new setting, manufacturing many essential goods consumed by the family, nurturing children, and carrying out a myriad of domestic chores.

Evelyn Nakano Glenn, "Women and Labor Migration," *Issei, Nisei, War Bride: Three Generations of Japanese-American Women in Domestic Service,* Philadelphia: Temple University Press, 1986: 3–5, 8–12.

As keepers of the home and socializers of children, they struggled to maintain their cultural traditions, often under harsh conditions. Additionally, many migrant women were forced into a new form of labor—wage work outside the home. In a period when the ideal for middle-class married women was to remain at home cultivating domestic virtues, migrant wives had to leave their homes to seek wage employment. Long before employment became a major issue for native white women, migrant women faced the double day.

What kinds of jobs did they find? Their options were limited. Handicapped by language, lacking industrial skills, and burdened by heavy household responsibilities, they also faced a race- and gender-stratified labor market that confined them to the lowest-paid and most degraded jobs. The particular forms of low-wage employment open to them varied according to time and place, ranging from agricultural field labor to operative jobs in manufacturing. Yet one field of employment epitomized the migrant woman's experience—domestic service. From the mid-nineteenth century until the advent of World War II, domestic service was the most common employment for migrant women and their daughters. Live-in servants, laundresses, and day workers accounted for half of all nonagriculturally employed foreign-born females[1] and over 80 percent of black women during this period.[2] The long hours, heavy work, lack of freedom, and, worst of all, low status made such employment distasteful to native women, while the incessant demand for household help and the absence of specific job qualifications made it easily accessible to newcomers.[3] Even today, domestic service remains one of the largest fields of initial employment for recent migrants.[4]

Servitude in domestic employment was an experience common to the immigrant generation of many ethnic groups, European and non-European alike. The legacy for subsequent cohorts differed, however, for voluntary immigrant groups (primarily European in origin) and labor migrant groups (primarily non-European people of color).

For European ethnics, who were not strictly set apart from natives or barred from movement on purely racial grounds, the pioneer generation's sweat was an investment that benefited subsequent generations. Daughters of European immigrants moved up and were absorbed into the more advanced sectors of the labor force. High school education, often financed in part by the mother's employment, enabled many an American-born daughter of European stock to take advantage of expanding opportunities for white-collar employment.[5] As men in these groups moved into the crafts or other secure jobs in primary industries, wives began to emulate the middle-class ideal of womanhood by leaving the labor force after marriage or motherhood. In short, domestic service was a temporary way station for European immigrant groups, a job that bridged the transition from the old country to the new.

The experience of racially distinct migrant groups differed. Recruited to fill temporary labor needs, they were denied basic political and legal rights and were hemmed in by almost impermeable "color" barriers to mobility. People of color were routinely barred from the skilled crafts, sales, clerical work, and even the "light" manufacturing jobs that were the steps up for sons and daughters of European immigrants. Domestic service and its close relative, laundry work, were often the only options outside of agriculture for black women in the North, Chicanas in the Southwest, and Japanese American women in Northern California, regardless of education or generation.[6] Settlement in the United States for these groups meant not assimilation, but transition to the status of a racial-ethnic minority. Women in these groups had to work outside the home even after marriage and motherhood, and they continued to be restricted to the same menial occupations as the immigrant generation.

For racial-ethnic women, then, employment in domestic service became a long-term proposition, not a temporary expedient. Their concentration in domestic service in turn reinforced their degraded status in society. They came to be seen as particularly suited for, and

only suited for, degraded work. Racial-ethnic status and occupational position became more or less synonymous badges of inferiority. The black cleaning woman, the Mexican maid, the Japanese housecleaner, became stereotyped images that helped to rationalize and justify their subordination.

The universality of domestic service among migrant women and its divergent consequences for later cohorts make it a pivotal occupation for understanding the role of women's work in ethnic migration, settlement, and adaptation. The study of individual and group involvement in domestic work can shed light on the way migrant and ethnic women are incorporated into the urban economy, the effects of employment on particular sectors of women, their families, and communities, and the factors that determine mobility.

[. . .]

Processes of Labor Migration and Settlement

The experiences of Japanese American women are a microcosm of a worldwide phenomenon—the movement of people from less developed regions to fill labor demands in more advanced economic centers. This phenomenon has been widely discussed recently as a result of the large-scale influx of foreign workers into the advanced industrial countries of the west.[7] By the mid-1970s foreign workers from Africa, the Middle East, and Southern Europe constituted about 10 percent of the workforce in Western Europe.[8] The exact size of the foreign labor force in the United States is unknown because of the large number of undocumented workers from Latin America and the Caribbean region.[9] Estimates in the mid-1970s ranged from 2 million to 12 million. The size and scope of modern labor migration has led some economists to conclude that migrant labor is essential to development of advanced capitalist economies.[10]

Though seen as primarily a post-World War II phenomenon linked to the drive for capital accumulation in postindustrial societies, labor migration from less advanced regions has been a critical element in the development of American capitalism since at least the mid-nineteenth century. The source of immigrants, the regions to which they are drawn, and the

sectors of the economy into which they have been recruited have changed to meet the shifting demands of
capitalist development. In the mid-nineteenth century, when the infrastructure of the American Far
West was being built, hundreds of thousands of Latin
American and Asian men were recruited to that region for "dirty" manual work. During World War I,
black men and women from the rural South were
drawn to the industrial North to fill the need for manual and service labor, and Mexican nationals were recruited to perform seasonal agricultural work in the
Southwest. In the 1970s and 1980s, female migrants
were being recruited from the Caribbean region and
Latin America to fill low-wage service and manufacturing jobs in the urban Northeast.[11]

Despite differences in time and place, observers
have noted striking continuities in the process of labor
migration and settlement.[12] First, labor migrants are
drawn from "backward" areas whose economies have
been disrupted and subsequent development distorted
by western colonial incursions. The distortion of the
economy leaves large segments of the population with
their usual means of livelihood interrupted. Many are
thus free to be torn from their roots and recruited to fill
labor needs in the advanced regions, often the source
of the original incursion. Second, migrants are recruited by receiving countries strictly to fill labor
needs, not to become permanent members of the society. Thus, policies are designed to prevent long-term
settlement. This intention is matched by the orientation
of the migrants, who see themselves as sojourners,
working abroad temporarily for economic reasons.
Third, migrants serve as a reserve army of flexible and
cheap labor. The jobs they fill are those shunned by native workers because they are insecure, seasonal, arduous, low-paying, or degraded. Typically, legal and
administrative barriers are devised to ensure that migrants remain in these jobs and do not compete with
native workers. Thus, at least in the initial stages of migration and entry into the labor market, the needs and
intentions of the dominant society and the orientations
and expectations of the migrants are complementary:
both see the migrant primarily as a laborer, temporarily residing abroad and willing to take whatever job is
available in order to earn enough to return "home" as
quickly as possible.

An underlying contradiction soon becomes apparent, however. Because they are relegated to insecure,
low-wage employment, migrants often find it difficult
to amass sufficient capital to go back with a stake.
Many thus stay longer than they intended. Willy-nilly
they begin to develop a sense of community. Separated
from kin, they congregate with compatriots for living
accommodations, job referrals, and sociability. Those
with a little capital open stores and restaurants catering
to ethnic tastes. In an effort at self-help and comfort,
they build institutions such as credit associations and
churches. Finally, as their stay stretches into an unde-
fined future, they may begin marrying or sending for
spouses. The rise of a second generation whose formative years are spent in the host society solidifies the
transition from sojourner to settler.[13]

During the transition the migrant's orientation toward employment undergoes change. As jobs begin to
be seen as long-term occupations, degrading work becomes more distasteful and insecurity less tolerable.
Thus occurs the often-observed rise in aspirations—
the desire for a better job, a piece of land, a business of
one's own. These changed aspirations clash with the
ostensible reasons for the migrant's recruitment in the
first place. It is at this point that hostility to migrants
often erupts. In confronting attempts of migrant labor
to move up, the interests of capital, independent producers (small farmers, entrepreneurs, and craftspeo-
ple), and native labor coincide. Capitalists in the
competitive sector want migrants only as long as they
remain highly exploitable; independent producers and
native workers want to forestall competition for jobs,
land, and markets. Antimigrant movements and exclusion drives thus find wide support. Measures to keep
migrants and their children in their "proper place"
range from mob violence to closed apprenticeship programs to legislation aimed at prohibiting entry.[14]

All immigrant groups in the United States have encountered some degree of hostility and discrimination,
but people of color have confronted more absolute and
systematic restrictions. Non-European immigrants
were concentrated in industrially backward regions of
the United States—the South, Southwest, and West—
where they were slotted into pre-industrial niches,
such as agriculture, mining, and domestic service.[15] It
was difficult to move from these niches into the indus-

trialized sector. Moreover, wherever Asian, latino, and black migrant labor was used, a two-tiered, or colonial, labor system operated. The system was based on the superiority of white laborers, who monopolized the more skilled, secure, clean, and supervisory jobs and who were paid on a separate and higher wage scale.[16]

The development of a two-tiered labor system requires that groups be initially distinguishable, ethnically or in other ways. Such a system can be more easily maintained beyond the immigrant generation when groups are racially, as well as ethnically, identifiable. Because of racial distinctiveness, later cohorts of nonwhite immigrant groups had different labor market experiences from later cohorts of white immigrant groups. Whereas the children and grandchildren of European immigrants became dispersed throughout the occupational hierarchy, latinos, blacks, and Asian Americans tended to remain at the bottom of the ladder even after several generations in the United States.

Given the barriers to mobility, how are migrants of color to escape dead-end jobs? Self-employment is the main possibility. Rather than remain wage workers, some migrants turn to entrepreneurial activity in farm-ing, retail trade, services, or small-scale manufacturing. The Chinese and Koreans have been notable for their concentration in small businesses, as have Cubans in Miami.[17] To the extent that it relies primarily on family labor, ethnic enterprise is a throwback to precapitalist modes of production in which the household was the unit of production. The smallest of these enterprises employ only immediate family members and are profitable only because all members, women and children included, work long hours without pay. Self-exploitation is substituted for exploitation through wage labor.[18] Larger ethnic enterprises are part of the competitive sector in that they may employ considerable outside labor—typically recent immigrants willing to work for low wages just to get a start. In this case the ethnic entrepreneur is a middleman who provides low-cost goods and services by exploiting his or her compatriots. The exploitation is mitigated by the opportunities for mobility that exist in ethnic enterprise in contrast to the rest of the competitive sector.[19] The experience gained, as well as sponsorship by the employer, often enables the workers to start their own businesses.

NOTES

1. Amey Watson, "Domestic Service," *Encyclopedia of the Social Sciences* (New York: Macmillan, 1937), 5:198–207.

2. U.S. Bureau of the Census, *Negro Population, 1790–1915* (Washington, D.C.: U.S. Government Printing Office, 1918), table 20.

3. David M. Katzman, *Seven Days a Week: Women and Domestic Service in Industrializing America* (New York: Oxford University Press, 1978).

4. Charles B. Keely, "Effects of the Manpower Provision of the U.S. Immigration Law," paper presented at the Population Association of America Annual Meeting, 1974.

5. George J. Stigler, "Domestic Servants in the United States, 1900–1940," Occasional Paper 24 (New York: National Bureau of Economic Research, 1946).

6. Segregated job markets for blacks and Chicanos are discussed in chap. 9, "The Job Ceiling," in St. Clair Drake and Horace R. Cayton, *Black Metropolis: A Study of Negro Life in a Northern City* (New York: Harcourt Brace, 1945); and Mario Barrera, *Race and Class in the Southwest* (Notre Dame, Ind.: University of Notre Dame Press, 1979). For a discussion of parallels in the employment patterns of black, Chicana, and Chinese American women, see Evelyn Nakano Glenn, "Racial Ethnic Women and Work: Towards an Analysis of Race and Gender Stratification," in Liesa Stamm and Carol D. Ryff (eds.), *Social Power and Dominance in Women* (Boulder, Colo.: Westview Press, 1984), pp. 117–50.

7. Discussions of immigrant labor in Europe are found in Ronald E. Krane (ed.), *International Labor Migration in Europe* (New York: Praeger, 1979), and Stephen Castles and Godula Kosack, *Immigrant Workers and Class Structure in Western Europe* (London: Oxford University Press, 1973).

8. Michael J. Piore, *Birds of Passage: Migrant Labor and Industrial Societies* (Cambridge: Cambridge University Press, 1979).

9. David S. North and Marion Houstoun, *The Characteristics and Roles of Illegal Aliens in the U.S. Labor Market: An Exploratory Study* (Washington, D.C.: Linton, 1976), p. 27.

10. Piore, *Birds of Passage.*

11. Latin American and Caribbean women and labor migration are discussed in Delores M. Mortimer and Roy S. Bryce-Laport (eds.), *Female Immigrants to the United States: Caribbean, Latin American and African Experiences,* Occasional Papers, no. 2, Research Institute on Immigration and Ethnic Studies (Washington, D.C.: Smithsonian Institution, 1981).

12. See Introduction, in Lucie Cheng and Edna Bonacich, *Labor Immigration under Advanced Capitalism: Asian Immigrant Workers in the United States before World War II* (Berkeley: University of California Press, 1984), and Piore, *Birds of Passage.* The following description applies to labor migrants, who in the United States have tended to be people of color; the process was different for voluntary white European immigrants.

13. Piore, *Birds of Passage,* pp. 65–67, notes a major difference in orientation between immigrants who spent their formative years in the sending society and those who spent those years in the host society. S. Frank Miyamoto, in "An Immigrant Community in North America," in Hilary Conroy and T. Scott Miyakawa (eds.), *East across the Pacific* (Santa Barbara, Calif.: ABC Clio Books, 1972), says that the rise of an American-born and -educated generation was a major turning point for the issei, who subsequently began to view their stay as long term or permanent.

14. Making a slightly different point, Edna Bonacich talks about exclusion movements resulting from the conflict between "high-priced" (in this case native) labor and "low-priced" (in this case migrant) labor in her classic article, "A Theory of Ethnic Antagonism: The Split Labor Market," *American Sociological Review* 37 (1972): 547–59.

15. Robert Blauner, *Racial Oppression in America* (New York: Harper & Row, 1972, pp. 51–82), argues that this feature is one of several differentiating the experience of people of color ("colonized minorities") from that of European immigrants ("immigrant minorities").

16. Characteristics of a colonial labor system are discussed by Barrera, *Race and Class in the Southwest,* pp. 34–57.

17. Light, *Ethnic Enterprise in America,* discusses the Japanese and Chinese propensity for small business. Edna Bonacich, Ivan Light, and Charles Choy Wong, "Small Businesses among Koreans in Los Angeles," in Emma Gee (ed.), *Counterpoint* (Los Angeles: Asian American Studies Center, University of California, Los Angeles, 1976), pp. 436–49, and Kenneth Wilson and Alejandro Portes, "Immigrant Enclaves: An Analysis of the Labor Market Experiences of Cubans in Miami," *American Journal of Sociology* 86 (1980): 295–319, discuss ethnic enterprise among Koreans and Cubans respectively.

18. Edna Bonacich, "United States Capitalism and Korean Small Business," paper presented at the Conference on New Directions in the Labor Process, Binghamton, New York, 1978.

19. Wilson and Portes, "Immigrant Enclaves."

A Maid by Any Other Name: The Transformation of "Dirty Work" by Central American Immigrants

LESLIE SALZINGER

Sociologist Leslie Salzinger studies immigrant women who do domestic work in the United States. She argues that diversity among these workers' experiences can be explained by the loss of manufacturing jobs and the increasing need for service workers. Domestic service jobs, Salzinger says, are needed not only by the wealthy but also by the elderly and by working parents. These demands create new incentives as well as new problems for working women.

I spent the fall of 1988 observing and sometimes participating in the meetings, gossip, English classes, and job-reception work of two immigrant Latina domestic worker cooperatives in the Bay Area. As the months passed, a few questions began to surface with increasing frequency. Many of these women had been in the

Leslie Salzinger, "A Maid by Any Other Name: The Transformation of 'Dirty Work' by Central American Immigrants," in Michael Burawoy et al., *Ethnography Unbound: Power and Resistance in the Modern Metropolis,* Berkeley: University of California Press, 1991: 139–41, 150–52.

United States for close to a decade. Why were they doing domestic work after so many years here? Domestic work is a paradigmatic case of immigrant "dirty" work—of work that is irredeemably demeaning.[1] Why did some of these women speak with such pride of their work? And even more puzzling, what accounted for the dramatically different attitudes members of the two groups held toward their work? As my attention was drawn to these anomalies, I realized that many of the explanations were to be found not within the cooperatives that had generated them, but in the market for domestic work. In this chapter I look at the occupational strategies of these women and locate them in the structural context within which they were formed. I argue that the human capital resources they brought—or failed to bring—with them account for little of their work experience in this country. Rather, it is within the context of the constraints and opportunities they encountered here that we can understand their occupational decisions, their attitudes toward their work, and ultimately their divergent abilities to transform the work itself.

Key Term

Fair Labor Standards Act In the United States, the Fair Labor Standards Act of 1938 provides minimum standards for both wages and overtime entitlement and includes provisions related to child labor and equal pay.

⟶ Why Domestic Work?

Although many immigration theorists emphasize the role of culture or human capital in explaining occupation,[2] such arguments provide us with little help in accounting for the occupational strategies of many of the women in Choices and Amigos. Teachers, cashiers, peasants, laundresses, housewives, recent immigrants, long-time residents, persecuted organizers, jobless mothers, documented recipients of political asylum, undocumented refugees, Nicaraguans, Guatemalans, Colombians, Salvadorans, single women, wives, widows, mothers . . . the most striking thing about the women I encountered was their diversity. No group seemed to lack its representatives. There are some whom we might expect to find: those who did domestic work in their countries of origin, or who come from rural areas, or who never obtained legal documents. However, we find others whose presence is harder to account for: urban, previously professional women who have been here long enough to obtain work permits. Why are they doing domestic work after so many years in this country?

The work of Saskia Sassen-Koob[3] moves away from the characteristics of individual women, or even of individual ethnic groups, to focus directly on the structural context entered by contemporary immigrants to American cities. During the last 20 years, immigrants have entered the United States' "declining" cities in ever-increasing numbers, and contrary to all predictions, they continue to find enough work to encourage others to follow them. Sassen-Koob asks how these immigrants can be absorbed by an economy that is rapidly losing its industrial base. Her explanation for this apparent anomaly is that while these cities are losing their place as manufacturing centers, they are simultaneously undergoing a rebirth as "global cities," dedicated to the coordination of scattered factories and to the production of "producer services" such as banking and insurance for an international corporate market. Retaining her focus on the niche filled by immigrant workers in contemporary cities, she emphasizes the direct support services and one-of-a-kind luxury goods financed by this new, export-directed service economy. Thus her analysis points not only to the financial analysts but to the clerical workers who

punch in their data, not only to the advertising executives but to the workers who stuff their futons and sew their quilts, not only to the commodity brokers but to the workers who clean their offices, buildings, and apartments. Like early analyses of household labor, her schema makes visible the denied: the work that enables the smooth operation of both the offices and the lives of those who run them.

[. . .]

⟶ A Bifurcated Market

Sassen-Koob points to the contemporary emergence of a two-tiered service economy composed of professionals and those who serve them, both at work and at home. What this analysis overlooks is the two-tiered nature of the domestic services market itself. For not only is there an increasing demand for domestic services from single, elite professionals (the "yuppie" phenomenon), but there is also an increasing demand for such services from the rising number of elderly people living alone on fixed incomes, from two-earner working-class families, and from single mothers who need cheap child care in order to work at all. These groups can afford very different pay scales and thus have different requirements and standards for their employees. Together they constitute a dual labor market within the bottom tier of the larger service economy.

In the Bay Area today, Latin American domestic workers are routinely paid anywhere from $5 to $10 hourly. Live-in salaries range between $300 and $1,000 monthly. In her study of Japanese-American domestic workers, Evelyn Nakano Glenn notes similarly broad discrepancies in pay among her respondents.[4] She attributes this to personalistic aspects of the negotiating process between domestic workers and their employers. However, such an explanation begs the question of how this tremendous range for negotiation came to exist in the first place. The variation is made possible in part by the social isolation of the work and by the lack of organization among both workers and employers. This atomization is compounded by ineffective state regulation; domestic work was not covered by the Fair Labor Standards Act until 1974, and even today it is often done under the table. However, hourly wages that vary routinely by factors of two or three must be produced as well as tolerated. What is the structure of demand for domestic work that has kept some wages so low, while allowing enterprising businesses to consistently raise the ceiling on prices at the other end of the spectrum?

Over the past 30 years, women have entered the paid labor force in ever-increasing numbers. This movement is a response both to the economic shifts mentioned by Sassen-Koob—the decline of (primarily men's) manufacturing jobs paying a "family wage" and the increasing availability of "feminized" service jobs—and to cultural shifts that have made paid work an acceptable choice for women even in the absence of financial need. This has led to the increasing commodification of what was once unpaid household labor, visible in the boom in restaurants and cleaning agencies and the increasing demand for child care during the last two decades.

Like all large-scale shifts in a stratified society, these developments have had a differential impact on the lives and options of people located at different levels within it. Working-class and lower-middle-class women, having entered low-paid service occupations themselves, generally can afford to pay very little to replace their household labor if they are to gain anything at all from their own salaries. Professional women raising children alone often find themselves in a similar quandary. Women in such situations show up regularly at Amigos. A single mother who works part-time at the post office comes in to interview live-in help. She wants to pay only $400 a month. "I can't afford any more," she says, looking desperate. "All I need is someone strong and trustworthy who can look after the kids while I'm gone." Elderly people living alone on fixed incomes, another growing sector of the population, also need domestic help and have little leeway in what they can pay for it. A manager for a seniors' apartment building calls. "My boss gave me your flyer," he says. "I'm always on the lookout to find cheap cleaning help for them. The most important thing is that people be honest." For these groups, the search for domestic help is less a negotiation process with a single worker than it is a desperate search for anyone willing to accept the inevitably exploitative salary they have to offer.

At the other end of this spectrum are single professionals of both genders, an increasingly significant segment of urban consumers in an era of delayed marriage and childbearing. This group faces very different constraints in their relationships with domestic workers. Regardless of the hourly cost, a weekly housecleaning will absorb only a minuscule portion of any middle-class budget. And even middle-class couples seeking full-time child care can afford to negotiate for particular skills and services. There is considerable plasticity in the amount these employers can pay for domestic work.

Not surprisingly, recent years have seen an explosion of entrepreneurs focused on convincing such people that there is something worth paying more for. Young white middle-class women hang advertising posters in trendy restaurants implying that they are just like employers and so can "make your home feel like a home." Professional advertisements for personalized cleaning agencies abound. "Maid-to-Order" promises an ad in the local Yellow Pages: "Your chores are our business. Bonded and Insured." "You've Got It Maid," asserts another: "We'll do the cleaning, run your errands, wash the laundry, drop off and pick up the cleaning." In a community accustomed to professionalized personal services of all sorts—therapy, home decorating, personal shoppers—this rhetoric finds fertile ground.

Beneath the seemingly random pattern of wage variations among Bay Area domestic workers there lies a dual labor market constituted by two distinct sets of potential employers: the elderly, working-class parents, and single mothers with the little money to spare; and professionals already accustomed to paying relatively high wages for work packaged as a personalized and professional service. What is remarkable is that the work done in these homes—vacuuming, dusting, scrubbing—remains similar. Insofar as there is any difference, it lies in the addition of child care to other duties in the *bottom* sector of the market.[5] It is the nature of the employer, rather than of the work, that is most significant in determining wages.

NOTES

1. Michael Piore, *Birds of Passage;* Judith Rollins, *Between Women.*

2. One of the foremost proponents of this position is Thomas Sowell. For instance, in *Ethnic America,* he attributes the fact that Irish immigrants often worked as domestic servants, whereas Italian immigrants generally did not, due to a divergence in cultural attitudes toward gender and family. See Stephen Steinberg, *The Ethnic Myth,* for an alternate explanation of this history based on dramatic differences in the gender composition of the two immigrant flows.

3. Saskia Sassen, *The Mobility of Labor and Capital;* Saskia Sassen-Koob, "New York City: Economic Restructuring and Immigration," "Changing Composition and Labor Market Location of Hispanic Immigrants in New York City, 1960–1980," "Labor Migrations and the New International Division of Labor," and "Immigrant and Minority Workers in the Organization of the Labor Process."

4. Evelyn Nakano Glenn, *Issei, Nissei, War Bride.*

5. Others have noted that an important strategy in transforming domestic work is the elimination of certain tasks. In "Sisterhood and Domestic Service" Mary Romero comments: "Chicana domestics use several methods to define themselves as professional housecleaners. One method involves eliminating personal services, such as babysitting, laundry and ironing" (p. 339).

REFERENCES

Piore, Michael. (1980). *Birds of Passage: Migrant Labor and Industrial Societies.* Cambridge: Cambridge University Press.

Rollins, Judith. (1985). *Between Women: Domestics and Their Employers.* Philadelphia: Temple University Press.

Romero, Mary. (1988). "Chicanas Modernize Domestic Service." *Qualitative Sociology* 11, 319–34.

———. (1988). "Sisterhood and Domestic Service: Race, Class and Gender in the Mistress-Maid Relationship." *Humanity and Society* 12, 318–46.

Sassen, Saskia. (1988). *The Mobility of Labor and Capital.* Cambridge: Cambridge University Press.

Sassen-Koob, Saskia. (1983). "Immigrant and Minority Workers in the Organization of the Labor Process." *Journal of Ethnic Studies* 8, 1–34.

———. (1983). "Labor Migrations and the New International Division of Labor." In *Women, Men and the International Division of Labor,* J. Nash and M. P. Fernandez-Kelly, eds. pp. 175–204. Albany: State University of New York Press.

Sowell, Thomas. (1981). *Ethnic America: A History.* New York: Basic Books.

Steinberg, Stephen. (1981). *The Ethnic Myth: Race, Ethnicity and Class in America.* Boston: Beacon Press.

FIGURE IV.3   ADVERTISEMENTS FOR DOMESTIC WORKERS.
The Trade in Domestic Workers, Noeleen Heyzer et al, eds. London: Zed, 1994: 55.

THE DREAM

Kim Kyong-ae, 1990

Private Room

THE REALITY

SPMMF, 1992

FIGURE IV.4   THE DREAM AND THE REALITY.
The Trade in Domestic Workers: Causes mechanisms and consequences of International migration Vol. 1 eds. Noeleen Heyzer et al, eds. London: Zed, 1994: 1.

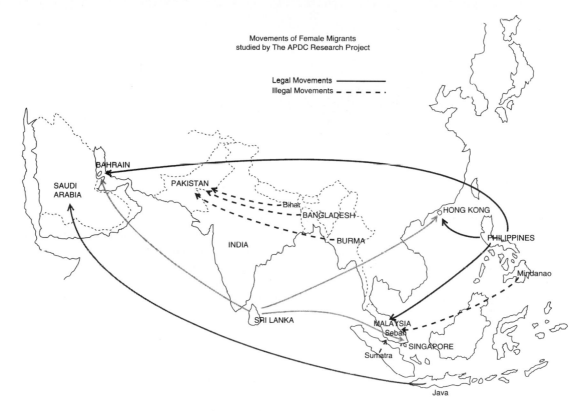

FIGURE IV.5   MOVEMENTS OF FEMALE MIGRANTS
The Trade in Domestic Workers, Noeleen Heyzer et al, eds. London: Zed, 1994: xiv.

Reading C

"A Maid in the Capital"
RIGOBERTA MENCHÚ

Human rights activist and 1992 Nobel Peace Prize winner Rigoberta Menchú relates her experience as a domestic servant in Guatemala City. Her memoir shows how young indigenous women are treated in a system that relies on their availability to do domestic work.

When we left the *finca,* the landowner's guards traveled behind him. And they were armed. I was terrified! But I told myself, "I must be brave, they can't do anything to me." My father said: 'I don't know if anything will happen to you, my child, but you are a mature woman.'

So we reached the capital. I remember that my clothes were worn out because I'd been working in the *finca:* my *corte* was really dirty and my *huipil* very old. I had a little *perraje,* the only one I owned. I didn't have any shoes. I didn't even know what wearing shoes was like. The master's wife was at home. There was another servant girl to do the cooking and I would have to do all the cleaning in the house. The other servant was also Indian, but she'd changed her clothes. She wore *ladino* clothes and already spoke Spanish. I didn't know any; I arrived and didn't know what to say. I couldn't speak Spanish but I understood a little because of the *finca* overseers who used to give us orders, bully us, and hand out the work. Many of them are Indians but they won't use Indian languages because they feel different from the labourers. So I understood Spanish although I couldn't speak it. The mistress called the other servant: "Take this girl to the room in the back." The girl came, looked at me with indifference, and told me to follow her. She took me to the other room. It was a room with a pile of boxes in the corner and plastic bags where they kept the rubbish. It had a little bed. They took it down for me and put a little mat on it, with another blanket, and left me there. I had nothing to cover myself with.

The first night, I remember, I didn't know what to do. That was when I felt what my sister had felt although, of course, my sister had been with another family. Then later the mistress called me. The food they gave me was a few beans with some very hard *tortillas.* There was a dog in the house, a pretty, white, fat dog. When I saw the maid bring out the dog's food— bits of meat, rice, things that the family ate—and they gave me a few beans and hard *tortillas,* that hurt me very much. The dog had a good meal and I didn't de-

Rigoberta Menchú, "A Maid in the Capital," from *I, Rigoberta Menchú: An Indian Woman in Guatemala.* Elizabeth Burgos Debray, ed. Ann Wright, trans. London: Verso, 1984: 91–97, 101.

Key Terms

corte Multicolored material that Guatemalan women use as a skirt.
finca A plantation.
huipil Embroidered blouse worn by Indian women.

Ladino Person of mixed blood or non-Indian.
perraje Colored cotton cloak.
Quetzal Guatemalan currency (100 centavos).

serve as good a meal as the dog. Anyway, I ate it, I was used to it. I didn't mind not having the dog's food because at home I ate only *tortillas* with chile or with salt or water. But I felt rejected. I was lower than the animals in the house. The girl came later and told me to go to sleep because I had to work in the morning and they got up at 7 or 8. I was in bed awake from 3:00. I didn't mind about the bed either because at home I slept on a mat on the floor and we sometimes didn't even have anything to cover ourselves with. But I had a look at the other girl's bed and it was quite comfortable because she wore *ladino* clothes and spoke Spanish. Later on, however, we got to know each other well. She used to eat the masters' leftovers, what they left in the dish. They'd eat first and she'd get what was left. If there wasn't any left, she'd also get some stale beans and *tortillas* or some leftovers from the fridge. She ate that and later on when we knew each other she'd give me some.

At 3 in the morning, I said: "My God, my parents will be working and I'm here." But I also thought, I must learn, and then go home. I always said that I must go home.

[. . .]

Of course, I was in the city but I didn't know the first thing about it. I knew nothing about the city even though I'd been there with my father. But then we'd only gone to one place and to some offices. I didn't know how to find my way around and I couldn't read the numbers or the streets.

So I did what the lady told me to do and afterwards, about 11:00, when they finished eating, they called me. "Have you eaten?" "No." "Give her some food." So they gave me what was left of their food. I was famished. At home we don't eat as much as we should, of course, but at least we're used to eating tortillas regularly, even if it's only with salt. I was really worried. At about 11:30, she called me again and took me into a room. She said: "I'm going to give you two months' pay in advance and you must buy yourself a *huipil,* a new *corte,* and a pair of shoes, because you put me to shame. My friends are coming and you're here like that. What would that look like to my friends? They are important people so you'll have to change your ways. I'll buy you these things but you stay here because I'm ashamed to be seen with you in the market. Here's your

two months' pay." Well, I didn't know what to say because I didn't know enough Spanish to protest or say what I thought. But in my mind I insulted her. I thought, if only I could send this woman to the mountains and let her do the work my mother does. I don't think she'd even be capable of it. I didn't think much of her at all.

She went off to the market. She came back with a *corte.* It was about a couple of yards long. The simplest there was. She also brought a simple *huipil* which must have cost her 2.50 or 3 *quetzals.* She must have got the *corte* for 15 *quetzals* or even less, perhaps only 12 *quetzals.* She didn't buy me another belt, I had my old one. And she said she didn't buy me shoes because two months' pay wasn't enough. Then she gave me the *corte.* I had to tear it into two so that I could keep one of them to change into. I tore it into two parts. Now, I'm one of those women who can weave, embroider, and do everything. When the other girl became more friendly, she asked me: "Can you embroider?" "Yes," I said. "Can you make blouses? I'll give you some material. I've got some thread and if you like you can make a blouse." And she gave me some material to make a blouse. Anyway, I tore that *corte* in two and changed right away. The mistress said, "When you've changed, go to my room and make my bed." I went to change, and she made me have a bath. I came back and started making her bed. When I'd finished she came to check my work and said, "Do this bed again, you didn't make it properly." And she began scolding the other girl: "Why didn't you show her how to do it? I don't want mobs of people here who can't earn their keep." We started to make the bed again. I didn't know how to dust because I'd never done it, so the other girl taught me how to dust, and how to clean the toilets.

And that was when I discovered the truth in what my grandmother used to say: that with rich people even their plates shine. Well, yes, even their toilets shine. At home we don't even have one. I was really very distressed, remembering all my parents' and my grandparents' advice. I learned to dust, wash, and iron very quickly. I found ironing the hardest because I'd never used an iron before. I remember how the washing and ironing used to pile up. The landowner had three children and they changed their clothes several times a day. All the clothes they left lying around had to be washed again, and ironed again, and then hung up in the right place. The mistress used to watch me all the time and was very nasty to me. She treated me like . . . I don't know what . . . not like a dog because she treated the dog well. She used to hug the dog. So I thought: "She doesn't even compare me with the dog." They had a garden and I sowed some plants. I used to do this at home so I got on really well with that. That's what I saw every day. The time came when I was working really well. I did all my jobs in a trice. I didn't find it difficult. I had to work for the two months that the mistress spent on my clothes without earning a *centavo*.

I didn't go out either, although on Saturdays the mistress said I had to go out; "Come on, out of here. I'm fed up with servants hanging around." That made me very angry because we worked, we did everything. We probably didn't work as hard for our parents as we did for that rich old woman. But on Saturdays, she'd say: "Out of here. I don't want to see heaps of maids around." That's what happens to Indian girls in the capital. On Saturdays we were allowed out in the evenings, but it was preparing their maids for prostitution because we were ordered out and then we had to find somewhere to sleep. We went out on Saturdays and came back on Sundays. Thank Heavens the other girl was really decent. She said; "I've got some friends here. We'll go to their house." I went with her. But what if I'd been on my own? I wouldn't have had anywhere to stay, only the street, because I couldn't even speak to the mistress to tell her not to throw me out. I couldn't find my way around the city either. So the other girl took me to her friend's house. We went there every Saturday to sleep. On Sundays, we'd go back at night because during the day we were allowed to go dancing, to the dance halls and all the places where maids go in the capital.

[. . .]

There were times when we'd really had enough. One day the other maid and I agreed we'd start being difficult. She said; "If the mistress complains, let her complain." And we stopped doing certain things just to annoy her. So she got up and shouted at us, but the more she shouted the more stubborn we became, and she saw that that wasn't any use. The other maid said:

"Come on, let's leave and find another job." But I was worried because I couldn't just decide like that; I didn't know the city and if I counted on her, she might take me somewhere worse. What was I to do? Soon I realized that the mistress spurned this girl because she wouldn't become the boys' lover. She told me later: "That old bag wants me to initiate her sons. She says boys have to learn how to do the sexual act and if they don't learn when they're young, it's harder for them when they're older. So she put in my contract that she'd pay me a bit more if I taught her sons." That was the condition she'd imposed, and that was why she was so hard on the girl: because she'd refused. Perhaps she nursed the hope that one day I'd be clean—she always said I was dirty—so that one day I'd be all right to teach her sons. That's what she hoped, that lady. She mistreated me and rejected me, but she didn't actually throw me out.

I remember that after I'd been in that rich man's house for two months, my father came to visit me. I'd been praying to God that my father wouldn't come, because I knew that if he did, what a dreadful reception he'd get! And I couldn't bear my father to be rejected by that old hag. My father was humble, poor, as I was. He came, not because he had any time to spare to visit me, but because he was left in the city without a single *centavo* in his pocket. He'd been to see about the business of our land. He said they'd sent him to Quetzaltenango, then to El Quiché and then they'd asked to see him in the capital and the money he'd brought for the trip had run out. So he hadn't got a penny. When my father rang the bell, the other maid went to see who it was. He said who he was. She told him to wait a minute because she knew what her mistress was like. She told her: "Rigoberta's father is here." "All right," said the lady of the house and went out to see my father. She saw how poor he was, of course. He was all dirty. Well, he would be because he'd been traveling to many places. That's what it's like for the poor. She went out to look and came straight back. She told me: "Go and see your father but don't bring him in here, please." That's what she said and I had to see him outside. She told me plainly not even to bring him into the corridor. He had to stay out in the yard and I explained the situation to him. I said the mistress was very nasty and that it disgusted and horrified her to see my father and that he couldn't even come into the house. He understood very well. He was used to it because we're rejected in so many different places. My father said: "My child, I need money. I've nothing for anything to eat or to get home with." But I still hadn't finished the two months that I owed and hadn't a penny to my name. I said; "The mistress had to buy clothes for me and docked me two months' pay for it. I haven't earned a single *centavo*." My father began to cry and said: "It can't be true." "Yes," I said, "everything I'm wearing the mistress bought for me." So I went to the other maid and told her my father had no money and I didn't know what to do; I couldn't ask the mistress for money as I couldn't speak Spanish. Then she spoke to the mistress for me and said: "Her father hasn't got a single *centavo* and needs money." The girl was very tough and would stand up to anyone and anything. She was really angry with our mistress and said: "She needs money and must be given some money for her father." Then the mistress started saying that we were trying to get all her money off her, trying to eat her money up, and we couldn't even do our jobs properly. All maids are the same. They've nothing to eat in their own homes, so they come and eat us out of ours. She opened her bag and took out 10 *quetzals* and threw them into my face. I took the 10 *quetzals* and told my father that I thought she'd take another month's pay. It will be another debt, but this is what I can give you. So my father went home with 10 *quetzals*. But the other girl just couldn't stomach this. She was really hurt by it and she often said that if the mistress complained, she would stand up for

me. She had a plan, because she was leaving anyway. She began a resistance campaign against the mistress.

I worked for more than four months, I think, and received no money. Then she paid me a little. She gave me 20 *quetzals* and I was very happy. I wanted to keep them for my father. But she told me that I had to buy shoes, because she was ashamed to have anyone in her house go barefoot. I had no shoes. But I said to myself: "I'm not going to buy any. If she wants me to have some, let her buy them."

[. . .]

December passed. And I went on working. All the work from Christmas set me back by two weeks. All the new clothes and all the new china they'd got out just piled up. The house was dirty. I had to do everything. The mistress pretended she didn't notice. She'd get up and go out. She didn't even complain so much, because she knew she needed me to do it all. That's when I thought: "I must get out of this house. I must go home to my parents." She gave me two months' money. It was 40 *quetzals*. With this and with what I'd already saved, I thought, I can go home to my parents satisfied. It wasn't very much, perhaps, but it would help them. I told the mistress: "I'm leaving. I'm going home." She said: 'No, how can you? We're so fond of you here. You must stay. I'll put your wages up, if you like. I'll give you a *quetzal* more.' "No," I said, "I've made up my mind to go." I was announcing my departure, unfortunately. I say unfortunately because a terrible thing happened: one of my brothers arrived and said: "Papá is in prison."

"WHAT THEY WERE THINKING"

FIGURE IV-6   LYNNE SCHWARTZBERG, GWENDOLYN MILLETTE, AND CALVIN SCHWARTZBERG, NEW YORK, APRIL 19, 1999.

SCHWARTZBERG: *"Calvin was 8 months old. At that time, I was working full time, and I was basically thinking that I was leaving him, and I was dreading that. When I first went back to work, leaving Calvin with a virtual stranger was so scary. Someone else was raising my child. It was hard to justify. In the beginning it was a real struggle to balance my life. I only had three hours a day with him. It was difficult. And it's always tough for a baby sitter to be with a mother and a child. The mother wants to be doing it. As the mother, I had to know when to let go and give over the power. I would not say Gwendolyn and I are friends. It's more of a professional relationship. Gwendolyn is a little quiet. She keeps to herself, which is fine."*

MILLETTE: *"I was thinking, Is he going to eat? For me, I'd rather be alone with Calvin, because it's uncomfortable being with parents. With him, I can jump and dance and do silly things. I don't like to be silly around grown-ups. And it's strange for me to get to know a new family. Lynne and I get along because we do a job together, but we are not quote-unquote friends. No matter how I look at it, I'm her subordinate. But I'm Calvin's friend. We just get along. I do have family of my own. I have four kids. My mother takes care of them in St. Vincent. Of course, I wish I was there, but the primary reason I'm here is to make a living. Being around kids helps me, because I'm not around my kids. I write to them a lot and talk to them a lot too. They know about Calvin."*

Interviews by Catherine Saint Louis, photograph by Lauren Ronick, *New York Times Magazine*, April 2, 2000, p. 34.

From Thailand to Japan: Migrant Sex Workers as Autonomous Subjects

SATOKO WATENABE

Satoko Watenabe studies women's migration and works as an agricultural economist at the International Development Center in Japan. In this essay, she explains that the Thai women who migrate to Japan to work in the sex industry do so for economic reasons. Immigration laws and economic conditions in Japan and Thailand affect the women's decisions to work in Japan in order to support themselves and their families, who remain in Thailand.

Satoko Watenabe, "From Thailand to Japan: "Migrant Sex Workers as Autonomous Subjects," in Kamala Kempadoo and Jo Doezema, eds., *Global Sex Workers: Rights, Resistance, and Redefinitions*. New York: Routledge, 1998: 114–23.

I could speak about my work to those Japanese women who protest against prostitution. If they said "Quit the work and go back home," I'd reply, "I'll

Key Terms

autonomous subject In the subject/object division, the subject acts and has power; the object is acted upon and is powerless. Marxist, feminist, and cultural theorists often discuss how workers, women, and people of color, respectively, often lack power in culture and thus are treated as objects rather than as subjects who can think and act independently even in inequitable legal and social conditions.

decriminalization Literally, removal from the criminal code of a law against something. Advocates for sex workers often urge governments to decriminalize prostitution rather than to legalize it. Legalized prostitution usually results in severe restrictions on sex workers' living and employment conditions, often furthering the social stigma associated with sex work. In contrast, decriminalization removes the threat of arrest and incarceration without requiring governmental involvement in sex workers' personal lives.

Hinode–Kogane belt An area in the city of Yokohama between two train stations (Hinode-cho and Kogane-cho), where many bars and hostess clubs are located.

Isezaki-cho Area A district in Yokohama.

sex worker A person who engages in sexually explicit performance and/or sexual acts for pay. "Sex work" includes a wide range of activities such as erotic dancing, hostessing, sensual massage, and prostitution. This term emphasizes the labor that women and men engage in when performing sexual services for pay, in contrast to words like *stripper* and *hooker,* which potentially carry an implicit moral judgment.

yakuza A powerful network of organized crime in Japan, or an individual involved in that network.

go back if you give me enough money." What should I do back in Thailand? There is no good work for a woman like me.

—Meow

Introduction

The following is a summary of my research on Thai sex workers in Japan conducted through interviews in Yokohama, Tokyo, and Chiba between December 17, 1995, and March 31, 1996. The five Thai women interviewed were Lak, Sai, Meow, Pet, and Nok. The ages of the five women fall into the category of 20 to 34, the largest age group of Thai women apprehended for violating the immigration control act in 1989 (the latest available figures). In this summary, the interviewed women are given fictitious nicknames, names common among Thai women, in order to maintain anonymity due to the nature of this study.

[. . .]

Because of problems in approaching Thai sex workers, I worked as a "hostess," though unpaid, for a week at a snack bar that employed undocumented migrant women. Above all, the experience in the bar has convinced me that entertaining a male client is nothing but work, which is quite tiring and stressful to the woman entertainer. This is in contrast to the prevailing view that merely "sitting with a man and pouring drinks" is not something deserving of a high wage.

[. . .]

Migration to Japan

None of the five women had visited Japan before. Each entered the country three to four years before the time of the interview on a "temporary visitor" visa, which permitted a stay up to 90 days. Accordingly, all of them overstayed their visas. All of them said that they obtained some information on prospective jobs and general working conditions in Japan before they made a decision about the migration. However, the quantity, as well as the quality, of information they had prior to their migration varied. The extent and quality of information a woman had access to before migration seemed to have determined the manner in which she migrated and found work in Japan, and therefore, the degree to which she would be exploited in both Thailand and Japan.

It is widely reported that many Thai women who migrate to work in Japan make a verbal contract with recruiters or brokers. This contract gives little detail of the actual terms of employment, working conditions, and the repayment of charges for recruitment, travel, and placement within an establishment. Thus, women under contract may find themselves in debt upon arrival.

[. . .]

Three of the women interviewed knew through their friends and/or the mass media that they would end up heavily indebted and in a situation in which they had little control over their work if they went to Japan under this type of contract. Lak, advised by her friend who was already working in Japan, turned down the offer of a Thai broker, who said, "You don't need even 100 yen ($1) to go to Japan. We'll get you everything necessary." Instead, she borrowed 300,000 yen ($3,000) from the friend and obtained a passport and a visa with the help of another friend.

[. . .]

The recruiter and the broker in Thailand may or may not be the same person. Women are recruited in cities or rural areas in Thailand, sold to brokers who have contacts in Japan, and brought, usually by the brokers, to their first workplaces in Japan. Recruiters and brokers in Thailand include various kinds of people, such as members of organized crime syndicates, travel agents, small business owners, and Japanese businessmen. Even when they are aware of the disadvantage of such a deal, many Thai women depend on recruiters and brokers to obtain their passports and visas because they do not know what to do with the paperwork. Migrant women, as well as the recruiters, are usually unaware of the involvement of international organized crime syndicates in their migration.

None of the women reported that they were forced by anybody to migrate. Pet, however, was under pressure from her mother, who had repeatedly "asked" her to go since she was 17 years old. None had learned Japanese prior to their migration to Japan. They learned the language mainly from their Thai colleagues and friends, and partially from their clients, employers, and language textbooks, after arrival in Japan.

Working Conditions in Japan

Sai, Pet, and Lak were bar hostesses, while Meow and Nok were "authentic" sex workers—that is, they specialized in having sex. "Hostess" is the term used in Japan for a female worker who entertains a customer by chatting, pouring drinks, singing, dancing, hugging, and so on, in bars and nightclubs. The work of bar hostesses ranges from menial service through intellectual entertainment to providing physical and emotional comfort. Sexual intercourse is not unusual, though it usually takes place outside the establishment. What kind of work is actually required of a hostess depends on the client and the establishment. A high-class bar expects its hostesses to be not only attractive and elegant but also intelligent and knowledgeable about various things, from art to economy and politics, since its clientele often include corporate executives and high-ranking officials. There are more casual bars that welcome working-class customers and make them feel at home; there are also bars that force hostesses to have sex with the customers. "Bar hostesses" are far from being a homogeneous group in terms of work they do and pay they receive. It is equally true that not all migrant women who work as bar hostess are engaged in prostitution or forced into prostitution.

[. . .]

A bar hostess usually works six hours a day and six days a week in the bar. Sunday is a holiday at most establishments. In order to maintain a certain number of clients, however, she has to spend much of her free time calling her clients and/or having meals with them. Moreover, a bar hostess has to "work" to prepare herself for the bar work for at least an hour. This includes makeup, hairdressing, and changing clothes. Therefore, on average their actual working hours are longer than six hours a day. The more clients a hostess has, the more power she has vis-à-vis the management. Among migrant women, however, only experienced or skillful workers can establish a steady clientele.

[. . .]

Women working in the bars on the Hinode–Kogane belt, as well as street prostitutes in the Isezaki-cho area, cannot work safely without paying a "security fee," the term used by *yakuzas*. If they do not pay it, on one hand, they will be harassed by the *yakuza* to whom they are supposed to pay the fee. On the other, they will have no protection against harassment (e.g., abusive acts, rape, murder, theft, nonpayment) by their clients. Clearly, they would not have to pay the fee if their work and overstay were not criminalized. Some of their immediate supervisors, usually called the *mamasan* or "mama" in a bar, are migrant workers themselves. Thai women often called their *mamasan* the "boss." But in some cases the boss designates an overseer who loans contracted women to establishments, supervises their work, and collects their earnings as a payment for the debt. The five women I interviewed did not have this kind of serious trouble with their mamasans and bar owners, mainly because they were not working on contract. If they had, they said, they would change their workplace. Sai, for example, had a conflict about her pay with the bar owner, who reduced her daily wage from 10,000 yen to 8,000 yen because of stagnant sales at the bar. However, he agreed to pay her at the previous rate when he learned that she was about to quit and move to another bar.

Meow and Pet reported that some Thai sex workers have sex for pleasure with Thai "hosts," a Japanese term for male sex workers working in "host clubs" whose customers are mainly women, female sex workers in particular. The price for such a sex service ranges from a few hundred dollars to $1,000 per night or per "session," depending on their relationships and/or the need of both the woman (for sexual and emotional care) and the man (for economic gain). If a woman wishes to "rent" such a male sex worker, she has to pay him 500,000 to 700,000 yen ($5,000–$7,000) per month.

[. . .]

According to Lak, Sai, and Meow, sex work assured them of freedom from marriage and men. Meow contradicted the general view that a prostitute sells not only her sexual service but also her personality. To her, the "sale of sexual access" was not the same as the "sale of self." Her view was similar to that of an "ordinary" worker: "I sell my time but not myself."

Home Links

Once or twice a week or whenever necessary, the Thai women called their families in Thailand. They were more likely to call than write a letter because they were busy and did not have much time to write. On average they spent 10,000–20,000 yen ($100–$200) per month on telephone calls to their families. In their calls and letters, they talked about life in Japan and their families' life in Thailand. Those with new houses under construction in Thailand (Sai, Meow, Pet, and Nok) often talked with their parents about the new house and the additional money needed for its construction. Their parents also asked them to send money for buying various goods, siblings' school expenses, and/or festivals. The money they sent home ranged from 10,000 yen ($100) to 400,000 yen ($4,000) monthly, depending on the type of work they did, its ups and downs, and how they lived. But they had all sent a considerably large sum of money to their families. Nok had remitted about 5 million yen ($50,000) in two years. Sai, Pet, and Meow had sent "more than 3 million yen ($30,000)" and Lak "more than 2 million yen ($20,000)," since she had been in Japan.

None of the women had visited their families since their arrival in Japan. It was clear that they would have liked to be able to visit their families in Thailand and then to return to work in Japan, but it was simply not possible. As they had overstayed their visas, they would first have to "surrender" to an immigration office and then, most probably, be deported if they wished to go back home. The women reported that it had become impossible for ordinary Thai people like them to obtain a tourist visa for Japan. According to them, the Japanese Embassy in Thailand granted tourist visas only to "rich" Thais who could present required documents such as a proof of property ownership and an income certificate. Before issuing a visa to her/him, the Embassy had to be convinced that the applicant was wealthy enough to go to Japan as a tourist, not as a worker. "Imagine that you can't go back home when you want to. It's so hard for me," Sai lamented.

What they wished to have most in their life in Japan was a "visa," more precisely, a work permit. They feared being caught by the police or the immigration control and being deported back to Thailand before their savings hit the target or before they felt it was time to return. Meow had even stopped going to the bar, having seen almost every day two or three Thai workers being caught in police and immigration raids on the Hinode–Kogane belt. She was seriously checking the possibility of forged marriage to a Japanese so that she would not have to fear immigration raids, though she would have to pay the "husband" probably 1.2 million yen or more every year.

Each of the five Thai women interviewed, as well as most Thai women I met during the fieldwork, had developed some form of social network through which they shared support and information. Such networks were formed primarily among Thai workers themselves, who came to know each other through work, by meeting and/or by telephone. In some cases, as Sai did, older or more experienced workers took care of younger or new workers, providing accommodation, taking them to clinics, finding them jobs, introducing prospective clients to them, and the like. Lak said it was difficult to develop such peer support for women working under contract but they still helped each other, hiding from their bosses. Unlike the general view that Thai women are the most vulnerable group among migrant workers in Japan due to a lack of social networks, these women have a network of friends, though it may be less overt compared to such formal networks as churches and women's organizations (e.g., the Filipino Wives of Japanese Associations).

Conclusion

The five women, as well as most of the Thai migrant women I met during the fieldwork, spent a significant part of their earnings on purchasing houses, often of western style, and other goods, notably automobiles, for their families and themselves. This suggests that working-class Thai people's demand for consumption far exceeds the income domestically available to them, particularly in rural areas. By migrating to work in Japan for higher wages instead of working in factories or agricultural fields in Thailand, they reject the existing international division of labor and the international wage hierarchy. As illustrated in the experiences of the Thai women, migrant workers partially contributed to creating new consumption habits, but the rapid economic expansion since the 1980s has had a larger impact on consumption patterns. While the surge of the urban economy has swelled the size of the professional and skilled white-collar workforce and enabled them a higher level of consumption, workers in rural areas and lower-waged urban sectors have become increasingly dissatisfied with the lower level of consumption and thus demand higher wages.

The case studies indicate that Thai migrant workers find more favorable class conditions in Japan even though they have to endure the undocumented, thus often exploitative, circumstances. In becoming accustomed to the work and life in Japan, the migrant women achieve a higher level of bargaining power vis-à-vis their employers. They may be creating a new wage division within Japan's sex industry as well as in the sector of women in general, but they can also be understood as multinational workers who, by moving across the artificial barriers of nation-state borders, are, at least to some extent, breaking down the international wage hierarchy and recomposing the structure and distribution of power within the working class against capital's control.

While regarding sex work as immoral, the five women did the work because it was far better paid than any other job available to them in Japan as well as in Thailand and, for some, because it provided independence from marriage and men. The money they earned in Japan expanded the choices available to them, to educate themselves or their children for other types of work and to begin their own businesses upon returning home. They differentiated between the sex they had for money from sex for their own emotional and physical satisfaction. They may not have thought of themselves as rebels against male power and social control, but at the same time, they did not view themselves as sexual slaves, either. As one of the bar prostitutes clearly described it, they sell sexual access to their bodies but not themselves. Even for the sexual access, they tried to minimize it for maximum gain and to reduce the chances of being exploited and abused by their customers. The sex workers were all subject to disease, injury, mistreatment, indignity, physical and psychological abuse, and coercion, but these conditions are not unique to sex work. Other types of work also involve at least some of them, if not all. [. . .] Thai migrant women choose sex work of particular forms despite the unfavorable conditions.

Since mainstream feminists in Japan view all forms of female migration from other Asian countries into the sex industry as traffic in women, sexual exploitation, and abuse, their campaigns tend to reinforce the police and immigration control over the migrant women and thus further endanger and limit the choices of those whose lives they aim to protect. Unless they have no other choice (e.g., being sent by the Thai Embassy), the Thai sex workers would not approach Japanese women's organizations, knowing they would only be told to quit the job and go home immediately. They also assumed that Japanese women did not welcome them because their work was related to sex. From the sex workers' experiences, the best way to "protect" their lives from exploitation and abuse would be to support the decriminalization of sex work and legitimize the migration for such employment.

REFLECTING ON THE SECTION

Glenn and Salzinger both discuss the ways in which race and gender come to matter in the kinds of jobs available for migrant workers. We also learn that immigration and migration laws are structured in relation to race, gender, class, sexuality, religion, and nationality. Menchú and Watenabe show the personal costs of the struggle for livelihood when women leave their homes and families, either forcibly or voluntarily, for work. What are some of the factors that contribute to women migrating for work? What are some advantages and challenges of migrating to work? We know that many migrant women end up doing either domestic or sex work. What do the readings tell you about why women continue to do such work in particular locations? How do the essays and graphics in this section challenge or reinforce the ways that women's labor is traditionally viewed and analyzed?

The Gender Politics of Economic Globalization

Reading A

Welcome to the Border

AUGUSTA DWYER

Journalist Augusta Dwyer describes the conditions prevalent in the maquiladoras *found on the U.S.– Mexico border. Pointing to the unhealthy and substandard living and working conditions of the* maquila *workers, who are primarily female, Dwyer shows how recent trade agreements such as* NAFTA *(the North American Free Trade Agreement) have benefited multinational corporations.*

Colonia Roma is typical of the living conditions of *maquiladora* workers and the low wages that characterise the industry. Those wages—a fraction of what workers in the United States and Canada earn—are the bottom-line advantage to setting up a *maquiladora* on the Mexican border.

American Chamber of Commerce estimates for 1992 show *maquiladora* wages ranging from a low of 57 cents an hour in Torreón to U.S. $1.95 in Matamoros. The average for the *maquiladora* industry throughout Mexico barely exceeds $1 an hour.

Yet even though wages are so low, prices are often higher than in the United States and *maquiladora* workers frequently cross the border to shop, bringing a large percentage of their wages back to the U.S. economy. In

Augusta Dwyer, "Welcome to the Border," in *On the Line: Life on the U.S.–Mexican Border,* London: Latin American Bureau, 1994: 4–8.

Hidalgo County, *maquila* employees add over U.S. $9 million to the economy; in Del R;iao, Texas, across the river from Ciudad Acuñta, shoppers spent U.S. $10.5 million in 1989, according to Chamber of Commerce estimates. In El Paso, retail sales to Mexican shoppers now add $1 billion a year to the local economy, according to that city's Chamber of Commerce.

Small-time vendors can buy goods across the river, sell them at double the price back on the Mexican side, and still undercut Mexican shopkeepers. Business fell drastically in American border towns and riots broke out in Nuevo Laredo in late 1992 when the Mexican government announced a new law reducing the value of duty-free goods people could bring back across the border from U.S. $300 to U.S. $50. When the Mexican currency was devalued in 1982, days after then-president José López Portillo had said he would "defend the peso like a dog," a large number of shops in American cities like Brownsville and El Paso went out of business as Mexican shoppers suddenly found U.S. prices impossibly high.

Just as the *maquiladoras* cluster along the southern side of the border, secondhand clothing stores dot the American side, selling castoffs by the pound rather than by item. Enterprising Mexicans cross the border regularly to purchase large bundles, or *pacas,* of bound clothing, displaying them along fences or under trees in poor Mexican *colonias* from the Gulf of Mexico to the

---

Key Term

colonias Unincorporated communities along the U.S.–Mexico border.

Pacific. As one woman *maquila* worker in Tijuana puts it, when asked how she copes with such low wages, "Well, you don't really. It barely gives you enough for food. I just say thank God that even though they're secondhand from the States, you can still buy clothes."

Transport to and from work in the industrial parks which house the *maquiladoras* is usually chaotic and expensive. Some companies provide old school buses, but in cities like Reynosa or nearby Matamoros, workers, students, and shoppers alike must crowd into tiny converted vans, paying 30 cents a trip. Anyone with an inside line to either the mayor or the local progovernment union can set up a bus service, providing uncomfortable transport devoid of safety and antipolluting measures.

Ever since *maquiladoras* became popular with American and other foreign business, suburbs of shacks began spreading all along *la frontera,* reaching farther and farther beyond the border cities' limits. Crowded, dirty, and dusty, they transform the varied northern landscapes into scenes of unalloyed misery. Few homes have running water, sanitary drainage, or electricity. In winter they are freezing and in summer, stiflingly hot. Mothers who work on the assembly lines often have no choice but to leave their children at home to look after themselves, and they often turn to drugs or gang violence as they grow older.

Open ditches run with human and toxic industrial wastes, while only the most progressive of municipal authorities will admit that because the foreign companies pay no local taxes, they have no money to provide services for the thousands of new residents flooding into their cities every year. The air swirls with the residues of burning plastics and chemicals, as well as fecal dust picked up by the wind from the inadequate drainage trenches in the poor *colonias.* Respiratory problems are becoming increasingly common and the environmental degradation quickly spreads. River water containing factory runoff is used to irrigate crops and pasture, potentially contaminating food that is eaten throughout Mexico and even exported. Gas or chemical leaks in Mexican towns float across the border to their American neighbours.

Health and safety violations abound in the myriad Fortune 500[1] factories that cluster at or near the border. Mexican law absolves foreign companies from legal suits for work-related accidents, confining awards to a government-set minimum, thus relieving corporations of the kinds of hefty payments for which they might be liable in the United States or Canada. Instead, injuries are summarily dealt with by even more strained state health and pension budgets. All kinds of unfair labour practices—everything from firing workers for trying to organise to firing those who have earned seniority and reasonable severance payments—are common. So is sexually harassing female workers, hiring minors, and closing up and leaving town without bothering to pay the final week's wages or severance pay.

Mexico now has more than 2,180 *maquiladoras* throughout the country. They are also known as inbond plants, because their components enter Mexico temporarily without duty, or "in bond" for assembly. To offset the image of *maquiladoras* as runaway plants, avoiding U.S. wages and health and safety standards, they are also referred to as twin plants, a name which suggests a manufacturing process involving both U.S. and Mexican plants working in partnership. The *maquiladoras,* however, are more often paired with warehouses or offices across the border than with factories.

According to the country's National Institute of Geography and Statistics (INEGI), 83 percent of the *maquiladoras* are spread along Mexico's 2000-mile-long border with the United States, employing almost 86 percent of the total workforce. Some companies favour big cities like Matamoros at the mouth of the Río Grande, across from Brownsville, Texas, or Ciudad Juárez, across from El Paso, or Tijuana, across the land border from San Diego, California. But the evergrowing need for labour has also forced them to set up in small towns, barely locatable on a map before the *maquila* boom, such as Piedras Negras and Ciudad Acuña, across the river from Eagle Pass and Del Río, Texas, respectively, or Agua Prieta and Nogales, neighbouring Douglas and Nogales, both in Arizona. *Maquiladoras* are now springing up in central cities such as Guadalajara and can be found as far south as the Yucatán.

The *maquiladora* programme, also known as the Border Industrialization Programme, is based on the quick assembly in Mexico of parts and raw materials from either the United States or other countries. The word *maquiladora* comes from the share of grain a miller would keep in payment for milling grain during colonial times in Mexico, and refers to the idea of a single step in a longer process going on elsewhere.

Mexico's Trade Secretariat (SECOFI) defines a *maquiladora* as any plant where the machinery and raw materials are "temporarily imported," only to be assembled and shipped back out again. Companies are exempt from the 2 percent assets tax charged everywhere else in Mexico, paying only a small tax on the value added to the product. Both American and other companies have a further advantage that their assembled product can come back into the United States duty free, thanks to a 1962 U.S. Customs regulation.

The *maquiladoras* in northern Mexico now assemble almost every imaginable item in use in modern society—from car parts, clothing, and electrical appliances to hospital materials, furniture, and computer parts. Even missile components for the U.S. Department of Defense are assembled in Circuitos. Binacionales de Tijuana, a *maquila* belonging to Hughes Aircraft Co., a subsidiary of General Motors.

Collectively these plants are part of an industrial process known as globalisation, whereby manufacturing has been broken down into a thousand tiny steps, each worker at times spending no more than a few minutes on each part of the production process, and those workers are spread out all over the world. This kind of offshore manufacturing plays an increasing role in keeping hundreds of American companies, and by extension a fair section of the American economy, afloat.

Service industries, such as entering data into computers, are also becoming popular. A close look at the fine print on any coupon offering discounts on all kinds of Canadian and U.S. products, for example, almost invariably instructs merchants to redeem costs by sending them to places like Del Río or El Paso. Across the river legions of young women are sorting and entering numbers for companies such as Carolina Coupon Processing, Seven Oaks, and A. C. Nielsen, which buy the coupons from merchants for the discount price and then get the money back from the various manufacturers.

Over half a million Mexicans now work in this vast chain of plants and workshops, according to INEGI, a figure that currently fluctuates between 14 and 16 percent of the country's entire manufacturing sector employment. In terms of output and exports, the *maquiladoras* easily constitute the fastest-growing sector in industry in Mexico. The number of plants increased at a rate of over 9 percent in 1992, and at 4.7 per cent for the first 10 months of 1993, down from the 16 percent annual growth rate registered between 1983 and 1990 due to the knock-on effect of the U.S. recession. Over the first three quarters of 1993, however, the value of *maquila* exports grew by 17.6 percent compared to the same period in 1992, according to the Bank of Mexico, reaching U.S. $15.6 billion. By October 1993, employment in the *maquila* industry had grown by 7.2 percent over the first 10 months of the previous year.

Most of the *maquiladoras,* 68 percent according to 1991 American Chamber of Commerce statistics, are wholly owned by U.S. firms. Another 25 percent of total investment comes from Mexican entrepreneurs, most of whom work with an exclusive contract to supply assembled parts to a U.S. company. Japanese investment increased greatly in the late 1980s but still represents only 4 percent. There are now 50 Japanese-owned *maquilas,* mostly based in Tijuana and Mexicali in Baja California state, compared to just five in 1985. The remainder of the investment comes from small numbers of European, Canadian, and Korean companies.

The reason so many foreign companies, especially from the United States, move their plants to Mexico is simple. They are close to American markets and transport costs are minimal. The Mexican workforce is young, hard-working, literate, and skillful. Unions are practically nonexistent, or where they do exist, pliant to the wishes of either *maquiladora* owners or the ruling Institutional Revolutionary Party (PRI). Caught up in the evolution from simple assembly plants to more high-tech plants, Mexican workers have also adapted to Japanese work techniques. Besides their greater flexibility. Mexican workers are cheap, often earning an average of only U.S. $5 or $6 a day.

After the 1982 devaluation, American dollars bought more pesos, making the *maquiladora* worker among the least expensive in the world. Furthermore, the 1987 wage and price control pact negotiated between the government, unions, and the private sector severely depressed wages in Mexico's fight to reduce inflation. It is this combination of low wages, flexibility, and skill, American company owners hope, that will allow them to regain an edge over their ever more able competitors in the Far East, and to hold their own with the European Union. For such companies, the most important aspect of the North American Free Trade Agreement (NAFTA), which came into force in 1994, is that it "locks in" Mexico's probusiness reforms, seemingly forever.

General Electric, based in Fairfield, Connecticut, opened its first plant in Ciudad Juárez in 1971. Its electrical appliance division in Louisville. Kentucky, was finding that making the electrical cables which go inside its appliances was becoming too costly. Because of the time needed to make them, they were expensive and also, explains a GE spokesman in Mexico, "the workers didn't like the job. If they could get moved to another department in the plant they would always take the opportunity." With the success of the Juárez plant, GE decided to expand in Mexico; it now has eight plants there, employing 8,500 people. Various GE divisions now operate in cities such as Nogales, Juárez, Chihuahua City, Ciudad Acuña, and Reynosa, where workers make circuit breakers, motors, coils, and pumps, allowing GE to compete not only with other American companies that have *maquiladoras* in Mexico but with the so-called Pacific Rim countries of Japan, Taiwan, and South Korea.

Ironically, the Reynosa plant is the only GE plant that is unionised. But even GE admits that those who run the union, which is progovernment and proemployer, have shown themselves to be far more intent on attempting to earn extra money through "purchasing arrangements and other contracting matters" than representing their dues-paying members.

Nor is it hard to figure out why the Mexican government is so happy to see such explosive growth in the twin-plant industry. Originally they were set up to provide jobs and economic opportunities in the traditionally poor and underdeveloped border area. The border had long attracted immigrants or temporary workers looking for jobs in the United States. When there was no work available, many came back to wait on the Mexican side of the border, usually in severe states of destitution. A workforce was therefore ready and waiting for the promotors of the industry. Yet it was rarely unemployed men who were hired to work in the new plants, but local women—new to industrial work, apparently docile, and cheap—who worked on the assembly lines.

NOTE

1. The list of 500 largest companies published annually by *Fortune* magazine.

Reading B

Sex Discrimination in the Maquiladoras

HUMAN RIGHTS WATCH

The group Human Rights Watch reports that sex discrimination in maquiladoras is contrary to Mexican law as well as international human rights conventions. For instance, the use of pregnancy tests to screen job applicants and the poor treatment of pregnant workers seem to be widespread.

"You indicated that women applicants are required to take pregnancy tests as a condition of employment. This is simply not true." That was the terse response by American Zettler, an electronics multinational, to accusations made by the U.S. organisation Human Rights Watch, which claims that its Mexican subsidiary, Zettler Mexico, based in Tijuana in the export-processing zone that stretches the length of the border with the United States, complies fully with Mexican labour legislation.

Twenty-eight-year-old Paula would dispute that. When she applied for a job on the Zettler Mexico assembly line two years ago, she had to take a pregnancy test, carried out by a doctor employed by the factory. The test was for all female applicants, she says. It's certainly not the only case. Human Rights Watch met hundreds of women in Mexico who, like Paula, were tested when they were hired. Bonita, who works at Deltronicos in Matamoros, a subsidiary of General Motors; Graciela, employed by Panasonic in Tijuana; and Rebecca at MagneTek in Matomoros . . . all had to take the test. Absence of pregnancy has become a condition of employment in most of the factories in the zone, the maquiladoras, which employ a total of half a

million workers, 70 percent of whom are women, and earn the Mexican state $20 million in export income.

In its report[1], Human Rights Watch cites a woman doctor, Adela Moreno, who works at Matsushita-Panasonic. "When I first started working at Matsushita, the director of personnel told me to make sure that I tested every single female applicant for pregnancy because pregnant women were too costly to the company. It seemed it was all I did. I was appalled" she continued.

Keeping costs down is precisely the reason companies insist on the test, which is contrary to Mexican law and international conventions. One company has even recognised as much. In a letter addressed to Human Rights Watch, Denis Winkleman, vice president of the Zenith electronics corporation, states his case bluntly. "The reason companies conduct pregnancy screening is because, historically, many women applicants not enrolled in Mexican social security have sought employment after learning of their pregnancies, took advantage of company-funded maternity benefits, and ended their employment after these benefits ran out. In effect, these women were not true job applicants, but women seeking maternity benefits which social security would not provide."

While the text speaks volumes about the companies' motives, the reason they give as justification is far from the truth. Zenith's vigilance doesn't end when the person is hired. Patricia worked for Zenith for four years before she became pregnant. "I waited three months before announcing my pregnancy because the doctor told me I risked having a miscarriage" says Patricia. But when she asked to change tasks because of her condition, she was pressured into resigning and lost all her rights. Patricia's case is far from isolated. The Human Rights Watch report is full of examples of

Human Rights Watch, "Sex Discrimination in the Maquiladoras," in *Free Labor World* 12, December 1996.

pregnant workers who have been bullied, transferred to heavier work, or forced to work the night shift, all aimed at pressuring them into resigning. When Maria Elena Corona Caldero, employed at Plasticos Bajacal in Tijuana, learned she was pregnant, she asked for a job she could perform sitting down. Maria Elena wraps frames in plastic that she puts in boxes, which she then lifts up to put on the assembly line. The work became too tiring for her but her supervisor turned down her request for a transfer. "This same day, I started bleeding soon after the shift began. My husband, who also works at the plant, asked my supervisor if he could take me to hospital. He said no. . . . I did not leave the plant until 6.30 A.M., when my shift ended. I went di-

rectly to the doctor, but I had haemorrhaged so much that I had lost the fetus."

Maria Elena kept her job. While she was in the hospital she underwent an operation to tie her fallopian tubes. "I didn't want any more problems" she confides.

Pregnancy tests for applicants, pressure on pregnant workers, and ill treatment—most of the 2,100 maquiladoras systematically violate women's fundamental rights, while the Mexican authorities turn a blind eye. A government official in Matamoros responsible for ensuring enforcement of the labour code admitted that he knew pregnancy tests took place, but that he was unable to prove it. Today the proof exists.

NOTE

1. "Sex Discrimination in Mexico's Maquiladora Sector," Human Rights Watch, 1996. Human Rights Watch, 485 Fifth Avenue, New York, NY 10017-6104, USA. Brussels office: 15, rue Van Campenhout, 1000 Brussels.

FIGURE IV.7   THE WORLD ACCORDING TO NIKE

"NIKE'S BUSINESS"

Let us take one set of such hands—an actual case study of a woman who labors in one of Nike's six Korean-run Indonesian shoe factories. Sadisah (the pseudonym provided by *Harper's* magazine, which first told the tale) earns about 14¢ an hour, raking in just under $40 each month by laboring 60-plus-hour workweeks manufacturing athletic shoes.[1] The shoes she makes sell for about $80 a pair, of which her value-added contribution is a full 11¢. There are various types of arithmetic that can be performed on these data. For example, it is easy to compute that it would take Sadisah two months to earn enough money to buy back the shoes she makes, although it is unclear where she would find the time for cross-training at the local athletic club. An even more interesting calculation is that Sadisah would only have to work an estimated 44,492 years to earn the $20 million, multiyear endorsement fee Michael Jordan commanded before his short-lived retirement from professional basketball. It should be pointed out in this regard that Nike's 1991 profits reached $287 million on $3 billion in sales, a figure that is of course calculated after Michael Jordan and all of Nike's designers, advertising agencies, marketing services, managers, and owners have taken their cut.

From: Richard P. Appelbaum, "Multiculturalism and Flexibility. Some New Directions in Global Capitalism," in *Mapping Multiculturalism,* Avery Gordon and Christopher Newfield, eds, University of Minnesota Press. 1996: 303.

1. Jeffrey Ballinger, "The New Free Trade Hell: Nike's Profits Jump on the Back of Asian Workers," Harper's (August 1992): 46–47.

Reading C

Our Policies, Their Consequences: Zambian Women's Lives under Structural Adjustment

AMBER AULT AND EVE SANDBERG

Amber Ault and Eve Sandberg describe the effects of the economic policy of "structural adjustment" on women in Zambia. Since the global economic system connects the First and Third Worlds, Ault and Sandberg argue that those of us in the First World have an obligation to educate ourselves about the policies and programs initiated by wealthy countries and enforced by international organizations.

Women around the globe share many concerns, including meeting basic subsistence needs, improving the prevention and treatment of diseases like AIDS, providing for reproductive health and freedom, reducing infant mortality and childhood illness, preventing violence against women, ensuring gender equity in labor, law, and education, and increasing women's ability to exercise sexual self-determination. Because wealthy countries and poor countries occupy very different positions in the global economic system, however, the social, economic, and political oppression experienced by women in poor countries differs in form from that experienced by women in wealthy countries. Furthermore, the oppression of women in Third World countries does not exist in a vacuum that begins and ends at national borders. Indeed, much of the poverty, discrimination, disease, and violence experienced by Third World women results from the ex-

Amber Ault and Eve Sandberg, "Our Policies, Their Consequences: Zambian Women's Lives under Structural Adjustment," *Feminist Frontiers V,* Laurel Richardson, Verta Taylor, and Nancy Whittier, eds. New York: McGraw-Hill, 2000: 503–6.

ploitation of their countries by wealthier countries and the international organizations that they control. As feminist scholars and activists in wealthy Western countries, we must educate ourselves about our roles in supporting the systems of domination which perpetuate the exploitation of women elsewhere.

We do not argue that all women in industrialized nations enjoy vast, substantial advantages over all women in Third World countries. Indeed, many women in the United States live in extreme poverty, without decent housing, steady health care, stable employment, or any assurance of personal safety, while some women in poor nations enjoy relatively high standards of living. Nonetheless, because wealthy Western countries benefit from the labor of exploited Third World workers, Western feminists need to understand the roles their governments play in women's oppression in other countries.

In this brief report, we use a case study to demonstrate how the self-interested practices of wealthier countries in one international organization exacerbate and sometimes create the oppression of Third World women as women, citizens, and workers. To explicate the connections between the United States government, one powerful international organization, and the lives of women in Third World countries, we recount the impact of an International Monetary Fund (IMF) Structural Adjustment Program in the African country of Zambia.

The International Monetary Fund constitutes an international agency designed to promote a stable world economy. As part of its mission, it provides loans to countries with failing economies. Capital for such loans comes from deposits made by the countries participating in the International Monetary Fund. The conditions each borrowing country must meet to secure a loan are contingent on the ultimate approval by the board of directors of the Fund, which includes representatives of the member states, whose votes are weighted relative to their countries' financial contributions; wealthy nations like the United States make large contributions and therefore enjoy great influence over the contingencies attached to loans the agency makes, as well as its policies and actions. Not surprisingly, the terms of loans to Third World countries reflect the economic and political interests and values of the world's wealthiest nations.

The "Structural Adjustment Program" constitutes one kind of loan package managed by this organization. The International Monetary Fund makes financial assistance to Third World countries contingent upon borrower countries' willingness to make significant adjustments in their economic systems. The adjustments required by the International Monetary Fund reflect Western capitalist economic ideologies. In addition, they often reflect a disregard for the structural, cultural, social, and technological features of the borrowing country. As a result, Structural Adjustment Programs administered by the International Monetary Fund frequently result in dramatic and devastating changes in the countries that adopt them. Nonetheless, because the International Monetary Fund constitutes one of the few sources of loan capital to which an indebted country can turn, countries suffering severe economic difficulty often accept the terms of Structural Adjustment Programs.

Such was the case of Zambia, a Black-governed country in South-Central Africa that implemented an IMF Structural Adjustment Program in October 1985 and wrestled with it in various forms until its termination in May 1987. Before we describe the policies and outcomes of the Structural Adjustment Program in Zambia, we offer a brief description of some features of the country, so that readers may more fully grasp the ramifications of the program on the lives of citizens in general and women in particular.

At the time it instituted its IMF Structural Adjustment Program, Zambia reported that its population numbered about 6.7 million citizens. About 3.81 mil-

lion Zambians over the age of 11 were working or actively seeking work, but only about 71 percent of these people could find jobs. While some urban Zambian women worked as teachers, nurses, secretaries, and waitresses, many more were self-employed as food sellers, street vendors, and charcoal producers, or in other jobs in the "informal sector"; in rural areas, women usually worked as farmers.

Then, as now, Zambia imported many goods. Government controls on foreign exchange rates held in check the cost to consumers of food and other goods imported by retailers before the implementation of the Structural Adjustment Program. Such controls helped to allow families in both urban and rural areas to meet their basic subsistence needs and were especially beneficial for women, upon whom rests most of the responsibility of supporting the family.

Other government policies and programs helped to make life in Zambia manageable for its citizens before the Structural Adjustment Program. For example, the Zambian government made heavily subsidized health care available to all citizens and ensured access to basic education. Zambian governmental policies also kept domestic tensions in check by equitably distributing government-subsidized resources to the four separate geographic areas occupied by the country's four major ethnic groups.

Before it would disburse a loan to Zambia, the IMF required the Zambian government to promise to make major changes in the structure of its economy. According to the IMF, the required changes would allow the country to participate more successfully in the world market and, as a result, would allow it to repay its loan. Although many of the wealthy countries with controlling interests in the IMF do not have balanced national budgets, the IMF's Structural Adjustment Program packages are designed around the idea that Third World countries should achieve balanced budgets, and that they should do this in part by suspending support to domestic programs.

The International Monetary Fund required Zambia to devalue its currency, discontinue its subsidization of food, health, and education, suspend social welfare programs, lay off federal employees, and turn its attention to both diversifying and increasing its exports for international markets. The result: a socioeconomic nightmare for the country's people. The changes required by the IMF produced widespread unemployment; inflation of astronomical proportions; the suspension of the education of many people, especially girls; a dramatic decrease in access to health care; an increase in violence; conflict between the country's ethnic groups; and increased class stratification. While these problems affected most citizens, they made life especially arduous for women.

Overnight, the devaluation of Zambian currency and the suspension of government subsidies on imported goods produced massive inflation. The consumer prices of domestically produced products and services, including health care, school fees, and transportation, rose by 50 percent; the prices of many imported goods doubled. Women and girls were especially hard hit by inflation. For example, because women are primarily responsible for feeding and clothing their children, the dramatic increases in the cost of food and household goods took a great toll on their limited incomes; with the increase in household expenses, and the end of nationally subsidized health care and education, medicine and schooling became increasingly beyond the means of most families. As a result, families made difficult decisions about who would receive the benefit of increasingly limited resources, and those decisions reflected entrenched patriarchal values. In the case of education, for example, families often reverted to traditions that promoted the education of male children over that of girls.

Sudden, massive unemployment exacerbated the problems resulting from inflation. The IMF required the Zambian government to lay off scores of government workers as a means of reducing expenditures. As a result of reduced consumer spending, private businesses and industry also let large numbers of workers go. In both spheres, women suffered great losses because their positions were frequently regarded as the most expendable. Joblessness, coupled with inflation, left Zambians destitute; sexist social structures disadvantaged women, even relative to men, who were suffering greatly.

For example, while the inflated price of gasoline made the cost of public transportation beyond most citizens' means and forced those who retained jobs to walk long distances to and from work, after-work hours were very different for men and women. Because they are responsible for feeding their families, many women had to extend their days either with extra income-producing activities or by obtaining land on which to create family gardens. Women's "double burden" of work and child care became even greater under the hardships of the Structural Adjustment Program.

Women also suffered directly at the hands of men as a result of the social stress the country experienced during the Structural Adjustment Program. Men, pressed to their limits, took advantage of women's resources and patriarchal social structures which allowed them to succeed in such efforts. For example, one woman farmer interviewed recounted how her brother had stolen from her: their father had willed them an ox to share, and every year she and her brother took turns using the animal to plow their fields; in the first year of the Structural Adjustment Program, the brother took the ox, refused to return it, and rented it to others for extra income, saying that his family could not survive if he did otherwise; the woman, in turn, could not plant enough to feed her family that year, and since customary law in the area did not recognize women's right to property, had no recourse. Such situations were not uncommon.

Nor was physical violence. In the years of the Structural Adjustment Program, the rate of violent crime in Zambia rose sharply. Women's increased activity away from home, as a result of their need to have extra income-generating activities, made them increasingly vulnerable to attack; women walking to and from work or their gardens, often distant from their homes, were fearful of being assaulted. At home, too, people were wary. One interviewee described how she and her husband took turns staying awake at night to protect themselves from prospective robbers.

These problems were further exacerbated by increasing conflict between groups in Zambia. As a result of IMF conditions, the government suspended its policy of distributing agricultural resources equitably throughout the country. Some areas of the country began to receive more and better supplies, setting the stage for conflicts between the ethnic groups living in different geographic regions. The Structural Adjustment Program also indirectly produced increased stratification among the country's women: those women farmers who happened to live along the country's supply roads received many more resources than those who lived in remote territories. While such women were among the few to benefit financially from the Structural Adjustment Program in Zambia, their prosperity rested on the deprivation of others.

Clearly, the imposition of the conditions of the IMF Structural Adjustment Program in Zambia wreaked havoc on the lives of the country's people. Similar IMF Structural Adjustment Programs throughout the Third World have produced equally devastating effects. We note that some IMF Structural Adjustment Programs in other impoverished countries have included a feature missing from the Zambian program: special encouragement for multinational corporations to promote exports. The mistreatment of women workers by such corporations has been well documented by other feminist scholars. (Nash and Fernandez-Kelly 1983; Fuentes and Ehrenreich 1983; Ward 1990)

A small number of women entrepreneurs benefit from the free-market conditions created by IMF adjustment programs, and some women find empowerment and forge coalitions with other women in their efforts to resist the hardships the programs impose. Generally, however, throughout the Third World, people suffer greatly as a result of the conditions their governments must accept in order to procure loans designed to relieve the economic instability of their countries.

As voting members in the IMF, western governments, including that of the United States, condone and encourage the policies that so disrupt the lives of so many millions in Third World states. The United Nations Economic Social and Cultural Organization (UNESCO) and the United Nations Africa Economic Committee (UNAEC) have criticized the extraordinary toll that citizens in Third World states, especially women, are paying for their governments' Structural Adjustment Programs. Today, other organizations and individual citizens in Western countries are also attempting to alter IMF policies. Friends of the Earth, for example, a Washington, D.C.-based nongovernmental organization concerned primarily with the environment, began a campaign in 1991 to urge the U.S. Congress to use the U.S. voting position in the International Monetary Fund to alter IMF Structural Adjustment Programs.

Western feminists can join or initiate efforts to alter the IMF's programs. Women from wealthy countries must recognize our collaboration in the global system that oppresses women. As citizens of the countries intimately involved with the implementation of international policies which foster the exploitation of women in the Third World, we can seek to change the system. Indeed, we must: to fail to act on behalf of the women suffering as a result of our government's involvement in the IMF is to perpetuate the oppression of others, even as we seek to relieve our own.

REFERENCES

Fuentes, Annette, and Ehrenreich, Barbara, eds. (1983). *Women in the Global Factory.* Boston: South End Press.

Nash, June, and Fernandez-Kelly, Patricia, eds. (1983). *Women, Men, and the International Division of Labor.* Albany: State University of New York Press.

Ward, Kathryn, ed. (1990). *Women Workers and Global Restructuring.* Ithaca: Cornell University Press.

QUESTIONS AND ANSWERS ABOUT THE IMF

■ What is the IMF?

The International Monetary Fund, headquartered in Washington, D.C., has 182 member countries and membership is nearly universal. Its mission is to maintain currency stability so world trade can flourish.

■ How does it work?

The IMF lends money to members who do not have enough cash to pay their debts to other members. The loans are repaid with interest.

The IMF uses its leverage by making the loans contingent on economic reform. The conditions usually call for strict monetary and fiscal policies. The required reforms are usually strongly market-oriented and are directed at opening economies to trade and competition.

Although not technically a world central bank, the IMF does act as a lender of last resort to countries in financial distress. It can alleviate a liquidity crisis by offering credit when other lenders are calling in their loans.

■ Where does it get its money?

The IMF lends from a $210 billion pool of money contributed by members. Member "quotas" vary by country. The bigger the quota, the more voting rights the member has and the more money it can borrow. The United States has 18 percent of the quota—about $39 billion—and the largest voting share.

The relationship between the IMF and its member countries is similar to that of a bank and its customers. The members deposit money, which can be withdrawn, and earn interest on the balance.

■ Who runs the IMF?

The fund is governed by a board with a representative from each country. A 24-member executive board supervises operations. The fund employs 2,300 staff members, mainly professional economists. Every year, a team of four or five fund economists visits member countries for two weeks to gather information and review the country's economic policies with government officials.

■ Why was the IMF created?

The IMF was created in July 1944 at Bretton Woods, New Hampshire, by world leaders hoping to avoid the economic calamities of the Great Depression and World War II.

The Bretton Woods institutions, which also include the United Nations, the General Agreement on Tariffs and Trade (renamed the World Trade Organization), and the World Bank, were created to stabilize the world economic and political order— and to prevent countries from resorting to the counterproductive actions so many of them took during the 1930s.

■ Who are its critics?

Both left- and right-wing conspiracy theorists oppose the IMF, which was the brainchild of British economist John Maynard Keynes and Harry Dexter White, a U.S. Treasury official later alleged to be a Soviet spy. Right-wing theorists contend that it is a secret tool to promote world socialism. Leftists blast it as an imperialist scourge that promotes capitalist exploitation in developing nations.

Some critics also argue that the IMF is too secretive and that its decision-making should be opened to public scrutiny. Supporters contend that this would politicize the fund and that, like the Federal Reserve and other central banks, its decision-making should be shielded from political pressure.

San Francisco Chronicle, January 13, 1998, A4.

The Gendered Politics and Violence of Structural Adjustment: A View from Jamaica

FAYE V. HARRISON

Anthropologist Faye Harrison looks at the upheaval caused by the process of structural adjustment in the life of one woman in Jamaica over the last 20 years.

An Ethnographic Window on a Crisis

"The ghetto not'ing but a sad shanty town now." This is what one of my friends and informants sadly remarked to me upon my 1992 visit to "Oceanview," a pseudonym for an impoverished slum neighborhood with a roughly 74 percent formal unemployment rate in the downtown district of the Kingston Metropolitan Area. Times were so hard that the tenements had deteriorated beyond repair. The conspicuous physical decline was a marker of the deepened socioeconomic austerity accompanying what some critics (e.g., *Race*

Faye V. Harrison, *"The Gendered Politics and Violence of Structural Adjustment: A View from Jamaica,"* in Louise Lamphere, Helena Ragoné, and Patricia Cavella, eds. *Situated Lives: Gender and Culture in Everyday Life,* New York: Routledge, 1997: 451–55.

& Class 1992) now consider to be the "recolonization" of Jamaica by "the new conquistadors"—the policies and programs that the International Monetary Fund (IMF), the World Bank, and the Reagan and Bush administrations of the United States government designed to "adjust" and "stabilize" the country's revived export-oriented economy. These strategies for delivering third-world societies from collapsing economies are informed by a development ideology that euphemizes the widening social disparities that have been the outcome of policies imposing an unbearable degree of austerity on living conditions. Hence, these policies have sacrificed ordinary people's—especially the poor's—basic needs in health care, housing, education, social services, and employment for those of free enterprise and free trade.

Since 1978, I have observed and conversed with Oceanview residents about the social, economic, and political conditions shaping their lived experiences and struggles for survival in this neighborhood (e.g., Harrison 1987a,b; 1988; 1991a,b). The late 1970s was a time of economic hardship and political turbulence, a time when the People's National Party's (PNP) democratic socialist path to economic development and social transformation was vehemently contested, blocked, and destabilized by political opponents both within and without the country and by the concerted economic force of an international recession, quadrupled oil prices, and a massive flight of both domestic and foreign capital. Life was certainly hard then, but, as one resident commented, "Cho, mahn [sic]; tings worse now." Despite the bright promises of political and economic "deliverance" made by the Jamaica Labour Party (JLP) and its major backer, the Reagan and later Bush administrations of the U.S. government, the 1980s and early 1990s— under the leadership of a much more conservative PNP—brought only a deepened poverty to the folk who people the streets and alleys of slum and shantytown neighborhoods like Oceanview. This deepening poverty is reflected, for example, in a serious decline in the conditions of public health. The implementation of structural adjustment policies has brought about alarming reductions in government health care expenditures and promoted the privatization of more costly and less accessible medical care (Phillips 1994, 137). Those most heavily burdened by the impact of these deteriorating social conditions and capital-centered policies are women (Antrobus 1989) who serve as the major "social shock absorbers" (Sparr 1992, 31; 1994) mediating the crisis at the local level of households and neighborhoods. Nearly 50 percent of all Kingston's households are female-headed, giving women the major responsibilities for making ends meet out of virtually nothing (Deere et al. 1990, 52–53). Concentrated in the informal sector of the economy, these women along with their children are most vulnerable to the consequences of malnutrition, hunger, and poor health: rising levels of morbidity and mortality (Phillips 1994, 142; Pan American Health Organization/World Health Organization 1992).

To appreciate and understand the effects, contradictions, and meanings that constitute the reality of a structurally adjusted pattern of production and trade, we must examine the everyday experiences, practices, discourses, and common sense of real people, particularly those encouraged to wait—and wait—for

social and economic benefits to trickle down. In the interest of an ethnographically grounded view of Jamaica's current economic predicament, I present the case of Mrs. Beulah Brown, an admirable woman whose life story I collected over several years, to help elucidate the impact the ongoing crisis has on the everyday lives of ordinary Jamaicans, particularly poor urban women and those who depend most on them. A longtime household head and informal-sector worker like so many other Jamaican women, Mrs. Brown was once a community health aide with a government program that provided much-needed health services to a population to whom such care would not have been available otherwise. Mrs. Brown would not have gotten or held that job for the years that she did without "the right political connections," something, unfortunately, that too few poor people ever obtain. Although visible benefits from membership in the local PNP group may have set her apart from most of her neighbors, the centrality of patronage-clientelism in local and national politics makes a former political client's experience an insightful window on the constraints and vulnerabilities built into Jamaica's political and economic policies.

Highlights from Mrs. Brown's life story lead us to the more encompassing story of postcolonial Jamaica's experience with debt, export-led development, and structural adjustment, and their combined impact on women workers as well as on neighborhood-level negotiations of crisis.

A Hard-Working Woman's Story within a Story

In the 1970s Beulah Brown, then a middle-aged woman responsible for a two-generation household and extended family, worked as a community health aide under the combined aegis of a government public health program and a local urban redevelopment agency, two projects that owed their existence to the social-policy orientation of the reformist PNP administration. Mrs. Brown had begun her employment history as a worker in a factory manufacturing undergarments. However, she preferred household-based self-employment over the stringent regimentation of factory work. A woman with strong civic consciousness and organizing skills, she had worked her way into the leadership of the PNP group within the neighborhood and wider political division. By the late 1970s, she was no longer an officer; however, her membership in the party was still active.

Mrs. Brown was so effective at working with patients and exhibiting good citizenship that she was widely recognized and addressed as "Nurse Brown," the term "nurse" being a title of utmost respect. When Mrs. Brown made her daily rounds, she did more than expected of a health aide. She treated her patients as whole persons with a range of basic needs she felt obligated to help meet. To this end, she saw to it that they had nutritional food to eat, clean clothes to wear, and neat and orderly rooms in which to live. She was especially devoted to the elderly, but she also invested considerable energy in young mothers, who were often merely children themselves. She shared her experiences and wisdom with them, admonishing them to eat healthy foods, read good books, and, given her religious worldview, "pray to the Lord Jesus Christ" so that their babies' characters and personalities would be positively influenced while still in the womb.

When I initially met her, Mrs. Brown was responsible for caring for her elderly father, her handicapped sister, her sister's three daughters, and her own two daughters. At earlier times she had even minded a young niece, who eventually joined her other siblings and mother, another of Mrs. Brown's sisters, in Canada. Despite many hardships, Beulah managed her household well enough to see to it that the children were fed, clothed, and schooled. Indeed, one of her nieces, Claudia, is now a nurse in New York City, and—"by the grace of God"—her eldest daughter, Cherry, is a graduate of the University of the West Indies. Unfortunately, Marie, the daughter who still remains at home, had difficulty getting and keeping wage work, whether in an office or a factory, so she decided to make and sell children's clothes so she could work at home while minding her children. Despite the economic uncertainty of informal-sector work, Marie appreciates its flexibility and the freedom from the "downpressive" (oppressive) industrial surveillance,

about which a number of former factory workers in Oceanview complain.

Because the community health aide job did not bring in enough income to support the household, Mrs. Brown found ways to augment her income. Mainly she made dresses, a skill and talent she had cultivated over most of her life. Years ago she had even had a small shop in Port Antonio that catered to locals as well as foreign tourists. That was before she gave up everything—her shop and her husband—to return home to Kingston to care for relatives who were going through some hard times. Besides her dressmaking enterprise, Mrs. Brown also baked and sold meat patties, bought and sold cheese, and sold ice from the deep freezer she had purchased with remittances from her twin sister in England and help from her church. Through political party connections gained through her earlier activism in the local PNP group, she also saw to it that her sister got a job cleaning streets in the government Crash Programme. Although her family managed better than most of their neighbors, survival was still an everyday struggle.

In the mid-1980s, Mrs. Brown lost her health aide job. The Community Health Aide Program suffered massive losses due to the retrenchment in public-sector employment stipulated by the structural adjustment and stabilization measures imposed by the IMF and World Bank. Luckily, the layoff came around the time when the girls she had raised were coming of age and could work to support themselves and their families. By 1988, the household was made up of only Beulah, her second daughter, Marie, and Marie's three small children. Everyone else had moved on to independent residences in Kingston or emigrated to the United States and Canada to live with relatives, "a foreign," overseas. This dispersal relieved the household of considerable financial pressure, but to make ends meet Beulah still had to intensify her informal means of generating income. She did more dressmaking and added baking wedding and birthday cakes to her list of moneymaking activities.

No matter how much work she did, she never seemed to be able to do more than barely make ends meet. With the devaluation of the Jamaican dollar and the removal of subsidies on basic consumer items like food, the costs of living had increased dramatically. What more could she do to keep pace with the inflationary trend designed to make Jamaican exports more competitive on the international market? She knew that she would never resort to the desperate illicit measures some of her neighbors had taken by "tiefing" ("thiefing") or dealing drugs. She simply refused to sell her soul to the devil for some of the "blood money" obtainable from the activities of local gangs—now called posses—that move from Kingston to the United States and back trafficking in substances like crack cocaine. Increasingly, especially with political patronage becoming more scarce, drug trafficking has become an important source of local subsistence and small-scale investment. However, the price paid for a life of crime is too high. She lamented that too many "youts"(youths) involved in the drug economy make the trip home to Jamaica enclosed in deathly wooden crates.

Like most Caribbean people, Mrs. Brown has long belonged to and actively participated in an international family network extending from Jamaica to Great Britain, Canada, and the United States (Basch et al. 1994). Her sisters abroad had often invited her to visit them, and they had also encouraged her to migrate so that she, too, could benefit from better opportunities. Before the mid-1980s, Mrs. Brown had been determined to remain at home caring for her family. More over, she loved her country, her church, and her party, and she wanted to help shape the direction of Jamaica's future. She strongly felt that someone had to remain in Jamaica to keep it going on the right course. Everyone couldn't migrate. "My home is here in Jamaica," she insisted adamantly.

These were her strong feelings *before* structural adjustment hit the heart of her home: her refrigerator, deep freezer, and kitchen table. In 1990 alone, the cost of chicken—a desirable entree to accompany rice and peas on Sunday—went up three times. The cost of even more basic staples also rose, making items such as fresh milk, cornmeal, and tomatoes (whose price increased 140 percent) more and more unaffordable for many people (Statistical Institute of Jamaica 1991).

Between 1987 and 1992, Mrs. Brown traveled abroad twice for extended visits with relatives in England, Canada, and the United States. While away for nearly a year at a time, she "did a likkle babysitting and ting" to earn money that she was able to save for her own purposes. Her family treated her "like a queen," buying her gifts ("good camera, TV, radio, and ting"), not letting her spend her own money for living expenses, and paying for her air transportation from point to point along her international itinerary. The savings she managed to send and bring back home were key to her Oceanview household's survival. Her transnational family network, and the geographic mobility it offered, allowed her to increase her earnings by taking advantage of the marked wage differential between Jamaica and the countries where her relatives live (Ho 1993, 33). This particular financial advantage has led even middle-class Jamaican women to tolerate an otherwise embarrassing and humiliating decline in social status to work as nannies and domestic helpers in North American homes. International migration within the Caribbean region as well as between it and major metropoles has been a traditional survival strategy among Jamaicans since nineteenth-century postemancipation society.

Harsh circumstances forced Mrs. Brown to join the larger wave of female emigrants from the Caribbean who, since the late 1960s, have outnumbered their male counterparts (Deere 1990, 76; Ho 1993, 33). Thus far, Mrs. Brown has remained a "visitor," but she acknowledges the possibility and perhaps even the probability that some day soon she will join her sisters as a permanent resident abroad. Meanwhile, she continues to take care of business at home by informally generating and allocating resources within the kinship-mediated transnational social field within which her local life is embedded.

Mrs. Brown's story and many others similar to it are symptomatic of the current age of globalization, marked by a deepening crisis that policies such as structural adjustment and its complement, export-led development strategy, attempt to manage in favor of the mobility and accumulation of transnational capital.

REFERENCES

Antrobus, Peggy. (1989). "Crisis, Challenge and the Experiences of Caribbean Women." *Caribbean Quarterly* 35(1&2):17–28.

Basch, Linda, Nina Glick Schiller, and Cristina Szanton Blanc. (1994). *Nations Unbound: Transnational Projects, Postcolonial Predicaments, and Deterritorialized Nation-States.* Langhorne, PA: Gordon and Breach Science Publishers.

Deere, Carmen Diana, et al. (1990). *In the Shadows of the Sun: Caribbean Development Alternatives and U.S. Policy.* Boulder: Westview Press.

Harrison, Faye V. (1987a). "Crime, Class, and Politics in Jamaica." *TransAfrica Forum* 5(1):29–38.

———— (1987b). "Gangs, Grassroots Politics, and the Crisis of Dependent Capitalism in Jamaica." In *Perspectives in U.S. Marxist Anthropology.* David Hakken and Hanna Lessinger, eds. Boulder: Westview Press.

———— (1988). "The Politics of Social Outlawry in Urban Jamaica." *Urban Anthropology and Studies in Cultural Systems and World Economic Development* 17(2&3):259–77.

———— (1990). "Jamaica and the International Drug Economy." *TransAfrica Forum* 7(3):49–57.

———— (1991a). "Ethnography as Politics." In *Decolonizing Anthropology: Moving Further toward an Anthropology for Liber-* *ation.* Faye V. Harrison, ed. Washington, D. C.: American Anthropological Association.

Ho, Christine G. T. (1993). "The Internationalization of Kinship and the Feminization of Caribbean Migration: The Case of Afro-Trinidadian Immigrants in Los Angeles." *Human Organization* 52(1):32–40.

Race & Class. "The New Conquistadors." (1992). 34(1) (July/Sept.):1–114.

Pan American Health Organization/World Health Organization. (1992). *The Health of Women in the English Speaking Caribbean.*

Phillips, Daphene. (1994). "The IMF, Structural Adjustment and Health in the Caribbean: Policy Change in Health Care in Trinidad and Tobago." *Twenty-first Century Policy Review* 2(1&2):129–49.

Sparr, Pamela. (1992). "How We Got into This Mess and Ways to Get Out." *Ms.* March/April, 130.

———— ed. (1994). *Mortgaging Women's Lives: Feminist Critiques of Structural Adjustment.* London: Zed Books.

Statistical Institute of Jamaica. (1991). *Statistical Yearbook of Jamaica.* Kingston: Statistical Institute of Jamaica.

REFLECTING ON THE SECTION

The North American Free Trade Agreement (NAFTA) and the International Monetary Fund's structural adjustment programs are designed to increase and facilitate global trade. The impact of these policies on women differs according to their class and nationality across national boundaries and also according to race and class (among other factors) within specific countries. Can you discuss some of these differences between First and Third World nations, and within a particular nation?

The readings also tell us about women as consumers and as producers of goods: is it accurate to say that globalization has turned First World women into consumers and Third World women into producers? What is left out of this viewpoint? How do women intervene in, consent to, and resist international and national trade policies that affect their lives? Ault and Sandberg assert that people in the First World must "educate ourselves about our roles in supporting the systems of domination which perpetuate the exploitation of women elsewhere." What are these roles? What roles do you think feminists should play in labor policies and politics as workers, consumers, employers, and/or educators?

Global Food Production and Consumption

Tomasito's Guide to Economic Integration: A Whirlwind Tour with Your Guide Tomasito, the Tomato

ECUMENICAL COALITION FOR ECONOMIC JUSTICE

The Ecumenical Coalition for Economic Justice, a nongovernmental group, describes the circuit taken by a popular commodity, the tomato, from field to table.

This piece highlights the exploitation of labor and the environment by multinational corporations in alliance with structural adjustment programs.

Ecumenical Coalition for Economic Justice, "Tomasito's Guide to Economic Integration: A Whirlwind Tour with Your Guide Tomasito, the Tomato," *Economic Integration of the Americas: An Education and Action Kit*. Toronto: 1994©.

"Tomasito's Guide to Economic Integration:

A Whirlwind Tour with Your Guide *Tomasito,* the Tomato,"

La guía de Tomasito para la integración económica:

Un tur por los molinos de viento, con su guía *Tomasito,* el tomate

1.

Our tour begins on land acquired by the U.S.-based jolly Green Giant Co. Mexican farmers used to work this land together on communally owned cooperative farms. 1960s structural adjustment reforms opened up Mexican agriculture to large-scale private investments and pushed small landholders off the land.

Nuestro tur comienza en tierras adquiridas por la compañía estadounidense, (el feliz Gigante Verde) Green Giant Co. Antes de que llegara este 'gigante', estas tierras eran cooperativas campesinas, propiedad comunal de los campesinos mexicanos. Las reformas en los ajustes estructurales de 1980 abren las puertas de la agricultura mexicana a inversiones extranjeras a gran escala que terminan por echar a los pequeños agricultores de su propia tierra.

2.

To prepare for mass cultivation and export of tomatoes, the land is first fumigated with methylbromide. This takes us to St. Louis, Missouri, headquarters of the Monsanto Corp. who produces the pesticides and is one of America's largest polluters.

Para preparar el cultivo masivo y la exportación de los tomates, se fumiga primero la tierra con metilio de bromo. Esto nos trae a St Luis de Missouri, casa matriz de la Corporación Monsanto quien produce estos pesticidas y es uno de los mayores causantes de la contaminación ambiental de todas lasAméricas.

3.

Our tour takes us to Emelle, Alabama—a poor, predominantly African-American community. Production waste from Monsanto is shipped here to the world's largest hazardous waste landfill.

Nuestro tur nos lleva ahora a Emelle, Alabama, una comunidad de origen predominantemente Afro-Americano. Aquí llegan los desechos tóxicos producidos por Monsanto. Emelle es al basural tóxico mas grande del mundo.

4.

Back in Mexico, we meet local farmworkers, who now make approximately U.S. $2.50 a day. They are given no protection from the pesticides: no gloves, masks, or safety instructions. The tomatoes are produced for export. Structural adjustment reforms promoted food exports to earn foreign exchange. The result: Mexican people are no longer producing their own food and cannot afford these tomatoes on the ages they earr.

De vuelta a México, ncs reunimos con los campesinos locales que ganan aproximadamente $2.50 USA por día. Los campesinos no tienen protección alguna en contra de los pesticidas: ni guantes, ni máscaras, tampoco reciben ningún tipo de instrucciones con respecto a su seguridad personal.

Los tomates se producen para la exportación. Las reformas de ajustes estructurales promovieron la exportación de alimentos para ganar moneda extranjera. El resultado de estas reformas: actualmente los mexicanos no producen su propio alimento y ni siquiera ganan lo suficiente como para comprar los tomates que ellos mismos producen.

5.

Next stop: Davis, California, headquarters of Calgene Inc. The tomato seed is a hybrid, patented and owned by this transnational company. It was originally developed from a Mexican strain. Transnational companies are fighting for long and stronger protection of patents for plants like this tomato.

Nuestro próximo paradero es la casa matriz de Calgene Inc. una compañía transnacional localizada en Davis, California. Calgene Inc. es propietaria de la patente de la semilla de tomate. Esta semilla es un híbrido y fue desarrollada originalmente de una especie mexicana. Las compañias transnacionales están peleando por conseguir el derecho a patentes como las de este tomate por períodos mas largos aún y con una protección todavia mas fuerte.

6.

Back in Mexico, the tomatoes are harvested, placed on plastic trays, covered in plastic wrap, packed in cardboard boxes, and driven in refrigerated trucks to wholesale distributors throughout North America, where they compete with tomatoes produced by local farming communities.

De vuelta a México, los tomates se cosechan, se ponen en bandejas plásticas, se cubren con un plástico, se embalan en cajas de cartón y se llevan en camiones refrigerados a los distribuidores al por mayor a lo largo de toda América del Norte, donde deben competir con otros tomates provenientes de comunidades agrícolas de la zona.

7.

Some of the tomatoes reach the Mexican maquiladora zones, where they are canned and made into sauce. Workers here earn U.S. $1.50-4.50 per day. Like their rural companeros, they don't earn enough to buy the goods they produce.

Algunos de estos tomates llegan hasta la zona de las maquiladoras de México donde se les envasa y se les convierte en salsa. Los trabajadores de esta zona ganan entre $1.50 USA y $4.50 USA diarios. Al igual que sus compañeros campesinos, no ganan lo suficiente como para comprar los bienes que ellos producen.

8.

The final stop is a Canadian restaurant where an unsuspecting customer looks forward to a juicy tomato salad. The waitress who took the order used to be employed in a food-processing plant that closed down and moved to Mexico. Workers in Canada and the United States are losing their jobs because they cannot afford to compete with low Mexican wages.

The waitress is now working part-time for minimum wage with no benefits. Like her Mexican sisters, she also cannot afford to order her food in this restaurant.

La última parada es un restaurante canadiense en el cual un ingenuo cliente se prepara para comer una rica y jugosa ensalada de tomates. La camarera trabajaba en una planta procesadora quo cerró y se trasladó a México. Los trabajadores en Canadá y en los Estados Unidos están perdiendo sus trabajos porque no pueden competir con los bajísimos salarios méxicanos.

La camarera trabaja ahora a media jornada y sin ningún subsidio laboral. Como sus hermanas mexicanas, ella tampoco puede pagar el precio que pide el restaurante por los all-mentos que ellas sirve a la clientela.

FIGURE IV.8

Globalization from a Consumer's Perspective: The Exciting Relationship between the World and Me

JUNKO ARIMURA

Consumer activist Junko Arimura outlines her objections to the globalization of the food industry. Arimura argues that agribusiness and international trade agreements that mandate standardization support multinational corporations at the expense of local food traditions, small farmers, and the environment.

Junko Arimura, "Globalization from a Consumer's Perspective: The Exciting Relationship between the World and Me," *Women's Asia 21: Voices from Japan,* No. 4 (1998): 30–38.

At the International Seminar on Sustainable Consumption Patterns, held on February 7 and 8, Dr. Song Bo-gyoun, representative of the Citizens' Alliance for Consumer Protection of Korea, reported how consumption patterns were changing in the midst of the

Key Terms

Food and Agriculture Organization (FAO)
Established in 1945, this United Nations agency is charged with raising levels of nutrition and standards of living, improving agricultural productivity, and bettering the condition of rural populations.

General Agreement on Tariffs and Trade (GATT) First signed in 1947, this international agreement facilitated "free trade" between United Nations members through reduction of trade barriers and tariffs.

harmonization International harmonization of food safety standards seeks to universalize the standards of the most powerful countries for all other countries, regardless of specific needs and concerns.

United Nations Development Program (UNDP)
The United Nations program dedicated to carry out development programs in alliance with governments.

Uruguay Round At the GATT meeting held in Uruguay in 1986, an agenda was created that addressed the trading system, intellectual property rights, agriculture, and textiles. Environmental issues entered negotiations for the first time at this round of meetings. It was not until 1993 that the agenda established in Uruguay was finalized.

won crisis In 1997, the currency crisis of South Korean financial markets led to instability and high unemployment rates.

World Health Organization (WHO) Established in 1946, this United Nations agency seeks to prevent the spread of disease worldwide.

World Trade Organization (WTO) Organization established in 1995 after approval of the declaration introduced at the Uruguay Round. The WTO monitors agreements and resolves disputes between member nations.

won crisis in South Korea. . . . South Korea has an extremely low food self-sufficiency ratio, just like Japan.

Her voice was filled with anger when she spoke about the suffering of farmers engaged in food production in South Korea. She said in the won crisis people could buy rice at the same price as before, because of the government's self-sufficiency policy on rice. But, the prices for other food commodities—including flour, beef, and pork—have all jumped up. In South Korea, hog, cattle, poultry, and dairy farms largely depend on imported feed grain. As the won's value dropped and the price for animal feed went up, farmers could not feed their animals. As a result, the animals starved to death. . . .

Her speech taught me that for a country with a low self-sufficiency ratio that is largely dependent on imported food, not only natural disasters and abnormal weather but also a currency crisis can be a major cause of food crisis. In fact, such economic factors should more realistically affect consumers.

As consumers, we became aware of the issue of self-sufficiency after the Uruguay Round of GATT. In 1992, when only the liberalization of the Japanese rice market was emphasized, the proposals on the full liberalization of the agriculture market and international harmonization of food safety standards (hereafter known as "harmonization") were under discussion during the Uruguay Round negotiations. Since then, both Japan and South Korea, under the theory of the international division of production, gave up the right to pursue food self-sufficiency policies except for that of rice.

Consumer organizations called for a nationwide protest against harmonization, saying that it would lead to more dependency on imported food at the cost of local agriculture, deprive citizens of the right to food security, and deprive local authorities of their sovereign right to establish food safety standards.

—Harmonization of Food Standards Is the Logic of Transnational Corporations

I began to work on this issue with my friends at the Seikatsu Club after attending a lecture by Mrs. Katsuko Nomura. She lectured on the harmonization proposal and the newly emerging international economic order called the World Trade Organization. After the lecture, we felt our right to food safety was threatened.

To maintain a food culture built on tradition and the local environment is a basic human right. It is the sovereign right of a country and local authorities to determine food safety by democratic procedures. We simply felt that it would be a violation of our sovereign right to have food safety standards harmonized internationally under the name of globalization.

In Kanagawa Prefecture, we formed a group called "No! to Harmonization Action Committee." We worked with other consumers and farmers' organizations to lobby the Ministry of Health and Welfare; we joined a lawsuit and a petition campaign asking the government to cancel lowered restrictions on pesticide residual levels. At the same time, we organized public seminars, teach-ins and other similar types of campaigns. However, the Uruguay Round came to the final agreement in December 1993.

Since then, the pesticides' residual levels were relaxed one after another. The government also permitted, under the Food Hygiene Law, application of post-harvest pesticides and other chemicals as a kind of food additives. The post-harvest application of pesticides is done by mixing chemicals into grain bins just like food additives. This deregulation was part of an effort to harmonize local food standards to international norms, because Japan's stringent food safety standards might be attacked as "nontariff trade barriers." Harmonization of food safety standards enabled Japan to import more agricultural produce from all over the world.

In enforcing the Uruguay Round commitment to establish free markets under WTO, Japan as the world's largest food importer (in dollars) has taken major steps of deregulation:

- April 1992: The application of lowered restrictions on residual levels for 34 pesticides was submitted to the government's committee (i.e., permission of post-harvest application). Numerous restrictions on pesticide residual levels have been lowered since then.
- January 1993: Food inspections from Europe enforced since the Chernobyl nuclear accident were lifted except for a few cases.
- January 1994: Antibiotics, growth hormones, and other veterinary drugs used in cattle, hog, poultry and dairy farming are now under review and the standards for setting the residual level have been

started. Previously, such drugs were set at zero-residual level.

- April 1995: The mandatory labeling of the date of production on processed food was abolished and instead, the labeling of the expiration (shelf-life) date was set.
- July 1995: The residual levels of six veterinary drugs were set.
- July 1996: The committee of the Ministry of Health and Welfare reported that genetically engineered crops met requirements of the government's safety guidelines. In essence, this means unofficial permission for importing such kinds of crops.[1]

—It Is "Safe" until the Evidence of Risk Is Shown

We lost the lawsuit against relaxed pesticides' residual levels in spring of 1997. At court, the discussion was focused on the residual levels of organophosphate pesticides in wheat. For example, the new level was set at 8 parts per million (ppm) for malathion, which was 80 times the level permitted in rice. In the case of phenetolothion, it was set at 10 ppm, 50 times the level permitted in rice. These levels are the highest residual levels that can be detected in wheat imported from the U.S. or Australia. It was the natural aim of the government to be able to import wheat anytime from anywhere in the world.

It was part of the effort of our government to build a firm infrastructure for the international division of production: Japan is to export industrial products and import all food commodities except rice. Under this agenda, there is no perspective to ensure a safe and secure food supply for Japanese consumers. Rather, the food security that our government is pursuing is to secure a certain volume of food regardless of the quality, bought by strong yen from wherever available.

During the latter half of the Uruguay Round negotiations, there was a nationwide propaganda campaign involving the mass media: "Because consumers can enjoy tasty and cheaper food from around the world, what's the reason for complaining?" This concept was so widespread that it finally became a kind of a national agreement. Another form of propaganda that we heard at that time was: "The Japanese farmers are spoiled by farm support programs. They have became too lazy to compete and don't want to solve their prob-

lems by themselves. Thus, Japanese farmers need to compete internationally to overcome their problems." But, actually, the main argument was: "In order to export industrial goods, we must import farm produce. It is the only way for Japan to survive."

The globalization of food is to distribute food produced at the lowest cost in a uniform world market. To do this, food safety standards needed to be standardized, just like industrial products, because with harmonized standards, producers could export food commodities to any country. Politically, the issue remained only one of national affairs. The food globalization promoters were not able to include perspectives of food culture, environment, and consumers' rights in the discussion.

[. . .]

—The Nature of Cash Crops Is to Exploit the Environment and Extract Social Costs

Five years have passed since the completion of the Uruguay Round. Now, we see countless numbers of fruits from all over the world in the supermarkets. The date of production has disappeared from packages, leaving us only the expiration dates. Since the date of production is unknown, many food products are thrown away, even if they are still good enough to eat.

What has rapidly increased is "certified organic" labels. Behind this trend, there is the trend to harmonize organic certification standards at the international level. Because consumers in a "free" international market exercise their freedom of choice and choose organic food, its standards should be internationally uniform. For example, once the international organic standard is set at the lowest common denominator, cattle grown on large-scale ranches that have been developed on huge tracts of land cleared in the rainforest in the Amazon could be certified organic as long as they satisfy the international standards. In fact, the proposed national organic standards by the U.S. Department of Agriculture included genetically engineered crops, irradiated food, and industrial sludge. If the proposed standards were adopted, it is clear that they would be the international standards eventually. As the breadbasket of the world, the United States is powerful in setting international standards. Now, it is becoming more and more clear that globalization means Americanization.

There is the growing trend of international direct trading that the Japanese consumers' movement should be proud of. One major direct trade is Balangon bananas from Negros Island in the Philippines. They are totally chemical-free with blackened tips. The price is 460 yen for 1 kilogram. Bananas are usually found on sale at most shops. Chiquita bananas are sold for around 100 yen for 1 kilogram. Chiquita started to sell organic bananas recently. However, the gap between the bananas from Negros and Chiquita is unbelievably huge. How can Chiquitas sell at such low prices? No matter how cheap the land is in banana-producing countries compared to Japan, how can they be so cheap after such a long journey to Japan? How can they be cheaper than other fruit grown in Japan? We need to really look behind these cheaper prices.

[. . .]

On banana plantations, no protection is provided to the workers who spray the pesticides in large amounts. The workers are intricately tied to management, shutting out any possibility for them to become economically independent. The ultimate goal of commercial cash crops is to dominate the market with cheaper commodities from mass production. Of course, there is no room for social, environmental, and workers' health costs to be internalized.

Cheaper Imported Food Is the Preliminary to Wage Cuts

During the Uruguay Round negotiations, there was the claim that cheaper food imports as a result of the total liberalization of the agricultural market mean an increase in income in real terms for workers. What is happening in the agricultural sector is now happening across the industrial sector in Japan. Lowered food prices brought about by expanded agricultural imports may have been the preliminary to wage cuts.

In regard to the global environment, I believe that people in countries of overconsumption must be "poor" in terms of self-controlled consumption. In the world, there is not only the gap between the South and North, but also between rich and poor within the overconsuming North.

[. . .]

Whose Economy Is It?

When we started the movement to reject the harmonization proposal, we asked the public, "Whose harmonization is it?" Now I would like to ask, "Whose economy is it?" The premise of globalization is to globally harmonize the consumers' market, not to correct the unfairness in the labor market. For the economy whose primary aim is to produce for the free market, the needs of the people who want to survive within the local communities are not relevant. Economic globalization essentially can be built only on discrimination and inequality.

At present, the consumers' movement in the world is working on the safety and labeling issues of genetically engineered food. The coming food crisis in the twenty-first century is the most pressing threat to the global environment. In the name of solutions to this crisis, agribusiness corporations are promoting genetically engineered food and its technologies as their strategic weapons to overcome the worsening natural environment.

For example, a soybean was developed to be tolerant of the herbicide Roundup, a product of Monsanto Corporation. The Bt-corn incorporates a bacterium gene that is harmful to pests and insects. The patent was given not to the new technology but to the specific gene of the bacterium. The artificial gene technology that manipulates beyond the boundaries of its pieces (i.e., genes) is now causing unexpected disruptions in farm ecology systems.

The genetic engineering crop technologies are in the same territory as those of cloning animals and other artificial animal factories, such as the insertion of human genes into pigs for producing organs needed for transplants. Frequently, corporate activities are not directed to eliminate root causes of problems in order to enhance the public welfare; often, they work toward creating social and environmental problems. As a result, the corporations must find solutions to the problems created by themselves. Often, they are short-term or temporary solutions that allow or justify further expansion of production or re-production. This is a typical business production cycle, which could be called the fate of huge corporations.

[. . .]

To strengthen consumer power, we can develop boycott campaigns. I believe stronger boycotts by consumers are practical and can effectively stand against the global corporate power that is currently enjoying overwhelming domination in the market.

NOTE

1. Seikatsu to Jichi, February 1997.

Reading C

The Obesity of the Food Industry
NANCY WORCESTER

Professor of nutrition Nancy Worcester discusses the role of the food industry in the poor nutrition habits of women in Europe and North America. Pointing to the millions of dollars spent to advertise foods high in saturated fat and calories, Worcester argues that the same industry that profits from selling such foods then profits from marketing diet foods and remedies.

It is ironic that while women in Europe and North America are intentionally starving themselves in order to lose weight and better fit the prized slim image, in other parts of the world (e.g., parts of Africa) the daughters of rich families are sent to special fattening houses, fed rich foods, and allowed no exercise. The fatter a girl grows, the more beautiful she is consid-

Nancy Worcester, "The Obesity of the Food Industry," in *Women's Health: Readings on Social, Economic and Political Issues* (2nd ed.). Nancy Worcester and Mariamne H. Whatley, eds. Dubuque, IA: Kendall/Hunt Publishing Company, 1996: 394–97.

ered.[1] Wherever there is a limited food supply or an unequal distribution of resources, fatness and obesity become status symbols because only the wealthy or powerful have access to ample food supplies.

The food industry makes certain that we have access to an abundance of food, but in the process of making itself a fat profit, the food industry also ends up making us fat.

In our affluent society, we are assured a steady, plentiful food supply. We have more nutritional information than ever before and have a clearer understanding of the relationship of food to health. We should be eating the healthiest diet[2] of all time. Instead we are now eating too much of the wrong foods and our pattern of food consumption is a major cause of ill health and death. Incongruously, the change in the balance of nutrients which is recommended to us today to promote health and prevent illness is very similar to the pattern which was consumed at the turn of the century (see Table 1) before the food industry became so influential in determining food habits.

TABLE I   NUTRITION RECOMMENDATIONS VS. REALITY

	(PERCENT OF DIET FROM DIFFERENT NUTRIENTS)		
	1909–1913	Current	Dietary Goals*
Protein	12%	12%	12%
Fat	32%	42%	30%
Carbohydrate	56%	46%	58%

*Dietary Goals for the U.S. 1977. Senate Select Committee on Nutrition and Human Needs

With an increased awareness of what is good for us, there is a tendency to blame the individual, or more specifically the woman of the family, for not choosing the healthiest foods. Such "victim blaming" ignores the tremendous pressure on everyone to eat in certain ways and overlooks the fact that consumers have little voice in choosing the choices available to them.

The food industry simply sets out to make a profit, but the food industry has a peculiar problem.[3] Unlike other consumer industries, the food industry cannot count on us buying more of its products as our incomes rise. Even if we are encouraged to overeat and are wasteful of food, there is a limit to the amount of food we can consume. In order to maximize their profits, the food companies must gain a greater share of the market and entice us to buy the foods with the highest profit margin.[4]

To gain the greatest share of the market, the food industry is now dominated by monopolies. For example, three corporations, Kelloggs', Weetabix, and the National Biscuit Company, control nearly 90 percent of the breakfast cereal market in the United Kingdom.[5] Similarly, Kelloggs', General Mills, and General Foods dominate over 90 percent of the breakfast cereal market in the United States.[6] Food companies are now a part of giant multinationals so ITT executives are making decisions about Hostess CupCakes, Wonder Bread, and Morton Frozen Foods, and Beatrice Foods owns Dannon yogurt, LaChoy oriental foods, and Samsonite luggage.[7] The health implications are obvious: the food industry gets further removed from consumers and is less and less responsive to the quality or quantity of foods which consumers want or need. Mo-

nopoly power results in extra profits for the food industry—at our expense. Frances Moore Lappé, in *Diet for a Small Planet*, estimates that every single North American overpays $90 per year for food compared to what prices should be in a more competitive food economy.[8]

In order to increase sales, a food company offers a number of variations of the same products, and it benefits whether we choose product A or B. In the 1950s, U.K. consumers had 1,500 lines of processed foods from which to choose.[9] Today there are more like 12,000 lines of processed foods. Whether being able to choose between bar-b-qued, sour cream, and au gratin flavored potato chips improves the quality of one's life may be a matter of debate: it certainly does not improve our access to healthy foods.

In an article on women and food (Women may have freed themselves from the kitchen, but at what cost?), Joan Dye Gussow comments, "The average supermarket has more than 12,000 items, the purpose of many of which would be unclear if it were not explained by advertising."[10] Through advertising, the food industry manages to exert a tremendous influence on food habits, aggressively promoting those foods which are most profitable. It is no coincidence that Quaker Oats was the first reputable company to appoint a full-time advertising manager. In the late 1800s, Quaker introduced the use of trademarks to establish brand loyalty. This denoted a radical change in the marketing of foods. "Food was no longer something people simply needed; for the first time it was defined as something people needed to be persuaded to buy."[11] More is spent on advertising food products than any other product category. In the United Kingdom, 42 percent of the total advertising expenditure is spent advertising food, drink, and tobacco; nearly one-quarter of all advertising is especially for food products.[12] In the United States, the food industry spends 3 percent of the cost of the food directly on advertising and promotion; another 13 percent of the food cost goes for packaging, which can be viewed as another form of advertising.[13] If we ate foods in proportion to the amount spent on advertising them, our diet would be made up of sweet foods, breakfast cereals, margarine, and potato chips.[14] A U.S. study found that ads for presweetened breakfast cereals outnumbered ads for meat, vegetables, milk, or cheese by a ratio of 1,800 to 1 on daytime television.[15] This puts tremendous pressure on women to buy unhealthy foods for their children.

Advertising turns out to be a major source of nutrition information for many people. This is a shame because advertising at its best is a poor source of nutrition information. At its worst, it deliberately confuses the consumer, exaggerates small differences between products without addressing real nutritional issues, and employs clever techniques to stay within the guidelines established to prevent false advertising. For example, enormous quantities are spent confusing the consumer about the benefits of polyunsaturated fatty acids compared to saturated fatty acids, trying to get the consumer to switch between butter and margarine or different types of margarine (usually all made by the same company). The urgent message which intentionally gets lost is that we need to cut down on *both* butter and margarine in order to reduce total fat consumption.

The consumer is deliberately encouraged to believe that there is little agreement about what constitutes a good diet and that so-called experts totally disagree with one another. Consumers are left feeling that they need not bother trying to modify their food habits because nutritional theories may change tomorrow. While there remain a number of nutritional questions which are being researched and debated, there is in fact overwhelming agreement among nutritionists and scientific, health, and governmental agencies about major constituents of a healthy diet. There is general agreement that for a healthier diet, we must[16]

- eat a variety of foods.
- increase consumption of complex carbohydrates (starch and fiber).
- restrict sugar intake.
- restrict fat intake (especially saturated fat).
- restrict cholesterol intake.
- restrict salt.
- use alcohol in moderation.
- maintain a good body weight.

Those most influenced by food advertising are exactly the same people who could most benefit from getting the maximum nutritional value from their money. Tests gauging nutrition knowledge have found the worst scores among those with the lowest income and in the highest age groups (though overall nutrition knowledge is disappointingly low in *most* groups.) The effects of poverty and lack of education tend to exaggerate each other, so it is not surprising to find the U.S. Senate Select Committee on Nutrition and Human Needs stating, "It is likely that those most influenced by food advertising are low-income and elderly consumers."[17]

We know there are class differences in health patterns and access to health care. Poor people have less chance of being healthy than middle-class or wealthy people. There are good reasons to believe that class differences in health patterns are related to diet. Poor people consume a less healthy diet than middle class people. The 1980 Household Food survey (U.K.) compared poor and middle-class families. Individuals in the poorer families were found to consume only 75 percent as many fresh vegetables, only 56 percent as much fresh fruit, but 150 percent more sugars than individuals in the better-off families.[18] One can guess how much the influence of food advertising contributes to this situation.

The high-profit foods are those with inexpensive ingredients and a long shelf life. Sugar and wheat are promoted by the food industry because they are cheap and easy to handle. White flour is more profitable than brown because the bran (fiber) and germ that have been removed can be sold separately and white flour products are less satisfying to the appetite, so people consume more of them.[19] Processing of food inevitably increases the profit margin, even though nutrients are inevitably lost in the process. Salt adds to the taste and coloring adds to the appearance without adding much cost to the industry. People have learned to like the flavors carried by fats and the texture of fats, so it is particularly profitable to process foods in a way which increases the fat content. (Adding animal fats inevitably means also adding cholesterol.) Food additives are an inexpensive way of prolonging shelf life. So we end up with a diet low in fiber and high in sugar, salt, fat, cholesterol, and food additives even though we know that a healthy diet is high in fiber and low in sugar, salt, fat, cholesterol, and food additives. A diet low in fiber and high in fat will lack bulk and will be very concentrated—literally will not take up much space. This is exactly the kind of diet which encourages one to eat more than one's body needs.

The fat story is a good one to use as an illustration of how we end up eating a diet which may make us unhealthy and fat while the food industry simply works at making its profit. Table 2 compares the price we pay for potatoes marketed in different ways and the caloric value of each style of potato. In each case, the added fat is responsible for the added Calories. Calories are a unit of measure for the energy content of food. Fats are the most concentrated form of energy. Every ounce of pure fat we eat gives us a whopping 250 Calories, compared to the 112 Calories per ounce in any carbohydrate or protein. This is why every *good* slimming diet works by directly or indirectly cutting down on the amount of fat consumed. People gain weight when the energy (Calorie) intake is greater than the energy being used by the body. It is easy to see how simply increasing the fat content of the diet (without increasing our energy output) has been the equivalent of sending us all to special fattening houses. Unfortunately, our high-fat diet also seems to be a cause of heart disease and breast and colon cancer.

The food industry certainly does not set out to deliberately sell us unhealthy foods. In truth, no one would be happier than the food companies if they could manage to get us to pay $3.18 per pound for baking potatoes without their increased costs of adding fat, processing, and packaging. They are as willing to make money from healthy foods as from any other product line.

The response of the food industry to the interest in healthier foods has been a good way to see how food

TABLE 2   PAYING A LOT FOR FAT!

Product	Price/pound	Calories/ounce
Baking potatoes	20¢	23
French fried potatoes	99¢	68
Sour cream potato chips	$2.85	90
Stacking potato chips	$3.18	117

companies actually work. They spend large sums on research trying to predict health trends which can be exploited as new markets. Nearly 20 years ago, doing product development for a food company, I was working to create "nutritious instant breakfast products children can fix for themselves." Market research had indicated that an increase in the number of mothers working outside the home combined with increased nutrition awareness could create a demand for such products.

Indeed, the so-called health-food market has turned out to be a big moneymaker for the food industry, though there is usually a gigantic gap between what the industry labels as health foods and what a nutritionist would identify as healthy eating. Much of what are passed off as health foods are merely variations of regular processed foods with a new packaging image emphasizing naturalness, purity, and old-fashioned goodness, and a new price tag. The choice of which vitamins and minerals are added to products is more often based on what "sounds good" (e.g., for which the consumer will pay a disproportionally higher price) rather than which nutrients are low in the diet or have been removed in processing that particular foodstuff.

The food companies were especially quick in offering a huge range of products to fit in with information showing the advantages of a high-fiber diet. Why not? They already had the fiber, which *they* had removed in processing. Instead of looking for another buyer, the manufacturer simply had to add it back, label the product "high in fiber" or "added fiber," and charge the consumer. Consumers have been willing to pay extraordinary amounts for high-fiber foods because they finally hit upon a way to improve their diet without having to make any basic changes in their eating patterns. As an added attraction, on a high-fiber diet the body gives immediate feedback that the changes in the diet are having the desired effect. (Bowel movements become larger and softer and are easily eliminated, indicating the absorbed water has facilitated the waste products to pass smoothly through the digestive tract. In the long term, this process probably helps prevent diverticulosis, colon cancer, and other diseases.) In contrast, one has to be satisfied with only *knowing,* not seeing, the beneficial effects of reducing saturated fats, reducing cholesterol, or giving up cigarettes. The fact that it is difficult to find high-fiber foods without sugar is a reminder that the consumer is being offered this new range of supposed health foods because it sells well rather than for health reasons.

This all leads up to a look at how the food industry benefits as much as anyone from the obsession for slimming. In fact, we will have to question the role that the food industry has in specifically creating the obsession for slimming. In a pattern which should now sound familiar, the food industry makes huge profits on special slimming products. The same companies which have encouraged us to buy fattening foods now offer us virtually the same products, with a slightly reduced fat content and calorie information, at a higher slimming-product, lite-version, price.

NOTES

1. Hilde Bruch, *Eating Disorders—Obesity, Anorexia Nervosa. and the Person Within,* New York: Basic Books 1973, pp. 14–15.

2. *Diet* is used as a term to denote one's usual pattern of eating and does not refer to a slimming diet unless specifically stated. Consistent with common usage of the word, *dieting* will be used to indicate the process of being on a reducing diet.

3. The Politics of Health Group, *Food and Profit—It Makes You Sick,* London: POHG, 1980, p. 7.

4. Chris Wardle, *Changing Food Habits in the U.K.,* London: Earth Resources, 1977, p. 29.

5. Wardle, *op. cit.* p. 25.

6. Frances Moore Lappé, *Diet for a Small Planet,* New York: Ballantine Books 1982, p. 43.

7. Brett Silverstein, *Fed up! The Food Forces That Make You Fat, Sick, and Poor,* Boston, MA: South End Press 1984, pp. 4–5.

8. Lappé, *op. cit.*

9. Wardle, *op. cit.* p. 26.

10. Joan Dye Gussow, "Women and Food;" *Country Journal,* February 1985, pp. 52–57.

11. Naomi Aronson, "Working Up an Appetite," in Jane Rachel Kaplan (ed.) *A Woman's Conflict—The Special Relationship between Women and Food,* Englewood Cliffs, NJ.: Prentice Hall 1980, pp. 215–16.

12. Wardle, op. cit. p. 31–33.

13. Letitia Brewster and Michael F. Jacobson, *The Changing American Diet,* Washington, D.C.: Center for Science in the Public Interest, 1978, p. 2.

14. POHG, op. cit. p. 11.

15. Aronson, op. cit. p. 216.

16. Marion Nestle, *Nutrition in Clinical Practice,* Greenbrae, CA.: Jones Medical Publications, 1985, pp. 42–44.

17. U.S. Senate Select Committee on Nutrition and Human Needs, *Eating in America—Dietary Goals for the United States,* London: MIT Press 1979, p. 63.

18. Ministry of Agriculture, Fisheries and Food, *Household Food Consumption and Expenditure,* 1980, Table 20, pp. 104–6, quoted in Hilary Graham, *Women Health and the Family,* Brighton, Sussex: Wheatsheaf Books 1984, p. 124.

19. POHG, op. cit. pp. 6–7.

REFLECTING ON THE SECTION

The politics of food—its production, distribution, and consumption—ties together many of the themes and concepts explored in this book. These themes include the interactions of science and culture, national and international politics, marketing and advertising, histories of travel and migration, and the interaction of race, class, and gender. Consider how the food we eat is affected by all of these forces. How do these systems affect women and gender relations? What kinds of actions, movements, and organizations are needed to address the gender politics of food?

CONCLUSION

Feminist Futures: Transnational Perspectives

There are different ways of imagining a feminist future. One way is utopian—to focus on the best and most ideal world possible, based on what we know about the past and the present. Another way is to create programs and projects as concrete means toward eliminating subordination and inequalities based on gender. We have chosen, however, a way of approaching the future by thinking about how we live in an imperfect world and how we struggle to negotiate the different powers and institutions within it. Such an approach means acknowledging both our power and our privilege, as well as our limits and marginalizations.

For those of us involved in women's studies, the task of internationalizing our curriculum and studies is an ongoing process in which awareness of these limits and privileges brings with it new opportunities. Since it is futile to be satisfied solely with our own identities in an era of globalization and continued colonization, the need to create links and coalitions across national and cultured boundaries remains paramount. Such links and coalitions force us to learn why and how difference matters. Although we may not find a common world of women in the future, we may find a world of meaningful connections based on all kinds of histories, knowledges, and politics. It is up to all of us to seek out these connections.

Reading A

Beyond the Global Victim
CYNTHIA ENLOE

Feminist political scientist Cynthia Enloe argues that feminists need to pay attention to international issues not only because international politics affects our futures but also because patriarchy creates gendered divisions of labor. In this context, international politics leads to both inequalities among women and the possibilities of organizing against those inequalities.

Some men and women active in campaigns to influence their country's foreign policy—on the right as well as the left—have called on women to become

Cynthia Enloe, "Beyond the Global Victim," in *Bananas, Beaches, and Bases: Making Feminist Sense of International Politics Feminist.* Berkeley: University of California Press, 1990: 15–17.

more involved in international issues, to learn more about "what's going on in the world": "You have to take more interest in international affairs because it affects how you live." The gist of the argument is that women need to devote precious time and energy to learning about events outside their own country because as women they are the objects of those events. For instance, a woman working in a garment factory in Ireland should learn more about the European Economic Community because what the EEC commissioners do in Brussels is going to help determine her wages and maybe even the hazards she faces on the job. An American woman will be encouraged to learn the difference between a Cruise and Pershing missile because international nuclear strategies are shaping her and her children's chances of a safe future.

Key Terms

Central Intelligence Agency (CIA) U.S. intelligence organization established in 1947 to protect U.S. military, political, and financial interests abroad. During the Cold War, the CIA supported dictatorships and totalitarian rule in many parts of the world in its efforts to fight Communism.

European Economic Community (EEC) Until 1993, this was the term for what is now called the European Union (EU). The political and economic alliance between the nations of Western Europe, the EU facilitates trade and deregulation of some border controls.

greenhouse effect The occurrence of increased solar radiation in the earth's atmosphere due to

trapped gases emitted by industries, technologies, cars, and other elements.

North Atlantic Treaty Organization (NATO) Established in 1949, this organization worked for the defense of Western Europe and North America, primarily against the Soviet Union. Since the end of Soviet rule, several former Soviet republics and Eastern European nations have joined NATO.

The Warsaw Pact Signed in 1955, this pact between Eastern European countries and the Soviet Union served to organize a defense against the West and NATO.

Two things are striking about this line of argument. First, the activists who are trying to persuade women to "get involved" are not inviting women to reinterpret international politics by drawing on their own experiences as women. If the explanations of how the EEC or nuclear rivalry works don't already include any concepts of femininity, masculinity, or patriarchy, they are unlikely to after the women join the movement. Because organizers aren't curious about what women's experiences could lend to an understanding of international politics, many women, especially those whose energies are already stretched to the limit, are wary of becoming involved in an international campaign. It can seem like one more attempt by privileged outsiders—women and men—to dilute their political efforts. If women are asked to join an international campaign—for peace, against communism, for refugees, against apartheid, for religious evangelism, against hunger—but are not allowed to define the problem, it looks to many locally engaged women like abstract do-gooding with minimal connection to the battles for a decent life in their households and in their communities.

Second, the typical "women-need-to-learn-more-about-foreign-affairs" approach usually portrays women as victims of the international political system. Women should learn about the EEC, the United Nations, the CIA, the IMF, NATO, the Warsaw Pact, the "greenhouse effect" because each has an impact on them. In this worldview, women are forever being acted upon; rarely are they seen to be actors.

It's true that in international politics women historically have not had access to the resources enabling them to wield influence. Today women are at the bottom of most international hierarchies: women are routinely paid less than even the lowest-paid men in multinational companies; women are two-thirds of all refugees. Women activists have a harder time influencing struggling ethnic nationalist movements than do men; women get less of the ideological and job rewards from fighting in foreign wars than do men. Though a pretty dismal picture, it can tell us a lot about how the international political system has been designed and how it is maintained every day: some men at the top, most women at the bottom.

But in many arenas of power, feminists have been uncovering a reality that is less simple. First, they have discovered that some women's class aspirations and their racist fears lured them into the role of controlling other women for the sake of imperial rule. British, American, Dutch, French, Spanish, Portuguese women may not have been the architects of their countries' colonial policies, but many of them took on the roles of colonial administrators' wives, missionaries, travel writers, and anthropologists in ways that tightened the noose of colonial rule around the necks of African, Latin American, and Asian women. To describe colonization as a process that has been carried on solely by men overlooks the ways in which male colonizers' success depended on some women's complicity. Without the willingness of "respectable" women to see that colonization offered them an opportunity for adventure, or a new chance of financial security or moral commitment, colonization would have been even more problematic.[1]

Second, feminists who listen to women working for multinational corporations have heard these women articulate their own strategies for coping with their husbands' resentment, their foremen's sexual harassment, and the paternalism of male union leaders. To depict these women merely as passive victims in the international politics of the banana or garment industries doesn't do them justice. It also produces an inaccurate picture of how these global systems operate. Corporate executives and development technocrats need some women to depend on cash wages; they need some women to see a factory or plantation job as a means of delaying marriage or fulfilling daughterly obligations. Without women's own needs, values, and worries, the global assembly line would grind to a halt. But many of those needs, values, and worries are defined by patriarchal structures and strictures. If fathers, brothers, husbands didn't gain some privilege, however small in global terms, from women's acquiescence to those confining notions of femininity, it might be much harder for the foreign executives and their local élite allies to recruit the cheap labor they desire. Consequently, women's capacity to challenge the men in their families, their communities, or their political movements will be a key to remaking the world.

1. See, for instance, "Western Women and Imperialism," special issue of *Women's Studies International Forum,* Margaret Strobel and Nupur Chaudhun, eds. vol. 13, no. 2, 1990.

Reading B

Cross-Border Talk: Transnational Perspectives on Labor, Race, and Sexuality

TERESA CARILLO

One of the organizing strategies for feminists in a global world has been the creation of cross-border alliances. As feminist political scientist Teresa Carillo argues, these transnational coalitions are vital if the inequalities

Teresa Carrillo, "Cross-Border Talk: Transnational Perspectives on Labor, Race, and Sexuality," in *Talking Visions,* Ella Shohat, ed. Cambridge, Mass.: MIT Press, 1998, 391, 393–96, 403–408.

of globalization are to be addressed. Yet national agendas often prevent feminists from creating coalitions.

The *frontera* between the United States and Mexico is one of the world's most fluid international boundaries. A constant flow of people, goods, and services traverses that 2,000-mile border and links the two countries of my birth: Mexico and the United States of America. Yet, in many ways, Mexico remains separate from the United

Key Terms

comedores populares Community kitchen/canteen.
communidad Community.
encuentros Meeting.
frontera Border.
mujeres Women.
raza Spanish word for "race," used to refer to Chicano and Chicana communities in the struggle for recognition and civil rights in the United States.

Zapatista In 1994 the EZLN (Zapatista National Liberation Army) was formed to defend the rights of indigenous and poor people in the Mexican state of Chiapas. The government responded with armed force and the conflict escalated under the leadership of Ernesto Zedillo, president of Mexico during the mid-90s. EZLN leader Marcos promoted the use of the Internet to organize worldwide support for the Zapatistas.

States; the border demarcates a divide between rich and poor, English and Spanish speakers, Mexican and "American." As Chicanas, our lives straddle the border and are embedded in the crisscross of communities. We are therefore uniquely positioned to create channels of communication and collaboration with women in Mexico. As regional integration fosters economic homogeneity and reinforces capitalist hegemony, it is imperative that we do so.

This is an essay about *mujeres* talking to *mujeres:* Chicana/Latina women North of the border, and Mexicana women to the South. In this era of economic restructuring, trade agreements like the NAFTA and GATT raise expectations that increased trade and investment will bring an increase in transnational communication and network building, not only among business leaders but also among North American citizens. Progressive visionaries have predicted that transnational networks at the grassroots will have a hand in shaping economic and political outcomes in the Americas. *Cross-Border Links,* an alternative, grassroots directory of North American organizations, for example, opens with these words: "From grassroots groups in border towns to labor union headquarters in New York, Toronto, and Mexico City, people are sharing experiences and ideas, fostering mutual understanding, and developing strategies to advance their interests. These social contacts are helping to shape the new economic structures being built on the continent."[1] This and other sources offer an optimistic view of the possibilities for a global society in which citizens, grassroots movements, and nongovernmental organizations (NGOs) communicate and build networks across borders in response to an increase in shared interests and concerns.[2] But can we, as workers and women, keep pace with the changes brought about by regional economic integration? While capital is eliminating tariffs and knocking down barriers to international trade, investors are positioning themselves in an extremely advantageous position in relation to labor and the communities providing human and natural resources for their investments. It is often low-cost female labor that attracts foreign investors to Mexico. How can we, as women activists, gain access to transnational networks so that we can come up with our own response to economic restructuring? How is economic restructuring affecting women on both sides of the border and what is standing in the way of building a collaborative response to these changes? These are some of the

questions framing this discussion of contemporary transnational organizing among Chicana/Latina and Mexican women in a post-cold war context.

Between Chicanas and Mexicanas

When an organized tour of Mexicana garment workers visited the garment district in Los Angeles and San Francisco, they were amazed to find that the conditions were similar to those in Mexico City, leading to a radically altered perspective of the U.S. garment industry. "Conditions in Los Angeles," said one of the tour members, "were worse than here in Mexico. Garment workers there have to deal with being undocumented on top of everything else. There are women from all over the world, from Asia, Mexico, Central America, trying to make their living in the garment district. It seems like clothes can be sewn anywhere and the [industry] owners are just looking for the cheapest labor. . . . Seeing all this for myself helped me to realize that making our own little union is not enough, we need to go beyond a national union and figure out how to get together with other garment workers who, like us, are trying to make a living by sewing clothes, whether they work in Los Angeles, the Philippines, or Mexico."[3] Rafaela, another tour participant, commented, "At least at home we can't get deported."[4] Rafaela and her colleagues often discuss the forces of globalization and their place within that process. Their tour through Los Angeles, Watsonville, and San Francisco eroded the lines dividing Mexican and U.S. workers, and the Mexicana women returned to Mexico with a new determination to organize across borders. U.S. workers who met with the Mexican garment workers were likewise inspired and determined. They talked about the futility of striking for higher wages and better working conditions if a victory would eventually lead to plant closures and relocation across a border so that management could exploit other women. They reaffirmed their commitment to transnational organizing with Mexican and Canadian workers.

Little happened, however, after the tour. The contact dropped off to almost nothing, the flow of information ceased, and the joint actions that had been discussed never took place. This pattern is not uncommon in attempts to build transnational links among women of the Americas. There have been numerous attempts to create transnational links between U.S. Latinas and other women of the Americas. In some cases, women have attempted collaborative actions such as drafting statements of women's rights in the U.N.-sponsored International Covenant of Human Rights and the 1995 Women's Conference in Beijing, or participating in labor protests and international boycotts of products (e.g., Gallo wine, Nestlé, Levi Strauss). But the majority of contacts across the border have not yet reached a point of collaborative action, remaining instead in a beginning step of establishing contact and discussing common ground. While U.S. Latinas readily express a need and a desire to establish transnational networks at the grassroots level, they, as individuals and organizations, have experienced substantial roadblocks, largely because of a lack of resources as well as differences in the central focus and agenda. Part of the daunting nature of the enormity of the task of transnational organizing is that Mexicanas and Latinas have distinct ways of defining their agendas. Chicanas and Latinas in the United States have focused on questions of race and ethnicity, while Mexicanas have focused on class issues and survival. Adding to these differences is a widespread perception that the interests of U.S. workers are at odds with the interests of workers in Mexico.

Combing through the various attempts to build alliances among Latinas, a two-sided problematic emerges. North of the border, the "multicultural women's movement" tends to privilege race, ethnicity, culture, and national origin, arguing that women of color experience a four-way intersection of oppressions based on race, class, gender, and sexual orientation; given the centrality of racism in the experience of women of color, the multicultural women's movement privileges above all the discussion of racial difference. South of the border, the popular women's movement focuses on family survival. A broad-based popular women's movement emerged in Mexico after the 1985 earthquake and defined what has been called a "popular" women's agenda centered around issues that have a great effect on "women's work" within a traditional division of labor, such as housing, basic nutritional needs, and public services.[5] Residentially based organizations such as neighborhood groups and renters' unions constitute the bulk of the popular women's movement, formed to survive the "lost decade" of the 1980s. The losses continued during the first half of the 1990s with Mexicans experiencing a constant erosion of their buying power, standard of living, and employment opportunities. Compounding these losses is a climate of political instability and violence punctuated by a string of political assassinations, rebellion in Chiapas, and a collapse of the economy. Within this setting, women have organized around issues of survival and their domestic responsibilities of caring for their homes and families—around what has been called "feminine consciousness" or "militant motherhood."[6]

To Mexican activists, the most immediate needs of housing, food, and services are not adequately addressed in the U.S. multicultural women's movement. When they have searched for counterpart organizations in the United States, Mexican women have found organizations not readily identified in the United States as "women's" groups, but rather as serving the poor: homeless shelters, welfare rights groups, labor groups, and church communities. To U.S. Latinas, meanwhile, the popular women's movement in Mexico appears to be confined to a domestic or private sphere, with little attention specifically directed to what is perceived to be the central problem: the interplay of race and ethnicity with gender. U.S. Latinas find hardly a mention of race, ethnicity, or colonialism among Mexicana women activists in the popular urban movements. The color/culture line, an essential starting point for "women of color" in the United States, is seemingly ignored by the Mexican popular women's movement. Race and ethnic differences exist between upper middle-class and educated feminists, and poor, working-class women in the popular movements, but the topic is largely skirted, as is the related topic of domestic service. Although Mexico is racially stratified, women activists disregard racial hierarchies among themselves, falling back on the revolutionary ideology of *mestizaje*—that all Mexicans are of mixed race.[7]

On a number of occasions, the centrality of race and ethnicity for U.S. Latinas has become an issue for Mexican women in various transnational forums. In one international exchange, for example, Mexicanas voiced a concern that too much attention to racial and ethnic difference was going to derail the alliance discussion, while U.S. Latinas demonstrated impatience with having to argue, yet again, that race indeed matters. Neither U.S. Latinas nor Mexicanas found comparable developments in women's organizing in the two countries, making it difficult for the movements to identify with counterpart groups and thus reach out to them across the border.[8] Despite these obstacles to establishing transnational alliances and collaborative actions be-tween U.S. Latinas and Mexican women, there are many examples of positive connections between women of color across the Americas. And in spite of the divisive spin of the NAFTA debate, women have been quick to re-alize that the benefactors of neoliberal economic reform are neither women nor workers on either side of the bor-der, but investors and employers on all sides. While there are many points of contradicting interests in the short term, Chicana, Latina, and Mexicana women have voiced an interest in creating cross-border links around their increasingly shared interests as women, workers, and community activists. Some of the most effective links between Chicana and Mexicana women have emerged around the very issue that has been at the heart of popular women's organizing in Mexico: community survival. Alliances between women in border commu-nities, for example, have resulted in transnational coali-tions within the environmental justice movement. Even women separated by thousands of kilometers are begin-ning to define a type of politics that is residentially or domestically based, but globally linked.

[. . .]

—Comunidades in Cyberspace

One of the groups that succeeded in establishing a sub-stantial and extended network of communication and ex-change between women was the School for International Organizers, developed by Mujer a Mujer in Mexico.[9] During 1992, twenty Mexican women from the labor and popular urban movements participated in a weekly train-ing seminar that examined the process of regional eco-nomic integration and its effects on U.S. Latinas and Mexican women. Each participant went on at least one international tour to the United States and gained first-hand knowledge of women's organizations in the United States. Another of the group's accomplishments was to establish communication with Latina women in the United States via email. Participants in the school, espe-cially those already familiar with computers in their workplaces, learned how to use the Internet system and the World Wide Web and established electronic ad-dresses on PeaceNet.

We use electronic mail to exchange ideas and infor-mation, plan things, and access a wide international

public. During the Trinational Encuentro of Work-ing Women, we were able to instantly disseminate the results of the conference, in Spanish and En-glish, to electronic addresses on our mailing list. Within days we were receiving responses and mak-ing new contacts. We got over that old feeling that the conferences we organized were like a tree falling in the woods with no one around to hear it. Now we have a way to send information about what we are doing and receive immediate responses from women in this and other continents.[10]

In September 1995, daily summaries of the International Women's Conferences in Huairou and Beijing, China, were instantly disseminated in Mexico and the United States by a joint team of Mexican and U.S. activists.

Instant and widespread dissemination of information via electronic mail was extremely important in the case of the 1994 Zapatista rebellion in Chiapas, Mexico. Sub-commandante Marcos communicated with the world via his laptop computer and modem. His communiqués gained popular support for the rebels and helped to pres-sure the Mexican government into a cease-fire, tempo-rary amnesty for rebel leaders, and peace negotiations. For women, access to a public via electronic mail will diminish the problems of isolation and silence. With the capability of instantly and affordably spreading informa-tion and analysis, women gain the protection offered by vigilant eyes and ears in the international community. This vigilance has helped to limit army abuses in Chia-pas, environmental abuses in the borderlands, and sexual abuse by government agents, most notably by Drug En-forcement agents in Mexico City. Although access to electronic communication is still extremely limited among U.S. Latinas and Mexicanas, there are some Raza women cruising the Internet, creating a transnational sense of *communidad* in cyberspace.

A transnational level of organization is more likely to be built around some issues than others. Neighborhood and housing issues, for example, are more difficult to frame within a global context than environmental, labor, or trade issues. Many Latina and Mexicana women ac-tive in popular movements involved in these localized concerns have had a difficult time addressing them through regional and global networks. One Mexican feminist faulted her organization's lack of resolve to cre-ate transnational channels of communication: "We haven't laid out a clear objective to establish transnational links. Projects have been determined by the necessities of the moment . . . and although we know it's important in the long run, in the short run, we don't have the energy to carry through on a project like that. . . . With the Free Trade Agreement comes a more urgent need for communication and more concrete initiatives."[11]

Women have been most effective in building networks around specific regional or single-issue causes. Women in the *maquiladoras,* for example, are part of the Coalition for Justice in the Maquiladoras and the Tri-National Commission for Justice in the Maquiladoras. Women's labor groups have collaborated in a number of trade-related bi- and tri-national coalitions, including the Mexican Free Trade Action Network, the U.S.–Mexico–Canada Labor Solidarity Network, and Common Frontiers. Transnational collaborations among women in specific industries have been organized by Fuerza Unida in San Antonio; La Mujer Obrera of El Paso; Trabajadoras Desplazadas (a committee of Mexicana workers laid off by Green Giant in Watsonville, California, when the company shifted production to Irapuato, Mexico); and Mujeres en Acción Sindical and the Frente Auténtico de Trabajo in Mexico D.F.[12] Mujer a Mujer in Mexico D.F. has been especially active and successful in facilitating transnational exchange among women through *encuentros,* conferences, tours, and correspondence. They have greatly expanded their work in connecting activist women in the region through various networks, including an electronic mail network (via PeaceNet) and participation in bi- and trinational coalitions. Once women gain the facility to communicate across borders, they are faced with the challenge of addressing the many contradictions and conflicts of interests, real or perceived, that exist among women— Chicanas/Latinas and Mexicanas, white women, and women of color. Whether the conflicts arise from distinctions based on race, national origin, immigration status, or culture, they present formidable obstacles to alliance building between women.

One activist comments that "globalization has started to erase the barrier of disinterest" in other women.[13] Time and time again women showed a strong interest in making connections and taking a more active role in establishing the rules and regulations of the process of regional integration. The frustration voiced by both Chicana/Latina and Mexicana women was that no one knew exactly how to take the next step in transnational network building after establishing initial contact. Women's movements lack a unifying focus or initiative around which groups can find common ground and take collaborative action. On every front, the move from communication and contact to collaborative action was not clearly defined.

The in-between step of increasing mutual awareness and understanding between U.S. Latinas and Mexican women has been one of the most consequential aspects of transnational communication and exchange. Exposure to the vibrant and multifaceted women's movements of Latin America has offered U.S. Latinas a valuable lesson in examining the gendered nature of citizenship and broadening the basis of support for our own movements. Sonia Alvarez writes, "We in the U.S. have much to learn about how to promote and reinforce the process of empowerment and gender consciousness among low-income and minority women who are involved in welfare rights struggles, in our own growing numbers of *comedores populares* and collective survival strategies, in our own government make-work programs, and permanent "emergency" relief programs."[14] The extensive engagement between popular women's groups and feminist advocacy groups in Mexico, and in Latin America in general, has advanced our consciousness and analysis of how class and gender issues are intertwined. In the United States, the connection between gender, race, and class consciousness needs to be established within the mainstream feminist movement, especially now that Congress is legislating welfare reform and retreating from affirmative action. Organizations formed by U.S. women of color have come into the forefront of feminism in the United States, demonstrating how issues of race and ethnicity are integral to women's empowerment. During the 1970s and 1980s, Latin American feminists drew on a rich and abundant source of criticism and analysis from feminists in the industrialized countries of Europe and North America. But in the 1990s, Latin American women's movements may capture the attention of U.S. feminists in search of a mass base of support for both gender issues and problems of community survival. In the past few years, collaboration and exchange between U.S. Latina and Mexican women has become a busy two-way street.

NOTES

1. From Ricardo Hernandez and Edith Sanchez, eds., *Cross-Border Links* (Albuquerque, NM: Inter-Hemispheric Education Resource Center, 1992). See also Milton H. Jamail and Margo Gutiérrez, *The Border Guide: Institutions and Organizations of the United States-Mexico Borderlands,* 2d ed. (Austin, TX: CMAS Books, 1992). Both guides provide comprehensive listings of organizations and agencies that seek to create links and promote collaborative action between peoples and communities of Mexico and the United States.

2. Cathryn L. Thorup examines the link between free trade and the need for coalition building in her article "The Politics of Free Trade and the Dynamics of Cross-Border Coalitions in U.S.–Mexican Relations," *Columbia Journal of World Business* 26, no. 2 (Summer 1991): 12–26.

3. Octavia Lara, Secretary of External Relations of the "19th of September" Garment Workers Union, interview by author, March 25, 1989, San Francisco.

4. Rafaela Dominguez, Secretary of Sports and Culture of the "19th of September" Garment Workers Union, interview by author, March 25, 1989, San Francisco.

5. See Marta Lamas, Alicia Martínez, Maria Luisa Tarrés, and Esperanza Tunon, "Junctures and Disjunctures: The Women's Movement in México, 1970–1993" (unpublished paper, sponsored by the Ford Foundation, Mexico).

6. Temma Kaplan argues that in line with a traditional sexual division of labor, women accept the responsibility for "preserving life" and act on what she calls "female consciousness," forming mass mobilizations in defense of their right and obligation to maintain a home and provide for the basic needs of their families. See Temma Kaplan, "Female Consciousness and Collective Action," *Signs: Journal of Women in Culture and Society* 7, no. 1: 55–76. For a related discussion of "militant motherhood," see Sonia Alvarez, *Engendering*

Democracy in Brazil: Women's Movements in Transition Politics (Princeton, NJ: Princeton University Press, 1990).

7. See Alan Knight, "Racism, Revolution and Indigenismo in Mexico," in Richard Graham, ed., *The Idea of Race in Latin America* (Austin: University of Texas Press, 1990).

8. The groundbreaking text on feminism among women of color in the United States is Cherrie Moraga and Gloria Anzaldúa, eds., *This Bridge Called My Back* (Watertown, Mass.: Persephone Press, 1981). A more recent collection, *Making Face, Making Soul/Haciendo Caras,* edited by Anzaldúa, was published in 1990 (San Francisco: Aunt Lute Books). For a discussion of the differences in women's agendas across national boundaries, see Chandra Mohanty's "Introduction" and "Under Western Eyes," in Mohanty, et al., *Third World Women and the Politics of Feminism* (Bloomington: Indiana University Press, 1991).

9. For more on this and other programs of Mujer a Mujer, see *Correspondencia,* a bilingual newsletter containing information and analysis about the impact of globalization and economic restructuring on women's lives and struggles. It is published three times a year by Mujer a Mujer, AP 24–553, Colonia Roma 06701, Mexico D.F.

10. Elaine Burns, Mujer a Mujer interview by author, August 25, 1992, Mexico D.F.

11. Itziar Lozano, CIDHAL, a feminist service organization, interview by author, June 30, 1992, Mexico D.F.

12. For more information on these and other cross-border networks, see Hernandez and Sanchez, eds., *Cross-Border Links.*

13. Elaine Burns, August 25, 1992.

14. Sonia Alvarez, "Redibujando el Feminismo en las Americas and 'Redrawing' the Parameters of Gender Struggle" (paper presented at the conference "Learning from Latin America: Women's Struggles for Livelihood," University of California, Los Angeles, February 28, 1992), TMs, p. 8.

REFLECTING ON THE SECTION

Teresa Carillo asks, "How can we, as women activists, gain access to transnational networks so that we can come up with our own response to economic restructuring?" Cynthia Enloe asserts that "women's capacity to challenge the men in their families, their communities, or their political movements will be a key to remaking the world." Do you think there is a single key to unlock or remake the world? What factors contribute to social change. Consider the tools that you have acquired while reading and using this book. Which tools are the most useful to you right now? How are you planning to use these ideas and information in your workplace, your school, your family, and other contexts in your daily life?

Bibliography: Works Excerpted

Abelson, Elaine. "Urban Women and the Emergence of Shopping." In *When Ladies Go A-Thieving: Middle-Class Shoplifters in the Victorian Department Store.* New York: Oxford University Press, 1989, pp. 14–15, 18–25, 37–40.

Abu-Habib, Lina. "Welfare Rights and the Disability Movement." In *Gender and Disability: Women's Experiences in the Middle East.* London: Oxfam, 1997, pp. 3–8.

Abusharaf, Rogaia. "Unmasking Tradition." *The Sciences,* March/April 1998, pp. 23–27.

Alloo, Fatma. "Using Information Technology as a Mobilizing Force: The Case of the Tanzania Media Women's Association." In *Women Encounter Technology: Changing Patterns of Employment in the Third World,* eds. Swasti Mitter and Sheila Rowbotham. London: Routledge, 1995, pp. 303–13.

Appelbaum, Richard P. "Multiculturalism and Flexibility: Some New Directions in Global Capitalism." In *Mapping Multiculturalism,* eds. Avery Gordon and Christopher Newfield. Minneapolis: University of Minnesota Press, 1996, p. 303.

Arimura, Junko. "Globalization from a Consumer's Perspective: The Exciting Relationship between the World and Me." *Women's Asia: Voices from Japan,* no. 4 (1998), pp. 30–38.

Arnold, David. "Women and Medicine." In *Colonizing the Body.* Berkeley: University of California Press, 1993, pp. 254–61, 265–66.

Ault, Amber, and Eve Sandberg. "Our Policies, Their Consequences: Zambian Women's Lives under Structural Adjustment." In *Feminist Frontiers V,* eds. Laurel Richardson, Verta Taylor, and Nancy Whittier. New York: McGraw-Hill, 2000, pp. 503–6.

Badran, Margot. "Competing Agenda: Feminists, Islam and the State in Nineteenth- and Twentieth-Century Egypt." *Women, Islam and the State,* ed. Deniz Kandiyoti. Philadelphia: Temple University Press, 1991, pp. 201–7.

Balsamo, Anne. "Feminism for the Incurably Informed." *Flame Wars: The Discourse of Cyberculture,* ed. Mark Dery. Durham, NC: Duke University Press, 1994, pp. 125–26, 143–47.

Barker-Benfield, Ben. "Sexual Surgery in Late-Nineteenth-Century America." *International Journal of Health Services* 15, no. 2 (1975), pp. 285–89, 293–95.

Bearak, Barry. "Ugliness in India over Miss World." *San Francisco Chronicle,* November 21, 1996, p. C1.

Berger, John. *Ways of Seeing.* Harmondsworth: Penguin Books, 1977, pp. 7–11, 16–17, 45–64.

Blee, Kathleen M. "The First Ku Klux Klan." In *Women of the Klan: Racism and Gender in the 1920s.* Berkeley: University of California Press, 1991, pp. 12–16, 24, 39–41.

Blocker, Jane. Excerpt from *Where Is Ana Mendieta?: Identity, Performativity, Exile.* Durham, NC: Duke University Press, 1999, pp. 1–4.

Bocock, Robert. "Gender and Consumption." *Consumption.* London: Routledge, 1993, pp. 95–108.

Bohlen, Celestine. "Italians Contemplate Beauty in a Caribbean Brow." *New York Times.* September 10, 1996, p. A3.

Burke, Peter. "We, the People: Popular Culture and Popular Identity in Modern Europe." In *Modernity and Identity,* eds. Scott Lash and Jonathan Friedman. Oxford: Blackwell Publishers, 1992, pp. 298–301.

Carillo, Teresa. "Cross-Border Talk: Transnational Perspectives on Labor, Race, and Sexuality." In *Talking Visions,* ed. Ella Shohat. Cambridge, MA.: MIT Press, 1998, pp. 391, 393–96, 403–8.

Carovano, Kathryn. "More than Mothers and Whores: Redefining the AIDS Prevention Needs of Women." *International Journal of Health Services* 21, no. 1 (1991), pp. 131–35.

Cervantes, Lorna Dee. "Refugee Ship." *Revista Chicano-Riquena* 3.1 (Winter 1975), p. 20.

Chant, Sylvia. "Female Employment in Puerto Vallarta: A Case Study." *Gender, Work, and Tourism.* ed. M. Thea Sinclair. London: Routledge, 1997, pp. 136–37, 139–43.

Committee on Women, Population and the Environment. "Call for a New Approach." In *Reproductive Rights and Wrongs,* ed. Betsy Hartmann. Boston: South End Press, 1997, pp. 126–27.

Coward, Rosalind. "The Body Beautiful." In *Female Desires.* New York: Grove Press, 1985, pp. 39–46.

Crenshaw, Kimberlé. "Mapping the Margins: Intersectionality, Identity Politics, and Violence against Women of Color." *Stanford Law Review* 43 (July 1991), pp. 1241–52, 1262–65.

Davidov, Judith Fryer. "Prologue." In *Women's Camera Work: Self/Body/Other in American Visual Culture*. Durham, NC: Duke University Press, 1998, pp. 3–6.

Davin, Anna. "Imperialism and Motherhood." *History Workshop Journal,* (Spring 1978), pp. 9–14.

Davis, Angela. "Reproductive Rights." In *Women, Race and Class*. New York: Vintage Books, 1983, pp. 215–21.

Davis, Susan E. "Contested Terrain: The Historical Struggle for Fertility Control." In *Women under Attack: Victories, Backlash, and the Fight for Reproductive Freedom,* ed. Susan E. Davis. Boston: South End Press, 1988, pp. 7–14.

Dean, Pat. "Literacy: Liberation or Lip Service?" *Connexions* 21 (Summer 1986), pp. 18–19.

Devi, Rassundari. "The Sixth Composition." In *Women Writing in India: 600 B.C. to the Present,* vol I, eds. Susie Tharu and K. Lalitha. New York: The Feminist Press, 1991, pp. 199–202.

Dikkoter, Frank. "Race Culture: Recent Perspectives on the History of Eugenics." *American Historical Review,* (April 1998), pp. 467–68, 470, 472 73, 476 77.

Duggan, Lisa. "Making It Perfectly Queer." *Socialist Review* 22, no. 1, (1992), pp. 11, 13–22, 26–31.

Dwyer, Augusta. "Welcome to the Border." In *On the Line: Life on the U.S.–Mexican Border*. London: Latin American Bureau, 1994, pp. 4–8.

Eastman, Crystal. "A Program for Voting Women." In *On Women and Revolution,* ed. Blanche Wiesen Cook. Oxford: Oxford University Press, 1978, pp. 266–67.

Ecumenical Coalition for Economic Justice. "Tomasito's Guide to Economic Integration: A Whirlwind Tour with Your Guide Tomasito, the Tomato." *Economic Integration of the Americas: An Educator's Kit.* 1994.

Ehrenreich, Barbara, and Dierdre English. "Exorcising the Midwives." In *For Her Own Good: 150 Years of the Experts' Advice to Women*. Garden City, NY: Anchor Press, 1978, pp. 84–88.

Elmadmad, Khadija. "The Human Rights of Refugees with Special Reference to Muslim Refugee Women." In *Engendering Forced Migration: Theory and Practice,* ed. Doreen Indra. New York: Berghahn Books, 1999, pp. 261–66.

Enloe, Cynthia. "Beyond the Global Victim." In *Bananas, Beaches, and Bases: Making Feminist Sense of International Politics*. Berkeley: University of California Press, 1990, pp. 15–17.

Enloe, Cynthia. "Nationalism and Masculinity." In *Bananas, Beaches, and Bases: Making Feminist Sense of International Politics*. Berkeley: University of California Press, 1990, pp. 45–46, 52–59.

Enloe, Cynthia. "On the Beach: Sexism and Tourism." In *Bananas, Beaches, and Bases: Making Feminist Sense of International Politics*. Berkeley: University of California Press, 1990, pp. 19–24, 28–32, 40–41.

Ewen, Stuart, and Elizabeth Ewen. "The Bribe of Frankenstein." In *Channels of Desire: Mass Images and the Shaping of American Consciousness*. Minneapolis: University of Minnesota Press, 1992, pp. 3–7.

Farah, Nadia. "The Egyptian Women's Health Book Collective." *Middle East Report* 21, no. 6 (November/December 1991), pp. 16–17, 25.

Fausto-Sterling, Anne. "The Biological Connection." In *Myths of Gender*. New York: Basic Books, 1992, pp. 8–10.

Furth, Charlotte. "Androgynous Males and Deficient Females: Biology and Gender Boundaries in Sixteenth- and Seventeenth-Century China." *Late Imperial China*. 9, no. 2 (December 1988), pp. 3–9, 12–14, 15–16.

Glenn, Evelyn Nakano. "Women and Labor Migration." In *Issei, Nisei, War Bride: Three Generations of Japanese-American Women in Domestic Service*. Philadelphia: Temple University Press, 1986, pp. 3–5, 8–12.

Gluckman, Amy, and Betsy Reed. "The Gay Marketing Moment: Leaving Diversity in the Dust." *Dollars and Sense* 190 (November/December 1993), pp. 16–18, 35.

Gordon, Linda. "Magic." In *Woman's Body, Woman's Right: Birth Control in America*. New York: Penguin, 1976, pp. 29–33.

Gordon, Linda. "Malthusianism." In *Woman's Body, Woman's Right: Birth Control in America.* New York: Penguin, 1976, pp. 73–77.

Gould, Stephen Jay. "Women's Brains." In *The Panda's Thumb: More Reflections in Natural History.* New York: W. W. Norton, 1980, pp. 152–59.

Graham-Brown, Sarah. *Images of Women: The Portrayal of Women in the Photography of the Middle East, 1860–1950.* London: Quartet Books, 1988, pp. 18–23, 71–74.

Gross, Joan, David McMurray, and Ted Swedenburg. "Arab Noise and Ramadan Nights: Rai, Rap, and Franco-Maghrebi Identity." *Diaspora* 3, no. 1 (Spring 1994), pp. 3–7, 9–11, 17–20, 27–28.

Guy, Donna J. " 'White Slavery,' Citizenship and Nationality in Argentina." *Nationalisms and Sexualities,* eds. Andrew Parker, Mary Russo, Doris Sommer, and Patricia Yaeger. New York: Routledge, 1992, pp. 201–6, 214.

Hagiwara, Hiroko. "Women of Conformity: The Work of Shimada Yoshiko." In *Generations and Geographies in the Visual Arts,* ed. Griselda Pollock. London: Routledge, 1996, pp. 254–58.

Hall, Stuart. "From 'Routes' to Roots." *A Place in the World,* eds. Doreen Massey and Pat Jess. New York: Oxford University Press, 1995, pp. 206–7.

Hammonds, Evelynn M. "New Technologies of Race." In *Processed Lives: Gender and Technology in Everyday Life,* eds. Jennifer Terry and Melodie Calvert. New York: Routledge, 1997, pp. 108–9, 111, 113–21.

Harrison, Faye V. "The Gendered Politics and Violence of Structural Adjustment." In *Situated Lives: Gender and Culture in Everyday Life,* eds. Louise Lamphere, Helena Ragone, and Patricia Zavella. New York: Routledge, 1997, pp. 451–55.

Harry, Debra. "The Human Genome Diversity Project: Implications for Indigenous Peoples." *Abya Yala News,* South and Meso American Indian Rights Center (SAIIC) 8, no. 4 (Winter 1994), pp. 1–5.

Hartmann, Betsy. "Family Matters." In *Reproductive Rights and Wrongs.* Boston: South End Press, 1997, pp. 5–12.

Human Rights Watch. "Sex Discrimination in the Maquiladoras." *Free Labor World* 12 (December 1996), np.

Jacobs, Sylvia M. "Give a Thought to Africa: Black Women Missionaries in Southern Africa." In *Western Women and Imperialism: Complicity and Resistance,* eds. Nupur Chaudhuri and Margaret Strobel. Bloomington, IN: Indiana University Press, 1992, pp. 207–11, 221–24.

King, Catherine. "Making Things Mean: Cultural Representations in Objects." In *Imagining Women: Cultural Representations and Gender,* eds. Frances Bonner, Lizbeth Goodman, Richard Allen, Linda Janes, and Catherine King. London: Polity Press, 1992, pp. 15–20.

Kollontai, Alexandra. "Feminism and the Question of Class." In *The Selected Writings of Alexandra Kollontai,* trans. Aliz Holt. London: Allison & Busby, 1977, pp. 58–62.

Laderman, Carol. "A Welcoming Soil: Islamic Humoralism on the Malay Peninsula." In *Paths in Asian Medical Knowledge,* eds. Charles Leslie and Allan Young. Berkeley: University of California Press, 1992, pp. 276–78.

Larkin, Maureen. "Global Aspects of Health and Health Policy in Third World Countries." In *Globalization and the Third World,* eds. Ray Kiely and Phil Newfleet. London: Routledge, 1998, pp. 92–99, 106–10.

Lazreg, Marnia. "Feminism and Difference." In *Conflicts in Feminism,* eds. Marianne Hirsch and Evelyn Fox Keller. New York: Routledge, 1990, pp. 330–32.

Lippard, Lucy R. *Mixed Blessings: New Art in a Multicultural America.* New York: Pantheon, 1990, plates 1, 4.

López, Ian F. Haney. "The Social Construction of Race." *Harvard Civil Rights –Civil Liberties Law Review* 29, no. 1, (1994), pp. 11–12, 13–15, 16–17, 27–33.

Lutz, Catherine A., and Jane L. Collins. *Reading National Geographic.* Chicago: University of Chicago Press, 1993, pp. 4–6, 166–68, 172–75.

Mankiller, Wilma, and Michael Wallis. *Mankiller: A Chief and Her People.* New York: St. Martin's Press, 1993, pp. 67–74.

Marchand, Roland. "Grotesque Moderne." In *Advertising and the American Dream: Making Way for Modernity, 1920–1940*. Berkeley: University of California Press, 1985, pp. 179–85.

Marfleet, Phil. "The Refugee." In *Globalization and the Third World,* eds. Ray Kiely and Phil Marfleet. London: Routledge, 1998, pp. 70–71.

Martin, Emily. "The Egg and the Sperm: How Science Has Constructed a Romance Based on Stereotyped Male-Female Roles." In *Gender and Scientific Authority,* eds. Barbara Laslett et al. Chicago: University of Chicago Press, 1996, pp. 324–28, 337–39.

Menchú, Rigoberta. "A Maid in the Capital." In *I, Rigoberta Menchú: An Indian Woman in Guatemala,* ed. Elizabeth Burgos Debray, trans. Ann Wright. London: Verso, 1984, pp. 91–97, 101.

Mladjenovic, Lepa, and Vera Litricin. "Belgrade Feminists 1992: Separation, Guilt, and Identity Crisis." *Feminist Review,* no. 45 (Autumn 1993), pp. 113–19.

Mlahleki, M. S. "Literacy: No Panacea for Women's Problems." *Connexions* 21 (Summer 1986), pp. 19–20.

Morsy, Soheir. "Biotechnology and the Taming of Women's Bodies." In *Processed Lives: Gender and Technology in Everyday Life,* eds. Jennifer Terry and Melodie Calvert. New York: Routledge, 1997, pp. 168–72.

National Latina Health Organization. "Norplant Information Sheet." In *Women's Health: Readings on Social, Economic and Political Issues.* 2nd ed., eds. Nancy Worcester and Mariamne H. Whatley. Dubuque, IA: Kendall/Hunt Publishing Company, 1996, pp. 274–76.

Nava, Mica. "Karen Alexander: Video Worker." *Feminist Review* 18 (1984), pp. 28–34.

Norsigian, Judy. "The Women's Health Movement in the United States." In *Man-Made Medicine: Women's Health, Public Policy, and Reform,* ed. Kary L. Moss. Durham: Duke University Press, 1996, pp. 79–85, 93.

Oudshoorn, Nelly. "Sex and the Body." In *Beyond the Natural Body: An Archaeology of Sex Hormones.* New York: Routledge, 1994, pp. 6–11.

Panos Media Briefing. No. 16. "The Internet and the South: Superhighway or Dirt-Track?" October 1994.

Parker, Rozsika. "Feminist Art Practices in 'Women's Images of Men,' 'About Time,' and 'Issue.' " *Art Monthly* 43 (1981), pp. 16–19.

Pettman, Jan Jindy. "Women and Citizenship." In *Worlding Women: A Feminist International Politics.* New York: Routledge, 1996, pp. 17–21.

Pettman, Jan Jindy. "Women, Gender and the State." In *Worlding Women: A Feminist International Politics.* New York: Routledge, 1996, pp. 5–18.

Pollock, Griselda. "Women and Art History." In *Vision and Difference: Femininity, Feminism and the History of Art.* New York: Routledge, 1988, pp. 23–24.

Potts, Lydia. Excerpt from *The World Labor Market: A History of Migration,* trans. Terry Bond. London: Zed Books, 1990, pp. 6–7, 200, 203, 206, 213–15.

"Questions and Answers about the IMF." *San Francisco Chronicle,* January 13, 1998, p. A4.

Ramphele, Mamphela. "Whither Feminism?" In *Transitions, Environments, Translations: Feminisms in International Politics,* eds. Joan W. Scott, Cora Kaplan, and Debra Keats. New York: Routledge, 1997, pp. 334–38.

Rowbotham, Sheila. "Feminist Approaches to Technology: Women's Values or a Gender Lens?"In *Women Encounter Technology: Changing Patterns of Employment in the Third World,* eds. Swasti Mitter and Sheila Rowbotham. New York: Routledge, 1995, pp. 52–59.

Rupp, Leila J. "The International First Wave." In *Worlds of Women: The Making of an International Women's Movement.* Princeton: Princeton University Press, 1997, pp. 3–4, 14, 34, 47–48.

Saint Louis, Catherine (text) and Lauren Ronick (photograph). "What They Were Thinking," *New York Times Magazine,* April 2, 2000, p. 34.

Salzinger, Leslie. "A Maid by Any Other Name: The Transformation of 'Dirty Work' by Central American Immigrants." In *Ethnography Unbound: Power and Resistance in the Modern Metropolis,* ed. Michael Burawoy et al. Berkeley: University of California Press, 1991, pp. 139–41, 150–52.

Samuels, Allison. "Black Beauty's New Face." *Newsweek,* November 24, 1997, p. 68.

Scanlon, Jennifer. *Inarticulate Longings: The Ladies' Home Journal, Gender, and the Promises of Consumer Culture.* New York: Routledge, 1995, pp. 4–9.

Schuklenk, Udo, Edward Stein, Jacinta Kerin, and William Byne. "The Ethics of Genetic Research on Sexual Orientation." Hastings-on-Hudson, NY: Hastings Center, *The Hastings Center Report.* (July/August 1997), pp. 1–4.

Seacole, Mary. *Wonderful Adventures of Mrs. Seacole in Many Lands.* New York: Oxford University Press, 1988, pp. 1–5, 82–86.

Shaheed, Farida. "Controlled or Autonomous: Identity and the Experience of the Network, Women Living under Muslim Laws." *Signs: Journal of Women in Culture and Society* 19, no. 4 (Summer 1994), pp. 997–1019.

Shohat, Ella. "Dislocated Identities: Reflections of an Arab Jew." *Emergences* 3/4, Fall 1992, pp. 39–43; *Movement Research: Performance Journal* 5 (Fall/Winter 1992), p. 8.

Smith, Lois M., and Alfred Padula. "Reproductive Health." In *Sex and Revolution: Women in Socialist Cuba.* New York: Oxford University Press, 1996, pp. 78–81.

Squires, Judith. "Public and Private." In *Gender in Political Theory.* Cambridge: Polity Press, 1999, pp. 24–30.

Tempest, Rone. "Barbie and the World Economy." *The Los Angeles Times,* September 22, 1996, pp. A1, A12.

Vance, Carole S. "Social Construction Theory: Problems in the History of Sexuality." In *Homosexuality, Which Homosexuality: International Conference on Gay and Lesbian Studies,* eds. Dennis Altman et al. London: GMP Publishers, 1989, pp. 13, 14, 16–17, 18, 23, 29–30, 31.

Watenabe, Satoko. "From Thailand to Japan: Migrant Sex Workers as Autonomous Subjects." In *Global Sex Workers: Rights, Resistance and Redefinitions,* eds. Kamala Kempadoo and Jo Doezema. New York: Routledge, 1998, pp. 114–23.

Weeks, Jeffrey. "Power and the State." In *State, Private Life and Political Change,* eds. Lynn Jamieson and Helen Corr. New York: St. Martin's Press, 1999, pp. 40–44.

Weiss, Andrea. "Female Pleasures and Perversions in the Silent and Early Sound Cinema." In *Vampires and Violets: Lesbians in Film.* Harmondsworth: Penguin Books, 1992, pp. 7–11.

Williams, Claudette. "Gal. . . You Come from Foreign." In *Charting the Journey: Writings by Black and Third World Women,* eds. Shabnam Grewal et al. London: Sheba Press, 1988, pp. 145–56.

Williams, Patricia J. "Owning the Self in a Disowned World." In *The Alchemy of Race and Rights.* Cambridge: Harvard University Press, 1991, pp. 183–85.

Williams, Raymond. "Community." In *Keywords.* New York: Oxford University Press, 1983, pp. 75–76.

Williamson, Judith. "Woman Is an Island." In *Studies in Entertainment,* ed. Tania Modleski. Bloomington, IN: Indiana University Press, 1986, pp. 111–13, 116–18.

Wollstonecraft, Mary. Excerpt from *A Vindication of the Rights of Woman,* ed. Miriam Brody. London: Penguin, 1992, pp. 108–9, 120, 122, 130–1, 132, 133–34.

Woodward, Kathryn. "Concepts of Identity and Difference." In *Identity and Difference,* ed. Kathryn Woodward. London: Sage, 1997, pp. 24–28.

Worcester, Nancy. "Nourishing Ourselves." *Women's Health: Readings on Social, Economic and Political Issues.* 2nd ed., eds. Nancy Worcester and Mariamne H. Whatley. Dubuque, IA: Kendall/Hunt Publishing Company, 1996, pp. 385–87, 389–93.

Worcester, Nancy. "The Obesity of the Food Industry." *Women's Health: Readings on Social, Economic and Political Issues.* 2nd ed., eds. Nancy Worcester and Mariamne H. Whatley. Dubuque, IA: Kendall/Hunt Publishing Company, 1996, pp. 394–97.

Wresch, William. "World Media." In *Disconnected: Haves and Have-Nots in the Information Age.* New Brunswick, NJ: Rutgers University Press, 1996, pp. 23–24, 33–38.

Zavella, Patricia. "Reflections on Diversity among Chicanas." *Frontiers* XII, no. 2 (1991), pp. 73–81.

Zenani, Nongenile Masithathu. Excerpt from " 'And So I Grew Up': The Autobiography of Nongenile Masithathu Zenani," researched and translated by Harold Scheub, in *Life Histories of African Women,* ed. Patricia W. Romero. London: Ashfield Press, 1988, pp. 43–45.

Zha, Jianying. "Yearnings." In *China Pop.* New York: The New Press, 1995, pp. 25–28.

List of Illustrations

Photo Credits

Figure I-2. "What Color is Black," *Newsweek,* February 13, 1995, cover. Photos by Anthony Barboza. Reprinted with permission.

Figure I-3. "The New Face of America," *Time Magazine,* Special Issue, Fall 1993, cover. © TimePix.

Figure I-4. "Time's Morphies," *Time Magazine,* Special Issue, Fall 1993, p. 67-68. © Ted Thai and Kin Wah Lam/TimePix.

Figure II-1. "Three Women" Shimada Yoshiko, etching, 1993. © Shimada Yoshiko. Reprinted with permission.

Figure II-2. "Hara Setsuko, Before and After." Shimada Yoshiko, etching, 1993. © Shimada Yoshiko. Reprinted with permission.

Figure II-3. "White Aprons," Shimada Yoshiko, etching, 1993. © Shimada Yoshiko. Reprinted with permission.

Figure II-4. "Shooting Lesson," Shimada Yoshiko, etching, 1993. © Shimada Yoshiko. Reprinted with permission.

Figure III-1. "Reclining Bacchante" (*La Bacchante*), Félix Trutat (1824-1848). Copyright - Musée des Beaux Arts de Dijon.

Figure III-2. "The Venus of Urbino," Titian (c. 1488-1576). Uffizi, Florence, Italy. Credit: Scala/Art Resources, NY.

Figure III-3. "Olympia," Edouard Manet (1832-1883). Musée d'Orsay, Paris, France. Credit: Réunion des Musées Nationaux/Art Resources, NY.

Figure III-5. "Untitled, 1982-1984." Drawing on leaf, 6 × 3 1/2 inches. Ana Mendieta. Courtesy of the Estate of Ana Mendieta and Galerie Lelong, New York.

Figure III-6. "Migrant Mother," Dorothea Lange.

Figure III-7. T. Fuente. *Dia de las Madres [after Migrant Mother, Nipomo, California]* c. 1964 as published in *Bohemia Venezolanna,* May 10, 1964. Courtesy the Dorothea Lange Collection, Oakland Museum of California.

Figure III-8. Malik. *Poverty is a Crime, and Our People Are the Victims [after Migrant Mother, Nipomo, California].* c. 1972 as published in *The Black Panther Intercommunal News Service,* December 7, 1972. Courtesy the Dorothea Lange Collection, Oakland Museum of California.

Figure III-9. The POND'S CREAM AND COCOA BUTTER "Discover the tropical secret for softer skin" Print Ad is reproduced courtesy of Cheesebrough-Pond's USA Co.

Figure III-10. The Hawaiian Tropic "The Natural Tan of the Islands" print advertisement is used with permission by Hawaiian Tropic, Daytona Beach, FL.

Figure III-11. "Lesbians Coming Out Strong," cover, *Newsweek,* June 21, 1993. Photograph courtesy of Shooting Star. © Newsweek, Inc. All rights reserved. Reprinted by permission.

Figure III-12. "The Fisher Body Girl," *Saturday Evening Post,* Nov. 24, 1928. Used with permission by the GM Media Archives.

Figure III-13. "His first love," *McCall's,* March 1928. Historic print advertisement used with permission by Colgate Palmolive Company, New York.

Figure III-14. "The Eureka Man Leaves You Health . . ." *Saturday Evening Post,* Dec. 8, 1928. Historic print advertisement used with permission by Eureka Company, Bloomington, IL.

Figure III-15. "All Eyes on Alek." Photographs courtesy of Dan and Corina Lecca.

Figure III-16 ."Denny Mendez, Miss Italy." Rome, Italy. September 7, 1996. © Reuters, 1996.

Figure III-17. "Disabled Girls Protested the Miss World Pageant in Bangalore," Bangalore, India. November 21, 1996. © Reuters, 1996.

Figure III-18. "Toys are Serious Business for U.S." Greg Hester, *The Los Angeles Times,* Sunday, September 22, 1996, p. A1. © Los Angeles Times, 1996.

Line Art Credits

Figure 0-1. Bill Griffith, "Catch You Later, Mercator." *From A to Zippy*. New York: Penguin Books, 1991, p. 183. © 1990 Bill Griffith.

Figure I-1. "Traditional American Values," Carol Simpson, "Impact Visuals," in *Women Under Attack* ed. Susan E. Davis, Boston: South End Press, 1988, p. 13. © South End Press. Reprinted by permission.

Figure I-5. "The Price of an Abortion," Susan Davis," Contested Terrain: The Historical Struggle for Fertility Control," in *Women Under Attack* ed. Susan E. Davis. Boston: South End Press, 1988, p. 13. © South End Press. Reprinted by permission.

Figure I-6. "How the Recession Reaches the Child," Jeanne Vickers, *Women and the World Economic Crisis*. London: Zed Books, 1991, p. 30. Reprinted by permission.

Figure I-7. "Default Isn't Ours!" Jeanne Vickers. In *Women and the World Economic Crisis*. London: Zed Books, 1991, p. 30. © Zed Books. Reprinted by permission.

Figure III-4. "Top Ten Ways to Tell if You're an Art World Token" Guerrilla Girls, *www.guerrillagirls. com/posters/poster_index.html*. © Guerrilla Girls.

Figure III-20. "Thanks, Ken." *San Francisco Chronicle,* Wednesday, November 19, 1997, page A22. © San Francisco Chronicle. Reprinted by permission.

Figure III-21. "TAMWA Organizational Chart," Fatma Alloo. In "Using Informational Technology as a Mobilizing Force." In *Women Encounter Technology: Changing Patterns of Employment in the Third World,* eds. Swasti Mitter and Sheila Rowbotham, London: Routledge. 1995, p. 306. Used with permission by Taylor and Francis Books, Ltd. and Swasti Mitter.

Figure III-22. "TAMWA Economic Unit." Fatma Alloo. In "Using Informational Technology as a Mobilizing Force," In *Women Encounter Technology: Changing Patterns of Employment in the Third World,* eds. Swasti Mitter and Sheila Rowbotham, London: Routledge. 1995, p. 308. Used with permission by Taylor and Francis Books, Ltd. and Swasti Mitter.

Figure III-23. "TAMWA Publishing Unit," Fatma Alloo. In "Using Informational Technology as a Mobilizing Force." In *Women Encounter Technology: Changing Patterns of Employment in the Third World,* eds. Swasti Mitter and Sheila Rowbotham, London: Routledge. 1995, p. 311. Used with permission by Taylor and Francis Books, Ltd. and Swasti Mitter.

Figure IV-4. "The Dream and the Reality." In *The Trade in Domestic Workers*. Noelleen Heyzer et al. (eds.) London: Zed, 1994, p. 1. Reprinted with permission.

Figure IV-5. "Movements of Female Migrants." In *The Trade in Domestic Workers*. Noelleen Heyzer et al. (eds.) London: Zed, 1994, p. xiv. Reprinted with permission.

Figure IV-6. "The World According to Nike." *Christian Science Monitor*/Los Angeles Times Syndicate," © Tribune Media Services, Inc. All rights reserved. Reprinted with permission.

Figure IV-8. "Tomasito's Guide to Economic Integration: A Whirlwind Tour with your Guide, Tomasito, the Tomato." Ecumenical Coalition for Economic Justice. *Economic Integration in the Americas: An Education and Action Kit*. Toronto:1994. © Ecumenical Coalition for Economic Justice.

Index